ROUTLEDGE LIBRARY EDITIONS:
ACCOUNTING HISTORY

Volume 36

REPORT OF THE TRIAL OF THE DIRECTORS AND THE MANAGER OF THE CITY OF GLASGOW BANK

REPORT OF THE TRIAL OF THE DIRECTORS AND THE MANAGER OF THE CITY OF GLASGOW BANK

CHARLES TENNANT COUPER

LONDON AND NEW YORK

First published in 1984 by Garland Publishing, Inc.

This edition first published in 2021
by Routledge
2 Park Square, Milton Park, Abingdon, Oxon OX14 4RN

and by Routledge
52 Vanderbilt Avenue, New York, NY 10017

Routledge is an imprint of the Taylor & Francis Group, an informa business

British Library Cataloguing in Publication Data
A catalogue record for this book is available from the British Library

ISBN: 978-0-367-33564-9 (Set)
ISBN: 978-1-00-304636-3 (Set) (ebk)
ISBN: 978-0-367-50600-1 (Volume 36) (hbk)
ISBN: 978-0-367-50602-5 (Volume 36) (pbk)
ISBN: 978-1-00-305047-6 (Volume 36) (ebk)

Publisher's Note
The publisher has gone to great lengths to ensure the quality of this reprint but points out that some imperfections in the original copies may be apparent.

Disclaimer
The publisher has made every effort to trace copyright holders and would welcome correspondence from those they have been unable to trace.

Report of the Trial of the Directors and the Manager of the City of Glasgow Bank

Charles Tennant Couper

with an introduction by
E. A. French

GARLAND PUBLISHING, INC.
NEW YORK & LONDON
1984

For a complete list of the titles in this series see the final pages of this volume.

This facsimile has been made from a copy in the Yale University Library.

Library of Congress Cataloging in Publication Data

City of Glasgow Bank.
Report of the trial of the directors and the managers of the City of Glasgow Bank.

(Accounting history and the development of a profession)
Reprint. Originally published: Report of the trial before the High Court of Justiciary, Her Majesty's advocate against the directors and the manager of the City of Glasgow Bank. Edinburgh : Edinburgh Pub. Co., 1879.
1. City of Glasgow Bank—Trials, litigation, etc.
2. Trials (Fraud)—Scotland—Edinburgh (Lothian).
3. Banking law—Scotland. 4. Banks and banking—Scotland—Accounting. I. Couper, Charles Tennant.
II. Scotland. High Court of Justiciary. III. Title.
KDC186.C57C57 1984 345.413'40263 83-49106
ISBN 0-8240-6320-1 (alk. paper) 344.13405263

The volumes in this series are printed on acid-free, 250-year-life paper.

Printed in the United States of America

INTRODUCTION

The collapse of the City of Glasgow Bank, on 2nd October 1878, came as a great shock to the general public. The Bank had displayed to the outside world the appearance of a stable, well managed and increasingly profitable concern. Since 1859 its annual dividend had risen steadily from 3% to 12% and the price of its shares (nominal value £100) had grown from £88 to £243. It had pursued an aggressive expansion policy and had attained a position of considerable significance in the Scottish Economy. In 1878 it had 133 branches, more than any other Scottish Bank, and reported gross assets of £12 million, translating into approximately £600 million by today's prices.

The immediate cause of the crash was the inability of the Bank to meet its commitments following the destruction of its credit in the London Discount Market. This, however, was rooted in a history of gross mismanagement which had been concealed from all but the directors and a handful of the Bank's officials by deceits facilitated by the absence of an independent audit. In broad terms, in defiance of the canons of sound banking, half of the Bank's assets had been lent to just four firms. These firms, the management of which was of the lowest imaginable standard, had largely used the loans to finance unsuccessful speculation in commodities (cotton, teak, rice, etc.) and textiles. Totally inadequate and inappropriate security had been taken by the Bank for these loans and the losses, in consequence, fell on it. In addition, the Bank had financed railway construction in North America and purchased land in Australia. Both investments, while holding out reasonable prospects of good returns in the long run, were currently yielding very little.

The loans to the four firms were mainly made on the authority of the manager of the Bank who did not tell most of the directors of his action. When he retired, due to ill-health, in 1875, his successor immediately informed the board of the position. Despite the precarious financial state of the Bank it was decided to keep it in operation and take steps to right matters. Rescue plans were devised for some customers. The Bank lent them further sums so that they could purchase land in Australia. The expected return from this land was significantly greater than the interest the Bank would charge and it was intended that the debts owed to the Bank would be reduced by the surplus so generated. Finance for these loans was obtained by manipulating the discount market. Accommodation bills were accepted by the Bank, which received the cash for them when the arrangements it had made for their discount were complete. Just before these bills fell due for payment a second set was issued, the discount of which provided the funds necessary to meet the original acceptances. This process continued until the collapse of the Bank. These operations, which were far beyond the pale of regular banking, had to be hidden. This, in part, was achieved by the establishment of The Edinburgh Pastoral Association, in which some of the land holdings were vested.

Carrying out these schemes required time. This was obtained by a policy of concealment. The hazardous financial position of the Bank was kept secret by a variety of deceits. False balance sheets, designed to mislead the discount market, government officials and the financial community, were issued for several years. The Bank purchased its own shares, through nominees, in order to maintain their market value. By 1878 this had been indulged in to the extent that the Bank held over 15% of its own shares. Profits, from which the increasing dividends had ostensibly been paid, were manufactured, inter alia, by taking credit for the interest (which had not been paid for several years) due on the major accounts, by treating as revenue the increase in market value above the price paid for the Bank's holding of its own shares, and by not writing off, or making provision for, bad debts.

As a result of these practices the Bank survived for a surprisingly long time. Despite some doubts its credit remained good until 1878. However, in March of that year the London Discount Market became more cautious following the collapse of Willis, Percival & Co., a small London Bank. Acceptances were scrutinised more carefully and those of the Bank, which were being discounted in large numbers, came under suspicion. Dealers asked for and obtained a premium above market rate for handling them. Lack of confidence increased, so much so that by September a number of Indian banks, which held large numbers of bills accepted by the Bank, experienced great trouble in negotiating them. They instructed their agents to take no more such bills. The Bank's credit was destroyed and it collapsed.

The economic consequences of the crash were momentous. The shareholders were badly affected. At that time the ramifications of large scale joint stock activity were still being worked out. It had not been fully appreciated that the shareholder in a large undertaking is essentially a purchaser of income who has little to do with the management of the concern and so needs the protection offered by limited liability. Thus, although limited liability had been generally available for over 20 years, the directors of banks, who believed that the unlimited liability of their shareholders increased their customers' confidence in them, had made little use of this new concept. This was highly dangerous for shareholders, as the nature of banking ensures that the ratio of creditors to share capital is extraordinarily high. If the assets of a bank are worthless, and limited liability does not exist, the claims on its shareholders can be enormous. In these circumstances the position is exacerbated by another aspect of business failure, the fact that most proprietors have but modest means. Where a concern is small, and the number of partners not great, any wealthy partners can usually cope with the liabilities transferred to them through the bankruptcy of their fellows. But in large businesses, where partners are numbered by the thousand, the effect of the failure of the less wealthy is geared up enormously. This leverage tends to ruin even rich partners.

The City of Glasgow Bank was an unlimited company. The consequences of these phenomena, together with the Bank's holdings of its own shares, were visited upon its shareholders. An original call of £500 per share was made, followed by a second call of £2,250 per share, a total of 27.5 times the nominal value. Of the 1819 shareholders only about 250 remained solvent after the Bank's creditors had been paid in full. The impact of the leverage effect on these 250 was striking, the Bank's deficit amounting to £850 per share. Those ruined included many (widows, retired persons, children, etc.) who had little prospect of recovering and the human misery involved makes calling the collapse a national tragedy no exaggeration.

The presence or absence of limited liability probably has little effect on the overall volume of business losses, but it vitally affects the incidence of their consequences. Whether these should fall on proprietors, creditors or some combination of the two is largely a subjective matter on which views can legitimately differ. However, the sufferings of the Bank's shareholders touched the public conscience. A committee to raise and administer a relief fund for them was established and attracted money from many quarters. In the longer term the shareholders' plight made investors keen to seek the protection of limited liability, so greatly encouraging its spread, and made the concept far more generally acceptable.

The impact of the Bank's collapse on the Scottish economy was striking. In 1879 over a thousand firms were sequestered, almost double the next highest yearly total in the seventy-five years before 1914. Interest rates plummeted. The other Scottish banks, which at the time of the collapse had taken some small measures to protect the integrity of the country's banking system, by continuing to accept the notes of the City of Glasgow Bank, reviewed their own administrations. They became ultracautious, keeping rigidly to accepting deposits from the public and lending them strictly on the short term, an attitude that was to persist for many years.

The Government's response to the Bank's failure was contained in the Companies Act of 1879. This can only be described as panic legislation intended to still public disquiet. In the early stages of its enactment the measure attempted wide-ranging reforms of the banking system. However, opposition from vested interests and the lack of Parliamentary time considerably reduced its scope. Its major effect was to remove the difficulties in the way of unlimited companies re-registering as limited. As it was believed that many of the malpractices of the Bank could not have taken place had its accounts been subject to independent audit, the Act also provided for the compulsory audit of banks registered as limited companies. However this safeguard could have been considerably strengthened. The auditors were not allowed to enter into questions of valuation, there was no requirement that they should be professional accountants, their appointment and remuneration were left, de facto, very much to the discretion of the directors and no penalties were prescribed for failure to have an audit.

Despite this, the collapse of the Bank was a great benefit to the infant profession of Accountancy. The liquidation of the Bank, which was entrusted to certain Scottish Chartered Accountants, was performed speedily, efficiently and at a very reasonable cost, so winning universal praise. More importantly, the failure dramatically illustrated the need for the independent verification of financial reports made available to the public. It emphasized the significance of the information in such reports. It provoked discussion and development of auditing techniques. It led to suggestions that the presence of professional accountants would improve decisions and so avoid the economic waste involved in gross blunders. In short, it greatly helped in establishing the auditor in the central position he occupies in U.K. Company Law as the shareholders' watchdog.

The Bank's collapse provided a field day for lawyers. The liquidators were involved in 420 civil cases, being successful in all but 56. At least 19 appeals were taken to the House of Lords. Prominent among such cases were attempts by shareholders to have their names removed from the list of contributors. Those who held shares as gratuitous trustees attracted considerable sympathy, but the test case of Muir and Others v The City of Glasgow Bank and Liquidators established their liability; the Law Lords argued that it was impossible to hold, in the circumstances of the case, that there were two classes of shareholders, those with, and those without limited liability. Other litigation involved the title of the Bank to securities (the schemes of concealment had created obscurities), disputes between the shareholders and the liquidators over fees and actions against directors for breach of the partnership contract. This, incidentally, had provided that the Bank was to be wound up in the event of one quarter of its capital being lost, an attempt by the shareholders to protect themselves which was defeated by the fraudulent over-valuation of the assets. It was, however, the criminal proceedings against the directors and manager of the Bank which gripped the public's attention. Couper's report is comprehensive and enables the reader to trace much of the detail of the collapse. Some additional information may help him to a better understanding of the case.

A reading of the report suggests that the prosecution was somewhat hastily assembled. This is explained by a right given to the accused (which they exercised) under a Statute of William and Mary, to be brought to trial within 100 days. Whether this constraint made sense when applied to a modern complex commercial fraud is debatable. The prosecution brought three charges: fraud, embezzlement and theft. On the seventh day of the trial the second and third were unexpectedly withdrawn. Part of the explanation for this was the desire of the Lord Advocate to prevent the accused obtaining bail. Popular feeling against them was high and one of the major debtors and ex-directors of the Bank, James Nicol Fleming, had fled to Spain. The theft alleged was not bailable as of right and the maintenance of this charge against the accused ensured they remained in custody from October 1878.

Until 1887 Scottish indictments were in a syllogistic form, containing a major and minor premise and a conclusion. The major premise set out the general crime, the minor premise contained details of the acts the accused was alleged to have committed and the conclusion reasoned that from the acts alleged the accused was guilty of the crime charged. This procedure accounts for the arguments on relevancy which appear in the case. The major premise had to be relevant in that it contained a crime known to the law or described a situation which the judges would hold to be criminal.

The minor premise had to give sufficient detail of the facts the Crown intended to prove and these had to be relevant in that they amounted to the crime in the major premise. Another procedural point of significance was that at the time of the trial it was still the rule of Scots law that the accused could not give evidence. This explains the absence of the directors from the witness box.

The sentences were considered far too light by an angry public. The *Glasgow News* assured them ". . . at least these masterful rogues will be usefully employed for 10 hours each day in the making of sacks and the teasing of old rope. They will wear prison clothes and as to diet, breakfast and evening meals will be oatmeal porridge with soor dook (sour milk) and midday meals of bread (wheaten) and pea soup or barley broth. This is more than they deserve." Readers will be able to judge whether this was fair comment.

E. A. French
University College,
Cardiff.

REPORT OF TRIAL

OF THE

CITY OF GLASGOW BANK DIRECTORS.

REPORT OF THE TRIAL

BEFORE

THE HIGH COURT OF JUSTICIARY

HER MAJESTY'S ADVOCATE

AGAINST

THE DIRECTORS AND THE MANAGER

OF

The City of Glasgow Bank

AND OF THE PROCEDURE UPON

THE PETITION FOR BAIL;

WITH LITHOGRAPHS OF THE SCROLL ABSTRACTS OF ACCOUNTS
AND THE REPORT OF THE INVESTIGATORS.

BY

CHARLES TENNANT COUPER,
ADVOCATE.

The Speeches and Opinions Revised by the Counsel and Judges, and the Charge by the Lord Justice-Clerk.

EDINBURGH:
THE EDINBURGH PUBLISHING COMPANY.
LONDON: SIMPKIN, MARSHALL, & CO.

1879.

CONTENTS.

ERRATA.

On the third line from the bottom of page 27, in the Abstract Balance-Sheet for 1876, for £10,589,785, 15s. 6d. *read* £10,539,785, 15s. 6d. Also, opposite the heading "VI. Profit and Loss," for £136,865, 10s. 3d. *read* £136,365, 10s. 3d.

HIGH COURT OF JUSTICIARY.

PETITION FOR BAIL

BY

THE DIRECTORS OF THE CITY OF GLASGOW BANK.

November 14th and 15th, 1878.

Present—

FULL BENCH.

THE LORD JUSTICE-GENERAL (INGLIS).

THE LORD JUSTICE-CLERK (LORD MONCREIFF).

LORDS DEAS, YOUNG, MURE, CRAIGHILL, AND ADAM.

LEWIS POTTER, *Petitioner*—Balfour and Asher.
ROBERT SALMOND, *Petitioner*—Balfour, Asher, and Dickson.
JOHN INNES WRIGHT, *Petitioner*—J. Guthrie Smith and Dickson.
WILLIAM TAYLOR, *Petitioner*—Balfour and Mackintosh.
ROBERT SUMMERS STRONACH, *Petitioner*—The Dean of Faculty (Fraser) and Darling.
CHARLES SAMUEL LERESCHE, *Petitioner*—Balfour, Brand, and M'Kechnie;—

HER MAJESTY'S ADVOCATE, *Compearer*—The Lord Advocate (Watson), the Solicitor-General (Macdonald), and Burnet, A.D.

BAIL—Statute 1701, c. 6 (for the prevention of wrongous imprisonment)—*Furtum grave*—Capital Offence—Breach of Trust and Embezzlement—Bills deposited for Collection—Bank.

Certain of the directors of a joint-stock bank having been committed for trial on a charge of theft under a complaint which set forth that the bank having, by their reckless and fraudulent dealing, been to their knowledge brought to a state of hopeless insolvency; and bills to a large amount, which were not yet due, having been deposited with the bank for the sole purpose of being collected when due, they, the accused, in pursuance of a conspiracy to continue the business of the bank and make it appear solvent, did, for their own pecuniary ends, endorse and make over said bills to a London bank before they became due, in order that the proceeds might be credited to their own bank, and thus stole the said bills. And the Lord Advocate having refused to admit the accused to bail, they presented a petition to be admitted thereto to the High Court of Justiciary, on the ground that the *species facti* in the complaint did not amount to theft, appealing also to the discretionary power of the Court.

Held (*dissentiente* Lord YOUNG)—That the accused having failed to satisfy the Court that the facts alleged in the complaint were insufficient to sustain a charge of *furtum grave* in the form of an indictment, and it not being alleged that bail had been refused in order to secure other than the ends of justice, there was no ground for the Court interfering with the exercise of the discretion vested in the Lord Advocate; and the petition refused accordingly.

The City of Glasgow Bank commenced business as a banking company in the year 1839, having its head office in Glasgow, and numerous branches throughout Scotland. It continued to carry on business until the end of the year 1857, about the time at which the Western Bank of Scotland closed its doors, when it also suspended payment; but it again resumed business in the beginning of the year 1858. It was registered under the Joint Stock Companies Act of 1862, in November of that year, and continued its operations until it finally ceased to do business and closed its doors on 2d October 1878.

On the day following, the directors placed the books of the Bank in the hands of Alexander Bennet M'Grigor, Esq., LL.D., of the firm of Messrs M'Grigor, Donald, & Company, writers in Glasgow, and William Anderson, Esq., chartered accountant, of the firm of Messrs Kerr, Andersons, Muir, and Main, accountants there, with instructions to investigate into and prepare a report of the state of the affairs of the Bank, to be laid before a meeting of the shareholders to be subsequently convened. These firms prepared a report, which was dated and issued upon the 18th of October following, from which it appeared that besides the capital of the Bank, amounting to £1,000,000 sterling, and the reserve fund, amounting to £450,000, the sum of £5,190,983, 11s. 3d. sterling had been lost by the Bank. (*See Appendix, No. I.*)

On the 19th of October the directors, manager, and secretary of the Bank were apprehended by the orders of the Lord Advocate, and taken before the Sheriff of Lanarkshire, when they were remanded for forty-eight hours, and a petition and complaint at the instance of Wm. Alexander Brown, Esq., advocate, the Procurator-Fiscal of Lanarkshire, was thereupon prepared and presented to the Sheriff on the 21st October, charging them with falsehood, fraud, and wilful imposition. And declarations with reference thereto having been emitted by the accused, the Sheriff, after considering the same, and the evidence so far as taken, of same date committed them for trial.

Thereafter a second petition and complaint at the instance of said Procurator-Fiscal was presented to the Sheriff on 29th October 1878, charging the said Lewis Potter, William Taylor, Henry Inglis, and John Stewart, directors of said Bank, from and since the year 1872, and John Innes Wright and Robert Summers Stronach, the former a director, and the latter a director and also the manager of said Bank, from and since the year 1875, and Charles Samuel

Leresche, the secretary of said Bank, from and since the year 1870, with the crime of theft. And the accused having been brought before the Sheriff, they each of them emitted a declaration having reference thereto, and were of same date, viz., 29th October 1878, committed in the following terms:

Glasgow, 30th October 1878.—Having resumed consideration of the foregoing Petition, with the declarations of Robert Salmond, Lewis Potter, John Innes Wright, William Taylor, Henry Inglis, John Stewart, Robert Summers Stronach, and Charles Samuel Leresche, complained upon, and precognition led, Grants warrant to imprison the said Robert Salmond, Lewis Potter, John Innes Wright, William Taylor, Henry Inglis, John Stewart, Robert Summers Stronach, and Charles Samuel Leresche, in the prison of Glasgow, therein to be detained until liberated in due course of law. F. W. CLARK.

The present petitioners, Lewis Potter, Robert Salmond, John Innes Wright, William Taylor, Robert Summers Stronach, and Charles Samuel Leresche, together with John Stewart, thereupon applied to the Sheriff to be admitted to bail; and from the latter bail to the extent of two sureties to the amount of £5000 each was accepted, with the consent of the Lord Advocate; and Charles Samuel Leresche was subsequently liberated. The application of the other petitioners was refused by the Sheriff, upon the ground that the offence for which they had been committed amounted to *furtum grave*, and that bail could not be accepted without the consent of the Lord Advocate, which had not been obtained. They accordingly presented the present petition to be admitted to bail to the High Court of Justiciary, and founded on the terms of the commitment and of the complaint upon which it was pronounced, which latter was in the following terms:

Glasgow, 29th October 1878.

Unto the Honourable the Sheriff of Lanarkshire, or his Substitutes, the PETITION of WILLIAM ALEXANDER BROWN, Advocate, Procurator-Fiscal of Court for the public interest.

Humbly sheweth,—

THAT from information received by the petitioner, it appears, and accordingly he charges, that Robert Salmond, Lewis Potter, William Taylor, Henry Inglis, and John Stewart, all at present prisoners in the prison of Glasgow, having been directors of the City of Glasgow Bank, incorporated under Act of Parliament from and since the year 1872, and John Innes Wright and Robert Summers Stronach, also presently prisoners in the prison of Glasgow, having been—the said John Innes Wright, a director, and the said Robert Summers Stronach a director and the manager of the said Bank from and since the year 1875, and Charles Samuel Leresche, also presently a prisoner in the prison of Glasgow, having been secretary of said Bank from and since the year 1870, and the said Bank having been in the years 1877 and 1878, and also during the years 1873, 1874, 1875, and 1876, or one or more of said years, by reason of the culpable, reckless, and fraudulent trading and mismanagement by the directors thereof, in a state of hopeless insolvency and unable to meet its liabilities, and the fact of the said insolvency of the said Bank being well known during the years 1873, 1874, 1875, 1876, and 1877, and the bypast part of 1878, or one or more of said years, to the said Robert Salmond, Lewis Potter, William Taylor, Henry Inglis, John Stewart, and Charles Samuel Leresche, and to the said John Innes Wright and Robert Summers Stronach, during the years 1875, 1876, and 1877, and the bypast part of 1878, or one or more of said years, and more particularly the said Bank being—as the said Robert Salmond, Lewis Potter, John Innes Wright, William Taylor, Henry Inglis, John Stewart, Robert Summers Stronach, and Charles Samuel Leresche well knew—as at 5th June 1878, in a state of hopeless insolvency and unable to meet its liabilities, and the said Robert Salmond, Lewis Potter, John Innes Wright, William

Taylor, Henry Inglis, John Stewart, Robert Summers Stronach, and Charles Samuel Leresche, or one or more of them, having, on or about the dates set forth in the first column of the schedule hereunto attached, at the offices of the said Bank described in the second column of said schedule, received from the respective persons, firms, and companies mentioned in the third column of said schedule, the several bills of exchange, specified in the fourth column of said schedule, for the special and sole purpose of collecting payment of the same when due from the debtors therein, on behalf of the said persons, firms, and companies mentioned in the third column of said schedule, none of whom were at the time indebted or under any obligation to the said Bank, and the said Robert Salmond, Lewis Potter, John Innes Wright, William Taylor, Henry Inglis, John Stewart, Robert Summers Stronach, and Charles Samuel Leresche not being entitled to make use of the said bills of exchange for any other purpose than that of collecting payment thereof when due, yet nevertheless the said Robert Salmond, Lewis Potter, John Innes Wright, William Taylor, Henry Inglis, John Stewart, Robert Summers Stronach, and Charles Samuel Leresche, or one or more of them, did, actors or actor or art and part, in pursuance of a wicked conspiracy devised by them to continue the business of the said Bank and make it appear to the shareholders and creditors thereof and the public as a solvent concern, for accomplishing their own personal and pecuniary ends, time or times and place or places above libelled, wickedly and feloniously steal and theftuously away take the said several bills of exchange, for sums amounting in all to £23,693, 11s. 7d. sterling or thereby, the property of the said several persons, firms, and companies mentioned in the said third column of said schedule, and did endorse and make over the said several bills of exchange before they had become due to the London Joint Stock Bank, London, in order that the proceeds thereof might be credited to the City of Glasgow Bank in account between them and the said London Joint Stock Bank, and the same were accordingly credited by the said London Joint Stock Bank as payments made on behalf of the said City of Glasgow Bank.

MAY IT THEREFORE please your Lordship to grant Warrant to search for and apprehend the said Robert Salmond, Lewis Potter, John Innes Wright, William Taylor, Henry Inglis, John Stewart, Robert Summers Stronach, and Charles Samuel Leresche, and to bring them for examination, and thereafter grant warrant to imprison them within the prison of Glasgow, therein to be detained for farther examination, or till liberated in due course of law: Farther, grant warrant to search the persons, repositories, and domicile of the said delinquents, and the house or premises in which they may be found, and to secure for the purpose of precognition all articles found therein, importing guilt or participation in the crime foresaid; and to cite all persons likely to have knowledge of the premises, in order to be precognosced thereanent, and to make production for the purposes foresaid of such writs and evidents pertinent to the case as are in their possession: And recommend to the Judges of other Counties and Jurisdictions to grant the warrants of concurrence necessary for enforcing that of your Lordship within their respective territories.

According to Justice, &c.,

W. A. BROWN, *P.F.*

[SCHEDULE.

SCHEDULE.

Dates when Received.	Places where Received.	Persons, Firms, and Companies, from whom Received.	Bills of Exchange.	
1878.				
June 26.	At Head Office of City of Glasgow Bank, Virginia Street, Glasgow.	Wright & Brackenridge, timber merchants, Glasgow.	One accepted by Dobie & Company, shipbuilders, Govan, amounting to	£321 4 4
July 11.	West End Branch of said Bank, Argyle Street, Glasgow.	John Ramsay, of Kildalton, distiller in Islay and Glasgow.	One accepted by Edward Young & Company, amounting to	252 7 0
July 11.	The place last mentioned.	The said John Ramsay.	One accepted by W. & A. Gilbey, wine importers, London, amounting to	496 12 2
September 3.	The place last mentioned.	The said John Ramsay.	One accepted by said W. & A. Gilbey, amounting to .	489 14 2
August 20.	At Anderston Branch of said Bank, Gusset House, Anderston, Glasgow.	Charles Connell & Company, shipbuilders, Scotstoun, Whiteinch.	One accepted by Alexander & Rawcliff, amounting to .	3000 0 0
" "	The place last mentioned.	The said Charles Connell & Company.	One accepted by said Alexander & Rawcliff, amounting to	3000 0 0
" "	The place last mentioned.	The said Charles Connell & Company.	One accepted by said Alexander & Rawcliff, amounting to	3000 0 0
" "	The place last mentioned.	The said Charles Connell & Company.	One accepted by said Alexander & Rawcliff, amounting to	3000 0 0
" 26.	The place last mentioned.	The said Charles Connell & Company.	One accepted by said Alexander & Rawcliff, amounting to	3000 0 0
" "	The place last mentioned.	The said Charles Connell & Company.	One accepted by said Alexander & Rawcliff, amounting to	3000 0 0
" 21.	At Head Office of said Bank, as aforesaid.	The Marbella Iron Ore Company (Limited), London.	One accepted by E. J. Wait & Company, Cardiff, amounting to	525 0 0
" "	The place last mentioned.	The Company last mentioned.	One accepted by the Panteg Steel Works Company, amounting to	358 13 8
" 31.	The place last mentioned.	The Company last mentioned.	One accepted by said E. J. Wait & Company, amounting to	800 0 0
September 5.	The place last mentioned.	The Company last mentioned.	One accepted by the Ebbw Vale Steel Company (Limited), amounting to	1187 11 3
" 21.	The place last mentioned.	John M'Pherson & Company, engineers, Mountblue, Glasgow.	One accepted by the Chartered Bank of India, Australia, and China, amounting to	562 10 0
" 13.	The place last mentioned.	James Baird, merchant, Newfoundland.	One accepted by Walter Grieve, Son, & Company, Greenock, amounting to.	700 0 0
				£23,693 12 7

W. A. BROWN, *P.F.*

At the Calling of the Petition before the High Court,

Mr ASHER—I appear for Mr Potter in support of the present application for bail. The accused applied to the Sheriff to be liberated on bail, but his application was refused upon the ground that he was committed on a charge of *furtum grave*, and therefore it was not within the power of the Sheriff to grant it, without the consent of the Crown. The accused thereupon applied to the Lord Advocate, and offered to find bail to the extent of £10,000, but the Lord Advocate refused his consent. His Lordship having been asked to state whether his refusal was in consequence of the amount offered being insufficient, I understand it has been intimated that bail will not be accepted in the present case. In these circumstances the present application is made to your Lordships, on the two-fold ground—first, that the petition upon which the commitment has proceeded does not set forth facts inferring a crime not bailable by law; and, secondly and alternatively, that, under the equitable power which the Court undoubtedly possesses, bail ought to be accepted in the circumstances of the present case. The commitment by the Sheriff is in the usual terms. It does not specify the charge on which the accused is committed, except by reference to the complaint; and although theft is charged in the complaint, it does not follow, I submit, that the accused is committed for theft. He is committed merely for trial upon the facts stated in the complaint. The question, therefore, is, whether the facts stated in the complaint do or do not amount to a case of *furtum grave*, and therefore to a crime which is not bailable by law. I have to ask your Lordships' attention to the terms of the complaint. It bears that the accused for whom I appear, and several others, having been directors of the Bank from the year 1872, and the Bank having been in the years 1877 and 1878, by reason of the culpable, reckless, and fraudulent trading and mismanagement by the directors thereof, in a state of hopeless insolvency and unable to meet its liabilities, and the fact of the insolvency of the Bank being well known to the accused during the years 1873, 1874, 1875, 1876, 1877, and part of 1878—more particularly, the Bank being, as was well known to the accused, at 5th June 1878, in a state of insolvency and unable to meet its liabilities; and they having, on or about the date, set forth in the first column of the schedule annexed to the charge, received from the respective persons, firms, and companies mentioned in the third column of the said schedule, the several bills of exchange specified in the fourth column of said schedule for the special and sole purpose of collecting payment of the same when due from the debtors therein, on behalf of said persons, firms, and companies mentioned in the third column of said schedule, none of whom were at the time indebted or under any obligation to the said Bank; and the Bank not being entitled to make use of the said bills of exchange for any other purpose than that of collecting payment thereof when due; "yet, nevertheless, "the said Robert Salmond, Lewis Potter, and the other persons named, or one "or more of them, did, actors or actor or art and part, in pursuance of a wicked "conspiracy devised by them to continue the business of the said Bank, and "make it appear to the shareholders and creditors thereof and the public as a "solvent concern, for accomplishing their own personal and pecuniary ends, "time and place above libelled, wickedly and feloniously steal and theftuously "away take the said several bills of exchange for sums amounting in all to "£23,693, 12s. 7d. sterling or thereby, the property of the said several persons, "firms, and companies mentioned in the said third column of said schedule, "and did endorse and make over the said several bills of exchange, before they "had become due, to the London Joint Stock Bank, London, in order that the "proceeds thereof might be credited to the City of Glasgow Bank, in ac-"count between them and the said London Joint Stock Bank, and the same "were accordingly credited by the London Joint Stock Bank, as payments "made on behalf of the said City of Glasgow Bank." That charge, my Lords, I think in substance amounts to this, that Mr Potter being a director of this Bank, and knowing that the Bank was insolvent as the result of reckless trading on the part of most of the directors, and having conspired with his co-directors to continue the business of the Bank and make it appear solvent, and having certain bills in the possession of the Bank for the purpose of collection, endorsed those bills to the London Joint Stock Bank, by which Bank the proceeds were placed to the credit of the City of Glasgow Bank.

Lord YOUNG—Were the bills endorsed at all to the City of Glasgow Bank?

Mr ASHER—I have not seen the bills. But I was just going to state that the bills must have been endorsed to the City of Glasgow Bank, because the charge is, that they were transferred by that Bank by endorsation to the London Joint Stock Bank, which could not have been done unless they had been endorsed to the City Bank. The Sheriff having committed the accused for trial on the *species facti* I have mentioned, the question is whether these *species facti* constitute a case of *furtum*. It is true that the line which separates breach of trust and embezzlement from theft has frequently been said to be somewhat shadowy; it is equally clear that theft and breach of trust and embezzlement are two distinct crimes in the eye of the law. Nothing could more thoroughly illustrate this than the consideration, that if this crime is theft—looking to the number and amount of the charges—it is a capital offence; if it is embezzlement it is not a capital offence. It has also been said, in applications like the present, that where the facts of the particular case are such as to bring it close to the margin which divides breach of trust and embezzlement from theft, the Court will not at this stage decide to which category it belongs, but leave it for decision on the indictment at the trial. On the other hand, it is quite plain that there are cases in regard to which there can be no doubt as to which category they belong to. The thief who walks into a shop, and theftuously lifts an article and appropriates it to his own uses and purposes, could never be said to have committed breach of trust and embezzlement. On the other hand, the mercantile agent who receives goods on consignment for sale, and having sold them, appropriates the price to his own uses, could never be said to have committed theft. If in such a case the mercantile agent were committed for theft, and so was deprived of his right to bail, he would be entitled, I submit, to come to this Court and say, "The facts on which I have been committed "have been improperly designated theft; they do not in law constitute theft; "and I am therefore entitled to bail." On behalf of the accused in the present case, I now prefer a like demand, and on the same grounds. The *species facti* in the complaint in the present case never can be construed as amounting to the crime of theft. The question is not doubtful in the present case. It is clear, and therefore I contend the accused are entitled to have it decided now. There are two points which appear to be conclusive against the case being one of theft. First, it is not said that the proceeds of these bills were appropriated by the accused either for their own uses and purposes, or, through their instrumentality, for the uses and purposes of the institution of which they were the directors. It is not said that the proceeds of these bills when collected in London were not immediately credited, and ultimately paid to those who had deposited them for collection; and in the absence of any allegation to that effect, I am entitled to assume that the case against the accused is merely this: That having bills in their possession for collection, they prematurely sent them to London for that purpose, and that when collected the proceeds were credited or paid to the parties to whom the bills originally belonged. The second point which, I submit, is conclusive against the case being one of theft is, the nature of the accused's possession of the things said to have been stolen. What they are said to have stolen are bills—pieces of paper having that written upon them which made them bills.

Lord YOUNG—A written document.

Mr ASHER—Yes, documents are the things said to have been stolen. That gives rise to the question, Was Mr Potter's possession of them such as to make his appropriation of them, even assuming that he did so, to his own uses and purposes, an act of theft, or was his possession not such as to make that appropriation merely breach of trust? My Lords, I know of no case in which facts at all resembling those of the present case have been held to amount to theft. The Bank were indorsees of the bills in question. Now, there is no case, so far as I am aware, in which a person possessing a thing, under such a title as an indorsee has to an indorsed bill, has been held to be the custodier of the thing in such a sense as to admit of the possibility of his committing theft in regard to it. A person who appropriates to his own use the property of another of which he has the custody merely, commits theft. But if the property so appropriated is in his lawful possession, he does not commit theft, but breach of trust. This distinction is recognised in several cases. For example, in the cases of Hugh Climie, High Court, May 21, 1838, Swint., vol. ii., p. 118, and George Brown, High Court, July 3, 1839, Swint., vol. ii., p. 394. The rubric of Climie's case is as follows: "A panel being charged with having, while a "servant in the employment of a company, received, from one of the partners, "the sum of £17 sterling, or thereby, in notes and silver money, for the special "purpose of paying £9 to one individual, and £8, being the balance of said "sum of £17, to another, and having appropriated it—this found not to be a "relevant charge of theft, principally on the ground that it was not set forth "that the money was to be delivered by him *in forma specifica*." It has occasionally been remarked on this case, that there was not an absolute unanimity on the part of the Judges who presided. But there was no difference of opinion in regard to the point for which I quote the case. All the learned Judges were of opinion that if the money given to the servant was not to be applied *in forma specifica* for the purpose for which it was given, then it was not theft. The only doubt expressed by any of the Judges was, whether the libel did not make it plain that the money was to be applied *in forma specifica*. Two of the learned Judges doubted whether the language of the libel did not make that plain. But there was unanimity of opinion that if the money was not to be applied *in forma specifica*, then the crime was not theft, but breach of trust. The case of Brown illustrates the same principle. That was the case of a watchmaker who received a watch for repair and appropriated it, and that was held to be theft and not breach of trust; and the ground on which that judgment proceeded was very clearly stated in the opinion of Lord Meadowbank, who said, "Now, it appears to me, in "this case, that when a party puts his watch into the hands of a watchmaker to "be cleaned or repaired, he only parts with the custody, that the possession of "the watchmaker is the possession of the owner, and that the watchmaker, in "appropriating it, takes it out of the lawful possession of the owner, and is so "guilty of theft. If we so decide the question now before us, it appears to me "that we shall be relieved of difficulty in all future cases of a similar nature." In all such cases—the case of the carrier, for example, the case of the servant having custody of his master's wine, and such similar cases, in which appropriation by the custodier is held to be theft, and not breach of trust—the possession has been of the nature of custody merely, and did not exclude the owner's possession. Applying that principle to the present case, the question arises whether the possession by the City of Glasgow Bank of the bills endorsed and delivered to them for collection was at all akin to that of the watchmaker who receives the watch for repair, under contract to return the very article he has received, or whether it was not, as in the class of cases represented by Climie, such possession as that of the servant who received money to pay particular accounts, not under an obligation to apply the money so received *in forma specifica* in payment of the accounts, but to expend an amount equal to that which he had received, in payment of the accounts. The bills here were put by the owners into the possession of the Bank for a purpose which excluded the idea of the possession of the owner continuing, and the Bank being merely a custodier. It was no part of the contract under which the bills were endorsed and delivered to the Bank that the bills—the things stolen—should be returned to the owner *in forma specifica.* It is against the whole theory and practice of banking that such a thing should ever happen. The purpose of a bill being endorsed and put into the hands of a bank is that the bank may have a title to negotiate it, and when this has been done, it is not the bill *in forma specifica* that comes back to the owner, but the proceeds which are realised from its negotiation.

Lord YOUNG—What, according to the contract, is it the duty of the bank to do with the money?

Mr ASHER—To credit or remit the amount to the person to whom it belongs.

Lord YOUNG—If it were a customer of the bank, of course he would be credited with the amount.

Mr ASHER—Precisely. The purpose of the transaction was that the bills should be negotiated. All the bills, with the exception of two payable in Govan, were payable in London. Now, what was the duty of the Bank in such a case? Was it not part of the contract, and according to the intention of such a transaction, that the Bank should, sometime prior to the date of payment, take the necessary steps for having the bill presented to the party by whom it was due, and at the place where it was payable? That surely does not imply that the Bank is to send an official to London carrying the bill with him, for the purpose of collecting the money and bringing the money back in a bag, and delivering it *in forma specifica* to the owner of the bill. The transaction is this. The City of Glasgow Bank having a correspondent in London has in due course to endorse the bill to the correspondent, by whom the money is collected, and when received it is placed to the credit of the Glasgow Bank, leaving the Glasgow Bank to account to the person from whom they received the bill, either by putting it to the credit of his account, or paying over the money when it is wanted.

Lord YOUNG—Not paying it of course *in forma specifica.*

Mr ASHER—Clearly not.

Lord YOUNG—According to the theory of this petition, if the City of Glasgow Bank were guilty of theft, the London and Joint Stock Bank, if it knew the character of the bills, would be art and part.

Mr ASHER—Doubtless they would be so. I submit that this is a case about which there is no doubt as to which category it belongs. The facts stated may amount to breach of trust, but clearly can never be theft, the Bank having been lawfully in possession of the bills for the purpose of negotiating them, and with a title to negotiate them. I know that this is not the stage of the case at which the relevancy of the charge falls to be determined. But, on the other hand, this Court, I submit, will not allow any one to be deprived of his legal right to bail where the facts disclosed in the petition plainly and distinctly do not constitute a non-bailable crime, merely because in the petition they are put under a *nomen juris* which belongs to that class. That is distinctly stated in the case of Joseph Dawson Wormald, High Court, December 3, 1875, Couper, vol. iii., p. 191, to which I refer now, as I have no doubt it will be mentioned by my learned friend, as a case in which it was held that the question, whether the charge was breach of trust or theft, should not be decided on an application for bail. That was the case of a law-agent who had received instructions from his client to invest in heritable security certain sums which were at the time deposited in two banks in Edinburgh. Before the security was obtained he uplifted the funds, and appropriated them to his own uses and purposes. He applied for bail, on the ground that it was a case of breach of trust, and not a case of theft; but your Lordships held that he was not entitled to bail, on the ground that, looking to the facts set forth in the petition on which he was committed, it might turn out at the trial to be a case of theft.

Lord YOUNG—They thought they might support a charge of theft.

Mr ASHER—And that expectation was fully realised in the future progress of the case. When the accused was brought to trial, he objected to the relevancy of the indictment in so far as he was charged with theft, and the relevancy was sustained upon the ground that the money was said to have come into the possession of Wormald without the authority of the person to whom it belonged, he having, without authority, and contrary to his duty, uplifted it before he got a heritable security, and in so uplifting it having stolen it. I ask your Lordships to observe the marked distinction between that case and the present. In the case of Wormald the thing stolen was the money so viciously acquired; here the thing said to have been stolen is a bill admittedly endorsed and delivered to the Bank for collection. I submit it is not within the range of possibility that at the trial of this case facts can possibly come out which will establish that there was vice in the acquisition by the Bank of the bills in question, at all analogous to the vice which existed in the acquisition of the money in Wormald's case? It would be contrary to the whole case set out in the petition that such a result should happen. That case is simply this, that the bills were endorsed and delivered to the Bank for collection. They were therefore in the lawful possession of the Bank, with no obligation to return them *in forma specifica;* on the contrary, with a duty to negotiate them,—to convert them into cash, and account for the proceeds. It is impossible that a case of that nature ever could at the trial turn out to be theft.

Lord CRAIGHILL—What is the distinction between that and the case of the watchmaker?

Mr ASHER—The watchmaker has merely the custody of the watch for a temporary purpose, and is bound to return it *in forma specifica* to the owner.

The LORD JUSTICE-CLERK—Are there any cases of this nature where bail has been granted?

Mr ASHER—I am unable to refer your Lordship to any case. But my explanation of that is, that I do not find in the books any case where the name of theft was put upon *species facti* in the least like those of the present case. I do find in cases, where bail is applied for, this doctrine constantly enunciated —that the Court will look at a complaint for the purpose of seeing that there is not introduced into it a *nomen juris* to which the *species facti* do not properly belong, for the purpose of excluding a right to bail otherwise belonging to the accused. Baron Hume, vol. ii., pp. 90-92, mentions several cases in which the Court have exercised its equitable power of admitting to bail where there was a capital charge.

The LORD JUSTICE-GENERAL—These were cases, I think, in which the prosecution was at the instance of the private party. Nothing is said about the Lord Advocate.

Mr ASHER—That appears to have been so. But in the case of Wormald, which, of course, was a prosecution at the instance of the Lord Advocate, it was stated by the Lord Justice-Clerk, and concurred in by the other learned Judges, that "if the charge of theft had been inserted in the petition in order "to prevent the offence from being bailable, without any reasonable ground in "the facts stated, we might interfere." My contention is that in the present case the *species facti* in the complaint have been misnamed,—that they do not afford any reasonable ground for a charge of theft, and therefore that my client is entitled to bail. I have further to ask attention to the Act 52 Geo. III., chap. 63, which is an Act passed to prevent bankers embezzling securities or documents which are placed in their custody. I refer to that Act for the purpose of showing that the legislature, when dealing with a crime of that nature, and making statutory provision for its punishment at a time long subsequent to the Act 1701, attached to it a sentence which in law makes it a bailable offence. This statute refers to Scotland, and the second section of it deals with a case resembling, but much more aggravated, than that charged in this complaint. It provides as follows:—"And whereas it is usual for persons having dealings with "bankers, merchants, brokers, attornies and other agents, to deposit or place "in the hands of such bankers, &c., sums of money, bills, notes, drafts, "cheques, or orders, for the payment of money with directions or orders to "invest," &c., "in the purchase of stocks or funds, or in or upon Government "or other securities for money, or to apply and dispose thereof in other "ways or for other purposes, and it is expedient to prevent embezzlement "and malversation in such cases: Be it therefore enacted," "that if any "such banker, merchant, or agent," &c., "in whose hands any sum or sums "of money, bill, note, &c., shall be placed for such investment, shall in "any manner apply to his own use or benefit any such sums of money in "violation of good faith, and contrary to *the special* purposes specified in the "direction or order in writing of the depositor, with intent to defraud the "owner or owners of any such sum or sums of money or orders, shall be "guilty of a misdemeanour, and being convicted thereof, according to law, "shall suffer such punishment as is hereinbefore mentioned." And the punishment provided is that "every person who shall commit in Scotland any "offence against this Act shall be liable to be punished by fine or imprison-"ment, or by either, or both, or by transportation for any term not exceed-"ing fourteen years." Now, the legislature in that statute makes the act of a banker, entrusted with negotiable documents, fraudulently appropriating them to his own uses and purposes, a statutory crime, and attaches to it a sentence which makes it a bailable offence. The charge in the present case is not under the statute but at common law. Indeed, the facts in the complaint would not have warranted the statutory charge. The statute deals with the case of a banker who, being entrusted with a negotiable document, defrauds the party from whom he got it, and defrauds him for the purpose of taking the benefit to himself. Whereas it is not said in the present case either that the banker by endorsing the bill prematurely, or sending it to London, benefited himself or the institution of which he was the servant to the extent of one single shilling, or defrauded the person from whom he got the bill to the extent of a single shilling either. I contend, therefore, that the more aggravated statutory crime being bailable by law, it would be a denial of justice to treat the charge in this complaint as constituting a crime not bailable by law. These are the remarks I have to make in support of the petition, in so far as vested on the legal right of the accused to bail.

But I put the case secondly and alternatively on this ground, that possessing, as your Lordships undoubtedly do, an equitable power to grant bail, when it cannot be demanded as matter of right, this is a case, looking to the circumstances, in which that equitable power should be exercised. The first ground on which I make that application is that, if I have failed in satisfying your Lordships that this is a case in which the offence charged is bailable, I should hope I have at least established that it is very doubtful whether, on such *species facti* as are here stated, there really can be a well-founded charge of theft; and if that is so, I submit, that in regard to such a matter, as withholding from a man his statutory right to bail, he should have the benefit of that doubt, and get his liberation until the time of his trial. My Lords, I have a further ground to state, and it is this: that upon the *species facti* of this petition there are no less than five or six persons detained in jail upon a charge of theft, which could only have been the act of one man. The theft is said to have been committed by endorsing and transmitting the bills to the London Joint Stock Bank. It is scarcely conceivable that that should have been the act of all the directors.

It was the ordinary mode of passing to the London banker the title to the bills which had to be collected in London, and would presumably be done by an official of the Bank in discharge of his ordinary duty.

Lord YOUNG—Probably none of the directors were there, as the *locus* where the theft is said to have been committed was an obscure banking office.

Mr ASHER—It is out of the question to suppose that a body of directors who met at stated periods could see to the endorsing of every bill that might be sent to London for collection. Has the Crown any evidence which *prima facie* connects the directors with the act? I ask your Lordships to require information as to that subject, for the purpose of seeing if there is anything of the kind against my client.

Lord YOUNG—Is there any instance of this Court having interfered with the decision of the public prosecutor?

Mr ASHER—I am not aware of any case in which it has been done. But the power of the Court has, I think, never been doubted. It was expressly recognised in the case of William Hamilton Thomson, High Court, 10th July 1871, Couper, vol. ii., p. 103. I have only further to point out, in support of my appeal to the equitable power of the Court, the great importance to the accused of being at liberty for the purpose of assisting in the preparation of his defence for the trial. The case will necessarily involve much complicated detail; and the importance to the accused of having free access to those acting for him is too clear to require to be stated. The age also of the accused, viz., seventy-two, and his social position, are elements not to be overlooked. On the whole matter, I submit that the accused is entitled to bail as matter of right; but if your Lordships should be of a different opinion, then, I submit, the circumstances of the case are such as to call for the exercise by the Court of its equitable power to allow liberation, on bail being found to such an amount as your Lordships may think proper.

The LORD ADVOCATE—I have hitherto considered this as a non-bailable offence; but even if I had entertained the opposite view, I would have refused the offers of bail that have been made, simply because I did not think that their acceptance would have enabled me to rely upon the attendance of the accused on the day of trial. It is very obvious that matters of this kind depend upon considerations,—nay, upon suspicions or surmises,—which it would be highly inexpedient, and certainly improper, to state in open court. There are two points raised on behalf of the prisoners. The first is that the crime or offence described in the complaint before the Court does not amount to theft; and the second is that, assuming that it does, the circumstances of the case are such that the Court ought to use their discretion and liberate the accused on bail. As regards the first point, the Court will not, I apprehend, deal with the question at this stage, as one purely of relevancy, but will view the crime charged as one purely falling within the category to which the public prosecutor has assigned it, unless the contrary plainly appears on the face of the complaint. And I would first call attention to what is alleged in the complaint against the accused, and then advert to the authorities cited in favour of the contention that the charge made is not one of theft. The allegation in the complaint is to the effect that, the accused being directors of the Bank, and, as such, well aware of its insolvency and inability to meet its debts and obligations; and having delivered to them the bills specified in the schedule by the persons or firms named as depositors, that they the accused, in that knowledge, received the bills for the special and sole purpose of collecting payment of the same when due, on behalf of these depositors, none of whom at the time were indebted to the Bank. That nevertheless, although not entitled to use the bills for any other purpose, they, in pursuance of a conspiracy to continue the business of the Bank and make it appear solvent, and for their own pecuniary ends, did endorse the bills to a

London Bank before they became due, in order that the proceeds might be credited to the City of Glasgow Bank, and so stole the said bills. That is a charge, not of the theft of money, but of the theft of the *corpora* of the bills. The sole purpose for which the accused were entitled to use the bills, was to hold them for the depositors until they had matured, and then to present them to the acceptors by whom they fell to be paid. The Bank's title to the bills plainly implied that they were to remain with the Bank up to the date of maturity, when, if they were paid, the proceeds should either have been paid to the owners of the bills, or credited to their accounts with the Bank; and if they were not paid, the bills themselves should have been delivered back o the owners. No doubt, in the ordinary course of dealing between the Bank and its customer, the money received from the acceptor would be put to he credit of the customer's account with the Bank. But my allegation is that the Bank had no right to deal with the bills otherwise than by collecting their amounts. They were not entitled to negotiate the bills, and thereby rear up an entirely new set of obligations; because the moment a bill is endorsed by the Bank, either to a banking company or to an individual, the result is that the depositor, who wants nothing more than that the money shall be collected from the acceptor, and who gives it for that purpose, becomes personally liable. The bill when negotiated (being endorsed by the Bank) becomes a ground of personal liability against the depositor as an endorser. The purpose for which the bills were deposited with the Bank was for collection, and that they might not go—according to commercial phrase—into the circle. The question raised here is not whether, if the mandate given to the Bank had been followed out, and the money received by the Bank, that money was the property of the customer of the Bank, and whether it was stolen; because it is quite clear in criminal law that you may have the theft of a document or obligation upon paper given for the purpose of collection, even although the result of following out instead of acting in breach of the mandate to collect would be to make the collector accountable, and only accountable, for the money. What is here complained of is the appropriation of the *ipsissima corpora* of the documents of these depositors, and in breach of the contract under which they were delivered to the Bank, and the appropriation of the same by the Bank. And, I contend, that is an act of theft, and theft only. The cases of Climie and Brown, in ii. Swinton, which have been cited, merely illustrate certain well-known principles of the criminal law, and do not exhaust the whole principles of the law on the point. The case of Climie was that of an alleged theft of money—there being no allegation by the public prosecutor, and nothing on the face of the libel to show that the money was to be paid back *in forma specifica;* and that was held not to constitute a good charge of theft, because, according to the contract and agreement between the parties, the accused might have put the money received into his own pocket, and paid the accounts (which he had been directed to pay) with his own money. And I need not refer to the case of Brown, as it has been cited for years in this Court in every case of the kind. But the principle of these cases was carried a good deal further, in the direction I am contending for, by the case of Robert Michie, High Court, January 28, 1839. Swinton, vol. ii., page 319. The second alternative charge in that case was in these terms:—"The said James Laurie having, time and place "above libelled, delivered to the said Robert Michie a bank or banker's "note for £20 sterling, in order that he might get the same changed, "and return with and deliver the change thereof to the said James "Laurie, the said Robert Michie did then and there, or at some other "time and place to the prosecutor unknown, wickedly and feloniously steal "and theftuously away take the said bank or banker's note for £20 ster-"ling, the property or in the lawful possession of the said James Laurie." Thus the mandate given to Michie, the accused, along with the note, and the contract upon which he got it, being that he should get it changed and return with the twenty pounds in cash, it was contended that his appropriation of the note could not amount to theft, because he had the authority of Laurie to change it, and that made him simply liable to account for the twenty pounds, the proceeds of the note. But the bench, of three judges, were clearly of opinion that the libel was relevant; and when the case went to trial, the only defence made was an attempt to prove that Michie had changed the note, and, in point of fact, had stolen the change. Lord Cockburn said: "I was of opinion even in the case of Climie that the charge amounted "to theft, and I am decidedly of the same opinion here. If the panel had "received from his master money to use for the general purposes of the shop, "and had been told, whenever he required change to get it, and if he had in "these circumstances changed some of the money and appropriated it, his "crime would have been breach of trust. The case would even have been "different if he had got the £20 note changed, and then kept the change. "But as the charge of theft is laid, I can have no doubt as to its relevancy." That case goes this length, that the theft of a note given for the special purpose of getting change and returning the change, is a relevant charge of theft, even although the theft of the change might not have amounted to that crime.

Lord YOUNG—A note is currency, which a bill is not.

The LORD ADVOCATE—I submit that that fact makes the present an *a fortiori* case. A note passes from hand to hand, and no fresh obligation can thereby be raised against the original owner of it; but in the case of a bill, the result is not merely that the owner loses its amount, but when endorsed it becomes converted from a document constituting a debt payable to him into a document of obligation by him, which the holder can enforce. There is also the case of John Mooney, High Court, November 17, 1851, J. Shaw, page 496. In that case the accused, of whom certain articles had been purchased, received from the purchaser a £1 note, that he might retain the price and return the balance. He appropriated the whole sum, and it was held that it was a theft of the £1 note, and not of the balance. The charge in the libel was that he took the note and appropriated it to his own use without changing it for the purpose of accounting for the balance. In the present case we have, in like manner, the felonious and theftuous appropriation of the bills to the purposes of the Bank before the stage of accounting was reached, and in this respect the case of Mooney is more analagous to the present than that of Brown.

Lord YOUNG—I presume that what you say is, that the directors stole the bills while the owners thereof were still entitled to demand them back *in forma specifica*.

The LORD ADVOCATE—My contention is that the bills were deposited with the Bank for collection, and collection merely. For the sole purpose of the Bank collecting payment of the proceeds of the same when due, from the debtors. That was a mandate which might be recalled at any time. The bills themselves might have been redemanded *in forma specifica* before the date of payment; and if their amounts were not paid by the acceptors, the duty of the Bank was to redeliver the bills to the owner. But what the accused did was, while the Bank was insolvent, they endorsed the bills to their London agents, that the proceeds might be credited to the City Bank in account between the latter and the London Joint Stock Bank.

The LORD JUSTICE-CLERK—You say that the endorsing of the bills to the London Bank was a breach of contract. If they sent them to that Bank for collection, would not that be the ordinary course followed?

The LORD ADVOCATE—This is not a case of sending the bills to the London Bank for collection. What is averred is that instead of retaining them in their hands for the purpose of collection, they paid them into their account with the London Bank. If the bills had been sent to London for collection, the London Bank would have been directly liable to the creditors in the bills, and they would have accepted the mandate given to the City Bank, and would not have put the proceeds to the credit of the account between them and the City Bank.

The LORD JUSTICE-CLERK—Take the case of a person who had an account with the City Bank, sending to the Bank a bill for collection; would the Bank, on receiving the bill, not at once place the amount to his credit?

The LORD ADVOCATE—Not till collected. The Bank might never get the money. If the Bank was discounting a bill for the customer it would be different. The amount of the bill would be at once placed to the credit of the customer's account, less the amount of the discount, and the bill would become the property of the Bank. But the depositor of a bill for collection does not contemplate that he is to pay money on that bill. He is to get money for it. I do not say that the bills should not have been collected through London, but that the City Bank ought not to have endorsed the bills to the Joint Stock Bank, in breach of their contract of collection, as a payment into that Bank on their, the City Bank's, own behoof.

The LORD JUSTICE-CLERK—Do you say that the putting the amounts of the bills to the credit of the City of Glasgow Bank necessarily implies appropriation?

The LORD ADVOCATE—It implies that the bills became the property of the London Bank,—held by them in satisfaction of any debt or bills due by the City of Glasgow Bank, and with a direct claim of personal liability for the amounts of the bills against the persons who endorsed them for collection merely. It makes these persons debtors upon their own bills to the holders of them. They become liable as endorsers, and are converted against their will into debtors upon their own bills for their full amounts. And I maintain that that is complete appropriation by the Bank of the *corpora* of the bills to their own purposes. The question is not one of accounting, but a question of what the Bank has done with the price of the movable property which the bills represented. In the case of Wormald, the documents were deposit-receipts; in this, they are bills lodged with the Bank for collection; and the accused had no more right to use these bills in payment or satisfaction of their liabilities to the London Bank than the watchmaker Brown had to take the watch that was given him to repair. The Bank were mandatories to cash the bills in a particular way, get the money from the acceptors, if they had it to give, and if they had not the money, to negotiate them against them, or await the commands of their customers, the owners.

Lord YOUNG—We are dealing with a familiar banking transaction of daily occurrence, viz., of the customers sending their bills to the bankers for collection. When a customer sends bills to his banker for collection they are really a bond of credit in his favour. I do not mean formally or necessarily, but practically they are so—practically it is the case that the depositor is at once credited with the amount. In other words, according to the value the banker puts on these bills he will allow the customer to draw in the meantime. Well, these bills being in the possession of the banker upon that lawful and familiar contract, the question is, can he steal them. The exigency no doubt of the contract is, that when he collects them he shall put their amounts to the customer's credit. But is a transaction of that kind consistent with a document or documents being stolen by the bank into whose hands they may have been placed. Grievous injury may no doubt be done to the customer. It may be a breach of confidence; but can it be said to be theft?

The LORD ADVOCATE—I do not consider that these bills were in the City Bank on that footing, and that the customers who deposited them would be immediately credited with their amounts. What I aver is that none of these customers were indebted or under any obligation to the Bank, and they were lodged therefore, not as a fund of credit, but simply in order that the money might be got for them. If it could be said that the Bank had any lien over them, I should still maintain that the Bank had no power to use them in the way I allege they did. But that is not the present case. You have here a thing given on a certain footing, and in entire disregard of that, you have a complete appropriation by the Bank.

The only remaining question is as to whether the Court ought, in the circumstances, to admit the accused to the privilege of bail. I do not in the least dispute that the Court has such a discretionary power, and I do not suppose that any public prosecutor would ever think of interposing himself between the discretion of the Court and the accused, if the Court felt disposed to exercise it; but, my Lords, I am bound to say, upon the authorities reported, that I can find nothing to justify bail on the arguments stated for the accused. It is said by Mr Asher that he has failed to find any such rule as to refusal of bail applied to such *species facti*. My answer to that is, that I have also looked through the books, and have failed to find any such *species facti* out of which any such rule could have arisen. And with regard to the Act of Geo. III. cited, I say that you cannot under it in the least derogate from the common law, as is shewn in many instances, such as the Post Office Acts, and others; and I do not suppose that when the legislature passed this Act, they thought it necessary to displace the common law of Scotland. In the case of John Wilson, High Court, October 1875, Couper, vol. iii., p. 169, Lord Ardmillan laid down the law upon an application to be admitted to bail thus:—"I do not think this application "incompetent. I do not say that the Court could not, in the exercise of their "discretion, authorise the liberation on bail in this case, if they thought that "the circumstances of the case really required it. But, while I think there is "nothing to preclude the Court from granting the prayer of this petition, were "they satisfied that it was right to do so, still, I must keep in view that a "large discretion rests on the Lord Advocate, and that the Court trusts him, "and has every confidence that he exercises that discretion well." I think it due to the office which I hold to say that much. With reference to the suggestion that the Court should require something like proof from the public prosecutor. That has evidently been founded upon a dictum to be found in Hume; but it has never been required in the case of a public prosecutor. The dictum referred to was intended to apply, and applies only to the case of a private prosecutor. I have only to say that, if your Lordships should come to think such a proof necessary, the Court will have to undertake a very large and serious enquiry. I shall not shrink from giving your Lordships, in that enquiry, all the assistance in my power, but I must enter my protest against such a course being followed in a case like the present.

Mr BALFOUR, for Lewis Potter, Robert Salmond, William Taylor, and Charles Samuel Leresche—I will deal shortly with the two grounds upon which this application is rested—viz., first, that the offence set out in the complaint is not an offence in respect of which the Crown can refuse bail,—that there is no relevant charge of theft so as to make an unbailable offence; and the second point, that even if the offence set out be an unbailable offence, we are entitled to make an appeal to the discretion of the Court for liberation on bail, as we now do. Of course, as regards the second point, the Court would require to be satisfied, through its clerk or otherwise, that the bail was sufficient to ensure the attendance of the accused; but that is a matter on which we are perfectly ready to satisfy your Lordships in any way that may be thought right. The first point depends upon whether the complaint clearly sets out a charge of theft. or, to give the Crown the benefit of the argument, whether it sets out that which, with any reasonable modification, could be converted in any indictment into a charge of theft. We maintain that it does not, and that although the facts may constitute a crime, that crime is breach of trust and embezzlement, and not theft. The distinguishing boundary between these two crimes is, whether the subject that is said to have been stolen has been entrusted to the person who is said to have stolen it, so as to give him the possession, as distinguished from the custody of it. I do not dispute that wherever a person who has received an article from another holds it on what merely amounts to custody as distinguished from possession, he may be guilty of the crime of theft if he appropriates the article to his own use. On the other hand, if the facts bearing on the delivery of the article to the person who holds it be such that his obligation is not to deliver it in *forma specifica*, but only to account for money or the like, that takes you into another category altogether. It may be the crime of breach of trust and embezzlement. In the cases referred to by the Lord Advocate you have the element of custody merely, and you have the allegation made in the indictment that the thing which is said to be stolen was in the possession of the true owner of it. In the case of the boy sent to get the change of the £20 note, it was distinctly stated that the bank-note was the property or in the lawful possession of Laurie, the sender; and it stands to reason and common sense that a boy simply sent to change a £20 note, does not become the possessor of it in the sense in which a factor or agent, or any such person, is the possessor. He merely gets it to do a particular thing with it, and instantly to go back with the change. I take it that this is true of all articles in the possession of servants. They are simply holders of the articles for their masters. In the case of Mooney, referred to by the Lord Advocate, the same thing occurred. There the thing stolen was said to be the property or in the lawful possession of the owner. I ask your Lordships to apply this principle to the present case, because in it the Crown have carefully and intelligibly abstained from saying that these bills were in the lawful possession of their owners. They have omitted from the complaint the usual words, "or in the lawful posses- "sion of the owners." They only say they were the property of the said several persons and firms and companies mentioned in the schedule. They could not predicate with any propriety that the bills were in the possession of the owners; because the bills had been placed in the hands of the Bank under a contract which made the Bank the possessors of the bills, and undoubtedly liable to execute the mandate or commission in respect of the bills, and to deliver the proceeds to the owners.

Lord YOUNG—If a merchant hands a bill of exchange to his banker for collection, does he thereby cease to be the holder of the bill?

Mr BALFOUR—I do not maintain that in all circumstances the depositors might not have asked their bills back; but how completely defective this complaint is in supporting the contention of the Lord Advocate is shown by the fact that there is nothing said in it about anyone having asked his bills back, nor is it alleged that it was a breach of duty to send the bills to London too soon. I take it to be a matter of common knowledge with respect to banking transactions, and which may be appealed to fairly, that when you have bills which are not to be collected in the city or place where the bank carries on its business, it falls within the mandate of that bank to transmit the bills to the place where they are to be collected. And so I take it that these bills, being all, with the exception of two only, London bills, would, in the ordinary course of business, be sent to London to be collected there by the London correspondent of the City of Glasgow Bank, as the Bank's subordinate agent.

The LORD JUSTICE-CLERK—Did the City of Glasgow Bank not discount the bills?

Mr BALFOUR—No, that is not stated. It is merely said that, having transmitted them to the London Bank, the City Bank got credit to account for the amount of the bills. The bills might have been transmitted in the ordinary course of business. Nothing is said as to the time that had to elapse before the bills became due. All that the Crown alleges is, that the City Bank did endorse and make over the said several bills of exchange before they had become due to the London Joint Stock Bank, for the purpose which the Lord Advocate has stated. Take the case that the bills had been due two days hence. For anything that appears, these bills may have been sent up to the London Bank within such short time before they became due, and that it was in perfect order to send them up. I could understand that it would be a different case if it had been set forth that, at the beginning of the currency of a four month's bill, it was sent out of the Bank. According to ordinary banking usage, that bill should have remained in Glasgow till it was about to mature, so as to be subject to the call of the customer. I am not saying that the facts set forth in the complaint might not be libelled as a crime; but the bills mentioned in it, for anything that appears to the contrary, may have been sent up at the right time—within a day or two of the date at which the mandate which was to enable the London Bank to execute its agency with the City Bank fell to be carried out.

The LORD JUSTICE-CLERK—In the act of collection a bank does not create a new liability against its customer.

Mr BALFOUR—That is no doubt the case because the bank is itself simply an agent.

The LORD JUSTICE-CLERK—What do you say is the effect of the allegation that the "proceeds might be credited to the City of Glasgow Bank in account "between them and the London Joint Stock Bank?". Is that in the ordinary course?

Mr BALFOUR—It is ordinary banking practice to send bills to the place where their amounts are to be ingathered, and to send the money back to the place where the customer is. They do not send it in a bundle or a bag, but by giving credit in account between the Banks. The bills are said to have been carried to the credit of the City Bank, and that might have been done in perfect consistence with this other step—that the City Bank would credit the customer. The London Bank would credit the proceeds to the City Bank, and debit itself with them. That could not be done until the bills were paid, and so it is only the proceeds and not the bills that are credited; but the Lord Advocate defines his charge as being a theft of the bills and not a theft of the proceeds. It would at all events be according to ordinary banking rules, for anything that appears, that these credits should be passed through the different accounts, and not that a bag of money should be sent. There is no allegation that the customer had asked back any one of his bills. I could have conceived this case, that the customer had said, "Give me back my bills; I will collect them myself." But there is no allegation that the customers ever withdrew their mandates, or said that the bills were not to be collected and delivered to the persons who were the debtors under them in respect of receiving the money for them. The bills, although sent to London, were sent with instructions to execute the agency, and the London Bank had the same duty to perform to the customer as the Glasgow Bank had undertaken. Then in regard to the allegation about the proceeds of the bills, I would refer to the case of Margaret Mills, High Court, 10th July, 1865, Irvine, vol. v., p. 196. The charge there was that a bank-note was delivered to the panel for the purpose of being changed; and the indictment was found irrelevant in respect that it was not clearly set forth that the panel had failed to give the change to the owner of the note. And that was a case in which the crime charged was the theft of the note. I quite admit that the charge in a complaint like the present is not to be scanned so critically as an indictment would be; but I take it to be quite clear that the present is so far parallel with that case, that while it was held fatal to that indictment that there was an omission to state that the money had not been got by the owner, there is in the present case no exclusion of the idea that the London Bank may have got the money from the debtors under the bills, and that by passing of credits in account, the customers may have got their money from the City of Glasgow Bank. If the customer did not and could not get his money, that should have been alleged. But the charge in the complaint breaks off in the middle, and simply says that the proceeds were directed to be credited to the City Bank, and there it stops.

The LORD JUSTICE-CLERK—We are not here considering the relevancy of an indictment, but are proceeding upon a complaint presented with a view to commitment in order to trial. It appears to me that the real question is whether the *species facti* disclosed admit of a charge of theft being stated.

Mr BALFOUR—On that question I have to submit that the Lord Advocate's contention that the theft which he has charged is a theft of the *ipsissima corpora* of the bills precludes him from saying that the *species facti* can be so stated; because the whole sting of the misappropriation charged is not of the bills, but of what was to be got in respect of the bills. It is charged that "they did endorse and make over the said several bills of exchange before "they had become due to the London Joint Stock Bank, London, in order "that the proceeds thereof might be credited to the City of Glasgow Bank," &c. The bills, so far as what is stated in the complaint is concerned, were to be used for the purpose which was intended when they were lodged with the Bank—viz., to collect the money—and the allegation is that the London Bank would keep them, and would not get the proceeds until they matured. What is said in the complaint is not that the amount of the bills was to be placed in the City Bank account instantly, but "that the proceeds thereof might be "credited to the City of Glasgow Bank," &c. That just means this,—that when the London Bank has executed its office of collector of the proceeds of the bills, then the instructions of the City Bank are that it is to treat these proceeds in a particular way. But that is a crime which has relation to the proceeds of the bills, and not to the bills themselves. And down to the time of the collection of the bills they might have been in the hands of the London Bank to do the very thing with them which the customers desired—viz., to collect their amounts. Therefore I say that the Lord Advocate's argument regarding the theft of the bills is not well-founded. The charge assumes that the London Bank was directed to use the bills—the bills as distinguished from the proceeds—that it was to treat them in the way the customer intended; and that the customers were to get the money. It is only after the money is got that there is anything to be done which which was contrary to the directions of the customer. I have to submit, therefore, that without drawing any fine distinctions, but taking the case in its substance, this is not a well-laid charge, and that there is no reasonable prospect that Crown counsel could turn it into anything that would affect its substance, and make it a good charge of theft.

The only other matter is as to the discretion of the Court. I shall say very little on that. I quite admit that in a matter of this kind the law officers of the Crown have a large discretion; and, moreover, we do not seek to do, what would not be proper, to call upon the law officers of the Crown to state impressions, which may or may not be of a very delicate nature. But there is one thing I venture to say we should know. I think it is only reasonable that we should know this—Is there to be bail or no bail taken for these men, and if so how much? That is to say, we are entitled to have some idea whether the objection is to the insufficiency of the bail that has been offered, or what. Most of the accused can go to almost any amount—at least to a very large amount indeed. This is a matter which of course rests with the Court. I make no complaint. But I do submit that when we are here appealing to your Lordships' discretion, and are able to offer such bail as to make it reasonably certain that the accused will appear, we are doing all that we can be called on to do in the circumstances. It is necessary that the accused should get out of prison in order to prepare for their defence. The charge is not one which is like a simple case of theft. The accused must have an opportunity granted to them of having access to the books of the Bank, and many explanations will require to be made by them to their law advisers. Even, therefore, if it should be held to be not clear that this is a bailable offence, I contend that its doubtful character affords us strong ground for appealing to the discretion of the Court, because if it should turn out that the Crown cannot frame a relevant indictment, charging the mode on which the Bank dealt with the bills as a theft, or prove that charge if relevantly framed, then great hardship will have been inflicted on the accused, by keeping them in prison when they should have been out. The interests of justice, I submit, will be satisfied, if such bail be exacted and given as shall secure the attendance of these persons to answer to the charge.

The LORD JUSTICE-GENERAL—The Court will pronounce judgment to-morrow morning.

At the calling of the case on November 15th,

The LORD JUSTICE-GENERAL asked—Is the Court to understand that the arguments we have had submitted to us on the previous day apply to all the petitioners?

Mr BALFOUR—That is the understanding. They are all in the same position, with some minor differences, such as duration of office, and that two of the petitioners were officials of the Bank; but subject to this explanation, and to the further explanation, that the bail which has been offered is larger in some cases than in others, the same argument applies to all.

The LORD JUSTICE-GENERAL then addressing the Court said—The petitioners have been committed for trial by warrant of the Sheriff of Lanarkshire, granted on a petition by the Procurator-Fiscal, charging the petitioners with the theft of certain valuable securities, being bills of exchange for the aggregate amount of £23,693, 11s. 7d. No such warrant is ever granted by a Sheriff without full and deliberate consideration of the declarations of the prisoners, and of the precognitions of the witnesses examined for the prosecution. The Procurator-Fiscal did not content himself with stating the charge in the general terms which I have just used, which would be quite sufficient, and according to practice in ordinary cases of theft; but most properly, in so serious and important a case, set out the *species facti*, which he contends amount to an act of theft, committed by all the petitioners in pursuance of a wicked conspiracy. The offence thus charged, if it amount to theft, is, on the admission of the counsel for the petitioners, not bailable. But it is open to the petitioners still to demand that they shall be admitted to bail as a matter of right, if they can show clearly that the *species facti* alleged against them can in no view amount to the crime of theft charged. But we are not under such an application to deal with the question as if we were judging of the relevancy of an indictment. Unless the petitioners can satisfy the Court that the facts stated, even when cast into the more precise and detailed form of the minor proposition of an indictment, will be clearly and undoubtedly insufficient to sustain a charge of theft, they cannot demand liberation. I am not satisfied of this. It is in my opinion far from being clear. This being so, it seems to me that it would be quite improper to go further for the present, or to state or indicate any impression I might possibly entertain, as an individual judge, as to the future course or prospect of the prosecution; for that would be to prejudge to some extent questions which may hereafter arise as to the relevancy of indictments or criminal letters which may be served on the petitioners. Such a course would not be fair either to the prosecutor or to the accused. The petitioners further appeal to the discretion of the Court to liberate them on such bail as may be sufficient to ensure their appearance hereafter to answer the charges made against them. That we possess such discretionary power cannot be disputed. But in prosecutions conducted by the public prosecutor the discretion is vested, in the first instance at least, in the Lord Advocate; and unless it can be alleged that the Lord Advocate has refused bail, not for the purpose of securing the ends of justice, but for some other and therefore illegitimate purpose, I think the Court ought not to interfere, because such interference would be nothing less than relieving the Lord Advocate of the responsibility attaching to his high office. He is subject to this responsibility, and vested with the corresponding discretion, because he has means and appliances for obtaining information and forming a judgment which are not within the reach of any other official, and are not possessed by this Court. But it has not been suggested that the Lord Advocate is not discharging his important and responsible duties with fairness and impartiality, and with a sole view to the public interest, and to secure the ends of justice. For the Court to interfere in such circumstances with his discretion would be inconsistent with the whole previous practice of the Court, and in the last degree inexpedient.

The LORD JUSTICE-CLERK—I concur entirely in the observations your Lordship has made; and coming to that resolution, it seems to me that it is desirable that we should not enter at all into the questions that have been so ably argued. As I come to the same resolution as that indicated in your Lordship's observations, I have nothing to add.

Lord DEAS—I need hardly say that in common with all your Lordships I have very earnestly and seriously considered the question which is now before us. I not only agree in the result arrived at by your Lordship, but I concur in every sentence of the clear and distinct opinion which has now been delivered; and that being so, it would be worse than superfluous for me to add another word.

Lord YOUNG—The law of bail in Scotland stands on an enactment of the Act 1701 in these words—"That all crimes not inferring capital punishment "shall be bailable." The petitioners contend that the crime for which they stand committed does not infer capital punishment, and so demand, as matter of right, that they shall be admitted to bail; and the demand is clearly irresistible, if the contention on which it rests is sound. The question for us, then, is whether the crime for which the petitioners are in prison infers capital punishment or not, and we must judge of it on the facts as they are stated in the warrant of commitment, or, as it happens in this case, in the petition of the Procurator-Fiscal, to which the warrant refers. These facts are, that certain current bills of exchange having been deposited in the City of Glasgow Bank by customers for collection when due, the petitioners, being directors of the Bank, used them, while still current, for the Bank's purposes, by endorsing them to the London Joint Stock Bank, in order that the proceeds might be placed to the credit of the City of Glasgow Bank, in breach of the confidence in which they had been deposited with and received by that bank. These are the facts, however they may be characterised, or whatever crime they may import. That the conduct of the petitioners, assuming the truth of the statement, was in violation of good faith, and contrary to the directions which accompanied the deposit of the bills, and which they undertook to obey, is clear; and that it amounts to an indictable offence may be assumed. But the proposition which we have now to consider is, that the alleged conduct amounts to a capital offence—or, to use the language of the Act 1701, to a crime "inferring capital punishment." This proposition would be very shocking if it were taken to mean what it expresses; but even taking it as unreal, except in so far as it may signify that an old barbarity of the criminal law had not been repealed by statute, but had disappeared under the influence of advancing civilisation, I cannot assent to it. For I am of opinion, first, that at no period of our history did such facts as are here alleged import a capital crime; and second, that they assuredly do not now. Down to the date of Mr Hume's work, and probably for some short time thereafter, theft, if attended with any aggravating circumstance—and the great value of the thing stolen might be one—was by the custom of Scotland punishable with death, if the Judge in his discretion saw fit. That it was customary law only, and subject in its application to the discretion of the Judge, Mr Hume announces emphatically and repeatedly. He introduces the subject with these words—"to come now to the *practice* of Scotland"—and treats of the whole law of punishment in cases of theft as depending on—I quote his expressions—"ancient custom," "equitable discretion," "the course of practice," "custom and practice," "the ordinary course "of justice for such offences." As the conclusion of the whole matter, he leaves, as he doubtless intended, his readers with the impression that the law of punishment for theft was customary, and, to a large extent, discretionary, and that there had been, and was, "a variable course of practice "in which the instances are numerous to the side of mercy," although grave thefts always brought the panel "into hazard of his life." The law on this head is still customary, but the custom has greatly changed, and it is not, and has not for a long while been true, that by the custom of Scotland theft infers capital punishment, or that any theft, however grave, brings the panel "into "hazard of his life." In Hume's time the older custom was on the wane, but had not died out. It is now dead, not to be revived, unless, indeed, we should relapse into barbarism. Theft is not, and, indeed, never was, capital by statute; and although the common law, which Hume refers to by the expressions which I have quoted from his book, such as "custom and practice," "the "ordinary course of justice," &c., once permitted, or, it may be, enjoined the graver sorts of it to be punished with death, these, viz., custom, practice, and the ordinary course of justice, and with them the common law, which rests on them, and is, indeed, another expression for them, are, and have for a long while, been changed. I am therefore of opinion that theft is a crime not "inferring capital punishment." But, further, I am of opinion that the facts alleged against these petitioners do not amount to the crime of theft. I quite understand the argument employed to bring them within that category, and, understanding it, reject it as too subtle. To constitute theft there must be a felonious taking of property out of the owner's possession, and the bills here in question were, I think, clearly not so taken. Mr Hume touches the case in hand very clearly when he says (vol. i. p. 58):—"Put the case even that "the owner does deliver the thing, but on some lower title than that of pro- "perty, as in the case of a watch given in loan, or a horse let to hire, or a "pack of goods sent by a carrier to be delivered at a certain place; still the "after conversion of this thing to the possessor's own use, by selling the "watch or horse, or opening the pack and taking the contents, though it is a "wrong, and even a criminal act, does not however amount to the crime of "theft. The reason is obvious, that there has been no felonious taking out "of the owner's possession. The man, in all these instances, had at first "obtained the thing honestly, by a fair contract, in the ordinary course of "business, and meaning, as at that time, to restore or deliver it in terms of "his agreement. At the instant, therefore, of the delivery made him in "pursuance of that contract, the owner's possession ceased. The receiver "was thenceforward in the lawful possession; and when he converts the "thing to his own use, in pursuance of a purpose which is only taken "up afterwards, and is probably suggested by his command of the thing, "he only breaks his contract, and abuses his powers as possessor." It is true that since Hume's time, and since we have ceased to punish theft with death, we have by a rather refined process of reasoning on the distinction between custody and constructive possession, brought within the category of theft cases which he and our older lawyers, who regarded it as a capital crime, excluded. Nevertheless, the Lord Advocate was unable to adduce any decided case more available for his argument than that of a man appropriating and running off with a sovereign or bank note which he had got to change. I will not now enter on an examination of the decisions, but content myself with saying that I think they are all inapplicable to the facts here presented to us. Nor do I think it immaterial to observe that in an archaic inquiry regarding acts, which by the custom of our ancestors were punishable capitally as theft, we are not at liberty to extend their definitions, or to make them more comprehensive by nice arguments which were not used, or at least found no favour, until a change in our customs had rendered it immaterial in the matter of punishment whether a dishonest act was called by one name or another. I notice as also material, in my opinion, that misappropriations, exactly such as we are now dealing with, by bankers of securities entrusted to them, are provided for by statute here as in England in a manner which shows that the legislature did not regard them as thefts, and most assuredly not as "crimes inferring capital punishment." I have cited the enactment of the

Act 1701, which embodies the whole law of bail. The expediency of it may be questionable, but it is certainly clear; and I cannot approve of any attempt to control or modify its operation by a fanciful and altogether unreal extension of capital crimes according to customs which have long ceased to be observed, and which no one would for a moment think of attempting to revive. "That "all crimes not inferring capital punishment shall be bailable" is an injunction addressed to us now, and we are, in my opinion, bound to obey it with reference to the law as it now exits, whether by statute or custom, meaning, of course, existing custom. I am not ignorant of the more recent cases, certainly not numerous, in which this Court held that *furtum grave* was capital, and so not bailable. The most recent is that of Wormald. With reference to them, I venture to point out that it is from the nature of the case impossible to determine the exact time when one custom is completely destroyed and superseded by another and different custom—just as impossible as t is to determine the day, or even year, when a man ceases to be young and becomes old. Such changes do, however, take place, and are quite recognisable when complete, notwithstanding the impossibility of assigning an exact date to them. Now the question to which I have addressed myself, in a matter of purely customary law, is whether now in this year 1878 it can be safely and truly affirmed that the former custom of Scotland, according to which theft was punishable capitally, has been completely superseded by another custom, now as firmly established, and on as good authority, as ever it was, whereby (that is without violating the custom) death may not be inflicted for that crime. This question no former decision can hinder me from answering as I have done in the affirmative. I think it not doubtful, and do not suppose any one does, that to punish any of the petitioners with death for the misappropriation of these bills would violate the custom of Scotland, as it would that of any other civilized country in the world. The result is that, in my opinion, the crime for which the petitioners stand committed is not a crime inferring capital punishment, and that it is, therefore, bailable. I have only to add that I think the law of bail is unsatisfactory and requires amendment, and that if I could have dealt with this application as made to the discretion of the Court, I should have concurred with your Lordships in refusing it.

Lord MURE—I entirely concur in the short, but very clear and sound, exposition which your Lordship in the chair has given of the law, and of the rules by which this Court should be guided, in dealing with the important question now before us; and in the wisdom of the course which your Lordship has adopted of not entering into any minute examination of the question of relevancy at this stage of the proceedings. I have nothing therefore to add, except to say that I concur in opinion with the majority of your Lordships.

Lord CRAIGHILL—I also entirely concur in your Lordship's opinion. I must add, however, that I do not concur in the opinion come to by Lord Young, because that appears, so far as I understand it, to be an opinion not on the question presented to us from the bar, but upon a question which has not been agitated at the bar, or on the bench, in the course of these proceedings. The opinion which he has indicated seems to me to apply an entirely different test from anything which has hitherto been applied by the law of Scotland as to what is or is not a crime inferring capital punishment. What my brother, Lord Young, seems to take as his test is this—whether a capital sentence would in this or any particular case be pronounced and carried into execution. This is not a test by which, I think, any question like that which we are called upon to decide can be determined. The point for consideration here is, not whether if the accused should be found guilty they would be visited with a capital sentence, but whether, in the light of authority, and as the case has been presented to us by the counsel for the accused, the crime is one inferring, according to the rules of the common law, a capital punishment. The course of the argument at the bar ought, I think, for all purposes requiring to be served in the present occasion, be taken to settle this question. The counsel for the accused did not dispute—on the contrary, they admitted—that if the *species facti* set forth in the complaint against them warranted a charge of theft, the crime was *furtum grave*, and consequently was one inferring a capital punishment. The point and the only point which they endeavoured to make was that the *species facti* did not amount to theft, and as to this, as already explained, I concur in the opinion which your Lordship in the chair has delivered. Perhaps I may be permitted to add that the result to which the opinion of Lord Young would lead, if adopted, demonstrates to me in a practical way the unsoundness and danger of that opinion; because, if this case is one in which the accused are entitled to be liberated on bail as a matter of right, such of them as are not landed men must, by the terms of the Act 1701, be liberated upon a bail bond for not more than £300, and those of them who are landed men, on a bond for not more than £600 at the most. No one can seriously say that the ends of justice in a case like the present would be reasonably or sufficiently protected by an obligation for sums so small.

Lord ADAM—I entirely concur with the observations made by your Lordship in the chair, and also with the remarks that have fallen from Lord Craighill.

The following was the Interlocutor pronounced:—

Edinburgh, 15*th November* 1878.—The Lord Justice-General, Lord Justice-Clerk, and Lords Commissioners of Justiciary: Having considered this Petition, and heard counsel for the parties, refuse the Petition.

(Signed) JOHN INGLIS, *I.P.D.*

Agents for Robert Salmond—J. & J. Ross, W.S.; and WRIGHT, JOHNSTONE, & MACKENZIE, Writers, Glasgow.

" Lewis Potter—J. & J. Ross, W.S.; and MACLEAY, MURRAY, & SPENS, Writers, Glasgow.

" William Taylor—R. A. BROWN, L.A.; and J. & J. BOYD, Writers, Glasgow.

" John Innes Wright—RONALD & RITCHIE, S.S.C.; and MACGEORGE, COWAN, and GALLOWAY, Writers, Glasgow.

" Robert Summers Stronach—COWAN & DALMAHOY, W.S.; and BORLAND and KING, Writers, Glasgow.

" Charles Samuel Leresche—A. KIRK MACKIE, S.S.C.

TRIAL OF JOHN STEWART, &c.

First Day—Monday, 20th January 1879.

Present—

THE LORD JUSTICE-CLERK (LORD MONCREIFF).

LORDS MURE AND CRAIGHILL.

HER MAJESTY'S ADVOCATE—The Lord Advocate (Watson), the Solicitor-General (Macdonald), Burnet, A.D., and Pearson;

AGAINST

JOHN STEWART—Trayner and MacLean.
LEWIS POTTER—Balfour and Jameson.
ROBERT SALMOND—Asher and Goudy.
WILLIAM TAYLOR—Mackintosh and Omond.
HENRY INGLIS—J. P. B. Robertson and Maconochie.
JOHN INNES WRIGHT—J. Guthrie Smith and Dickson.
ROBERT SUMMERS STRONACH—The Dean of Faculty (Fraser), and Darling.

THE INDICTMENT.

JOHN STEWART, now or lately residing in Moray Place, Edinburgh, and LEWIS POTTER, ROBERT SALMOND, WILLIAM TAYLOR, HENRY INGLIS, JOHN INNES WRIGHT, and ROBERT SUMMERS STRONACH, all now or lately prisoners in the prison of Glasgow, you are indicted and accused, at the instance of the Right Hon. William Watson, Her Majesty's advocate for Her Majesty's interest: that albeit, by the laws of this and of every other well-governed realm, falsehood, fraud, and wilful imposition; as also the wicked and felonious fabrication and falsification, by directors or officials of a joint-stock banking company, of any balance-sheet, or statement of affairs, for the purpose of concealing and misrepresenting the true state of the company's affairs, with intent to defraud, and wickedly and feloniously using and uttering the same as true, for said purpose, with intent to defraud, and whereby members of the company and of the public are deceived, imposed upon, and defrauded; as also the wickedly and feloniously using and uttering, as true, by the directors or officials of a joint-stock banking company, any fabricated and falsified balance-sheet or statement of affairs, knowing the same to be fabricated and false, for the purpose of concealing and misrepresenting the true state of the company's affairs, with intent to defraud, and whereby members of the company and of the public are deceived, imposed upon, and defrauded; as also theft; as also breach of trust and embezzlement, are crimes of an heinous nature and severely punishable:

Yet true it is and of verity, that you, the said John Stewart, Lewis Potter, Robert Salmond, William Taylor, Henry Inglis, John Innes Wright, and Robert Summers Stronach are, all and each or one or more of you, guilty of the crimes above libelled, or of one or more of them, actors or actor, or art and part,

In so far as you, the said John Stewart, Lewis Potter, Robert Salmond, William Taylor, and Henry Inglis having been, during the years 1876, 1877, and 1878, and during several previous years, directors of a joint-stock banking company, registered under the Companies Acts, 1862 and 1867, and carrying on the business of banking in Glasgow and elsewhere throughout Scotland under the name or firm of the City of Glasgow Bank, with a paid-up capital of £1,000,000 sterling; and you the said John Innes Wright, having been, during the years 1875, 1876, 1877, and 1878, a director of the said Company, and you the said Robert Summers Stronach having been, during the years 1876, 1877, and 1878, manager, and also, *ex officio*, a director of the said Company; and it being your duty, as directors and manager aforesaid respectively, to see that regular books were kept for the business of the Company, in which all its transactions, affairs, and obligations were duly entered; and it being farther your duty to see that every year a true and accurate abstract or statement of the Company's affairs, made up from the Company's books, as balanced on the first Wednesday of June in each year, was prepared and duly examined, and thereafter at each annual general meeting of the members of the Company, held on the first Wednesday of July in each year, reported for the satisfaction of all concerned:

Yet, nevertheless (I.), on one or more days in the month of June 1876, or of May immediately preceding, or of July immediately following, the time or times being more particularly to the prosecutor unknown, in or near the head office of the City of Glasgow Bank in Virginia Street, Glasgow, or elsewhere in or near Glasgow, to the prosecutor unknown, you the said John Stewart, Lewis Potter, Robert Salmond, William Taylor, Henry Inglis, John Innes Wright, and Robert Summers Stronach, did, all and each or one or more of you, wickedly and feloniously, with intent to defraud the members of the said Company and the public, and for the purpose of concealing and misrepresenting the true state of the affairs of the said Company, concoct and fabricate, or cause or procure to be concocted and fabricated, a false and fictitious abstract balance-sheet or statement of affairs, purporting to represent the true condition of the Bank's affairs as at 7th June 1876, in the following or similar terms, videlicet:—

CITY OF GLASGOW BANK.—ABSTRACT BALANCE-SHEET, AS AT 7TH JUNE 1876.

Dr. Liabilities.		
I. Deposits at the head office and branches, and balances at the credit of banking correspondents,		£8,364,056 18 5
II. Bank notes in circulation in Scotland and the Isle of Man,		860,355 0 0
III. Drafts outstanding, due, or with a currency not exceeding 21 days,	£326,853 14 1	
Drafts accepted by the bank and its London agents on account of home and foreign constituents,	988,520 3 0	
		1,315,373 17 1
Liabilities to the public,		£10,589,785 15 6
IV. Capital account,	£1,000,000 0 0	
V. Reserve fund,	450,000 0 0	
VI. Profit and loss,	136,865 10 3	
Liabilities to partners,		1,586,365 10 3
		£12,126,151 5 9

Cr.	**Assets.**		
I.	Bills of exchange, local and country bills, credit accounts, and other advances upon security, ...		£8,787,804 17 9
II.	Advances on heritable property, and value of bank buildings and furniture, ...		256,665 10 7
III.	Cash on hand—viz., gold and silver coin and notes of other banks at head office and branches,	£862,812 4 4	
IV.	Government stocks, Exchequer bills, railway and other stocks and debentures, and balances in hands of banking correspondents,	2,218,868 13 7	
			3,081,680 17 11
			£12,126,151 5 9

which abstract balance-sheet or statement of affairs was false and fictitious, and was known by you to be so, in the following particulars or part thereof, videlicet—(1) The amount of deposits at the head office and branches, and balances at the credit of banking correspondents, under Article I. on the debtor side, was understated to the extent of £1,006,216, 12s. 10d. or thereby; (2) the amount of drafts outstanding, and drafts accepted by the Bank and its London agents, under Article III. on the debtor side, was understated to the extent of £973,300 or thereby; (3) the amount of bills of exchange, local and country bills, credit accounts and other advances under Article I. on the creditor side, was understated to the extent of £2,698,539, 10s. 4d. or thereby; (4) the amount of cash on hand—viz., gold and silver coin and notes of other banks, under Article III. on the creditor side, was overstated to the extent of £29,095 or thereby; (5) the amount of Government stocks, Exchequer bills, railway and other stocks and debentures, and balances in hands of banking correspondents, under Article III. on the creditor side, was overstated to the extent of £753,211, 2s. 6d. or thereby; (6) the earnings of the Bank during the year were overstated, under the head of profit and loss, to the extent of £125,763, 12s. 8d. or thereby; (7) a reserve fund to the extent of £450,000 was stated to exist, while in reality no such fund existed; *(8) bad and irrecoverable debts to an amount far exceeding the whole capital stock of the Bank were included under Article I. on the creditor side, and so treated as subsisting and available assets of the Company. Farther, on or about the 5th day of July 1876, in or near the Chamber of Commerce, *in or near West George Street*, Glasgow, you, the said John Stewart, Lewis Potter, Robert Salmond, William Taylor, Henry Inglis, John Innes Wright, and Robert Summers Stronach, did, all and each or one or more of you, wickedly and feloniously, and with intent to defraud, use and utter the said false and fabricated abstract balance-sheet or statement of affairs as true, by then and there reporting the same to the members of the said Company at their annual general meeting, along with a report on the Bank's affairs, in which you did, wickedly and feloniously, and falsely and fradulently, represent and pretend that the said Company was in a sound and prosperous condition, and capable of paying to its members a dividend at the rate of 11 per centum per annum, free of income-tax, and of carrying forward to the credit of the next year's profit and loss account a sum of £21,365, 10s. 3d., and by thereafter causing the said report and abstract balance-sheet or statement of affairs to be printed and published, and circulated throughout Scotland; and all this you did, well knowing the said abstract balance-sheet or statement of affairs to be false and fabricated, and for the purpose of concealing and misrepresenting the true state of the said Company's affairs; by all which, or part thereof, you did, wickedly and feloniously, deceive, impose upon, and defraud members of the said Company and of the public, and induce said members of the Company to retain the stock held by them therein, and many of the public, including

Robert Craig, papermaker, residing at Craigesk House, in the parish of Newbattle, and county of Edinburgh; the Rev. John Pulsford, Dalrymple Crescent, Edinburgh; James Ritchie, stationer, High Street, Edinburgh; and Thomas Brownlee, Gresham Cottage, Uddingston, Lanarkshire, to acquire stock in the said Company, and others of the public, including Thomson and Porteous, tobacco manufacturers in Edinburgh; Honeyman & Wilson, wholesale grocers in Edinburgh; Hamilton & Inches, jewellers in Edinburgh; Mossman & Watson, provision merchants in Edinburgh; Renton and Kerr, stockbrokers in Edinburgh; and Robert Christie, grocer in Edinburgh, to deposit money in the said Bank, to the great loss and prejudice of the said members of the Company and of the public.

LIKEAS (II.), on one or more days in the month of June 1877, or of May immediately preceding, or of July immediately following, the time or times being more particularly to the prosecutor unknown, in or near the said office of the City of Glasgow Bank in Virginia Street, Glasgow, or elsewhere in or near Glasgow, to the prosecutor unknown, you, the said John Stewart, Lewis Potter, Robert Salmond, William Taylor, Henry Inglis, John Innes Wright, and Robert Summers Stronach, did, all and each or one or more of you, wickedly and feloniously, with intent to defraud the members of the said Company and the public, and for the purpose of concealing and misrepresenting the true state of the affairs of the said Company, concoct and fabricate, or cause or procure to be concocted and fabricated, a false and fictitious abstract balance-sheet, or statement of affairs, purporting to represent the true condition of the affairs of the said Bank as at 6th June 1877, in the following or similar terms, videlicet:—

CITY OF GLASGOW BANK—ABSTRACT BALANCE-SHEET, AS AT 6TH JUNE 1877.

Dr. LIABILITIES.		
I. Deposits at the head office and branches, and balances at the credit of banking correspondents,		£8,382,711 12 10
II. Bank notes in circulation in Scotland and the Isle of Man,		763,894 0 0
III. Drafts outstanding, due, or with a currency not exceeding 21 days, and drafts accepted by the Bank and its London agents on account of home and foreign constituents,		1,350,335 1 1
Liabilities to the public,		£10,496,940 13 11
IV. Capital account,	£1,000,000 0 0	
V. Reserve fund,	450,000 0 0	
VI. Profit and loss,	148,501 12 6	
Liabilities to partners,		1,598,501 12 6
		£12,095,442 6 5

Cr. ASSETS.		
I. Bills of exchange, local and country bills, credit accounts, and other advances upon security,		£8,758,838 17 8
II. Advances on heritable property, and value of bank buildings and furniture at head office and branches,		257,689 0 6
III. Cash on hand—viz., gold and silver coin and notes of other banks at the head office and branches,	£891,018 0 2	
IV. Government stocks, Exchequer bills, railway and other stocks and debentures, and balances in hands of banking correspondents,	2,187,896 8 1	
		3,078,914 8 3
		£12,095,442 6 5

which abstract balance-sheet or statement of affairs was false and fictitious, and was known by you to be so, in the following particulars, or part thereof, videlicet:—(1) The amount of deposits at the head office and branches, and balances at the credit of banking correspondents, under Article I. on the debtor side, was understated to the extent of £1,151,518, 13s. 5d. or thereby; (2) the amount of bank notes in circulation under Article II. on the debtor side, was understated to the extent of £76,110 or thereby; (3) the amount of drafts outstanding, and drafts accepted by the Bank and its London agents, under Article III. on the debtor side, was understated to the extent of £1,330,712, 19s. 1d. or thereby; (4) the amount of bills of exchange, local and country bills, credit accounts, and other advances under Article I. on the creditor side, was understated to the extent of £3,227,154, 12s. 8d. or thereby; (5) the amount of cash on hand—viz., gold and silver coin and notes of other banks, under Article III. on the creditor side, was understated to the extent of £30,000 or thereby; (6) the amount of Government stocks, Exchequer bills, railway and other stocks and debentures, and balances in hands of banking correspondents, under Article III. on the creditor side, was overstated to the extent of £751,775, or thereby; (7) the earnings of the Bank during the year were overstated, under the head of profit and loss, to the extent of £128,998, 19s. 9d. or thereby; (8) a reserve fund to the extent of £450,000 was stated to exist, while in reality no such fund existed; *(9) bad and irrecoverable debts to an amount far exceeding the whole capital stock of the Bank were included under Article I., on the creditor side, and so treated as subsisting and available assets of the Company. FARTHER, on or about the 4th day of July 1877, in or near the Trades' Hall, Glassford Street, Glasgow, you the said John Stewart, Lewis Potter, Robert Salmond, William Taylor, Henry Inglis, John Innes Wright, and Robert Summers Stronach, did, all and each or one or more of you, wickedly and feloniously, and with intent to defraud, use and utter the said false and fabricated abstract balance-sheet or statement of affairs, last above libelled, as true, by then and there reporting the same to the members of the said Company at their annual general meeting, along with a report on the Bank's affairs, in which you did, wickedly and feloniously, and falsely and fraudulently, represent and pretend that the said Company was in a sound and prosperous condition, and capable of paying to its members a dividend at the rate of 12 per centum per annum, free of income-tax, and of carrying forward to the credit of next year's profit and loss account a sum of £18,501, 12s. 6d., and by thereafter causing the said report, and the said abstract balance-sheet or statement of affairs, last above libelled, to be printed and published, and circulated throughout Scotland; and all this you did, well knowing the said abstract balance-sheet or statement of affairs to be false and fabricated, and for the purpose of concealing and misrepresenting the true state of the said Company's affairs, by all which, or part thereof, you did, wickedly and feloniously, deceive, impose upon, and defraud members of the said Company, and of the public, and induce said members of the Company to retain the stock held by them therein, and many of the public, including James and William Russell, residing in Carrick Park, in or near Ayr; Peter Hume, warehouseman, residing in Salisbury Place, Great Western Road, Glasgow; Matthew Jarvis Dick, book-keeper, residing at Glenclelland, in the parish of Shotts, Lanarkshire; Robert Dick, coalmaster, residing in Garturk Street, Govan Hill, in or near Glasgow; and Edward M'Callum, residing at Plewlands House, Spylaw Road, in or near Edinburgh, to acquire stock in the said Company; and others of the public, including the said Thomson and Porteous, Honeyman & Wilson, Hamilton & Inches, Mossman & Watson, Renton & Kerr, and Robert Christie, to deposit money in the said Bank, to the great loss and prejudice of the said members of the Company and of the public.

LIKEAS (III.), on one or more days of the month of June 1878, or of May immediately preceding, or of July immediately following, the time or times being more particularly to the prosecutor unknown, in or near the said office of the City of Glasgow Bank, in Virginia Street, Glasgow, or elsewhere in or near Glasgow, to the prosecutor unknown, you the said John Stewart, Lewis Potter, Robert Salmond, William Taylor, Henry Inglis, John Innes Wright, and Robert Summers Stronach, did all and each or one or more of you, wickedly and feloniously, with intent to defraud the members of the said Company and the public, and for the purpose of concealing and misrepresenting the true state of the affairs of the said Company, concoct and fabricate, or cause or procure to be concocted and fabricated, a false and fictitious abstract balance-sheet or statement of affairs, purporting to represent the true condition of the affairs of the said Bank as at 5th June 1878, in the following or similar terms, videlicet :—

CITY OF GLASGOW BANK.—ABSTRACT BALANCE SHEET, AS AT 5TH JUNE 1878.

Dr. LIABILITIES.

I. Deposits at the head office and branches, and balances at the credit of banking correspondents, ...	£8,102,001 0 4	
II. Bank notes in circulation in Scotland and the Isle of Man, . . .	710,252 0 0	
III. Drafts outstanding, due, or with a currency not exceeding twenty-one days, and drafts accepted by the Bank and its London agents on account of home and foreign constituents, . . .	1,488,244 18 6	
Liabilities to the public, . .		£10,300,497 18 10
IV. Capital Account, ...	£1,000,000 0 0	
V. Reserve fund, ...	450,000 0 0	
VI. Profit and loss, ...	142,095 12 10	
Liabilities to partners, . .		1,592,095 12 10
		£11,892,593 11 8

Cr. ASSETS.

I. Bills of exchange, local and country bills, credit accounts, and other advances upon security, ...		£8,484,466 9 2
II. Advances on heritable property, and value of bank buildings and furniture at head office and branches, ...		265,324 9 0
III. Cash on hand—viz., gold and silver coin and notes of other banks at head office and branches, ...	£845,963 1 0	
Government stocks, Exchequer bills, railway and other stocks and debentures, and balances in hands of banking correspondents, . . .	2,296,839 12 6	
		3,142,802 13 6
		£11,892,593 11 8

which abstract balance-sheet or statement of affairs was false and fictitious and was known by you to be so in the following particulars, or part thereof, videlicet : —(1) The amount of deposits at the head office and branches and balances at the credit of banking correspondents, under Article I. on the debtor side, was understated to the extent of £941,284, 13s. 5d. or thereby; (2) the amount of bank notes in circulation, under Article II. on the debtor side, was understated to the extent £89,031 or thereby; (3) the amount of drafts outstanding, and drafts accepted by the Bank and its London agents, under Article III. on the debtor side, was understated to the extent of £1,393,008 or thereby; (4) the amount of bills of exchange, local and country bills, credit accounts, and other advances, under Article I. on the creditor side, was under stated to the extent of £3,520,913, 11s. 8d. or thereby; (5) the amount of cash in hand—viz., gold and silver coin and notes of other banks, under Article III. on the creditor side, was overstated to the extent of £219,522, 5s. 10d. or thereby; (6) the amount of Government stocks, Exchequer bills, railway and other stocks and debentures and balances in hands of banking correspondents, under Article III. on the creditor side, was overstated to the extent of £926,764 or thereby; (7) the earnings of the Bank were overstated, under the head of profit and loss, to the extent of £125,875, 9s. or thereby; (8) a reserve fund, to the extent of £450,000, was stated to exist, while in reality no such fund existed; *(9) bad and irrecoverable debts to an amount far exceeding the whole capital stock of the Bank were included under Article I. on the creditor side, and so treated as subsisting and available assets of the Company. FARTHER, on or about the 3d day of July 1878, in or near the Trades' Hall, Glassford Street, Glasgow, you, the said John Stewart, Lewis Potter, Robert Salmond, William Taylor, Henry Inglis, John Innes Wright, and Robert Summers Stronach, did, all and each or one or more of you, wickedly and feloniously, and with intent to defraud, use and utter the said false and fabricated abstract balance-sheet or statement of affairs, last above-libelled, as true, by then and there reporting the same to the members of the said Company at their annual general meeting, along with a report on the Bank's affairs, in which you did, wickedly and feloniously, and falsely and fraudulently represent and pretend that the said Company was in a sound and prosperous condition, and capable of paying to its members a dividend at the rate of 12 per centum per annum, free of income-tax, and carrying forward to the credit of the next year's profit and loss account a sum of £13,222, 12s. 10d., and by thereafter causing the said report and the said abstract balance-sheet or statement of affairs, last above-libelled, to be printed and published and circulated throughout Scotland, and all this you did, well knowing the said abstract balance-sheet or statement of affairs to be false and fabricated, and for the purpose of concealing and misrepresenting the true state of the said Company's affairs; by all which, or part thereof, you did, wickedly and feloniously, deceive, impose upon, and defraud members of the said Company and of the public, and induce said members of the Company to retain the stock held by them therein, and many of the public, including John Gillespie, Writer to the Signet in Edinburgh; Thomas Paterson, Writer to the Signet in Edinburgh; Alexander Fergusson, treasurer to the Caledonian Railway Company, residing in Elmbank Crescent, Glasgow; William Shearer, storekeeper, residing at Chapel, in the parish of Cambusnethan, Lanarkshire; William Howe, residing at Ferndean Cottage, Uddingston, Lanarkshire; and James Drummond, residing at Mollinsburn, in the parish of Cadder, Lanarkshire, to acquire stock in the said Company, and others of the public, including the said Thomson & Porteous, Honeyman & Wilson, Hamilton & Inches, Mossman & Watson, Renton and Kerr, and Robert Christie, to deposit money in the said Bank, to the great loss and prejudice of the said members of the Company and of the public.

LIKEAS (IV.), you, the said John Stewart, having been during the years 1874, 1875, 1876, 1877, and 1878 a partner of the firm of Stewart, Pott, & Co., wine merchants, Glasgow, and also a director of the said City of Glasgow Bank; and you the said John Stewart, and the said firm of Stewart, Pott, & Co. respectively, having had during the said period, or part thereof, an account or accounts current, or a credit account or accounts, with the said City of Glasgow Bank, and it being your duty as director foresaid not to allow overdrafts on such accounts to be made without any security, or upon wholly inadequate security, and in particular, not to allow any such overdraft to be made without security, or upon wholly inadequate security, as aforesaid, by you the said John Stewart, or by any firm whereof you were at the time a partner; and you the said John Stewart, having in your capacity as director foresaid, along with the other directors and officials of the said City of Glasgow Bank, received from the depositors and other creditors of the said City of Glasgow Bank, and been entrusted by them with large sums of money in order that the same might be employed in the ordinary business of banking: YET, NEVERTHELESS, you the said John Stewart, did, taking advantage of your official position as director foresaid, on several or one or more occasions during the years 1874, 1875, 1876, 1877, and 1878, the time or times being more particularly to the prosecutor unknown, in or near the head office of the said City of Glasgow Bank, in or near Virginia Street foresaid, or elsewhere in or near Glasgow to the prosecutor unknown, overdraw, or cause or procure to be overdrawn (1), the account current or credit account standing in the books of the said City of Glasgow Bank in the name of you, the said John Stewart, to the extent of £11,521, 3s. 10d. or thereby; and (2), the account current or credit account standing in the books of the said City of Glasgow Bank in the name of the said firm of Stewart, Pott, & Co., to the extent of £23,717, 7s. 4d., or thereby, and that without any security, or at least upon wholly inadequate security; and you, the said John Stewart, did thus, then and there, wickedly and feloniously, and in breach of the trust reposed in you as aforesaid, and in breach of your duty as director foresaid, embezzle and appropriate to your own uses and purposes, or to the uses and purposes of the said firm of Stewart, Pott, & Company, of which you were at the time a partner, the said sums of £11,521, 3s. 10d., and £23,717, 7s. 4d. sterling, or thereby, or part thereof, received by and entrusted to you as aforesaid, the property of the said City of Glasgow Bank, or of the depositors and other creditors of the said Bank.

LIKEAS (V.), you, the said William Taylor, having been during the years 1874, 1875, 1876, 1877, and 1878, a partner of the firm of Henry Taylor and Sons, grain merchants, Glasgow, and also a director of the said City of Glasgow Bank; and the said firm of Henry Taylor & Sons having had during the said period, or part thereof, an account or accounts current, or a credit account or accounts with the said City of Glasgow Bank, and it being your duty, as director foresaid, not to allow overdrafts on such accounts to be made without any security, or upon wholly inadequate security; and, in particular, not to allow any such overdraft to be made without security, or upon wholly inadequate security, as aforesaid, by you, the said William Taylor, or by any firm whereof you were at the time a partner; and you, the said William Taylor, having, in your capacity as director foresaid, along with the other directors and officials of the said City of Glasgow Bank, received from the depositors and other creditors of the said City of Glasgow Bank, and been entrusted by them with large sums of money, in order that the same might be employed in the ordinary business of banking: YET, NEVERTHELESS, you, the said William Taylor, did, taking advantage of your official position as director foresaid, on several, or one or more occasions during the years 1874, 1875, 1876, 1877, and 1878, the time or times being more particularly to the prosecutor unknown, in or near the head office of the said City of Glasgow Bank, in or near Virginia Street foresaid, or elsewhere in or near Glasgow to the prosecutor unknown, overdraw, or cause or procure to be overdrawn, the account or accounts current, or credit account or accounts, standing in the books of the said City of Glasgow Bank in the name of your said firm of Henry Taylor and Sons, to the extent of £73,460, 19s. 3d. or thereby, and that without any security, or at least upon wholly inadequate security; and you, the said William Taylor, did thus, then and there, wickedly and feloniously, and in breach of the trust reposed in you as aforesaid, and in breach of your duty as director foresaid, embezzle and appropriate to your own uses and purposes, or to the uses and purposes of the said firm of Henry Taylor & Sons, of which you were at the time a partner, the said sum of £73,460, 19s. 3d. sterling or thereby, or part thereof, received by and entrusted to you as aforesaid, the property of the said City of Glasgow Bank, or of the depositors and other creditors of the said bank.

LIKEAS (VI.), you, the said Henry Inglis, having been, during the years from 1862 to 1878, both inclusive, a partner of the firm of H. & A. Inglis, Writers to the Signet, Edinburgh, and also a director of the said City of Glasgow Bank, and you, the said Henry Inglis, and the said firm of H. & A. Inglis respectively, having had during the said period, or part thereof, an account or accounts current, or a credit account or accounts with the said City of Glasgow Bank; and it being your duty, as director foresaid, not to allow overdrafts on such accounts to be made or continued without any security, or upon wholly inadequate security; and in particular not to allow any such overdraft to be made or continued without security, or upon wholly inadequate security as aforesaid, by you, the said Henry Inglis, or by any firm whereof you were at the time a partner; and you, the said Henry Inglis, having, in your capacity as director foresaid, along with the other directors and officials of the said City of Glasgow Bank, received from the depositors and other creditors of the said City of Glasgow Bank, and been entrusted by them with large sums of money, in order that the same might be employed in the ordinary business of banking: YET, NEVERTHELESS, you, the said Henry Inglis, did, taking advantage of your official position as director foresaid, on various occasions during the years from 1862 to 1878, both inclusive, the times being more particularly to the prosecutor unknown, in or near the said head office of the said City of Glasgow Bank, or elsewhere in or near Glasgow, to the prosecutor unknown, or in or near the branch office of the said City of Glasgow Bank, in or near Hanover Street, Edinburgh, overdraw, or cause or procure to be overdrawn (1), the account or accounts current or credit account or accounts standing in the books of the said City of Glasgow Bank in the name of you, the said Henry Inglis, to the extent of £44,625, 16s. 2d. or thereby; and (2), the account or accounts current, or credit account or accounts standing in the books of the said City of Glasgow Bank, in the name of the said firm of H. & A. Inglis, to the extent of £7,125, 3s. 10d. or thereby, or did allow the overdrafts on the said accounts, in name of you and of your said firm, to be continued and increased to the said amounts respectively, and that without any security, or at least upon wholly inadequate security; and you the said Henry Inglis did thus, then and there, wickedly and feloniously, and in breach of the trust reposed in you as aforesaid, and in breach of your duty as director foresaid, embezzle and appropriate to your own uses and purposes, or to the uses and purposes of the said firm of H. & A. Inglis, of which you were at the time a partner, the said sums of £44,625, 16s. 2d. and £7125, 3s. 10d. sterling or thereby, or part thereof, received by and entrusted to you as aforesaid, the property of the said City of Glasgow Bank, or of the depositors and other creditors of said Bank.

LIKEAS (VII.), you, the said John Innes Wright, having been during the years 1875, 1876, 1877, and 1878, a partner of the firm of John Innes Wright & Co., merchants, Glasgow, and also a director of the said City of Glasgow Bank; and you, the said John Innes Wright, and the said firm of John Innes Wright & Co. respectively, having had, during the said period, or part thereof, an account or accounts current, or a credit account or accounts, with the said City of Glasgow Bank, and it being your duty, as director foresaid, not to allow overdrafts on such accounts to be made or continued without any security, or upon wholly inadequate security; and in particular not to allow any such overdraft to be made or continued without security, or upon wholly inadequate security as aforesaid, by you the said John Innes Wright, or by any firm whereof you were at the time a partner; and you the said John

Innes Wright having, in your capacity as director foresaid, along with the other directors and officials of the said City of Glasgow Bank, received from the depositors and other creditors of the said City of Glasgow Bank, and been entrusted by them with large sums of money, in order that the same might be employed in the ordinary business of banking: YET, NEVERTHELESS, you, the said John Innes Wright did, taking advantage of your official position as director foresaid, on several, or one or more occasions, during the years 1875, 1876, 1877, and 1878, the time or times being more particularly to the prosecutor unknown, in or near the said head office of the said City of Glasgow Bank, or elsewhere in or near Glasgow to the prosecutor unknown, overdraw, or cause or procure to be overdrawn—(1), the account current or credit account standing in the books of the said City of Glasgow Bank, in the name of you the said John Innes Wright, to the extent of £2746, 8s. 4d., or thereby; and (2), the accounts current or credit accounts standing in the books of the said City of Glasgow Bank, in the name of the said firm of John Innes Wright & Company, or did allow the overdrafts of your said firm to be continued and increased to the amount of £340,210, 7s. 3d., or thereby, and that without any security, or at least upon wholly inadequate security; and you, the said John Innes Wright, did thus, then and there, wickedly and feloniously, and in breach of the trust reposed in you as aforesaid, and in breach of your duty as director foresaid, embezzle and appropriate to your own uses and purposes, or to the uses and purposes of the said firm of John Innes Wright & Company, above designed, of which you were at the time a partner, the said sums of £2746, 8s. 4d. and £340,210, 7s. 3d. sterling, or thereby, or part thereof, received by and entrusted to you as aforesaid, the property of the said City of Glasgow Bank, or of the depositors and other creditors of the said Bank.

LIKEAS (VIII.), you, the said John Stewart, Lewis Potter, Robert Salmond, William Taylor, Henry Inglis, John Innes Wright, and Robert Summers Stronach, or one or more of you, having, on the 11th day of July 1878, or on one or other of the days of that month, or of June immediately preceding, or of August immediately following, in or near the branch office of the said City of Glasgow Bank, in or near Argyle Street, Glasgow, received from John Ramsay of Kildalton, Islay, distiller in Islay and Glasgow, and now or lately residing at Kildalton aforesaid, and been entrusted by him with a bill of exchange for the sum of £252, 7s. sterling, dated Glasgow, 13th June 1878, drawn by the said John Ramsay upon and accepted by the firm of Edward Young & Co., then and now or lately spirit merchants, Seal Street, Liverpool, and payable four months after date, at the office of Williams, Deacon, & Co., bankers, London, for the special and sole purpose of retaining the said bill in your custody till due, and of collecting payment of the same when due from the debtors therein on behalf of the said John Ramsay, who was not then or afterwards indebted or under obligation to the said City of Glasgow Bank; and you, the said John Stewart, Lewis Potter, Robert Salmond, William Taylor, Henry Inglis, John Innes Wright, and Robert Summers Stronach, not having authority to make use of the said bill of exchange above libelled for any other purpose than that of collecting payment thereof when due as aforesaid; YET, NEVERTHELESS, you, the said John Stewart, Lewis Potter, Robert Salmond, William Taylor, Henry Inglis, John Innes Wright, and Robert Summers Stronach, did, all and each or one or more of you, on the 11th day of July 1878, or on one or other of the days of that month, or of June immediately preceding, or of August immediately following, in or near the said branch office of the said City of Glasgow Bank, in or near Argyle Street, Glasgow, or in or near the said head office of the said City of Glasgow Bank, wickedly and feloniously steal and theftuously away take the bill of exchange for the sum of £252, 7s. above libelled, the property of the said John

Ramsay; and did endorse and make over, or cause or procure to be endorsed and made over, the said bill of exchange above libelled, before it had become due, to the London Joint Stock Bank, London, in order that the proceeds thereof might be credited to the said City of Glasgow Bank in account with the said London Joint Stock Bank as a payment made on behalf of the said City of Glasgow Bank, and the said proceeds were credited accordingly: OR OTHERWISE, you, the said John Stewart, Lewis Potter, Robert Salmond, William Taylor, Henry Inglis, John Innes Wright, and Robert Summers Stronach, did, all and each or one or more of you, time and place last above libelled, wickedly and feloniously, and in breach of the trust reposed in you as aforesaid, embezzle and appropriate to your own uses and purposes, or to the uses and purposes of the said City of Glasgow Bank, the said bill of exchange last above libelled, received by and entrusted to you as aforesaid, or the proceeds of the said bill, the property of the said John Ramsay.

LIKEAS (IX.), you, the said John Stewart, Lewis Potter, Robert Salmond, William Taylor, Henry Inglis, John Innes Wright, and Robert Summers Stronach, or one or more of you, having, time last above libelled, in or near the said branch office of the said City of Glasgow Bank, in or near Argyle Street, Glasgow, received from John Ramsay above designed, and been entrusted by him with a bill of exchange for the sum of £496, 12s. 2d. sterling, dated Glasgow, 26th June 1878, drawn by the said John Ramsay upon, and accepted by, the firm of W. & A. Gilbey, then and now or lately wine and spirit importers, Pantheon, Oxford Street, London, and payable four months after date at the Bank of England, Western Branch, London, for the special and sole purpose of retaining the said bill in your custody till due, and of collecting payment of the same when due from the debtors therein, on behalf of the said John Ramsay, who was not then or afterwards indebted or under obligation to the said City of Glasgow Bank; and you, the said John Stewart, Lewis Potter, Robert Salmond, William Taylor, Henry Inglis, John Innes Wright, and Robert Summers Stronach, not having authority to make use of the said bill of exchange last above libelled, for any other purpose than that of collecting payment thereof when due as aforesaid: YET, NEVERTHELESS, you, the said John Stewart, Lewis Potter, Robert Salmond, William Taylor, Henry Inglis, John Innes Wright, and Robert Summers Stronach, did, all and each or one of more of you, on the 11th day of July 1878, or on one or other of the days or that month, or of June immediately preceding, or of August immediately following, in or near the said branch office of the said City of Glasgow Bank, in or near Argyle Street. Glasgow, or in or near the said head office of the said City of Glasgow Bank, wickedly and feloniously steal and theftuously away take the bill of exchange for the sum of £496, 12s. 2d., above libelled, the property of the said John Ramsay, and did endorse and make over, or cause or procure to be endorsed and made over, the said bill of exchange last above libelled, before it had become due, to the London Joint Stock Bank, London, in order that the proceeds thereof might be credited to the said City of Glasgow Bank in account with the said London Joint Stock Bank, as a payment made on behalf of the said City of Glasgow Bank, and the said proceeds were credited accordingly: OR OTHERWISE, you, the said John Stewart, Lewis Potter, Robert Salmond, William Taylor, Henry Inglis, John Innes Wright, and Robert Summers Stronach, did, all and each or one or more of you, time and place last above libelled, wickedly and feloniously, and in breach of the trust reposed in you as aforesaid, embezzle and appropriate to your own uses and purposes, or to the uses and purposes of the said City of Glasgow Bank, the said bill of exchange last above libelled, received by and entrusted to you as aforesaid, or the proceeds of the said bill, the property of the said John Ramsay.

LIKEAS (X.), you, the said John Stewart, Lewis Potter, Robert Salmond, William Taylor, Henry Inglis, John Innes Wright, and Robert Summers Stronach, or one or more of you, having, on the 3d day of September 1878, or on one or other of the days of that month, or of August immediately preceding, in or near the said branch office of the said City of Glasgow Bank, in or near Argyle Street, Glasgow, received from John Ramsay, above designed, and been entrusted by him with a bill of exchange for the sum of £489, 14s. 2d. sterling, dated Glasgow, 24th July 1878, drawn by the said John Ramsay upon, and accepted by, the said firm of W. & A. Gilbey, and payable four months after date, at the Bank of England, Western Branch, London, for the special and sole purpose of retaining the said bill in your custody till due, and of collecting payment of the same when due from the debtors therein, on behalf of the said John Ramsay, who was not then or afterwards indebted or under obligation to the said City of Glasgow Bank; and you, the said John Stewart, Lewis Potter, Robert Salmond, William Taylor, Henry Inglis, John Innes Wright, and Robert Summers Stronach, not having authority to make use of the said bill of exchange last above libelled, for any other purpose than that of collecting payment thereof when due as aforesaid: YET, NEVERTHELESS, you, the said John Stewart, Lewis Potter, Robert Salmond, William Taylor, Henry Inglis, John Innes Wright, and Robert Summers Stronach, did, all and each or one or more of you, on the 3d day of September 1878, or on one or other of the days of that month, or of August immediately preceding, in or near the said branch office of the said City of Glasgow Bank, in or near Argyle Street, Glasgow, or in or near the said head office of the said City of Glasgow Bank, wickedly and feloniously steal and theftuously away take the bill of exchange for the sum of £489, 14s. 2d. above libelled, the property of the said John Ramsay; and did endorse and make over, or cause and procure to be endorsed and made over, the said bill of exchange last above libelled, before it had become due, to the London Joint Stock Bank, London, in order that the proceeds thereof might be credited to the said City of Glasgow Bank, in account with the said London Joint Stock Bank, as a payment made on behalf of the said City of Glasgow Bank, and the said proceeds were credited accordingly: OR OTHERWISE, you, the said John Stewart, Lewis Potter, Robert Salmond, William Taylor, Henry Inglis, John Innes Wright, and Robert Summers Stronach, did, all and each or one or more of you, time and place last above libelled, wickedly and feloniously, and in breach of the trust reposed in you as aforesaid, embezzle and appropriate to your own uses and purposes, or to the uses and purposes of the said City of Glasgow Bank, the said bill of exchange last above libelled, received by and entrusted to you as aforesaid, or the proceeds of the said bill, the property of the said John Ramsay.

LIKEAS (XI.), you, the said John Stewart, Lewis Potter, Robert Salmond, William Taylor, Henry Inglis, John Innes Wright, and Robert Summers Stronach, or one or more of you, having on the 20th day of August 1878, or on one or other of the days of that month, or of July immediately preceding, or of September immediately following, in or near the Anderston branch office of the said City of Glasgow Bank, in or near Anderston, Glasgow, received from Charles Connell & Company, then and now or lately shipbuilders, Scotstoun, Whiteinch, near Glasgow, or from Charles Connell, the only partner of said firm, then and now or lately residing at Rozelle, Broomhill Drive, Partick, in the county of Lanark, and been entrusted by them, or him, with two several bills of exchange, each for the sum of £3000 sterling, and each dated Glasgow, 3d April 1878, drawn by the said Charles Connell & Company upon, and accepted by the firm of Alexander & Radcliffe, then and now or lately shipowners, Liverpool and London Chambers, Exchange, Liverpool, and each payable six months after date at the office in London of Barnetts, Hoares, and Company, bankers there; and having, time and place last above libelled, received from the said Charles Connell & Company, or from the said Charles Connell, and been entrusted by them, or him, with two several bills of exchange, each for the sum of £3000 sterling, and each dated Glasgow, 28th May 1878, drawn by the said Charles Connell & Company upon, and accepted by the said firm of Alexander & Radcliffe above designed, and each payable six months after date at the office in London of Barnetts, Hoares, & Company, above designed; and having, on the 26th day of August 1878, or on one or other of the days of that month, or of September immediately following, in or near the said Anderston branch office of the said City of Glasgow Bank, received from the said Charles Connell & Company, or from the said Charles Connell, and been entrusted by them, or him, with two several bills of exchange, each for the sum of £3000 sterling, and each dated Glasgow, 2d June 1878, drawn by the said Charles Connell & Company upon, and accepted by the said firm of Alexander & Radcliffe, above designed, and each payable six months after date at the office in London of Barnetts, Hoares, & Company, above designed, all for the special and sole purpose of retaining the said bills in your custody till due, and of collecting payment of the same when due, from the debtors therein, on behalf of the said Charles Connell & Company, or of the said Charles Connell, neither of whom was, at the dates when the said six bills of exchange last above libelled were respectively received as aforesaid, or afterwards, indebted or under obligation to the said City of Glasgow Bank; and you, the said John Stewart, Lewis Potter Robert Salmond, William Taylor, Henry Inglis, John Innes Wright, and Robert Summers Stronach, not having authority to make use of the said six bills of exchange last above libelled, or any of them, for any other purpose than that of collecting payment thereof when due, as aforesaid: YET, NEVERTHELESS, you the said John Stewart, Lewis Potter, Robert Salmond, William Taylor, Henry Inglis, John Innes Wright, and Robert Summers Stronach, did, all and each or one or more of you, on the 20th day of August 1878, or on one or other of the days of that month, or of July immediately preceding, or of September immediately following, as regards the four first above mentioned of the six bills of exchange last above libelled, and on the 26th day of August 1878, or on one or other of the days of that month, or of September immediately following, as regards the two last above mentioned of the six bills of exchange last above libelled, in or near the said Anderston branch office of the said City of Glasgow Bank, or in or near the said head office of the said City of Glasgow Bank, wickedly and feloniously steal and theftuously away take the six bills of exchange last above libelled, or part thereof, the property of the said Charles Connell & Company, or of the said Charles Connell, and did endorse and make over, or cause or procure to be endorsed and made over, each of the said six bills of exchange last above libelled, before it had become due, to the London Joint Stock Bank, London, in order that the proceeds thereof might be credited to the said City of Glasgow Bank, in account with the said London Joint Stock Bank, as a payment made on behalf of the said City of Glasgow Bank, and the said proceeds were credited accordingly: OR OTHERWISE, you, the said John Stewart, Lewis Potter, Robert Salmond, William Taylor, Henry Inglis, John Innes Wright, and Robert Summers Stronach, did, all and each or one or more of you, time or times or place or places respectively above libelled, as regards the six bills of exchange last above libelled respectively, wickedly and feloniously, and in breach of the trust reposed in you as aforesaid, embezzle and appropriate to your own uses and purposes, or to the uses and purposes of the said City of Glasgow Bank, the six bills of exchange last above libelled, or part thereof, received by and entrusted to you as aforesaid, or the proceeds of the said bills, or part thereof, the property of the said Charles Connell & Company, or of the said Charles Connell.

LIKEAS (XII.), you, the said John Stewart, Lewis Potter, Robert Salmond, William Taylor, Henry Inglis, John Innes Wright, and Robert Summers Stronach, or one or more of you, having, on the 21st day of August 1878, or on one or other of the days of that month, or of July immediately preceding, or of September immediately following, in or near the said head office of the said City of Glasgow Bank, received from the Marbella Iron Ore Company (Limited), having its registered office in London, and been entrusted by the said Marbella Iron Ore Company (Limited) with a bill of exchange for the sum of £525 sterling, dated London, 7th July 1878, drawn by the said Marbella Iron Ore Company (Limited) upon and accepted by the firm of E. J. Waite & Company, Bute Docks, Cardiff, and payable four months after date at the office of Glyn, Mills, Currie, & Company, bankers, London, for the special and sole purpose of retaining the said bill in your custody till due, and of collecting payment of the same when due from the debtors therein on behalf of the said Marbella Iron Ore Company (Limited), which was not then or afterwards indebted or under obligation to the said City of Glasgow Bank; and you, the said John Stewart, Lewis Potter, Robert Salmond, William Taylor, Henry Inglis, John Innes Wright, and Robert Summers Stronach, not having authority to make use of the said bill of exchange last above libelled, for any other purpose than that of collecting payment thereof when due as aforesaid: YET, NEVERTHELESS, you, the said John Stewart, Lewis Potter, Robert Salmond, William Taylor, Henry Inglis, John Innes Wright, and Robert Summers Stronach, did, all and each or one or more of you, on the 21st day of August 1878, or on one or other of the days of that month, or of July immediately preceding, or of September immediately following, in or near the said head office of the said City of Glasgow Bank, wickedly and feloniously steal and theftuously away take the bill of exchange for the sum of £525 above libelled, the property of the said Marbella Iron Ore Company (Limited), and did endorse and make over, or cause or procure to be endorsed and made over, the said bill of exchange last above libelled, before it had become due, to the London Joint Stock Bank, London, in order that the proceeds thereof might be credited to the said City of Glasgow Bank, in account with the said London Joint Stock Bank, as a payment made on behalf of the said City of Glasgow Bank, and the said proceeds were credited accordingly: OR OTHERWISE, you, the said John Stewart, Lewis Potter, Robert Salmond, William Taylor, Henry Inglis, John Innes Wright, and Robert Summers Stronach, did, all and each or one or more of you, time and place last above libelled, wickedly and feloniously, and in breach of the trust reposed in you as aforesaid, embezzle and appropriate to your own uses and purposes, or to the uses and purposes of the said City of Glasgow Bank, the said bill of exchange last above libelled, received by and entrusted to you as aforesaid, or the proceeds of the said bill, the property of the said Marbella Iron Ore Company (Limited).

LIKEAS (XIII.), you, the said John Stewart, Lewis Potter, Robert Salmond, William Taylor, Henry Inglis, John Innes Wright, and Robert Summers Stronach, or one or more of you, having, time and place last above libelled, received from the said Marbella Iron Ore Company (Limited), and been entrusted by them with a bill of exchange for the sum of £358, 13s. 8d. sterling, dated London, 13th August 1878, drawn by the said Marbella Iron Ore Company (Limited), upon and accepted by the Panteg Steel Works and Engineering Company (Limited), Panteg, near Pontypool, Monmouthshire, and payable four months after date at 77 Lombard Street, London, E.C., Messrs Fuller, Banbury, Nix, & Mathieson, for the special and sole purpose of retaining the said bill in your custody till due, and of collecting payment of the same when due from the debtors therein, on behalf of the said Marbella Iron Ore Company (Limited), which was not then or afterwards indebted or under obligation to the said City of Glasgow Bank; and you, the said John Stewart, Lewis Potter, Robert Salmond, William Taylor, Henry Inglis, John Innes Wright, and Robert Summers Stronach, not having authority to make use of the said bill of exchange last above libelled for any other purpose than that of collecting payment thereof when due as aforesaid: YET, NEVERTHELESS, you, the said John Stewart, Lewis Potter, Robert Salmond, William Taylor, Henry Inglis, John Innes Wright, and Robert Summers Stronach, did, all and each or one or more of you, time and place last above libelled, wickedly and feloniously steal and theftuously away take the bill of exchange for the sum of £358, 13s. 8d. above libelled, the property of the said Marbella Iron Ore Company (Limited), and did endorse and make over, or cause or procure to be endorsed and made over, the said bill of exchange last above libelled, before it had become due, to the London Joint Stock Bank, London, in order that the proceeds thereof might be credited to the said City of Glasgow Bank in account with the said London Joint Stock Bank, as a payment made on behalf of the said City of Glasgow Bank, and the said proceeds were credited accordingly: OR OTHERWISE, you, the said John Stewart, Lewis Potter, Robert Salmond, William Taylor, Henry Inglis, John Innes Wright, and Robert Summers Stronach, did, all and each or one or more of you, time and place last above libelled, wickedly and feloniously, and in breach of the trust reposed in you as aforesaid, embezzle and appropriate to your own uses and purposes, or to the uses and purposes of the said City of Glasgow Bank, the said bill of exchange last above libelled, received by and entrusted to you as aforesaid, or the proceeds of the said bill, the property of the said Marbella Iron Ore Company (Limited).

LIKEAS (XIV.), you, the said John Stewart, Lewis Potter, Robert Salmond, William Taylor, Henry Inglis, John Innes Wright, and Robert Summers Stronach, or one or more of you, having, on the 31st day of August 1878, or on one or other of the days of that month, or of July immediately preceding, or of September immediately following, in or near the said head office of the said City of Glasgow Bank, received from the said Marbella Iron Ore Company (Limited), and been entrusted by them with a bill of exchange for the sum of £800 sterling, dated London, 14th July 1878, drawn by the said Marbella Iron Ore Company (Limited), upon, and accepted by the said firm of E. J. Wait & Co. above designed, and payable four months after date, at the office of Glyn, Mills, Currie, & Co., bankers, London, for the special and sole purpose of retaining the said bill in your custody till due, and of collecting payment of the same when due from the debtors therein, on behalf of the said Marbella Iron Ore Company (Limited), which was not then or afterwards indebted or under obligation to the said City of Glasgow Bank; and you, the said John Stewart, Lewis Potter, Robert Salmond, William Taylor, Henry Inglis, John Innes Wright, and Robert Summers Stronach, not having authority to make use of the said bill of exchange last above libelled, for any other purpose than that of collecting payment thereof when due, as aforesaid: YET, NEVERTHELESS, you, the said John Stewart, Lewis Potter, Robert Salmond, William Taylor, Henry Inglis, John Innes Wright, and Robert Summers Stronach, did, all and each or one or more of you, on the 31st day of August 1878, or on one or other of the days of that month, or of July immediately preceding, or of September immediately following, place last above libelled, wickedly and feloniously steal, and theftuously away take the bill of exchange for the sum of £800 above libelled, the property of the said Marbella Iron Ore Company (Limited), and did endorse and make over, or cause or procure to be endorsed and made over, the said bill of exchange last above libelled, before it had become due, to the London Joint Stock Bank, London, in order that the proceeds thereof might be credited to the said City of Glasgow Bank, in account with the said London Joint Stock Bank, as a payment made on behalf of the said City of Glasgow Bank, and the said proceeds were credited accordingly: OR OTHERWISE, you, the said John Stewart, Lewis Potter, Robert Salmond, William Taylor, Henry Inglis, John Innes Wright, and Robert Summers Stronach, did, all and each or one or more of you, time and place last above libelled, wickedly and feloniously, and in breach of the trust reposed in you as aforesaid, embezzle and appropriate to your own uses and purposes, or to the uses and purposes of the said City of Glasgow Bank, the said bill of exchange last above libelled, received by and entrusted to you as aforesaid, or the proceeds of the said bill, the property of the said Marbella Iron Ore Company (Limited).

LIKEAS (XV.), you, the said John Stewart, Lewis Potter, Robert Salmond, William Taylor, Henry Inglis, John Innes Wright, and Robert Summers Stronach, or one or more of you, having, on the 5th day of September 1878, or on one or other of the days of that month, or of August immediately preceding, place last above libelled, received from the said Marbella Iron Ore Company (Limited) and been entrusted by them with a bill of exchange for the sum of £1187, 11s. 3d. sterling, dated London, 10th July 1878, drawn by the said Marbella Iron Ore Company (Limited), upon and accepted by the Ebbw Vale Steel, Iron, and Coal Company (Limited), Ebbw Vale Works, Monmouthshire, and payable four months after date at the office of the Consolidated Bank, London, for the special and sole purpose of retaining the said bill in your custody till due, and of collecting payment of the same when due from the debtors therein, on behalf of the said Marbella Iron Ore Company (Limited), which was not then or afterwards indebted or under obligation to the said City of Glasgow Bank; and you, the said John Stewart, Lewis Potter, Robert Salmond, William Taylor, Henry Inglis, John Innes Wright, and Robert Summers Stronach, not having authority to make use of the said bill of exchange last above libelled for any other purpose than that of collecting payment thereof when due, as aforesaid: YET, NEVERTHELESS, you, the said John Stewart, Lewis Potter, Robert Salmond, William Taylor, Henry Inglis, John Innes Wright, and Robert Summers Stronach, did, all and each or one or more of you, on the 5th day of September 1878, or on one or other of the days of that month, or of August immediately preceding, place last above libelled, wickedly and feloniously steal, and theftuously away take, the bill of exchange for the sum of £1187, 11s. 3d. above libelled, the property of the said Marbella Iron Ore Company (Limited), and did endorse and make over, or cause or procure to be endorsed and made over, the said bill of exchange last above libelled, before it had become due, to the London Joint Stock Bank, London, in order that the proceeds thereof might be credited to the said City of Glasgow Bank in account with the said London Joint Stock Bank, as a payment made on behalf of the said City of Glasgow Bank, and the said proceeds were credited accordingly: OR OTHERWISE, you, the said John Stewart, Lewis Potter, Robert Salmond, William Taylor, Henry Inglis, John Innes Wright, and Robert Summers Stronach did, all and each or one or more of you, time and place last above libelled, wickedly and feloniously, and in breach of the trust reposed in you as aforesaid, embezzle and appropriate to your own uses and purposes, or to the uses and purposes of the said City of Glasgow Bank, the said bill of exchange last above libelled, received by and entrusted to you as aforesaid, or the proceeds thereof, the property of the said Marbella Iron Ore Company (Limited).

LIKEAS (XVI.), you, the said John Stewart, Lewis Potter, Robert Salmond, William Taylor, Henry Inglis, John Innes Wright, and Robert Summers Stronach, or one or more of you, having, on the 13th day of September 1878, or on one or other of the days of that month, or of August immediately preceding, place last above libelled, received from James Baird, merchant at St John's,

Newfoundland, and then residing in Glasgow, and been entrusted by him with a bill of exchange for the sum of £700 sterling, dated St John's, Newfoundland, 21st August 1878, drawn by Walter Grieve and Company, merchants at St John's aforesaid, upon Walter Grieve, Son, & Company, merchants, Greenock, and payable in London sixty days after sight, to the order of the Union Bank of Newfoundland, and endorsed by the said Union Bank of Newfoundland to the said James Baird, and accepted by the said Walter Grieve, Son, & Company, of date 2d September 1878, as payable at the Union Bank of London, and that for the special and sole purpose of retaining the said bill in your custody till due, and of collecting payment of the same when due from the debtors therein, on behalf of the said James Baird, who was not then or afterwards indebted or under obligation to the said City of Glasgow Bank; and you, the said John Stewart, Lewis Potter, Robert Salmond, William Taylor, Henry Inglis, John Innes Wright, and Robert Summers Stronach, not having authority to make use of the said bill of exchange last above libelled for any other purpose than that of collecting payment thereof when due, as aforesaid: YET, NEVERTHELESS, you, the said John Stewart, Lewis Potter, Robert Salmond, William Taylor, Henry Inglis, John Innes Wright, and Robert Summers Stronach, did, all and each or one or more of you, on the 13th day of September 1878, or on one or other of the days of that month, or of August immediately preceding, place last above libelled, wickedly and feloniously steal and theftuously away take, the bill of exchange for the sum of £700 above libelled, the property of the said James Baird, and did endorse and make over, or cause or procure to be endorsed and made over, the said bill of exchange last above libelled, before it had become due, to the London Joint Stock Bank, London, in order that the proceeds thereof might be credited to the said City of Glasgow Bank in account with the said London Joint Stock Bank, as a payment made on behalf of the said City of Glasgow Bank, and the said proceeds were credited accordingly: OR OTHERWISE, you, the said John Stewart, Lewis Potter, Robert Salmond, William Taylor, Henry Inglis, John Innes Wright, and Robert Summers Stronach, did, all and each or one or more of you, time and place last above libelled, wickedly and feloniously, and in breach of the trust reposed in you as aforesaid, embezzle and appropriate to your own uses and purposes, or to the uses and purposes of the said City of Glasgow Bank, the said bill of exchange last above libelled, received by and entrusted to you as aforesaid, or the proceeds of the said bill, the property of the said James Baird.

LIKEAS (XVII.), you, the said John Stewart, Lewis Potter, Robert Salmond, William Taylor, Henry Inglis, John Innes Wright, and Robert Summers Stronach, or one or more of you, having, on the 21st day of September 1878, or on one or other of the days of that month, or of August immediately preceding, place last above libelled, received from John M'Pherson and Company, then and now or lately engineers and ironfounders, Mount Blue Works, Camlachie, in or near Glasgow, and been entrusted by them with a bill of exchange for the sum of £562, 10s. sterling, dated Hong Kong, 9th August 1878, drawn by the Chartered Bank of India, Australia, and China, Hong Kong upon the Chartered Bank of India, Australia, and China, Hatton Court, Threadneedle Street, London, and payable thirty days after sight to the order of, and endorsed to the said John M'Pherson and Company, and accepted by the said Chartered Bank of India, Australia, and China, Hatton Court aforesaid, of date 23d September 1878, as payable at the City Bank, London, and that for the special and sole purpose of retaining the said bill in your custody till due, and of collecting payment of the same when due, for the debtors therein on behalf of the said John M'Pherson & Company, which firm was not then or afterwards indebted or under obligation to the said City of Glasgow Bank; and you, the said John

Stewart, Lewis Potter, Robert Salmond, William Taylor, Henry Inglis, John Innes Wright, and Robert Summers Stronach, not having authority to make use of the said bill of exchange last above libelled for any other purpose than that of collecting payment thereof when due as aforesaid: YET, NEVERTHELESS, you, the said John Stewart, Lewis Potter, Robert Salmond, William Taylor, Henry Inglis, John Innes Wright, and Robert Summers Stronach, did, all and each or one or more of you, on the 21st day of September 1878, or on one or other of the days of that month, or of August immediately preceding, place last above libelled, wickedly and feloniously steal and theftuously away take the bill of exchange for the sum of £562, 10s., above libelled, the property of the said John M'Pherson & Company, and did endorse and make over, or cause or procure to be endorsed and made over, the said bill of exchange last above libelled, before it had become due, to the London Joint Stock Bank, London, in order that the proceeds thereof might be credited to the said City of Glasgow Bank, in account with the said London Joint Stock Bank, as a payment made on behalf of the said City of Glasgow Bank, and the said proceeds were credited accordingly: OR OTHERWISE, you the said John Stewart, Lewis Potter, Robert Salmond, William Taylor, Henry Inglis, John Innes Wright, and Robert Summers Stronach, did, all and each or one or more of you, time and place last above libelled, wickedly and feloniously, and in breach of the trust reposed in you as aforesaid, embezzle and appropriate to your own uses and purposes, or to the uses and purposes of the said City of Glasgow Bank, the said bill of exchange last above libelled, received by and entrusted to you as aforesaid, or the proceeds of the said bill, the property of the said John Macpherson & Company; and you, the said John Stewart, having been apprehended and taken before Francis William Clark, Esq., advocate, Sheriff of Lanarkshire, did, in his presence at Glasgow, on the 22d and 29th days of October 1878 respectively, emit and subscribe a declaration; and you, the said Lewis Potter, having been apprehended and taken before the said Francis William Clark, did, in his presence at Glasgow, on the 22d, 25th, and 29th days of October, 1878 respectively, emit and subscribe a declaration; and you, the said Robert Salmond, having been apprehended and taken before the said Francis William Clark, did, in his presence at Glasgow, on the 22d and 29th days of October 1878 respectively, emit and subscribe a declaration; and you, the said William Taylor, having been apprehended and taken before the said Francis William Clark, did, in his presence at Glasgow, on the 22d, and on two several occasions on the 29th days of October 1878 respectively, emit and subscribe a declaration; and you, the said Henry Inglis, having been apprehended and taken before the said Francis William Clark, did, in his presence at Glasgow, on the 22d, and on two several occasions on the 29th days of October 1878 respectively, emit and subscribe a declaration; and you, the said John Innes Wright, having been apprehended and taken before the said Francis William Clark, did, in his presence at Glasgow, on the 22d, and on two several occasions on the 29th days of October 1878 respectively, emit and subscribe a declaration; and you, the said Robert Summers Stronach, having been apprehended and taken before the said Francis William Clark, did, in his presence at Glasgow, on the 22d and 29th days of October 1878 respectively, emit and subscribe a declaration, which several declarations being to be used in evidence against each of you by whom the same were respectively emitted, as also the books, letters, documents, excerpts, prints, and other articles enumerated in an inventory thereof, hereunto annexed and referred to, being to be used in evidence against all and each, or one or more of you, the said John Stewart, Lewis Potter, Robert Salmond, William Taylor, Henry Inglis, John Innes Wright, and Robert Summers Stronach, at your trial, will for that purpose be in due time lodged in the hands of the Clerk of the High Court of Justiciary, before which you are to be tried, that you may respectively have an opportunity of seeing the same, all which, or part thereof, being found proven by the verdict of an assize, or admitted by the respective judicial confessions of you, the said John Stewart, Lewis Potter, Robert Salmond, William Taylor, Henry Inglis, John Innes Wright, and Robert Summers Stronach, before the Lord Justice-General, Lord Justice-Clerk, and Lords Commissioners of Justiciary, you, the said John Stewart, Lewis Potter, Robert Salmond, William Taylor, Henry Inglis, John Innes Wright, and Robert Summers Stronach, ought to be punished with the pains of law to deter others from committing the like crimes in all time coming.

(Signed) JOHN BURNET, *A.D.*

The diet having been called,

The LORD JUSTICE-CLERK asked—Is there any objection to the relevancy?

The LORD ADVOCATE—Before any objections are stated to relevancy, I desire, with the leave of the Court, to delete six words occurring on page four of the indictment, at the foot of the page. The description of the *locus* there runs, "in or near the Chamber of Commerce in or near West George Street, "Glasgow." I propose, with your Lordships' leave, to amend the libel by striking out these six words, "in or near West George Street." [See page 27 these words printed in italics.] I don't know whether there is any objection to this proposal.

The LORD JUSTICE-CLERK—Is there any objection?

Mr TRAYNER—No.

Mr BALFOUR—No.

Mr MACKINTOSH—On behalf of the panel Mr Taylor, I have to state certain objections to the relevancy of the libel, and I may say that these objections are concurred in by my learned friends who represent the other prisoners, it being, however, understood that any of my learned friends may supplement my observations upon any matter which they think material to their respective clients. The indictment is a somewhat extensive document, and it will be proper that I begin by asking your Lordships' attention to its general scheme. The major proposition sets out five separate charges, which it affirms to be crimes severely punishable by the law of Scotland. The first three are the well-known and nominate charges of (1) falsehood, fraud, and wilful imposition; (2) theft; and (3) breach of trust and embezzlement. The other two are innominate charges, falling under no recognised legal category, and they immediately follow the charges of falsehood, fraud, and wilful imposition, and are as follow:—"As also the wicked and felonious "fabrication and falsification, by directors or officials of a joint stock "banking company, of any balance-sheet or statement of affairs, for the "purpose of concealing and misrepresenting the true state of the company's "affairs, with intent to defraud, and whereby the members of the company "and of the public are deceived, imposed upon, and defrauded; as also "the wickedly and feloniously using and uttering as true, by the directors "or officials of a joint stock banking company, any fabricated and falsified "balance-sheet or statement of affairs, knowing the same to be false and "fabricated, for the purpose of concealing and misrepresenting the true state "of the company's affairs, with intent to defraud." Your Lordships will observe that the distinction between these two last charges is this,—the one assumes that the accused both prepared and issued the alleged false balance-sheets, while the other alleges that they issued them knowing their false character. That is the major. The minor proposition sets out in the usual form that the accused are, all or one or more of them, guilty of the said crimes, or one or more of them, in so far as, during the period mentioned, they committed a number of acts, which are set forth under seventeen separate counts in the minor. It will, I think, be found that these seventeen counts divide themselves into three sets or series, the charges in each set of the series being substantially identical. The first set are counts 1 to 3 inclusive, the substance of which is that they charge the accused with issuing false balances of the City of Glasgow Bank during the years 1876-77-78. That is the first series of charges, and they apply to all the accused. The second series of counts or charges are those numbered 4 to 7 inclusive, and they, in substance, charge what I may call for brevity the overdrawing of accounts by directors, or certain of them. The charge is not common to the whole of the accused, Messrs Potter, Salmond, and Stronach not being included. The third set of charges, those numbered 8 to 17, are charges of stealing or otherwise embezzling certain bills, which had been sent to the Bank for collection. And this set of charges is directed against all the accused. That is the general scheme of the indictment, and that being so, I proceed to consider its relevancy. And, first, as to the major proposition, I do not know that it is necessary to enter upon any detailed discussion. Questions, of course, suggest themselves in regard to the two innominate charges to which I have referred, and I must say that, construing these charges upon their terms and according to the ordinary rules of construction, I think a very serious question suggests itself as to the relevancy of these charges. In one view, the charges in question are simply charges of uttering untruths in a particular form, and for the purpose and with the result of producing a particular state of public opinion. In another view, they are not distinct and separate charges at all, but simply charges of falsehood, fraud, and wilful imposition, with this remarkable peculiarity, that although it appears that the alleged fraud was committed for the benefit of the company, it at the same time appears that the effect of the fraud was to injure, not merely third parties, namely, members of the public, but also members of the company. But while these criticisms may be made, it must be kept in view that, in dealing with innominate charges, it is always possible to construe them by reference to the more detailed statement which is to be found in the minor. And therefore it will be convenient to take, at least in the first instance, the whole argument upon the relevancy of the minor, upon the construction of which I am to maintain to your Lordships that from first to last it contains no relevant charge of falsehood, fraud, or wilful imposition, or breach of trust or embezzlement, or theft, or any other crime, nominate or innominate, known to the law of Scotland.

My Lords, I begin with counts one, two, and three [pp. 26, 28, and 29], which I have described as charges of issuing false balance-sheets, and I propose to take as a specimen the first charge, which your Lordships will find between pages 1 and 3 [see p. 26], and which deals with the balance-sheet of 1876. I take that charge as a specimen, because in substance the other two charges are substantially the same, and raise substantially the same questions. The charge begins by narrating that the accused were directors of the City of Glasgow Bank, an institution having a capital of one million, and that during certain years which are mentioned it was their duty as directors and managers to see that the books were properly kept and all transactions duly entered; and that it was further their duty to see that every year an abstract or statement at 1st June was prepared and submitted to the shareholders. It then sets forth that nevertheless, "on the " first or one or more of the days of the month of June 1876, or July imme- " diately following, the time or times being unknown, in or near the head " office of the City of Glasgow Bank, you, the said John Stewart," and so on, " did all, or one or more of you, wickedly and feloniously, with intent to " defraud the members of the company and the public, and for the purpose " of concealing and misrepresenting the true state of the affairs of the said "company, concoct and fabricate, or cause and procure to be concocted and "fabricated, a false and fictitious abstract balance-sheet or statement of "affairs, purporting to represent the true condition of the Bank's affairs as at "7th June 1876, in the following or similar terms." Then follows a copy of the balance-sheet, which I need not read. Then there follows an enumeration of the particular misrepresentations or falsehoods which it is said to have contained, which are set forth under eight heads or articles, it being premised that the prosecutor does not bind himself to prove that the whole of these eight misrepresentations were false and fictitious, but only, as the indictment expresses it, that the balance-sheet was false in the eight paticulars mentioned, "or part thereof." The eight heads are—"(1) The amount of "deposits at the head office and branches, and balances at the credit of "banking correspondents, on the debtor side, is understated to the amount "of £1,006,216, 12s. 10d., or thereby; (2) the amount of drafts outstanding, "and accepted by the Bank and its London agents, in article 3 of the debtor "side, is understated to the amount of £973,000, or thereby; (3) the amount "of bills of exchange, local and country bills, credit accounts; and other "advances upon security, on the creditor side, is understated to the amount "of £2,698,539, 10s. 4d.; (4) the amount of cash on hand, viz., gold and "silver coin and notes of other banks, was overstated to the extent of "£29,090, 10s., or thereby; (5) the amount of Government stocks, Ex-"chequer bills, and other debentures, under article 3 of the creditor side, "was overstated to the amount of £753,211, 2s. 6d.; (6) the earnings of the "Bank during the year were overstated, under the head of profit and loss, to "the extent of £125,763, 12s. 8d., or thereby; (7) a reserve fund to the "extent of £450,000 was stated to exist, while in reality no such fund "existed; and (8) bad and irrecoverable debts"—and I call your Lordships' special attention to this item—"to an amount far exceeding the whole capital "stock of the Bank, were included under article 1 on the creditor side, and "so treated as subsisting and available assets of the company." [See asterisk on p. 28.]

These, my Lords, are the averments of the falsehood of the balance-sheet. Then the minor proposition goes on to aver the publication of the balance-sheet, the purpose for which it was published, and the result of its publication in these terms:—"Further, on or about the 5th day "of July 1876, in or near the Chamber of Commerce in Glasgow, you, the "said John Stewart," and so on, "and all and each, or one or more of "you, wickedly and feloniously, and with intent to defraud, did use and utter "the said false and fabricated abstract balance-sheet, along with the report "of the Bank's affairs, in which you did wickedly and feloniously represent "that the said company was in a sound and prosperous condition, and "capable of paying to its members a dividend at the rate of 11 per cent. per "annum, and of carrying forward to the credit of next year's profit and loss "account the sum of £21,361, 10s. 3d., and thereafter caused it to be printed "and circulated throughout Scotland. And all this you did, well knowing "the said abstract balance-sheet and report to be false and fictitious, for the "purpose of concealing and misrepresenting the true state of the company's "affairs, and by all which, or part thereof, you did wickedly and feloniously "deceive, impose upon, and defraud members of the company and of the "public, and induce said members of the company to retain the stock held "by them therein, and many of the public, including persons mentioned, to "deposit money in the said Bank, to the great loss and injury of the members "of the company and to the public." That is the purpose, and these are the results of the publication. That is all that it is necessary to read in connection with the charges of issuing false balance-sheets. And the first question which arises on the relevancy of these charges is, whether the *falsehood* of the balance-sheet or balance-sheets is relevantly averred. I submit to your

Lordships that on this head the libel is irrelevant—(1) As wanting in specification; and (2) as being contradictory and unintelligible.

My Lords, as I have already pointed out, the balance-sheet in question is said to have been false in eight several particulars, that is to say, it is said to have contained eight several false statements. The first observation which occurs is that we are here left altogether in doubt as to the sense in which the statements complained of are said to be false. Are they false in the sense of being disconform to the books, or in the sense of being disconform to the facts? or are some of them false in one sense and some of them in the other? and if so, which are false in the one sense and which in the other? This is not an unimportant observation, as your Lordships will at once see, because it is quite manifest, upon the most cursory examination of the eight enumerated falsehoods, that they are not and cannot all be false in the same sense. It is quite plain, for example, upon comparing article 3 with article 8, that they cannot be both false as disconform to the books, or both false as disconform to the fact; the one must be false in the one sense, and the other false in the other; and for aught that can be ascertained, the same may be the case with regard to several of the articles. The truth is, that on the face of it this enumeration appears to have been made up on two different and inconsistent principles, without any attempt at discriminating between them. My observation is, that no information is conveyed to me as to the standard of truth in this matter—as to the sense in which the statement is false—whether it is false as disconform to the fact, or only false as disconform to the books of the Bank.

Passing, however, to the particulars, I first ask your Lordships' attention to the eighth article. What I have to submit to your Lordships is, that that eighth article is altogether wanting in that specification to which the accused were entitled. The statement there is that this balance-sheet is false in respect that it includes, as good, bad and irrecoverable debts to an amount far exceeding the whole capital of the Bank. It is here necessary to be borne in mind, first, that the capital of the Bank thus said to have been lost amounts to one million; and, secondly, that the whole debts which are thus stated to have been overstated amount, as I read the indictment, to something like £11,000,000. There is £8,000,000 in the balance-sheet, and £2,000,000 more should have been added; so that it comes to this, that out of £11,000,000 of outstanding debts the prosecutor alleges that upwards of £1,000,000 were bad and irrecoverable; and he proposes to leave the accused to find out, as best they may, among this £11,000,000 of debts, which million he means to found upon as bad and irrecoverable. I submit that that is altogether unprecedented—that it is unjust to the accused—and that the effect of this want of specification must at least be to delete this part of the charge from the indictment. In this matter I am not speaking without authority. I do not know that this precise question has ever come up in a criminal case, but I don't suppose that the prosecutor will contend that he is entitled to greater latitude than the pursuer in an action founded on the same *media* would be entitled to in a civil cause. Now, we have a judgment of the First Division of the Court of Session in a civil cause founded upon precisely the same *media* as those libelled here, and in that case the same point was carefully considered, and judgment pronounced upon it. I refer to the case of Inglis against the Western Bank, 22 Dunlop 505. In that case, Mr Inglis, one of the shareholders of the Western Bank, who had purchased shares shortly before the Bank stopped, brought an action against the directors of the Bank, claiming damages in respect that he had been induced to purchase shares by false and fraudulent misrepresentations made by them, these false and fraudulent misrepresentations being contained in the two last balance-sheets issued by the company. He said that these two last balance-sheets were false in certain particulars, and that he was thereby defrauded into purchasing certain shares; and he sued the directors of the company for reparation in respect of their fraud. There were other conclusions directed against the Bank and the liquidators, in which he concluded that it ought to be found that he was not a shareholder; but these conclusions were subsequently departed from, as were also all the grounds of action against the directors not founded on fraud, and the case, as I have said, thus came to rest precisely upon the same *media* as this part of the present libel with which we are now dealing, the only difference being that a civil remedy was there sought to be obtained, whereas in this case punishment is what is asked. Now, what were Mr Inglis' averments in that case? I find that they were much more specific than the averment here. In his condescendence he first states generally "that since the issue of the "balance-sheets particularized, it has been discovered and has come to the "knowledge of the pursuer that the statements contained in the said balance-"sheets, as well as the statements and representations contained in the said "reports, on which the pursuer relied, were false, and misrepresented the "position of the affairs of the Bank; that the Company, so far from being in "a sound and prosperous condition, as it was there said, was at the time in a "state of the greatest embarrassment; and that, in place of dividends being "paid out of profits which had accrued throughout the year, they were paid "out of moneys which ought not to have been devoted to that purpose, there "being, in fact, no profits out of which dividends could have been paid." He then goes on to state that in the balance-sheets of 1856 and 1857 there were included large sums as assets of the Bank which ought not to have been so regarded, and which were truly losses, among which were several irrecoverable debts. This is the averment by which the condescendence No. 28 is introduced. Then the pursuer thinks it necessary to become more specific, and he becomes more specific. "In particular," he states, "in the balance-"sheets submitted to the meetings in 1856 and 1857, desperate and irre-"coverable debts were included as good assets, under the head of sundry "debtors' account, to the amount of £350,000; under the head of protested "bills, £26,000; under the credit account, £860,000; and under the "deposit account, £18.000; and that there was besides included in one of "these balances the sum of £38,000 as due at other agencies." Now, your Lordships will see that Mr Inglis' general averment was almost identical with the one we are here considering. There were there debts to the extent of one million which were bad and which were treated as good; and if the averment had stopped there we should have been precisely in the same condition here that the pursuer was there. But the pursuer in the case of Inglis went somewhat further. He specified the accounts in which the bad debts could be found. He did not specify the debts themselves, but he referred the defenders to certain accounts, and said that in such and such an account you will find one bad debt, and in such and such another you will find other bad debts. The question came to be whether these averments were relevant, or rather whether they were sufficiently specific, and upon that point there was a unanimous judgment of the First Division of the Court, which, if it had been prepared and pronounced for the purpose of this case, he ventured to say, could not have been more apposite. I shall take leave to read one or two passages from the opinions of the Judges.

In the first place, Lord Colonsay, then Lord President, observes as follows:—"But, farther. even in regard to what remains, I think that in some "parts of this record that are very important—I would say material parts—"there is a want of that specification and that information to the opposite "party which I think is necessary towards the safe conduct of a trial in such "a cause. I have said that the basis, or one great basis, of the alleged mis-"representation is stated to be the assumption of certain balances or "accounts as good assets of the company when truly they were bad and irre-

" coverable debts, and ought to have been written off as such and deducted, " instead of being assumed as good assets. We find, in particular, in article " 28, a statement of these. That article is all-important to this case; every " word of it almost is important; it runs thus"—and then it reads as I read it to your Lordships. Then a little further on he says—"This is said to " arise from having included in certain accounts debts of a desperate and " irrecoverable character in the 'sundry debtors' account, £350,000, and " in the protested bills account, £26,000," and so on. "Now, what " accounts included in the protested bills account, amounting to £26,000 are " alleged to have been desperate and irrecoverable? The accounts included " in the protested bills account in the balance-sheet amount to £123,000. " It is said that, in that large sum, there was included £26,000 which was " desperate and irrecoverable. Now, what were the particular accounts or " bills that were desperate and irrecoverable? How does the defender know, " or how can he be prepared to show that any one of these accounts or " bills which is said to have been desperate and irrecoverable, was not so " regarded at the time, or was not known at the time, or could not have " been known to him to be so at the time? There is no specification here. " And so in the credit accounts, £368,000 are said to have been in that state. " The credit accounts amount to £1,844,000. Which of the accounts in that " £1,844,000 are said to have been desperate and irrecoverable? Then, " again, the sum of £178,000 in the books of the Paisley agency, and £38,000 " 'at other agencies,' are said to have been in the same condition. At what " agencies? And what were the particular balances at these agencies? The " balances at the whole of the agencies appear to have been £481,000. " Which of these are said to have been desperate and irrecoverable? It " appears to me that as the foundation and the great basis of the misrepre- " sentation as set forth on this record is said to consist of including, as assets, " those debts which were truly bad and irrecoverable, the pursuer ought to " have pointed out the balances and debts which are alleged to have been " bad and irrecoverable, in order that the defenders might meet that case. Mr " Horne complained of the want of specification in this record. I do not " suppose that it would have been difficult to be specific in regard to that, " which is the great basis of the case; indeed, I think that at the late stage at " which this record was closed, it might have been easy, because I suppose " the liquidators have been at work for a long time, and probably the figures " that are put down here are deduced from some pretty good source."

Then Lord Ivory says—" I entirely agree with your Lordship in the observa- " tions which you have now made;" and Lord Curriehill, who followed, put the matter thus:—"Above all, there are two things which, in this class of " cases, must be carefully ascertained; in the first place, that the directors " have been guilty of falsehood in making such reports; and, secondly, that " they were at the time in the knowledge of the falsehood. These are essen- " tial elements of a case of fraud." "Then there must be in the record an un- " equivocal specification of the facts in which the falsehood so imputed to the " directors is said to consist, in order that they may have a full opportunity " of meeting them at the trial. This is indispensable, even in cases of in- " vestigation by proof on commission. And where the investigation is by trial " by jury, where the defenders must come fully prepared to meet the case that " is made against them, they must have full notice beforehand of the falsehoods " which they are alleged to have been knowingly guilty of, so as to enable " them to make such preparation. I agree with your Lordship in thinking that " there are in this record general averments, from which probably we might be " able to extract all the elements which are necessary to make such a case of " falsehood. But the defect in this record appears to me to be that the " directors have not got such a specification of the falsehoods which are attri- " buted to them, and of their knowledge of these falsehoods, which is indis-

"pensable to enable them to meet the accusations which are made against them, "and to secure justice being fairly administered in this case." "The general "allegation is only that the parties who were owing these debts, had not "sufficient funds to pay them, and that their inability to do so was known "to the defenders. The defenders, as denying that allegation, are called "upon by the pursuer to go before a jury to have its truth investigated." But they said they could not meet it without knowing what the debts were to which the pursuers referred. That they were stated to be only part of other debts, which amounted in all in round numbers to about three millions; and how was that part to be identified and distinguished from the other two millions? I ask your Lordships, in passing, to note the application of this last sentence to the present case. In round numbers, the debts which are alleged to be bad here amount to over a million, and the debts of which that million is a part are said to be eleven millions.

The LORD JUSTICE-CLERK—What is the specification here which you desiderate—the individual debts, or the amount?

Mr MACKINTOSH—The individual debts; and I have not got the individual debts here, nor the amounts, nor anything else. In the case quoted, Lord Curriehill concurred with the Lord President and Lord Ivory that a suitable record should be of new made up, and that the revised condescendence lodged should be withdrawn. That was what was ultimately done. Lord Deas, I should add, also concurred with the other Judges that it was impossible to require the defenders to go to trial without having the particular debts which were alleged to be bad and irrecoverable, and known to be bad and irrecoverable, set forth, so that they might prepare their defence.

Now, my Lords, that being the case of Inglis, is there any distinction between that case and the present, except that we are here not in a civil but in a criminal case? If the defenders in that civil case were entitled to know which million of the three millions of debts there in question were to be brought against them as bad and irrecoverable, surely, *a fortiori*, we are entitled to know which million of the eleven millions of debts which are here in question are said to be bad and irrecoverable. This is a case of the directors being charged with, both in books and balance-sheets, representing a million and upwards of bad and irrecoverable debts as subsisting assets; and the question is whether, that being charged, the accused are not entitled to know what the debts are to which the charge applies, and what the accounts in the books are that are founded on, or to know in some other way what is the nature of the case to be made against them.

Without, therefore, going further, I submit to your Lordships that article 8 falls for want of specification, and if that is so, then the next point is, that article 8 falling, articles 6 and 7 must fall along with it. Because it is impossible, comparing the balance-sheet with page 28, not to see that the alleged loss of the reserve fund, and the alleged absence of any profits made during the year, depend entirely on the estimate to be made of the assets of the company—that is to say, upon the estimate made of the outstanding debts. It is not said that, treating all the outstanding debts as good, there was yet no reserve fund and no profits. It is not said that the books do not show a reserve fund, or that the books do not show profit to the amount stated; and it is plain that the books must have brought out these amounts, or they would not have been able to make a balance. Therefore the charges really depend on each other. If your Lordships hold that article 8 is bad for want of specification, articles 6 and 7 must fall on the same ground; for it would not do for the Crown, after being shut out from proving under article 8 bad debts of which they had given the accused no specification, to bring in the same evidence without notice as regards articles 6 and 7.

I have next, however, to submit that the averments of the falsehood of this balance-sheet are irrelevant, not merely from want of specification, but in respect that they are contradictory and unintelligible. And I begin with article 1 of the enumeration [see p. 28], premising what I have already mentioned, that under this indictment the prosecutor puts forward each of his eight particulars as being each by itself sufficient to entitle him to a conviction. Now, what is the falsehood set forth in article 1? It is this—that the deposits of the Bank are said to have been understated. Now is that intelligible as a basis for a charge of fraud? How, standing by itself, can an understatement of the deposits in a bank tend to defraud either the shareholders, or depositors, or anybody else?

Lord CRAIGHILL—By understating debts due by the Bank, and making it understood that its affairs were better than they were.

Mr MACKINTOSH—I should say that was a matter of opinion. A bank with ten millions of deposits may very well have appeared more prosperous than a bank with eight millions. I don't see how that could be the basis of a charge of fraud. I have already shown that, in order to test the relevancy of this part of the charge, you require to take each item as it stands alone. On the theory of this indictment, the prosecutor would be entitled to a verdict if any one of those particulars in the balance-sheet was inaccurate, and was published with the result of inducing persons to become depositors.

Lord CRAIGHILL—You over-estimate the assets, and you under-estimate the liabilities.

Mr MACKINTOSH—But I am taking the case as if article 1 stood alone, and what I say is that, standing alone, it is not an intelligible basis for a charge of fraud. Passing, however, from that, I come to article 3 and article 8 [p. 28]. These articles are contradictory. The amount of bills of exchange, credit accounts, &c., it is said in article 3, were understated to the extent of £2,698,000, or thereby. That is to say, the assets were understated by two millions and upwards. But then in article 8 it is said that these same assets were overstated to the extent of over a million. How is this to be explained? The contradiction is demonstrable. For observe what it comes to. The Crown complains in article 3 that the accused understated the assets of the Bank, and understated a particular class of assets—namely, those under head 1. But when it comes to article 8, the Crown complains that the accused overstated the assets of the Bank, and overstated that same particular class of assets, being those under head 1 of that balance-sheet. The Crown says in one breath you have understated, and in the next breath you have overstated. It is for my learned friend to say how he explains this. I conjecture that his explanation may be something of this sort—that article 3 states a disconformity between the balance-sheet and the books, and article 8 states a disconformity between the books and the facts. But if that is so, that just brings us back to and illustrates the general objection with which I started, that the falsehoods here alleged are false in different senses, and that there are no means of ascertaining in what sense any particular falsehood is said to be false.

Lord MURE—They say you understated the assets.

Mr MACKINTOSH—Yes; outstanding debts are assets.

The LORD JUSTICE-CLERK—In the way in which the books are kept, all current bills of exchange, and advances to customers on security, are treated as assets, just as if they were all realized.

Mr MACKINTOSH—Just so. If your Lordships give effect to article 3, the item of £8,787,000 ought, according to the Crown, to have been £11,000,000. But then, coming down to article 8, the item in question ought to have been only £7,000,000 odds; so that in one breath the Crown says as to head 1 of the balance-sheet, that it ought to have been £11,000,000, and in another it says it ought to have been £7,000,000.

The LORD JUSTICE-CLERK—It comes to this,—those assets, consisting of current bills and other advances, were in truth bad and irrecoverable to the extent stated, and therefore you contend the balance-sheet was correct?

Mr MACKINTOSH—That is consistent with the averments.

The LORD JUSTICE-CLERK—I understand your argument to come to this, that if the bad and irrecoverable debts had been stated along with the assets, they would substantially have represented the assets of the Bank in the same way as the balance-sheets that are said to be false.

Mr MACKINTOSH—It comes to that for anything that appears. As I have said, however, it is a quite possible explanation of the confusion which pervades this part of the indictment, that the list of items on page 4 [p. 28] is made up on two different principles—the first five items being said to be false as being disconform to the books, and the last three items false as disconform to the facts. But that, of course, makes the indictment not better but worse, for the reasons I have already stated.

So far, my Lords, I have endeavoured to show that the averments of the *falsehood* of this balance-sheet are irrelevant. But now the next question which arises is this, Whether, assuming the falsehood, it appears from the indictment that the balance-sheets were issued for the *purpose* and with the *result* required to constitute the crime of falsehood, fraud, and wilful imposition. or any other cognate offence? It is here necessary to say a word or two upon a matter of principle.

The LORD JUSTICE-CLERK—You have been assuming that the major proposition is good. You say these details are not relevant, however good the major proposition is.

Mr MACKINTOSH—I am going to submit, my Lord, that even assuming the balance-sheet is false, the libel is irrelevant, in respect that it does not set forth that the balance-sheets issued were issued for the purpose and with the result which the law requires in order to constitute the crime of falsehood, fraud, and wilful imposition, or any other offence of the same character, nominate or innominate. It is here necessary, as I said before, to say a word or two on a matter of principle. We have not here, your Lordships will see, to deal with documents which are said to be false in the sense in which forged documents are false. Language no doubt is used in the major proposition—loosely and improperly used, I think—which is only appropriate to the case of forged documents. I refer to such passages in the major proposition as that in which the directors are accused of fabricating the balance-sheets. But it is plainly not there meant, however loose may be the language, that the balance-sheets were other than genuine balance-sheets. The alleged falsehood of the balance-sheets consists simply in this, that they are said to be mendacious.

Lord CRAIGHILL—You mean that the balance-sheets were issued by parties who were entitled to issue them?

Mr MACKINTOSH—Yes: they were not fictitious documents issued by somebody who had no right to issue them. In short, the balance-sheet is said to be false and fraudulent simply in the sense that it purports to set out truly certain facts in regard to the assets and liabilities of this Bank, and yet sets forth those facts untruly, and is therefore a mendacious document. That being so, we are not dealing, as I have said, with a case of falsehood in the sense of forgery; neither, again, are we dealing with another kind of case with which your Lordships are familiar, the case of false statements put forward by persons holding public offices, in violation of public duty. Familiar instances of the latter kind of crime are the cases of messengers returning false executions, of notaries making false docquets, and of doctors issuing false vaccination certificates. We have nothing of that kind here. These directors are simply managers of a trading company, and that being so, you have in these balance-sheets simply certain false statements made by certain private persons to the shareholders, and it may be to the public, in regard to the state of this City of Glasgow Bank. The case would not be in the least degree different if the alleged false statements had been made in the report, or in the chairman's speech at the shareholder's meeting. Now, that being so, the question comes to be, under what conditions is simple falsehood recognised as a crime according to the law of Scotland? I submit that, upon a review of the whole authorities, it will be found that falsehood can only be a relevant basis for a criminal charge when it is used as the means of obtaining to the accused, or to some institution which the accused represents, patrimonial gain or advantage, at the expense and to the injury of some other person or persons. In other words, where you exclude forgery and breach of *munus publicum*, the only remaining category under which criminal proceedings founded upon falsehood of this sort can be brought is what Hume describes as "fraud or cheating." He says (vol. i. p. 172)—"The same is even true of "those offences of a private and patrimonial nature, which fall under the "description of what is known in England by the name of swindling; and "are committed by some false assumption of name, character, commission, or "errand, for the purpose of obtaining goods or money, or other valuable "thing, to the offender's profit." And then he goes on to quote a number of instances of this kind of crime, the essential elements in all of them being—(1) falsehood (2) patrimonial gain and patrimonial loss resulting from the falsehood, and (3) the employment of the falsehood for the purpose of obtaining the patrimonial gain and producing the patrimonial loss. I do not know that I need go into a citation of the authorities. Your Lordships know them very well. I may just mention one case, which brings out very distinctly the necessity of the falsehood being first proved for the purpose of obtaining the resulting advantage. I refer to the case of Wilkie, tried before your Lordship in the chair and Lord Cowan at Stirling Circuit on 13th September 1876, and which is reported in Couper, vol. ii., p. 353. The libel was there held irrelevant, in respect that it did not sufficiently appear that the false representations were made in order to obtain the patrimonial advantage which the accused was said to have obtained.

Now, my Lords, if that be so, let us see here what are the advantages or *results* which are said to have been produced by these fraudulent balance-sheets. Your Lordships will find these results set forth on page 5 [see foot of p. 28]. They are three in number, and I shall take them separately. The first result said to have been produced is this, that members of the company were induced to *retain* the shares held by them therein. Now, is it a relevant statement in a charge of this kind to say that by means of false balance-sheets made by the directors of a joint stock company, issued to the members of the company, the members were induced to retain their shares?

Lord Mure—Can you separate that from the allegation that they were made for the purpose of misrepresenting the state of the company?

Mr Mackintosh—I am at present assuming that the false balance-sheets were issued for a fraudulent purpose, but it is essential, in libelling a crime of this sort, that the indictment shall set out some wrongful result or results as following from the falsehood. And I am at present considering whether the results which are set out as produced by the publication of these balance-sheets are results involving patrimonial gain on the one hand or patrimonial loss on the other. It is not easy at first to see what the Crown means by this statement—inducing shareholders to retain their shares. That did not import any gain either to the directors or to the company; and, in the next place, it did not import any loss or injury to the persons said to have been defrauded. For what does it amount to? Is it suggested that if the truth had been told, anybody would have been found to buy these shares? Or is it suggested that if the truth had been told to the shareholders, but concealed from the rest of the world, a shareholder might, by going into the market, have found an ignorant third party, and deceived him into taking the shares at an undue price? Clearly that is an advantage to which the shareholder was not entitled. He was not entitled to have information for the purpose of enabling him to get an advantage over others, and no wrong was committed by that information being withheld. I am not in the least suggesting that it was defensible in any view to issue these balance-sheets. But that really brings one back to the proposition with which one started, that the law of Scotland does not recognise the telling of untruths as criminal; and it does not recognise the publication of untruths as criminal unless something follows, involving, on the one hand, injury to the person deceived, and, on the other, patrimonial gain to the person deceiving. I therefore ask whether there is an averment here of this fraud having been effectual to that effect. It is quite plain that if the truth had been told, the shareholder must have retained his shares, as nobody would have bought them. Therefore it is impossible to say that he suffered any loss. He had to retain them as it was, and he would all the more have had to retain them if the truth had been told; and if it be necessary, in order to complete the charge of falsehood, fraud, and wilful imposition, or any cognate charge, that there shall have been a wrong produced to a third party by the fraudulent act, then this averment is irrelevant in respect that it does not involve the allegation of any wrong as sustained by the party said to have been defrauded.

The LORD JUSTICE-CLERK—You say it is no loss to the shareholders that these false representations were made, but it is a loss to the persons who bought shares.

Mr MACKINTOSH—I am coming to the second averment in regard to persons purchasing, but this first averment relates exclusively to members of the company, who are said to have been defrauded in this respect, that having shares they retained them. They could have suffered loss only by deceiving somebody else. It will not do to say that they might have taken steps to get the company wound up; that is not what the prosecutor means. If he had meant anything of that sort, he would have required to say so. The retaining of shares is plainly spoken of as in opposition to selling or transferring them. The case stated clearly points to the shareholders being deprived of the remedy of selling their shares. Retaining the shares is used in opposition to transferring them to somebody else; and if it be once assumed that the shares were unsaleable consistently with good faith on the part of the shareholders, why, then, what wrong was suffered? It follows that nobody took any harm, and that it was all one to the company.

The LORD JUSTICE-CLERK—Suppose the shares had not been saleable at all, the shareholders would have been manifestly wronged.

Mr MACKINTOSH—They might have been wronged by being lulled into a false security, but one does not see of what remedy they were deprived.

The LORD JUSTICE-CLERK—To realise the property and pay the debts.

Mr MACKINTOSH—That is to say, winding up the company. That is a very special remedy indeed; and, as I have already said, if the depriving the shareholders of that remedy was the wrong meant to be alleged, the indictment should and would have been quite differently framed. I therefore submit that it is not relevant to allege that by the issue of these balance-sheets shareholders were induced to *retain* their shares. And I may say that the question thus raised is not a new one. It arose in Dobie *v.* The Directors of the Edinburgh and Glasgow Bank, 21 D. 624, where the present Lord President pronounced the proposition now put forward by the prosecutor "as of a startling nature." It also came up in Cullen *v.* The Directors of the same Bank; but, so far as I know, there is no example anywhere in the books of the averment being held relevant that shareholders were induced by fraud to retain their shares, as here alleged.

The LORD JUSTICE-CLERK—In the Royal British Bank case, was there not a charge of this kind?

Mr Mackintosh—The charge there was altogether different, for it was a charge of conspiracy.

The Lord Justice-Clerk—There was a distinct allegation there that the fraud consisted in inducing the shareholders to retain their shares.

Mr Mackintosh—That was one of the elements of the charge in the Royal British Bank case. But the circumstances were so entirely special, and the charge so entirely different from anything we have here, that I have not thought it worth while to refer your Lordship to that case. With us an attempt to commit fraud is no crime; in England it becomes a crime if you have associated with it the element of conspiracy. The next result said to have been produced by the issue of these false balance-sheets is this. It is said that "many of the public, including Robert Craig, &c., were induced to acquire "stock in the said company" [last line p. 28]. Now, my Lords, I do not dispute that this would have been quite a relevant averment, if it had borne that many of the public were induced to purchase stock in the company from the company. We know that there are at present many persons pursuing actions of reduction in the Court of Session, who found their actions upon the averment that they were induced by false balance-sheets to purchase from the company, or from certain parties who held as trustees for the company, stock in this Bank, to their loss and prejudice. If that had been the averment here, I should have been unable to resist the contention that there was not merely the element of falsehood, but also the element of patrimonial gain to the company, on the one hand, and patrimonial loss to the public, on the other. But the averment here does not suggest that. All that it comes to is that the directors of this company issued certain false statements as to its affairs, with the result of inducing certain transactions between third parties.

Lord Craighill—That is to say, members of the company.

Mr Mackintosh—No.

Lord Craighill—How can one sell what he does not hold?

Mr Mackintosh—The member of the company was not prejudiced. The member of the company was benefited.

Lord Craighill—I know that quite well.

Mr Mackintosh—The charge is that members of the public were induced to acquire shares from members of the company. That comes to this, that by means of false statements the directors of this company induced transactions between third parties, whereby one of these parties was benefited, viz. the seller, while the other, viz. the buyer, was injured. Now, that has never hitherto been recognised as a crime, or as partaking of the character of a crime, by the law of Scotland.

The Lord Justice-Clerk—The law of joint stock companies is of comparatively recent development, and it may well be that the criminal law of Scotland is elastic enough to meet cases as they arise.

Mr Mackintosh—But it cannot be said that the law of joint stock companies is now to be developed for the first time more than any other branch of the law. There is no case that can be pointed out where falsehood—that is to say, misrepresentation of the nature here alleged—has been held to constitute a crime, unless you have the element of patrimonial gain on the one side, and patrimonial loss on the other.

The Lord Justice-Clerk—Take the case of a managing partner and another partner; that the one partner issues a false balance-sheet to his other partner. Is not that falsehood?

Mr Mackintosh—It may be, if the result would be gain to the person who issued the false balance-sheet

The Lord Justice-Clerk—The person was induced to believe that his concern was thriving, while it was not. Would that not be falsehood?

Mr Mackintosh—That would be analogous to the case of a shareholder being induced to abstain from taking action to have the company wound up.

Lord CRAIGHILL—Do you contend that it is necessary that there should bc an allegation of personal gain?

Mr MACKINTOSH—I do not say that it was necessary there should have been personal gain to the directors. It was only necessary that there should have been patrimonial gain to the institution they represented. My proposition is, that no charge is relevant which does not set forth at least patrimonial gain to the Bank; and in regard to the case of persons induced to purchase shares, which is the case I am now dealing with, I say it has never been suggested to be a crime in the law of Scotland, that a person by misrepresentation induces a transaction between third parties in which the alleged offender has no interest. If that were so, it would follow that every person publishing a *canard* in a newspaper would be liable to be indicted for falsehood, fraud, and wilful imposition, or some similar offence. That has never been suggested; and I say it was no interest of the Bank whether members of the public bought shares as members of the company or not. It was all one to the company whether transfers took place or not. If they lost the transferer, they gained the transferee; and it was quite as likely that the transferee should be a better man than the transferer, as it was that the transferer should be a better man than the transferee.

But then, my Lords, we now come to the third result said to have been produced by these balance-sheets, viz., that members of the public were thereby induced to deposit money in the Bank, to the great loss and prejudice of the said members of the public. There is here undoubtedly an averment of patrimonial gain to the company—the averment that by false representations the company obtained what I may concede to be a benefit. But two questions here arise—First, Is there any averment that the depositors suffered injury? and next, Is there any averment that the false representations were made in order that depositors might make deposits, and the company thereby benefit? My Lords, it is a remarkable fact that, from first to last of this indictment, if you except a statement in subdivision 8, on page 4 [p. 28], which I have already submitted is bad, there is not anywhere an averment that this company is insolvent; there is not anywhere even an averment that it has stopped payment; and that being so, the question arises, whether the averment that by means of these false balance-sheets depositors were induced to deposit money in a Bank, which for anything alleged is perfectly solvent, is an averment which implies injury to the depositors. I think I was entitled to have information as to wherein the loss consisted. There can be no loss if the depositors are paid out; and for aught that appears, they may be paid out as soon as they demand payment. It would have been easy, if loss existed, to have specified that loss; but there is nothing but a vague and general averment applicable to the whole of the preceding statements under this charge. In regard, therefore, to the depositors, the averment, I submit, fails in respect there is no averment of patrimonial injury sustained. But apart from that, there is another point. As I have already observed, it is necessary, in order to found a criminal charge upon a false representation, that not only shall certain results be produced, but also that it shall appear that the false representations were made for the purpose of producing those results. Now, where is it here averred that the directors of the Bank published these balance-sheets for the purpose of inducing depositors to deposit with them, or for the purpose of otherwise inducing any patrimonial gain to themselves or the company? The only averment on that subject is in the middle of page 5 [see foot of p. 28], where it is said in general terms that the balance-sheets were issued "for the purpose of concealing and misrepresenting the true state of the company's affairs." But this is not an averment that the directors had it as their purpose to induce depositors to make deposits. That is not said; and it by no means follows from or is implied in what is said. Let us suppose the case of man producing a general opinion that he was a person of wealth, and issuing extravagant statements about his affairs

—doing that verbally and in writing—and, as an indirect result of that, tradesmen come and offer him credit, and persons come and lend him money or deposit, is he guilty of falsehood, fraud, and wilful imposition? Is he guilty of any offence against property? The essence of this charge is that it is an offence against property. It is there that the element of patrimonial gain and patrimonial loss comes in. It may be very undesirable that persons should be under a false impression about anything, or that parties should suppose a company is rich when it is poor, and dwell thereby in a state of false security.

The LORD JUSTICE-CLERK—Suppose the company were insolvent?

Mr MACKINTOSH—In the case of the depositors, that would supply the element of patrimonial loss, but I am now dealing with the question of purpose; and it is necessary, as I said, that the false representations should have been made not merely with the result, but for the purpose of inducing patrimonial gain on the one hand and loss on the other.

Lord CRAIGHILL—In nine cases out of ten, the forger intends to pay the loss in the end.

Mr MACKINTOSH—But in this case, as soon as the false document is uttered the offence is complete. Forgery is simply a mode for obtaining a certain patrimonial benefit at the expense of somebody else. It may be the forger intends to pay, but there can be no question that he forges the document with the intention that in the meantime, at all events, there shall be a certain patrimonial gain to him on the one hand, and, on the other, patrimonial loss or the liability to loss. But there was nothing like forgery in this case. I endeavoured, at the outset, to define it as being quite distinct from forgery or breach of *munus publicum*. It was essential to my argument that it was distinct from these things. If it was not, my argument was at an end. What I am contending now is, that this is a case of simple falsehood—not falsehood said to have been published for a criminal purpose. My present point is, that assuming that the falsehood is relevantly alleged, and assuming that the results which the law requires for the constitution of the crime are also relevantly alleged, yet there is no relevant averment of connection between the issuing of the fraudulent statements and the fraudulent results; for your Lordship laid down, in the case of Wilkie, as a matter of familiar law, that you require to show that falsehood was used in order to obtain the benefit in fact obtained.

The LORD JUSTICE-CLERK—Suppose the Bank issued these balance-sheets for the purpose of tiding over a difficulty?

Mr MACKINTOSH—That may be wrong, but it is not an offence against property, unless the result is to cause patrimonial loss to some person and patrimonial gain to another.

The LORD JUSTICE-CLERK—They run the risk of exposing persons to loss in the event of their not succeeding.

Mr MACKINTOSH—Suppose that the directors of a company desire to maintain the *status quo*—that they desire to prevent new depositors coming in, and desire to prevent transactions in shares, and for that purpose they issue to their shareholders a certain report, which is primarily intended for them alone. And then suppose results follow which were not intended by the directors at all, and not desired by them, viz., new depositors and new shareholders coming in in the place of the old; is it to be said that they are guilty of the crime of falsehood, fraud, and wilful imposition? The argument your Lordship suggests might have been put with equal force in the case of Wilkie. A man goes into a lodging-house and makes a false statement about his affairs, and about the purpose for which he is in the place, and as a result, not the indirect but the direct result of this false statement, he gets food and lodgings; there it might be thought the offence was complete, but your Lordship held that unless it could be shown that the man intended to obtain these results by the false statements, it was no crime. The peculiarity of all these cases is that they cannot be other than crimes against property, and when that is once recognised, it follows as a necessary consequence, that all such cases necessarily involve the element of patrimonial loss on the one hand, and patrimonial gain on the other. I do not think I need say more upon this part of the case, and I now come to the second set of charges.

The LORD ADVOCATE—I would ask your Lordships to dispose of this part of the objection first.

Mr MACKINTOSH—According to the argument which I am to maintain, the different charges in the minor reflect light upon each other, and I should certainly deprecate any division of the discussion.

The LORD JUSTICE-CLERK—I should not think that a desirable course. But it is another question whether we should call for a reply on that part of the case.

The LORD JUSTICE-CLERK—What do you say to the relevancy of the innominate charges in the major?

Mr MACKINTOSH—My Lords, in regard to the innominate charges in the major proposition, my case is this. I said at the outset that according to the construction put upon the language used in the major, the innominate charges might either amount to falsehood, fraud, and wilful imposition, or might resolve into no crime at all; and I explained that the question between these two constructions would depend very much on what was found in the amplified statement in the minor proposition. I now say, as the result of my examination of the minor, that the indictment throughout, both in the major and in the minor, must be construed as omitting the elements of patrimonial gain or patrimonial loss, and as therefore failing to set forth what is necessary in order to constitute an offence of the class libelled, viz., an offence against property. I have further, however, to point out in regard to the innominate charges in the major, that it is an essential part of those charges as laid that "members of the company" are defrauded; and as the only respect in which members of the company are said to be defrauded is by their being induced to retain their shares. it will follow, if my argument as to the irrelevancy of the part of the minor is successful, that the innominate charges in the major must fall, upon the separate ground that in any view there is no relevant case stated of fraud committed on "members of the company." But I pass now to the charges of *overdrawing*, and I shall take as a specimen of those charges the one affecting my own client, Mr Taylor [see p. 33].

Lord MURE—Are the charges all the same?

Mr MACKINTOSH—All the same, except that in Mr Wright's case he is charged with continuing, after he became a director, to overdraw—that is to say, with failing to pay up his overdraft as soon as he became a director. But I am taking the charge as against Mr Taylor, because it is a fair enough specimen of the others, with the exception I have mentioned. The charge in question is as follows. [Reads at p. 33.] The question is whether this is a relevant charge according to our law. I pray your Lordships, in the first place, to notice some things which this charge does not aver. In the first place, it does not aver that Mr Taylor obtained those advances otherwise than in the ordinary course of business. It is not said that the Bank had not the protection of the other directors and of its officials. Neither is it said that the directors of the Bank conspired together to allow each other to overdraw at pleasure. I do not say that, if the facts had permitted, a relevant case might not have been stated, founded upon some such allegations as these; but there are no such allegations made. Then, again, it is not said that Mr Taylor or his firm was insolvent. It is not said that any loss arose to the Bank in connection with these advances. It is not even said that the advances were not duly or even immediately repaid. For all that appears, the advances may have been paid the day after they were obtained. Then, in regard to the matter of security, your Lordships will observe there is no averment that there was no security. All that the prosecutor says is that the security was wholly inadequate; and that being the case, it is not said that Taylor & Sons, or Mr Taylor, knew that the security was inadequate. It is not even said how the securities came to be inadequate—whether they came to be inadequate from defect of value or from defective conveyancing; or whether, being adequate at the time, they became inadequate by change of circumstances. The proposition involved in this charge is, in short, the broad and bald proposition, that if a member of a firm, however wealthy and respectable, happens to be a director of a bank in which his firm keep their account, and he, in conjunction with the other directors, allows for a month or a day his firm to overdraw their account to the amount even of a single shilling, he thereby becomes guilty of the crime of embezzlement.

The LORD JUSTICE-CLERK—On inadequate security for the advance.

Mr MACKINTOSH—On inadequate security, it may be,—he becomes guilty of the crime of embezzlement, and becomes liable to be placed at the bar, and put to satisfy a jury that the advances were made on what, in the opinion of the jury, judging *ex post facto*, was adequate security. My Lords, I say with all deference that such a proposition is preposterous, and that such a charge savours of the burlesque. Is it not matter of common knowledge that it is the ordinary business of bankers to give advances upon what in the proper sense of the term is no security? I take it that it is their business and constant practice to make such advances. I do not profess to know, but I imagine that there is scarcely a great legal firm in Edinburgh which does not at certain periods of the year, for a longer or shorter time, overdraw its bank account; and the suggestion is, that if such a firm happens so to overdraw its account with a bank where one of its partners is a director, the result is to subject that partner to a charge of embezzlement, and, I suppose, also all the other partners to a similar charge as being art and part in the offence, and all this although the money was duly paid back within a month or a week, or within even a shorter period.

The LORD JUSTICE-CLERK—The repayment of the money is quite indifferent to the charge of embezzlement.

Mr MACKINTOSH—I think I am justified in saying that the embezzlement alleged might be committed, although the party paid back the money the very next day; and, in point of fact, there is nothing upon the face of this charge to suggest that these advances, extending, some of them, in the case of Mr Inglis, from the year 1862, were not paid back from time to time, and at very short periods. That brings one to regard with some curiosity the averment of the duty resting on directors which is said to lead to this singular result. It is the general duty, and set forth in the middle of page 13 thus [see p. 33]:—"It being your duty as director foresaid not to allow overdrafts on such "account to be made without security, or on wholly inadequate security; and, "in particular" (your Lordships will observe that what follows is only set forth as a particular example of the general duty)—"and, in particular, not to "allow any such overdraft to be made without security, or upon wholly inade-"quate security, as aforesaid, by you, the said William Taylor," or your firm. Now, where is the duty thus alleged to be found? It must arise under the contract of the company or at common law. The contract not being alleged, for the very good reason that it could not be alleged, we are forced to look for the alleged duty at common law. And is it suggested that at common law there is an absolute obligation upon the directors of joint stock banking companies to refuse advances without security—that is, security other than the personal credit of the borrower?

Lord MURE—Are directors to be allowed to overdraw as much as they like without security?

Mr MACKINTOSH—The directors have no right to allow overdrafts to anybody without regard to amount and circumstances. It is the duty of the directors not to act recklessly in any matter. The mere amount, however, of the advances cannot be any indication of the duty of the directors, because, in order to make the amount a proper indication, we must know the means of the party. An advance to the amount of £70,000 to a man worth £100,000, and turning over in business a sum of £500,000 a year, and in possession of an established business—such an advance as that is not to be characterised as reckless. Your Lordships cannot send this case to a jury unless you are to declare that the proposition, as a proposition, is sound —that it is the duty of the directors to refuse advances upon anything except securities in the proper sense of the word—that is to say, upon property or something of that kind. I can quite understand its being said that there is an averment of duty, but in dealing with this averment of duty you are really dealing with an averment in point of law. It is not said that the directors violated the contract. If so, the contract should have been set forth, and the particular clause in the contract; or it should have been set forth that under the contract of copartnery it was the duty of the directors to do so and so. That is not set forth or suggested, and therefore my point is, that it is inconsistent both with common law and common knowledge that there shall exist in bank directors the disability here alleged; and here, again, I am in a position to quote an authority which, although a civil case, is good for the purpose here—I refer to the case Baird *v.* The Western Bank, 24 D. p. 905, per the Lord Justice-Clerk. In dealing with the question of relevancy in that case, the Second Division of the Court laid down that a charge of the character in question was altogether irrelevant. It was there alleged that advances of the Bank funds were made to a large amount to persons or companies and firms, without having obtained security therefor, and that the directors were debarred from doing this by the contract of copartnery and the common law and practice of banking; and, further, that the advances were in great part irrecoverable—a statement which we have not here. It was held, however, in reference to this general averment, that there was no prohibition in the contract of copartnery, and still less in the ordinary practice of banking, against making advances without security. Indeed, the Court put it that it was the main business of bankers to make advances without security in the ordinary sense of the term. There the pursuers regarded it as a matter of obligation to set forth the source of duty. They set forth that the duty arose upon the contract, and also upon the civil law. The Court, however, taking the contract, said there was no duty in the contract; and then they said that at common law it was nonsense to say that bankers are debarred from making advances without security. It was, it was said, the ordinary business of banking to make such advances; and the Court were not going to hold as relevant any such averment. I therefore put it to your Lordships that here the averment of the duty, which is at the root of the prosecutor's case, is not a relevant averment; but supposing the duty existed, I say that these gentlemen are not said to have known that the security was inadequate. It is not stated that there was no security. It is not stated that any loss was occasioned to the Bank. It is not stated that the security was inadequate in respect of value. For aught that appears, it may have been inadequate in this way only, that they accepted security which was not value according to the strict rules of conveyancing. All is left absolutely vague in the indictment. I submit to your Lordships that this charge, in respect of the absence of the various essential elements to which I have referred, is altogether bad.

I now come to the last charge—that relating to the bills; and here I don't anticipate that I shall require to detain your Lordships long, because your Lordships are fresh in the recollection of the argument which was presented by my learned friends Mr Asher and Mr Balfour on the occasion of the recent discussion as to the question of bail. The charge in regard to the bills is as follows. [Reads Count VIII., see p. 35.] Your Lordships will notice that this is substantially the same charge as that set forth in the petition on which the former discussion was taken, with just two differences—(1) That in the petition the Bank was averred to be hopelessly insolvent at the time of the alleged theft, while here we have no such averment; and (2) That in the petition it appeared that some of the bills were payable elsewhere than in London, while here it appears that they were all payable in London.

Now, what I am to submit in the first place is, that there is here no relevant charge of any crime, in respect that, upon the fair reading of the charge, all that it necessarily involves is that the bills were sent up to London prematurely. Let me ask, to begin with, What it is that appears to have been in the contemplation of parties when these bills were handed to the Bank? It is certain that the bills were endorsed to the City of Glasgow Bank by Mr Ramsay, and that they were put by him into the Bank's hands with the view of being sent up to London. It is further undoubted that when the bills were endorsed to the Bank and handed over to the Bank, it was the intention of all parties that they should be sooner or later sent up to the Bank's correspondents in London. It is also certain that at the same time nobody contemplated that the correspondent should, on collecting the money, send it down in a bag to to the City of Glasgow Bank. What was intended was, that the proceeds should be credited to the account of the City of Glasgow Bank, and thereafter be credited by the City of Glasgow Bank to the customer of it in Glasgow. That being what was contemplated; what is averred contrary to that contemplation? Here, again, it is important to consider what is not averred. It is not averred that the proceeds of these bills were not credited to the customer as soon as the Bank got them credited to themselves.

Lord CRAIGHILL—At what time were these bills sent by the City of Glasgow Bank to their London correspondents?

Mr MACKINTOSH—There is no averment that they were credited at any other than the proper time. The libel says that the proceeds were credited—that means that the bills had to be collected before the proceeds arose. You cannot credit the proceeds of a bill till it is collected.

Lord CRAIGHILL—But the bills were sent up the moment they were received, and the money placed to the credit of the City Bank.

Mr MACKINTOSH—It comes then to this, that these bills, being in the hands of the City of Glasgow Bank, are sent up to London to remain there till they are due. They are then collected, and the proceeds put to the credit of the City of Glasgow Bank; and, for all that appears, the proceeds are at the same time credited to the customer in the books of the City of Glasgow Bank. That is the state of the facts according to the averment. And the only thing not contemplated which appears to have been done was this, that instead of keeping the bills in their own safe in Glasgow till they fell due, the Bank sent them up to London prematurely for collection. There is nothing to show here that the Bank got any benefit from those bills till they fell due; and there is nothing to show that when the bills fell due and the proceeds were collected, the customer did not get credit for the full amount of the proceeds. Therefore, prematurely sending them up to London amounted to no more than if the Bank had sent up one of its clerks to London to keep the bills in his possession till they became due. The only element remaining was that in sending the bills up to London the Bank endorsed them. It may be said that this was inconsistent with the idea of their being sent up for collection; but that could not be maintained in the face of the indictment, because it appeared that ordinary endorsation was regarded as quite appropriate by the holder of the bill, when he was sending the bill to the City of Glasgow Bank for collection. There was therefore nothing but the statement of premature transmission to London.

Lord CRAIGHILL—But it says in the indictment, "Did cause or procure to "be endorsed and made over the said bill of exchange above libelled, before "it became due, to the London Joint Stock Bank, London, in order that the "proceeds thereof might be credited to the City of Glasgow Bank." Now, supposing a balance was due by the City of Glasgow Bank to its London correspondents, would the City of Glasgow Bank have been entitled to ask that these bills they got for collection should be credited to them?

Mr MACKINTOSH—The same result would equally arise if the bills had not been sent up until a day before they became due.

The LORD JUSTICE-CLERK—You say that in any case they would have been credited to the City of Glasgow Bank?

Mr MACKINTOSH—Yes. It might be that in sending them up prematurely for collection, they exposed the holders to the inconvenience of a new set of creditors, but nothing else. It is not suggested that the City of Glasgow Bank was insolvent at the time, or that its members are not well able to pay a great deal more money than the money said to have been stolen. Mr Ramsay had barred himself from saying there was an irregularity in endorsing the bills, because he did the same thing himself. The irregularity came entirely to depend upon the endorsation. It may be admitted that there was an irregularity; but admitting that, an irregularity of that description would surely be a long way from the crime of breach of trust and embezzlement. And if your Lordships are therefore satisfied that, apart from the endorsements, all that took place was just what was contemplated by the parties, I submit that no crime is relevantly alleged. But supposing your Lordships should be of opinion that there was a crime of some sort committed, as of breach of trust and embezzlement, the next question is—Does what is here charged amount to theft? Now, here the question just turns upon the distinction between custody and possession. The rule of law is that where bills are in the lawful possession of the customer, and merely in the custody of the Bank, that will amount to theft; but that, on the other hand, if it can be held that the Bank are in the lawful possession of the bills, they cannot steal them. Therefore the question turns upon a question as between possession and custody, and in regard to that there are three things that require to be adverted to. The first thing is the relation between the Bank and the customer. That relation is not the least like the relation of master and servant. It is much more like the relation between agent and principal. It is the relation of banker and customer, that being a complex relation, comprising the relation of agent and principal, of lender and borrower, and of buyer and seller, according to circumstances. It is a relation arising under a mercantile contract, or a series of mercantile contracts, and a relation which certainly is not suggestive on the face of it of the Bank being simply the hand of the customer with regard to any pecuniary transaction between them. The second thing to be attended to is this, that the title which was obtained by the Bank from the customer is inconsistent with mere custody. They obtained from Mr Ramsay—indeed, they must have obtained from Mr Ramsay, if the statement of the Crown is correct—a title of property to these bills.

The LORD JUSTICE-CLERK—If the endorsation to the Bank was merely for realisation, it would not have that effect.

Mr MACKINTOSH—But in the meantime I think the endorsation is important, as tending to show the footing on which the Bank held the bills.

The LORD JUSTICE-CLERK—It depends upon the terms of the endorsation.

Mr MACKINTOSH—Of course you may take off the effect of the endorsation, just as you may take off the effect of anything else. But in ascertaining whether the Bank's connection with this bill was custody on the one hand, or possession on the other hand, it is a most material element to keep in view that they did not merely get the bills put into their hands, but that they obtained what is *ex facie* a title of property to the bills.

The LORD JUSTICE-CLERK—That is explained, because the endorsation might be necessary to enable them properly to obtain payment when they fell due.

Mr Mackintosh—But it is an element in the question as between custody and possession. When your Lordships refer to cases in which persons holding lawful possession have been held guilty of theft, you find that they were all cases where the persons stood in the relation of master and servant. I do not by any means say, on the question as between custody and possession, that you must take this matter of endorsation as conclusive of the relations between the two parties, but it is one of the elements which may go to determine the relation between the parties. I am not putting it by itself, but along with the relation between the Bank and its customer as an element, and one must take these things in their order. And, *prima facie*, it is inconsistent with mere custody. But then, my Lords, the third element of importance is this, that it is quite plain on the face of this indictment that it was not contemplated that this bill should ever again reach the hands of the customer. It might do so, if he chose to withdraw his mandate, but the contemplation of the parties was that the customer should never see the bill again. Not only so, it was further in the contemplation of the parties that even the proceeds of the bill should never reach the customer *in forma specifica*. What was contemplated was, that the Bank should get the bill, should dispose of it in London, and should get the proceeds, and, having got the proceeds in London, should give the customer credit for the proceeds in Glasgow. That necessarily follows from the relation of the parties, and from circumstances set forth in the indictment. It would not have been possible to do it in any other way. And that being so, can it be said that it was beyond the contemplation of parties, when these bills were entrusted to the Bank, that the Bank should take the course of sending the bills to London, and, having got them collected in London, should get them paid to their account in London to-day, and credit the proceeds in accounting with Mr Ramsay in Glasgow to-morrow? Surely, upon the facts stated, it is open to the accused to maintain that the transaction was, if not in all respects regular, yet one which in any view did not import custody, but imported possession.

The Lord Justice-Clerk—But you get the bills solely for the purpose of collection. Suppose I send my servant with instructions to collect an account and pay in the money to my bankers, and the servant appropriates the money, is that theft or breach of trust?

Mr Mackintosh—That is just the same case as if the servant were instructed to get the money and bring it back to his master. The master's banker is just the master himself. He is the master's agent to receive the money, and that being so, the servant's offence would very probably amount to theft. But why? Because the servant is a mere hand, whose possession is his master's possession, and who is bound to restore the money received by him *in forma specifica*. We have no case of that sort here. The relation is not that of master and servant. There is no obligation to account *in forma specifica*. There is possession under a title, and not mere custody. Mr Ramsay was not and could not be described as being in the lawful possession of these bills, which he had endorsed and parted with, in the manner explained. And if the bills were not in his lawful possession, but in the lawful possession of the Bank, they may have been embezzled, but they could not be stolen.

On these grounds, and without detaining your Lordships further, I submit on behalf of the accused, that this indictment is irrelevant.

Mr Guthrie Smith—I appear on behalf of Mr John Innes Wright, and while I concur in the exceptions taken to the relevancy of the indictment by Mr Mackintosh, I desire to give special emphasis to the objection referring to overdrafts so far as regards Mr Wright. The charge is on pages 15 and 16 [see pp. 34 and 35] under the seventh count, and is generally in the same terms as the similar charges in respect to other directors, viz., that Mr Wright obtained for his own purposes £2746, 8s. 4d., and allowed overdrafts to his firm of £340,210, 7s. 3d. to be continued and increased. In discussing the relevancy of this charge, I am entitled to found not only on what is averred, but also on what is not averred, because I think there is authority for saying that, if what is averred is insufficient to constitute a criminal charge, the public prosecutor is not to be allowed to add anything which is not averred to make that sufficient which otherwise would be insufficient. The substance of this charge is that during the last three years of the Bank it was Mr Wright's duty as a director not to allow any account to be overdrawn—in particular, his own account or his firm's—and in breach of this duty he suffered sums to be drawn from the Bank without any adequate security. I submit, for the reasons already alleged by Mr Mackintosh, that if the whole of what is said there was true, it does not amount to a crime cognisable by the law of Scotland. The material elements of a criminal offence are wanting. In the first place, it is not said that Wright at the time he became a director and obtained this advance was insolvent, or that he knew himself to be insolvent; and, in the next place, it is not said that the security, which was alleged to be inadequate, and upon the faith of which this advance was made, was known to him to be insufficient. I take it that the duty which he is charged with violating arises from the office of director simply. It could only arise either from the contract of copartnery, or from the terms of Mr Wright's appointment, or from some bye-law of the corporation. If it had been upon any of these three things which I have referred to, then I think it was required by the rules of criminal pleading that it should have been so stated in the indictment. None of them being averred, it must be assumed that the duty charged is averred to flow from the directors' office as such; the indictment, in short, simply represents what is familiar to us in such language as *qua* director of this Bank. In other words, there is attached to the office of director of any public company, in particular any banking company, the obligation here charged. That is a question which your Lordships are entitled to deal with on the relevancy. I put it whether the law of Scotland really attaches any such obligation,—any such qualification, as to the manner in which banking business is to be conducted. The most profitable of all banking business is the making of advances upon cash credit, provided, of course, the security offered is sufficient. Having made this remark, I would direct attention to the distinction which is made between the first sum—the sum given, or alleged to be taken by Mr Wright personally—and the other sum which is alleged to be given to his firm. The only allegation of active misconduct on the part of the defender is as regards the money taken personally; as regards the firm's money, what is charged is simply passive. Although I am not at liberty, dealing with a matter of relevancy, to explain what it is, I shall put it as a hypothetical case. There are many instances, we know, in which a person of experience and proper capacity for the office is not qualified to become a director, because he is not possessed of any stock in the concern sufficient to constitute qualification. In order to give him that qualification, and in order that the company may avail itself of his services, it is matter of experience that the stock is found for him, and he grants an obligation for the price. Your Lordships will see afterwards how far the case here has any relation to the hypothetical case I am putting. But I put this case in order to show that really there would be nothing criminal in a transaction of that nature. I say it would not have been criminal to have placed to his credit in the books of the Bank a sum of money representing the stock he held, and yet here something like that is in effect charged as criminal against the prisoner at the bar. I apprehend that. in order to make a relevant charge, the public prosecutor should have descended to particulars. Your Lordships will see that what is charged in respect of the second portion of the charge is simply and peculiarly passive. It is said, in the first place, that when he was appointed a director he was doing business through his firm with the Bank; that the result of his firm's operations was to leave a large balance against him standing in the books of the company, and that it was a crime on his part not at once to pay off that balance. That is simply what is meant when it is said that he allowed this balance to continue. That may have been a matter of imprudence on the part of a director, or he may have been chargeable with negligence, but surely not of embezzlement, by not paying off at once the balance standing against him in the books of the Bank prior to becoming a director. I want to know how the element of criminality arises. Why did the accused allow the balance to be continued? It is not said there was any reason for paying it off.

Lord CRAIGHILL—It is said in the indictment that there were entrusted to him large sums of money, and that he not only abused the trust, but embezzled the money. And he allowed in this particular matter the account due by his firm to lie over.

The LORD JUSTICE-CLERK—The money had been advanced to the firm, and was in the pocket of the firm, and the real question is—A member being in this position as a debtor, what are his obligations as a director? The balance was incurred before he became a director.

Lord CRAIGHILL—He became a director, leaving the debt unpaid.

Mr GUTHRIE SMITH—I say that the relation is simply the relation of a debtor to a creditor, and this relation was not in any way altered by his becoming a director. A director is not in possession of the bank funds, which are held by the proper officials. He is a trustee of powers but not of property, so as to make any misapplication of it on his part a breach of trust criminally punishable. There is then, I maintain, nothing to import criminal responsibility. In the next place, the second branch of this charge is that he allowed the overdraft to be increased. Now, if the public prosecutor is going to found upon this circumstance, I want to know the extent to which that increase is laid. The whole sum stated is £340,210, 7s. 3d. Supposing the increase to be 7s. 3d., will that make a criminal charge?

Lord CRAIGHILL—There is no distinction in that way between what is relevant and irrelevant.

Mr GUTHRIE SMITH—In corroboration of what I have now submitted, I would remind your Lordships of what fell from your Lordship in the chair in the case of Rae against Linton, High Court, December 11, 1874, Couper, vol. iii., p. 67. In that case your Lordship said it had been decided that where the act set forth in the criminal libel is not of itself criminal but innocent, the libel will not be rendered relevant merely by the addition of epithets or objections, but there must be specified the circumstances which give the act a criminal character. Now, I take my stand on that proposition, and I submit upon this point that the acts specified are not of themselves of a criminal character. The case in which these observations occurred just illustrates the propriety of attending to those ancient rules of procedure. A person from Annan came into Edinburgh and passed a cheque in the Bank of Scotland offices here, drawn upon the bank in Annan. The clerk, assuming that he had an account with the bank at Annan, at once paid the money; and it having come to the knowledge of the bank that there were no assets in Annan, the accused was brought before the Court upon a charge of fraud and embezzlement, and convicted and sentenced; but on appeal to this Court the sentence was quashed, because of the irrelevancy of the charge of theft which had been ultimately proceeded upon. The rubric of the case is in these words—"Held "that a complaint which set forth that the accused had wickedly and feloni- "ously, falsely and fraudulently presented a cheque at the bank, well knowing "that he had then no money in said bank, and did in that manner impose upon "and deceive said bank, and obtain the amount of the said cheque, which he

" appropriated, did not amount to a relevant charge of falsehood, fraud, and " wilful imposition. and sentence pronounced by a magistrate under Edinburgh " Provisional Order thereon suspended accordingly." The judges who decided this case were Lord Neaves, Lord Young, and your Lordship in the chair; and I think a few remarks which I find reported in the judgment of Lord Neaves well illustrates the proposition which I have submitted for your Lordships' consideration. Lord Neaves says—" I do not say that there are " not cases where the use of such words as falsely and fraudulently is suffi- " cient. without any specific statement that the thing done amounted to a " criminal act, by reason of the state of matters existing when it was done. " Some acts are in themselves inconsistent with innocence, and where that is " the case there is no necessity for further explanation in the libel of the way " in which they assume their criminal character. Now, in the present case, " the complainer is charged with having drawn a cheque upon his own account " with a bank in Annan, and with having caused it to be presented to a bank " in Edinburgh; and it is sought to be inferred that he was thereby guilty of a " crime because he had then no money at his credit with the bank at Annan. " That is not a fair libel. You must specify in what respect the act of draw- " ing and presenting the cheque was fraudulent. There is nothing stated in the " libel which is not consistent with perfect innocence on the part of the com- " plainer of all fraudulent design. The having money at his credit with a bank " is not the only ground on which a man may draw a cheque. He may be " directly authorised by the bank to draw on credit, either by reason of having " granted a cash credit bond, or by reason merely of his undoubted solvency; " or being obliged to overdraw his account in a temporary emergency, he " may be as morally certain that the bank will honour his draft as he would " be if he knew that he had money at his credit. Or he may even be in " ignorance that he has overdrawn his account at all. Yet in this indictment " there is nothing but the use of the words falsely and fraudulently to convert " that into a criminal act which is perfectly consistent with innocence." With these remarks Lord Young concurred; and on the same grounds I say that there is nothing to show that the act in question was inconsistent with innocence. If there had been intention on the part of the procurator-fiscal to make this a fraudulent breach of trust, then he should have averred something to that effect,—either that the security offered in this case was inadequate, or that the act in itself was fraudulent, the party being at the time insolvent; or something, at all events, to make him not an innocent man.

The LORD JUSTICE-CLERK (To the Lord Advocate)—On the first of the objections, namely, the question of specification under the first head, especially as regards the 8th subdivision of that part of the indictment, we should like to have a few observations, and also on the question to which Mr Smith has just addressed himself. In regard to the relevancy of the innominate offence, and in regard to the charge of theft, while we, of course, do not at all shut out any further observations that may be hereafter made on the part of the prisoners, we do not at present wish your Lordship to say anything.

The LORD ADVOCATE—After what your Lordship has just said, I apprehend that my duty is a very simple and very short one, because I am no longer bound to argue against what appeared to me to be really one of the most serious contentions for the accused—serious, not as involving a difficult question of law or libel, but as involving very serious consequences to the prisoners and also the public—viz., the contention that what is set forth in the major and minor propositions of the libel in its first three counts, constituted merely an exaggerated instance of moral delinquency, and not a grave commercial crime. In regard to that one point, the 8th particular, if I may call it so, I shall be glad to save the time of the Court by consenting to its being struck out. It is a question which I cannot promise your Lordships you will get rid of altogether, because it may turn out that, on an examination of the books, what appears there may yet be made matter of discussion. But as constituting a separate statement I withdraw it, because I do not know, and I cannot tell at this moment precisely, *quo animo* the manipulation or fabrication of the accounts connected with this proceeded, and it may be that the £2,000,000 odds understated in stating the amount of debts due to the Bank may have been intended to include bad debts.

Mr TRAYNER asked if the particular in question was to be struck out of the indictment as regarded the three years.

The LORD ADVOCATE—Yes; I understood the argument to apply to all. The only question with which, therefore, I have to deal is the relevancy of the minor,—because no objection is stated to the relevancy of the major proposition in the second class of charges—first, as in the case of William Taylor; and secondly, assuming the libel in that case to be relevant, as in the case of John Innes Wright. In consequence of the distinction drawn by counsel——

Mr ROBERTSON—I understood that it was not necessary that the counsel for each panel should point out where the cases coincided, but the Lord Advocate will understand the case of Mr Inglis falls under the same category as that of Mr Innes Wright.

The LORD ADVOCATE—I quite understood that. I did not think it necessary to repeat it—it was so distinctly announced by Mr Mackintosh that what he did say upon the case of Taylor applied to all the others, without exception, as regards this second class of charges. In the case of Mr Innes Wright there are some peculiarities, distinguishing that case from the others, and Mr Inglis is in substantially the same position. Now, let me call to mind the character of the major in this case before I proceed to consider the minor proposition; and first, taking the case of Taylor, I quite admit that it is the duty of the public prosecutor, having set forth a charge in the major proposition of breach of trust and embezzlement, to set forth in the minor the particulars of that charge as against each panel, so as to give them fair notice of the case to be brought against them. A good deal of what is necessary to be alleged in such a case depends upon the circumstances of the case, and upon the practice of the Court. In the case of Taylor, the allegation made by the Crown is simply this—first, that Taylor was a director of the company during the later years of its existence; and secondly, that in his capacity of a director a certain duty was incumbent upon him—not to allow overdrafts upon an account or accounts current or a credit account without any security, or upon wholly inadequate security. And inadequate security plainly means and is certainly intended to signify a security inadequate not only from the outset but throughout.

The LORD JUSTICE-CLERK—Manifestly inadequate.

The LORD ADVOCATE—Obviously and unmistakably inadequate. I don't think it is either necessary or usual in a criminal indictment to libel the source from which the duty springs.

The LORD JUSTICE-CLERK—The directors had power to allow overdrafts. Is the allegation here that one of them by himself made an overdraft on his own account?

The LORD ADVOCATE—I take it that the meaning is that he drew upon the Bank for himself or his firm.

The LORD JUSTICE-CLERK—The overdraft was by his own hand; but did the other directors allow it? Where does that come in?

The LORD ADVOCATE—My allegation is that he did it alone, whether the others were willing or not.

The LORD JUSTICE-CLERK—How does that imply breach of trust on the part of the other directors.

The LORD ADVOCATE—The meaning is, that being a director, and assuming the authority of a director, he used that power to overdraw his account.

The LORD JUSTICE-CLERK—Or managed it without.

Lord CRAIGHILL—That is as if the money had been committed to him individually.

The LORD ADVOCATE—Being a director, he used that power for a particular purpose. My allegation is that he did it alone—that, being a director, armed with the authority of a director, he used that power simply to overdraw his account without giving security, whether the other directors were willing or unwilling. Being one of several directors, each of whom was under a certain duty to the shareholders of the Bank in regard to the money of the Bank, he, simply availing himself of his position, took the money by overdrafts. That is the allegation unquestionably, and it is one which appears to me to be perfectly plain in the indictment. Of course the public outside rely upon the checks which the directors ought to have interposed in conducting the affairs of the Bank, and my allegation is that, being one of the body entrusted with money, he has simply taken it for himself. It is just the same thing as if I had alleged that certain persons, being trustees on a trust estate, and having the whole estate and effects of the truster, belonging to them in a sense, in their possession, subject solely to the trust, one of them helped himself to the money, or silver plate, or other property of the trust. The case of the Western Bank *v.* Baird might have been an authority against me had it stood exactly where my learned friend Mr Mackintosh appears to think that it does. Reference was made to the contract of copartnery of the Bank, and of course that will be put in evidence, should your Lordships sustain the relevancy of these charges; and all that I say at present on this point is, that the duty of the directors is a matter to be instructed by evidence, and that if the evidence offered by the Crown in support of the allegation of duty is insufficient to support the statement in the libel, there is an end to the case, because the prosecutor has failed to prove that which is the basis of the charge. But my learned friend mistakes the meaning of the words "personal "security." He used the words "personal security" in their looser and more popular sense. When there is a stipulation in the contract of a bank for an overdraft of an account current or a cash credit, it is simply a liberty to overdraw—there being no money in the account necessarily. When that is granted by the bank, there is a provision that that shall not be done—taking a case by way of illustration, for it is not the case here—without real or personal security. In a case like that, personal security does not mean personal credit. Personal security there means that there shall be surety taken in the form of an obligation by some other person, that if the debtor fails to pay, that person will make payment forthcoming. In any other sense "personal security" is without meaning.

The LORD JUSTICE-CLERK—You are taking the case of cash credits?

The LORD ADVOCATE—Yes. There are observations made by the Lord President with regard to the particular case of Baird and the Western Bank, which, I venture to say, if read in any other light than for the purposes of that case, are not well founded in law. You may have personal security upon bills, and there is no commoner instance than that. A wishes the bank to take his draft, and the answer is, We will not take your draft unless other persons, as B or C, will become liable along with you for repayment, either *subsidiarie* or conjunctly, but in that case we will take it. I refer to this, because it leads up to another point in that case which entirely distinguishes it from the present. The allegation in that case was this: "The said directors and members "of the committee of management, through the periods of their respective "tenures of office, habitually and systematically and grossly violated and neglected their duty to the Bank and to the shareholders thereof, exceeded "their powers, and contravened the provisions of the contract of copartnery, "inasmuch as they made large advances to persons and companies and firms "without having obtained security therefor, as required by the provisions of "the contract of copartnery, as well as by the ordinary rules and practice of "banking." The observation which the then Lord Justice-Clerk makes upon that matter has been already read to your Lordships by Mr Mackintosh. But in that case the pursuers proposed to amend their record by altering that general statement, including documents of debt of every class and description, into a substantive statement, to the effect that certain cash credit accounts had been allowed to be overdrawn by the directors, in breach of their duty, and specifying the amount of the overdrafts which had been fraudulently sanctioned. The observation of the Court upon that was that that new and amended allegation was an allegation of a character so entirely different from that made in the record, and so completely altered the case from irrelevancy in the direction of relevancy, that they refused to permit the amendment to be made. Your Lordships will find this in the passage following that read by my learned friend. I will read it, because it makes the view of the Court exceedingly plain. "In the course of the argument the pursuers became so much satisfied of the irrelevancy of this part of their case, that they asked leave to "alter the averment now under consideration by adding the statement that "those advances were made by way of giving cash credits without security, "in violation of the 28th clause of the contract of copartnery. This, however, "involves so complete a change on the nature of the charge here made, that "I think the amendment quite inadmissable. It amounts to nothing less "than substituting a definite charge of the violation of a particular clause of "the contract, instead of a vague and utterly irrelevant allegation of breaking "the contract and transgressing the ordinary rules of banking, by doing what "is in truth nothing else than pursuing the ordinary business of banking." Now I think it unfortunate that my learned friend, in addressing his argument to the Court, should have assumed that the statement here was made in that loose and irrelevant form which, in the case of the Western Bank against Baird, the Court refused to recognise as relevant. and did not advert to the fact that the present case is stated in terms of the alternative case which it was proposed to place upon the record. Because, whether or not it is an authority going the whole length of holding that to be a relevant allegation, the case of Baird is at all events a very plain authority to this effect, that the statement made in this libel is entirely different from that which was held irrelevant in the other. Now, in the case of Taylor, you have the averment of duty quite distinctly made; and you have the statement that that which was a plain duty in the case of a third party is a very plain duty in the case of a director. Does that make the statement irrelevant, that a director ought not to do a certain thing in dealing with a third person, and that he ought not to do it in his own case? Does the law allow to directors of such companies this latitude of action, that they may give themselves banking accommodation upon terms on which they cannot give it to anybody else?

The LORD JUSTICE-CLERK—Would what you have said have been a good charge against the other directors?

The LORD ADVOCATE—If I was to allege that they had sanctioned this overdraft, it would; but it is of the essence of the charge that one director took upon himself to do in his own favour that which the directors collectively could not have done, because it would be beyond their right. I could not have made the charge of embezzlement against them unless I had alleged that it had been done in fraudulent concert with the other parties. If the directors had authorised it by minute, that would have raised many questions. If they had done it upon the solicitation of the individual director who got the credit, that is one case. If it was done without his knowledge, and he availed himself of it subsequently, that is another case. In such a case, treating it as an offence by the directors against the terms of their duty, on the one hand it might amount to simple fraud, but, on the other hand, they might be so bound up with the person getting the money as to make them art and part in enabling him to embezzle. Suppose the case of a number of directors sitting round a table. A wants an overdraft of £10,000, B wants £15,000, C £20,000, D £25,000, and so on. If that were done by a series of minutes, and done collectively and at once, I should not hesitate to say that the minutes thus signed, with the consent of the whole of them, to enable A, B, C, and D to get their advances without security, would constitute a case of general embezzlement by the whole body of directors. But we must take the case as we find it. I have no desire to press unduly this view, but the accusation I make in setting forth the particular breach of duty which I say was committed, is that he took advantage of his official position as a director to get overdrafts.

Lord Craighill—Where does the element of breach of trust come in?

The Lord Advocate—It begins with the words "taking advantage of "your official position."

Lord Craighill—If he presented a cheque and obtained value for it, that would not be a breach of trust. It would not be embezzlement of money. The money was, rightly or wrongly, given him for his own purposes.

The Lord Advocate—I quite admit that this belongs to a class of cases which are fortunately rare. The money is not given to him only. You have a joint ownership on the part of trustees. The real question of difficulty which your Lordship appears to suggest is this, that when one trustee takes upon him, by virtue of his *pro indiviso* right in the property, to take it out of the trust of the other person, that is not taking what is embezzled out of his own trust. But with all deference, I must submit that it is not so.

Lord Craighill—By whom was it received and entrusted?

The Lord Advocate—It was received by and entrusted to him by the Bank corporation in their distinctive corporate capacity.

Lord Craighill—In return for his cheque?

The Lord Advocate—Not at all. The indictment sets forth—"You, the "said William Taylor, having in your capacity as director foresaid, along with "the other directors and officials of the said City of Glasgow Bank, received "from the depositors and other creditors of the said City of Glasgow Bank, "and been entrusted by them with large sums of money, in order that the "same might be employed in the ordinary business of banking." Let me put this illustration :—A body, say, of three trustees, are vested in the property of a trust estate which they are to hold for, it may be, a person unborn. The beneficiary is not in existence, and therefore they are co-proprietors, although not beneficially interested. Suppose that under the custody of the servant of the deceased truster there is trust plate, and that one of the trustees, who is a *pro indiviso* proprietor, goes and tells the butler to give him a teapot, and that, having got the teapot, he goes and pawns it, and spends the money, is not that theft from the lawful possession of the trustees, and breach of duty at the same time? The difference between that case and the present, is that it would be held to be a theft because it was the appropriation of a specific article—an article which he was bound to deliver in *forma specifica* to the beneficiary. But take the case of a clerk to trustees. The funds in that clerk's drawer are as much in his custody as the money in the teller's custody for the day to enable him to conduct the business of the bank. Whose property are these funds? They are the property of the corporation in one sense, but are under the direct control of all the officials, who are under the control of the directors, because the corporation itself is a mere legal entity, and can do nothing. It has nothing but a legal and mythical existence as a legal *persona*, and cannot finger money, appoint a teller or dismiss a teller, or give instructions as to the disposal of the property of the bank. The directors are the persons who hold the funds of the bank, who are answerable to the corporation for the funds of the bank. They may, like any other trustees, be exempt from liability for factors who may have been guilty of embezzlement.

They are not liable to the bank if any official does wrongly. But if, in the case of a private trust, or the case of a bank, a trustee, *qua* trustee, goes to one of the officials of the trust and says, Give me £50 of the trust funds—and there are very few officials of the trust who would decline to give it—and if he gets the money and applies it to trust purposes, he has discharged himself of the obligations which he was under.

Lord CRAIGHILL—But were these funds entrusted to him in his possession?

The LORD ADVOCATE—They were in his possession, and that was the point I was proceeding to illustrate. They were in his possession in the same sense that trust funds were in the possession of the trustees. My contention is that each man is in possession of the whole. He may not have a right to possess them; but if he possesses himself of them wrongfully, and uses them wrongfully, he is violating the trust obligation as much as if he were acting along with the whole body of the trustees. The real question is simply this—If a trustee commits an act which would be a breach of duty in every single member of the body were they to do it collectively, is that less an act in contravention of the trust that he does it singly, without the aid, and it may be against the wishes, of the other trustees? Does it not simply come to this—a *pro indiviso* right to property covers the whole, and may be quite sufficient to entitle any one director to handle the money of the bank or control the officials of the bank? If it does not put them in that position, then he was not taking advantage of his official position as a director at all. The allegation is that he took advantage of his position as a director—that he did that to obtain money which he would have tried or attempted to do in vain but for the fact that he was at the time a director of the Bank. And if I cannot prove to the satisfaction of a jury, under the direction of the Court, that he took advantage of his position as a director to obtain money, I shall not have proved the minor of this indictment. On the other hand, if I succeed in satisfying a jury, under the direction of the Court, that in obtaining that money, which was the property of the corporation or the Bank, he did take advantage of his official position as a director, is it possible to allege that that is not a breach of the trust reposed in him as a director? In connection with this matter, the question arises—Could a bank director not steal? I maintain that a bank director might be guilty of a charge of theft. Of course there is always a difficulty arising from this, that he takes what he is only bound to use in a particular way—and the speciality is this,—the liability to account. The question always arises—whether he is taking *in forma specifica;* and is so bound to restore. But here is simply a case of taking money, and he takes advantage of his trust capacity in order to take it. If he had got it rightly as a director, his obligation would not have been to pay it back *in forma specifica*, he might have paid it back in the notes of any solvent bank, or in gold. He may not have got the money at all. An entry in a book would have the same effect, of giving him a credit. It is immaterial in what shape it comes; but a legitimate overdraft simply implied an obligation to account. If he had legitimately done so, that would have met his obligation; but, having obtained money or a credit illegitimately, at his own hand, under the cover of the position he holds, I have to submit to your Lordships that the crime is relevantly libelled as embezzlement. In other words, the persons to whom he is liable to account are truly the shareholders of the Bank. There is no obligation on the part of the directors to find funds in any particular shape; so long as they legitimately hold funds in their hands, they are entitled to convert them and use them as they choose. Their liability is a liability to account. They may set forth that they hold so much consols, so much gold, so many bills, so much in heritable security, so many obligations covered by the guarantee of others. So long as they account for them in some form or other, there is no obligation on their part to deliver them *in forma specifica*. It is also so with persons entrusted with the collection of money, and whose liability is simply one to account. He can pay the money into the Bank to the credit of the owner, unless there is something in his mandate preventing him from doing so. A man in that position could not be charged with theft if he appropriated the money, because he is not bound to restore that which he collected *in forma specifica;* neither is there any such obligation on the part of bank directors. The only alternatives in such a case are either theft or embezzlement, and as it is impossible to affix the charge of theft to a credit, the only other alternative is a charge of embezzlement, because there is not what must be present in every charge of theft—an appropriation of a specific thing, but an appropriation to his own purposes or to his own advantage of a sum got by using his trust character as a director of the Bank. Then, upon the case of Mr Wright and Mr Inglis, the allegation there is that when they became directors they were owing money to the Bank, but that instead of reducing that they increased it.

Lord CRAIGHILL—But there was a sum already due by Mr Wright's firm to the Bank. Now, where does the misappropriation begin? The overdraft existed previously to his becoming a director. Do you hold Mr Wright responsible for the whole amount overdrawn?

The LORD ADVOCATE—It comes to this, that as soon as this debtor of the Bank became a director, an entirely different duty arose. What had been done by him, with the consent of the directors for the time, when he became a director he came under an obligation not to permit; and the allegation they had here is that he not only continued his debt, but increased it.

The LORD JUSTICE-CLERK—Take the case of a director whose firm had an overdraft before he assumed office.

The LORD ADVOCATE—As a director he had undertaken to do one thing, while he had done precisely the reverse. He had undertaken a trust in a question with the Bank, and it was his duty in the capacity of a director to guard it.

The LORD JUSTICE-CLERK—Do you reply for the whole of the prisoners, Mr Trayner?

Mr TRAYNER—Yes, my Lord, upon the question of overdraft. A clear and short question has been raised by my friend Mr Mackintosh on this part of the indictment—Whether, even supposing the jury should find proven everything stated in the charge of overdraft, there should follow any punishment against the prisoners, in respect of this not being in itself a relevant point of dittay. It appears to me that the learned Lord Advocate has applied himself more to illustrate and enforce views which do not necessarily arise upon this charge at all, than meet the case very clearly put by Mr Mackintosh, which, to my mind at least, bore no trace of confusion at all. If I read this indictment aright, without following exactly every technical expression in it, it amounts to this: The prisoner—I am just now taking Taylor's case, although I shall advert particularly to Mr Stewart's case by and by—having been elected a director of the City of Glasgow Bank, and in respect of the election having had imposed upon him a certain duty, he, in violation of that duty, allowed an overdraft on an account current on the Bank, and that particularly he violated that duty by allowing an overdraft to himself or to his firm. I think your Lordships have heard, and we have all heard, for the very first time, that an overdraft upon a Bank, allowed by directors to themselves or any customer of the Bank, is a crime according to the law of Scotland. I should be very much astonished to hear any one maintain that abstract proposition before your Lordships, especially after the very clear and emphatic expression of opinion which fell from the present head of the Court in the case which has already been referred to. I ask, in the first place, what is the duty that is said here to have been violated? Whence did that duty arise? Is it a duty at common law, or is it a duty upon contract? The Lord Advocate said he would make it matter of proof, that by the Bank's contract of copartnery it was forbidden. But, my Lords, I beg to say with all submission, that the learned Lord Advocate will not be allowed to make anything matter of proof in this case that he has not first made matter of averment, and that unless he can point to the page and line in this indictment which charges me and warns me in what respect I have violated the duty which by contract I entered into and undertook, he will not be allowed to prove the existence of the contract, and consequently cannot be allowed to prove its violation. Did the Lord Advocate know of the existence of this contract? He says he will make it matter of proof. Then there is no excuse for the prosecutor not having warned the prisoner of everything he intended to prove. Again I say, that if this alleged duty arising out of contract is not made matter of averment, it cannot be made a matter of proof. Is it then a matter of duty at common law? This is of so great moment that I will again trouble your Lordships with a reference to Baird's case, especially as I think the Lord Advocate has failed to appreciate the importance of the Lord President's observations. The case there was in the civil court, and raised the question whether the directors had violated their duty as directors under the contract of copartnery towards the parties who had elected them to that particular office. The question raised by the action, and settled by the Court, was just as essentially and clearly a question of relevancy as that now being debated. It was not in the least degree with reference to the proposed alteration on the record that the Lord President made the observation to which I am about to refer. The averment was that the said directors and members of committee of management, during the respective periods when they held office, were guilty of gross and culpable neglect of duty, excess of power, contravention of the contract of copartnery, and of wrongous and fraudulent conduct in the superintendence and management of the business of the company, whereby great loss was sustained by the shareholders of the company. Then condescendence 43 went on to specify the particulars of violation of duty alleged—that the said directors and members of the committee of management, during the periods of their respective tenures of office, habitually and systematically, culpably and grossly, violated and neglected their duty to the Bank and its shareholders, and also exceeded their powers and contravened the provisions of the contract of copartnery, inasmuch as they made advances of large amounts to persons and companies or firms without having obtained security therefor, as required by the provisions of the contract of copartnery, as well as by the ordinary rules and practice of banking. That article had appended to it two different schedules, in which were set forth the names of the persons to whom the advances were given, and the amounts so given, which the pursuer averred were irrecoverable from the persons in question. The Lord President said—The foresaid article alleged that sums were advanced without having obtained security, as required by the provisions of the contract of copartnery. "It is said these advances have in great part proved irrecoverable, and been lost to the Bank. In this general form the averment "is altogether valueless; for there is no absolute prohibition in the contract of copartnery, and still less any to be derived from the ordinary "practice of bankers, against making advances without security. It is the "main business of a banker to make advances without security in the ordinary "sense of the term, as by discounting bills to traders in good credit. But the "43d article professes to follow up this averment by detail."—"I have no "hesitation in saying that this is not a relevant allegation of a contravention "of the contract, or of the ordinary rules of banking, or of anything else "than mere misfortune in the conduct of the Bank's affairs, unless, indeed, "it may be indirectly implied from the amount of the losses that the management was imprudent." Let me compare the *species facti* there with the *species facti* set forth in the indictment. The panel is said to have allowed overdrafts upon certain accounts, and specially to have allowed an overdraft to his own firm, which under any circumstances he should not have allowed. The averments in Baird's case, in which the directors were sought to be made personally responsible in the civil courts for loss, were just as broadly put as it is possible to put them in words. It was that, contrary to the contract of copartnery—which we have not here—and contrary to the ordinary principles and rules of banking, they allowed overdrafts without any security at all. But the Court there held that that was not enough. Why? They held it was not enough, because it was thought that to allow overdrafts without security was not contrary to the general practice and principles of banking; and, in the second place, because there was not, in the contract of copartnery libelled on, any special prohibition against their doing so. I do not know, and I cannot tell—because the contract is not here—what may be the effect of clauses in the contract of copartnery on this question. If it had been here, I should have been prepared to argue upon it. But for the purpose of this discussion we do not know that there is a contract at all, and we do not know that the clauses of the contract impose any duties upon the directors in this matter, and that they may not give overdrafts at their pleasure.

The LORD JUSTICE-CLERK—You are quite entitled to assume that you do not know anything here about a contract, but you cannot assume anything further.

Mr TRAYNER—I am entitled, my Lord, to assume that, as the prosecutor has not averred the contract, I have done nothing in violation of my duty so far as contract is concerned. I think the words of the Lord President in Baird's case put it beyond argument, that what I may have done was not contrary to the principles of banking, for that which the Court was there dealing with was this, that overdrafts were alleged to have been given to different persons, in different and large sums that were irrecoverable, and that without any security at all. What more can the Lord Advocate aver against Mr Taylor, or the other prisoners at the bar, except that they advanced money without security? But I go further, and I find that the Lord Advocate does not confine his case to the panels' giving advances without security, but goes on to this, that if this was not the fact, and if there was always some security in the case, yet he would be entitled to a verdict if the overdraft was allowed on wholly inadequate securities. Who is to be the judge of that? What is the point of time at which the inadequacy is to be ascertained? That is a very general expression. Is it to be "inadequate" in the opinion of the person who gave the advance, or in the opinion of the jury who are now to try this question? And then it is to be observed that, although the Lord Advocate in the course of his argument stated that by inadequate security he understands and means a security manifestly or obviously inadequate at the time it was tendered, yet this is not stated in this indictment. And yet that is a matter which he was just as much bound to libel as that we gave the advances without security or without sufficient security. It is not enough for him to come forward in the most general terms, and say that we gave advances without security, or without adequate security, but he must say that we advanced this money, and allowed these overdrafts, not only on what was obviously an inadequate security, but what we knew to be an inadequate security. And I look in vain on the face of this indictment for an averment that the directors in this matter, acting however imprudently, however unwisely, however foolishly, as the event might prove, did not act in perfect *bona fide*, dealing with the security in each case as it came up. Let me put a case further, just to show still more clearly—if that really can be done—the irrelevancy of this averment. It is said that the directors violated their duty, as having employed money contrary to the ordinary business of banking, and that thus they were guilty of breach of trust and embezzlement in respect of their putting to their own uses money which they had as directors obtained. The Lord Advocate has said—and it is one of the many things he has said which might fairly enough, perhaps, be stated in argument, but which did not enter into the pure question of relevancy—that, according to his reading of it, this charge amounts to this—that they took unjust and unfair advantage of their official position, and got money in an irregular manner, not by overdraft on an open account. That is not the case which is put here, any more than is the instance, which he also used by way of illustration, of half-a-dozen directors sitting round the table, and telling each other their wants, and consenting and agreeing to supply them—B agreeing to consent to an overdraft of £500 to A, if he will consent to an overdraft to B for £1500. That would be a direct violation of their duty as directors. But that is not the case put here. Baldly stated, the case put here is, that a person appointed to be a director was to be prevented having those banking facilities which any other man in Edinburgh or Glasgow might freely have. That is so in the case of Mr Stewart, and I have promised to come back to the case of Mr Stewart for the special bearing that it has on this point. Mr Stewart was partner of a firm having a large account with the Bank, and as a director is charged with breach of duty and embezzlement because of the large amount of the overdraft which was allowed to his firm. Let it be supposed that Mr Stewart's firm—and, so far as the indictment bears, nothing appears to the contrary—consisted of a dozen members. Well, then, because that firm, consisting of a dozen members, obtains from the Bank an overdraft to the extent of I don't care how much money, Mr Stewart is to be charged with breach of trust and embezzlement, and to answer for it at the bar of the High Court of Justiciary, because the rest of the directors are quite willing to trust that firm, although he comes forward and says, "You had better not do so." That would be reducing the case to an absurdity. You have it reduced to an absurdity in the case of Mr Wright. He is a member of a firm having a good credit with the Bank, or any other of the banks in Glasgow. He or his firm are debtors to the Bank to the extent of £20,000, but, having been elected a director, it is clear from the contention in this case that if he does not pay up every shilling owed by his firm immediately on taking his seat, he is guilty of embezzlement. Nothing can more completely show the absurdity of this charge than taking the case of Mr Wright as put in that way. I ask your Lordships to consider whether or not the charge can stand when you take this into account. The Bank advances money to Stewart & Co., or to John Stewart, or any one, and John Stewart, because of his having got money from the Bank, and used it for his own purposes, is charged with embezzling it. What are the essentials of embezzlement? That money must have been put into a man's hands or his custody for one purpose, while he appropriates it to another. How can it be said that Stewart, or his firm, embezzled one shilling of this money? It may have been imprudent to give it, and it may not have been unwise to allow overdrafts, but how can it be embezzlement? The money was not entrusted by the depositors to Stewart. Mr Stewart, although a director, had no money entrusted to him in his individual capacity. The corporation has a quantity of money committed to its care for certain purposes—for banking purposes. I pass here from the fact that one of the highest authorities has declared that to give money in some cases without security was one of the parts of the business of banking.

Lord CRAIGHILL—It must have been a great part of the City of Glasgow Bank system.

Mr TRAYNER—I suppose the City of Glasgow Bank was not, in that respect, different from the other banks. We have heard a great deal lately of the difficulty of getting trustees to act under voluntary trusts, but I think if it is to be held that a bank director who allows an overdraft without security is to incur a criminal charge of embezzlement, you will have hereafter as much difficulty in getting directors of banks as trustees in an ordinary settlement. Whether this was the practice of the City Bank I am not to inquire. What

I say is, that the money was not entrusted to Stewart, Potts, & Co., and therefore that it has not been embezzled.

The LORD JUSTICE-CLERK—The conversion of money to what it was not intended by the truster may mean embezzlement.

Mr TRAYNER—Possibly so; but I am maintaining now that it is essential to know to whom the money was entrusted, because if it was not entrusted to Stewart, then he could not embezzle it.

The LORD JUSTICE-CLERK—If the security was insufficient, and the transaction not a right one, then in taking the money he broke his trust.

Mr TRAYNER—Then in that case the proper charge would be that the directors sitting when the overdraft was granted were all guilty of the charge.

The LORD JUSTICE-CLERK—But the Lord Advocate does not mean that it was done by Stewart alone.

Mr TRAYNER—I should like to have that stated by the Lord Advocate. It is not what the Lord Advocate means that I am concerned with; it is rather, what is the plain meaning of the words in the indictment? Money had been entrusted, so says the indictment, by the creditors of the Bank to the Bank, for the purpose of being employed in the ordinary business of banking. The indictment does not say the money was entrusted or delivered to Mr Stewart. One man standing in the position of a director may have a different *persona* as a director and as a man. What is averred here is, that the money having been entrusted to the Bank, part of it was given out to Stewart, and that he embezzled the money so entrusted to the Bank. I venture to think that is upon the face of it an answer to the charge of embezzlement. Before you can make Stewart or any one else guilty of embezzlement, you must have the money entrusted to him for a particular purpose, and devoted by him to a different purpose.

I submit upon the whole matter that the charge is quite irrelevant, and I will sum up what I think the grounds of that irrelevancy are. In the first place, it is not averred how the duty, said to have been violated, arises; in the second place, if it is the right of the directors at common law to give advances, to do so without security or without adequate security is not in itself a breach of the banking practices and principles of the country, and I quote as an authority in support of this, the opinion of his Lordship at the head of the Court. As to breach of duty on contract, that is untenable; no such case is stated, and no such case can be proved. As to embezzlement, the indictment cannot be sustained, because one cannot embezzle money not entrusted to him; and to give money to the Bank by way of deposit was not putting it into Mr Stewart's hands, but putting it into the Bank. I say, further, the Lord Advocate is not entitled to go to a jury on this part of the case, because he has not averred when the overdrafts were made. He says the panel allowed an overdraft on his account or his firm's account upon inadequate security, but he has not averred that the overdraft was known to the panel at the time it was obtained. Further, it is not said that the overdraft has not been repaid. I think it is putting the case in a slovenly shape to say that after a great many years' transactions it was found out that when the Bank's doors were closed there was a balance of so much against Mr Stewart and Mr Taylor. Let me suppose that Mr Stewart or Mr Taylor were members of firms with large and extensive business in Glasgow, with great and almost unbounded credit, well known to commercial circles, and of high trust. Suppose that these men in 1872 had an overdraft of £30,000, and that in 1873, instead of having an overdraft of £30,000, they had £30,000 at their credit. Then, in the year 1875, their overdraft came again to £30,000, and so on, and that it just happens that at the time when the Bank's doors are closed the balance is against them instead of being in their favour. There is nothing contrary to banking principles in that; and so far from that being embezzlement, the next year the balance might have turned out the other way.

I think it can fairly be said that the men, in the circumstance supposed, are dealing honestly with the Bank. And are these men to be charged with embezzlement when the balance is against them, while if the Bank had closed its doors twelve months before, or kept them open for twelve months longer, it would not have been embezzlement at all? Then there is no averment that the Bank has not been repaid, and no averment that these gentlemen are not quite ready to pay every penny due to the Bank. Neither is it averred that, as individuals or as members of firms, they are not solvent, and ready to meet every engagement to the Bank and otherwise.

Mr MACKINTOSH—All the overdrafts in Mr Taylor's case were overdrafts by his firm.

Mr TRAYNER—In the case of Mr Stewart, there are certain overdrafts on his individual account, apart from the firm's account. I submit that there is no relevant case here against the panels on the averments as laid. I submit that it is on these averments, and these averments only, as they appear on the face of the indictment, and according to the plain and ordinary meaning of the language there used, not upon what, as was explained, it is intended to prove by them, and what it is intended to express by them, which the Court is to go. If your Lordships affirm that this is a relevant charge, it will come to this—In the first place, that the moment a man becomes a bank director he is not to have the banking facilities that any other person has; and, in the second place, that the moment a bank director allows an overdraft, no matter how small the amount, without security, or what years afterwards may be considered a wholly inadequate security, he is guilty of embezzlement, and liable to be placed at the bar of a criminal court.

Mr BALFOUR—There is only one point to which I would direct attention—it is a short one, but nevertheless of very great importance—and that is the effect upon the relevancy of this indictment of the withdrawal by the Lord Advocate of the 8th particular contained in the charge relative to the falsification of the balance-sheets. I take the 8th particular in the year 1876 [see asterisk, p. 28], and the corresponding particulars in the other years. Now, the Lord Advocate has withdrawn, and therefore has disabled himself from proving, the allegation that this balance is false, in respect that "bad and irrecoverable debts to "an amount far exceeding the whole capital stock of the Bank were included "under article 1 on the creditor side, and so treated as subsisting and available "assets of the company." That being withdrawn, I submit that it necessarily follows that the sixth and seventh particulars must go along with it; and if the Lord Advocate does not withdraw them, I should ask your Lordships to find them irrelevant, because it is quite plain, as Mr Mackintosh pointed out in his opening, that Nos. 6 and 7 are inseparably bound up with No. 8. No. 6 sets out that the earnings of the Bank during the year were overstated under the head of profit and loss to the extent of £125,763, 12s. 8d. or thereby, and No. 7 that a reserve fund to the extent of £450,000 was stated to exist, while in reality no such fund existed. Now, of course, this bears to set out what appears upon the balance-sheet; and as your Lordships have the balance-sheet before you, you will see how these two items, the statement of profit and the statement of reserve fund, are made in that sheet. By turning to the balance-sheet, your Lordships will see that those items do not appear on the assets or credit side at all; they appear only on the debit side as two of the items of liability to the partners. It is important first to see what the scheme of this balance-sheet is, and I think that when the form of the balance-sheet is once noticed and apprehended, it will come out perfectly clear that Nos. 6 and 7 must go with 8. I would ask your Lordships just to take first the left-hand or debtor side. [See foot of p. 27.] You have there the liabilities. The first three heads of liabilities are liabilities to the public, and they amount in the aggregate to £10,539,785, 15s. 6d.

Then you have, fourth, the capital account of £1,000,000; fifth, the reserve fund, £450,000; and, sixth, profit and loss, £136,365, 10s. 3d. These three items together make up liabilities to partners, the total liabilities to partners being £1,586,365, 10s. 3d. Now, the sum which is thus stated under three heads as the amount of the liabilities to partners is simply the sum which is necessary to make the liability side and the asset side balance, and the point I ask attention to is this. There is no statement in this balance-sheet of the capital as such, or of the reserve fund as such, or of the profits as such on the assets side; they are simply ingredients under the different heads of assets—that is to say, they are not in any way severed. I could have quite understood the meaning of the Lord Advocate's indictment, if on the assets side there had been an allegation that there was a reserve fund of £450,000 in a separate coffer, or if that fund had appeared in some way severed from the rest of the assets. But that is not the case. These sums only appear as liabilities, and therefore the only place where they are, or where they can be, on the creditor side is under some one or other of the three heads on that side. That being so, it was quite intelligible, so long as the Lord Advocate alleged and offered to prove that there was an amount of bad and irrecoverable debts on the assets side to an extent, as the indictment says, far exceeding the whole capital stock—meaning, I suppose, the capital, the reserve fund, and profits, and possibly something more—so long as he gave notice of that allegation, he gave notice of an undertaking to prove that there were items among the assets which should not be among the assets; but since he has given up article 8, I would ask attention to the only statement which his indictment contains of any error on the assets side. The only error on the assets side which remains alleged is in article 3, and that is not an allegation that the assets are overstated—it is an allegation that the assets are understated. According to that article (article 8 being out), the only thing that is wrong on the assets side is that the amount is made too little, not that it is made too much. The complaint of the Crown thus comes to be that there is an under-statement of the assets to the extent of £2,698,539. Then the Crown says the amount of notes is overstated by £29,000; and, further, that the amount of Government stocks is overstated to the extent of £753,211. Now, if your Lordships add together these over-statements in 4 and 5 to the statements in 1 and 2, where there are under-statements on the debit side, the sum total will be found to be £2,761,822.

The LORD JUSTICE-CLERK—What do you exactly mean, Mr Balfour, by adding these under-statements and over-statements together?

Mr BALFOUR—What I mean is this. The two first heads relate to the debtor side, and are under-statements. Then, the next two—4 and 5—are over-statements on the credit side. If you add together 1 and 2, which are under-statements on the debit, and 4 and 5, which are over-statements on the credit side, the total you will get is £2,761,822.

The LORD JUSTICE-CLERK—What is the effect of this addition?

Mr BALFOUR—If your Lordships put these four items, which are items making the company appear better than it was, against the statement in article 3, which makes the company appear worse than it was, you will find there is only a difference of about £63,283 between the two totals. So that the result is this, that the Lord Advocate cannot possibly, on his own figures, prove away the reserve fund and the profits except by going back on bad debts. Our complaint with reference to that point is, that there is a want of specification of what the bad debts are that are said to be entered in the assets side. The only possible way that the reserve fund and the profits can be wiped off, is by showing that the assets given on the credit side comprehended bad and irrecoverable debts amounting to at least £525,000—that is to say, to the amount of the sum of the reserve fund and of the profit and loss. The reserve fund is £450,000; and the total profit and loss £136,365.

The LORD JUSTICE-CLERK—That would at all events imply manipulation.

Mr BALFOUR—If the public prosecutor is content to go simply to the jury with this, that there has been, as your Lordship has said, manipulation, by which I understand the handling or altering of sums which appeared in the books—if he will limit himself to that, I am content. But I am showing that the prosecutor can never prove 6 and 7 without taking out of the assets side something in it which he can only take out of it by proving that it contains bad and irrecoverable debts; or, if we are wrong in that idea, we are entitled, I apprehend, to know how it was that profits were not earned, or how it was that the reserve fund was wiped away. All that was quite intelligible so long as article 8 stood, under which the Lord Advocate undertook to prove that there were bad and irrecoverable debts far exceeding the capital, the interest on which was alleged to be profits. Your Lordships are aware that a great part of the profit of a banking business consists in interest due on debts owing to it; but if these debts are bad and irrecoverable, one can easily see how interest on them should not have been treated as the profits. So long as the Lord Advocate adhered to article 8, one could see how article 6 could be proved. But when I have put these figures together, I have shown your Lordships that the only complaint made against the two sides of this account, taken as a whole, will not even wipe off the profits, still less wipe off the reserve fund, unless by proving debts irrecoverable, which the Lord Advocate is no longer entitled to do. I say, therefore, we are entitled either to have articles 6 and 7 struck out, as article 8 was struck out, or we are entitled to have an admission from the Crown that they do not intend to prove them by proving bad and irrecoverable debts; because, if they mean to prove bad debts for the purpose of destroying the reserve fund and the profits, our objection as to want of specification at once comes in. The purpose for which a thing is to be proved is immaterial. An accused person is entitled to have notice of the particular things which he is alleged or charged with having misrepresented—what assets he treated as good which should have been treated as bad. Your Lordships will see that the theory of the Crown here is, that on the assets side there ought to have been upwards of £11,000,000—I mean under the first head of the assets—while the amount actually stated is £8,787,000 odds. The Crown says, in particular, there is £2,698,000 short, so that when the first head of the assets side is rectified—as the Crown says it should be rectified—it will be brought up to £11,484,237. We are put in this position, that the Crown may select and prove any £450,000 of these alleged assets to be bad without notice. Now, I submit that is a very startling result.

The LORD ADVOCATE, in reply, said—I think that the fallacy which pervades the contention of my learned friend is very much this—he assumes that because I have pointed out several errors on both sides of it, I have undertaken to convert this false and fabricated balance-sheet into a perfectly true balance-sheet. I certainly do not contemplate anything of the kind. The alterations made upon the balance-sheet are in these two directions—first, in setting forth as assets of the company gold which was not in their coffers, Government stocks which they did not hold; and, on the other hand, in diminishing their actual bad assets by cutting off a large quantity of outstanding bills, sums due on open account, and other obligations of that class. The object which I shall suggest the accused had in view in making these alterations will be this, that from the state of their own books, and of various accounts in these books, they had a very plain and intelligible purpose in striking off that part which may be called assets, but may represent liabilities, and, on the other hand, of rearing up assets where none existed. I allege that the balance-sheet, from the beginning to the end of it, is a falsehood, and brings out results which are not true results. In the knowledge the panels had—because if there was no knowledge I don't conclude guilt—this statement was made, instead of a true statement, for the purpose of keeping concealed the true state of the affairs of the Bank, and leading persons to believe that the capital was not only intact, but that the Bank was in a position to meet all claims against it. What is legitimate evidence against these gentlemen is their own books, and the question will be how far knowledge of the facts therein stated is brought home to them. I distinctly intimate that my purpose is not to convict the accused of certain errors of statement, but to show from the state of the books of the Bank, and the condition of the Bank as appearing from these books, that they had within their knowledge that which led them to make these false representations with a criminal intent.

The LORD JUSTICE-CLERK intimated that the Court would give judgment to-morrow.

Second Day—Tuesday, 21st January 1879.

The Court met at half-past ten.

The LORD JUSTICE-CLERK—The question we have to decide is whether the public prosecutor has stated in this indictment facts which are relevant to go to proof—whether the facts stated here are to be inquired into by a jury. My Lords, a great many important and serious matters were raised by the counsel for the prisoners. Many of them were considerations of very great weight, which will require to be carefully dealt with when the case goes to the investigation of the facts, and for that reason I think, probably, it will be desirable not to enter at length into these considerations, which, though they had a material bearing upon the question of relevancy, will have also a material bearing upon the question of the facts when disclosed; and at a later stage of these proceedings, it may be necessary to resume them at length, but in the mean time I shall simply announce my own opinion, and, I believe, that of your Lordships, on the various objections that have been taken to the different heads of this indictment in their order. The indictment itself deals substantially with three classes of offences. I forbear at present to go into them technically; but I simply state them as they appear upon the general complexion of the indictment. The first of these is the falsification of the balance-sheets of this joint stock banking company, and the making of false statements to the shareholders of the Bank and the public. The second is the obtaining of advances, on the part of the directors, of the funds committed to their care, for the purposes of the banking company, on terms and conditions not authorised by the duty which they held towards the company; and the third is the theft of certain bills of exchange which were entrusted and confided to the directors for the purpose of collection by creditors in these bills. To the charges, under these three heads, objections have been taken in this discussion on the relevancy. In regard to the first of them, which is a charge of falsifying the statements made to the shareholders of the state of the finances of the Bank, the main objection that was taken in regard to the specification of the offence related to the 8th subdivision of the first charge, which embraces the accounts for the year 1876, the other charges for the other succeeding years being in the same terms. That 8th section charges the whole of the directors with falsely stating the bad and irrecoverable debts to an amount far exceeding the whole capital stock of the Bank. It was admitted that the debts were not specified. The objection certainly appeared to be formidable, and the Lord Advocate has accordingly expunged that charge from his indictment. What the effect of that may be upon the evidence in support of that charge is a question on which I do not at present give any opinion. But it was objected by Mr Balfour that if that subdivision of the 8th charge were missed out, it would then be necessary also to omit others of the charges that are contained there, because, he says, when the figures are looked to they will be found to be inconsistent with each other. Mr Lords, I think it was very plain, upon Mr Balfour's own statement, that that was a matter for proof, and not a matter on relevancy. We cannot sit here and judge without evidence of the effect of the manipulation of the figures which is here in question. It may quite well be that the affairs of the Bank have been entirely misrepresented, and yet when you come to add the misrepresentations together, the sum total may be the same, or nearly the same. For instance, it is not the same thing to say that there were eight millions of floating assets, and no bad or irrecoverable debts, and to say that there were eleven millions of floating assets, and a large amount of irrecoverable debts. These are two different things. I give no further opinion, but I have come to the conclusion that the objection taken by Mr Balfour, whatever weight it may have when the facts come to be ascertained, is not truly an objection to the relevancy. Then it was said by Mr Mackintosh, still farther on this head, that on page 5 [see p. 28] of the indictment there was not a sufficient specification of injury done to the shareholders by the alleged falsehood, and that it was a falsehood without injury. My Lords, I think that that was perhaps not the most forcible part of the observations of my learned friend; because it really comes to this,—if a man is entrusted with the business of another, and makes false reports to him as to the amount of his finances, he suffers nothing. Mr Mackintosh said that the shares would not have been saleable if the truth had been known. My Lords, I don't think that goes far. It is quite clear that every shareholder was entitled to know how the finances stood, in order that he might know how he stood himself; and what was the effect of the false statement upon the different shareholders, and of the reliance which they necessarily placed upon these false reports, it is impossible for us now to say; but it must be quite manifest that a very large and important patrimonial interest was thereby endangered; and that is alleged in the indictment. So much for the first part of these charges; and the same considerations apply to the charges as to 1877 and 1878. And then we come to a very important part of this indictment, which has given us a great deal of anxiety. These charges are directed against individual directors and are contained in the sixth and seventh charges of the indictment. They are charges against individual directors of obtaining or taking from the Bank certain large advances by way of overdrafts on their own individual accounts out of the moneys with which they were entrusted for the purposes of the Bank. There is no doubt that that is a most important portion of this very formidable indictment, and I am anxious not to say more upon it at present than is necessary for the discharge of the immediate duty on hand, and the decision of the question of relevancy. It is quite manifest that it embraces many topics of immense importance to the prisoners at the bar, and also of immense importance to the public. I must own that I have had a great deal of difficulty in regard to the question of relevancy here, as I believe your Lordships have also had. I think, I may say, without speaking too strongly on the subject, that, perhaps, the use of more precise and definite expressions might have saved some at least of the difficulties that we have felt. My general opinion upon the matters submitted for discussion yesterday is, that it is not every violation or excess of the rights of directors or persons in that position of trust which will ground a criminal prosecution. It may quite well be that directors violate the conditions on which they hold their office, by doing acts which are not sanctioned by the terms of their appointment. Such cases occur every day in the civil courts, and if directors in that position act beyond their powers, or in violation of their powers, they will be responsible in the civil consequences, and their acts will not have the validity of legal acts of the directors. But before this can be raised into a criminal offence, and be the subject of a criminal indictment, there must be superadded to the illegality of the act—the invalidity of the act—some element of bad faith, some corrupt motive, some guilty knowledge, some fraudulent intent, which shall raise that which, although illegal, was not a crime, into the category of a crime. These are familiar and elementary principles; and in cases of that kind the corrupt motive, the bad faith, is essential to the crime itself, and without it there is no crime. Now, here I should not have been satisfied, although the duty of the directors had been clearly charged, and the trust reposed in them clearly expressed, and the obligation not to allow overdrafts on open account without security quite precise, and the insufficiency of the security on which these advances were made clearly alleged, unless there had appeared in the charge something beyond these elements—namely, an element of want of faith, which would give a colour and character to all the rest; and I must fairly say that I could have wished that this had been more clearly and specifically expressed, nor do I altogether see why it was not so. But, my Lords, upon further consideration of the whole of that argument, I am satisfied that, assuming those principles which I have now announced, and which I consider both elementary and important, such is not truly the nature of the charge that is made here, because there are some words which override all the facts alleged, and seem to me completely to raise the element of bad faith throughout the whole transaction, or, what is the same thing, to exclude the good faith of the parties in the proceeding,—and that is, that these advances were obtained by taking advantage of the position of the accused as directors. Now, no doubt that places upon the prosecutor a very heavy burden of proof, but, I take it, these words signify that the directors obtained these advances under conditions in which, but for their character as directors, they could not have obtained them; in other words, that they used their characters as directors to obtain advantages in regard to the money entrusted to themselves which an ordinary customer could not have obtained. That is the element which has led me to come to be of opinion that there is a sufficiently relevant case stated under these charges for investigation by a jury. Doubtless the public prosecutor has a heavy task before him, because he must not only prove the trust, and prove the duty as he alleges it, and prove that the security which was offered or existed was manifestly insufficient, but he must also prove what he has alleged, I think in sufficient language, that all these things were done solely and entirely by taking advantage of the position of a director, and abusing that position to the effect of a result for which it never was conferred. If these things are proved—if it be shown that these advances were not in the ordinary course of business, and were not made in good faith, but were made solely and entirely in consequence of the position which the directors had on that board—if it be proved that these were advances which no ordinary customer could have obtained, and which therefore no director was in good faith to accept, I think that the logic of the indictment on this head is sufficient. There is a minor point upon two of these charges, in relation to Mr Inglis and Mr Wright, which is of this nature. It would rather appear from the statement in the charge against Mr Inglis, on pages 14 and 15 [see p. 34], that some part at all events of these advances had been obtained prior to his becoming a director of the concern. We are of opinion that the advances to that extent are not properly or relevantly brought within the charge stated in the indictment, and that, therefore, it will be necessary in Mr Inglis' indictment to expunge the words on page 15, "or did allow the overdrafts on the said accounts in name of you and of "your said firm to be continued and increased;" [see p. 34] and in the case of Mr Wright, the words, "or did allow the overdrafts of your said firm to be con- "tinued and increased." [See p. 35.] In other words, we do not hold that this charge can apply to advances which had been already made when the accused became a director. Of course, any increase in the advance is another matter. That is a question that will arrive upon the proof; but in the meantime we think that these words are not relevant, and therefore they must be expunged. My Lords, the only other point relates to the charge of theft of a number of bills mentioned in the indictment. My Lords, the distinction between theft and breach of trust is a very fine and subtle one, and, I think, depends more upon words than upon substance; but I have no doubt at all that the *species facti* alleged in this particular case, if proved in its terms, amounts to theft. One can quite well see that there are elements contained in it that might come to have a very material bearing on the question whether it did or did not amount to theft. But as stated, it is nothing but this, that the Bank directors having been entrusted with certain bills of exchange for the purpose of collecting these bills—that is to say, of obtaining payment for the creditor when due, as mandatories of the creditor—used the bills for their own purposes by endorsing them to correspondents and creditors of the Bank—viz., the London Bank. Now, that case taken by itself, on that bare statement of it, is simply the same thing as if instead of being a bill of exchange, it had been a bond or any other document of obligation, which, having been put into the hands of a man for the purpose of making it effectual against the debtor for the benefit of the creditor, is used directly for his own purposes, to increase his own credit. It was said in the argument, and of course it will have great weight when we come to the inquiry, that what is alleged here was in truth done in the process of collection, and for no other object. But that does not appear on the indictment, nor can we assume it; and consequently at the present stage I am not prepared to say that that charge is irrelevant, although very important matters will remain for the investigation when we come to the Jury. My Lords, these are the views upon which, to the extent which I have now indicated, I am prepared to sustain the relevancy of this indictment. I forgot to explain upon the first of these charges, that a reference was made to the case of Wilkie, which was decided at Stirling, in regard to the connection between the injury and the false representation. I think that if that case is studied it will be found that there was in the subsumption of the indictment a passage to this effect—"And you having induced so-and-so to receive you as a "lodger by these representations or by other representations," such-and-such happened; and it was upon that ground, if I recollect aright, that the judgment proceeded. The first part of the indictment was clear enough, but it was the subsumption which left it doubtful whether it was these representations or the other representations which were the means of inducing the lodging-house keeper to accept the lodger. My Lords, with these views I propose that we should sustain the relevancy of the indictment.

Lord MURE—I concur with your Lordship in the result of your opinion, and shall therefore state my views very shortly. On the first point referred to—viz., the relevancy of what have been called the innominate charges in the major proposition of the indictment, of wickedly and feloniously preparing false balance-sheets, and uttering the same with intent to defraud, &c.—I have not, and never had, any doubt; neither have I entertained any doubt that the facts relative to those charges, as set forth in the minor proposition, are relevant, and would, if proved to the satisfaction of a jury, amount to the crimes charged in the major proposition. The criticisms on subdivision 8 of the objections to the balance-sheet were important; but we have been relieved from the necessity of dealing with them by the Crown having withdrawn that item of the account; and I agree with your Lordship that the objections since raised to several of the other subdivisions of the same charge founded on the fact of that withdrawal, are not strictly speaking objections to relevancy, but must be disposed of on the evidence.

On the second question—viz., the charge of breach of trust and embezzlement relative to the overdrafts—I have experienced the same difficulties as your Lordship; and it is not without hesitation that I have come to the conclusion that it should be sent to proof substantially as it stands. I have no doubt of this as a general proposition, that a bank agent or bank manager, entrusted with the money of the bank of which he is manager, who avails himself of his position to get cheques passed on his own account with the bank to a large amount, without any regular security given to the bank, and without having any money at his credit, and who applies that money to his own uses and purposes, commits a criminal offence, if he does all this when in the knowledge that he has no money at his credit. That, I think, is quite settled; and the latest case I at present recollect was that of the manager of a bank at Stirling, who, when he had no money at his credit with the bank, and the bank held no security, drew on his own account, and received a large sum of money from the teller who had charge of the cash, and appropriated the money to his own uses and purposes. But in that case it was very distinctly alleged that what was then done by the manager, was done he "well "knowing" that he had no money at his credit in the bank, and was not entitled to draw the money or any part of it. That was the case of a manager. Here we have to deal with that of directors. But in this respect I do not think there is any essential distinction between the cases, if what the four directors are here charged with doing amounts substantially to what I have stated to be the law, in my view of it, as regards bank managers. Now, it is here distinctly alleged, and the Crown undertakes to prove, that the directors were entrusted with large sums of money to be employed in the ordinary business of banking, and that it was their duty not to allow overdrafts to be made on their own accounts without adequate security, which it is alleged they nevertheless did, or caused or procured to be done, to a very large extent, in the way set out in the indictment, and did embezzle and appropriate the money to their own uses and purposes. But then there is an omission of the important words I have referred to—that they did this well knowing they had no money at their credit; and the main difficulty I have felt has been to satisfy myself that there are in this indictment any equivalent words. After anxious consideration, I have come to be of opinion with your Lordship that there are; for, in the first place, they are charged with procuring overdrafts, which necessarily implies that when the draft was made no money stood at their credit with the Bank; and they are charged with doing this by "taking advantage of their official position as directors" to obtain the drafts, which will, I presume, also be proved. Now, these combined allegations of largely overdrawing their accounts, and using their position as directors to enable them so to get money which they would not otherwise have been able to obtain, appear to me to introduce an element of fraud which, if distinctly proved, is sufficient to stamp their acts with the character of a criminal offence.

With reference to the words "or did allow the overdrafts on your said "accounts to be continued," that is after they became directors, as I understand the allegations in the charges against two of the accused, I am very clearly of opinion that those words ought to be struck out. For, as at present advised, I am unable to see how a party can be said to have embezzled, through his position as a bank director, moneys which were advanced to him or to his firm, and spent before he became a director of the bank.

On the question of theft or embezzlement, I agree with your Lordship that this will depend mainly upon the proof, and that on the evidence it may be one or other of those crimes, according to the precise nature of the facts disclosed.

Lord CRAIGHILL—I concur, and I think it unnecessary to say more than refer to the opinions delivered by your Lordships as a true statement of the views which I entertain on this indictment.

The following was the interlocutor pronounced :—

Edinburgh, 21st January 1879.—The Lords having heard counsel for the pannels on the objections stated to the relevancy of the libel, and Her Majesty's Advocate in reply, Repel the objections to the first, second, and third charges of the libel; Direct the words "or did allow the overdrafts on "the said accounts, in name of you and of your said firm, to be continued "and increased to the said amounts respectively," occurring on the twelfth, thirteenth, and fourteenth lines of the indictment, page fifteen; as also the words "or did allow the overdrafts of your said firm to be continued and "increased," occurring on the twentieth and twenty-first lines of page sixteen of the indictment, to be deleted; thereupon Repel the objections to the fourth, fifth, sixth, and seventh charges of the indictment; Repel the objections stated to the remaining charges of the libel; and Find the libel, as thus limited, relevant to infer the pains of law.

MONCREIFF, *I.P.D.*

The LORD JUSTICE-CLERK then asked the prisoners in succession, "What do "you say—are you guilty or not guilty?" when each answered, "Not Guilty."

Before the empannelling of the jury commenced,

The DEAN OF FACULTY asked their Lordships to intimate that if any of those called were shareholders or depositors in the Bank, they should not come forward or act as jurors.

The LORD ADVOCATE—I have no objection to that whatever. I think it is perfectly proper.

The LORD JUSTICE-CLERK (addressing the jurymen)—The Dean of Faculty has made a request, which I think is a very proper one, that I should intimate to you that if any of you are shareholders or depositors of the City of Glasgow Bank, you ought to intimate that to the Court if you should be called in the ballot to-day.

The first juror called was Mr James M'Kenzie, chemist, 16 Glengyle Terrace.

Mr M'Kenzie pleaded that, as he was a chemist, he was exempted, owing to the responsibility of his position, from acting on the jury.

The Lord Justice-Clerk relieved him from attendance.

The following were sworn to try the case —

1. James Jamieson, brewer, 22 Douglas Crescent, Edinburgh.
2. William Small, outfitter, 4 Bernard Terrace, Edinburgh.
3. Robert Simpson, builder, Pilrig Cottages, Leith Walk, Edinburgh.
4. Alexander Wallace, innkeeper, Peebles.
5. David Aikman, manager, Shotts Iron Company, 32 Restalrig Terrace, Leith.
6. Alexander Thomson, ironmonger, 6 Gilmore Place, Edinburgh.
7. James Binnie, innkeeper, Slateford.
8. James Potter, 21 Gillespie Crescent, Edinburgh.
9. Thomas Forbes, road surveyor, Mid-Calder.
10. William M'Ewan, painter, 16 Lothian Road, Edinburgh.
11. George Rosie, mason, 1 Livingstone Place, Edinburgh.
12. Joseph Powrie, chairmaker, 14 Upper Grove Place, Edinburgh.
13. Joseph Chapman, draughtsman, 9 London Row, Leith.
14. John Gray Jack, jeweller, 24 Lady Menzies Place, Edinburgh.
15. David Donaldson, commission merchant, 23 Gordon Street, Easter Road, Leith.

Mr Asher said—Before any witnesses are called, I ask to be allowed to lodge a special defence for Mr Salmond.

The Clerk of Court then read the defence, as follows:—"The said Robert "Salmond pleads not guilty; and, further, with reference to the first charge "in the indictment, pleads that he was not in Scotland from 5th June till 6th "July 1876, having been resident in London from the said 5th till 12th "June, when he left London for Homburg, Germany, where he thereafter "resided, in consequence of the state of his health, till the said 6th July "1876; (2) With reference to the second charge in the indictment, pleads "that he was not in Scotland between the 3d and 15th June 1877, nor "between the 6th and 15th July 1877, having been resident during both these "periods at the Burlington Hotel, London; (3) With reference to the third "charge, pleads that he was not in Scotland from 24th May till 25th July "1878, having been resident in the Burlington Hotel, London, from the said "24th May till 20th June, on which date he went to Buxton, Derbyshire, in "consequence of the state of his health, and resided at the Palace Hotel "there from 20th June till 5th July 1878."

EVIDENCE FOR THE PROSECUTION.

Sheriff CLARK.

Francis William Clark, Esq., advocate, Sheriff of Lanarkshire, on being examined by the Solicitor-General with reference to the declarations, deponed,—That they were each of them emitted before him of the dates they bear by the prisoners at the bar, while in their sound and sober senses, and after being duly cautioned and admonished in the usual way.

By Mr Mackintosh—The first declarations of the accused were emitted on the same day. The taking of them began about noon, and continued till about five minutes before twelve o'clock midnight. I do not remember whose declaration was taken last. I do not remember whether it was Mr Taylor's. The accused were brought to my chambers about midday, and they were kept in the buildings till midnight.

By Solicitor-General—There was no reason for taking all the declarations that day, except that I have always regarded it to be the duty of the magistrate to give accused persons the earliest possible opportunity of making any statement they may desire to make, because if they make a statement such as may warrant the magistrate in releasing them, which may sometimes be the case, the sooner it is made in their interest the better. On this occasion, I may say, I sat on at considerable personal inconvenience, so as to give them that benefit. I inquired, and was told that they were properly taken care of in the building. No complaint was made to me of any exhaustion on their part; if such had been made, I certainly would have attended to it.

GEORGE BRANDER.

By the Solicitor-General—I am a clerk in the Sheriff-Clerk's office, Glasgow. I attended as a witness when the prisoners emitted their declarations. [Shown two declarations by Mr Stewart, dated 22d and 29th October 1878; three by Potter, 22d, 25th, and 29th; two by Salmond, 22d and 29th; three by Taylor, 22d and 29th (two); three by Inglis, 22d and 29th (two); three by Wright, 22d and 29th (two); and two by Stronach, 22d and 29th.] I was present at the emitting of these declarations, and wrote them. They were freely and voluntarily emitted. The prisoners were in their sound and sober senses. I heard them duly cautioned and admonished by the Sheriff in the usual way.

WILLIAM ALEXANDER BROWN.

By Mr Burnet—I am procurator-fiscal at Glasgow. On 21st October, 1878, I went to the City of Glasgow Bank, and recovered from Dr M'Grigor, one of the investigators into the affairs of the Bank, the documents numbered in the inventory 124, 125, 127, and 128. After the meeting of shareholders on 22d October, I had a conversation with Dr M'Grigor as to the necessity of taking over the books of the Bank for the purposes of the prosecution; and on the following day (23d October) I met Dr M'Grigor (then agent for the liquidators) and the liquidators in the Bank, and arranged with them that they should minute the arrangement by which the Crown was to take possession of the whole books and documents of the Bank. Since 23d October, accordingly, the books have been in the possession of the Crown, subject to the uses of the Crown and of the liquidation. They were not duly marked until immediately before they were brought to Edinburgh, but I became so convinced of the necessity of providing for their safe custody that the whole books of the Bank have been under charge of an officer under my supervision daily. There was a mark put on after 22d October to draw the distinction between the books of the Bank prior to that, and the time when the liquidation began. A stamp was put on to show that on 22d October the Bank went into liquidation. It was put on the books as they were when the liquidators took them over. The same books have been continued by the liquidators since. Nos. 1 to 123 of the inventory are books of the Bank, or excerpts from them. Nos. 508 to 514, both inclusive, are also books of the Bank recovered in the Bank. Nos. 129 to 184, both inclusive, are documents which I recovered from Dr M'Grigor from time to time, or prints of them since made. Nos. 185 to 190, and No. 191A, I recovered in the Bank from Mr Morris, private secretary of the late manager, Mr Stronach. Under my instructions, Mr Boyd, superintendent of police made a search in the Bank for further documents; and on 28th October he brought to me two locked boxes. In these I found the documents from No. 192 to 248 inclusive. They were selected from these boxes; also No. 290. On 14th November I instructed Mr Boyd to make a further search, and he brought me a tin box, from which were recovered Nos. 249, 250, and 324. On 4th December I instructed him to make a further search in the Bank, and he took possession of a locked drawer, from which I recovered Nos. 251 to 260 inclusive, and Nos. 273 to 277 inclusive, and No. 295. I recovered Nos, 578 and 579 from Mr Harding, the receiver on Smith, Fleming, and Co.'s estate, and on James Morton's estate. I also received Nos. 191, 191C, and 292 from Mr Harding. From the officers of Inland Revenue in London I recovered Nos. 305 to 320 inclusive. Nos. 325 to 348 inclusive, I got in the Bank. No. 359 I got from John Wardrop, a clerk in the Bank. I recovered Nos. 448 and 455 from Mr Aikman, the law secretary of the Bank. These books and documents have all been brought here.

Cross-examined by Mr Balfour—(Q.) What was the total number of books and documents which you had through your hands in preparing the case for the Crown? (A.) It is rather difficult to answer that question without a little more time—a considerable number. (Q.) A very large number? (A.) A considerable number is, I think, a better way of expressing it. (Q.) Hundreds or thousands? (A.) Certainly not thousands, nor hundreds either. Those which I had were selections made by my instructions from still larger numbers. Besides the books and documents of the Bank, I had also through my hands a considerable number of documents—not many books—relating to other matters.

Cross-examined by the Dean of Faculty.—No. 298 is a writing which was found on Mr Stronach when he was apprehended, and which was handed to me by Mr Superintendent Boyd. I was not present when it was taken from him, but I was told by Mr Boyd that it had been.

DAVID MACKENZIE.

By Mr Burnet—I am in the employment of Messrs Johnston, lithographers, Edinburgh. [Shown Nos. 124, 125, 127, and 128.] These are abstracts of accounts of the City of Glasgow Bank. There is a great deal of printing, and black ink, red ink and pencil marking on them. We were employed to make correct copies of these four documents, and we did so of three of them, A, C, D. We did not make a copy of B. [Shown Nos. 127A, 128A, and 124A.] [See Appendix No. II.] These are the lithograph copies that we made. They are correct. [Shown No. 131.] That bears to be abstract of accounts of City of Glasgow Bank at head office, 6th June 1877. No. 131A is our lithographic copy of it. It also is a correct copy.

Cross-examined by the Dean of Faculty—[Shown No. 124.] I see that throughout that paper there are a number of pencil marks imperfectly delineated. They appear to have been rubbed out—whether intentionally or unintentionally, I don't know. That is also made to appear, as well as we could do it, on the lithograph copy. No. 124A is a *facsimile* of the original, as near as we could make it. [Shown No. 127.] I see that there are also a number of pencil figures on that paper. We have also represented them in our lithograph copy, No. 127A, as nearly as we could. They are not so much rubbed out in that paper as in No. 124. (Q.) Do these figures exhibit the same kind of calculations that you think were in the other paper? (A.) I never addressed myself to that particular point.

By the Lord Justice-Clerk—Our lithographs are *facsimilies* of the originals, as nearly as we could make them. They indicate the print, the MS. part, and the pencil jottings. They are, as nearly as we could make them, a faithful representation of the originals.

JOHN BOYD.

By Mr Burnet—I am a superintendent of police in Glasgow. I apprehended several of the prisoners, and among others Mr Stronach. I found on him a pencil document beginning with the words, "Until for some time before "my brother left the Bank," &c. [Shown No. 298.] That document was given up by Mr Stronach on his apprehension to me in the police office, and also the letter No. 297. It bears to be a letter from D. Bell, 11 Queen Victoria Street, London. After the prisoners were apprehended, I was instructed by the procurator-fiscal to search for documents in the Bank. I went there first on 28th October, when I found a great many. I locked them up in two boxes, and took them to the procurator-fiscal's room. Nos. 192 to 248 inclusive in the list of documents appended to the indictment, were a portion of the documents which were in these two boxes; they were all recovered by me in the secretary's room, and also No. 290. I again visited the Bank on 14th November, and took possession of a tin box in the manager's room, which I also took to the Fiscal's office, and handed to Mr Brown. In that box were the documents Nos. 249, 250, and 324. On 4th December I again visited the Bank, and took possession of two bundles of papers, which were also taken to Mr Brown. In these bundles were found the documents Nos. 250 to 260 inclusive, 273 to 277 inclusive, and 295. The documents now spoken to were all initialed by me, and handed to the procurator-fiscal.

JAMES RODEN.

By Mr Pearson—I am a sheriff-officer in Glasgow. I was instructed by the procurator-fiscal to take charge of the books of the Bank. They have been under my charge since 30th October last. I recovered certain documents in the Bank at various dates in October and November. [Shown Nos. 249, 250, 278 to 283, 296, and 324.] I recovered these documents. They are all initialed by me as part of the documents I recovered in the Bank.

The declarations of the prisoners were then read.

FIRST DECLARATION OF JOHN STEWART.

At Glasgow, the twenty-second day of October, eighteen hundred and seventy-eight, in presence of Francis William Clark, Esquire, advocate, Sheriff of Lanarkshire.

Compeared a prisoner, and the charge against him having been read over and explained to him, and he having been judicially admonished and examined, declares and says—My name is John Stewart. I am a native of Glasgow, sixty-one years of age, and I reside at 34 Moray Place, Edinburgh. I am a wine merchant.

I declare that I am not guilty of the charge of falsehood, fraud, and wilful imposition preferred against me, of having falsified the books of the City of Glasgow Bank, and prepared and issued false and fabricated balance-sheets, during the years from 1873 to 1878 inclusive, while the Bank was in a state of insolvency, and well known to me to be so, so as to conceal the true state of the affairs of the Bank from the shareholders and creditors, and of declaring false dividends, in order to deceive said shareholders, creditors, and the public.

I farther declare that, as I have been advised, I decline at this stage to make any farther statement, or answer any farther questions. All which I declare to be truth.

J. STEWART.
F. W. CLARK.

W. A. Brown,
Geo. Brander,
B. M'Lauchlin, } *Witnesses.*

SECOND DECLARATION OF JOHN STEWART.

At Glasgow, the twenty-ninth day of October, eighteen hundred and seventy-eight years, in presence of Francis William Clark, Esquire, advocate, Sheriff of Lanarkshire.

Compeared John Stewart, presently prisoner in the prison of Glasgow, and a charge of theft now preferred against him having been read over and explained to him, and he having been judicially admonished and examined, declares and says—I am not guilty of the charge made against me of stealing a number of bills, amounting to twenty-three thousand six hundred and ninety-three pounds twelve shillings and sevenpence, or thereby.

I am advised to make no farther statement at this stage than that I am not guilty. All which I declare to be truth.

J. STEWART.
F. W. CLARK.

W. A. Brown,
Geo. Brander,
B. M'Lauchlin, } *Witnesses.*

FIRST DECLARATION OF LEWIS POTTER.

At Glasgow the twenty-second day of October, eighteen hundred and seventy-eight years, in presence of Francis William Clark, Esquire, advocate, Sheriff of Lanarkshire.

Compeared a prisoner, and the charge against him having been read over and explained to him, and he having been judicially admonished and examined, declares and says—My name is Lewis Potter. I am a native of Falkirk, seventy-one years of age; and I reside at No. 7 Claremont Terrace, Glasgow. I am a retired merchant.

I declare that I am not guilty of the charge of falsehood, fraud, and wilful imposition preferred against me, of having falsified the books of the City of Glasgow Bank, and prepared and issued false and fabricated balance-sheets during the years from 1873 to 1878 inclusive, while the Bank was in a state of insolvency, and well known to me to be so, so as to conceal the true state of the affairs of the Bank from the shareholders and creditors, and of declaring false dividends in order to deceive said shareholders, creditors, and the public.

I have nothing farther to say in the meantime, and I decline to answer any questions that may be put to me. All which I declare to be truth.

Lewis Potter.
F. W. Clark.

W. A. Brown,
Geo. Brander,
B. M'Lauchlin,
} *Witnesses.*

SECOND DECLARATION OF LEWIS POTTER.

At Glasgow, the twenty-fifth day of October, eighteen hundred and seventy-eight years, in presence of Francis William Clark, Esquire, advocate, Sheriff of Lanarkshire.

Compeared Lewis Potter, presently prisoner in the prison of Glasgow, and the declaration emitted by him before the said Sheriff, of date the twenty-second day of October current, having been read over to him, and he having been judicially admonished and examined, declares and says—

I am now brought before the Sheriff at my own request.

I considered that the City Bank was in a solvent state when the last balance-sheet was struck. I was under the impression that all the securities were sufficient. I signed the last balance-sheet. I did this under the impression that it was correct. It was done while I and the other directors were at luncheon, and I signed it at their request. I think I had just come from Ayr at the time, where my time was spent in country quarters, and my mind was entirely off business. Before signing I had not examined any of the books or documents, so as to test the accuracy of the balance-sheet. I acted on the impression that others had done so.

Shown a document, titled on the back, "City of Glasgow Bank, Abstract "of Accounts at June 5, 1878, B." [See Appendix No. II.] I cannot say whether I had seen that before I signed the balance-sheet or ledger. I don't recollect of going over the foresaid document along with Mr Stewart and Mr Robert Stronach before signing the balance-sheet. I may have seen it at the Bank. It is likely I did.

I observe that in the foresaid document the indebtedness of the Bank is stated under "bills payable" at £2,881,252, 18s. 6d., and that there is deducted from that, under "bills payable," a sum of £973,300. I don't know why that was done, and I understand nothing about it.

On the other side of the document I see an entry showing the amount lent by the Bank on credit accounts No. 1, a sum of £2,009,752, 11s. 2d., and that there is deducted from that a sum of £680,614. I do not know how that was done, and I don't understand it.

Interrogated—Did you think it was properly done? Declares—I cannot say. I am unable to give explanations regarding the said document, because, though I may have seen it, I have never thoroughly examined it.

I have been about twenty years a director of the City Bank. I came into the direction soon after the stoppage in 1856. I did this at the urgent request of parties.

I do not think I or my firms were indebted to the Bank at that time. Ever since that time, and certainly latterly, I and my firms abstained from doing business with the Bank. What business we did was almost all transacted with the National Bank and the British Linen. We got some credits from the City Bank, but I think these did not exceed £30,000 at the outside. I explain that we have considerable credits from the Bank, but these are principally on its own account.

The City Bank wished to acquire certain lands in New Zealand, and they gave us credits to pay for the same, to be held on their account.

I have no doubt this proposal originated at a meeting of directors, and was sanctioned by them, and I suppose will appear in the minutes. I know that lands were bought, but cannot say as to the form of the title. I don't think the Bank has any title to the lands. These purchases were made within the last six or nine months, and we should be glad to give up the titles to the Bank as soon as the credits are paid.

The Bank also wished my firm to acquire shares for them in the New Zealand and Australian Land Company, and they gave us credits in order to purchase these. The title was taken in name of my son John Alexander and Cunningham Smith, both partners of Potter, Wilson, & Co. There were also some shares taken in my own name.

Interrogated—Why were those titles not taken directly to the Bank instead of your and your partners' names? Declares—I cannot explain that. I and my partners have held these shares for about five years. We have not disposed of them or trafficked in them. They were held by us for the Bank in the hope that a large profit might be secured for the Bank in a short time.

During the time of our holding, the only securities held by the Bank against us I believe to be letters which have passed between us and the Bank. These letters, if they exist, were addressed by us to the directors or the manager. I don't suppose such letters came before the weekly meetings of the Bank, but I am not sure. The transaction was perfectly well understood, and it was unnecessary to revert to it at the meetings. Even in the event of the stoppage of my firm, the Bank would suffer no prejudice, because I suppose the minutes would bear that such shares or property were held by us from the Bank, and my private estate remained accountable. I suppose even yet I shall have a considerable reversion.

I do not know personally of any advances made by the Bank to Smith, Fleming, & Co., without the sanction of the board. There may have been; and if so, that was the manager's affair.

I know nothing, even yet, about the amount of advances to James Morton and Co., but I was aware that advances had been made. The advances to that firm were never brought before us, to the best of my belief.

I never knew anything of the amount of the advances to John Innes Wright and Co. till shortly before the stoppage, but I knew that some advances had been made.

It certainly was our duty, as directors, to inquire into the advances which we knew were being made to the above firms, but we did not do so, from the faith we had in the manager. For all that I knew, the Bank might have advanced £2,000,000 to James Morton & Co.

I understood they had securities, but I knew nothing of their amount.

Interrogated—Do you consider that £2,132,453 was a large or moderate sum for the Bank to be liable in on acceptances? Declares—I think moderate, considering the probability that a good part of that was for its own benefit.

Shown a book, titled on the back, "City of Glasgow Bank Cash Book, "Private, No. 6." and being referred to the cross entries under heads "Foreign "and Colonial Credits, No. 2," and "Bills Payable, No. 2,"—I never saw those entries before, and was confounded when I saw a reference to them in the Investigators' Report. I don't think I knew that such a book existed before. I can give no explanation of how, in the balance ledger of the Bank, under date June 4, 1873, foreign and colonial credits are only entered to the amount of £1,159,153, 2s. 3d. I was not aware of the fact that in the balance ledger of the Bank they were so credited.

At the date of the stoppage, I think I held about twelve shares. The shares were converted into stock about 1856. I don't think I ever held more.

I did not think, and never considered, that the Bank was in an insolvent state till its stoppage.

About a month before, I thought I saw tightness in money. I was present at the meeting in Edinburgh which resolved on stoppage. The meeting in Edinburgh was composed of myself, Mr Stewart, and the manager, as deputed by the board. We resolved on stoppage, for want of the usual facilities to carry on the business. It had been arranged by the directors in Glasgow that a stoppage should take place if we failed to get facilities. The account of Smith, Fleming, & Co. was talked of among the directors before the stoppage.

The immediate want of money was the cause of the stoppage. Latterly the manager found it difficult to negotiate the Bank's paper in the market. I do not know any reason why the Bank lost its credit, unless it were the undue amount of credit given to customers.

From 1873 to 1878, I have not taken a greater amount of interest in the Bank than the other directors. We were all much the same in that respect.

James Nicol Fleming did not take a greater share in the management than other people.

I cannot say that during the years from 1873 downwards I have made no examination of the Bank books. I have not had conferences with the manager in going over the books.

I don't think there is a special meeting of the directors generally called to go over the balance-sheet, but I think they should see it is correct. We had full faith in the manager when he presented a document.

Very likely we went over it in a sort of way; but latterly I was getting old, and was not attending to business as formerly. Since I became a director I never said to any one that I had suspicions of the Bank's stability.

The foresaid declaration, document, and Private Cash Book No. 6, are docqueted and subscribed as relative hereto. All which I declare to be truth.

Lewis Potter.
F. W. Clark.

W. A. Brown,
Geo. Brander,
B. M'Lauchlin, } *Witnesses.*

THIRD DECLARATION OF LEWIS POTTER.

At Glasgow, the twenty-ninth day of October, eighteen hundred and seventy-eight years, in presence of Francis William Clark, Esquire, advocate, Sheriff of Lanarkshire.

Compeared Lewis Potter, presently prisoner in the prison of Glasgow, and a charge of theft, now preferred against him, having been read over and explained to him, and he having been judicially admonished and examined, declares and says—I am not guilty of the charge preferred against me, of stealing a number of bills, amounting to twenty-three thousand six hundred and ninety-three pounds twelve shillings and sevenpence, or thereby.

I was not aware that the City Bank was in the habit of receiving bills for collection, and endorsing and handing them over to the London Joint Stock Bank before they had become due.

These bills received for collection were not the property of the Bank, and therefore the Bank was not entitled to retain them, or have them discounted on their own account.

As a director, I could not know that any such practice was followed in the Bank. We had such full confidence in the manager, that we never thought he would do such a thing. We only discovered after the stoppage that such things had been done, and we were recommended to the best of my belief, by our law agent, not to interfere.

If any such practice as that above referred to existed, and known to the directors to exist, it would never have been sanctioned by the directors, but would have been repudiated with indignation. All which I declare to be truth.

LEWIS POTTER.
F. W. CLARK.

W. A. Brown,
Geo. Brander,
B. M'Lauchlin, } *Witnesses.*

FIRST DECLARATION OF ROBERT SALMOND.

At Glasgow, the twenty-second day of October, eighteen hundred and seventy-eight years, in presence of Francis William Clark, Esquire, advocate, Sheriff of Lanarkshire.

Compeared a prisoner, and the charge against him having been read over and explained to him, and he having been judicially admonished and examined, declares and says—My name is Robert Salmond. I am a native of Inveraray, seventy-four years of age, and I reside at Rankinston, Ayrshire. I am director of several concerns in England.

I declare that I am not guilty of the charge of falsehood, fraud, and wilful imposition preferred against me, of having falsified the books of the City of Glasgow Bank, and prepared and issued false and fabricated balance-sheets during the years from 1873 to 1878 inclusive, while the Bank was in a state of insolvency, and well known to me to be so, so as to conceal the true state of the affairs of the Bank from the shareholders and creditors, and of declaring false dividends in order to deceive said shareholders, creditors, and the public.

To the best of my recollection, I was appointed director of the Bank about 1861 or 1862.

Interrogated—Did you consider the Bank in a solvent condition when the last balance-sheet was issued? Declares—Certainly I did so, to the best of my knowledge and belief. I signed it after the meeting was over, and the dividend declared twelve or fourteen days after. I had been absent from Glasgow and the Bank while the balance-sheet was being prepared. Before signing the balance-sheet I did not examine the accounts of the Bank to ascertain if they were correct. I signed in the full belief of the accuracy of the statements made in the balance-sheets. Ever since my appointment as director I have pursued the same course. My attendance at the examination of the books was more a matter of form than anything else. The only thing I examined specially was the branch accounts or returns, and that I think only on two occasions. The manager was perfectly aware that I did not examine the books or accounts; and the other directors acted as I did myself, confiding in our own innocence and honour, and in the statements of the manager. I think it was through my recommendation that Mr Innes Wright became a director. I am not aware that I ever asked any one to take shares.

I think the shareholders might have regarded my name as a guarantee for the Bank, and for its being properly conducted.

Being shown a book titled on the back "City of Glasgow Bank Cash Book, "Private, No. 6," and my attention being drawn to two entries, dated respec- "tively June 4, 1873," under the heads "Foreign and Colonial Credits No. "2," and "Bills Payable, No. 2"—I declare that I knew nothing about these entries, and never saw them until they were in the hands of the investigators some days ago, when they showed them to me.

During the years 1873, 1874, and 1875, I subscribed the balance ledger before the balance-sheets were issued to the shareholders. The accounts therein appearing were all summed up by the directors, and found to be arithmetically correct; but beyond that we made no inquiry. I now see my name at the annual balances in the current balance ledger, commencing "June 4, "1873." Shown a document titled on the back "City of Glasgow Bank Abstract "of Accounts, 5 June 1878, A." [See Appendix II.] I never saw that until I saw it in the hands of Mr M'Gregor.

Is is quite useless to ask me any questions relative to the books of the Bank, as I know nothing about them.

My present indebtedness to the Bank will range between £130,000 and £140,000, but this is entirely covered by my securities, to the extent of about £200,000, which are first-class.

I did not advise, nor was I ever consulted, in relation to the advances by the Bank to James Morton & Co., Smith, Fleming, & Co., James Nicol Fleming, and John Innes Wright & Co. I was not aware that such advances had been made till eighteen months ago. The names had often been before me, but I was not aware till that time that the advances had been made.

At the striking of the last balance-sheet, I knew that some advances had been made to these parties, but I had no doubt that ultimately they would prove quite good. There was some concealment regarding the advances to James Morton & Co., which, so far as I was concerned, was never cleared up till very recently.

Before the stoppage of the Bank, I was never aware that its capital had been lost.

I was aware of the extent to which the directors were buying their own stock, but I understood that this was done under the provisions of the contract of copartnery.

Meetings of the directors were held once a week. I regularly attended them. At these meetings the advances made to the afore-mentioned parties were not specially stated. The statements were merely *pro forma* bills, discounts, deposits, and the like.

The first manager of the bank was Henry Paul. I succeeded him in 1842, and remained manager till 1861 or 1862, when Alexander Stronach succeeded me.

I am not an annuitant of the Bank. I left the management without claiming anything.

I first came to know that the Bank was not in an easy position some three or four years ago, but I thought nothing of it, believing it would all come right in a short time. The real cause of the unsatisfactory state of the Bank was the absorption of the capital by the foresaid advances; and though I did not know the amount of the advances, I was satisfied that the accounts must have been in a very unsatisfactory state to require such absorption. I suspected or inferred that there was something wrong with these advances, without knowing what it was.

Declares further—As regards what took place at the weekly meetings, I explain that the advances made to the parties before-mentioned came up in the ordinary way, but were not specially stated. They came up just in the ordinary general way, the same as advances to other customers.

The book, entries, and document before referred to, are now docqueted and subscribed as relative hereto. All which I declare to be truth.

ROB. SALMOND.
F. W. CLARK.

W. A. Brown,
Geo. Brander,
B. M'Lauchlin, } *Witnesses.*

SECOND DECLARATION OF ROBERT SALMOND.

At Glasgow, the twenty-ninth day of October, eighteen hundred and seventy-eight years, in presence of Francis William Clark, Esquire, advocate, Sheriff of Lanarkshire.

Compeared Robert Salmond, presently prisoner in the prison of Glasgow, and a charge of theft now preferred against him having been read over and explained to him, and he having been judicially admonished and examined, declares and says—I am not guilty of the charge preferred against me of stealing a number of bills, amounting in the aggregate to the sum of twenty-three thousand six hundred and ninety-three pounds twelve shillings and sevenpence, or thereby.

I explain that I never even heard of the existence of such bills until the stoppage of the Bank, and even then I only heard of them from the fact that inquiries were made regarding them.

Interrogated—Were you aware that it was the practice of the City of Glasgow Bank to receive bills of exchange from customers of the Bank for the special and sole purpose of collecting payment of the same, and thereafter endorsing and making over said bills before they had become due, in order that the proceeds thereof might be credited to the City of Glasgow Bank? Declares—I knew that this was the practice of all the banks in Scotland, but I was not aware that there was any speciality in the practice of the City Bank in this respect. I cannot say whether any discrimination was made by the City Bank between bills for collection and bills for discount sent up to London. I consider that the City Bank was quite entitled to follow this practice in relation to bills received by them for collection. There was no other way by which said bills could be collected in London.

Interrogated—What, then, is the position of the creditors in these bills, now that the Bank is stopped? Declares—That is a very awkward question, insomuch that I consider the liquidators bound to pay back the money so received. I think that such moneys never were the property of the Bank. All which I declare to be truth.

ROB. SALMOND.
F. W. CLARK.

W. A. Brown,
Geo. Brander,
B. M'Lauchlin, } *Witnesses.*

FIRST DECLARATION OF WILLIAM TAYLOR.

At Glasgow, the twenty-second day of October, eighteen hundred and seventy-eight years, in presence of Francis William Clark, Esquire, advocate, Sheriff of Lanarkshire.

Compeared a prisoner, and the charge against him having been read over and explained to him, and he having been judicially admonished and examined, declares and says—My name is William Taylor. I am a native of Glasgow, sixty-six years of age; and I reside at Langbank, Newton-Mearns.

I am a merchant in Glasgow.

I am not guilty of the charge of falsehood, fraud, and wilful imposition preferred against me, of having falsified the books of the City of Glasgow Bank, and prepared and issued false and fabricated balance-sheets during the years from 1873 to 1878 inclusive, while the Bank was in a state of insolvency, and well known to me to be so, so as to conceal the true state of the affairs of the Bank from the shareholders and creditors, and of declaring false dividends in order to deceive said shareholders, creditors, and the public.

I believed the City of Glasgow Bank to be solvent when the last balance-sheet was issued, and since I became a director I believed all the balance-sheets to be correct that were issued. I always believed the statements put before us by the Bank officials to be correct. I never heard anything to the contrary.

I don't exactly know who constituted the officials, except that they included Mr Leresche, Mr Turnbull, and Mr Murdoch. Mr Aikman, the accountant, and Mr Morris, were probably conversant with the details. I have been a director since 1872, I think.

I don't think we ever compared the balance-sheets with the Bank books, so as to test their accuracy. We just took the statement of the officials on trust.

No books were ever submitted to us along with the balance-sheets. We subscribed the latter on the faith of the representations made to us by the officials.

I don't think I ever examined any of the Bank books with the view of testing the accuracy of the balance-sheets. I did not think it my duty as a director to do so. Such an examination would have involved the work of an accountant. My duty as a director, I thought, consisted in attending the weekly meetings, and dealing with the questions submitted for our consideration.

I would add, that shortly after my appointment as director, Mr Stewart and I were detailed to take charge of the branches, and to visit them occasionally, and this we did. At each weekly meeting a book was brought up showing a statement of all the branch accounts, with the deposits and advances in detail. We examined these items, and if in any case a branch seemed to exceed their limit of advances, we took a note of it, and their attention was called to it. At the time when we were detailed for this duty, which was in 1872, Mr Salmond and Mr Potter were appointed to take charge of the head office accounts.

Sometimes they made reports to the officials, which were brought up as part of the weekly business, and sometimes they drew the attention of the meeting to anything special in relation to the accounts.

My firm was indebted to the Bank at the time of the stoppage about £70,000. That represented advances made by the Bank at different times to our firm. We did not make application to the directors for those advances. I understood they were arranged with the manager, Mr Stronach, and he would afterwards report them to the directors individually, but not at a meeting of the board.

The Bank never held any securities against those advances. Mr Stronach knew personally that I and my firm held property in Hope Street, in relation to which we laid out part of the advances; but there was no mortgage or other security created over such property in favour of the Bank. I also gave Mr Stronach some scrip of the South-Western Railway, to the value of £2500.

Interrogated—Were you ever aware that the Bank had made heavy advances to the firms of James Morton & Company, Smith, Fleming, & Company, James Nicol Fleming, and Potter, Wilson, & Company. Declares—No. On Mr Stronach's appointment as manager, he called the attention of the directors to certain advances or accounts which had been gone into in his brother's time, which he said were covered by securities, but for which he did not wish to be held responsible.

These had been gone into before my time, and that was the first notice I got of them.

I think the minutes of the directors will show what was done with those accounts when brought under the notice of the board by Mr Stronach.

With the exception of certain advances made to Smith, Fleming, & Co. since 1876, and which in the aggregate might amount to £75,000, and against which there were special securities, I am not aware of any advances made to the above-mentioned firms since that time.

Interrogated—Can you explain how one of these firms comes to be indebted to the Bank in a sum amounting to nearly £2,000,000, and another in a sum over £2,000,200? Declares—I am unable to explain that. The directors never in my time authorised such advances. There were never any applications to the board for advances such as those; and if they were got, I am unable to explain how.

I was not aware of the Bank being in difficulties until, at the farthest, ten days before its stoppage. I first heard of it at a meeting of directors called to consider a statement by Mr Morton that the Bank's acceptances could not be discounted in London.

It was then stated that some £500,000 would tide over the difficulty.

I was quite certain that if that money could be got the Bank would go on, and I thought that, but for that difficulty, the Bank was in a most prosperous condition.

Until the very morning when the Bank stopped, I was not aware that a stoppage was contemplated. The very day before, I directed some £700 or £800 to be deposited in the Bank. That sum belonged to my firm; and as we had an account with the Union Bank, I should have deposited it there if I had had any doubts of the City Bank. All the directors were present at the meetings which took place in Glasgow before the stoppage of the Bank, with the exception of one, at which I think Mr Inglis was not present.

From what passed at the meetings, it seemed to be the impression of the board, as certainly it was my own, that if we had got assistance from the Edinburgh banks, we should have been able to go on.

The directors did not latterly give orders for the purchase of the Bank stock by the Bank itself. I was not aware of such a practice. I did not know who the brokers for the Bank were in such purchases till after the stoppage.

To the best of my recollection, I held stock in the Bank at its stoppage to about £2200.

I beg to explain that I have been a shareholder in the Bank since its commencement, and added to my stock in 1856.

I again took additional stock when the new stock was issued in 1874. At the same time my son and brother, on my recommendation, took five shares each.

I have never sold a share since I was connected with the Bank.

I did not know of any gold being sent to London. All which I declare to be truth.

William Taylor.
F. W. Clark.

W. A. Brown,
Geo. Brander,
B. M'Lauchlin, } *Witnesses.*

SECOND DECLARATION OF WILLIAM TAYLOR.

At Glasgow, the twenty-ninth day of October, eighteen hundred and seventy-eight years, in presence of Francis William Clark, Esquire, advocate, Sheriff of Lanarkshire.

Compeared William Taylor, presently prisoner in the prison of Glasgow, and the declaration emitted by him before the said Sheriff, of date the twenty-second day of October, having been read over to him, and he having been again judicially admonished and examined, declares and says—I am now brought before the Sheriff at my own request, and wish to explain that when I formerly stated that I had not examined any of the books of the Bank, I should have added, what I now recollect, that I had looked over the balance ledger, but not critically, and that I took the statements in it as being substantially correct, coming as they did from the officials.

The aforesaid declaration is docqueted and subscribed as relative hereto. All which I declare to be truth.

William Taylor.
F. W. Clark.

W. A. Brown,
Geo. Brander,
B. M'Lauchlin, } *Witnesses.*

THIRD DECLARATION OF WILLIAM TAYLOR.

At Glasgow, the twenty-ninth day of October, eighteen hundred and seventy-eight years, in presence of Francis William Clark, Esquire, advocate, Sheriff of Lanarkshire.

Compeared William Taylor, presently prisoner in the prison of Glasgow, and a charge of theft now preferred against him having been read over and explained to him, and he having been judicially admonished and examined, declares and says—I am not guilty of the charge preferred against me, of stealing a number of bills, amounting to twenty-three thousand six hundred and ninety-three pounds twelve shillings and sevenpence, or thereby. I was not aware that such bills had been sent to London. If such bills were sent to London, it was without the authority of the board entirely. Bills left for the purpose of collection were not the property of the Bank, and the Bank had no right to dispose of them in that manner. I knew that the London Joint Stock Bank were agents in London for the City of Glasgow Bank, but beyond this I did not know of the details of the transactions between them. All which I declare to be truth.

William Taylor.
F. W. Clark.

W. A. Brown,
Geo. Brander,
B. M'Lauchlin, } *Witnesses.*

FIRST DECLARATION OF HENRY INGLIS.

At Glasgow, the twenty-second day of October, eighteen hundred and seventy-eight years, in presence of Francis William Clark, Esquire, advocate, Sheriff of Lanarkshire.

Compeared a prisoner, and the charge against him having been read over and explained to him, and he having been judicially admonished and examined, declares and says—My name is Henry Inglis. I am a native of Edinburgh, seventy-two years of age; and I reside at No. 1 Great Stuart Street, Edinburgh. I am a Writer to the Signet.

I declare that I am not guilty of the charge of falsehood, fraud, and wilful imposition preferred against me, of having falsified the books of the Bank, and prepared and issued false and fabricated balance-sheets during the years from 1873 to 1878 inclusive, while the Bank was in a state of insolvency, and well known to me to be so, so as to conceal the true state of the affairs of the Bank from the shareholders and creditors, and of declaring false dividends, in order to deceive said shareholders, creditors, and the public. Further, I beg to say, that about nine years ago or thereby, I was requested to become a director of the City of Glasgow Bank. I accepted the office, and upon taking my seat at the board, I found that my co-directors appeared to me to be a body of Glasgow gentlemen, irreproachable in character and in position. I also found that the manager of the Bank, at that period, was an officer who possessed their entire confidence, and that confidence gradually extended itself to myself, without any restriction whatsoever. I have only to add, that my crime, if crime it be, was the possession of the most entire confidence in every statement and in every figure which was laid before me. Not having the minute books of the directors before me at present, I do not feel myself justified in saying more, and I do not at present wish to answer any questions with reference to the charge. All which I declare to be truth.

HENRY INGLIS.
F. W. CLARK.

W. A. Brown,
Geo. Brander, } *Witnesses.*
B. M'Lauchlin,

SECOND DECLARATION OF HENRY INGLIS.

At Glasgow, the twenty-ninth day of October, eighteen hundred and seventy-eight years, in presence of Francis William Clark, Esquire, advocate, Sheriff of Lanarkshire.

Compeared Henry Inglis, presently prisoner in the prison of Glasgow, and the declaration emitted by him before the Sheriff, of date the twenty-second day of October current, having been read over to him, and he being again judicially admonished and examined, declares and says—I am now brought before the Sheriff at my own request, as I wish to state that during one of the years embraced in the charge I was absent for many months from the board of the Bank. The particular year I cannot specify at present, but it can be easily ascertained from the minute book of the directors.

During that year or period I was absent in Portugal, where I was attacked by a disease called gangrenous erysipelas, and operated upon severely and dangerously by Dr Barboza, of Lisbon. On returning home I was confined to the house. Thereafter I was further attacked by severe neuralgia in the face, and thereafter by congestion of the brain and congestion of the left lung. These circumstances will account for my absence from the Glasgow board, and I think it right to state them. All which I declare to be truth.

The foresaid declaration is now docqueted and subscribed as relative hereto.

HENRY INGLIS.
F. W. CLARK.

W. A. Brown,
Geo. Brander, } *Witnesses.*
B. M'Lauchlin,

THIRD DECLARATION OF HENRY INGLIS.

At Glasgow, the twenty-ninth day of October, eighteen hundred and seventy-eight years, in presence of Francis William Clark, Esquire, advocate, Sheriff of Lanarkshire.

Compeared Henry Inglis, presently prisoner in the prison of Glasgow, and a charge of theft now preferred against him having been read over and explained to him, and he having been judicially admonished and examined, declares and says—

I am not guilty of the charge preferred against me of stealing a number of bills, amounting to twenty-three thousand six hundred and ninety-three pounds twelve shillings and sevenpence, or thereby, and I take the liberty of saying that I consider the charge so absurd that I am constrained to believe that it has been made for some purpose which the prosecutor deems necessary, but which is not known to me.

I was not aware of any practice in the Bank of sending bills got for collection before they became due to London, and I was only made aware of the circumstance alluded to by being told of it after the stoppage by one of the investigators, Mr M'Grigor.

I do not know whether it is proper to send such bills to London before they become due. That and all other banking details were matters for the manager to consider, and they never came before the board of directors. All which I declare to be truth.

HENRY INGLIS.
F. W. CLARK.

W. A. Brown,
Geo. Brander, } *Witnesses.*
B. M'Lauchlin,

FIRST DECLARATION OF JOHN INNES WRIGHT.

At Glasgow, the twenty-second day of October, eighteen hundred and seventy-eight years, in presence of Francis William Clark, Esquire, advocate, Sheriff of Lanarkshire.

Compeared a prisoner, and the charge against him having been read over and explained to him, and he having been judicially admonished and examined, declares and says—My name is John Innes Wright. I am a native of Glasgow, sixty-eight years of age; and I reside at 10 Queen's Terrace, Glasgow. I am a merchant.

I declare that I am not guilty of the charge of falsehood, fraud, and wilful imposition, preferred against me, of having falsified the books of the City of Glasgow Bank, and prepared and issued false and fabricated balance-sheets during the years from 1875 to 1878 inclusive, while the Bank was in a state of insolvency, and well known to me to be so, so as to conceal the true state of the affairs of the Bank from the shareholders and creditors, and of declaring false dividends in order to deceive said shareholders, creditors, and the public.

When the last balance-sheet was issued to the shareholders, I believed the Bank to be in a solvent condition. I signed that balance-sheet and all balance-sheets since 1876. I became a director in 1875.

It is the duty of the directors to make such an examination of the Bank books as to ascertain that the balance-sheet is correct. With relation to all the balance-sheets which I signed as a director, I examined all the books that were laid before me. There was, I think, a special meeting always held in relation to the balance-sheet. So far as my experience goes, that was the practice of the Bank. I think it was the accountant of the Bank that laid the books before us. The cashier may also have brought some.

I suppose it was the manager, and not the directors, who desired these books to be laid before us. I understand that the manager would tell the accountant what were the proper books to lay before us. I cannot at present recollect what the books were, a bank has so many kinds of books. I have no recollection of seeing discount ledgers and abstracts thereof on such occasions.

I never saw the credit ledgers containing a record of the cash credits granted by the Bank.

I understood the cash credits were secured, but I did not ascertain that from the books.

When cash credits came before us, it was generally stated what were the relative securities. We learned this from the applications, which were read by the secretary. I never took any means to ascertain whether the securities possessed the values put upon them. I was new to the direction, and leant very much on the older members.

The only ledger we saw, so far as I recollect, was the balance ledger. I never saw the register of securities held by the Bank, nor the circulation register, to the best of my recollection.

I do not recollect of having seen a document entitled "Abstract of "Accounts."

The balance-sheets were correct, according to the books laid before me. Beyond that I did not think it requisite to inquire. I trusted very much to the good faith of the manager and the bank officials.

I did not become aware of the bank capital having been lost till the Investigators' Report was drawn out. I may say that I did not know the true state of affairs till it was issued. I never suspected until then the loss of the capital.

I was not aware that the Bank was to be stopped until I read the stoppage in the morning newspapers. I believed or thought up till that time that the Scottish banks would come forward and enable the City Bank to go on.

I don't know who decided on the stoppage. It was done in Edinburgh. I was not there, and was not consulted. I was a party to the communings of the directors which immediately preceded the stoppage. It was first intended to apply to the London Joint Stock Bank for aid. If we did not get aid, it was quite believed that we should have to stop.

The principal or only thing that would render a stoppage necessary was, so far as I know, the difficulty of discounting the Bank's acceptances in London. I am unable to say what was the amount of those acceptances. At one of the meetings before the stoppage it was supposed that £500,000 would tide us over the difficulties. It might be a year or more before the stoppage when I became aware that the Bank's paper was not so readily taken as that of other banks.

When I became a director in June 1875, my firm was indebted to the Bank somewhere about £400,000. My firm was John Innes Wright & Co., and William Scott was the partner who took charge of the finance. To the best of my belief, our indebtedness to the Bank at the time of the stoppage was not more than £403,000. That indebtedness was the result of advances by the Bank to our firm. The Bank had certain securities against those advances; for example, shares in companies. I did not consider the Bank wholly secured. The stocks of all kinds for some years past had very much depreciated. I don't think the Bank was ever entirely secured for the advances made to us, but I cannot say to what extent they were unsecured, even approximately.

During the term of my directorship those advances were not brought under the notice of the weekly meetings until latterly, perhaps within six or nine months of the stoppage.

Before that they might have been talked of occasionally.

I can't say whether the advances to my firm were made without the authority of the directors. They might have been consulted privately without my knowledge; and, in point of fact, these advances were substantially made before I became a director.

I understood that the Bank had granted open and marginal credits to Smith, Fleming, & Co., and Potter, Wilson, & Co., or their agents in Australia.

These credits were to a certain extent brought under the notice of the directors. I did not know the full extent of those credits. They may have exceeded what came before us. If there was any excess, it must have been granted by the bank officials unknown to me. All those open and marginal credits ought to have proceeded on application to the board of directors, and of course the directors would know the amounts contained in these applications.

I had no idea, at the time of the stoppage, of the extent of indebtedness of these firms as now brought out in the Report by the Investigators. Certain securities were held against these credits. We, the directors, as far as we could, endeavoured to ascertain the value of these securities. We went very much on the statements of the parties themselves. Of course, we had a general idea of their value ourselves. £1200 is, as I understand, the qualification for a director. I only held £1200 bank stock in my own name, but I held about £2600 in trust. I never held more than £1200 stock in my own name.

Being shown a book, titled on the back, "City of Glasgow Bank Cash "Book, Private No. 6," and my attention drawn to two entries, dated respectively, "June 4, 1873," under the heads, "Foreign and Colonial Credits, No. "2," and "Bills Payable, No. 2."

I have never seen these entries until now, and I am unable to explain their meaning.

I was not aware that these sums of £973,300 were regularly annually repeated since the year 1873, until I was told so by Mr M'Grigor.

Shown an entry, dated "June 4, 1873, by Cash per Cash Book, £973,300," at page 87 of the volume titled on the back, "City of Glasgow Bank Ledger "General Accounts, 1872-3."

That entry is quite beyond my comprehension.

I make the same remarks as touching the entry June 4th, 1873, "To Cash "p. Cash Book, £973,300," at page 95 of the said last-mentioned volume. I have no recollection of ever having seen the books at the Bank containing an abstract of the weekly balances.

The foresaid entries and volume referred to are now docqueted and subscribed as relative hereto. All which I declare to be truth.

John Innes Wright.
F. W. Clark.

W. A. Brown,
Geo. Brander,
B. M'Lauchlin, } *Witnesses.*

SECOND DECLARATION OF JOHN INNES WRIGHT.

At Glasgow, the twenty-ninth day of October, eighteen hundred and seventy-eight years, in the presence of Francis William Clark, Esquire, advocate, Sheriff of Lanarkshire.

Compeared John Innes Wright, presently prisoner in the prison of Glasgow, and the declaration emitted by him before the Sheriff of date the twenty-second day of October current, having been read over to him, and he being again judicially admonished and examined, declares and says—I am now brought before the Sheriff at my own request, as I wish to state distinctly that when I become a director in 1875 I owed the Bank nothing as an individual. I succeeded James Nicol Fleming as a director.

Prior to my becoming a director, my firm, John Innes Wright & Co., had had business relations with Smith, Fleming, & Co., London, and Nicol, Fleming, & Co., Calcutta; but, to a considerable extent, our relation with Smith, Fleming, and Co., and their foreign correspondents, had been broken off.

I had not the necessary qualification of stock when I was elected a director.

I stated this to the manager, but I obtained the qualification a few days afterwards. I also urged the condition of my firm's account as a reason against my having any connection with the board.

Stronach was apparently anxious that I should be a director, and Mr Salmond also urged me to consent.

The request to be a director came to me quite unexpectedly, and I am not aware what reason induced them to make the request. The stock necessary for my qualification was acquired for me by the Bank. No cash passed, but I gave a cheque for the amount, and that cheque stands against my account with the Bank to the present day.

I am not aware of a similar course being followed in the case of any other director.

The foresaid declaration is docqueted and subscribed as relative hereto. All which I declare to be truth.

JOHN INNES WRIGHT.
F. W. CLARK.

W. A. Brown,
Geo. Brander,
B. M'Lauchlin, } *Witnesses.*

THIRD DECLARATION OF JOHN INNES WRIGHT.

At Glasgow, the twenty-ninth day of October, eighteen hundred and seventy-eight years, in presence of Francis William Clark, Esquire, advocate, Sheriff of Lanarkshire.

Compeared, John Innes Wright, presently prisoner in the prison of Glasgow, and a charge of theft now preferred against him having been read over and explained to him, and he having been judicially admonished and examined, declares and says—

I am not guilty of the charge made against me of stealing a number of bills, amounting to twenty-three thousand six hundred and ninety-three pounds twelve shillings and sevenpence sterling, or thereby.

Bills sent in for collection, as these apparently were, never came before the directors at all. They were received by the officials and forwarded in the usual way, as we understood, but they did not come under the cognisance of the directors.

I was not aware, until after the stoppage of the Bank, of any bills sent in for collection having been forwarded in this irregular way. The matter came before us after the stoppage; and Mr Stronach then informed the board that these bills, along with various others sent in the usual way of business, had been forwarded to London without his being aware that a portion of the bills were for collection merely.

I am not aware that bills sent in for collection merely have a different marking from other bills. All which I declare to be truth.

JOHN INNES WRIGHT.
F. W. CLARK.

W. A. Brown,
Geo. Brander,
B. M'Lauchlin, } *Witnesses.*

FIRST DECLARATION OF ROBERT SUMMERS STRONACH.

At Glasgow, the twenty-second day of October eighteen hundred and seventy-eight years, in presence of Francis William Clark, Esquire, advocate, Sheriff of Lanarkshire.

Compeared a prisoner, and the charge against him having been read over and explained to him, and he having been judicially admonished and examined, declares and says—

My name is Robert Summers Stronach. I am a native of Lonmay, Aberdeenshire, 52 years of age; and I reside at 13 Crown Gardens, Dowanhill, Glasgow. I am a banker in Glasgow.

I am not guilty of the charge preferred against me of falsehood, fraud, and wilful imposition, in having falsified the books of the City of Glasgow Bank, and prepared and issued false and fabricated balance-sheets during the years from 1875 to 1878 inclusive, while the Bank was in a state of insolvency, and when I was well aware of that fact, so as to conceal the true state of the affairs of the said Bank from the shareholders and creditors, and in declaring false dividends in order to deceive said shareholders, creditors, and the public. I declare further that, from the state of my health, and my mind being worn out by the anxieties of the last twelve months, I do not at present feel myself in a position to make explanations, or answer questions relative to the charges made against me.

Farther, I desire to add that Mr Leresche, secretary to the Bank, has nothing to do with the balance-sheets, but that he simply appears at the annual meetings and reads the minutes, which is simply a matter of form. All which I declare to be truth.

R. S. STRONACH.
F. W. CLARK.

W. A. Brown,
Geo. Brander,
B. M'Lauchlin, } *Witnesses.*

SECOND DECLARATION OF ROBERT SUMMERS STRONACH.

At Glasgow, the twenty-ninth day of October, eighteen hundred and seventy-eight years, in presence of Francis William Clark, Esquire, advocate, Sheriff of Lanarkshire.

Compeared Robert Summers Stronach, presently prisoner in the prison of Glasgow, and a charge of theft now preferred against him having been read over and explained to him, and he having been judicially admonished and examined, declares and says—I decline to make any statements, or answer any questions, with reference to the charge made against me of stealing a number of bills, amounting to twenty-three thousand six hundred and ninety-three pounds twelve shillings, or thereby.

I am satisfied that I shall be able to clear myself of the same at the proper time. All which I declare to be truth.

R. S. STRONACH.
F. W. CLARK.

W. A. Brown,
Geo. Brander,
B. M'Lauchlin, } *Witnesses.*

ALBERT THOMAS APTHORPE.

By Mr Burnet—I am clerk in the office of the Queen's and Lord Treasurer's Remembrancer. I have charge of the department for the registration of joint stock companies. The City of Glasgow Bank was registered as an unlimited company, under the Companies Act of 1862, on 29th November 1862. [Shown Nos. 303 and 304.] One of these is the certificate of incorporation, and the other an office copy,—the one being dated in 1862, and the other in 1878, certifying that at that date the Bank was still registered under the Act.

ALEXANDER BENNET M'GRIGOR, LL.D.

By the Lord Advocate—I am a writer, carrying on business in Glasgow, and a partner of the firm of M'Grigor, Donald, & Co. My firm have acted as agents for the Royal and British Linen Co. Banks. On 2d October 1878, I got a message asking me to meet the directors of the City of Glasgow Bank in Mr Potter's offices in Gordon Street. I went there. There were present—Mr Potter, Mr Wright, Mr Stewart, Mr Inglis, Mr Taylor, Mr Leresche the secretary of the Bank, and afterwards Mr Stronach. Mr William Anderson, C.A., was present at the commencement of the interview. I found him there. Some of the directors mentioned that of course I understood the painful circumstances under which they were met, and a somewhat general conversation took place as to the course that should be followed, and as to the propriety of a meeting of the shareholders being called at once. I was consulted as to these, and as to the propriety of such a meeting being called, and then I was asked, in conjunction with Mr Anderson, to prepare a balance-sheet of the affairs of the Bank, in order that it might be submitted to such a meeting. That request was preferred to myself and Mr Anderson jointly, and I cannot say that any one of the directors more than another preferred it; it was a general request. They all took part in the conversation. Mr Stronach came into the room apparently from a side room, I think about five minutes after I arrived. We had been conversing in regard to the state of the Bank before he arrived. I can hardly say that he took any part in the conversation. He seemed completely overpowered, and almost unable to speak. Mr Leresche did take part, and he appeared—if one may use the expression—to have more his wits about him than any one else in the room. I at first demurred to acting in the preparation of a balance-sheet, in consequence of my connection with those other banks; and I may say that I would almost have been glad of any excuse to get rid of what promised to be a very painful piece of business. It occurred to me that there might be some complication arising from the fact that my firm acted for those two banks; but I was very urgently pressed, and after consulting with Mr Anderson, I said I would communicate with those banks. I subsequently did so, and they thought there was no objection to my acting in the way proposed. I doubt if I was with the directors on the occasion I have mentioned for more than a quarter-of-an-hour or twenty minutes altogether. At that meeting nothing definite was said while I was there as to the state of the Bank; the conversation proceeded on a general assumption that the crisis was very serious—that there was something very far wrong. None of the directors present at that time entered upon any explanation of the causes of the crisis. When I said that Mr Leresche appeared to have more his wits about him than any of the rest, I meant that he appeared to me to be there more in an official capacity. I may say that I had never seen Mr Leresche to my knowledge before, and the directors appeared very much overcome, agitated, while Mr Leresche presented the appearance of a man engaged in his ordinary official duties. I left the meeting in company with Mr Anderson, and having telegraphed to Edinburgh for the opinion of the cashier of the Royal Bank, I called at the British Linen Company's Bank and got their approval of my course of action. I ascertained there was no objection on their part to my acting, though I held the position of their agent. Having received that assurance from those banks, I proceeded to make an investigation for the purpose of drawing up a balance-sheet and report to be laid before the meeting of shareholders. I went down immediately that afternoon to the Bank, and I may say that Mr Anderson and I were there continuously from that day until we issued our report, which was on the 18th of October. Mr Anderson and I worked into each other's hands, doing particular parts of the work. Of course, what may be called the general accountant's part of the work devolved upon him and his partner. With respect to my portion of the work, in the first instance, having heard that a statement had been prepared as to some leading accounts, and submitted through Mr Auldjo Jamieson (now one of the liquidators) to the Scotch banks, I telegraphed to Mr Jamieson to send me that statement, and I received it from him that evening. I took that statement merely as a guide in my own investigation. I cannot say whether or not it was at the meeting with the directors that I had learned Mr Jamieson had been furnished with that information; I rather think it was at the British Linen Company's Bank. Upon receiving Mr Jamieson's notanda, Mr Anderson and I proceeded to investigate for ourselves. We looked over these notanda, and found that they embraced a note of four leading accounts, which had been the subject of conversation with the Bank directors. These were the accounts of James Morton & Company, Smith, Fleming, & Company, James Nicol Fleming, and John Innes Wright & Company. The statement embraced the balances at the debit of these several accounts, and the securities held against them, and as I understood that these securities were put down at the valuations which the Bank itself had furnished, we took the deficit as showing the minimum deficit. We very roughly endeavoured to correct off-hand the value of the securities from such facts as were patent upon the face of the accounts, and upon that information we became satisfied next day that we must advise the directors at once that there was no hope of the Bank continuing business. Within a day of receiving these notanda and examining them in the way I have described, I came unhesitatingly to the conclusion that the Bank could not possibly go on,—that it was hopelessly insolvent. John Innes Wright and Co. is the firm of which the panel Mr Wright is a partner, and he is a director of the Company. There was enough in the indebtedness of these firms to make it impossible, in our judgment, for the Bank to go on. After that we proceeded to make farther inquiry about those accounts. In conjunction with Mr Muir I made a detailed precognition of Mr Morison, the accountant of the Bank, and obtained from him a number of documents, in particular certain abstract balance-sheets. These documents were given to me by Mr Morison out of his custody, as an official of the Bank, and I got him to initial and mark them as he gave them. These documents are Nos. 124, 125, 127, and 128, and they were marked A, B, C, and D. [See Appendix, No. II.] From the time they were given to me by Mr Morison, they remained in my special custody until 21st October, when I handed them over to the procurator-fiscal. So far as we had time, between the receipt of Mr Jamieson's notes and the issuing of our report, we proceeded to check his notes upon those accounts to the best of our ability, and likewise to check the general abstract balance-sheet for 1878, which I had received from Mr Morison. When I say the general abstract balance-sheet, I do not mean the balance-sheet that was published; I mean the scroll abstract. That is the abstract which has just been shown to me. The prospects of the company did not get brighter as our examination proceeded. In the course of our investigation we came upon some facts which appeared to us so peculiar and likely to lead to such consequences in the way of charges against the directors' management, that we felt we would not be justified in putting these into print without intimating to them their nature and character, and I consequently asked the directors individually, one by one, to meet me, and narrated to them the conclusions at which we had arrived. I communicated with Mr Stronach on the same subject. The report was published on the evening of Friday the 18th, and I think it would be about the Tuesday or Wednesday preceding that these communications were made. In conversation with some of the directors previously, I had strongly urged them to employ an agent of their own, not only for their own private interest, but likewise an agent who could advise them in the management of the Bank, because the disposition at first was to consult Mr Anderson and myself about a great number of questions that necessarily occurred immediately after the stoppage, and we found that we had really no time to give to these. I communicated with each director separately in the beginning of the week which ended on 19th October. There was no joint communication made to more than one of the directors at that time. In the case of Mr Stronach, I said to him that I was going to put various questions to him in regard to subjects which would come up in this report, and we thought it our duty to put those before him as we had put them before the other directors, but that it was for him to consider whether, as I knew he was then in the hands of a private agent, it would not be right that, before entering on this matter, he should consult his agent. He said he would do so, and would see me next day. I saw him next day, and he then said that he had been advised that perhaps under the circumstances the less he said the better. I said that still I would not feel myself quite clear to publish this report until I had gone over the various items of it with him, not asking him to make any remark unless he chose, and I did go over the items with him. He made no remark, but remained silent; but I am bound in justice to Mr Stronach to say that he was thoroughly and entirely broken down during this period. I was not in the least surprised at the state in which he appeared to be; he had been confined to bed for several days. When I had those meetings with the directors singly I did not meet Mr Inglis, as he was in Edinburgh at the time; but after meeting the other directors singly, I had a meeting with the whole of them collectively, including Mr Inglis. I think that was on the morning of the day of the publication of the report—Friday the 18th. The board was assembled, and the object of my going up was this: We saw that we would be in a position to issue our report late that evening. We were satisfied that it was very desirable the report should be in the hands of the shareholders a day or two before the meeting, which had been summoned a week previously for Tuesday the 22d, and my object in going up to that meeting was to ask their permission to publish the report the moment it was ready. We had received our commission to prepare the balance-sheet for them, and we felt technically that we must get their permission before we could make it public. They gave their consent. While I was there, one or other of them—I cannot remember which it was—said that I had been going over various items with them singly, and it would be better that I should go over them with the whole board collectively. I happened to have the rough draft of the printed report in my hand. I had not been in communication with Mr Inglis previously upon this subject. Taking the rough draft, I went over item by item the notes on that draft which appeared to me to affect the directors personally. I did so without, so far as I remember, any remark being made; and the moment I had done it I was very glad to take the opportunity of leaving the room, from the unpleasant nature of the affair. No one spoke, unless there may have been an exclamation or two of astonishment. They all appeared to be very much surprised and astonished at the various items to which I referred, but there was no distinct or definite remark with which I can charge my memory. Mr Stronach was present. He was in the same state in which he had previously been.

By the Lord Justice-Clerk—This meeting took place in a small room in the Bank's premises.

Examination continued.—At this time we had not checked or finally ascertained the precise amount of the deficit, according to our calculation; the figures were not added up. Before I left the room I undertook to inform the directors of the amount the moment we had ascertained it. We did ascertain it about half-past three the same afternoon (Friday), and I went up to the board-room with a slip of paper, on which were the words, as nearly as possible—" Deficit, " upwards of five millions"—which I handed to Mr Naismith, who was acting as agent for the directors. (Q.) And that, I need hardly ask you, was, in point of fact, the actual deficit, so far as you could ascertain it? [Question objected to by Mr Asher. Objection repelled.] (A.) Yes. That result was never challenged by any of the directors as being an incorrect representation of the state of matters. I knew the abstract that had been published by the directors on 5th July 1878; we published that abstract as part of our report. It showed that the Bank had assets exceeding liabilities to the amount of a million and a half in round numbers. Our report brought out a balance of loss of £5,190,000, so that the difference between the two results—the one brought out in their report to the shareholders on 5th July, and the other in our report on 18th October in the same year—was something over six and a half millions. No. 576 is a copy of our report. [See Appendix, No. I.] Nos. 98, 99, 100, and 101 are minute-books of the Bank. We, as investigators, took possession of all the books of the Bank. These books we got from the secretary's department. The cashier's ledger, No. 95, and the circulation returns, No. 96, I got from Mr Turnbull. The book titled "Special Securities," No. 120, I got from Mr William Morris, who, I understand, was the confidential clerk of Mr Alexander, and afterwards of Mr Robert Stronach. All the other books were got from Mr Morison. We retained these books in our possession until we gave them over to the Crown. For convenience sake we continued to enter the operations of the Bank in these books. We found it would have put a practical stop to the liquidation if they had started a new set of books at once; but I arranged with Mr Brown a stamp which should be put at the end of every entry in a book that was in use, marking the time when the liquidators began, so that the books bear evidence of that wherever there was an entry made in continuation of the Bank's own operations. I, as law agent of the liquidators, was in possession of certain of the muniments of the Bank. The contract of copartnery of the City of Glasgow Bank, No. 299, was given over by me to the Crown; and also the supplementary contract, of dates from 22d May 1843 to 20th June 1844, No. 301, and the supplementary contract, of dates from 26th June 1844 to 28th September 1849, No. 302. No. 300 is a print which was prepared containing these three documents in full.

Cross-examined by Mr Trayner—Mr Anderson and I took sixteen days to make up the report which we issued on 18th October. During these sixteen days we were very busy the whole day, and more than the day, with the Bank's affairs. We got access to any and all of the books of the Bank that we desired, and we obtained every facility which the Bank clerks or the Bank officials could afford. (Q.) I suppose I may take it that you got up that report, with its results, just as quickly as two experienced business men could manage to do it? (A.) I think we did. We had other accountants' assistance besides the personal labour of Mr Anderson. All the partners of Mr Anderson's firm were employed, I may almost say continuously, and two at least of my own partners; and we had a staff of our own. We had a large number both of Mr Anderson's clerks and of mine employed during the whole time. I saw Mr Stewart several times between 2d October and the publication of our report. On 2d October, I met him and all the other directors, as I have already mentioned. He did not say anything on that occasion indicative of his acquaintance with the Bank's books or the entries therein. (Q.) Then the information which the directors gave you then, that there was a crisis at hand, was information, I suppose, just as general in their minds as the expression you have mentioned to us now? (A.) Very much so. (Q.) And no details were gone into to show you that Mr Stewart or anybody else knew what was the exact nature of the crisis that was expected? (A.) None. (Q.) That disposes of the 2d of October; what was the next occasion on which you saw Mr Stewart? (A.) I must have seen Mr Stewart at the first meeting or two of the Bank directors, but no particulars with regard to these meetings dwelt upon my mind. The first time that I remember Mr Stewart saying anything to me individually upon the subject was when I met him one day at the door of the Bank. That was before our report had been completed, and before I had spoken to the directors privately. (Q.) What took place between you? (A.) It was a mere shaking of hands; and he hurrying past in a state of great excitement, and saying that he was a broken-hearted man, and perfectly astounded at the state in which the Bank's affairs were found to have been. (Q.) Then, after that, you, I suppose, met him when you went over the draft report with him, as you did with each of the directors? (A.) I sent for him to come down to my room, and he came down alone, and I went over the various points with him. He stated then that he was entirely and totally ignorant of every fact that I brought before him. I believed him. I have known Mr Stewart for some time in business. He was a director of the old New Zealand and Australian Company, and I was a director of the Canterbury and Otago Company. About two years ago negotiations took place for the amalgamation of these two companies, and then and from that time, at the board of the united company, I have met Mr Stewart frequently. I must say that I always looked upon him as an essentially honourable man in every respect, and not a man who, so far as I could judge, would be likely to fabricate or falsify accounts. I knew him to be a man reputed to be of large means, and one who held a position of esteem in Glasgow. (Q.) What opinion have you formed with regard to Mr Stewart's character as an accountant? (A.) I can only give, in the most general terms, my own impression, and that is that I should think he had a peculiarly bad head for figures. [Shown Abstract of Accounts for 1878, No. 126.] (Q.) From what you know of his head for figures, do you think that is a document which Mr Stewart could readily comprehend? (A.) I think it is a document which he would require to give extreme and exceptional attention to before he could comprehend it. (Q.) Do you think if he had that document before him, and all the Bank's books at his hand, he could have checked it with any ordinary amount of care or labour? (A.) What I mean to say is this, that Mr Stewart is not a man that I would have employed to do it if I had any choice. I afterwards saw Mr Stewart at the meeting of directors, when our report was all but completed. (Q.) Did Mr Stewart on that occasion say anything to indicate to you what he knew or what he did not know of the Bank's affairs? (A.) No; he did not. (Q.) Was astonishment expressed by him at the results which you had reached? (A.) Astonishment had been expressed by him very strongly before, when I met him alone; and the same impression was left upon my mind that that astonishment was continued. (Q.) What was Mr Stewart's appearance when you told him at that private meeting the results of your investigation? (A.) I should say something like horror. (Q.) Did you at all suppose him to be feigning an ignorance which was not the fact? (A.) No; I did not. (Q.) In short, from what he stated, and from his manner, you believed his statement that your revelations were perfectly new to him? (A.) I did.

GEORGE AULDJO JAMIESON.

By the Lord Advocate—I am a chartered accountant in Edinburgh. I am now one of the liquidators of the City of Glasgow Bank. On the 30th of September 1878 I was sent for by the cashier of the Royal Bank, and was told that my services were required by himself and the other banks to investigate as well as I could, in a short time, the affairs of the City of Glasgow Bank, which had applied to the other Scotch banks for assistance. I was informed that the state of affairs, so far as disclosed, had occasioned considerable alarm to the other banks. I met the managers of the Scotch banks that evening, and next morning (Tuesday, 1st October,) I went to Glasgow. Mr Fleming, the cashier of the Royal Bank, had handed to me certain papers which had been left with him by the representatives of the

City Bank. On arriving at Glasgow I went to the office of Messrs Stewart, Pott, & Co., and afterwards to the City of Glasgow Bank. I went alone to the Bank. I met there the manager of the Bank, Mr Stronach, and Mr Potter, a director. I also saw the accountant of the bank, Mr Morison, and the secretary, Mr Leresche. Mr Potter was very strong in giving directions to the officials of the Bank that every possible information and explanation should be afforded to me; and these directions were thoroughly carried out by the officials. Mr Potter and Mr Stronach were together; but Mr Potter was spokesman. I asked for the balance-sheet of the year to 5th June 1878. [Shown No. 124.] I forget at this moment whether there were red ink figures on the balance-sheet shown to me; my impression is they were all in black; but this balance-sheet was certainly shown to me. If there be a balance-sheet showing these results in black figures, it was that which was shown to me. [Shown No. 125.] That is the one I saw. I asked explanations at the officials, especially as to gold. From the materials put into my hands by Mr Fleming, I had an index by which to examine the matters in the balance-sheet, and making use of that, I put the necessary questions to the officials. I also examined some of the accounts in the books. Some were large accounts. I went into the discount ledger and some of the other ledgers with the view of taking out and making notes on the largest and most important accounts I there found. In the course of the afternoon Mr Stewart and Mr Innes Wright, two of the directors, came to see me, and to see what was going on. Mr Potter had been there during a considerable part of the day, and was there when they arrived. They were anxious to know the result of my investigation, so far as it had gone. I did not communicate the result definitely to them, because I had not completed it. They asked me to communicate what would be the probable tenor of the report I should make to the banks in Edinburgh that afternoon, and I told them that I could hold out no expectation that I could recommend the banks to afford any assistance, because I had satisfied myself that the amount of probable loss greatly exceeded anything that the banks would venture to face. That conclusion was based on the rapid view which I had been enabled to take, by the information so readily supplied to me, of the position of the Bank with reference to important accounts, and to the disclosure of the affairs of the Bank contained in the balance-sheets. (Q.) In speaking of important accounts, do you mean advances, and to whom? [Objected to. Objection repelled.] (A.) I mean entries in the balance-sheet itself, and advances made to specific customers of the Bank, as laid before me at that time by the officials and in the documents then submitted to me. These specific customers of the Bank were James Morton & Co., Smith, Fleming, and Co., J. Nicol Fleming, and John Innes Wright & Co. As I made them up at that hurried time, the advances shown to these four firms amounted to £5,870,000. (Q.) Was it in respect of these advances that you formed your estimate that the Bank would not be able to go on? (A.) That, combined with some of the other elements in the balance-sheet of the Bank. I intimated my opinion to Mr Wright, Mr Stewart, and Mr Potter. I stated to them the advances as being about five millions. They appeared to be surprised at the amount, and I recollect Mr Potter turned to the manager and said, "Is it "possible"—I forget whether he said "we" or "you"—"have given so much "to those firms?" One of the firms was Mr Wright's own. He did not make any observation about the amount—not that I can recollect. Mr Stronach, in answer to Mr Potter, said he feared it was too true. I don't think Mr Stewart said anything. He appeared to be very much distressed and disturbed by the state of matters, but I cannot recollect that he said anything.

By the Lord Justice-Clerk—(Q.) Distressed by your information? (A.) By my information.

By the Lord Advocate—(Q.) Do you mean that he betrayed that state of mind upon receiving your information; or do you mean that he was in that state before he received it? (A.) I should say partly both. I took it for granted that, having asked me to give an indication of the report which I was to make to the banks,—on which so much depended,—he was distressed at finding that I was not prepared to report favourably. I returned to Edinburgh and laid my statement before the managers of the banks, who afterwards resolved to give no assistance. I was appointed a liquidator. We have made no final estimate of the assets and liabilities. The officials of the Bank and the books have been taken up so much in connection with the investigations for this trial, that it has been impossible, as yet, to complete such estimate.

WILLIAM MORISON.

By the Lord Advocate—I was accountant of the City of Glasgow Bank from 1871 to its stoppage. I had previously been a clerk in the same department. I succeeded Mr R. S. Stronach (afterwards manager) as accountant. I had charge of all the clerks in the accountant's department, and of the ledgers and other books in which the transactions of the Bank were entered. I had charge of the private cash-book, the general ledger, the weekly balance book, the balance ledger, and the contingent account ledger. The cash balance book was not kept by me, but I made certain entries in it, showing the amount in my general ledger. I kept a number of subsidiary books; amongst others a book titled "Credit Accounts, Nos. 3 and 4." [No. 31 of Inventory.] That book contains entries of cash advances to Smith, Fleming, and Co., and James Nicol Fleming. There is also an account in that book under the head "New Zealand and Australian Land Co. Stock." (Q.) When did you begin to keep that book? (A.) In June 1875. The annual balance of the Bank was struck on the first Wednesday of June, in terms of the contract. The contract was followed so long as I was an officer of the Bank. The general meeting of the shareholders took place on the first Wednesday of July each year. The preparation of the balance and report of the affairs of the company for the preceding year had to be completed between these two dates. It was my duty as accountant to take part in the preparation of the annual balance. I had to bring down balances from the general ledger, and the branches general ledger, and the correspondence general ledger, into the balance ledger. This was finished about ten days after the annual balance. When prepared, I submitted it to the manager. [Shown No. 130.] That is a scroll abstract of the accounts at the head office for the year ending 7th June 1876. It was prepared in the head office. No. 133 is an abstract of the accounts at the branches for the same period. It was prepared under the superintendence of Mr Miller, superintendent of branches department. These two abstracts showed the whole operations of the Bank of that class requiring to be brought into the balance-sheet for the year; and the full balance-sheet required to be made up from these. [Shown No. 128.] That is titled on the back "Scroll Abstract "of Accounts." [See Appendix, No. II.] It was prepared in the office. The black ink figures on it bring together the two abstracts I have just spoken to. They bring together the whole operations of the Bank and their results, at the head office and branches. As originally prepared by me, the figures in red ink were not on No. 128; but No. 128 was not the first scroll. There may have been more than one scroll before it. It was the final scroll. The black and red ink figures were put on No. 128 at the same time. (Q.) You start with an abstract for the head office, and an abstract for the branches; when you bring these two together you have a new scroll? (A.) Yes. (Q.) When you had simply brought the two together on the face of the sheet, what did you do with that? (A.) Submitted it to the manager. (Q.) When you submitted it to the manager what was done? (A.) There was an arrangement made that Mr Potter, one of the directors, should meet the manager and go over the separate items. (Q.) You are speaking of the balance-sheet of 1876? (A.) Yes.

By the Lord Justice-Clerk—(Q.) You arranged that with the manager? (A.) Yes. (Q.) Did Mr Potter meet the manager? (A.) Yes. (Q.) And yourself? (A.) Yes.

By the Lord Advocate—(Q.) What happened at the meeting? (A.) No. 128 was the result. (Q.) Were the red ink marks put on at that meeting, or had they been put on before? (A.) This [No. 128] is the effect of what was done at the meeting, but I cannot say that it is the scroll that it was done on. (Q.) Were the red ink marks on before the meeting? (A.) Not before the meeting. (Q.) The red ink marks represent the result of what was settled at that meeting? (A.) Yes. (Q.) Added to what you had prepared? (A.) Yes. (Q.) And the black ink marks show what you had prepared? (A.) Yes. (Q.) And the red shows what was agreed on at the meeting? (A.) Partly so.

By the Lord Justice-Clerk—The red ink marks are in my writing.

By the Lord Advocate—(Q.) Is the whole of it in your writing? (A.) Yes, the whole of it. (Q.) Were the alterations made on it in red ink made out of your own head, or upon instructions? (A.) By instructions. (Q.) Whose instructions? (A.) Mr Potter's and the manager's. (Q.) Did these two gentlemen go over that sheet for 1876 item by item? (A.) Yes. (Q.) Is that document, as it stands, giving effect to the alterations which you were instructed to make, in accordance with the books of the Bank that were under your charge? (A.) No. (Q.) Was the abstract which you formerly spoke of (No. 130) in conformity with the books of the Bank? (A.) Yes. (Q.) But the result of the instructions you got from Mr Potter and Mr Stronach was to make the balance-sheet which you framed, with red figures on it, disconform to the books of the Bank? (A.) Yes. (Q.) What did you do with the altered abstract after it was adjusted with Mr Potter and the manager? (A.) It formed the annual report. The annual report was made out from it. (Q.) Did you prepare the abstract and send it to the printer? (A.) I prepared the annual report and sent it to the printer. A proof of the report was sent to the directors. (Q.) Was it the practice that when a final proof of the balance-sheet was adjusted, it was laid before a meeting of the directors? (A.) I don't know as to that. (Q.) Did you not attend the meeting? (A.) No. (Q.) Did you not attend for the purpose of having the balance ledger adjusted and docketed? (A.) Yes. (Q.) When was that done, and for what purpose? (A.) For the purpose of going over the books,—to compare them, and see that they were the same as the balance ledger. This took place probably on the Wednesday or Thursday before the annual meeting day: (Q.) Was there any document intermediate between the abstract No. 128 and the abstract published to the shareholders in 1876? (A.) No. (Q.) How long were Mr Potter and Mr Stronach and you engaged in revising that balance-sheet, resulting in the red figures being put on? (A.) Perhaps an hour or two. On the left-hand side of No. 128 [see Appendix, No. 128A] there are entries S. F. and Co. (Smith, Fleming, & Co.), £200,875; J. N. F. (James Nicol Fleming), £100,300; and J. M. & Co. (James Morton & Co.), £450,600. These were credit accounts, entered in that part of the abstract which contains advances on credit. (Q.) But you bring them down and insert them among what? (A.) Government stocks, railway stocks and debentures, and other securities. (Q.) In the abstract for 1876 [see Indictment, p. 28], there is an entry under assets, "Government stocks, Exchequer bills, railway and other "stocks and debentures, and balances in hands of banking correspondents, "£2,218,868, 13s. 7d.;" so that the effect of that change was to represent that a debt due on credit account by these firms to the amount of £751,775 was either a Government stock or a security on a balance in the hands of correspondents of the Bank? (A.) Yes. (Q.) By whose instigation were these sums brought down? (A.) Mr Potter. (Q.) Was it by his directions it was done? (A.) Yes. (Q.) Did he assign any reason or justification for it? (A.) That the Bank held certain stocks against the debt of £751,775.

By the Lord Justice-Clerk—(Q.) And therefore treating them as good assets? (A.) Yes.

By the Lord Advocate—(Q.) Did Mr Potter seem to understand the different items that they were considering? (A.) Apparently so. (Q.) Did he appear to be quite conversant with them? (A.) Quite conversant. (Q.) Did the books of the Bank correctly show the operations of the Bank? (A.) Yes. (Q.) Were they in conformity with the actual fact? (A.) Yes. (Q.) How were the debts to the extent of £751,775 represented or stated in the abstract prepared by you, No. 130? (A.) As credit accounts. (Q.) Which they were? (A.) Which they were,—in the books. In No. 130 there is an entry on the right-hand side, "Deposit accounts, £455,444, 5s. 10d." shown as due by the Bank, and on the other side there is an entry of "Deposit accounts, "£1346, 16s. 6d." due to the Bank. These are correctly stated in No. 130. They are not correctly stated in the revised abstract. The £1346, 16s. 6d. only is put in it. The effect of this was to reduce the liabilities by the difference between £455,444, 5s. 10d. and the debtor balance of £1346, 16s. 6d. In No. 128, on the debtor side, under the head Foreign and colonial credits, there is an entry of £2,278,173, 17s. 1d. That is the actual amount, but £973,300 is deducted from that, leaving only £1,304,873, 17s. 1d.

By the Lord Justice-Clerk—It is reduced by nearly a million.

By the Lord Advocate—Shown No. 39A [excerpt from progressive ledger, foreign and colonial], and asked—Why was the sum of £973,300 deducted from the foreign and colonial credits? Depones—Because there was a credit account to that extent. (Q.) Did you get instructions from anybody to deduct it? (A.) No; it was in the ledger. (Q.) Why did you put it in the ledger? (A.) In June 1873, there was an entry made by the instructions of the late manager, Mr Alexander Stronach, which appears in the book titled "City of "Glasgow Bank cash book, private, No. 6," extracts from which are contained in No. 2A. I made that entry. It is in the following terms: "Foreign and "colonial credits, No. 2. The following credits to be retired as they mature, "and debited under the respective accounts to 'Credit accounts, No. 2,' "against which securities are now held by the Bank, and in process of real-"isation and payment of the proceeds, £973,300." That deduction from foreign and colonial credits was carried on in the books and in the balance-sheets from year to year thereafter down to 1878 inclusive, without any change being made. There was a note written by the late manager giving the particulars of that deduction, but I never got the particulars.

By the Lord Justice-Clerk—(Q.) Was it a right deduction? (A.) I would not like to say so. I would not like to give an opinion upon that.

By the Lord Advocate—The entry "Foreign and colonial credits" represents the liability side of the acceptances sent out by the Bank,—what the customer was due in respect of acceptances granted to him by the Bank. (Q.) So that, taking off £973,300 from that amount simply represented, amongst other things, that there were £973,300 less of the Bank's acceptances afloat or in the circle than was really the case? (A.) Yes.

By the Lord Justice-Clerk—(Q.) The foreign and colonial credits represented a sum of more than two millions? (A.) Yes. (Q.) Then in 1873 Mr Alexander Stronach directed that this £973,300 should be deducted in the books from these debits to the foreign and colonial customers? (A.) Yes. (Q.) That represented, I presume, on the books so much security held by the Bank against the two millions, and was therefore deducted? (A.) Yes. (Q.) Can you go further and say what the £973,300 was composed of. (A.) No. (Q.) You just took it from the notandum of Mr Alexander Stronach? (A.) Yes.

By the Lord Advocate—Being shown the book No. 2, from which the excerpts No. 2A were taken, depones,—There are two entries, one on each side of this book. There is on the one side the entry I have already read; on the other, there is the following entry: "Bills payable No. 2. The following amounts "under acceptance at this date, to be retired by the Bank under special "arrangements with the parties, of date 1st June 1873, against which certain "securities are now held by the Bank, and in process of realization and pay-"ment of proceeds, £973,300." The date of that is 4th June 1873; and the entry has been kept up for every successive year since that date. I am not aware whether there has been any realization of securities held by the Bank against the bills; but if so, it has not been taken off this entry. The entry has never been taken out of the books by any other entry applicable to this or any part of it. (Q.) Therefore the floating acceptances of the Bank, whether covered or not, have been yearly understated to the amount of £973,300? (A.) Yes.

By the Lord Justice-Clerk—(Q.) Unless there are securities for that amount? (A.) I don't know about that. I cannot say that there are such securities, or that there are not.

By the Lord Advocate—I had no charge of the securities. (Q.) Did you feel comfortable in making that entry in the books? (A.) No. (Q.) Why not. (A.) Because I had not the particulars of the entry in my cash-book. I had no means of knowing whether it was a correct entry or not. (Q.) Had you any written authority or evidence of who had authorised you to make it? (A.) I got a note or slip from the late manager to make the entry. (Q.) Did you speak to him about it frequently? (A.) At the annual balance I would speak of it. (Q.) Did you ever speak about that entry in going over abstract D with Mr Potter and Mr Robert Stronach in 1876? (A.) They would see it, and I have no doubt I would speak of it. I recollect speaking of it to Mr Robert Stronach; I have no recollection of speaking of it to Mr Potter. I recommended to Mr Stronach that it should be taken out.

By the Lord Justice-Clerk—(Q.) Why? (A.) Because there were no particulars in my cash book of the entry. I had no particulars of it. (Q.) Was it not because you did not believe there were these securities? (A.) No; that was not the reason.

By the Lord Advocate—(Q.) It was an unvouched entry so far as you were concerned? (A.) I had a voucher for it, or rather I was aware that the late manager had a statement of it. I have seen it. It was a memorandum, not of securities, but of the entry. (Q.) But did you ever see securities or anything of that sort that would have warranted you at your own hand in making such an entry? (A.) No. When I spoke to Mr Robert Stronach about having the entry taken out, I think he said it was there before he was appointed, and it would be better to leave it in the meantime. That took place in 1876. (Q.) Was that the occasion when Mr Potter was present? (A.) I could not say that. (Q.) On the creditor side of the abstract No. 130 [Scroll abstract of accounts at head office on 7th June 1876], at what sum are the liabilities of the Bank under credit accounts stated? (A.) At £147,468, 16s. 11d. That sum is altogether omitted from the scroll abstract No. 128, the result being to understate the liabilities to that extent. I cannot tell why it was left out. I left it out of the statement in consequence of instructions given to me by Mr Potter and the manager. I have no recollection whether they gave any reason for leaving it out. (Q.) On the creditor side of the abstract No. 130, what amount is there taken from the books and represented as due by the Bank to London, provincial, and foreign correspondents? (A.) £378,481, 8s. 5d. (Q.) Is that sum correctly transferred to the abstract No. 128? (A.) No. The amount there is £364,264, 13s. 3d., being a difference of £14,216, 15s. 2d. (Q.) How is that managed? (A.) The lesser amount is simply the balance betwixt the different amounts. (Q.) Was that in point of fact an under-statement of indebtedness to that amount? (A.) Not of indebtedness. (Q.) What then? (A.) Well, if you look at it in that light, it was.

By the Lord Justice-Clerk—(Q.) Does that mean a balance due to the London and provincial correspondents, or a balance due by them? (A.) The larger amount is the balance due by them. The original sum was the correct one; and therefore the last sum is wrong to the extent of £14,216.

By the Lord Advocate—(Q.) At the time you were adjusting the balance for 1875, had you anything to do with ascertaining the amount of bad debts? (A.) I was sent for by the manager; Mr Potter was there; and I was asked to make up a statement of the bad debts. I told him it was not for me to make up a state of the bad debts, but that I would make up a statement of accounts that were not bearing interest, that is, on which no interest was charged. That suggestion was adopted, and I made up such a statement. (Q.) Had you any interview with the directors about that, or any of them? (A.) I saw Mr Potter repeatedly about it. I went to his office and saw him there. (Q.) What was done as the result of that? (A.) My figures to the extent of £250,000 were adopted. (Q.) How much did you make it? (A.) It was either £300,000 or £350,000, but I think it was £300,000. (Q.) And how did you deal with them in the abstract? (A.) They are entered as assets. (Q.) How much was entered as assets? (A.) There was a balance of an old bad and doubtful debts account, and that was amalgamated with the £250,000, making up altogether £300,000, which was entered in my abstract under the heading of "Suspense account." (Q.) How much of that £300,000 was stated in the abstract from which the report was made up as bad and doubtful? (A.) You will find under the heading of bad and doubtful debts £50,000. The difference of £250,000 you will find entered amongst the other accounts in the abstract as good assets. That £250,000 consisted entirely of debts on which no interest had been paid: I could not say exactly off-hand for how long, but perhaps for five or six years. (Q.) Did you make it known to Mr Potter and Mr Stronach that these accounts had not borne interest for that time? (A.) Yes; they were quite aware of it. The three sums of £200,875, £100,300, and £450,600 already referred to as having been taken down from head 1 to head 3, were not taken out of the public books of the Bank in 1876. [Shown excerpts from cash book No. 2A.] (Q.) Did Mr Robert Stronach in 1875 give you directions with regard to certain accounts in that ledger? I refer to a sum of £683,263 credited to certain accounts of Smith, Fleming, & Co.? (A.) Yes; that was at 2d June, 1875. (Q.) What were you directed to do with regard to them? (A.) The accounts of Smith, Fleming, & Co. in credit accounts were transferred to credit accounts No. 3, to the extent of £761,265, 19s. 9d. The effect of that was to take them out of credit accounts, where they were seen by the clerks in the cheque box, and put them into credit accounts in No. 3 ledger, which was kept by me, and was accessible only to the manager and directors. (Q.) Why was that transfer made? (A.) I presume to bring all the accounts together. (Q.) Did no other reason suggest itself to you at the time? (A.) It would have the effect of keeping the accounts quieter. (Q.) What do you mean by keeping the accounts quiet? (A.) It would have the effect that no person would see them except myself. (Q.) And fewer people would know of the extent of the indebtedness to the Bank of Smith, Fleming, and Co.? (A.) Yes. (Q.) That was the amount in which they were indebted at that time, upon accounts kept in books to which the clerks had access? (A.) Yes. (Q.) These accounts were closed, and the accounts transferred to a book which was patent only to you and the manager? (A.) Yes. They were taken out by means of a cross entry. These accounts have since been kept by me, and they are entered in the same way yet. The balance-sheet for 1877 was prepared on the same principle as the other, so far as making up abstracts went. [Shown No. 129, Weekly balances in general ledger,

5th June 1878.] That was prepared in the same way from two abstracts, and then it was altered as before. (Q.) By whom was it altered, or by whose directions, in 1877? (A.) I cannot recollect about 1877 very well. (Q.) But so far as you do recollect? (A.) They were gone over by the manager, but I have no recollection of meeting any other person.

By the Lord Justice-Clerk—There are a number of alterations. (Q.) Did you prepare it according to the alterations of the year before? (A.) I prepared it in the usual way—the correct way. (Q.) So the same alterations would require to be made again? (A.) Yes. (Q.) And they were made? (A.) Yes.

Re-examined—These are shown partly in red ink and partly in pencil on this sheet. (Q.) Do I understand you to say that so far as it is yours it is taken from your abstract, which is correct? (A.) Yes. (Q.) And that so far as it differs from those two abstracts which were brought forward by you, it is owing to the directions of others? (A.) Yes. (Q.) But you cannot say who the others were? (A.) With the exception of the manager. (Q.) You cannot mention any other person than the manager? (A.) I have no recollection of that year. The deposit and credit accounts were dealt with on the same principle as they had been in the year before. (Q.) Was the £973,300 odds kept up again? (A.) There is one of the sheets from which I can show that. I refer to No. 131. [Abstract of accounts at head office on 6th June 1877.] In making up the statement, the £973,300 is set aside, and certain other sums are deducted. (Q.) Instead of putting in that £973,000 as a cross entry, what did you do on both sides? (A.) There was —cash lodged in C A, £94,368, 14s. 11d.; anticipations, £527,940; S. F. and Co., £552,704, 4s. 2d.; J. N. F., £158,000; making altogether, £1,333,012, 19s. 1d. "Cash lodged on credit account" would represent renewals of bills given out and the cash paid in. "Anticipations," I understand, were bills given out in the same way,—anticipations of credit; that is to say, two sets of bills given out,—bills upon which the Bank were debtors. (Q.) And in anticipation of credit coming in? (A.) In anticipation of other bills to the same extent falling due; and in order to meet those bills when they did fall due, a second set of bills would be given out. "S. F. & Co." means Smith, Fleming, & Co. The £552,704, I presume, would be bills payable that they would get. "J. N. F., £158,000," would represent bills given out to him. (Q.) Was there anything in your books to indicate these entries, or in any books you had access to; or were they merely suggestions? (A.) There were no entries made for these alterations. They were not made from any entries or any heading in the books. (Q.) Are they purely fictitious? (A.) There are no entries for them. (Q.) Then are they not fictitious entirely? (A.) So far as I know. The £1,333,012, 19s. 1d. was deducted from the amount of the bills payable by the Bank,—the Bank's acceptances. The Bank's acceptances that year amounted to £2,683,348, 0s. 2d., so that that took off about one-half. That was what was substituted in the year 1877 for the £973,300. (Q.) The old £973,000 disappeared, and this new invention was substituted? (A.) Yes. In my own abstract there is a clerical error to the effect of understating the amount of bills payable. I again prepared balance-sheets in 1878 with a view to the annual public abstract as in previous years. [Shown No. 124. Abstract of accounts at 5th June 1878.] That is the result, after adjustment [see Appendix No. II.],—the red ink draft. My own abstract was taken correctly from the books. The abstract I prepared as the basis of No. 124 was correctly made up from my own abstract and that furnished by Mr Miller, superintendent of branches, and was in conformity with the books. Alterations were made upon that abstract of 1878. These are shown upon the document before me. They were made by directions of the manager, Mr Robert Stronach.

By the Lord Justice-Clerk—I made them.

Re-examined—There was no other person concerned in it.

By the Lord Justice-Clerk—These alterations were almost on the same lines as before.

Examined—(Q.) Only you have the £973,000 back again instead of the sum in the previous year? (A.) Yes. A clean copy of that abstract was made, by instructions of Mr Stronach, after it was red-inked. He did not say for what purpose it was wanted. After it was made, Mr Stewart, Mr Potter, and the manager, met in the manager's room, and went over it. I was present, but I did not go over it with them. I was in the room. I do not think the annual abstract issued to the shareholders had been printed at that time. (Q.) Did these three gentlemen not compare the clean document with the abstract? (A.) They compared the clean document with the abstract published in the previous year's report. [Shown No. 125.] That is the clean copy which was made.

Third Day.—Wednesday, 22d January 1879.

WILLIAM MORISON—(*recalled*).

By the Lord Advocate—In the abstract balance-sheet issued to the shareholders at 5th June 1878, the first item on the debtor side is "Deposits at the "head offices and branches, and balances at the credit of banking correspond- "ents, £8,102,001, 0s. 4d." [See p. 31.] That is not correctly stated as from the books of the company. It is understated. (Q.) To what extent, and in what particulars? (A.) Deposit accounts, £440,738, 10s. 9d. [see Abstract of accounts at 5th June 1878, Appendix II.]; credit accounts, £346,336, 6s. 9d. Both these were due by the Bank.

By the Lord Justice-Clerk—(Q.) In other words, there were deposits to the extent of £440,000 due by the Bank which were not entered in the balance-sheet? (A.) Yes. (Q.) Is that all the deficiency? (A.) No.

By the Lord Advocate—(Q.) You had entered these sums as part of the liabilities of the Bank in your abstract? (A.) Yes. (Q.) Point out on the altered scroll balance-sheet how they were got rid of? (A.) Both sums are put into a debtor column on the creditor portion of the state. (Q.) In fact, they were taken out by a cross entry? (A.) Not by an entry. (Q.) The amount of bank notes in circulation is stated in the published balance-sheet at £710,252; was that correct? (A.) There is an under-statement of £89,031. (Q.) The next item in the balance-sheet is "Drafts outstanding "due, or with a currency not exceeding twenty-one days, and drafts accepted "by the Bank and its London agents on account of home and foreign con- "stituents, £1,488,244, 18s. 6d.;" is that sum correct according to the books? (A.) No. (Q.) To what extent is it incorrect? (A.) There is the bills payable credit account of £973,300 deducted. (Q.) That is the old entry? (A.) Yes; and there is also £419,708 deducted. [Shown No. 39A.] (Q.) That is an extract from the Foreign and colonial credits progressive ledger No. 1? (A.) Yes. (Q.) What was the true amount at that date? (A.) £2,881,252, 18s. 6d. (Q.) That item in the published abstract was reduced by about one-half? (A.) Yes. (Q.) These amounts are entered in the scroll abstract, No. 124? (A.) Yes. In that abstract there is a note in red ink, "Amount of bills on the circle, and against which an equal sum is at the "credit of J. M. & Co. on D/A." That note is in my handwriting. "J. M. "and Co." are James Morton & Co. I was directed to make that entry by the manager. I understood the note to mean that two sets of bills would be out for the same amount, and that the first set of bills would be discounted, and the proceeds paid in to the credit of James Morton & Co. (Q.) That is what you call anticipation? (A.) Yes. (Q.) What was the course of dealing in the case of these anticipations? (A.) I cannot speak personally as to that; I could only speak from hearsay. On the creditor side of the published balance-sheet for 1878 the first entry is, "Bills of exchange, local and "country bills, credit accounts, and other advances upon security, £8,484,466, "9s. 2d." (Q.) Was that sum fully and correctly stated? (A.) No. (Q.) What was wrongfully deducted from it? (A.) Under the head of credit accounts there is a sum of £680,614. That is written off upon the abstract in red ink. (Q.) Then there is a sum of? (A.) £346,336, 6s. 9d. (Q.) That is written off credit accounts, creditor balances? (A.) Yes. (Q.) Then there is the cross entry? (A.) There is first £440,738, 10s. 9d. (Q.) That same sum occurred on the other side of the account, but it was written off by being entered on both? (A.) Yes. Then there is a sum of £973,300, which was also a cross entry; and then £419,708, also a cross entry. Then there is a sum of £148,888 deducted from Credit accounts No. 3. These were Smith, Fleming, & Co.'s accounts. They stood in credit account ledgers Nos. 3 and 4. The total of their indebtedness is shown in the entry opposite, in black figures, on the left hand, as £891,762; and that was reduced by deducting from it that sum of £148,888. These were sums due by them on credit account. Below the last-mentioned sum there is a sum written off (in red figures) of £297,232. That is deducted from the sum (in black figures) of £512,192, 12s. 6d., which was taken from Credit accounts No. 4. That was the balance due by James Nicol Fleming. All these sums are deducted from head 1 on the assets side of the abstract balance-sheet. Referring next to head 3 in the abstract-sheet (p. 9 of indictment), there is the item, "Cash on hand, viz., gold and silver coin and notes of other "banks at head office and branches, £845,963, 1s." [See p. 31.] (Q.) What was stated by you as at that date as the true amount in your own figures? (A.) £845,963, 1s. (Q.) Was that correct according to the information from the books of the Bank? (A.) With the exception of the same entry of £89,031, which was on the other side.

By the Lord Justice-Clerk—(Q.) Where in your own abstract, before it was altered, do you find that sum of £845,963, 1s.? (A.) Under head 3. (Q.) The sum of £596,623, 6s. 11d. is given there? (A.) Yes; that is, at the head office. Then you have to add the branches, £249,339, 14s. 1d. (Q.) And that makes the £845,963, 1s.? (A.) Yes.

By the Lord Advocate—(Q.) Then there is a deduction made from that of £89,031; is that a proper deduction? (A.) Well, I consider it so. It was company's notes received at the exchange on the following morning before the commencement of business. I did not receive that information until after I had made up my abstract. If I had received it the night before, I would have given effect to it then. (Q.) Then there is still an over-statement, according to your statement, of £200,000 as to the gold: is that the sum which is interlined in red ink in the scroll abstract? (A.) Yes. (Q.) There is a cross in red ink opposite to it, and there is also a cross opposite the sum of £480,614 a short way below? (A.) Yes. (Q.) What is the meaning of that? (A.) It is to connect these two sums, which together make up the sum of £680,614. (Q.) Have these two sums any connection with the other sum of £680,614 deducted from credit account balances No. 1? (A.) Yes. (Q.) So that the operation you performed there was to bring down £680,614 which was due upon credit accounts, and to enter £200,000 of it as gold in the coffers of the Bank? (A.) Yes. (Q.) The remaining £480,614 is represented in the abstract issued to the shareholders as Government stocks, Exchequer bills, railway and other stocks and debentures in the hands of the Bank and correspondents? (A.) Yes. (Q.) These sums of £200,000 in gold, £480,614, £148,888, and £297,262 are all included in the third item of the balance-sheet? (A.) Yes. (Q.) Was that a correct statement in the published balance-sheet? (A.) So far as regards the deductions from the credit accounts, if they held absolutely the stocks that represented these amounts, I do not see much wrong in it. (Q.) Would it not have been more correct, even if they held securities, to state the amount that was due to them upon open account, and then to state also the securities held? (A.) If they had made an entry through the books, I would have considered it quite right if they had done so.

By the Lord Justice-Clerk—(Q.) If they held sufficient security, you think there is not much wrong in the entry? (A.) No. (Q.) What about the £200,000 in gold? (A.) I cannot say anything about that; I cannot justify that. (Q.) What did it represent—anything? (A.) Yes, the balance of the £600,000. (Q.) But was there any balance; I mean, did it represent any gold and silver? (A.) Not that I know of.

By the Lord Advocate—(Q.) Just take this case—Suppose a bank to have £100,000 due to them upon open account, and that they hold securities against it, do you think it is right, instead of stating that there is a debt of £100,000 due to them, and stating the securities covering it, that they should state that they have an asset of the value of £100,000 without disclosing the debt or the security? (A.) It would be the correct way to disclose both, but it is only figures that go into the report. (Q.) I suppose that, even according to your view, if assets to that full value were not held, that was a false entry? (A.) Yes; but, as I said yesterday, I had no means of knowing personally whether such securities were held or not. (Q.) Was any assurance given to you when you got directions to make these entries that such securities were held? (A.) From the conversation I understood so. (Q.) But what I want to know is whether you were simply directed to do this, and inferred from what you were told that there were securities, or were you distinctly given to understand that such things existed? (A.) I was never told that such things existed; I was told to make the alteration. (Q.) And you fancied that it was an honest transaction, at least that it had some degree of honesty about it, and inferred that there were securities? (A.) Exactly so. The alterations which I made upon these three abstracts prepared by me in 1876, 1877, and 1878, were all very much of the same class. (Q.) Did you receive any more explanations on any one of those occasions than on another? (A.) I remember the manager stating to me that he hoped this would be the last time that he would require to do such a thing. It was in the year 1878 that he said so, and, I presume, about the time we were making up the balance-sheet. I have no recollection of anything of that sort being said to me by the manager or Mr Potter in 1876. With regard to the clean copy of the abstract of 1878, of which I spoke in my evidence yesterday, it is not so easy on that copy to trace the under-statements and over-statements as in the red ink copy before me. (Q.) Whose duty was it to convert that clean copy of the document before you into the abstract that was published to the shareholders, and who did it? (A.) I would take the figures after they were examined by the directors and would get them printed; I mean, get the report printed. I see the entries of "Reserve gold in cash chest," and "Gold and silver coin on hand in the cash "chest," in No. 125. The reserve gold in cash chest, £200,000, was part of the sum due by Smith, Fleming, & Co., from the credit ledger. (Q.) Why do you call it reserve gold? (A.) The Bank is bound to hold a certain quantity of gold against its issue. That is what is meant by reserve gold. (Q.) Does this mean that £200,000 was held against issue, and that "gold and silver on "hand" was held for other purposes? (A.) No; they are both held against the issue. (Q.) But what is the difference between having gold on hand and having reserve gold? (A.) I do not think there is anything in the phrase at all.

By the Lord Justice-Clerk—I had no such heading as "Reserve gold" in the original abstract I prepared.

By the Lord Advocate—At the foot of the left-hand page of No. 124, on the debtor side, the three sums of £480,614, £148,888, and £297,262, are entered as balances brought down from credit accounts. They are not represented as Government stocks or anything else,—simply as Credit account No. 1 balance, and so on. (Q.) By whose authority were these represented in the abstract as being Government stocks, or something of that kind? (A.) It was a simple continuation of the arrangement made in 1876. (Q.) Who made the arrangement in 1876, that although these appeared as credit balances in the scroll balance, they were to be represented as Government stocks or debentures, or something of that kind, in the abstract? (A.) Mr Potter and Mr Robert Stronach, the manager. (Q.) And in transferring them and calling them Government stocks, debentures, or something else, you were merely following out in 1877 and 1878 the instructions you had got in 1876? (A.) Yes. When the clean copy, without the red ink marks, was submitted to the manager, Mr Stewart, and Mr Potter, I was in the room to give any information wanted. (Q.) Were you asked to give information about anything? (A.) The only information I was asked for was to compare the 1877 report with the 1878 one. (Q.) Which report? (A.) I mean the annual balance-sheet. I was asked to do so, I presume, in order to compare the different sums the one year with the other. (Q.) Simply for the purpose, I suppose, of stating what was the difference in the trading of the Bank between these two years? (A.) Yes. I was not asked to explain any entry in this account, merely to compare results. The time occupied in that examination by the manager and those two directors was perhaps an hour,—not so much. (Q.) Since you became accountant of the Bank, has the Bank been in the habit of dealing in its own stock? (A.) Yes. The entry of gold in the abstract which I prepared was taken from the cashier's ledger. [Shown No. 95.] I did not take it from there: I would get the amount from the cashier. There is a slip of paper in No. 95, which states the amount of gold at 5th June 1878 as £338,500. It was the duty of the directors to count the gold in the safe for the annual balance. That entry is initialed by a director. It was usual that this should be done. I think that entry bears Mr Stewart's initials, but I am not confident. I cannot say what the initials are. (Q.) But do you know that they are initials? (A.) They are checked off.

By Mr Balfour—The only balance signed by the directors was the balance in the balance ledger. That balance in the balance ledger was brought out by taking the sum of all the separate heads of accounts appearing at the head office and branches. (Q.) All the separate accounts appearing at the head office had their balances brought into the balance ledger? (A.) Yes. (Q.) And as regards the branches, the balance due by or to the Bank upon each branch was brought in separately? (A.) As a branch, yes. (Q.) The distinction is this, is it not, that in the case of the head office you had the balances of the separate heads of account; in regard to the branches you had just the aggregate balance of the branches? (A.) Yes. (Q.) And the sum total appearing on each side of the balance ledger was just the addition of these different items? (A.) Yes. (Q.) And the balance ledger was the same in principle in each of the years? (A.) Yes. (Q.) There were a large number of separate heads of accounts kept in the head office? (A.) Yes. (Q.) You did not bring in the balances from the individual accounts, but only from the classes? (A.) From the general accounts. (Q.) Look at the balance ledger for 1878 (12A): there appear to be about sixty separate heads on the left-hand of the debtor side? (A.) About that. (Q.) Besides that, you have on the left-hand side also five branches, Dumfries, Dundee, &c., which appear to have been debtors at that time? (A.) Debtors to the head office. (Q.) On the other side you have first on the creditor side somewhere about thirty-eight heads before you come to the branches? (A.) Yes. (Q.) Then you have balances brought in from the branches: you had about 133 branches? (A.) Yes. (Q.) What was signed by the directors was just the addition of these two sides? (A.) Yes. (Q.) Take an example: the second entry on the creditor side of the balance is notes issued £7,864,500? (A.) Yes. (Q.) That was the summation taken from the book applicable to notes, of all the notes that had been issued? (A.) It was taken from the general ledger, which would correspond with that book. (Q.) You took it directly from the general ledger, and indirectly from the book where it was entered? (A.) Yes. This referred to all the notes that had been issued from the beginning of the Bank. On the debtor side there is an entry of notes burned £5,700,710. These were burned when worn out. The difference between the £7,800,000 odds and the £5,700,000 odds was the actual number of notes in existence, whether in actual use at the time or not. (Q.) That £5,000,000 swelled the total sum at the end of each side of that account? (A.) Yes, it was summed in. (Q.) Therefore, though that was a cross entry, it swelled the total on each side? (A.) Yes. The total on each side is £16,189,231. (Q.) There are upwards of two millions of notes shown to be in existence? (A.) Yes. (Q.) Some of these might be in the coffers of the Bank, either at the head office or branches? (A.) Yes. (Q.) But if you wished to show the shareholders or the public the amount of notes that were out, you would require to make a further deduction for those from the two millions? (A.) Yes. (Q.) I suppose it would have been perfectly useless and misleading to bring into the abstract balance-sheet such entries as these cross entries applicable to burned notes? (A.) Quite so. (Q.) There may be other instances of the same kind of thing in the balance ledger? (A.) There may; I don't know. (Q.) I suppose that was quite a correct kind of balance for the purposes for which it was made, of showing the actual results of balances standing in the books? (A.) Yes. (Q.) If you wished to give information to the shareholders or the public, first deducting the notes burned and no longer in use, and then the notes which were not actually out, but which were in the coffers at the head office or branches, the difference would be what ought to go into an abstract? (A.) Yes. (Q.) And accordingly the amounts which we see in any of the published abstracts are very much smaller? (A.) Yes. (Q.) Being what were the notes out? (A.) What were in the hands of the public. (Q.) Deducting those burned or in the hands of the Bank? (A.) Yes. (Q.) Still talking of the balance ledger, look on the creditor side to the heading of deposit accounts, eight or ten entries down; do you see the entry "Deposit "accounts, £33,959, 14s. 8d."? (A.) Yes. (Q.) Is that entry the balance which is brought out on the deposit account, after crossing the different entries on the two sides of that account? (A.) Quite so. (Q.) So that this balance ledger, from its frame and the scheme on which it is made up, does not profess to show the details on the two sides, but merely to bring in a balance? (A.) Simply the balance found in the ledger. (Q.) You see Credit accounts No. 1 on the left-hand side of the same sheet, £2,009,072? (A.) Yes. (Q.) Is that also a balance arrived at by crossing the two sides of Credit account No. 1? (A.) Yes; a balance found in the general ledger. (Q.) It does not profess to show, and does not show, the aggregates of the two sides, but merely the balance brought out by deducting the one from the other? (A.) Yes. (Q.) When these different balances had thus been brought into the balance ledger, they were presented to the directors? (A.) Yes. (Q.) Assembled at a meeting? (A.) Yes. (Q.) And was the manner in which they were treated, by an official of the Bank—I think yourself—going with the weekly balance book, so that they might check the one against the other? (A.) Yes. (Q.) And you had a weekly balance book, one applicable to the head office, another to the branches, and another to correspondents? (A.) Yes. (Q.) And the directors got the balance ledger placed before them, did they not, and you read off from these balance books the items which appear in it? (A.) Yes. (Q.) The director having his eye on the balance ledger, and you reading off from these balance books? (A.) Yes. (Q.) That was the way in which the balance ledger was checked? (A.) Yes. (Q.) All you read off in such cases as I gave you was of course the balance? (A.) Of course the balance. (Q.) Checking by that method, the directors did not see, and, indeed, had not the means of seeing, the details, but just the balances? (A.) Simply balances. (Q.) Take as an instance the weekly balance of the general ledger of June 1878. [Shown No. 129A.] Is that the weekly balance applicable to the head office, from which you read off the corresponding entries to the directors when they checked the balance of June 1878? (A.) Yes. (Q.) That is the way that the balance ledger was checked, by the weekly balance applicable to the last week referring to the head office being taken? (A.) Yes. (Q.) And the branches? (A.) Yes; it is the head office balances with reference to branches. (Q.) But they were separate accounts? (A.) Yes. (Q.) The head office account was one and the branches another? (A.) Yes. I see the item about half-way down the left-hand page (129A), "Foreign "and colonial credits," and the sum £2,881,252 odds. That is a debtor entry. (Q.) Against that, under the creditor column, you have the sum of £973,300? (A.) Yes. (Q.) And you bring out as the balance of those two, deducting the latter from the former, £1,907,952? (A.) Yes. (Q.) Then looking to the balance ledger, the entry under foreign and colonial credits is that balance of £1,907,952? (A.) Yes. (Q.) That was the amount you read off when the balance ledger was under the eyes of the directors? (A.) Yes. (Q.) So that when the balance ledger was under their eyes you did not read off the £2,881,000, or the thing you deducted from it? (A.) No. Only the £1,907,000.

By the Lord Justice-Clerk—I read nothing but the £1,907,000.

By Mr Balfour—The balance ledger having been checked in that way, it was signed by the directors. I did not sign it, but I had read off the different items in the way I have explained. The docquet which the directors signed was a docquet certifying that the whole is correctly stated, and they do hereby approve and confirm the same, being satisfied that the whole is in accordance with the Bank's books. (Q.) And it was in accordance with the Bank's books, although what it brought in was balances in such accounts as I have put to you, and not the aggregates of the two sides? (A.) Yes. The balance ledger was the only thing the directors signed that I am aware of, or that they examined at that time. (Q.) The abstract of accounts which was to be put before the shareholders was, I suppose, intended to show the state of the Bank's business as a going business? (A.) Yes. (Q.) That was your understanding of its object? (A.) Yes. (Q.) I suppose it was not intended to show obsolete entries, like those five millions of burned notes, or anything like that? (A.) I should think not. (Q.) Was the abstract for the shareholders prepared from the weekly states—from the states applicable to the head office, the branches, and the correspondents? (A.) Yes. (Q.) Apparently to some extent that abstract, from its purpose, was upon a different principle from the balance signed by the directors? (A.) Yes. (Q.) And necessarily so? (A.) Necessarily so. (Q.) It did not profess to be an abstract of what was in the balance ledger? (A.) It corresponded with the balance ledger. (Q.) In result? (A.) Yes, in result. (Q.) But it contained in some cases, did it not, the totals of the entries in the accounts instead of containing merely balances as they appear in the balance ledger? (A.) Yes. (Q.) In some cases it contained balances? (A.) In certain cases it did. (Q.) But where it contained, instead of balances as they were in the balance ledger, the aggregates of the two sides, it necessarily was on a different principle from the balance ledger? (A.) Yes. (Q.) And properly so for its purpose? (A.) Properly so, I think. (Q.) Which was to give information to the shareholders of the Bank as a going concern? (A.) Yes. [Shown No. 124A, Abstract of accounts at 5th June 1878, see Appendix II.] (Q.) Were all the figures that appear in black ink upon that balance written by you before you say you took it to the manager? (A.) Yes. (Q.) All of them? (A.) All of them. (Q.) Nothing that is in red ink was put on before you took it to the manager, you say? (A.) This is not the first sheet that I presented to the manager.

By the Lord Justice-Clerk—This is the balance-sheet of 1878.

By Mr Balfour—(Q.) What I want to know with regard to No. 124A is—was everything in black ink put on by you before you took it to the manager, and was everything that appears in red ink put on after, or at the meeting? (A.) This is not the sheet that I presented to the manager; it may or it may not be. I may have made up five or six before I was done with it? (Q.) Is it or is it not the sheet you laid before the manager? (A.) I could not say. (Q.) Have you no idea? (A.) No. (Q.) I must really ask you to try and recollect this; it is very vital. Is this, which I understood you in your evidence to represent as altered at a meeting with the manager,—is it or is it not the sheet you had with you before the manager? (A.) I could not say. (Q.) Do you think it was or it was not? (A.) It is very probable it was. (Q.) But only probable? (A.) There might have been four or five written out for all that I recollect. (Q.) I don't want to know how many were written out; I want to know whether that is the sheet you had before the manager, or is it not? (A.) I could not say. (Q.) Is it so long ago that you have forgotten? (A.) I don't recollect.

By the Lord Justice-Clerk—(Q.) You said before that these alterations were made by the directions of the manager; was that so? (A.) Yes.

By Mr Balfour—Then if these alterations and deletions were made at that meeting, this must have been the sheet that you had before the manager? (A.) That is the effect of the meeting. (Q.) But I want to know were they made at the meeting or not? (A.) Do you mean, did I put these red ink figures in when I was along with the manager? (Q.) I want you to tell me, if you can recollect, whether that is the paper that you had before the manager or not? (A.) I cannot bring it to my memory. Would you show me the original? [Shown No. 124.]

By the Lord Justice-Clerk—(Q.) You prepared that abstract in 1878, on the same principles as that which you prepared in 1876? (A.) Yes. (Q.) And it was again altered in red ink figures, on the same lines, as you expressed it yesterday? (A.) Yes. (Q.) Had you any meeting for the purpose of going over that abstract before it was altered? (A.) Several meetings—often. (Q.) With whom? (A.) With the manager. (Q.) Was the alteration made before the first of these meetings, or afterwards? (A.) After the meetings. (Q.) Were they all made at the same time? (A.) I should think not.

By Mr Balfour—(Q.) Then do you mean to say that, with regard to this important matter, which happened in June of last year, you cannot say whether that (No. 124) is the paper you had before the manager or not? (A.) No; I cannot say. (Q.) Have you any recollection of putting away any other paper that was before the manager in 1878? (A.) No. (Q.) I do not mean putting away in the sense of wilfully destroying; but have you any recollection of laying any other paper before him which was not preserved? (A.) No; I have no recollection of it; but I might have done it. (Q.) Do you not think, when you look at that paper, and see that a great many of the black ink entries are scored out, and red ink entries substituted, that that must have been the paper that you had before the manager? (A.) I don't see it.

By the Lord Justice-Clerk—(Q.) It must have been; you would never think of making a new copy of your black ink original abstract after the red ink alterations were made? (A.) But there might have been two or three different sheets before all these alterations were made. These (showing on paper) might have been put in after these red ink figures on the same line. (Q.) Of course they might have been put in after, but that is not the question. You made up an abstract of the company's affairs; did you make more than one for the manager before it was altered? (A.) No—one. (Q.) Then, where is that one? (A.) I have not got it. (Q.) Just consider for a moment. Have you any doubt that that of which the lithograph is a copy is your original abstract? (A.) I have no doubt that this abstract was before the manager, but whether that was the first one, or the fifth, or the sixth, I cannot tell you. But that one would be before him. (Q.) You did not make more than one, did you? (A.) I may have made half-a-dozen; I don't recollect. (Q.) But did you make more than one identical copy of your original abstract? (A.) Yes. (Q.) For what purpose? (A.) Because there might have been alterations going on. (Q.) But an unaltered copy is what you were asked about. The question is whether that is the abstract that you laid before the manager. Do you mean to say you made various copies of the same abstract? (A.) I made various copies of the abstract with the alterations. (Q.) That is not the question. The question is whether you made more than one copy of your original abstract unaltered? (A.) I cannot answer that.

By Mr Balfour—(Q.) Are you not satisfied that if there were any alterations on any previous scrolls to this, you would give effect to them in black ink when you wrote out this? (A.) No. (Q.) Then, it comes to this, you cannot say whether that (No. 124) is the document or not? (A.) No. It is one of them. (Q.) Can you tell me now, were all the figures that are in black ink upon that paper written upon it by you, before you took it to the manager? (A.) Yes. (Q.) You are quite sure of that? (A.) Perfectly. (Q.) With reference to the first particular in connection with the balance-sheet of 1878, mentioned on page 10 of the indictment [see p. 31], amounting to £941,284, 13s. 5d., is that sum made up of the following sums:—1st, the sum of £440,738, 10s. 9d., entered in red ink in the debtor column on the right-hand page of the abstract [see abstract for 1876, Appendix II.]; 2d, the sum of £346,336, 6s. 9d., entered in red ink immediately below that; these two sums added together amounting to £787,074, 17s. 6d.; 3d, the sum of £154,090, 3s. 11d., entered in red ink opposite "Cross accounts" in the middle of the page; and a further sum of £119, 12s. which does not appear there? (A.) Yes. (Q.) What does the sum of £440,738 consist of? (A.) Deposit accounts, debtor balances. (Q.) What is the £346,336? (A.) Credit accounts, creditor balances. (Q.) I suppose the debtor balances on deposit accounts are overdrafts,—that is, sums due to the Bank by depositors on current account who have overdrawn? (A.) Yes. (Q.) Accordingly the £787,074 is the addition of overdrawn accounts of these two classes,—the deposit accounts and the creditor balances? (A.) Yes. The £787,074 is the sum of these two which I have explained. (Q.) Let there be no mistake. What is the £440,000? (A.) That is in the debtor column; these are deposit accounts —debtor balances. Debtor balances are overdrafts on current accounts. (Q.) What is the £154,000? (A.) Cross accounts at Edinburgh branches, £148,939, 18s. 11d. In the business of the Bank we have instances of the same customer having different accounts with the Bank. For example, coalmasters, who have businesses in different places, or companies, have sometimes different accounts in the head office. Where that is the case, the Bank is in the way of crossing these respective accounts and bringing forward only the balance. That is when the same man is both debtor and creditor. It would be idle to bring down the particulars of a man's account in two separate columns, and so we bring down his balance in a slump. (Q.) Does that £787,000 contain a large number of cross entries of that kind? (A.) Yes, I would say so. In 1878, I would say, about £300,000 of that sum consisted of proper cross accounts in the head office alone. (Q.) Then was it perfectly proper, in dealing with that item of the account, to cross at all events the accounts where the same person was debtor and creditor? (A.) Yes. (Q.) And it would be absurd to do anything else? (A.) I would say so. (Q.) You have crossed the whole of them here? (A.) Yes. (Q.) Why did you cross the whole, and not limit that to about £300.000. which you think was at the head office, instead of the £440,000? (A.) The crossing here has the effect of simply leaving the balance in the general ledger where it was, and takes the balance of a deposit ledger. (Q.) There is nothing wrong in that, is there? (A.) So far as regards assets and liabilities, I should say it was. (Q.) As regards the £300,000, if the man owes money on one account to you, and you owe him money on the other, is the natural and proper thing to cross it? (A.) So far as the cross accounts are concerned. (Q.) And there is about £300,000 in the head office alone? (A.) Yes. (Q.) In so far as that consists of cross accounts, it is all right? (A.) I should say so. (Q.) You cannot see anything to be said against it? (A.) Nothing. As regards the £154,000, that is out of my personal knowledge, with the exception of £5000 at the Glasgow West End branch, which I happen to know about. (Q.) But the £148,939 was given to you as proper cross accounts by the Edinburgh officials? (A.) By Mr Miller, superintendent of branches. He gave me that as proper cross accounts. I know that the West End branch had cross accounts to the amount of £5150. (Q.) Then was it perfectly right that those cross accounts to the amount of £154,090 should be crossed as they are here? (A.) That is my opinion. (Q.) And if you add that to the sum of about £300,000 of crosses at the head office, that would give you about £454,000 odds of properly crossed accounts? (A.) Yes. (Q.) And so far as you can see, there is no objection to the balance-sheet, so far as that is concerned? (A.) Not as regards the cross accounts.

By the Lord Justice-Clerk—(Q.) Do you mean that to that extent the red ink alterations are a proper rectification of your original account? (A.) Yes.

By Mr Balfour—With regard to the second particular on p. 10 [see p. 31] of the indictment, that "the amount of bank notes in circulation under article 2 "on the debtor side. was understated to the extent of £89,031 or thereby," and looking again to the abstract balance, that sum of £89,000 odds is made up of two sums, one of £41,085, and the other of £47,946, which appear on the left-hand side of the abstract in pencil, and on the right-hand side in red ink. (Q.) This balance-sheet professes to show the balance of gold and silver coin, notes of other banks on hand, and also your own circulation? (A.) Yes. In the course of banking we come to be possessed of the notes of other banks, and at regular intervals we exchange these for our own notes. (Q.) Was that done, at the time this balance was prepared, between business closing on Wednesday 5th June, and business beginning on Thursday 6th June? (A.) It would be. (Q.) About nine o'clock on the morning of the 6th? (A.) Yes. (Q.) Then is it the fact that before business hours on the 6th, though after business hours on the 5th, you got back at the head office in exchange from other banks £41,085 of your own notes? (A.) Yes. (Q.) And you got back at the branches £47,946? (A.) Yes. (Q.) So that the £89,031 complained of by the Crown in item 2 of the indictment was notes of your own, which were back into the Bank in the way I have stated between the afternoon of the 5th and the beginning of business on the 6th? (A.) Yes. (Q.) Although this abstract relates to the 5th of June, was it written up in the course of a week or so after 5th June? (A.) After 5th June. (Q.) You could not write it up on that day, because you had not all the particulars in? (A.) Quite so. (Q.) So before any part of the abstract was written the notes would be all back? (A.) They would be all back. (Q.) They would be back by nine o'clock on the morning of the 6th, although you did not actually write up even the original edition of this till after that? (A.) Quite so. (Q.) Now, as these notes were back into the Bank before business began for the new year, was it not quite right to make this deduction? (A.) I think so. (Q.) Because, before business began after the new year, they were not in circulation, but were back into the Bank? (A.) Quite so. (Q.) Why was that entry not made at the beginning when you wrote it out? (A.) The reason why a number of these alterations were made in red ink was simply to show that the alterations were not made in the books. (Q.) Was it merely to keep yourself in recollection? (A.) Quite so. (Q.) Then was it not the case that from the first time you did make up this abstract you did enter these notes? (A.) Yes. (Q.) In pencil first? (A.) I presume so—I cannot say. Being referred to the left-hand side of the abstract, opposite the word "Branches," I see figures there in pencil to the same amount. These are just the same figures. (Q.) I suppose you would write in pencil before you wrote in ink? (A.) Very likely. The next item in red ink, still on the left-hand side, is £41,000 odds deducted from £75,000 odds. (Q.) That is the notes at the head office; and you see again £47,000 deducted from £77,000? (A.) Yes. (Q.) And it is the differences which make the £89,000? (A.) Yes. These figures appear again on the right-hand side of the same page. (Q.) Were these entries about the notes not made by yourself from the very beginning? (A.) Yes. (Q.) Before you went to the manager at all? (A.) Yes. (Q.) And they were quite right entries? (A.) I consider them so. (Q.) And you merely made them in red ink as a notandum, and to keep yourself in mind that they did not go into the books? (A.) Yes. (Q.) Then that was not an entry made to falsify the balance-sheet, and the manager had nothing to do with it? (A.) I beg your pardon. (Q.) You have told us that these entries were made at your own instance, and that you think them right? (A.) Yes. (Q.) And that they were made from the first in red ink merely to keep yourself in mind of what they were? (A.) Yes; and in order to keep in my memory that there was no entry made through the books for the alteration. (Q.) Then it is not the case that everything that appears here in red ink was made at the request of the manager? (A.) In this instance it was not. (Q.) Was there anything else in red ink made of your own motion by yourself? (A.) No, nothing else. I am quite sure of that. (Q.) Did you make these entries before you went in to the manager, or after? (A.) I would say they would be made from the very first. (Q.) So when you took this in to the manager it was partly black and partly red? (A.) If this is the same sheet. (Q.) And if it was the predecessor of this sheet, it was red from the first as regards the notes? (A.) It would be. (Q.) Does the fact of your finding these calculations about the notes jotted here in pencil not rather suggest to your mind that this was the first sheet on which these were made? (A.) No. (Q.) Did you copy your pencil as well as your writing? (A.) These might have been made after—long after. (Q.) I thought you said you entered the notes in red ink on the first abstract you made up? (A.) There were so many people using these sheets, that in order to show the alterations these might have been put down in pencil long after. (Q.) What was in pencil might have been long after, but what was in red ink was there from the first? (A.) Yes. (Q.) And if this was not the original sheet, it was also in red ink on its predecessor? (A.) I should say so.

By Lord Justice-Clerk—What I mean to say is this, that the pencil marks might have been put on the sheet after the stoppage of the Bank, because there were so many people inquiring into these sheets that they might have been put down to explain the matter.

By Mr Balfour—(Q.) But the red ink was there from the first? (A.) Yes. (Q.) Then that is article 2 of the indictment, which in your judgment is all right? (A.) Yes.

By the Lord Justice-Clerk—The notes on hand of other banks represent what was actually in the Bank at the time. (Q.) Then when the £41,000 of returned notes came into your hands, did you make any allowance for the notes of other banks returned at the same time? (A.) The same amount was deducted on the one side as there was on the other side.

By Mr Balfour—(Q.) Is it this, that near the foot of the left-hand page, you have notes of other banks on hand, £75,000? (A.) Yes. (Q.) You deduct from that £41,000, and £34,000 is the balance? (A.) Yes. (Q.) So with respect to notes of other banks of the branches you have £77,000, and you deduct from that £47,000, and carry across the balance? (A.) Yes. (Q.) And so the matter was made right on both sides of the account? (A.) I think so. (Q.) You did not make it appear that while you had called in £89,000 of your own issue, you had a corresponding amount of the issue of other banks? (A.) No. (Q.) Then that entry is all right on both sides? (A.) Yes. The black ink was all written first, and the red ink all written afterwards. Being referred to the creditor column, top of right-hand page, I see a summation in black ink of £1,448,453. That summation includes two sums in red ink of £440,000 odds, and £346,000. It is also the case that there are black summations below which include what is written in red ink. (Q.) How is it possible that you summed up in black ink something that was only written on afterwards in red? (A.) Because this will be simply a copy of some other sheet. I cannot tell where that is. With regard to the third particular of the indictment, "amount of drafts outstanding," &c., understated to the extent of £1,393,008 or thereby [see p. 31], that amount is the summation of £973,300 and £419,708. The £973,300 is an entry which was raised in the books by Mr Alexander Stronach's orders in 1873, and which was carried forward and received effect in the balance-sheets always after that, except in 1877, when the exact amount was varied. (Q.) In preparing your balance-sheet for your abstract or scroll balance for each year, did you give effect to that without anybody's instructions? (A.) Yes. (Q.) You had it in the books? (A.) Yes. (Q.) And if you had not given effect to it in the scroll balance, you would have been missing out something which was in the books? (A.) Yes. (Q.) And that is the history of it, that, having been raised, and appearing in the books from 1873, it received effect ever after without your getting or needing to get anybody's instructions for it? (A.) Yes. [Shown No. 129A, Weekly balances in general ledger on 5th June 1878.] Being referred to the foreign and colonial credits on the debit side of that weekly state, there is a sum of £2,881,000 odds, from which there is deducted the £973,300. I only read out the balance £1,907,952 to the directors. (Q.) Then the directors would not know or see from what you read out that that balance was reached by deducting the £973,300? (A.) Not from reading it. (Q.) That is the head office weekly abstract for 1878? (A.) Yes. (Q.) Was that a correct statement of the weekly balance ending with 5th June 1878? (A.) A correct statement of the general ledger according to the books. (Q.) And without giving effect to anybody's alterations, for there were none? (A.) Quite so.

By the Lord Justice-Clerk—(Q.) You told us yesterday that in consequence of the directions of Mr Potter and Mr Stronach you made an alteration upon the original sums that you brought out in your black ink abstract in 1876. Now, was that sum of £2,800,000 consistent with your original black ink abstract, or was it consistent with the red ink alterations of 1876? (A.) The £2,800,000 was quite in accordance with the books. (Q.) With the books of 1876? (A.) Yes. (Q.) Was effect given in the weekly balance ledger to the alterations that you made in 1876? (A.) No.

By Mr Balfour—(Q.) Accordingly, from 1873 onwards, with the exception of one year, was the £973,300 treated just as it is here? (A.) Quite so. (Q.) And treated just as it is here, not only in the weekly balance for the week ending in June, but in the same way in the weekly balance of the other fifty-one weeks of the year? (A.) Yes. (Q.) In short, for the whole fifty-two weeks of the year, that was treated just in the same way? (A.) Yes. (Q.) And that was correct according to the books? (A.) Yes. (Q.) Can you say that before you had the meeting with Mr Potter and the manager in 1876 you had given effect to the entry of £973,300 as usual, just as it had been for the three years then past? (A.) Yes. (Q.) So they had nothing whatever to do with the mode of treating the £973,300? (A.) No. (Q.) Neither in 1876 nor at any time? (A.) No. (Q.) It was Mr Alexander Stronach, and nobody else? (A.) Just so. (Q.) You understood the reason for Alexander Stronach giving that direction to be that there was cash, or that there were securities in course of realisation, to work off those credits? (A.) The entry in the cash book represents that. Mr Stronach also had some slips which bore to show that. (Q.) If that was the case, was there anything wrong with the entry,—if these were in the course of realisation? (A.) It was an anticipatory entry. (Q.) And dependent upon whether the anticipations were realised or not? (A.) Quite so. (Q.) With regard to the other item of £419,780, the Bank, as I understand, had granted acceptances which were out in the circle to a certain amount? (A.) Yes. (Q.) These acceptances were about to mature? (A.) Yes. (Q.) With the view of taking up these acceptances, were other acceptances issued which it was intended to discount to lift the first set? (A.) I understand so. (Q.) Was that done within a few days before the first set of acceptances matured? (A.) I cannot tell you that; I cannot speak personally of it. (Q.) But it would be done within a few days? (A.) I cannot say. (Q.) So that for a time there were two sets of bills in the circle applicable to the same amounts? (A.) Yes. (Q.) That is to say, during the time between the maturity and the retirement of the first set of bills,—before that, and after the second set to lift them had been put out? (A.) Yes. (Q.) Now, the aggregate from which you deduct the £419,000 comprehends both of those sets of bills which were so out for a short time? (A.) The larger amount includes both sets. (Q.) Which were out for a short time though representing the same debt? (A.) Yes. (Q.) Would the total amount of the double set be just about £419,000? (A.) That was the amount I got as being out. (Q.) Now, if it is the case that the second set of bills were applied to the purpose for which they were issued—that is, to be discounted and lift the first set—and if the Bank had got the money so raised, was that entry quite right? (A.) If the money was in the cheque box. (Q.) If the discount for the second set had been got to lift the first, that entry was right? (A.) If that money had been lodged in the cheque box. (Q.) Do you know of your own knowledge whether that money was not in the cheque box? (A.) I do not know it was not in it. That was not a thing within my department. (Q.) Therefore you cannot say whether that entry of £419,000 odds was right or wrong, because you do not know whether the discount money had come in or not? (A.) Yes. With regard to the fourth head of the charge, "Amount "of bills of exchange, local and country bills, credit accounts and other ad- "vances under article 1 on creditor side, understated to the extent of "£3,520,913, 11s. 8d., or thereby" [pp. 31 and 32]—and being referred to the left-hand side of the scroll 124A [see Appendix No. II.], the first matters that enter into that are the entries of £346,336 and £440,738. I treated these as cross entries. The very same considerations which I have already given in dealing with the same entries on the other side would again apply here. In so far as they were proper cross entries they were not understated in the one place any more than in the other. (Q.) That is, to the extent of about £445,000? (A.) Yes. The next item complained of on that head is what is called the bringing down of the balances from the three credit accounts. The amounts as they originally appear at the top of the page contain the total amount of the overdrafts on the credit accounts there mentioned. What was done was to deduct a part of that and to bring it down under the general head where securities come. (Q.) If it was the case that to the extent of the sums so brought down there were securities held against that part of the accounts, was there anything wrong in bringing them down? (A.) I should say not. I do not know whether or not there were securities held against these. (Q.) Were you led to suppose there were securities held against these? (A.) In so far as that there were certain securities valued. (Q.) Was this the scheme of the alteration that the unsecured part of the overdraft was left at the top, and that the part for which securities was held was taken down with its securities under the head of securities? (A.) It does not follow. (Q.) Was that what was done? (A.) The balance might have been covered as well. (Q.) But was that what was done—it was brought down under the head of securities? (A.) I understood that the portion that was brought down was covered by stocks. (Q.) And if it was covered by stocks it was all right? (A.) I consider so, in my opinion. (Q.) The other might be covered by personal obligations, cash credits, bills or securities other than stocks? (A.) Quite so. (Q.) The Lord Advocate put it to you once or twice that these were Government stocks and the like. I observe in the published balance issued the enumeration is not limited to Government stocks; it is Government stocks, Exchequer bills, railway and other stocks. If there were stocks held against the parts which were so brought down, was it not quite a proper denomination to put them under other stocks? (A.) I consider so. (Q.) Did any of the alterations which you have described and explained, or any of the alterations which were made upon your scrolls, affect the profit and loss at all? (A.) No. (Q.) They did not affect the result of the accounts or the balance of the accounts as to profit and loss? (A.) No. (Q.) Or as to reserve? (A.) Or as to reserve. (Q.) Or as to capital? (A.) Or as to capital. (Q.) So from what you have said, the alterations which were made did not affect one of the amounts which entered the published balance as liabilities to partners? (A.) Quite so. (Q.) Now, those three things which you say were not affected by the alterations, viz., the capital account £1,000,000, the reserve fund £450,000, and the profit and loss £142,095, are the same in the published abstract as they are in the balance ledger signed by the directors? (A.) The same. They were not affected in any way by any of the things which I have explained. I signed the published balance as correct in 1877 and 1878. That balance was what I may call an abstract of the original scroll abstract. (Q.) That is to say, it epitomised further what had been already epitomised in the scroll abstract? (A.) Just so. (Q.) Is it the case that you have lost the sheet of the balance applicable to 1877? (A.) Yes, that is a clean copy; I cannot find it. (Q.) Are you able to give the same full explanations about 1877 that you have now given about 1878? (A.) Not so well. (Q.) Have you any doubt that the explanations which I have now got from you as to the different entries I have asked you about would be equally applicable to 1877? (A.) On the same lines.

By the Lord Justice-Clerk—(Q.) Are you quite sure that the entries were on the same lines in 1877? You said otherwise yesterday. If the £973,000 was treated in the same way in 1877 as in 1876, you may be right? (A.) The explanation that I made was that the first sheet was ignored, that is to say, the £973,000 was ignored, and other sums put in.

By Mr Balfour—(Q.) With that exception, was there any other difference in the principle, except that the £973,000 was treated as you have explained? (A.) Not that I recollect of; and I may add that the sums that were put in were simply following out the £973,000 entry. (Q.) Did they include it? (A.) They must have done so. (Q.) Did it receive effect in 1877, although it received effect with something added to it? Is that it? (A.) Quite so.

By the Lord Justice-Clerk—(Q.) You told us yesterday that the figures that were inserted in 1877 in order to fill the place of the £973,000 were not in the books? (A.) Yes. (Q.) And they were not in the books? (A.) They were not in the books. (Q.) Therefore that sum was not stated in the same way as in 1876? (A.) Quite so. (Q.) Therefore you must qualify your answer to that effect? (A.) Quite so.

By Mr Balfour—(Q.) Subject to that qualification, they were on the same lines? (A.) Yes. (Q.) By the year 1878 had you not for the first time got prepared a general printed scroll sheet to fill up the various items? (A.)

For 1877. (Q.) For the first time? (A.) For the first time. (Q.) And it was upon that sheet that you made the entries which you have explained to us in 1878 and also in 1877? (A.) Quite so. (Q.) By 1876 you had not, I think, got that large and complete sheet prepared? (A.) No. (Q.) And in 1876 was your general balance got by superinducing the balances from the branches and the correspondents' books on to the head office weekly balance? (A.) Quite so. (Q.) The principle of making out the balance was still the same? (A.) Still the same. (Q.) The total balance of the Bank was got from—1st, the weekly balance at the head office; 2d, the weekly balance at the branches; and 3d, the information from correspondents? (A.) Yes. (Q.) But not having the big sheet in 1876 you wrote the entries applicable to the two latter heads on to the weekly balance of the head office? (A.) Yes—wrote them together on the one sheet. (Q.) The totals? (A.) Yes. [Shown No. 130.] That is the head office weekly balance. (Q.) And it was the basis on which the others were superinduced? (A.) Yes. (Q.) What is No. 133? (A.) The branch weekly balance. (Q.) What was the paper from which you got the entries applicable to the correspondents? (A.) That is embraced in 130. (Q.) Does it come to this, that the weekly balance applicable to branches has also upon it the information relative to correspondents? (A.) Yes. (Q.) So that your balance of 1876 was made up from 130 and 133? (A.) Yes. (Q.) Now, I want to know a little more particularly about 128 [Abstract of accounts at head office on 7th June, Appendix No. II.] and its predecessors. You said yesterday that you took the scroll abstract to a meeting at which Mr Potter and the manager were present? (A.) Yes. (Q.) Was the scroll abstract which you took to that meeting, as prepared by yourself, written entirely in black ink? (A.) It would. (Q.) You have no doubt about that? I have no doubt about it. (Q.) That the scroll abstract that you took to those gentlemen was written entirely in black ink? (A.) Yes. (Q.) You said that alterations were made upon it in red ink? (A.) Not at the meeting; I did not say that. (Q.) Did the scroll abstract which you so took to the meeting, and which was written entirely in black ink, contain the entries brought from the sheet applicable to branches and to correspondents? (A.) Yes. (Q.) So that it focussed in black ink all the entries applicable to head office, branches, and correspondents? (A.) Yes. (Q.) Where did that meeting take place? (A.) In the manager's room. No one was present but Mr Potter, the manager, and myself. The meeting took place between the annual balance day and the annual meeting day—that is between the first Wednesday of June and the first Wednesday of July. I cannot give the date more particularly. (Q.) Were any alterations made in writing on that document at that meeting? (A.) I would take the different alterations and give effect to them in the balance-sheet. (Q.) Were any alterations made in writing at that meeting upon the black ink scroll that you took to it? (A.) Yes. (Q.) What alterations were made, and in what kind of ink? (A.) The sheet is not here at all. (Q.) Do you not recollect? (A.) It would be all in black ink or pencil.

By the Lord Justice-Clerk—(Q.) The alterations? (A.) Yes.

By Mr Balfour—(Q.) I thought you said yesterday that the alterations were made in red ink? (A.) No; I said the effect of the alterations. (Q.) Are you satisfied now that the alterations made on the black ink scroll were made in black ink or pencil, and not at all in red ink? (A.) Yes. (Q.) Was it done in black ink at the meeting, or in pencil at the meeting, or do you not recollect which? (A.) I have no recollection. (Q.) Then you don't recollect whether it was done in black ink, or pencil, or partly in the one and partly in the other? (A.) Quite so; it might have been either; I would rather say pencil. (Q.) Or both? (A.) Or both. (Q.) Now, where is that document which you say you took to that meeting? (A.) It would be destroyed when this one was made. (Q.) Then 128 is not the document that you had at that meeting? (A.) Oh, no. (Q.) Do you recollect what became of that document? (A.) I have no doubt it would be destroyed when a clean copy was made. (Q.) You have no doubt, but do you recollect? (A.) I have no doubt I destroyed it. (Q.) Who would destroy it? (A.) I would destroy it. (Q.) Do you recollect of that, or do you merely suppose so? (A.) I remember I did destroy it.

By the Lord Justice-Clerk—(Q.) From what is the lithograph taken? (A.) From this (128). (Q.) When was it made? (A.) After the meeting. (Q.) Did you write out again your black ink, and then put on it the red ink alterations? (A.) Yes. (Q.) That is what you did? (A.) Yes.

By Mr Balfour—(Q.) Does it come to this, that 128 shows in black ink what you took to the meeting, and the one you say you destroyed, and what is shown in red ink on 128 shows the alterations that were made at the meeting? (A.) I think there was a mistake made yesterday as to the red ink markings on this sheet (128). The red ink markings simply bring the two abstracts together. (Q.) Do you say, or do you not, that 128 contains in black ink what was in the abstract you took to the meeting in black ink, and that the red ink on 128 shows the alterations that you were directed to make? Do you now say that? (A.) No. (Q.) Then does 128 show anything in red ink which was altered in black ink at the meeting which you say you had with Mr Potter and the manager? (A.) This sheet (128) is the effect of the meeting. (Q.) Do the red ink markings, or any of them, on 128, show the alterations made at the meeting? (A.) They must have been brought together before that time. (Q.) Are not the entries applicable to the branches only brought in in red ink on 128? (A.) Yes. (Q.) Is not this just what you explained a little ago,—that the abstract of 1876 was made by taking as the basis the weekly abstract of the head office, and superinducing the entries relative to the branches and correspondents? (A.) Quite so. (Q.) And are not those entries relative to the branches and correspondents superinduced in red ink upon 128? (A.) Yes. (Q.) Then your evidence yesterday was not correct? (A.) Will you allow me to explain that we were referring to the three sums of £200,000, £100,000, and £450,000.

By the Lord Justice-Clerk—(Q.) You told us yesterday that your original black ink abstract which you took to the meeting was a proper abstract made up from the books, and was correct. Do you still say that? (A.) Yes; this one. (Q.) And all the red ink alterations were made upon the instructions of Mr Potter and the manager? (A.) In so far as these figures are concerned,—the £200,000, the £100,000, and the £450,000. (Q.) There were other alterations made in red ink which you made yourself, in order to make your original abstract entirely accurate? (A.) In order to bring the two abstracts together. (Q.) Which two? (A.) The branches one and the head office one. (Q.) You had done that; this original abstract was bringing them together? (A.) Oh, no. (Q.) I understood yesterday you told us the way in which you prepared your abstract for the directors was, first, that you prepared the abstract of the balances at the head office, and then the superintendent of branches prepared his abstract. Did you take the two and put them together in a general abstract which you took to the directors? (A.) Yes. (Q.) The thing you took to the directors was the general abstract embracing both branches and head office? (A.) Yes. (Q.) And on that the red ink alterations were made? (A.) Yes.

By Mr Balfour—(Q.) Do you desire to correct anything you said yesterday or not? (A.) I think I said yesterday that the alterations on the figures were made in red ink. If I said that these figures £200,000, £100,000, and £450,000 were made in red ink, I made a mistake. (Q.) You have told us that what you took to the directors contained both the entries as to the branches, and the other entries in black ink? (A.) Yes. (Q.) 128 contains the entries relative to the branches in red ink; why is that? (A.) This is not the sheet submitted. (Q.) But if you had the entries relative to the branches in black ink on the original scroll, why did you put the entries relative to the branches in red ink in the second scroll? (A.) In order to make it more distinct. (Q.) For whom? (A.) For myself. (Q.) Did you not know what related to the branches without putting it in red ink? (A.) But it was clearer: it brought out where the two were put together easier. (Q.) If it was clearer to have it in red ink in the second scroll for yourself, why did you put it in black ink for the manager and Mr Potter? (A.) It was quite a different sheet altogether the one presented in 1876. (Q.) Was not this (128) the first scroll you ever made out? (A.) Not the one I submitted to the directors. (Q.) Then did you copy in red ink on 128 about the branches what you had written in black ink on the original scroll? (A.) Yes. (Q.) Have you no farther explanation of why you did that than that it was clearer for yourself? (A.) No. (Q.) You say the thing you were told to do was to bring down £200,875, £100,300, and £450,000, from the top of the page to the bottom? (A.) Yes. (Q.) That alteration you have shown on 128 not in red, but in black ink? (A.) Yes. (Q.) Then does it come to this, that you have not shown anywhere in red ink the alterations which you say were made by direction of the manager and Mr Potter? (A.) There is nothing here (128) in red ink that I was desired to alter. (Q.) Then upon any sheet, either the first or the second, none of the alterations were carried out in red ink? (A.) No. (Q.) And the only thing that is in red ink is what relates to the branches, which was not an alteration? (A.) Quite so. (Q.) Did you not say yesterday that some part at all events of the alterations had been given effect to in red ink? (A.) On this sheet? (Q.) Upon any sheet? (A.) Not in 1876. (Q.) I am only speaking of 1876? (A.) There is no alteration. (Q.) But neither upon the original sheet nor upon this sheet have you given effect to any of the alterations that you were directed to make in red ink? (A.) Quite so. (Q.) Do you adhere to the statement that this is not the first abstract you made? (A.) Yes. (Q.) What is it that is different in black ink in 128, from what you took to the meeting in black ink on the scroll which you say you tore up? (A.) These amounts are brought down from credit accounts. (Q.) The three sums which I have mentioned? (A.) Yes.

By the Lord Justice-Clerk—(Q.) If that is not the thing you took to the meeting in 1876, what is it, and when did you make it? (A.) This was copied after the meeting.

By Mr Balfour—(Q.) What led to its being made? (A.) This was the first year that I had got it printed. (Q.) Why did you not just give effect to the alterations in red ink on the black ink scroll which you took to the meeting, in the same way that you did in 1878? (A.) It was simply for my own information that I put them in red ink at any time. (Q.) And the only thing you put in red ink here was what you had put in black at the first? (A.) Yes. (Q.) You did not put in red ink anything you were told to alter? (A.) Not in the 1876 one. (Q.) Were not these three amounts which appear here in black ink also written originally in that place in black ink in the scroll you took to the directors? (A.) No. They were not there at all in the scroll I took to the directors. (Q.) I think you said that another particular in which this scroll differs from the scroll that you took to the directors was in bringing out on the right hand page only balances instead of the £455,000 on the line? [See p. 114.] (A.) Yes. (Q.) You said you had in the original the items which the Lord Advocate put to you, and that here you brought out a balance of £1346, 16s. 6d.? (A.) Yes. (Q.) What is that balance? (A.) The balance in general ledger on deposit accounts and the total amount of deposit receipts. (Q.) Then is that entry of £1346 a correct balance taken from the books? (A.) It is taken from the general ledger. (Q.) Does that correspond to the sum which I read out to you from the statements of 1878 of £33,000 odds? (A.) Yes; it is on the same principle. It is the balance from the general ledger. (Q.) So that this is an entry brought from the books of the Bank? (A.) Yes. (Q.) And showing correctly the balance by deducting the larger from the smaller sums of the debtor and creditor sides? (A.) Quite so. (Q.) Then as to the sum which you say was carried down, that I think is just brought down to the head of securities in the same way as the corresponding items I asked you about in 1878? (A.) Yes. (Q.) Did you understand that there were securities held for these amounts? (A.) From the conversation I understood so. (Q.) And if there were securities held for these amounts, was it, in your judgment, quite right so to bring it down? (A.) Quite right. (Q.) Securities of the nature of stocks? (A.) Securities, and held absolutely by the Bank, so that they could sell them at any time. (Q.) And if there were securities of the nature of stocks held for those sums, it would be quite proper to class them under other stocks in the printed balance-sheet? (A.) Yes. (Q.) So that whether that was right or wrong depends upon a matter that you don't know? (A.) Yes. (Q.) On the right-hand page of the scroll abstract for 1876, Dr. No. 2, I see you have a good deal of figuring, by which you bring out a result of £860,355? (A.) Yes. (Q.) Is that the entry which was carried into the printed balance under head 2 of the debtor side—bank notes in circulation in Scotland and the Isle of Man? (A.) Yes. (Q.) Then that is quite correct? (A.) Quite. (Q.) In the red ink figuring under Dr. No. 3, near the foot of the left-hand page, and at the right-hand side of the page, there is a sum of £29,095 (page 4 of indictment, article 4). Does that sum represent your own notes which had been got in exchange for the notes of other banks between the afternoon of the Wednesday and the commencement of business on the Thursday, as you explained with reference to the £89,031? (A.) No. (Q.) What is it? (A.) There is a reference here to it, "Notes remitted by "branches." (Q.) Was that sum remitted from the branches? (A.) I have no doubt of it. (Q.) But were these notes then in the hands of the Bank? (A.) They would be in transmission. (Q.) That means going from the branches to the head office? (A.) Yes, and belonging to the head office. (Q.) But when a note is passing from a branch to the head office, it is in the hands of the Bank; it is not in circulation? (A.) No. (Q.) Then, if these notes were in that position, was it not a perfectly proper deduction to make? (A.) I should say so. (Q.) If you had stated these notes as in circulation, you would have stated what was wrong, if they were going between a branch and the head office? (A.) That is my opinion. (Q.) I suppose that, notwithstanding any alterations that were made upon the scroll sheet, the profit and loss, the capital, and the reserve fund are unaffected, just as you explained, as to 1878 and 1877? (A.) Yes. (Q.) If the notes were actually in transit, they were more clearly out of circulation than those of the £89,031, which were withdrawn? (A.) Yes. I was a shareholder of the Bank, and continued to be so till its stoppage.

By Mr Asher—The books were balanced annually as at the first Wednesday in June. The first Wednesday in June 1876 was the 7th, in 1877 the 6th, and in 1878 the 5th. I wrote up the entries in the balance ledger, which was docqueted by the directors. The balance so entered in the balance ledger showed the balances appearing in three separate books—the weekly balance book, the branches balance book, and the correspondents' balance book. In that balance each branch was treated as a debtor to or creditor of the Bank merely. There was only one sum entered opposite the name of each branch, representing the amount at the debit or at the credit of that particular branch. There did not appear in that balance ledger the amount of deposits at any branch, the bills discounted, or the cash in hand.

By the Lord Justice-Clerk—(Q.) Nor the transactions generally? (A.) No. (Q.) It was only the result that you entered in your books? (A.) Yes;

simply the balance between the head office and the branch as a branch. (Q.) As if they had been customers of the Bank? (A.) Yes.

By Mr Asher—(Q.) You prepared the abstract of accounts? (A.) Yes. (Q.) The balance ledger which I have just mentioned was the thing which was docqueted by the directors? (A.) Yes. (Q.) And to examine it, it was merely necessary to examine the balances in the three subordinate books I have mentioned? (A.) Yes. (Q.) Did any one of the subordinate books show the state of accounts between the Bank and any individual customer? (A.) No. (Q.) You were present at the examination of books by the directors? (A.) Yes. (Q.) Did the examination mentioned in the docquet refer merely to a comparison of the balances in the balance ledger with the balances in the weekly balance book, the agents' balance book, and the correspondents' balance book? (A.) Quite so. (Q.) That was the only examination made? (A.) The only one. (Q.) And with regard to 1876, 1877, and 1878, I understand you to say that the docquet is correct, in saying that everything in the balance ledger is in accordance with the Bank's books? (A.) Yes. I prepared the abstracts of accounts. In 1876 I would commence the preparation of the abstract immediately after 7th June, when the books were balanced, and the abstract would be completed within perhaps a fortnight afterwards. (Q.) In making up that document did you make it from the balance ledger which had been docqueted by the directors, or from other books? (A.) From the weekly balance book and other books? (Q.) The balance ledger alone would not enable you to make up the abstract of accounts? (A.) No. (Q.) You required to take the books showing the details of business at the various agencies, did you not; because in these abstracts you classed the deposits at the agencies along with the deposits at the head office, and the cash in hand at the agencies along with the cash in hand at the head office? (A.) Yes. (Q.) And so with regard to bills and other accounts? (A.) Yes. (Q.) Therefore the abstracts presented the state of the Bank's affairs as if the whole business at the head office, correspondents' offices, and agencies had been carried on under one roof? (A.) Yes. (Q.) The draft abstracts were prepared in the form you have spoken to, and they were further epitomised for publication? (A.) Yes. In 1876 the whole of the work of making up the balance and preparing the abstract balance-sheet for publication was completed before the annual meeting. The annual meeting took place on the first Wednesday of July, which was the 5th. (Q.) Was the balance ledger generally docqueted by the directors between the date down to which the books were balanced and the date of that meeting? (A.) If I had got them to sign it. (Q.) And they generally were got to sign it at some time during that interval, were they not? (A.) If possible. (Q.) You attended at the meeting at which the books were examined? (A.) Yes. (Q.) If a director happened to be absent from the meeting at which the examination of the books took place, did he generally sign the balance-sheet after he came back? (A.) Yes. (Q.) Was there any separate attendance of officials for the purpose of his making an examination if he had been absent before, or did he generally just attach his name to where the other directors had signed? (A.) He just signed the balance ledger at the usual place. (Q.) There was no second examination made by the director who happened to be absent when the examination took place? (A.) No. In 1877, also, the abstract would be prepared within fourteen days after the first Wednesday of June, which was on the 6th. The annual meeting in that year was on the first Wednesday in July, which was on the 4th. In 1878, in like manner, the abstract would be prepared within a fortnight after the date when the books were balanced. The annual meeting in that year was on 3d July. When the abstract balance which was to be published had been prepared, it was generally put into print, and I understand that a copy was sent to each director. (Q.) But it was not the practice, I believe, to communicate the draft to the directors? (A.) In 1876 and in 1878 were the only times when I met the directors for such a purpose. (Q.) You did not meet Mr Salmond in 1876 or 1878 for that purpose? (A.) I never met Mr Salmond. (Q.) Or showed him the abstract balance-sheet? (A.) No. (Q.) Whom do you mean by the directors that you met in 1876 and 1878? (A.) In 1876 Mr Potter, and in 1878 Mr Stewart and Mr Potter. (Q.) With that exception, was there ever submitted to any director, to your knowledge, anything except the abstract printed for publication with the report? (A.) No; not to my knowledge. (Q.) And you were the person who was engaged in the preparation of the draft, and converting it into the form in which it was published? (A.) Yes. (Q.) And you held your position of accountant from 1871 down to the close? (A.) Yes. (Q.) You were the custodier of the books of the Bank, except at the time when the weekly balance book, the branch balance book, and the correspondents' balance book were submitted to the directors for comparison with the balance ledger once a year: were the directors in the habit of examining the details of the books of the Bank? (A.) Not that I know of. (Q.) And you were the custodier of the books? (A.) Of the one I was. (Q.) Of which one? (A.) Of the weekly balance book. (Q.) So that the weekly balance book was not submitted at the weekly meetings? (A.) Not that I am aware of. (Q.) You spoke of a private cash book No. 6, in which an entry of £973,300 was made; were you the custodier of that book? (A.) Yes. (Q.) Did you ever show that book to Mr Salmond? (A.) No. (Q.) Did he ever see it so far as you know? (A.) Not that I know of. (Q.) Or any of the directors? (A.) No; I don't think they did. (Q.) Do you happen to know that during the years 1876, 1877, and 1878, Mr Salmond was much in the country, and was frequently absent from the meetings of the Bank? (A.) He was, for a year or so, but I could not mention the dates. (Q.) During these years, did you see him at the Bank at all, except when he was there at the weekly meetings he attended? (A.) Very seldom. (Q.) You are aware that he resided in Ayrshire? (A.) Yes. (Q.) Do you remember that Mr Salmond was not at the Bank at the time the books were examined in 1878 by the other directors? (A.) I am quite certain he was not. (Q.) And do you remember that he did not come to the Bank until after the general meeting? (A.) Yes. (Q.) Then, I see his name attached to the docquet in the books in 1878; was his signature put there at the same time as those of the other directors in that year? (A.) Mr Potter and Mr Salmond signed that docquet both on the same day. (Q.) When was that? (A.) I would say it would be after the annual meeting. (Q.) Was there any examination of the books made then? (A.) No. (Q.) I believe you cannot remember as to the years 1876 and 1877? Your memory does not enable you to say whether Mr Salmond was there at that time or not? (A.) No; I cannot recollect about that.

By the Dean of Faculty—Mr Robert Stronach became manager of the Bank in 1875. I cannot give the month. I cannot recollect whether it was at the end of the year. (Q.) You mentioned yesterday the transference of an account of Smith, Fleming, & Co. from one heading to another, which brought it under your jurisdiction: that took place in June 1875? (A.) It was of that date. (Q.) You stated certain reasons for that transference which seemed to me to be suppositions on your part? (A.) Quite so. (Q.) Were you informed in any way of the reason of the transference? (A.) No. (Q.) Were you aware that, about that time, an agreement had been come to between Smith, Fleming, & Co. and the Bank, whereby their account was put upon a new footing, under which they were to pay a certain percentage upon the debt? (A.) I have heard so. I know of that from having made up an account with that statement in it. (Q.) Was the entering into that agreement the ground for the change in the heading of the account, and the transference of it from the cheque box to the accountant's department? (A.) I cannot say. (Q.) The knowledge of such agreements did not, except incidentally, come before you? (A.) No. [Shown No. 127, Abstract of accounts in general ledger on 6th June 1877, Appendix No. II.] (Q.) In that paper you have got printed matter, figures in black ink, figures in red ink, and figures in pencil. Is the whole of the writing and the whole of the figuring in that paper in your handwriting? (A.) Yes. (Q.) Is that paper the first scroll that was prepared of the abstract of accounts for the year 1877? (A.) Yes. (Q.) Did you submit it to the manager and the directors? (A.) Not to the directors—to the manager. (Q.) Did you write what we have here—the black and the red—before you had any consultation with the manager or the directors? (A.) No. (Q.) What do the calculations in pencil on the right-hand side refer to? (A.) There is a part of it apparently in connection with the heading 1 of the assets in the abstract. (Q.) Can you tell me from that paper what was the amount of City Bank notes in circulation in Scotland in 1877? (A.) Yes,—£840,004. (Q.) And the amount that was published in the abstract (page 6 of the indictment) was £763,894? [See p. 29.] (A.) Yes. (Q.) There was thus a difference between the fact and what was stated in the abstract of £76,110? (A.) I will take it for granted; I cannot check it here. (Q.) You prepared that abstract? (A.) Yes. (Q.) And you inserted these figures—£763,894? (A.) Yes. (Q.) Where did you get them? (A.) I would require to get the other sheet before I could tell you that. (Q.) I think you will be able to get it from this sheet (No. 127, Abstract for 1877), all of which contains your own figuring. About three-fourths down the right-hand page of that abstract you have the true figures, £840.004. A little above that you will find, also in your own figures, £860,355, and underneath that you put £840,004, being, as we have seen, the true circulation for 1877. The first of the figures now given, £860,355, was the circulation for the previous year, as we see from page 3 of the indictment [see p. 37]; and in comparing the two you find that there is a difference of £20,355? (A.) Yes. (Q.) Thereafter, if you refer to the black ink markings in the middle of the same page, under the heading "Circulation," you seem to have gone on to compare the four years 1874, 1875, 1876, and 1877? (A.) Yes. (Q.) When did you make the pencil markings on that sheet? (A.) I could not well tell you that. I presume the most of them had been made when consulting with the manager. (Q.) Was not the whole of this calculation, until you brought out the sum that is published, gone through by you before you consulted with a human being? Is it not the result of the working of your own mind? (A.) No; certainly not.

By the Lord Justice-Clerk—(Q.) When do you say you made these pencil markings? (A.) I could not say for the whole of them. (Q.) Was it after the general meeting or before? (A.) It would be long before the general meeting.

By the Dean of Faculty—(Q.) To the left of the black ink figures, under the head "Circulation," in the middle of the page, are certain red ink figures, 214m, &c., meaning £214,000, £176,000, £197,000, and £126,000; what are these figures? (A.) That appears to be the difference betwixt the circulation on the Saturday and the circulation as shown on each annual balance day. The red figures under "Circulation" on the right-hand side of No. 127A indicate the Saturday issue of notes. The Wednesday issue is in black ink figures, £840,000 for 1877. I deducted the £714,000 from the £840,000, bringing out £126,000. I see the entry of £21,000 in pencil below the £714,000. I don't think that £21,000 represents the entry farther up, "B of M actual issue." I cannot say what that is. It has no relation to the Bank of Mona. (Q.) Is that £21,000 the £21,000 which you have added in pencil below the £714.000? (A.) I cannot follow it. I deducted the £735,000 from the £840,004, bringing out £105,000. (Q.) Then you say this: "Say make it £100,000 less;" were you experimenting then? (A.) Probably so. (Q.) What did you mean by "make "it £100,000 less?" (A.) I cannot tell you; it was not I that was experimenting. (Q.) But it is your writing? (A.) Yes, it is. (Q.) And it is your thinking which this writing indicates? (A.) No. (Q.) Whose thinking is it? (A.) The manager's. (Q.) Was the manager looking over your shoulder and telling you to write "make it £100,000 less?" (A.) Yes. (Q.) Then this paper was made in the manager's presence? (A.) Lots of it, and that amongst it. (Q.) Do you swear that, Mr Morison? (A.) I do. (Q.) Is there anything here your own original composition? (A.) The black figures are taken from the books. (Q.) That is all you acknowledge to as being your own? (A.) Yes. (Q.) Now, if you go to the right-hand side of the same page, immediately above the red ink figures £840,004, you will find an experiment of deducting the £100,000? (A.) Yes. (Q.) And there is brought to the left £740,000? (A.) Yes. (Q.) That was trying to see how it would look by taking off £100,000? (A.) It must have been. (Q.) Apparently you dropped that experiment, and you took to another; for if you look down on the right-hand page, about three inches from the bottom, you will find in pencil the true figure £840,004, and there is deducted from that £46,110? (A.) Yes. (Q.) What is that £46,110? (A.) Notes received at exchange on Thursday morning in Glasgow. (Q.) And you deducted that from the true sum in circulation? (A.) Yes. (Q.) And you brought out £793,894, the sum published in the abstract being £763,894. Now, how was £30,000 taken off the £793,000? (A.) I cannot explain that. (Q.) Did you not sign the balance-sheet as correct? (A.) Yes. (Q.) On the left-hand page you will find, under head 3, "gold and silver coin on hand, and "notes of other banks on hand," bringing out a total of £921,018, 0s. 2d.? (A.) Yes. (Q.) And there is this pencil marking in your handwriting, "Why "should this be so much?" Did that occur to your own mind, or was it suggested to you by anybody? (A.) It was suggested to me. (Q.) And you wrote it down? (A.) Yes. (Q.) "Why should this be so much?" (A.) Oh! I beg your pardon: I understand what you mean now; I was astonished to see the amount of gold and silver at the branches when it should have been at head office. (Q.) Then this astonishment was your own? (A.) It was. (Q.) You see £30,000 in pencil deducted from the £921,018? (A.) Yes. (Q.) Bringing out £891,018? (A.) Yes. (Q.) Where did you get that £30,000? (A.) I got it from the manager. (Q.) What is it? (A.) I cannot tell. (Q.) Is it not an answer to your own question, "Why this should be so "large?" (A.) No. (Q.) Did you not mean that it should be made less when you expressed your astonishment? (A.) I simply did what I was told. (Q.) Did you ask the manager where the £30,000 came from? (A.) No. (Q.) Did you form an idea at the moment whether it was an invention of his, or whether it represented an existing sum of money? (A.) All that I know about it is that it is taken off both sides. (Q.) Did you not ask him what the £30,000 represented which is deducted from the coin in hand. (A.) There might have been a conversation, but I cannot recollect about it. (Q.) You certified that that £30,000 was correct when you signed this abstract? (A.) Yes. (Q.) Then you took the £30,000 from the left-hand side to the right-hand side, and deducted it from the £793,894, and brought out the published sum of £763,000? (A.) That is so. (Q.) And then you deduct £30,000 from the coin on hand, £921,018, and bring out £891,018 as the coin on hand? (A.) Yes. That was published in the abstract balance-sheet. (Q.) And that is less than the true amount by £30,000? (A.) Yes. (Q.) Now, I ask again, is not the paper that I hold in my hand the working out of the operations of your own mind, before a human being saw it? (A.) No. (Q.) And were not all these experiments yours, and no other person's? (A.) No. (Q.) The paper is without any summation; it never was presented complete to anybody? (A.) Oh! yes, it is summed up. Both sides of it are summed up. I cannot tell when it was summed up without going over the summations. (Q.) You have said that the manager told you to put in certain things, and that certain things were your own; why did you tell Mr Balfour that you did not remember anything about the balance of 1877? (A.) I did not say I did not remember anything about it. (Q. You said there was a sheet wanting, and you could not give any explanations? (A.) Yes. (Q.) I show you the abstract for 1878; at the left-hand you see a number of pencil figurings not obliterated yet, in the fourth column; these figures are yours? (A.) Yes. (Q.) Was this paper covered with calculations of the same sort that we see in 1877? (A.) I cannot tell you. (Q.) Any figuring that was here was in your handwriting? (A.) Yes. (Q.) You recollect about 1878; do you recollect of making calculations in regard to the various items to be entered in the abstract? (A.) Yes; I made calculations. (Q.) And they were upon this paper? (A.) Yes. (Q.) Who obliterated the pencil markings here? (A.) I cannot tell you. (Q.) Did you do it? (A.) I might have done it; I cannot tell.

By the Lord Advocate—(Q.) I understand that in the balance abstracts furnished to you by the superintendent of branches there were entered the whole deposits at the branches, the bills floating, and all other details? (A.) Yes. (Q.) The same as in the case of the head office? (A.) Yes. (Q.) And you carried all these deposits, and bills, and others, into the final balance-sheet? (A.) Yes. (Q.) But in the balance ledger nothing is given except the balance at each branch. (A.) Yes; the item of balance at each branch. (Q.) Not the details bringing it out? (A.) Not the details. (Q.) Did you at the making up of any of these three balance-sheets for 1876, 1877, or 1878, of your own accord alter the balances so as not to be in conformity with the books under your charge? (A.) That is personally you mean? (Q.) Yes? (A.) No. (Q.) You were responsible for keeping the books? (A.) Yes. (Q.) But did you ever make up or complete a balance sheet without the aid and sanction of the manager? (A.) Never. (Q.) In bringing down to the heading No. 3 the balances from credit accounts and others, I think you said that you had no knowledge which would have enabled you to say that that was a right thing to do? (A.) I had no knowledge of the securities. (Q.) Or whether there were securities? (A.) Or whether there were securities. (Q.) But you certified the abstract as completed, bringing these down, although you had not that knowledge? (A.) Yes. (Q.) Upon what, then, did you rely in signing that abstract or balance-sheet containing such entries. (A.) I relied on the alterations made by the directors. (Q.) Including the manager? (A.) Including the manager, of course. (Q.) The directors, so far as you have spoken to them? (A.) Yes. (Q.) You have said that, in your opinion, where a debt is due in the form of an overdraft upon a current account or a bill, and there is security held by the Bank sufficient to cover that, in making out a balance-sheet, the directors, or the manager, or yourself, would be warranted in entering that not as a debt on the one side, with security upon the other, but simply as an asset of that amount? (A.) Simply an asset. (Q.) Do you think that would fairly inform a shareholder of the Bank of the state of the Bank? (A.) Do you refer to the sums taken down? (Q.) Yes? (A.) They were simply taken down from the one heading to the other; the securities, if any, would still have been there. (Q.) Suppose the Bank had lent five millions, and they held five millions of securities, would it be right to enter these as five millions lent, with securities against them, or simply as an asset of five millions? (A.) As an asset. (Q.) Of five millions? (A.) They are all assets; all that side are assets. (Q.) You see no difference between these two things? (A.) No. (Q.) Suppose the security were turning out bad within a week after the publication of the balance-sheet, would the balance-sheet be true in that case? (A.) It would not be true after they were bad. (Q.) You said that the alterations you made upon the accounts did not alter the balance? (A.) They did not alter the stock account, profit and loss, and reserve. (Q.) Do you think that an entry in a balance-sheet is legitimate, leaving out entries, so long as you don't affect the result? (A.) Oh! no.

(Q.) Those entries that were taken down, I understand, only appear as so taken down in that scroll balance-sheet, and in the abstract which you published? (A.) Yes. (Q.) Do they anywhere appear in the books of the Bank as so dealt with? (A.) No. (Q.) Or in the balance ledger? (A.) No. (Q.) You said Mr Stronach made a remark to you in 1878, that he hoped it would not be done again, or that he would not require to do it again: what did he refer to? (A.) I understood it to be some settlement of James Morton & Co.'s affairs. (Q.) What was it that it would not be necessary to do again? (A.) To understate the bills payable, and of course the foreign and colonial credits. (Q.) Did you understand why he hoped it would not be necessary to do it again? (A.) I understood that it was to be a settlement of James Morton & Co.'s affairs. (Q.) Did you think he was doing a right thing in so understating the bills payable and the foreign and colonial credits? (A.) No. (Q.) Why did you think it was not right? (A.) Because the amount in the balance-sheet did not correspond with the sum in the books. (Q.) Did you believe that he held securities against it? (A.) Yes. (Q.) Was it a wrong thing to enter the bills payable so, even if he held securities? (A.) Yes, in so far as it did not correspond with the Bank books. (Q.) And did you understand him then to allude only to its not corresponding with the Bank books? (A.) Quite so. (Q.) If you are right in your view, why did its non-correspondence with the Bank books make it a wrong thing to tell a shareholder? (A.) Because the amount shown to the shareholders differed from what was in the books. (Q.) If you were right in your view, what harm did the shareholders take from not seeing what was in the books, and seeing what was in the abstract instead? (A.) It understates their liabilities to the public. (Q.) It concealed their liabilities from the public? (A.) It certainly concealed them. (Q.) Do you think, or do you not think, that it is of importance to the public or to shareholders, to have a truthful statement of the liabilities of a bank? (A.) A truthful statement. (Q.) According to the books? (A.) According to the books. (Q.) Is it important to them or not? (A.) It should be important; it must be. (Q.) Important as influencing their judgment as to the state of the Bank? (A.) Quite so. (Q.) Does the amount of these things not affect the credit of the Bank? (A.) I should say so. (Q.) And do you still say that it was a legitimate thing to reduce them, although there was security held? (A.) You mean the bills payable? (Q.) Do you still say that it was a right thing, assuming there was security, to make them disconform to the books? (A.) I never said that it was right. (Q.) In regard to bills payable; but do you say it is a right thing in regard to these credit balances, to take them down in the way that was done,—as securities; is it a right thing for the public or the shareholders? (A.) I see no reason why they should not have been taken down, if they held securities. (Q.) And entered in the books? (A.) And entered in the books. (Q.) Is it a right thing to take them down without that appearing in the books, or the security appearing in the books as against them? (A.) The practice was not to bring them down. (Q.) But you departed from the practice. Was that departure, in your opinion, justifiable when there was no entry in the books to show it? (A.) I should have preferred an entry. (Q.) Why should you have preferred that? (A.) Because it would have made the amount agree with the general ledger. (Q.) Not because it was right, but only because it would make the amount agree with the general ledger? (A.) Because the amount would then agree with the general ledger. (Q.) Who suggested that departure from the general practice? (A.) In 1876, Mr Potter. (Q.) And thereafter? (A.) It was continued.

By the Lord Justice-Clerk—I made up an abstract balance for the head office, and the superintendent of branches made it up for the branches. I then made up a draft of a full abstract, combining the results of these. I then submitted that to the manager. I did so in 1876. I became accountant in 1871. In 1876, at the annual balance, I had a conversation with the manager and Mr Potter, and certain alterations were made at their suggestion. (Q.) Was that the first time that any such interview had ever taken place? (A.) Yes. (Q.) Were these alterations consequent on an examination of the books, or how did Mr Potter and the manager get at the sums you have mentioned? (A.) They got certain statements from me or some of the other gentlemen. (Q.) Had they anybody else at the meeting with them? (A.) No. (Q.) Had they come prepared with figures? (A.) They had no figures. (Q.) Then the figures that appear in red ink were not suggested by them? (A.) All the alterations were suggested by them. (Q.) Had they any figures to give you? (A.) Yes. (Q.) Your statement is that they mentioned sums to you which they instructed you to put into your abstract? (A.) Yes. (Q.) Were these sums which they had already jotted down, or which they had in their heads, or were they derived from an examination of the books at the time? (A.) I got certain information for them from certain of the clerks. (Q.) You mean that at that meeting they asked you for some information? (A.) Yes. (Q.) And that you went and got it? (A.) Yes. (Q.) Now, what information was that? (A.) As to the amount of the bills payable. The full amount of them was in my abstract, but they wanted information as to the separate accounts forming the gross amount of which this sum was composed. (Q.) For what purpose? (A.) It must have been in order to see if they could make any deductions from it. (Q.) Was it to see whether your sum total was correct or not? (A.) Oh, no. (Q.) You understood at the time that it was to see if they could make any deduction from it? (A.) At the time. (Q.) And you did get the details of the bills payable? (A.) Yes. (Q.) Did they make a deduction from the bills payable? (A.) They did. They deducted the £973,000. (Q.) What was the whole amount? (A.) £2,288,673, 17s. 1d. That was the amount appearing in my abstract, as taken from the books. (Q.) When did that £973,000 first appear, and what was the history of it up to 1876? (A.) It was an entry or entries made in Mr Alexander Stronach's time in June 1873. (Q.) Where was it made? (A.) First, in the private cash book, and then in the general ledger, and then in the weekly balance book. (Q.) What was it? (A.) I never got the particulars of it. (Q.) You said you were told to get the details of bills payable, and you understood the reason why they wanted the details to be that they might make some deduction from them. You also said that when you came back with the information, they directed you to deduct £973,000. Is that right? (A.) That is right. (Q.) Then what was that £973,000? (A.) You cannot reconcile the figures as any portion of the £2,288,673. (Q.) But what did the £973,000 represent? What was the original of it? (A.) It was an entry made the same as if certain bills payable had been taken out of the circle. (Q.) Who were the debtors in them? (A.) I cannot speak to that unless I saw the memorandum, which is still to be found. (Q.) Surely you know well enough what it was? (A.) No. I don't. (Q.) Well, the result was that they told you to strike out that £973,000 from bills payable, and you did so? (A.) Yes. (Q.) What was the effect of that on your abstract? (A.) To reduce the bills payable by that amount. (Q.) And the effect on the abstract was to diminish the liabilities of the Bank to that extent? (A.) To that extent. (Q.) Now, you are quite sure that you were told to do that by the manager and Mr Potter? (A.) Yes. (Q.) And did you do it in red ink? (A.) No. (Q.) Why? (A.) Because the amount was in the general ledger. (Q.) It was only the things that were not in the books that you put into red ink? (A.) Yes. (Q.) Was there anything else they told you to do? (A.) There are the three entries of Smith, Fleming, & Co., &c. These stood in my abstract as credit accounts. That was the place I thought they ought to be in. They directed me to take down £751,775 of them. They were in their right place under credit accounts, and this corresponded with the books. (Q.) What was their reason for putting that under the other head? (A.) I understood it was because they held certain stocks to that extent. (Q.) You mean that it was a good asset to the extent of the security held? (A.) Yes. (Q.) And that they thought the £751,000 represented the security? (A.) Yes. (Q.) Would that have been the right way of doing it if that had been the case, or were they not properly charged as in the credit accounts, whether there was security or no? (A.) It would have been quite right, at least I don't see anything wrong in it, had they made the entry. (Q.) Was the proper way of entering it as you did it at first? (A.) The amount was in the credit accounts ledger as at 7th June. (Q.) How were you in the habit of dealing with sums appearing in the credit accounts where there was security granted for them? (A.) The cash drawn out is simply shown. (Q.) But in your abstracts of the balances did you enter nothing under your credit account for which security was held? (A.) We understand that all credit accounts are covered by security. (Q.) Then why should the fact of there being security for this part of the credit account alter the way of stating it? (A.) I understood it was for stocks that were easily convertible into cash. (Q.) Is that any reason why it should not appear in the credit accounts? (A.) None. (Q.) Was the reason not to reduce the apparent amount of the credit accounts? (A.) It had that effect. (Q.) Was that not the object? (A.) I cannot say. (Q.) Was that not your impression? (A.) It increased the amount of advances which were easily convertible into cash, and reduced the amounts under the heading. (Q.) The effect was to reduce the apparent amount of the sums under credit accounts? (A.) That was the effect of it. (Q.) So that the shareholders should not see that that £751,000 had been advanced under credit account; that is the effect of it? (A.) That is the effect of it. (Q.) You won't say that that was the reason of it? (A.) I could not say. (Q.) Did the manager or Mr Potter suggest any other reason for it? (A.) That is the only one that I mentioned before,—that it would be brought down under the heading of stocks, thereby increasing the apparent assets under that head. (Q.) Do you know of any other instance where sums advanced on credit accounts with security were placed under that head? (A.) Not taken from credit accounts in the same way. (Q.) It is the only time you ever knew it done? (A.) The only time. (Q.) You are quite sure that that was directed by the manager and Potter? (A.) Perfectly. (Q.) Did you make that alteration in red ink? (A.) It is not made here in red ink. (Q.) Where is the alteration? (A.) [Shows.] It is just under the heading "Railway and "other stocks and debentures." It is in black ink there. (Q.) Then you say that this thing upon which the red ink marks are is not the original abstract that you made? (A.) No. (Q.) Not the one that was altered in terms of their instructions? (A.) No. (Q.) And you don't know where it is? (A.) No; I do not. (Q.) What is this [No. 127]? (A.) It is the clean copy of it. It would be made as soon after the other as I could. (Q.) You made it up and altered it in red ink yourself in order to be ready for the ultimate abstract? (A.) Yes. The red ink markings, you will observe, are simply bringing the head office abstract and the branches abstract together. (Q.) Were you told or did you understand that this conversation with the manager and Potter was to be confidential? (A.) I never was instructed so. Nothing was said to me on the subject. (Q.) You did not make any alteration on those accounts in the books that you have spoken to in consequence of what the directors or the manager had said to you in 1876? (A.) No. (Q.) But in 1877 you did not repeat in your abstract the entry of the sum of £973,300? (A.) No. (Q.) You omitted it? (A.) Yes. (Q.) Why? (A.) Because there were other sums adopted instead of it. (Q.) I want to know why you omitted the £973,300, and why you put in new sums? Were you told to do it? (A.) Yes, by Mr Stronach. I would not like to say Mr

Potter; I am not certain of that for 1877. (Q.) Had you any meeting in 1877, as you had in 1876, with the manager or Potter? (A.) I am not certain of 1877; I would not like to speak to it. (Q.) But that alteration in 1877 was made by the directions of Stronach? (A.) Yes. (Q.) And no reason was given for it? (A.) No. (Q.) Are you sure? (A.) There was no special reason given for it. (Q.) But the effect was that these sums were entered in the book and substantially filled up the amount of the £973,300, although apparently under different heads? (A.) Quite so. (Q.) Did these new sums represent any new transactions? (A.) Yes; a certain amount deducted from the bills payable. (Q.) But the sums which you put in in order to deduct it from the bills payable, did they represent any real debts? You said yesterday they were not altogether fictitious. (A.) The first amount deducted was cash lodged on credit account, £94,368, 14s. 1d. (Q.) I don't want you to go through the whole of it, but the effect was that £1,333,000 was deducted from the bills payable instead of the £973,000? (A.) Yes. (Q.) Next year the £973,000 was restored, and this sum of £1,333,000 disappeared from the abstract? (A.) Yes. (Q.) All that was by direction of the manager. (A.) Yes. (Q.) With regard to the cross entries, the sum of £973,300 appears on both sides of the account? (A.) Yes. (Q.) What is the effect of that? (A.) It reduces the amount of the indebtedness of the Bank to that extent, and on the other hand it reduces the amount of the assets. (Q.) They balance each other? (A.) Yes. (Q.) But if they are correct entries, you say they are rightly entered in the abstract? (A.) They are in the abstract because they are in the general ledger. (Q.) What was the general effect of the alterations in 1876 on the position of the Bank? (A.) By putting in the balance, or balances rather, of the deposit accounts, and the balance of the credit accounts, reducing on the one side the assets of the Bank, and on the other the liabilities. The £973,300 entry did the same on both sides. (Q.) It was to show a smaller amount of assets, and a smaller amount of liabilities than the actual fact? (A.) Yes. (Q.) Not affecting, however, the profit and loss account? (A.) No. Of course the £751,000 entry did not alter the liabilities at all. (Q.) With regard to securities, I suppose that sums that were fully covered are entered as assets in the credit accounts? (A.) They are entered whether they are secured or not. (Q.) Then what notice do you take of securities in your abstracts—in your balances? (A.) They are not referred to at all; there are simply the figures given. (Q.) When a debt is wholly unsecured, and the debtor is not supposed to be good for it, it goes into bad or doubtful debts, I suppose? (A.) It should do. (Q.) Or suspense account? (A.) Or suspense account. (Q.) But no notice is ever taken of securities in the abstract? (A.) No. There is a register of securities, but I do not consult it in making up my abstract. I have no concern with it whatever. (Q.) Therefore, whether there were or were not securities for the sums you have been speaking to you had no means of knowing? (A.) None. (Q.) Could you have ascertained from the securities' book, if you had chosen, whether there was security for the £973,300? (A.) If the law secretary had shown me the book, but I don't know that he would have shown it to me. The book was in his custody.

CHARLES SAMUEL LERESCHE.

By Solicitor-General—I have been secretary of the City of Glasgow Bank since 1870. I was appointed in October 1870, and took charge in December. The directors at the time I was appointed were Mr Inglis, Mr Potter, Mr Salmond, Mr Alexander Stronach, Mr Lorraine, and Mr James Nicol Fleming. Mr Alexander Stronach resigned as a director and also as the manager of the Bank in 1875, and he was succeeded as manager by his brother Robert, who was a director *ex officio*. Mr Lorraine died shortly after I entered the Bank, in the beginning of 1871. Mr Mackinnon had retired from the Bank a few months prior to my entering, and there were two directors elected shortly before the next annual meeting. They were Mr Stewart and Mr Taylor. I could not tell from memory when James Nicol Fleming retired, but he was succeeded by Mr Wright. My predecessor as secretary was Mr Low, who is now dead. When I entered on my duties in 1870, Mr Alexander Stronach spoke to me in a very marked manner, and told me that my predecessor, Mr Low, had made himself obnoxious to the directors by pushing himself forward, and asking for information about accounts which were in no way connected with his department, and that the feeling was so strong at the last that a letter which he had handed in to the board in connection with these matters the directors had refused to receive. (Q.) What effect had that on you or on your course of conduct after you became secretary? (A.) Mr Stronach spoke to me very plainly, and told me it was his own wish, as also the wish of the directors, that I should just confine myself to my own department. The duties of the office of secretary were to take charge of the general correspondence of the Bank; to keep the minute book of the directors, and to enter therein the minute of the weekly meeting of the board; to take charge of certain properties in the Western States of America in which the Bank at that time was largely interested; and to answer inquiries from correspondents as to the financial position of local firms. The meetings of the directors were held once a week. There was an agenda book kept, in which the business to be done was put on the one side, and the deliverance upon it in a rough form on the other. [Shown Nos. 554 and 556.] No. 554 is the agenda book commencing on 30th July 1874, and No. 556 is the agenda book commencing on 7th December 1876, and coming down to the date of the closing of the Bank. [Shown Nos. 100 and 101.] These are the minute books applicable to the period from 1st December 1870, when the first of them commences, down to the closing of the Bank. The usual course of proceeding with regard to business to be brought before these meetings was that I went down to the manager on the morning of each Thursday, and would ask him what business he would have to bring before the board that day. He would tell me whether there were any letters of credit or cash credits or anything connected with the branches, whatever the business was; and he would give me the letters and any papers connected therewith. I would take these and commence entering them in the agenda book, and afterwards bring the book with them to the meeting. After the meeting, those letters that were connected with letters of credit, such as Smith, Fleming, and Co.'s, I would generally take in to Mr Morris; and sometimes I would take them back, and leave them with the manager. Mr Morris was the private secretary of the manager. Where it is stated in any of the minutes that a letter was read, it was the practice when I was present really to have the letter read. That was always done. It was my duty as secretary to be present at the meetings. The names of the directors present at the meetings were generally put down in the agenda book by the chairman for the time being. I see from the agenda book that the directors present at the meeting on 23d December 1875, were Mr Taylor, Mr Stewart, Mr Wright, Mr Inglis, and Mr Salmond. Mr Robert Stronach, who was then assistant manager, was also present. Mr Taylor was the chairman. I remember about that meeting. (Q.) What was the usual concluding part of the business at these meetings? (A.) The reading of what was called the abstracts and statements. (Q.) Was there not the burning of notes which were to be cancelled? (A.) That was done at any time. (Q.) When that required to be done was it not the last piece of formal business? (A.) Yes. (Q.) On that occasion, 23d December 1875, were there notes which ought to have been burned? (A.) Yes. (Q.) What happened when that item of business came on? (A.) So far as I can remember, when these notes came forward to be burned they would say to me "We "will not take these up this week; we have some matters to talk over, and "it can be postponed for another week." I would then retire from the meeting. (Q.) Was it at their request that you retired? (A.) It was never said in so many words, but the usual custom was, after I had finished reading the abstracts and statements, I would say to the chairman, "That is all the "business I have to bring forward," and the chairman would bow me out, and I would retire. It was an understood custom. When there was nothing else to be done, I would take the agenda book away with me; but on other occasions they would say they had some matters to talk over, and would ask me to leave the agenda book. That was done on 23d December 1875. I would be called in afterwards. [Shown No. 206.] That is a letter which was handed to me when I came back, and which I was instructed to have engrossed in the minutes. It is a letter from Mr Alexander Stronach containing his resignation on account of ill-health. At the meeting on 30th December 1875, there were present, Mr Taylor, Mr Potter, Mr Stewart, Mr Salmond, Mr Inglis, and Mr Wright. Mr Alexander Stronach having retired, that was the whole board at that time. On that occasion the burning of notes was again adjourned, and I again left the room, but I cannot say whether I left the agenda book behind me or not. The board had a long deliberation that day. I should say it must have been two hours.

By the Lord Justice-Clerk—(Q.) Are you speaking from recollection alone? (A.) I remember it, because December 30th was the occasion when the letter of the manager was read accepting the appointment.

By the Solicitor-General—[Shown Nos. 208 and 209.] When I came back the letter No. 208 and the corresponding envelope No. 209 were handed to me by the chairman, who was Mr Taylor. It is a letter from Mr Robert Stronach to the directors. [Letter read.]

"City of Glasgow Bank, Glasgow, 28th December 1875.

"The Chairman and Directors of the
"City of Glasgow Bank.

"Gentlemen,—In thanking you for the offer of the managership of this Bank "which you have kindly made to me, I beg to state my willingness to accept it. "But before undertaking this responsibility, I deem it prudent to ask the board to "minute its approval of the policy which has been pursued of supporting several "accounts of an unsatisfactory character since my brother discontinued personally "to manage the Bank; and further, to appoint a committee to investigate and "place on record what may be found to have been the exact position of these ac- "counts and advances generally when my brother ceased to be manager,—and also "to act and guide me in any important detail therewith connected, as I am in no "wise responsible up to this date for the state of certain advances which I need not "here particularise.

"You will, I hope, admit the reasonableness of the precaution which this request "involves; and I feel you will the more readily do this when you consider that "whilst we are all hopeful that those advances may eventuate without loss, yet the "working out of them must of necessity be a work of some time. And when you "also consider that there may be changes in the board during this time, and I "should have to explain to new directors what you know regarding my connection "with the inception of these advances.—I am, gentlemen, your most obedient "servant, "R. S. STRONACH."

(Q.) Since that letter was read to the board of directors there has been no change in the directorate? The gentlemen who sat that day, with the exception of Mr Robert Stronach, are the gentlemen at the bar? (A.) Yes. Mr Stronach's name is not in the agenda book that day, but I see from the minute book that he was present. [Shown No. 205.] (Q.) Is that a draft resolution which was handed to you by the chairman on the same occasion after you were recalled? (A.) Yes. The first part of it is in Mr Taylor's, and the last of it in Mr Inglis's handwriting. It is—"A letter was read from Mr Robert Summers Stronach, of "date 28th December 1875, accepting the office of manager of the Bank, "and the same having been considered *and approved of*, is ordered to be "recorded in the minute book, and appoint all the members of the board of "directors a committee to comply with his request. The directors wish also "to record on their own behalf the fact that the matters alluded to in the "letter in question were not at any time brought before them by their late "manager." The three words "and approved of" in the first part of the document are also in Mr Inglis' handwriting, besides the part at the end. In the agenda book, under date 18th February 1875, there is an entry—"Appoint Messrs Potter and Salmond a committee to assist the manager in "arranging the securities and advances connected with the late firm of James "N. Fleming & Co., Calcutta, and Smith, Fleming, & Co., London, "with full powers." (Q.) Was that deliverance agreed to in your hearing, or after you had retired? (A.) After I had retired. (Q.) Was it handed to you to be entered? (A.) On this occasion I would be called up. That deliverance in the agenda book is in Mr Taylor's handwriting. Being referred to agenda book under date 1st June 1876,—there were present that day Mr Taylor, Mr Potter, Mr Salmond, Mr Inglis, Mr Wright, and the manager. There is an entry on the right-hand page, near the bottom, as follows:—"The committee appointed February 18, 1875, to look into the "accounts of Smith, Fleming, & Co., and J. N. Fleming & Co., reported that "they had seen that these accounts had been put into shape." That entry was made by me. I was told to make it. Mr Taylor was chairman. (Q.) Did he tell you to record it? (A.) No; my recollection is that Mr Potter said the committee had looked into these accounts, and had put them into order, and he wished to have that recorded; and this minute I took down probably from what Mr Potter said. (Q.) You heard Mr Potter make that statement, but do you remember whether the direction was given more specially than that, or not? (A.) It was just given verbally,—"We wish to "have that inserted in the minutes." It was inserted in the minutes from the agenda book. I did not ask that a draft should be made out; I just wrote it down. That deliverance is engrossed in the minute book of the directors of the same date. In the agenda book on 22d June 1876, the sederunt is Mr Taylor, chairman, Messrs Stewart, Wright, and Potter, and the manager. The last item of business on the left-hand page is "Appoint-"ment of committee to examine into the old accounts." The corresponding entry in the minutes of 22d June is engrossed as follows:—"It was resolved "to appoint Messrs Taylor and Potter a committee to examine into certain "old accounts of the Bank, and to assist the manager in arranging these "under one general heading, with full power." I cannot tell how that matter came up at the meeting of 22d June; it came up after I retired. Either the book had been left, or I had brought up the book. (Q.) Do you remember the manager saying anything while you were present on that occasion to the effect that he wished those old accounts looked into? (A.) I do remember now. I would write this in probably just at the time when I was at the meeting. I do not recollect anything more that took place on that occasion. The manager was desirous that certain old accounts of the Bank should be looked into. (Q.) It was on the suggestion of the manager that the committee was appointed? (A.) Yes. (Q.) Was any specification given of the accounts referred to, or were they just spoken of in that way? (A.) Just in a general way. In the agenda book, under date 13th July 1876, there were present Messrs Inglis, Potter, Taylor, Stewart, and Wright. The sederunt is taken in pencil by myself; it had been omitted by the chairman. [Shown No. 213.] That is a letter by Mr Scott, marked "Private," and addressed to Mr Stronach, dated 12th July 1876. It was read at the meeting of the 13th. Mr Scott is a partner of John Innes Wright & Co. "J. I. W. and Co." in that letter is intended for John Innes Wright & Co. The deliverance of the board upon that letter, in the agenda book, is in the handwriting of Mr Inglis, and it is as follows:—"Mr Potter and Mr Wright "appointed a committee with full powers to confer with the manager as to "the proposed re-arrangement, which is considered an advisable step; the "committee to report to the board when they consider necessary." The Mr Wright there referred to, and appointed a member of the committee, is a member of the firm of John Innes Wright & Co. In the agenda book, under date 3d August 1876, there were present Mr Stewart, chairman, Messrs Potter, Wright, and Taylor, and the manager. [Shown Nos. 214, letter, W. Glen Walker & Co. to J. Innes Wright, dated 26th July 1876, and 215 and 216.] No. 215 is a letter from John Innes Wright & Co., dated 2d August 1876. I cannot say in whose handwriting it is; it appears to be in the same handwriting as the letter read at the previous meeting. That was the first piece of business that followed upon Mr Scott's letter as to establishing a new firm. No. 216 is a letter from Mr James Morton, dated 2d August, produced and read at that meeting. (Q.) Was there any discussion of these letters in your hearing, or were they simply handed to you to be engrossed? (A.) They were simply handed to me to be put up with the other letters referred to. In the agenda book, under date 17th August 1876, there were present Mr Stewart, chairman, Messrs Wright, Taylor, and Potter, and the manager. [Shown Nos. 217, 218, two letters, W. Glen Walker to R. Stronach, dated 14th August 1876, and 219, letter, James Morton to the Bank, dated 16th August 1876.] These are letters which are referred to in the agenda book, under the date of that meeting, at the foot of the left-hand page. I do not remember hearing those letters read at that meeting. [Shown No. 198.] That is a draft resolution, dated 21st August 1876, in the handwriting of Mr Robert Stronach, the manager. (Q.) Was that handed to you by the manager? (A.) Yes; my recollection of it is that I was called down some days after the meeting of the 17th into the manager's room, and I was handed this draft resolution. I was asked to bring my agenda book down, and enter it therein as under the date of the 17th. So far as I recollect, Mr Taylor and Mr Inglis were present when Mr Stronach handed it to me; and my memory is confirmed by the fact that there are in Mr Taylor's handwriting the words "Read and agreed to," and in Mr Inglis' handwriting, "Insert in minutes deliverance of Board." (Q.) So you have no doubt that those two gentlemen were the two who were present? (A.) That is the impression I have at present. The words at the side of the memorandum, "As referred to in the minute of 30th December 1875," and "as referred to," are in my handwriting. The whole of the body of it is in the handwriting of Mr Stronach, except two lines which come in, "And "previously brought under the consideration of the Board by the present "manager," which is in the handwriting of Mr Inglis. In the minutes of 17th August, that memorandum is engrossed in full as I got it. There were present—Messrs Stewart, Wright, Taylor, Potter, and Stronach. That minute was approved of at next meeting, at which were present—Mr Inglis, chairman, Messrs Potter, Stewart, Salmond, Wright, Taylor, and Stronach. Referring to the agenda book, under date 24th August 1876, the ordinary business of that day closed with the appointment of an agent at the Brechin branch. (Q.) How do you know that? (A.) In this instance there are the initials of the chairman, Mr Inglis. Then there follows—"Report by John Innes "Wright and Lewis Potter in connection with deliverance at meeting of 13th "July." [Shown Nos. 192 and 193.] No. 192 is the report, and No. 193 is the envelope in which it was kept. I was not present when that report was brought before the meeting and considered; I had left after the business of the Brechin branch was over. It was afterwards handed to me to be engrossed. On 19th October there were present—Messrs Inglis, Potter, Salmond, Stewart, Wright, and Taylor, and the manager. There is a note in the agenda book in the following terms:—"Referred to manager, after having heard the observations of the Board." That is in the handwriting of Mr Inglis. (Q.) What was it about which observations had been made by the Board—you heard them? (A.) I believe I did, in this case. (Q.) Was it the credits of Smith, Fleming, & Co? [No reply.] [Shown Nos. 194 and 195.] No. 194 is a report by Messrs Taylor, Stewart, and Potter; it must have been handed in in a rough draft by them at that meeting. (Q.) Was the report handed to you afterwards in the form in which you see it there? (A.) My recollection of this is that it was a rough draft report which was handed in, and I was asked to copy it fair, which I did. It is in my handwriting. After it was written out from the rough scroll it was signed by Messrs Taylor, Stewart, and Potter. No. 195 is the envelope in which it was. (Q.) Does that recall to your recollection what was the matter that was referred to the manager on 19th October? Look at the agenda book; does that bring it to your recollection? (A.) I do not know it has any connection with this. (Q.) Had you to retire from that meeting? (A.) I cannot recollect anything in regard to this particular credit of Smith, Fleming, & Co. In the agenda book, under date 11th January 1877, there were present—Messrs Inglis (chairman), Potter, Salmond, Stewart, Wright, and Taylor, and the manager. The ordinary business of that meeting was closed by a letter from Mr Bain, and the initials of Mr Inglis are after that piece of business. The Board remained in deliberation after that for a considerable time. (Q.) A long time? (A.) Yes. I was called in, and a draft resolution was handed to me to be entered in the book. I cannot recollect in whose handwriting it was; probably it was in that of Mr Inglis. (Q.) It was not preserved? (A.) I have no knowledge of it. On the left-hand side, in the agenda book, is an entry—"Morton's account"—in the handwriting of Mr Inglis. It is put in as a separate piece of business from what had been made up by me for the use of the meeting. Morton's account was never spoken of in my presence. On 18th January 1877 Morton's account appears again. Mr Inglis was in the chair, and there were also present—Messrs Inglis, Potter, Taylor, Wright, and the manager. I was not present then when Morton's account was taken up. On 8th March 1877 there were present—Mr Inglis, chairman; Messrs Potter, Salmond, Stewart, Wright, and Taylor. An application of Smith, Fleming, & Co. for credit was brought up that day. (Q.) Were you present when that was discussed? (A.) I think I must have been. [After a short pause] No; the probability is, I should not have been present at that time. (Q.) Were you ever present at the discussion of credits of Smith, Fleming, & Co? (A.) Yes; I was present at the discussion of many of those to Law, Brown, & Co., and also to ———. I wish to say about this, that on reconsideration I believe I would be present at this meeting when this credit was brought up. (Q.) On 8th March? (A.) Yes; when Smith, Fleming, & Co.'s was brought up.

By the Lord Justice-Clerk—I was generally present when an application from Smith, Fleming, & Co., for a cash credit was discussed. I never was present when there was such an application from Morton, or Wright & Co., and never heard any discussion about that. That may be taken as applicable to all the minutes. I think on this occasion I must have been present, because I do not remember a credit to Law, Brown, & Co., when I was not present.

By the Solicitor-General—I remember the meeting of 21st June 1877, when the accounts for the year were taken up, and the dividend for 1877 was fixed. I was not present when the dividend was fixed. The dividend was increased 1 per cent. as compared with the previous year. It had been 11 per cent. in 1876, and it was raised to 12 per cent. (Q.) Was there a discussion upon that matter in private that day? (A.) The only knowledge I have about it is that the manager said he was going to bring up, on the morning of 21st June, the annual returns for the year to 6th June, and asked me to put that into the agenda book, but that he would not bring up the other statements as to the annual report as usual. At that meeting on 21st June, Messrs Inglis, Potter, Salmond, Stewart, Wright, and Taylor, and the manager, were present. I got from the manager, after they had met in private, the details necessary to enable me to make out the minute.

Fourth Day—Thursday, 23d January 1879.

CHARLES SAMUEL LERESCHÉ *(recalled).*

By the Solicitor-General—[Shown Nos. 235, 236, and 237]. No. 235 is a letter from W. C. Smith to Kinross & Co., dated 18th September 1877; No. 236, a letter from W. C. Smith to John Hunter, 20th September 1877; and No. 237, a letter from W. C. Smith to C. Smith, 28th September 1877. These three letters were read at the meeting of directors on 8th November 1877. The letters related to purchases of land in New Zealand. At the meeting on 26th July 1877, I see from the agenda book that Mr Stewart was chairman, and Mr Potter, Mr Inglis, Mr Wright, Mr Taylor, Mr Salmond, and the manager were present,—a full board. That was not the first meeting at which anything took place as to the purchase of property in New Zealand or Australia. That had been referred to as early as 17th August of the previous year. At the meeting on 26th July 1877, there was a deliberation by the directors, at which I was not present. There is an entry in the agenda book in the handwriting of Mr Inglis—" Purchase of property in New Zealand and Australia." When I was called in, I received a draft resolution which I would be instructed to engross in the book, and it is initialed by the chairman. It is as follows:

" With reference to the purchase of property in New Zealand and Australia, " an authority was given to Mr Potter, Mr Stewart, and the manager, on the " 21st June last, in the following terms:

" ' City of Glasgow Bank,
" ' Glasgow, 21st June 1877.

" ' Dear Sir,—As authorised by the meeting of directors held of this date, " ' you will be so good as instruct Messrs Potter & Stewart, two of our number, " ' to purchase freehold land in New Zealand, on behalf of this Bank, to the " ' extent of £50,000.

" ' Yours truly,
" ' HENRY INGLIS, Chairman.

" ' Robert Stronach, Esq., Manager;" '
" and on more mature consideration it was resolved that the power to purchase " land should be extended to Australia, and the sum to be invested in behalf " of the Bank to be increased, if considered necessary, by them and by Mr " Taylor, whose name is added as formerly to this acting committee, to " £100,000. These resolutions are adopted as a sequence to the board's " minute of 17th August 1876. The usual abstracts and statements were read " to the board." [Shown No. 230.] That is a letter of 29th August 1877, from Mr Glen Walker to the manager, which was read at the meeting of 30th August 1877.

" The Manager of " Glasgow, 29th Augt. 1877.
" The City of Glasgow Bank,
" Glasgow.

" Dear Sir,—A week ago I had a telegram from my partner, asking that the City " Bank should request the agency of the Commercial Banking Company of Sydney

"—address, 39 Lombard Street, London—to wire to Sydney an extension of the "credits which remain in the colony, and which expire about this time.

"There will be considerable sums to pay, for a/c of the recent purchase, and my "partner's only resource is these credits.

"Please, therefore, do not delay arranging that this credit be extended, or that it "be allowed to lapse, and a new one wired through the Bank referred to.

"You know my partner is not much accustomed to finance, and should be kept "—strong. If a new credit be sent, I think it better be for £20,000.—I am, faith-"fully yours,

"W. GLEN WALKER."

Mr Stewart (chairman), Mr Potter, Mr Wright, and the manager were present at that meeting. At the meeting on 6th September 1877, Mr Stewart (chairman), Mr Potter, Mr Inglis, Mr Wright, and Mr Taylor were present. (Q.) Was anything brought up by any one at that meeting about further investments in New Zealand or Australia? (A.) Yes. (Q.) By whom? (A.) By Mr Potter. I was present. (Q.) What was suggested? (A.) Mr Potter just said that the committee considered it advisable to authorise a further sum of £150,000 to be invested in property in New Zealand or Australia, and requested that that should be minuted, and I took it down from their dictation. (Q.) Was there any discussion before it was agreed to? (A.) No; the chairman just said, "I suppose that this is agreed to." That was all that passed. It was put down as agreed to. Mr Potter dictated the minute. The minute is—"It was considered advisable to authorise the committee to invest a further "sum of £150,000 in property in New Zealand or Australia. This investment, "in addition to the sums already authorised, will now therefore amount to "about £400,000; and this, in addition to the interest of about £100,000 "already held, completes an investment to about £500,000—say five hun-"dred thousand pounds." On 1st November 1877, there were present Mr Stewart (chairman), Mr Potter, Mr Wright, Mr Inglis, and the manager. I was absent from the meeting when some deliberation took place in connection with these properties. [Shown No. 196]. That is the report signed by Messrs Inglis, Taylor, and Salmond, which is engrossed in that minute. On 15th November 1877, there were present Mr Stewart (chairman), Mr Potter, Mr Salmond, Mr Inglis, Mr Wright, Mr Taylor, and the manager. I was absent from the meeting during the latter part of it, when they were deliberating on the New Zealand matters. Afterwards I was called in, and recorded the deliverance. (Q.) After you had engrossed the board's deliverance about the New Zealand and Australian advances, did the manager say anything in your hearing to the directors? (A.) Yes. He said he wished that a committee of the whole board should sit periodically to consider the various accounts of the Bank. (Q.) Did you hear what passed on that suggestion? (A.) Yes. It was agreed to, and I then entered in this resolution—"It was resolved "that a committee of the whole board should sit periodically to consider the "position of the various accounts of the Bank." A conversation then arose as to whether the manager wished this to be done at once, and a suggestion was made that it should begin six months afterwards. (Q.) Who said that? (A.) I cannot remember who said it. (Q.) Was it Mr Stronach or some one else? (A.) It would not be Mr Stronach. It would be one of the directors; and afterwards it was suggested, so far as I can recollect, by Mr Taylor, that it should be four months. (Q.) What was to be done in four months? (A.) The looking into these securities. (Q.) The sitting of this committee? (A.) Yes. (Q.) And accordingly it was minuted—"This not to take place for "four months?" (A.) No, I think that took place afterwards. (Q.) I was referring to what appears in the agenda book, while I think you are referring to the minute book. Would you read what is written in the agenda book? (A.) It says, "This is not to take place for four months." (Q.) In whose handwriting is that entry in the agenda book—"It was resolved that a com-"mittee of the whole board should sit periodically to consider the position "of the various accounts of the Bank?" (A.) It looks like Mr Taylor's handwriting. (Q.) That entry is—"It was resolved that a committee of the "whole board should sit periodically to consider the position of the various "accounts of the Bank. This not to take place for four months?" (A.) Yes. (Q.) How was the entry made in the minute book? (A.) It was entered in the minute book—"It was resolved that a committee of the whole "board should sit periodically to consider the position of the various accounts "of the Bank." I put nothing more in it, and then the usual abstract and statements were read to the board. I did not put in that part of it about the four months, but when the minute came before the board at their meeting on the 22d, they said it was agreed that that should not take place for four months. I gave some explanation that I thought that was more an understanding than a resolution, but they told me I had better engross it, and therefore it appears as it was entered afterwards. (Q.) That was inserted on revisal? (A.) Yes. It says—"The committee of inquiry above mentioned will meet "not later than four months from this date." (Q.) When did that committee meet for the first time? (A.) I have no knowledge of that committee meeting. About four months from that date, I think you will find that there was another committee formed. (Q.) You don't know of your own knowledge whether that committee met or not? (A.) No. (Q.) On 28th February 1878, there was a discussion in private that day,—I mean a discussion at which you were not present,—with regard to Innes Wright & Co.'s affairs? (A.) Yes. A draft was afterwards handed to me to be put in. It was handed to me on the Wednesday before the following meeting,—after they had deliberated in private,—and it was in the handwriting of the manager. Referring to the minute of meeting of 21st March 1878, I find there a reference to a committee appointed on Morton's account. (Q.) Had any such committee been appointed when you were present at the previous meeting, or were the instructions to write the minute given to you afterwards? (A.) This here would be given me probably after the meeting. (Q.) But you were not present? (A.) No; I would be called up and would engross it at the time, as it is initialed. Being referred to minute of 30th May 1878, and shown No. 191c,—that is a letter from Mr Stronach, the manager, to John Fleming of London, dated 23d May 1878. (Q.) Was that letter brought up at the meeting while you were there on the 30th? (A.) Yes. (Q.) Was that letter, or any answer to it by Mr John Fleming, brought up while you were present? (A.) I do not recollect that I was present then. On 6th June 1878 the minute bears that proceedings took place in regard to Innes Wright & Co.'s accounts. I was not present when Innes Wright & Co.'s affairs were discussed that day. On 20th June, what appears in the agenda book, and is recorded in the minute, took place after I had left the meeting. A rough memorandum was given to me, as had been done on former occasions. In the minute of 1st August 1878 a resolution appears as having been formed on that date. That was done after the formal business had been brought to a close, and the agenda book initialed. I was not present at what appears after the initials of the chairman; that was just given me to enter in. Since I was appointed secretary I have regularly attended the annual meetings of the shareholders, at which the election of the directors took place. I kept the minute book containing the reports of the annual meetings. That is No. 102 of the inventory. It contains a correct record by me of what passed at the meetings, up to the date of the last annual meeting. The minute is subscribed by the chairman, and the copy of the report is subscribed by all the directors. I never was present at any discussion that took place in regard to advances that had been made to James Nicol Fleming. I never was present at any discussion that took place in regard to advances that had been made to John Innes Wright & Co. I never was present at any discussion in regard to

James Morton & Co.'s advances. (Q.) You said yesterday that you were present when Smith, Fleming, & Co.'s affairs came up; were you ever present when any discussion took place in regard to their existing debts to the company, or was it only in regard to proposed new credits? (A.) I don't remember saying that. (Q.) I think you said you were present when Smith, Fleming, & Co.'s accounts came up? (A.) No; when the applications of Smith, Fleming & Co. for those letters of credit came up, I was generally present. I never was present when any discussion or deliberation took place in reference to the state of Smith, Fleming, & Co.'s account. (Q.) On those occasions when the board deliberated in private, and you afterwards were called in or received a draft to insert, did the sederunt of the meeting remain the same during the private deliberations? (A.) I cannot speak to that. (Q.) Do you remember on any occasion when you were recalled of the sederunt being different from what it was when you opened the meeting? I do not ask you to speak to every individual case, but was it usual that the whole board remained for those private deliberations after you retired? (A.) Yes, it was usual; that is, I would leave the whole of the board there. There were some exceptions, in the case, for instance, of Mr Taylor. He had to attend some insurance meeting on the same day, the Thursday, and he may have had to go away on many occasions. [Shown Nos. 604, 605, and 606.] These are the annual reports by the directors of the Bank to the shareholders for the years 1876, 1877, and 1878. These are prints which were circulated by me as secretary as the annual report of the directors. [Shown No. 95.] That is the cashier's ledger, commencing 6th June 1866. Being referred to the slip fastened into the board of the book, stating the amount of cash under date 5th June 1878,—that slip is initialed by Mr Stewart. The entry is dated 5th June 1878, and is as follows:—

"Cash in cashier's hands—	
"£100 notes,	£68,000
"£5, "	163,500
"£1, "	190,000
"Gold,	338,500
"Total,	£760,000"

Below there is a detail of the gold as follows:—

"In original safe,	£149,000
"In new safe below,	62,500
"In new safe above,	109,000
"In new safe, top,	18,000
"Total,	£338,500"

That memorandum is in the handwriting of Mr Turnbull, the cashier. Mr Stewart's initials in the first of these statements are placed to each item, so far as the notes are concerned, but apparently not to the gold; but they are placed to each item of the gold in the detailed list.

By Mr Trayner—[Shown cashier's ledger.] That book is kept by Mr Turnbull, the cashier. Being referred to page 376, I see there an entry of the money as ending 5th June 1878. That corresponds exactly with the statement initialed by Mr Stewart, to which I have been already referred—£338,500. The next entry beginning the account, cash in hand as at the year beginning 6th June 1878, commences again with that exact sum.

By Mr Balfour—(Q.) You were asked with regard to the agenda for 18th February 1875, and you read a note as to what was to be brought before that meeting: I should like to ask your attention to the terms of the whole of that minute? (A.) It is as follows:—"Notice of dissolution of partnership "between James Nicol Fleming and William Grant, under the firm of J. "Nicol Fleming & Co., Calcutta, having been reported to the board, it was "resolved to appoint Messrs Potter and Salmond a committee to assist the "manager in arranging the securities and advances connected with the late "firm of J. Nicol Fleming & Co., Calcutta, and Smith, Fleming, & Co., "London, with full powers." I saw from the documents given to the Bank that there had been a dissolution at that time, which made such a re-arrangement necessary. That was the cause of this re-arrangement.

By Mr Asher—Being referred to the agenda book, I observe that the sederunt of 1st June 1876 includes the name of Mr Salmond. The date of the next meeting at which his name is entered as present is 20th July 1876. There had been meetings in the interval on 8th, 22d, and 28th June, and 5th and 13th July, at none of which Mr Salmond was present. The meetings last mentioned were the meetings at which the business connected with the annual balance was dealt with. Mr Salmond was again absent on 3d and 17th August following. Looking at the same book for 1877, I find that Mr Salmond was absent on 18th January, 7th and 14th June, 12th July, 30th August, 6th September, 1st and 29th November. In 1878 he was absent on 10th January and 28th March. He was present on 16th May. The next meeting after that at which he was present was 11th of July. Between May 16th and July 11th, there had been meetings on 23d and 30th May, and 6th, 20th, and 27th June, from all of which he was absent. These last mentioned meetings were the meetings at which the business connected with the annual balance was transacted. The sederunt was noted in the agenda book by the chairman. (Q.) When business connected with your department had been transacted, you were in the habit, you told us, of withdrawing from the meeting? (A.) Yes, after I had read the abstracts and statements. (Q.) With regard to any business in the agenda book not connected with your department,—I suppose you cannot say whether all the directors mentioned in the sederunt continued to be present when that was being done? (A.) I cannot say that. (Q.) In short, with regard to the directors who were present, your sole means for giving evidence here is that you find their names noted in the sederunt in the agenda book? (A.) Yes. (Q.) To what extent they took part in the business noted in the agenda book, or whether they were present throughout the whole meeting or only a part, of course you are unable to say? (A.) I am unable to say. (Q.) It was the custom of the Bank board to divide the business to some extent amongst the directors. Can you tell me which of the directors were the committee on branches during 1876, 1877, and 1878? (A.) There was no committee formed to my knowledge during those years. (Q.) Was there not an acting committee during those years—a standing committee? (A.) No, I have no knowledge of that. (Q.) Perhaps that was not within your department? (A.) There was no minute of it. (Q.) But if there had been a committee appointed before these years which continued to act, that would not fall within your knowledge, I suppose? You would have nothing to do with it, unless it was in the minutes? (A.) Nothing to do with it except it was in the minutes. (Q.) There was no meeting of the directors, I suppose, at some part of which you were not present? You were always present, I suppose, at some part of their meetings? (A.) Except during my holidays. (Q.) You prepared a note of the business, I believe, which came before each meeting of the directors? (A.) Yes. (Q.) The directors met weekly, on Thursdays, at twelve o'clock? (A.) Yes. (Q.) So that you were familiar with the regular business that came before each meeting of the directors? (A.) Yes. (Q.) Had you any knowledge that there was anything wrong with the Bank until its suspension? (A.) I had no knowledge at all that there was anything wrong with the Bank until a few days before the suspension.

By Mr Mackintosh—(Q.) You mentioned that Mr Taylor was in the way of leaving your meetings to attend insurance meetings? (A.) Occasionally he was. (Q.) Was not that the case very generally? (A.) I could not remember of it myself more than four or five times. (Q.) But it may have been oftener? (A.) It may have been oftener; some of our meetings were short. My recollection is that his insurance meeting was held at one o'clock; our meeting was held at twelve. Our office was in Virginia Street; his insurance company was, I think, the Scottish Imperial: their office is in West George Street, about ten minutes' walk distant.

By Mr Robertson—(Q.) You have been referred to the meeting of 15th November 1877, already read. If you go on four months, that brings you to the middle of March 1878. Look at the minute of 14th March 1878; at the end of it you will see this—"In connection with the minute of 15th November last, it was agreed that Messrs Stewart, Potter, and Salmond be appointed a committee, along with the manager, to examine the advance accounts at head office weekly, and to deal in particular with the account of Messrs James Morton & Co."? (A.) Yes. (Q.) Were you present when that resolution was adopted? (A.) No. (Q.) But as matter of fact, was there ever any committee of the whole board sitting on that subject to your knowledge at this time, or did not the resolution of March 1878 supersede so far the resolution of November 1877? (A.) This was given to me after the meeting to be entered. It must have been some days after the meeting. The probability is that it would be as late as,—I think myself it was even on the Thursday of the next meeting. (Q.) But my question is, as matter of fact, no committee of the whole board sat on that subject to carry out the the resolution of 15th November? (A.) Not to my knowledge.

By the Dean of Faculty—(Q.) You have read the minute of 18th February 1875, where notice is taken of the dissolution of partnership between James Nicol Fleming and William Grant, and arrangements were made to appoint a committee to assist the manager in arranging the securities and advances connected with the late firm of J. Nicol Fleming & Co., Calcutta. Do you know that an agreement was entered into during the same year—1875—in the month of August, between the Bank and Smith, Fleming, & Co., of Calcutta and London, whereby their account was put upon a new and distinct footing? (A.) I have no knowledge of that, except from seeing it referred to in the minute book. (Q.) You do see it referred to in the books? (A.) I think I have seen it in the minute book, but I have no knowledge of it myself. [Shown Nos. 188 and 189.] No. 189 is a letter dated 26th; the rest of the date is torn off. No. 188 is a letter dated 24th August 1875, signed by Smith, Fleming, & Co., John Fleming, R. M'Ilwraith, and W. Nicol, and there is a schedule of properties that follows. (Q.) The opening passage of that letter begins—"Referring to the interview which the writer had," &c.; then there is a long agreement, consisting of no less than ten articles, whereby you see that Smith, Fleming, & Co. agree to pay 3½ per cent. for their account, and to hand over various securities, of which there is a schedule appended. (A.) Yes, I see that under Article No. 6A they are to pay interest at the rate of 3½ per cent. per annum upon the £100,000 as aforesaid. (Q.) Then the next item is to pay the whole surplus interest arising from the stock, after meeting the charge for interest as above, to the credit of our account with the Bank, and in the event of a sale to apply the proceeds first in liquidation of the foresaid advance of £100,000, the whole of the surplus over and above the said advance being put to the credit of our account with the Bank? (A.) Yes. (Q.) I am putting these questions with reference to the transference of the account in August 1875 from the cheque box to the accountant's office. If you will turn to the end of the letter, after the signatures of Smith, Fleming, & Co. and their partners, you will find a schedule of property belonging to Smith, Fleming, & Co. which was lodged as security in the City of Glasgow Bank. Did you know anything about this agreement at the time it was entered into?

(A.) No; I never saw this letter before. (Q.) You came to a knowledge of it through the books? (A.) I saw from some minutes that there had been some agreement entered into. (Q.) Do you know whether Smith, Fleming, & Co.'s account was changed from the ordinary open credit account dealt with in the cheque box to the accountant's department after this agreement was entered into? No; I have no knowledge. (Q.) In the minute of 22d June 1876, to which you have already spoken, the concluding paragraph is—"It was re- "solved to appoint Messrs Taylor and Potter a committee to examine into "certain old accounts of the Bank, and to assist the manager in arranging "these under one general heading, with full powers." You told us yesterday that the manager had required that these old accounts should be investigated into? (A.) Yes. (Q.) Can you tell what old accounts were there referred to? (A.) I have no knowledge. (Q.) Were you present when this resolution was come to? (A.) I think not. I don't think I would be present then. (Q.) Can you tell me the meaning of these words—"in arranging them under "one general heading"? (A.) No; this would be a draft that would probably be written out and handed to me. (Q.) Can you give me any notion of what general heading they were to be put under? (A.) No; I have no knowledge whatever. (Q.) Did the manager speak to you about his anxiety to have these old accounts looked into? (A.) No, not to me personally. (Q.) You had no conversation with Mr Stronach about the matter? (A.) No. [Shown minute of 17th August 1876]:—

> "Having in view the position of certain old accounts, and looking to the whole "circumstances, and particularly to the fact that the contemplated arrangements "for the working of the credits are largely part of transactions in existence for "many years, and previously brought under consideration of the board by the pre- "sent manager, the board deemed it expedient to come to their present decision— "as referred to in minute of 30th December 1875."

I cannot tell what are the old accounts there referred to; I have no knowledge of that. (Q.) Can you tell me when it was that the manager brought these old accounts under the consideration of the board? (A.) I would understand from this that it was on 30th December 1875; but the minute reads in this way, "brought under consideration of the board by the present "manager, as referred to in minute of 30th December 1875," the board deemed it expedient to come to their present decision. (Q.) You think it refers to his remonstrances of 30th December 1875? (A.) I cannot say whether there was any remonstrance then. (Q.) You think it refers to what took place at the meeting? (A.) I infer so; but I have no knowledge beyond the minute. (Q.) In the minute of 30th December 1875 there is engrossed a letter from Mr Stronach accepting the office of manager; where is that letter now? (A.) It is produced. (Q.) Was that the first letter that Mr Stronach submitted to the directors with reference to his acceptance? (A.) The first that I am aware of. (Q.) Did you see a draft of another letter? (A.) No. I have no knowledge of that. (Q.) Did you see a draft of any letter? (A.) No. I have no recollection of that. (Q.) Was this the only letter of Mr Stronach that you knew of as having been laid before the directors? (A.) On that occasion? (Q.) Yes? (A.) That was the only one. (Q.) Did any of the directors speak to you about another having been laid before them? (A.) On that occasion? (Q.) Yes? (A.) No. (Q.) On any occasion do you know of any other letter by Mr Stronach to the directors in reference to these accounts? (A.) No, nothing but what is minuted. (Q.) Did Mr Glen Walker speak to you about another letter that was given by Mr Stronach to the directors? (A.) No, I have no recollection of anything. (Q.) Had you any talk with any of the officials in the Bank about this letter of Mr Stronach's when you first saw it? (A.) No, I have no recollection of it. (Q.) Who gave it to you to engross in the minutes? (A.) The chairman, Mr Taylor.

(Q.) Did he make any remark when he gave it to you? (A.) No; he merely told me that it had been handed in by the manager; he made no remark as to the contents of the letter. I was not present at the meeting when the letter was considered.

By the Lord Justice-Clerk—(Q.) You have no recollection of hearing of any other letter addressed to the directors by Stronach in regard to these accounts at that time, or about that time? (A.) No, I have no recollection of that at all.

WILLIAM MORISON (*recalled*).

By the Lord Justice-Clerk—(Q.) On your first examination we were led to understand that the document No. 128, of which we have a lithograph, was the original abstract of accounts which you first submitted to the manager and Mr Potter: that is to say, without the red ink markings, and that the red ink markings denoted the alterations which you were instructed to make. Yesterday you corrected that, and you told us that this abstract, so far as it appears in black ink, was not the thing which you submitted to the manager, but was another copy made after your interview with the manager. Is that so? (A.) Yes. (Q.) Now tell me exactly what the figures are on No. 128,—go over them *seriatim*,—which you were instructed to alter, and which appear as altered on the document as it now stands? (A.) There is first the entry of Smith, Fleming, & Co., £200,875 on the left-hand side, J. N. F., £100,300, J. M. & Co., 450,600. (Q.) Amounting in all to £751,000? (A.) Yes. (Q.) That originally appeared in a larger sum; what was its amount? (A.) £3,467,689 14s. 11d. (Q.) And that £751,000 is deducted from that on the face of this? (A.) Yes. And the balance of £2,715,000 is carried out? (A.) Yes. (Q.) What becomes of the £751,000? (A.) It is brought down under the third heading. (Q.) In what sum is it included, and under what head? (A.) It is under the third head, Smith, Fleming, & Co., stocks, £200,875; James Nicol Fleming, stocks, £100,300; James Morton & Co., stocks, £450,600. (Q.) That is included in the Government stocks, railway stocks and debentures, London and provincial correspondents; you had originally an abstract of the accounts under that head? (A.) Yes. (Q.) Where did you get it? From what materials did you make it up? (A.) From the general ledger or the weekly balance book. (Q.) And these books contain all the accounts which ought to be under that head? (A.) All the accounts. (Q.) The head "Government stocks and other securities," means investments by the Bank? (A.) Government stocks Nos. 1 and 2. (Q.) These are investments made by the Bank? (A.) By the Bank. (Q.) And held by the Bank? (A.) Held by the Bank, I understand. (Q.) They don't mean securities held for advances or open accounts? (A.) No. (Q.) Or with credit? (A.) I can only speak from what I have heard; I don't know personally about the securities. (Q.) But you know what the book means? (A.) I understand they are held by the Bank. (Q.) The book from which you made up that part of head No. 3 was a book which contained nothing but investments by the Bank? (A.) I understand so. (Q.) You understood so when you made it up? (A.) Yes. (Q.) You said yesterday that it might be right to put these accounts into that head of the abstract? (A.) Yes. (Q.) Knowing that if they were securities, they were securities for advances upon credit? (A.) Yes. (Q.) Why did you say that? (A.) At the time of the alteration, from the conversation betwixt Mr Potter and the manager, I understood that these stocks were held by the Bank. (Q.) Did you understand that these were not advances on credit to these firms? (A.) They were under the heading in the credit accounts ledger as advances to these firms. (Q.) And therefore they were properly, in your opinion, entered in that account? (A.) In the credit accounts. (Q.) What difference did it make that there were securities held for them? (A.) It made no difference so far as regarded the credit accounts. (Q.) What difference did it make in regard to the place in the abstract in which they should be entered? (A.) By bringing them down here, it put them under the heading, or one portion of the heading, of cash held. (Q.) They were represented, in short, as being investments held by the Bank? (A.) Yes. (Q.) Which they were not? (A.) I cannot tell you that. (Q.) If they were credit advances, were they properly investments held by the Bank? You gave an opinion yesterday that if there were securities held for these credits, they might be properly entered under the investments of the Bank. Is that so? (A.) With the addition, I said, that if an entry had been passed through the books. (Q.) Then you did not mean to say that that might be a right entry? (A.) This entry here? (Q.) Yes? (A.) Unless an entry had passed through the cash book and general ledger. (Q.) You did not mean to say it was right as it stands? (A.) No. (Q.) What was the next alteration which the directors directed you to make on this sheet, still dealing with the debit side? (A.) Under the heading of heritable property account, there is a sum of £30,000 deducted. (Q.) You were directed to do that? (A.) Yes. (Q.) Is that in red ink or black ink? (A.) Black ink. (Q.) Then that must have been done after the meeting? (A.) Yes. (Q.) Is there not before that a sum of £430,000 struck out? (A.) No. (Q.) Well, what next? (A.) Under the heading of Foreign and colonial credits, there is a sum of £973,300 deducted from bills payable. (Q.) And that, you told us, reduced the apparent amount of bills payable? (A.) For foreign and colonial credits in the meantime. (Q.) By nearly a million of money? (A.) Yes; with the explanation that that £973,000 entry was in the general ledger. (Q.) Is there anything else material in that state which you were directed to alter by the directors? (A.) There is the same £30,000 that was deducted from the heritable property account brought down under the No. 2 heading, "Advances on heritable "property and value of Bank buildings and furniture." (Q.) Anything else? (A.) There is a sum of £29,095 added to the amount of notes of other banks on hand. (Q.) Are these the material alterations which you were told to make? (A.) Then there are the £200,875, £100,300, and £450,600 brought down that I spoke of before.

By Mr Balfour—(Q.) Under the first head from which these items were brought down, is there not an entry "City of Glasgow Bank stock, £356,825." Was that an investment of the Bank in its own stock? (A.) Yes. (Q.) And yet that appeared under the first head? (A.) Yes.

By the Lord Justice-Clerk [on the suggestion of a juryman]—(Q.) You have said that the effect of these alterations was to show a larger amount of assets and a smaller amount of liabilities than your original abstract would have shown, or than the books would have shown, and at the same time you said that the alterations did not affect the profit and loss for the year, or the reserve fund. Can you explain that? (A.) If the assets were reduced, the liabilities were reduced. I did not say the liabilities were reduced and the assets enlarged. They are both reduced. (Q.) You mean that the amount of assets is reduced, and the amount of liabilities is reduced, and therefore the amount of transactions is made apparently less than in point of fact they were. Is that so? (A.) Yes.

WILLIAM MILLER.

By the Lord Advocate—I was for some years, and down to the stoppage of the City of Glasgow Bank, superintendent of its branches. I was so from 1862. My duty was to conduct correspondence with the branches, and to examine the advances made at the branches, and report on them to the manager; also to take a general oversight of the business transacted at the branches. My duties never brought me into contact with the board of directors. (Q.) Were you ever present at their meetings? (A.) I have been asked to come in to answer a question occasionally, but I was not there habitually,—very seldom,—only when a question or explanation was asked as to something in my department. On the occasion of the annual balance being prepared, there was a form prepared and given to us by Mr Morison, on which we entered the figures from our own books, and returned the sheet to Mr Morison. The branch balance-sheets for the years 1876, 1877, and 1878, were prepared in that way under my superintendence. They contained a correct statement of the balances of the branches for these years. We got weekly returns from each branch, and the accuracy of these was checked by our inspectors. In each of these three years about £10,000 was written off for bad debts at the branches. I have made an analysis of that for the past five years, and I find that the average sum so written off for bad debts was £10,900 per annum. The business done at the branches was a very profitable one,—averaging £70,000 a year, after deducting the bad debts.

By Mr Asher—At the annual balance, Mr Morison, the accountant, sent me a form of abstract to be filled up in connection with the branches—a form having the same heads, I believe, as there are in the balance ledger at the head office. We allocated the returns from the branches under these various heads. We gave back the form to Mr Morison, to be incorporated in the general abstract, as I understood. I understood that the branch business and the head office business were brought together in that form only once a year.

By Mr Balfour—(Q.) Was it part of that return to show the cross accounts which existed at the branches? (A.) Yes. (Q.) What did you return as the cross accounts for 1878? (A.) I don't remember. (Q.) The amount entered in No. 124A—the abstract for 1878—under the head "Cross accounts," is "Edinburgh branch, £148,939, 18s. 11d." Have you any doubt that that was the amount you returned as the cross accounts of that branch? (A.) I have no doubt that is correct, but I have no means here of testing it. (Q.) Did you return the amount of cross accounts for 1876? (A.) I don't remember as to 1876: there was as to 1877 and 1878, but I am not sure that form was prepared before 1877. (Q.) Have you no books here that would refresh your recollection about that? (A.) I don't think there are any. I have seen the abstracts of branches in the hands of Mr Brown. The abstract branches' account of 1876, now shown me, has been filled up by one of our inspectors of branches. I have no doubt it is quite correct. The amount of cross accounts, branches, in 1876, was £376,334, 5s. 3d. No. 134 is the abstract of accounts of branches for June 1877. There is entered there under the head of cross accounts—Edinburgh branch, £268,692, 8s. 3d. (Q.) Before you go further, will you explain to the jury what is the meaning of cross accounts as appearing in these branches' abstracts? (A.) They belong entirely to the accounts of the North British Railway. The North British Railway Company kept several accounts for their own purposes; some of them were debtor and some were creditor. The mode of bringing out these was by deducting the debtor from the creditor balance, treating it as one account. I think that is a perfectly proper book-keeping operation.

By the Lord Justice-Clerk—The amount brought out for 1876 in that way was £376,000 odds. (Q.) It is the balance of a debtor and creditor account? (A.) You deduct the one from the other, and bring out the sum that should come in here.

By Mr Balfour—The only instance in which we so crossed accounts was in connection with the North British Railway. We never did it anywhere but at Edinburgh, and in connection with the North British Railway. (Q.) Is there not a similar entry applicable to the West End branch, Glasgow? (A.) Yes; that was a fictitious entry returned by me to the head office for the following purpose:—The West Calder Oil Company owed £5150. That originated at the West End branch, where they kept their account. There was also a debit account in the head office of the same kind; and it was resolved to bring up the West End balance to the head office, because, I understood, the head office had securities against these advances. Subsequently it was sent back to the West End branch in order that they might make a cross entry in their books for the purpose of keeping the debt before them. Had that not been deducted, the debt would have been entered twice. It was perfectly necessary and proper, having regard to the manner in which these accounts at the two offices were kept, to make that entry. The amount of cross accounts, as shown by No. 134, for the week ending Wednesday, 6th June 1877, was—Edinburgh branch. £268,692, 8s. 3d.; West End branch, Glasgow, £5150, 5s. In 1878, as shown by No. 135, the cross accounts amounted to —Edinburgh branch, £148,939, 18s. 11d.; West End branch, Glasgow, £5150, 5s.; total, £154,090, 3s. 11d. [Shown No. 133. Abstract of accounts at branches on Thursday, 1st June 1876.] That is the printed form which Mr Morison supplied to us in order that we might fill in these returns.

By the Dean of Faculty—I have been inspector of branches since 1862. In conducting the business of my department with the head office, I dealt only with the manager. I never came in contact with the accountant except when giving him these returns; I had no occasion to do so. Since Mr Robert Stronach was appointed manager, I have seen him every day, and several times every day. I thought him a particularly careful manager in all advances that we had to do with. I found him very careful, and, I would say, very strict in investigating into securities for proposed credits. I thought, up to 1st October 1878, that he was a perfectly conscientious honourable gentleman, —a man whom I would not have suspected of doing anything wrong.

By the Lord Advocate—The sum of £376,334 in 1876 was applicable entirely to the accounts of the North British Railway. I may explain that it to a large extent consisted of two accounts, the one called a general account, and the other an interest and dividend account. The general account was generally creditor, because into that went all the monies lodged, and as these came in from day to day and week to week, they were put to that credit. Then when interest and dividends were paid, they were debited to the other account in the first place. It was really a debtor and creditor account kept in the form of two accounts,—the one containing debit and the other credit entries. With regard to the two sums in each of the years 1877 and 1878, the larger of these was entirely applicable to the North British Railway, and the smaller to the West End branch relative to the West Calder Oil Company. I had nothing whatever to do with credits granted or transactions of any kind at the head office. I knew nothing that was done at the head office. (Q.) You had no means of ascertaining on what terms money was given there? (A.) Certainly not, and I never wished to know, that was more; not that I suspected anything wrong, but I did not want to be bothered about it; I had plenty to do with my own business, and wished to keep myself entirely to that. I never asked a question about the head office. (Q.) What do you mean by saying that the manager was very strict? (A.) I mean to say that when any proposal, for a credit account for instance, or an advance of any kind, came up to me and I showed it to him, he was particularly careful in seeing what he believed to be proper security lodged before it could be granted, and he was in the habit of investigating the returns of the advances himself, and looking at them.

WILLIAM MORRIS.

By the Lord Advocate—I was in the employment of the City of Glasgow Bank from the year 1864 down to the time of its stoppage, in various capacities. I was at first in the accountant's department, and in 1871 I was appointed private clerk to the manager, Mr Alexander Stronach. I acted in that capacity until Mr Alexander Stronach resigned, and on the appointment of Mr Robert Stronach, I continued to act under him in the same capacity. Alexander Stronach ceased to attend the Bank about December 1874. (Q.) Was he much about the Bank, or was he absent altogether from the Bank from that date down to December 1875? (A.) He was absent altogether. During that period his brother, Mr Robert Stronach, performed the duties of manager. My duties as private clerk to the manager were to attend to the manager's correspondence. (Q.) Were you employed by him to write, or did you merely write from his scroll or dictation? (A.) Both from scroll and to dictation. (Q.) You were not employed in any other sense to conduct correspondence? (A.) Well, there were official letters as well, such as Smith, Fleming, & Co's. (Q.) But what I want to know is this,—were you employed merely to write what was dictated or given you to copy, or were you employed to write letters from information given you? (A.) Latterly with Mr Robert Stronach from information given me. Before that date I wrote principally from scroll, with Alexander Stronach. With Robert Stronach I wrote from information given me. The official letters of the Bank were generally addressed to the City of Glasgow Bank. These letters, I understand, were opened by Mr Leresche. When letters were addressed to the manager by name, they were delivered to the manager himself. (Q.) Were there any particular letters which came addressed always to the manager? (A.) Yes; Smith, Fleming, & Co.'s. I wrote the replies to those letters. I had an apartment adjoining that of Mr Alexander Stronach. Shortly after I became his private clerk I directed a duplicate set of books to be kept by the bill clerk, Mr Laing. The two sets of books were a little differently arranged, but the results were the same. These books included a book titled on the back, "Ledger A, Open credit, No. 3;" another book, titled "Ledger B, Open or marginal credits, No. 3;" and a third book, "Ledger C, Open or marginal credits, No. 3." The entries contained in ledger A. were the credits granted to James Morton & Co., Matthew Buchanan and Co., and Potter, Wilson, & Co. Ledger B. contained credits granted to Smith, Fleming, & Co., and James Nicol Fleming. Ledger C. contained miscellaneous credits, including credits granted to Glen Walker & Co., and John Innes Wright & Co., amongst others. In working these ledgers I kept a book, titled "Daily list of bills payable." That contained a list of the bills payable by the Bank as they matured from day to day under each of the credits in these books.

By the Lord Justice-Clerk—The books were confined to the particular accounts I have mentioned. The duplicate set was applicable only to those accounts.

By the Lord Advocate—These credit accounts were accounts which involved acceptances by the Bank, on which the Bank's credit was interposed. Ledger C includes acceptances by the London Joint Stock Bank on behalf of the City of Glasgow Bank. (Q.) How would you describe the character of the credits entered in ledger A? (A.) Running credits. By a running credit I mean a credit that has been renewed and is kept renewed, kept continuing upon the circle, renewed from day to day. (Q.) Where the Bank issue new acceptances to retire those that are in the circle when they come due? (A.) Precisely. (Q.) Do you apply the term "open credits" also to these? (A.) Yes, they are classed amongst the open credits. (Q.) What was the common practice of the Bank in granting such credits—how did it begin? (A.) By a letter of application from the person requiring the credit. (Q.) And then, I believe, it was usual to issue a letter of credit? (A.) Sometimes it was, and sometimes it was not. (Q.) Was it not invariably the course pursued with the ordinary creditors of the Bank to require an application in writing? (A.) It was. (Q.) Was that course pursued with the credits that are entered in ledger A? (A.) In some instances it was, in others not. Ledger B contains open and marginal credits together. A marginal credit is almost a similar document to an open credit. A marginal credit is a margin attached to a bill, instead of a letter being granted; it is a set of bills, and the obligation of the Bank is attached to the bill, like a counterfoil, the obligation of the Bank being to accept the bill when presented against produce. In the case of marginal credits the bill attached to the counterfoil sets forth the sum that it is drawn for. In the case of an open credit, where there is a letter of credit (say) for £50,000, the customer can draw for any amount that suits his purpose up to the limit of £50,000 in bills of any amount. But when a marginal credit is granted, we issue five bills of £10,000 each. There were a number of firms connected with James Nicol Fleming, and Smith, Fleming, & Co., who operated upon the credits given to them. These were James Nicol Fleming and Co., Calcutta; William Nicol & Co., Bombay; Todd, Findlay, & Co., Rangoon; Fleming & Co., Kurrachee; and there was a Colombo credit that was operated upon by Fowlie, Richmond, & Co., at one time; but that firm came to grief along with Messrs Collie in 1875, and since then that credit has been operated upon by William Nicol & Co., Bombay. Ledger A showed that the operations of James Morton & Co. under these credits were very large. With the view of keeping up my information on the subject, I prepared folio sheets from month to month, showing James Morton & Co.'s liabilities as at the beginning of each month, on credits and discounts, past due bills, and open accounts. My object in ascertaining Morton & Co.'s liabilities at the beginning of each month, was to keep the manager supplied with information; it was such a large account that I thought that necessary. These sheets were submitted to him monthly. (Q.) Did you keep them after you prepared them, or how did you deal with them? (A.) The book lay with the manager, and I was in the habit of getting it at the beginning of each month to post up. It lay with him during the intervening month, and I got it back from him. It was to Mr Robert Stronach that I supplied that information,—not to Mr Alexander Stronach. I cannot remember whether it was his suggestion or mine that these monthly sheets should be prepared. [Shown Nos. 122, Analysis of securities, James Morton and Co., commencing 20th Sept. 1876, and 123.] No. 123 is titled "Weekly "abstract of credits, S., F., & Co., and J. N. F." It contains a weekly abstract. It is one of my own books, kept in the room I occupied. It was not patent to the other officers of the Bank. The weekly abstracts show *in cumulo* the state from week to week of the credits to those firms, as operated upon from the different places I have mentioned. The special credits granted to Smith, Fleming, & Co. were not entered in that book at all. They were never put through an abstract. The sheets produced here are only a part. No. 122 goes back to 1876. I retained Smith, Fleming, & Co.'s sheets,—No. 123. I also kept a book (No. 120), titled "Special securities, J. N. F., S., F., & Co., "J. M. & Co., and others." These initials mean James Nicol Fleming, Smith, Fleming, & Co., and James Morton & Co. That book was made up by me in June 1877. I had no special instructions to make it up. These things were recorded in loose sheets, and I thought it proper to have them embodied in a book. It shows the amount of liabilities by these parties, and the securities supposed to be held against these liabilities. (Q.) Did you always receive from Smith, Fleming, & Co. application letters for credits granted to them? (A.) As a rule. (Q.) Do you say the same thing with regard to the credits granted to Mr Morton? (A.) No. (Q.) Were there, as a rule, letters there? (A.) As a rule there were letters, but there were three or four credits without letters of application. (Q.) In some of Mr Morton's applications, he asks credits against securities annexed? (A.) He does. (Q.) Were securities annexed in these cases? (A.) Sometimes, and sometimes not. (Q.) How did you account for that? What occurred to you at the time as his reason for not annexing the securities? (A.) I cannot say; I have no idea. (Q.) Did Mr Morton deposit securities from time to time without applying for a credit at the time? (A.) Well, probably he did, before my time; sometimes. (Q.) You kept another book, I believe, containing the entries in connection with foreign and colonial credits, and the acceptances maturing of foreign and colonial bills? (A.) I don't remember that book. (Q.) When applications were sent in to the manager by Morton & Co., or Smith, Fleming, & Co., after the manager opened these letters, what did he do with them,—to whom did he give them? (A.) He sent them upstairs to me, or I called for them and got them in the manager's room. (Q.) Were they given to Mr Leresche? (A.) Sometimes they were. (Q.) Was that the general rule? (A.) No. (Q.) Were applications for credits from these firms handed to Mr Leresche? (A.) Yes; latterly they were. The application letters for the special credits were handed to him. (Q.) But was the correspondence with regard to the credits other than special handed to Mr Leresche? (A.) No. (Q.) Was there any document or letter sent from your office or from the manager with your knowledge to Mr Leresche which could inform him of the amount of Morton's credits or liabilities? (A.) No. (Q.) But you, as private clerk, had information upon the subject? (A.) I had. [Shown Nos. 185 to 188 inclusive.] No. 188 is a letter, dated 24th August 1875, from Smith, Fleming, and Co.. to R. S. Stronach. I am familiar with that letter; I have seen it. (Q.) You saw it at the time, didn't you? (A.) Probably I did. Nos. 185 to 187 are letters from John Fleming to the manager, and which were received by him. I never saw the minute books. [Shown No. 215.] That is a letter from John Innes Wright & Co. to the manager, R. S. Stronach, dated 2d August 1876, in the following terms:—

"115 St Vincent Street, Glasgow,
"2d Augt. 1876.

"R. S. Stronach, Esq.

"Dear Sir,—Referring to the letter addressed to you by the writer on 12th ulto., "we now beg to apply for marginal credits as undernoted, for one hundred thou- "sand pound (£100,000 stg.), to be drawn by Messrs Glen Walker & Co., of Mel- "bourne, the partners of which are Wm. Glen Walker, Wm. Geddes Borron, and "Ferdinand Spiro.

"In security for same, we engage to hold for, or lodge with you, the documents "for wool and other produce sent to us by Messrs G. W. & Co. as received (stipu- "lating that the same represents an excess of 20 per cent. over the amounts drawn), "or we shall pay you cash to the amount of your acceptances.

"We beg to enclose copy of letter received from W. G. Walker, Esq., requesting "the credits now applied for, and who purposes leaving this for Melbourne in a "few weeks, for the purpose of giving the business his personal attention.—We re- "main, dear sir, yours faithfully,

"JOHN INNES WRIGHT & Co.

"Marginal credits at 4 or 6 m/ st. Payable in London. In force for one year. "In 20 bills for £5000 each, and in triplicate."

"Triplicates" means in sets of three. (Q.) You did not see the minutes, I believe? (A.) I did not. (Q.) But you became aware by the issuing of bills that that credit had been granted? (A.) Yes. (Q.) Was the security mentioned in that letter given to the Bank? (A.) Not that I am aware of. The £100,000 marginal credit was drawn upon to the extent, I think, of £57,000. £25,000 was paid in in cash by John Innes Wright & Co., and the balance was paid by the Bank. (Q.) How did they deal with it in their books on retiring the acceptances? (A.) It would go into the debit of John Innes Wright and Co.'s open balance. (Q.) To the extent of £32,000? (A.) Yes. [Shown minute of directors of 17th August 1876, in the following terms]:—

"A letter from Messrs James Morton & Co., and two letters from Mr W. Glen "Walker, dated respectively Glasgow the 16th and 14th instant, in regard to the "drawing of credits in lieu of those now drawn by Messrs Holmes, White, & Co., "and others, and one of the latter as to the acquisition of certain pastoral properties, "were brought under the notice of the board, after full consideration the board "came to the resolution that it was advisable to adopt generally the suggestions "contained in these letters, and they accordingly requested the manager, associated "with Messrs Potter, Stewart, and Taylor, to arrange with Mr Walker as to all "details. While arriving at this resolution, the board were fully sensible of the "undesirableness of such investments as the purchases proposed in the letters; but "having in view the position of certain old accounts, and looking to the whole cir- "cumstances, and particularly to the fact that the contemplated arrangements for "the working of the credits are largely part of transactions in existence for many "years, and previously brought under consideration of the board by the present "manager, the board deemed it expedient to come to their present decision—as "referred to in minute of 30th December 1875."

(Q.) You were not cognisant of the terms of the minute at the time? (A.) I was not. (Q.) But you knew the transactions to which it related? (A.) I did. (Q.) There was a credit, No. 24/6 for £235,000? (A.) There was. (Q.) In whose favour? Explain what you know about it? (A.) The credit was granted to James Morton & Co., and was drawn under in favour of Holmes, White, & Co., of Melbourne. The limit of the credit was £235,400, but the credit was reduced to the extent of £100,000 by the drafts of Glen Walker and Co.; and the same securities that were held against 24/6 were put up as a security against the new credit for £100,000. That was the credit 38/47. (Q.) Then, was the original sum reduced? (A.) The original sum of the credit was reduced by £100,000 by the opening of the new credit. (Q.) That had just the effect of splitting it into two, had it not? (A.) Precisely. (Q.) I should have read you the other minute of 11th January 1877:—

"It was proposed and agreed to that the Bank should accept drafts by Glen "Walker & Company, to the extent of £20,000, in renewal of those retired for a "like amount due 1st instant on a/c Glen Walker & Co., Melbourne, per minute of "30th December 1875.

"Also, that the Bank should accept drafts by Glen Walker & Co., to the extent "of £100,000, to retire a like amount, drawn by Holmes, White, & Co., of Mel- "bourne, on account of James Morton & Co. The securities at present held "against Holmes, White, & Co.'s drafts to be placed as security against the drafts "of Glen Walker & Co. Letter to be obtained from James Morton & Co. to this "effect, and no drafts to be accepted until this letter is in possession of the "Bank."

(Q.) The original credit you say was for £235,000 to James Morton & Co.? (A.) Yes. (Q.) It was operated upon by Holmes, White, & Co.? (A.) It was. (Q.) And that was reduced to £135,000 by taking Glen Walker & Co.'s bills for Holmes, White, & Co.'s? (A.) Precisely. Glen Walker & Co.'s acceptances were discounted by John Innes Wright & Co., and the proceeds, so far as received by the Bank, were paid into the credit of credit 38/47. That was one of the credits into which 24/6 was split. (Q.) Did Innes Wright & Co. account to the Bank for the amount of these drafts? (A.) Not for the whole. (Q.) Who came to the Bank with regard to these drafts? (A.) Mr Inglis, a clerk of Potter, Wilson, & Co. (Q.) Did Inglis explain to you how he was taking charge of the matter? (A.) He said he had a general supervision over that credit of £100,000. (Q.) But he came on behalf of Innes Wright & Co.? (A.) On behalf of Potter, Wilson, & Co. (Q.) Was it Potter, Wilson, & Co. who were taking the supervision of that? (A.) Yes. (Q.) Did you call the attention of the manager, Mr Robert Stronach, to these short payments on the part of Innes Wright & Co.? (A.) I did. (Q.) Did he make any observation? (A.) He was very much displeased. (Q.) Were you sent by him on more than one occasion to Innes Wright & Co. to inquire about it. (A.) Yes, and I also spoke to Mr Inglis, Potter's clerk, regarding the matter, complaining of the short payments; for example, if they got drafts for £10,000, perhaps Mr Scott, of John Innes Wright & Co., would only pay one-half of that instead of paying in the £10,000. (Q.) Instead of paying in the proceeds that they got by discounting the bills, they only paid in a part? (A.) Yes. (Q.) And you were sent by Mr Stronach to remonstrate against that proceeding? (A.) Yes. (Q.) And you did so both to Mr Inglis, who was supervising, or at least who was saying he was supervising on behalf of Potter, Wilson, & Co., and also to Innes Wright & Co.? (A.) I did. (Q.) Whom did you see on these occasions when you went to Innes Wright & Co.? (A.) Mr Scott, as a rule; sometimes I saw Mr Wright also. (Q.) What did Mr Scott say when you saw him on these occasions, and you complained of him retaining these moneys? (A.) He made excuses, and said that he was waiting telegraphic advice or such like from London. (Q.) What did Mr Innes Wright say about it when you saw him? (A.) He stated that Mr Scott generally took charge of these things. (Q.) Was that all he said? (A.) There was one occasion when Mr Scott was from home in London, and Mr Wright said that when the short payments were made he was waiting till he got telegraphic advice from Mr Scott; the drafts had not been placed. (Q.) Did he seem to be aware that short payments had been made? (A.) Oh, yes. [Shown account No. 399.] I have seen that account before. It is an account current between Glen Walker & Co. and John Innes Wright and Co. and the Bank. I think it was Mr Inglis, Potter, Wilson, & Co.'s clerk, who brought it to the Bank. It refers to the drafts on 38/47, and the payments made to the Bank against them. The last date in the series is 25th January 1878. The accounts are signed by John Innes Wright & Co. The firm's signature there is in Mr Scott's handwriting. The ultimate debit against the firm of short payments retained by them is £48,668, 1s. 2d., being money belonging to the Bank which they had received and failed to pay into the Bank. The date of the beginning of the account is March 1877. [Shown minute of directors, dated 14th March 1878, and referred to the following passage] :—

"With reference to the minute of 28th February last, in regard to accounting "by Messrs John Innes Wright & Co. of proceeds of drafts in connection with the "credits therein named, Messrs Stewart and Potter, the committee appointed to "deal with the matter, reported that they had had an interview with Mr Wm. "Scott, of the firm of Messrs John Innes Wright & Co., and had arranged for a "settlement by cash and securities to be completed by 21st March current, as "detailed in the statement now submitted, and which was ordered to be lodged."

And also the minute of 21st March 1878, containing the following passage :—

"Mr Stewart reported that, as appointed by last meeting, Mr Potter and he had "had an interview with Mr William Scott, of the firm of Messrs John Innes Wright "and Co., which resulted in his promise to send to the Bank acceptances by his "London firm to the extent of £10,000 additional to those already held by the "Bank, to realise forthwith sugar to the extent of from £7000 to £8000, to be paid "to the Bank, and to meet the committee again on Wednesday next, at 12 o'clock, "for further and final arrangements."

I was aware that that committee had been appointed, although I had not seen the minutes, and I was present at a meeting of the committee which was held in Mr Potter's office in Gordon Street. There were present at that meeting Mr Stewart, Mr Potter, and Mr William Scott of John Innes Wright and Co. [Shown No. 400.] That statement was produced at the meeting. It was drawn up by me. It contains a statement of the short payments, £48,000, and a list of the payments to be made, and of the security to be lodged against the debt. The document is in the following terms :—

' J. INNES WRIGHT & Co.

" 1st March 1878.

" Arrangement as to settlement of G. W. & Co.'s balance.

" *Dr.*	
" To balance say	£48,000
" *Cr.*	
" London firms acceptances already in Bank's possession, viz :—	
" 1st acceptances due 26th April 1878	3000
" 26th July "	5000
" 26th Octr. "	7000
" 26th Jany. 1879	7000
	£22,000
" 2d Cash to Account on or before 21st March, ...	10,000
" 3d " or other approved mercantile security, on or before 21st March, ...	7500
" 4th London firm's acceptances, due end of June, to be handed to Bank on or before 21st March, ...	2500
" 5th Cash or securities before date above mentioned, . .	6000
	£48,000

" London firm's bills to be given to-day for £10,000. Wm. Scott to give " orders for sale of sugar to-day. Mr Scott meets us on Wednesday to " arrange the remainder." There are two different handwritings on that document. The body of it, down to the summation of £48,000, was written by me. The words, " London firm's bills to be given to-day for £10,000. " Wm. Scott to give orders for sale of sugar to-day. Mr Scott meets us on " Wednesday to arrange the remainder," are in Mr Stewart's handwriting. There was considerable discussion at the meeting about this matter. Mr Stewart took the leading part in the conversation for the Bank. (Q.) What did he say? Did he make any observation after that statement was produced? (A.) Yes; he remarked to Mr Scott that it was a very ugly matter indeed, and he could only characterise it by one name, and so long as he held the onerous and honourable position of the chairman of directors of the Bank, he would not allow such a thing to be permitted. (Q.) As so dealing with the funds of the Bank? (A.) As so dealing with the funds of the Bank. (Q.) After he said that did Mr Scott make any suggestion? (A.) Mr Scott wished evidently to make some remark, and he asked me to retire. I retired, with Mr Stewart's permission. (Q.) Did Mr Stewart seem to be really in earnest and angry? (A.) Yes, he was; he was very much heated. I remained out of the room for about ten minutes, when I was recalled, I think by Mr Potter. (Q.) When you returned to the room how were the three parties there engaged; what were they doing? (A.) They were on their feet, apparently dismissing. Mr Stewart made a remark to me. He said that I need not take any notice of what had passed. (Q.) Did he say what had passed? Did he refer to it in any other terms? (A.) The heat of the meeting —that I need not take any notice of the heat of the meeting while I was in the room. (Q.) Were these the words he used—that you need not take any notice of the heat of the meeting? (A.) Yes. (Q.) Did he say why? (A.) I forget now. (Q.) Did he say that they had come to any arrangement or anything of that kind? (A.) Yes,—that the matter had been arranged satisfactorily. (Q.) Did he say with whom? (A.) With Mr Scott. I then left. The Bank at that time had in its possession £22,000 of the acceptances of John Innes Wright & Co.'s London firm—drafts by the Glasgow firm accepted by the London firm. (Q.) One of the things to be given in settlement was cash to account on or before 21st March, £10,000; did the Bank get that? (A.) No. (Q.) Did they get anything instead of it? (A.) They got an additional £10,000 of the London acceptances of John Innes Wright & Co.

(Q.) More paper? (A.) More paper. (Q.) Did the Bank get the items, 3, 4, and 5, approved mercantile security, and so forth? (A.) Not that I am aware of. (Q.) You never saw or heard of it? (A.) No. (Q.) And it never was credited to them? (A.) No. (Q.) Mr Stewart says in his note, "Wm. "Scott to give orders for sale of sugar to-day;" I suppose you don't know whether he gave the orders or not? (A.) I am not aware. (Q.) But did any proceeds of such a sale come to the Bank? (A.) No. (Q.) Has any part of that £48,000 been paid to this day, so far as you are aware, or had any part of it been paid at the stoppage of the Bank? (A.) There was £8000 of the acceptances paid, leaving £40,000. (Q.) I believe from their failure to pay that money, the manager removed the conduct of the management of the £100,000 credit from them altogether? (A.) Yes. (Q.) He did not entrust them with discounting any further? (A.) No. (Q.) In what capacity were Innes Wright & Co. superintending that credit—in the interest of the Bank or whose? (A.) The credit, of course, was a portion of James Morton & Co.'s credit. (Q.) I know, but they took charge of it? (A.) They took charge of that portion of it? (Q.) The £100,000, being one of the portions into which the £235,000 was split? (A.) Yes.

By the Lord Justice-Clerk—(Q.) For their own interest, or Morton's interest, or the Bank's interest? (A.) I presume for Morton's interest.

By the Lord Advocate—(Q.) Did they charge commission? (A.) I am not aware.

By the Lord Justice-Clerk—(Q.) As I understand this marginal credit, the Bank undertook to accept within a certain margin the drafts of the customer, which were to be discounted and the proceeds paid into the account? (A.) Yes. (Q.) Innes Wright & Co. were employed to do that? (A.) They were employed to discount the bills. (Q.) And they only paid part of the discount received, and retained the rest? (A.) Precisely.

By the Lord Advocate—[Shown No. 191.] That is a letter written by the manager, Mr Robert Stronach, and addressed to John Fleming, Esquire, dated 21st December 1875, in the following terms :—

"City of Glasgow Bank,
"Glasgow, 21st December 1875.

"My Dear Sir,—I have your private note of yesterday, and am sorry to hear that "the indulgence shown by the directors respecting the Brown pro-note for £5000 "has not been sufficient to the requirements of the case. I can, therefore, only "bring the matter up again for the consideration of the directors on Thursday, but "I do so very reluctantly, I assure you, knowing the feeling which existed among "them when the matter was put before them last week, and of which you are "aware.

"Referring to the amount we have come under cash advance to you on the No. "2 cash account, £27 or thereby, and should be very glad if you could arrange to "relieve us of this or part at your earliest convenience.—Yours faithfully,

"R. S. STRONACH.

"John Fleming, Esq., London.

"*P.S.*—Please send me the two acceptances of Mr Brown p. £2500 each in the "meantime."

The body of the letter is in my handwriting. The P.S. is in the manager's handwriting. Letter No. 191C, Mr Stronach to John Fleming, 23d May 1878, read as follows :—

"City of Glasgow Bank,
"Glasgow, 23d May 1878.

"My Dear Sir,—I brought up your application for a renewal of credits 38/5 p. "£15,000 and 39/47 p. £25,000 at our meeting to-day; and, as I anticipated, great "dissatisfaction was expressed that no tangible reduction was made upon the "former, and that you should approach at all for a renewal of the latter, which was "quite a temporary transaction, & only to remain in force until such time as the "mails assumed their normal condition. And as we presume this difficulty has "now been got over, it is very much to be regretted, indeed, that you should find "it necessary to ask for an extension of this credit. Just to show you that the "directors have good cause for being aggrieved at the very marked manner in "which your credits on the circle have been growing these few years past, I send "you a comparative statement herewith of the amounts on the circle at the beginning of the Bank's financial year since 1875, which be good enough to peruse "carefully & return with any comments you may think necessary to make upon the "anticipated accounts & those informal in other respects.

"Particularly I would call your attention to anticipations on Bombay, Rangoon, "Fowlie's credit, and the two credits under consideration to-day, Yours very truly,

"R, S. STRONACH,
"Manager.

"John Fleming, Esq.,
"London.

"*P.S.*—Please let me have a formal application for the Mail Credit, dated "Tuesday, and restrict it to £25m/."

That letter and the postscript are in my handwriting. It is signed by Mr Stronach the manager. [Shown No. 186.] Letter, John Fleming, to Mr Stronach, 12th April 1875. Letter read as follows :—

"17 & 18 Leadenhall Street, London, E.C.,
"12th April 1875.

"R. S. Stronach, Esq.,
"City of Glasgow Bank, Glasgow.

"Dear Sir,—Referring to the meeting I had with your directors & yourself on "Thursday the 1st inst, respecting the state of our account with the Bank, I "now beg to detail the terms of the agreement come to, as I understood them.

"1. Smith, Fleming, & Co., as a firm, & the partners as individuals, pledge them- "selves to abstain absolutely from all speculative operations, unless specially "sanctioned by the Bank.

"2. They are to hold all property belonging to the firm, as per annexed state- "ment, as security or cover to the Bank for its various advances to them; but "inasmuch as it is of the greatest importance that the credit of the firm should not "be injured, but be carefully maintained, no public transfer of the property is mean- "while to be made. The realization of the property is to be left in S., F., & Co.'s "hands, who undertake faithfully to account for & pay over to the Bank the whole "proceeds of all property realized.

"3. The Bank's charge for commission for all the credits issued for S., F., & Co.'s "accommodation, as per list herewith, shall be at the rate of one-half per cent. "per annum, and this arrangement is to be retrospective as from 1st Jany. 1875.

"4. The Bank's charge for interest on all cash advances to S., F., & Co. shall be "at the rate of three & a half p, cent. p. annum as from 1st Jany. 1875.

"A statement of the balances of various accounts, as on 31st March last, is "appended.

"5. The Bank shall advance the sum of £100,000 at the rate of 3½ % p. annum, "for the requisition of £100,000 of the stock of the Canterbury and Otago Co., "£7800 of which is to be provided by me, credit for the equivalent of (£7800) being "given to Smith, Fleming, & Co. in account with the Bank at 1st Jany. 1875.

"6. The £100,000 of stock as above shall be held by trustees in trust for the "following purposes :—

"(1.) To pay interest at the rate of 3½ % p. annum to the Bank for the £100,000 "advanced for the purchase of the stock.

"(2.) To pay the whole of the surplus income arising from the stock, after meet- "ing the charge for interest as above, to the credit of S., F., & Co.'s a/c "with the Bank; and to continue doing so until all S., F., & Co.'s debts "to the Bank have been liquidated.

"(3.) Nothing was agreed as to the ultimate disposition of the stock, upon the "final liquidation of all S., F., & Co.'s obligations to the Bank, but I "venture to suggest that in that event the trustees be directed to re-transfer "the stock at cost price (viz., par) to the parties who furnished it, or their "assignees or heirs.

"7. A comparison of the charges on S., F., & Co.'s debt, with their probable in- "comings from all sources, as per memo. herewith, shows they have the command "of an annual surplus amounting at present to £25,000 applicable to the reduction "of their debts to the Bank. They accordingly undertake to pay £25,000 per

" annum in reduction of their debt to the Bank, in addition to paying punctually " all charges for interest & commission.

" The reduction is, in the first place, to be made on the credits, & as these involve " an annual charge of 5% for commission, stamps, exchange, and discount, each " reduction will be attended with a corresponding saving in future annual charges, " which saving shall be applied in further reduction of the principal of the debt; and " thus, starting with an annual payment of £25,000, applied to the reduction of the " credits, which involve an annual charge of 5%, there should be, in course of four- " teen years, an aggregate reduction in the debt of half a million sterling.

" The credits being duly liquidated shall be followed by the liquidation of the " cash advances.

" 8. Regarding the credits, W. Nicol & Co. have undertaken to pay off the Bom- " bay credit, now amounting to about £260,000, at the rate of £20,000 p. annum; " and Fleming & Co. have undertaken to liquidate their credit, now amounting to " £60,000, at the rate of £5000 p. annum; and they have undertaken to hold the " properties enumerated in the statement herewith under lien to the Bank, as " security for these credits.

" Todd, Findlay, & Co., of Rangoon and Moulmein, have undertaken to come " under obligation for the Rangoon credit, amounting to £90,000, and to liquidate " the same at the rate of £15,000 p. annum, but I am unable to place their under- " taking in your hands until arrangements now in progress for retiring certain " acceptances of ours to Todd, Findlay, & Co. against the debt to you as by the " old firm of Todd, Findlay, & Co. (*i.e.*, before Mr Mair became a partner). I am " in correspondence with Mr Morton about this matter, which I have not the " slightest doubt will be shortly arranged, when I shall be at liberty to place in " your hands Mr Mair's obligation, which is already in mine.

" I shall be glad to learn whether I have correctly stated the understanding come " to, and whether it be desired that it be reduced to a formal agreement.—I am, " dear sir, yours faithfully, JOHN FLEMING.

" 1.

" Property belonging to Smith, Fleming, & Co., pledged as security to the " City of Glasgow Bank.

" Tarapore Tea Gardens.
" 108 British India Steam Co. Shares.
" 150 Shares Great Eastern Telegraph Shares.
" 300 Shares West Calder Oil Co.
" 50 Shares North British & Mercantile Ince. Co.
" 400 Shares Universal Marine Ince. Co.
" 100 Shares Ocean Marine Ince. Co.
" 19 Shares Tuticorin Press Co. Shares.
" 10 Shares North China Ince. Shares.
" City of Glasgow Bank Stock, £1000.
" Antwerp Tool Factory.
" R. Duckworth & Co.'s debt.
" Gorst & Lance's debt.
" T. D. Findlay & Co.'s p/notes, £80,000.

" 13th April 1875.

" 2.

" Credits issued by the City of Glasgow Bank as on Smith, Fleming, & Co.'s " a/c, 31st March 1875.

" Bombay,	£254,564	3	5
" Kurrachee,	60,000	0	0
" Rangoon,	87,390	15	7
" Colombo,	90,500	0	0
" 33/50 our a/c,	60,000	0	0
" 36/35 Sawmill Shares,	10,000	0	0
	" £562,454	19	0"

Then there is No. 3—Cash Advances to Smith, Fleming, & Co., amounting to £771,581, 18s. 2d.

"4.

"Estimate of Debt Charges and Incomings.

"Credits aggregating £570,000 will cost p. annum for comn., stamps, "exchange, and discounts, 5%,	£28,500	
"Cash advance, say £770,000 @ 3½%,	23,485	
"Premium of Ince. on J. Fleming's life,	4,000	
	£55,985	

Incomings.

"Bombay & Kurrachee, interest on partners' capital & on balances,	£13,000	
"Proportion of profits,	28,000	
		£41,000
"Home securities,		10,500
"Interest on money engaged in working this business,		3,500
"Todd, Findlay, & Co.,		15,000
"Fowlie,		1,000
		£71,000
"Probable surplus from Canterbury & Otago stock,		9,000
		£80,000
"Charges as above,		55,985
		£24,015

"13th April 1875.

"JOHN FLEMING."

The total indebtedness of Smith, Fleming, & Co., as at 31st March 1875, was £1,334,000; and at the stoppage of the Bank £1,900,000, or thereby. (Q.) Do you see pencil marks on that document? (A.) Yes. (Q.) In whose handwriting? Some in Mr Stronach's? (A.) Some in Mr Stronach's. (Q.) What are they? Mention one or two of them? (A.) "The power to con-"tinue the credits from time to time." (Q.) At page 6 do you see another handwriting on it, near the foot? (A.) "Five years to hold securities, then "sell if required; £25 when due." (Q.) In whose handwriting is that addition? (A.) Mr Potter's. (Q.) On the next page is there not another addition in Mr Potter's handwriting? (A.) Yes; "Life Policies." (Q.) In the minute of the directors of date 11th January 1877, it is said :—

"It was proposed and agreed to that the Bank should accept drafts by Glen "Walker & Company, to the extent of £20,000 in renewal of those retired for a like "amount due 1st instant on a/c Glen Walker & Co., Melbourne, per minute of 30th "December 1875.

"Also, that the Bank should accept drafts by Glen Walker & Co., to the extent "of £100,000, to retire a like amount, drawn by Holmes, White, & Co., of Mel-"bourne, on account of James Morton & Co. The securities at present held against "Holmes, White, & Co.'s drafts to be placed as security against the drafts of Glen "Walker & Co. Letter to be obtained from James Morton & Co. to this effect."

I also read the minute of 30th December 1875 there referred to :—

"A letter was read from Mr W. Glen Walker, applying for an open letter of "credit for £20,000, in favour of Messrs Glen Walker & Co., Melbourne, to be "drawn at or under 6 mos/st, and depositing stock of the New Zealand and Austra-"lian Land Company, Limited, in security. The application was granted on the "usual terms and conditions, the details being left to the manager to arrange."

Was that credit granted? (A.) It was. (Q.) Was that New Zealand stock referred to in the minute of December lodged? (A.) No. (Q.) The security stipulated was not lodged. (A.) It was not lodged. (Q.) Was any other security lodged in lieu of it? (A.) Not that I am aware of. (Q.) Did the Bank ultimately come under cash advance for the whole of these credits? (A.)

It did. (Q.) To whom was the cash advanced by the Bank debited? (A.) £20,000 was debited to W. Glen Walker. (Q.) I call your attention to a minute of 28th Feb. 1878:—

"A letter was read from Messrs Smith, Fleming, & Co., dated London, 26th " February 1878, applying for letters of credit for £25,000 in favour of Messrs W. " Nicol & Co., Bombay, to be drawn at 3 mos.'/st., in terms of their letter—the " application was granted on the understanding that the drafts are to be retired at " maturity. The manager reported that the Bank had recently been brought into " cash advance to the extent of £48,000 from the proceeds of drafts being short " accounted for by Messrs J. Innes Wright & Co. in connection with the credit of " £100,000 granted to Glen Walker & Co. per minute of 11th January 1877, and " also £18,000 in the placing of the drafts of J. Nicol Fleming in liquidation. It " was resolved to appoint Messrs Stewart and Potter a committee to deal with this " matter, and to report."

Was the credit authorised by that minute carried out? (A.) The credit of £25,000 was. (Q.) Will you explain what you know of the shortcoming of £18,000 in regard to the drafts of Nicol Fleming? (A.) These were Calcutta drafts accepted by the Bank and discounted by John Innes Wright and Co.; £18,000 is the sum short paid from the draft they got away from the Bank. (Q.) Their duty was to pay the proceeds of the bills they got? (A.) Yes. (Q.) Into the Bank to the account of J. Nicol Fleming? (A.) Yes, to retire old drafts maturing. (Q.) And they failed to account for £18,000? (A.) Yes. (Q.) What was the date of that failure? About what time did they discount these bills? (A.) It was over a long period—throughout a considerable period. (Q.) For a considerable period prior to that report in 1878? (A.) Precisely. (Q.) Had you been sent to remonstrate against that shortcoming of £18,000? (A.) Yes, I had. (Q.) Sent by Mr Stronach? (A.) By Mr Stronach. (Q.) And whom did you see when you went to remonstrate with Innes Wright & Co.? (A.) Mr Scott. (Q.) Did you see Mr Innes Wright? (A.) I may have seen him, but I don't recollect. (Q.) What excuse was given? (A.) The excuse that he gave in regard to Glen Walker and Co.'s drafts,—he was waiting telegraphic advice from London, or some such excuse. (Q.) I suppose the Bank had to retire the whole of these acceptances eventually? (A.) Yes. (Q.) No, 400 is a pencil jotting by Mr Scott of the liabilities of his firm? (A.) Yes. (Q.) He there enters the shortcoming of £18,000 as due by the firm? (A.) He does. (Q.) Read it. (A.) "J. N. F. " account £18,000 securities for same will be handed to Mr R. S. S. on or before 21st March 1878 William Scott, 2/3/78: 21st March 78. This has not been done." (Q.) In whose handwriting are the words "This has not " been done?" (A.) Mr Robert Stronach, the manager's.

By the Lord Justice-Clerk—(Q.) What was the date of the meeting you described with Messrs Stewart, Stronach, and Potter, about Scott's short payment? (A.) About the beginning of March last.

By the Lord Advocate—(Q.) [Shown No. 120.] Where was that book kept? (A.) As a rule, the manager had it in his possession. It was made up by me. So far as I am aware, it was not communicated to Mr Morison, the accountant, or to any of the other officials of the Bank. It is titled on the outside—"Special securities, J. N. F., S., F., & Co., J. M. & Co., and others." The initials are those of James Nicol Fleming, Smith, Fleming, & Co., and James Morton & Co. That book was made up at the balancing period of June 1877. It contains statements in either ink or pencil of the whole indebtedness to the Bank of James Nicol Fleming, Smith, Fleming, & Co., and James Morton and Co. It includes their whole indebtedness, whether on open credits, cash advances, or past due bills. It also contains statements of the securities held against these credits in the case of each of them. James Nicol Fleming's account appears in that book as at 6th June 1877. His total indebtedness upon cash credits, bills, and otherwise at that date was £1,142,480, 11s. 7d.

The summation of the securities stated to be held against that is £1,142,480, 11s. 7d. The two sides balance.

By the Lord Justice-Clerk—(Q.) Do you mean that the securities were exactly equal in value to the debt? (A.) Yes, it is so stated. That is the meaning of the entry, as I read it. I made the entry myself.

By the Lord Advocate—The total indebtedness of Smith, Fleming, & Co. at the same date was £1,670,643, and the special securities stated to be held against that amount to £1,114,710, so that the advances were uncovered to the extent of (in round numbers) £560,000. The total indebtedness of James Morton & Co. at the same date was £1,858,294, 11s. 6d. and the securities are entered at £1,018,807, leaving a deficit (in round numbers) of £840,000. Taking these three firms together, the Bank was in advance, or had given credit to them to the amount of (in round numbers) £4,670,000, and against that the Bank are stated in that book to hold securities to the amount of £3,275,000, leaving a total deficit of securities as against advances of £1,395,000. The date at which that is taken is as at the commencement of June 1877. With regard to the securities stated to be held against James Nicol Fleming's indebtedness, the capital invested in his Manchester and Calcutta business is put down as a security granted to the Bank. The amount of that was £40,000. The Bank did not hold the capital embarked in his business, or any title to it. There is also entered a sum held in security by the British Linen Co. in course of being reduced, to the amount of £5814. The Bank had no title to that. Then there is an item of policies on Mr Fleming's life, stated as a security for £100,000,—that is the total amount of the policies. These were only realisable to that extent on Mr Fleming's death; there is no deduction made, and no estimate of their surrender or selling value. These are the insurances for which £4000 of premium appeared in a former account. (Q.) There is a sum of £796,000 brought out there among these securities; how do you get that out of the stocks that are stated there? (A.) The stocks were valued at 400 per cent. premium in order to make the two sides balance. These stocks consisted of New Zealand and Australian Land Company shares. Their par value was £62, 10s. I am not aware of their ever having reached 400 per cent. premium. (Q.) But that was done for the purpose of making the two ends meet? (A.) Yes. (Q.) The securities and the advances? (A.) Yes. (Q.) Who directed that to be done? (A.) Probably I did it myself. (Q.) Without directions? (A.) Without directions. (Q.) When you say that probably you did it, do you mean you may not have done it yourself? (A.) I did it myself; I may have got instructions from the manager. (Q.) What were your instructions in regard to the preparation of that statement of advances and securities? (A.) I don't think I had any particular instructions. (Q.) Had you any instructions in regard to it after you had begun the work? (A.) No, I don't remember. (Q.) Did you show Mr Stronach your valuation? (A.) Yes, I think I did. (Q.) And you gave him the book? (A.) He had the book. (Q.) In fact, he kept it after you made it up? (A.) Yes. (Q.) How did you come to make the securities balance with the amount due in the case of James Nicol Fleming, and not in the others? (A.) I cannot remember; I don't recollect why that was done. James Nicol Fleming's account was in liquidation at the time; I mean, we were realising the securities as fast as we could. (Q.) Did you expect to get 400 per cent. premium for those stocks in realising them? (A.) I had no idea of the value of the stocks. (Q.) Did you think at the time you made the entry that they would ever realise 400 per cent. in liquidation then? (A.) No. (Q.) Why did you put them at 400 per cent. when making up that account as in liquidation? (A.) I cannot tell. (Q.) In point of fact, when you made that entry, did you believe these stocks would bring that in liquidation at the time? (A.) No, I did not. (Q.) But you thought the account would look better if the two sides balanced? (A.) Probably. Taking next Smith,

Fleming, & Co.'s account, there are entered as securities policies of insurance on the life of John Fleming to the amount of £100,000. In the previous account the policies were on the life of James Nicol Fleming. The policies on the life of John Fleming are also stated at their full value as realisable at his death. Another special security stated is the estimated capital upon which Smith, Fleming, & Co. were trading, £254,000. That is put as a special security held by the Bank against those advances. It was not held by the Bank. They were supposed to be trading with it. (Q.) There is another special security in that list—a debt due of £60,000,—by whom was that due? (A.) By William Nicol & Co., and Fleming & Co., of Bombay and Kurrachee respectively, to Smith, Fleming, & Co. That is included in the £254,000. (Q.) In the £254,000 trading stock of those people which the Bank are stated to hold as security, how many elephants are included? (A.) There were six elephants upon a schedule attached to the Rangoon security. With regard to Morton & Co's account, there are included as special securities life policies to the amount of £48,000 and £17,000, in all £65,000. These are estimated at full value in the same way as the other policies. (Q.) Was there not £125,000 of policies? (A.) I was not aware there were £125,000. I observe in this book an entry of £25,000, and another of £120,000 in pencil. That £120,000 is not included in the total summation.

By Mr Smith—I know that Mr Wright has two firms—one in Glasgow and the other in London. I believe they are different firms. Mr Scott is a partner of the Glasgow firm. As a rule, it was Mr Scott whom I saw in my interviews about the accounts of the firm. The bills I believe were handed to the firm for the purpose of discounting. I am not aware how they were discounted. I know they were sent by Mr Scott to his brother in London. I am not aware whether they received a commission for these. (Q.) But they were given to Wright & Co. in order that Mr Scott might send them to his brother in London to be discounted? (A.) Yes; or to some other broker. (Q.) Then Wright & Co. acted the part of bill-brokers in the matter? [Shown No. 215, letter, J. Innes Wright & Co. to R. S. Stronach, dated Glasgow 2d August 1876.] That letter is in the handwriting of Mr Scott. It is apparently written on behalf of Glen Walker & Co., of Melbourne. The purpose of the transaction, I understood, was to enable Glen Walker & Co. to buy produce in Melbourne, which was to be shipped to this country. The proceeds were to go to pay these drafts. The application is for £100,000. Of these bills there were returned £40,000, and £3000 lapsed—that is to say, were not presented for acceptance.

By the Lord Justice-Clerk—To the extent of £43,000 they were never turned into money.

By Mr Smith—That left £57,000 under this application which was actually used. That account was entered in the books of the Bank under the name of John Innes Wright & Co. (Q.) Was there anything else at the heading of the account? (A.) Yes; "Wool Liens." Referring to the account, I find the drafts are favouring Glen Walker & Co., Melbourne. (Q.) That is to say, John Innes Wright & Co. were the primary debtors to the Bank under this letter, but Glen Walker & Co. were debtors also? (A.) Yes, as being the drawers of the drafts. (Q.) So that failing Wright & Co., the Bank would have a claim against Glen Walker & Co.? (A.) I presume so. (Q.) Do you know if £35,000 of these drafts was used in the purchase of wool? (A.) I cannot answer that. (Q.) Do you know that £25,000 was got upon wool liens to the value of £35,000, and paid into the Bank? (A.) John Innes Wright paid into the Bank £25,000, but I am not aware if it was got upon wool liens. (Q.) Do you know if Glen Walker & Co. paid for some land with these drafts by instructions of the Bank? (A.) I believe £17,000 was used by Glen Walker & Co. for the purchase of land on behalf of the Edinburgh Pastoral Association. I was not aware at that time, but I now know that that was the Bank. (Q.) Do you know also if a further sum was used in the purchase of tin and tallow? (A.) Yes; I have seen such a sum in Walker's statements to the amount of about £7000. (Q.) Was it not £8465? (A.) Perhaps so. I cannot tell whether that tin and tallow was sent direct to Wright & Co., London. The undertaking in the letter is to pay in the proceeds of the produce actually shipped to account of drafts. I am not aware whether there was any loss. With regard to the original credit of £235,000, the application letter, I think, is dated in August 1871. That credit was opened in favour of Holmes, White, & Co., who, I believe, were merchants in Melbourne. Their drafts were accepted by the Bank, and were discounted by James Morton & Co. The £100,000 in favour of Glen Walker & Co. was in substitution of part of these drafts. (Q.) So it was really the substitution of Glen Walker & Co. for Holmes, White. & Co. to the extent of £100,000 of the original credit opened in 1871? (A.) Yes. These drafts were handed to Potter, Wilson, & Co. for the purpose of discounting. Potter, Wilson, and Co. handed them over to Innes Wright & Co. to be discounted. They were drawn by Glen Walker & Co. (Q.) Whom did they represent? (A.) James Morton & Co., I should think.

By the Lord Justice-Clerk—It was on behalf of James Morton & Co.'s credit that Glen Walker & Co. did it.

By Mr Smith—You understood that Glen Walker & Co. were the same as Morton & Co.,—were acting on behalf of Morton & Co.? (A.) Yes. (Q.) Was there anything on the face of the bills to show that such was their true character? (A.) No. (Q.) Or anywhere else? (A.) No; I think not.

By the Lord Justice-Clerk—(Q.) Why were Glen Walker & Co.'s bills given to Potter? (A.) Potter apparently was financing—was arranging. He held the drafts. (Q.) As the financial agent of Glen Walker & Co. in this country. Was that so? (A.) I don't know, I am sure, whether they were financial agents or not. (Q.) Why did you give Glen Walker & Co.'s bills to Potter & Co.? (A.) I cannot say why they were given; they were given for discount to replace drafts maturing under Morton's credit. (Q.) Why were they given to Potter's firm? Were they acting for the Bank, or were they acting for the customer, Glen Walker & Co.? (A.) I cannot say who they were acting for. (Q.) But the fact is, the drafts were given to Potter's firm, and they gave them to Innes Wright & Co.? (A.) Yes. (Q.) To discount? (A.) To discount.

By Mr Smith—(Q.) What is the shortcoming upon these discounts at this date? How much is it reduced to? (A.) Upwards of £40,000 now. (Q.) There were some bills granted by the London firm in reduction of this balance? (A.) Yes. (Q.) To what extent? (A.) About £34,000 altogether, I think. (Q.) Supposing these London bills were paid, what would be the balance? (A.) £26,000. (Q.) Is it not £16,000? (A.) Yes, £16,000. (Q.) Did any one tell you if Wright & Co. had authority to retain any portion of these discounts? (A.) Yes, I understood that they were allowed to retain £15,000. (Q.) So that it comes to this, that if the bills were paid, the sum due now would just be £1000 in excess of the sum they were allowed to retain? (A.) Yes; but the sum they were allowed to retain was while they had the credit,—while they were discounting the drafts, and not after. (Q.) How was this account entered in the Bank books? (A.) I cannot say; the check clerk could answer that. (Q.) And you don't know how the account was closed? (A.) The account is not closed; there is still a balance standing. (Q.) A balance at the debit of whom? Glen Walker & Co.? (A.) I am not sure whether it is Glen Walker & Co.'s name that is the title of the account or not. (Q.) Wright & Co. had various accounts opened subsequently to June 1875? (A.) Yes. (Q.) If we except the wool lien credit, and these discounts, are these accounts now all closed? (A.) No. (Q.) Which of them are open? (A.) There are a great number of accounts open of John Innes Wright & Co. still. (Q.) Are there any of the accounts which have been opened since 1875 still open? (A.) Yes, they are still open. (Q.) The credit accounts? (A.) The credit accounts are open—that is to say, the cash credits are still open; you are perhaps confounding them with the foreign and colonial credits. (Q.) There are no foreign and colonial credits which have been opened since 1875 now open? (A.) No. (Q.) Do you know the indebtedness of Wright & Co. in June 1875? (A.) I think it is upwards of £400,000. (Q.) If you exclude the interest upon that sum, the wool lien credit, and these discounts, is the indebtedness now less or more? (A.) Do you mean less on the present balance? (Q.) That is what I mean? (A.) I cannot say whether it will be less on the present balance or not; that is to say, the balance at the stoppage of the Bank. (Q.) Do you know when the debt of £18,000 arose—the shortcoming in connection with J. Nicol Fleming's account? (A.) I think it commenced about 1876. It arose from short payments of the Bank's acceptances which they got from James Nicol Fleming to discount. (Q.) What was the form of these bills? (A.) They were John Innes Wright's bills. (Q.) Was he drawer or acceptor? (A.) They were drawn upon the Bank; they were all Bank's acceptances. (Q.) Were they given to Wright & Co.? (A.) Yes; through J. Nicol Fleming.

By the Lord Justice-Clerk—They were to have the bills discounted. I understood they were discounted; I believe they were sent to London.

By Mr Smith—(Q.) Did these bills not come to Wright & Co. from Nicol Fleming? (A.) Yes. (Q.) Then Wright & Co. will be responsible to Nicol Fleming for these bills? (A.) Yes, I should say so.

By Mr Trayner—(Q.) No. 400 contains a statement of "arrangement as "to settlement of G. W. & Co.'s balance," and it is headed "J. Innes "Wright & Co.?" (A.) Yes. (Q.) In whose handwriting is that account down to the summation of £48,000? (A.) In my own handwriting. It was written out by me prior to the meeting with Mr Scott in Mr Potter's office. It is dated 1st March 1878. I cannot say on what day the meeting was held,—perhaps the day after the preparation of this document. The portion of it "London firm's bills to be given to-day for £10,000. Wm. "Scott to give orders for sale of sugar to-day. Mr Scott meets us on Wed-"nesday to arrange the remainder," is in Mr Stewart's handwriting. I had that document with me at the meeting. (Q.) Was that last portion added by Mr Stewart after he had spoken in the angry terms in which you described him as having spoken to Mr Scott? (A.) I cannot say. It was not on the paper when I took it to the meeting. I did not get it back from Mr Stewart after I returned to the room. I next saw it sometime after; I may not have got it back till after the stoppage; I don't know when I got it back. When I next saw it, it had that last portion, "London firm's bills," &c., on it in Mr Stewart's handwriting. (Q.) Had you become aware that that was the arrangement before you saw that writing by Mr Stewart? (A.) Yes. (Q.) Have you any doubt that that is just the embodiment by Mr Stewart of the arrangement that took place when you were asked to retire? (A.) No. (Q.) Along with that state there is a pencil slip, "J. N. F.'s account, £18,000. Securities for "same will be handed to Mr R. S. S. on or before 21st March 1878"; that related to the same business, did it not? (A.) No, it did not. (Q.) Was that given by Scott on the same date when the other arrangement was entered into? (A.) I cannot say. (Q.) Had you that before you when you prepared this statement which was laid before the meeting? (A.) No, I think not. (Q.) The next letter, No. 401, by Mr Scott to Mr Stewart, dated 21st March 1878, says, "This is the Greenock fast-day, so the sugar market is closed. Business will, "no doubt, go on as usual on Monday or Tuesday first." Does that not enable you to come nearer the date of the meeting at which Mr Scott undertook "to give "orders for sale of sugar to-day"? (A.) Yes; it must have been about the 20th, apparently. (Q.) From this letter you think the meeting with Mr Stewart and

Mr Scott to which you spoke must have taken place about 20th March? (A.) Evidently from this letter. (Q.) The postscript is, "The above was sent us "in reply to our order to sell a cargo to-day"; so that Mr Scott had sent to Greenock an order to sell in terms of his undertaking? (A.) Apparently so. (Q.) And the reply comes back that it is the fast-day, and so he excuses the non-fulfilment of it that day. That is what it comes to, is it not? (A.) Yes.

By Mr Mackintosh—(Q.) Do you remember anything about the meeting referred to by Mr Fleming in his letter to Mr Stronach of 12th April 1875 (No. 186), "Referring to the meeting I had with your directors and yourself "on Thursday"? (A.) No; I remember there was such a meeting. (Q.) Look at the letter No. 78 from Mr Stronach to John Fleming, 5th April 1875, "In terms of the arrangement concluded at the meeting of the committee of "directors," &c. Does that refer to the same meeting? (A.) I should think so. (Q.) You see from that letter that the meeting referred to in the letter of 12th April as a "meeting of your directors" was a meeting with the "com-"mittee of directors"? (A.) Yes. I do not know who were the members of that committee. I believe that will appear from the minutes.

By the Dean of Faculty—(Q.) Was the arrangement in the letter of 12th April for the adjustment of Smith, Fleming, & Co.'s account carried out? (A.) I believe it was. (Q.) Was the account of Smith, Fleming, & Co. taken from the current accounts on which customers were operating, and put into the accountant's department in consequence of that arrangement? (A.) I am not aware whether it was in consequence of that arrangement or not. (Q.) But it was done at that time? (A.) There was a sum transferred about that time. (Q.) Do you remember writing the letter of 20th April 1875, Mr Stronach to John Fleming, "I would suggest with reference to the account, and the "majority of which appears to be dormant, that the inoperative should be "consolidated, and that one or two having occasional operations, such as the "No. 1 cash and the No. 1 trust, to remain as then, are for working purposes. "This arrangement would simplify our working considerably here, and would, "no doubt, I think, be equally advantageous to you"? (A.) I remember something of that letter. The dormant accounts were those upon which there were few or no operations going on. These were put in the accountant's department. I cannot give the indebtedness of Smith, Fleming, & Co., James Nicol Fleming, and Morton, as at 1st January 1876, or at June 1876. (Q.) What induced you to make up the indebtedness as at June 1877? (A.) Because previously these accounts were all kept upon sheets, and that was the date at which the book was made up; the balance was made up as at June 1877. The sheets are still in existence; some of them may have been destroyed. (Q.) Did Morton's indebtedness arise before January 1876? (A.) Yes. (Q.) He was very heavily indebted, was he not, at the time you became manager's clerk even? (A.) Yes, even then. (Q.) But still had not Morton in Australia and New Zealand properties that were looked on as exceedingly valuable? (A.) Yes, he had properties. (Q.) Have you not heard deliberations going on either amongst the directors, or between the directors and Mr Stronach, as to the probability of these properties rising very largely in value, and clearing off the whole of his debt? (A.) Yes; not clearing off the whole of his debt. (Q.) But clearing off a great part of it? (A.) Yes. (Q.) Down to what date did you hear these deliberations? (A.) The properties were always considered valuable. I heard that they were always considered valuable. (Q.) Had Smith, Fleming, & Co. any Australian and New Zealand properties? (A.) Yes; there were 1003 shares, I think. (Q.) I suppose you looked upon that property as having the same prospects as to rise as the property belonging to Morton? (A.) Yes. (Q.) Had Smith, Fleming, & Co. not pledged to the Bank properties at Bombay, Kurrachee, and in Rangoon? (A.) Yes. (Q.) And these were only taken as security for debt after valuation made?

(A.) Yes. I believe part of these properties has been realised in Bombay. Some of it has not been realised. Their property in Rangoon was valued in the books at £86,000, I think. I am not aware that any of the Rangoon property has been sold. (Q.) At the time you made up that book in June 1877, was the New Zealand stock quoted in the market lists? (A.) No, I think not. I quoted it at par. I cannot at present state the indebtedness of Smith, Fleming, & Co., as at 1st January 1876. (Q.) At the end of 1875 had there been incurred by Smith, Fleming, & Co. nine-tenths of that debt which they were owing to the Bank when it stopped? (A.) I should think so. The greater portion of James Nicol Fleming's debt was incurred before 1876. I don't think there was any advance made to him from the beginning of 1876 onwards, except in connection with the Australian and New Zealand properties. (Q.) The Bank ordered these properties to be bought in Australia and New Zealand as a speculation of their own? (A.) I don't know that. (Q.) But you know that they ordered these properties to be bought? (A.) No, I did not. (Q.) Don't you know that they did buy property in Australia and New Zealand? (A.) Not on behalf of James Nicol Fleming. (Q.) Did they buy property on their own account, in their own name, or in the name of others in trust for them? (A.) Yes. I had no particular instructions to make up the book in June 1877.

By the Lord Advocate—I made it up for the information of the manager, and to keep the state of accounts before him. (Q.) You said you heard some persons, in connection with the Bank, speculating as to the probable rise of Morton's securities? (A.) Yes. (Q.) Who were these individuals? (A.) The manager. (Q.) Any other? (A.) And Mr John Hunter. (Q.) But none of the directors of the Bank? (A.) And Mr Potter too, I think, was very sanguine as to the properties. (Q.) Are you making that statement from what you heard Mr Potter say in your presence? (A.) Yes. (Q. What was Mr Potter discussing at the time he made that statement as to his being sanguine, and with whom was he discussing? (A.) He was discussing in regard to the New Zealand shares, a statement of which was before him and the manager. (Q.) Were these the shares that the Bank themselves held. (A.) Yes, or were supposed to have held. (Q.) Was it in regard to their own shares that he expressed that hope, or was it both in regard to their own shares and those they held in security? (A.) I understood the observation as applying to both. (Q.) At the time he expressed a hope that the shares would rise, did he say anything as to how far they would extinguish Morton's indebtedness, or not? (A.) No; he said nothing about that. He spoke generally about the probability of the shares rising. About 1875 certain accounts were dormant,—that is, inoperative. There were debtor balances upon the whole of them. (Q.) And by dormant you mean that the debtor was not paying what was due to the Bank? (A.) Yes. (Q.) Was the interest not accumulating? (A.) Yes, I believe so; I am not aware whether interest was added when they were transferred or not. (Q.) You don't know whether it was entered, but I suppose you knew it was bearing interest? (A.) Yes. (Q.) Then what you meant by dormant was that the debtor was not paying, but that interest was accumulating and the debt swelling? (A.) Yes.

By the Lord Justice-Clerk—(Q.) In dormant accounts, which I suppose mean accounts where there are no operations, is interest charged generally? (A.) It is. (Q.) Is it kept on—charged—year after year in the account? (A.) Yes. (Q.) Or does it after a time cease to be charged? (A.) No; I think not. It is continued to be charged. (Q.) This additional set of books, —who directed you to keep them? (A.) Mr Alexander Stronach. (Q.) Why? (A.) For his own convenience. (Q.) With regard to these particular debts? (A.) Yes. (Q.) Where did you get the material that enabled you to keep the book? (A.) I got it from the register downstairs, kept in the public office. (Q.) It was a duplicate, you say? (A.) Yes. (Q.) So I suppose the same persons had their accounts in the ordinary accounts who had their accounts in your books? (A.) Yes; precisely. (Q.) Were they the same? (A.) They were differently arranged—a little. (Q.) But the materials were substantially the same? (A.) Precisely the same. (Q.) How did you come to value these securities at your own hand in the case of James Nicol Fleming? (A.) I did not value the whole of the securities for James Nicol Fleming. It was only the stock that I extended in a pencil jotting. (Q.) I think you said that the value you attributed to the security in the book was exactly the same as the amount of indebtedness? (A.) Yes. (Q.) Why did you do that? Had you any means of ascertaining that the value was the same, or that the securities were worth that amount? (A.) No, I had not. (Q.) Was it a mere random thing? (A.) Yes, a mere random thing. It was done upon the principle of making the two sides correspond. (Q.) Is that the only random sum in your book? (A.) No. (Q.) There may be others? (A.) Yes; there are securities that really did not exist. (Q.) And that was done entirely at your own hand? (A.) It was done from information obtained from the manager's sheets. (Q.) Without instructions? (A.) Yes; from drafts made out by the late manager. (Q.) Would you have made any of these entries without authority from the manager? (A.) Oh, no. (Q.) You had authority for them all? (A.) Yes. (Q.) Including that one of the valuation of the securities? (A.) Well, nothing was said when the book was lying with the manager—nothing was said with regard to the extension of the value of the stock. (Q.) But you assumed that was what you were meant to do? (A.) Yes. (Q.) When you say that you made these entries from sheets made up by the late manager, to whom do you refer? (A.) Mr Alexander Stronach. (Q.) It was from these sheets you made these entries? (A.) Yes; with respect to Smith, Fleming, & Co. and James Morton & Co. (Q.) Where were these sheets when you made up the book in 1877? (A.) They were in my possession. (Q.) Was Mr Robert Stronach aware that you had these things? (A.) Yes, I think so. (Q.) He had seen the sheets? (A.) Yes. (Q.) Just explain to me a little more distinctly about these marginal credits and the bills that were granted under them. If I rightly follow the course of the transaction it was this, that in consideration of securities the Bank undertook to accept bills to a specific amount, granting a variety of bills with the precise amount of the credit attached to them? (A.) Precisely. (Q.) These bills being granted to the drawer and accepted by the Bank, he then proceeded to discount them? (A.) Yes, but they were not always granted to the drawer. (Q.) But sometimes with the drawer's name on them, they were given by the Bank to be discounted, and the proceeds to be paid to them? (A.) Yes. (Q.) Was that uniform, that the proceeds of the discount were to be paid to the account of the drawer in the Bank? (A.) Not of the drawer,—to the endorser of the bill or the applicant for the credit. (Q.) But that was the mode of dealing? (A.) It was. (Q.) In this case the bills were drawn in favour of Glen Walker & Co. of Australia? (A.) Yes. (Q.) They were accepted by the Bank, and handed to Potter, Wilson, & Co. for the purpose of discounting them, and paying in the proceeds to the Bank? (A.) Yes. (Q.) And they again employed Innes Wright & Co. to get them discounted? (A.) Yes. (Q.) Innes Wright & Co. sent them to their London firm. Are the London firm brokers? (A.) Not to the London firm. (Q.) Where did they send them? (A.) To H. C. Scott, I think, as a rule. (Q.) As a bill broker? (A.) Yes. (Q.) In order that he might discount them in London, and transmit the proceeds here? (A.) Yes. (Q.) And that he failed to do to a certain extent? (A.) Yes.

JOHN TURNBULL.

By the Solicitor-General—I have been cashier to the City of Glasgow Bank for about eighteen years, and I was accountant before that. I have been in the service of the Bank since 1843. When I became a servant of the Bank Mr Robert Salmond was the manager. He ceased to be manager about 1858, when the Bank resumed after the stoppage in 1857. I cannot tell how long Mr Robert Stronach was in the employment of the Bank. He was there before the stoppage in 1857. It was my duty as cashier to take charge of making up the weekly returns of gold and silver coin. I kept two books—the cashier's ledger and the circulation ledger. [Shown Nos. 95 and 96.] These are the books which I kept. The cashier's ledger (No. 95) contains entries showing day by day the reserve stock of money as represented by gold and silver and bank notes—that is, the gold, silver, and bank notes which were not out in issue or in the hands of the tellers. The entries in that book are all correct. No. 96 is the circulation ledger, in which should be shown the gold and silver lying at the head office as against notes issued in excess of the authorised circulation. (Q.) In the beginning of 1878, did you find the Bank's credit being strained? (A.) Yes. (Q.) Did you find renewals of bills being refused in London? (A.) Yes. (Q.) Did that necessitate gold being sent to London from the Bank? (A.) Yes. During the week ending 5th January there had been £60,000 in gold sent to London. (Q.) From whom did you get the directions to send it up? (A.) From the manager, through Mr Murdoch, who is my assistant. (Q.) In making up the statement or figures of the entries for that week, was the amount correctly stated of what was in your hands? (A.) No. (Q.) What was the incorrectness? (A.) £60,000. (Q.) The £60,000 which was sent to London was not deducted? (A.) No. (Q.) Explain to me how that came about? (A.) I cannot give you any explanation further than the fact. (Q.) Who suggested it to you? (A.) I must do it. We are bound to do it to agree with the issue of notes. (Q.) Did you speak to Mr Stronach about that? (A.) Not upon that particular occasion. (Q.) Did you speak to him when you had to make the return to the commissioners of stamps and taxes? (A.) Not on that occasion. (Q.) When did you speak to him? (A.) Several times afterwards—frequently afterwards. (Q.) Had you sent several returns to the commissioners of stamps and taxes, stating the sum at the full amount without taking off the £60,000, before you spoke to him? (A.) I may have. (Q.) When did you speak to him first about it? (A.) I cannot give the date of that. (Q.) But nearly? (A.) I really cannot give the date. It may have been a week or a fortnight. (Q.) But a very short time after the thing was done? (A.) Yes. (Q.) What did you say to him? (A.) I expressed my regret that the thing should have been necessary or should have been done,—that it was wrong to do it. (Q.) What did he say? (A.) That it could not be helped. (Q.) Anything more? (A.) I think not—not at that time. Afterwards he said of course that he was responsible for it. (Q.) Between that date in January 1878, and down to the stoppage of the Bank, in how many weeks was the amount of gold overstated in the returns made? (A.) I think, during the whole time, except two weeks.—these two weeks being the week ending 16th February and the week ending 16th March. (Q.) That was down to 28th September, which was the last, about which I will ask you more particularly. Was the amount of over-statement increasing during that time? (A.) It varied. (Q.) But did it gradually increase? Did it gradually come up to £293,182 at the end? (A.) Yes, about that. (Q.) Will you look at the book, and say whether under the head of the amount of gold each day during these months there is not a double entry made? (A.) There is an interlining. (Q.) That is to say, within the space for the entry of gold for that day there is an interlining? (A.) Yes. (Q.) Does the large figure give the amount that was returned? (A.) No; it gives the actual cash, and the other gives the shortage. (Q.) Do those inserted figures give correctly the amount of shortage in each case? (A.) Yes. The last return that was made was for the week ending 28th September 1878. The amount in that return was stated correctly according to the amount in the coffers of the Bank. I did not sign that last return. I had signed all the previous ones, and sent them in. (Q.) Why did you not sign the last one? (A.) I had various reasons. I wished that the last return should not have been sent at all. (Q.) Because it corrected the previous ones? (A.) Not only that; but the Bank had stopped payment, and the right of issue was lost, and there was nothing to be gained by sending the return. (Q.) But the return was quite contradictory of the previous ones? (A.) Of course it was. (Q.) Who signed it? (A.) The manager. I remember of a meeting of the board on 11th October 1878, after the Bank had stopped. I was called in before the directors that day. (Q.) Who spoke to you? (A.) The chairman, I think. (Q.) Who was the chairman? (A.) Mr Salmond, I think. (Q.) What did he ask you? (A.) He asked my reasons why the return had not been made of the last week that the Bank was open. I am not sure it was Mr Salmond that spoke to me; but I think so; he was in the chair. [Shown No. 317.] That is a letter dated the same day, and addressed by me to Mr Cousins, Inland Revenue Office, London. It is as follows:—

"City of Glasgow Bank, 11th October 1878.

"W. W. Cousins, Esq.,
"Inland Revenue, London.

"Dear Sir,—I beg to acknowledge receipt of your letter of the 7th instant, and "to inform you that immediately on receipt, I handed it to the manager of the "Bank, under whose instructions I have hitherto made the returns to your office. "You may probably be aware that the Bank has stopped payment, and that its "affairs are under investigation.—I am, sir, your obedient servant,

"John Turnbull."

(Q.) Did you lay that letter before the meeting of directors? (A.) I sent them a copy. (Q.) You gave them a copy of it? (A.) Yes. (Q.) Was the statement in that letter true as to the instructions under which you had made the returns as you had made them? (A.) Quite true. (Q.) Did anything else pass between the directors and you after you showed them that letter? (A.) No, nothing more.

By Mr Asher—I think you said that it was in January 1878 that the gold was overstated for the first time in the return to the inland revenue? (A.) Yes. (Q.) And that return was so made, you said, by the instructions of the manager? (A.) All the returns were. (Q.) Did you get any instructions from the directors with regard to that matter? (A.) None. (Q.) When did the directors first know that the gold had been overstated in the return? (A.) I don't think they knew at all until after the Bank had stopped. I have been cashier of the Bank for about eighteen years; and before that I was in the employment of the Bank for about seventeen years. As cashier I had charge of several of the securities. (Q.) When did you first suspect that anything was wrong with the Bank? (A.) Never until the gold was meddled with. (Q.) Until the error was made in the return of the gold in January 1878, you, as cashier, had no reason to suspect that there was anything wrong with the Bank? (A.) None whatever. (Q.) And the error in the return of the gold was your only reason then for suspecting; is that so? (A.) That is so. I am a shareholder of the Bank for £1000 of stock. I still hold that stock. I have known Mr Salmond for a long time. He has lived in the country, in Ayrshire, for many years. I cannot give a date when he went to reside there, but I should think it must be twelve or fifteen years ago,—probably more. I think he has not had a house in Glasgow for a number of years. (Q.) So that he came up from the country for the weekly meetings of the Bank when he was able to attend? (A.) Yes. (Q.) How long did the weekly meetings last? (A.) I cannot tell that; I was never present at any of them. I should think about an hour usually, or an hour and a-half. (Q.) Was it only for the weekly meetings that Mr Salmond has been in the habit of coming to the Bank for a number of years? (A.) I think so.

By Mr Trayner—Would you look at some papers that are attached to the circulation ledger, in the inside of it. You will find there the amount of cash, as at 5th June 1878, initialed by Mr Stewart? (A.) Yes. (Q.) And different sums are distinguished there as being situated in different safes? (A.) Yes. (Q.) Was that, as initialed, a correct state of the cash in the Bank at the time? (A.) Perfectly correct. (Q.) You were cashier, and you know that that is in point of fact the correct amount of cash that was in the different safes as there put down? (A.) Perfectly correct.

By the Solicitor-General—Did Mr Stewart take that upon your statement without counting the gold himself or turning it out at all? (A.) He counted the notes. (Q.) But he did not count the gold? (A.) Not in 1878. (Q.) Did he take it on trust from you? (A.) Entirely. (Q.) And he initialed the amount that you had put down? (A.) Yes. (Q.) Were you aware at the end of 1877 that the directors of the Bank had advanced over five millions to three firms,—James Nicol Fleming, Smith, Fleming, & Co., and James Morton & Co.? (A.) No. (Q.) You knew nothing about the internal affairs of the Bank? (A.) No.

By the Lord Justice-Clerk—Why was it on that particular occasion in 1878 that Mr Stewart took your reason for not counting the gold? (A.) There are a number of reasons. It was generally done at the close of the business of the year, and of the day late in the afternoon; and the safe was a very small safe, and it was a very troublesome thing to take out such a large quantity of gold as that. It cost us a great deal of trouble; that was one reason. I volunteered to turn the gold out if Mr Stewart wished it, but he was satisfied. (Q.) You would have turned it out if he had wished it, but it was quite a correct state, you say? (A.) Yes, quite a correct state. (Q.) When was the gold first short? (A.) On 5th January 1878, or about that date. (Q.) And you were aware when you made the return that it was in excess of what you had? (A.) Yes, perfectly. (Q.) And you continued to do that until the end? (A.) Yes. (Q.) Was there no check upon the amount of gold in the ordinary management of the Bank? (A.) There was a check at the close of each year in the directors counting it. (Q.) But did the directors count the gold? (A.) In 1877, in 1876, and previous years, it was all counted. (Q.) They did so? (A.) Yes. (Q.) Did they do it in 1878? (A.) They did not count it in 1878. (Q.) Why? (A.) They took it upon my word. (Q.) But how did they come to give up the practice? (A.) There were several reasons. (Q.) Was it your doing? (A.) No. (Q.) Then how did they come to give up the practice? (A.) Well, I cannot tell. It used to be taken out and laid upon the floor of the manager's room, but in consequence of some alterations in the office. the directors came to sit in the manager's room, and they had their large table in the middle of the room. (Q.) Was there any reason in 1878 why they should not have done the same thing that they did in 1877? (A.) That was one reason. (Q.) Was that a reason applicable to 1878 only? (A.) To 1878 only. (Q.) However, the fact is that they did not count it? (A.) They did not count it. (Q.) The first short return, you say, was on 5th January 1878? (A.) I think so. (Q.) What had been returned the week before? (A.) In January 1878, the total amount of gold and silver in hand was £577.763; in the previous week it was £557,015. (Q.) What is the difference? (A.) About £20,000.

By Lord Craighill—(Q.) What was the amount of gold that was returned to the inland revenue office in the week before 5th June 1878? (A.) The amount of gold and silver returned on 1st June 1878 was £613,642. (Q.) And the amount initialed by Mr Stewart was what? (A.) £338,500. (Q.) When had that gold been counted? (A.) It was counted by the directors the previous year. (Q.) But when had that gold been counted, the sum of which you gave to Mr Stewart? (A.) It was counted at various times since I took it in. (Q.) When had it been last counted? (A.) The previous year. (Q.) Not since the previous year? (A.) No. (Q.) On what did you proceed in making your returns to the inland revenue? (A.) The returns to the inland revenue at that point show £200,000 of gold improperly stated. (Q.) But on what did you proceed in making your returns to the inland revenue? Were the sums all the same every week? (A.) They were altering every week. (Q.) On what did you proceed in making the alterations? (A.) I don't understand your question. (Q.) How did you come to know what was in the coffers of the Bank? (A.) By it being in my own possession. (Q.) When was it counted? (A.) By me? (Q.) Yes. (A.) I counted it every day as the gold came in and went out. (Q.) Was one of your reasons for not having the gold counted before Mr Stewart on 5th June 1878, that you were aware of the deficiency? (A.) No.

By the Lord Justice-Clerk—(Q.) I understand that the return you made to the inland revenue was a thing you did yourself,—the directors had nothing to do with it? (A.) Nothing whatever. (Q.) And you did not communicate with them before you made it? (A.) No; never. (Q.) Then the only thing that was wrong was the return you made? (A.) Yes. (Q.) And you returned it as if nothing had been taken out? (A.) Yes.

By the Solicitor-General—(Q.) The amount that was wrong stated has been entered in the space for the statement of the true figures every week in your book? (A.) Yes. (Q.) The erroneous figure has been put into the book, and it is the adding of the true figure and the erroneous figure that made up the amount sent in the return? (A.) Yes.

By the Lord Justice-Clerk—(Q.) That is the interlineation? (A.) Yes.

By the Solicitor-General—(Q.) What book is it in? (A.) The circulation book.

By the Lord Justice-Clerk—(Q.) So, as I thought before, there is a double entry in your circulation book,—one of which represents the actual gold, and the other represents the deficiency? (A.) Yes.

By the Solicitor-General—(Q.) For example, on 13th April 1878, the amount put down on the blue line is £316,500, and above that there is put £120,000? (A.) Yes. (Q.) And the return you made was the two together? (A.) Yes; it embraced them both. (Q.) And wherever that occurs it is the same thing? (A.) Yes. (Q.) That is in the circulation ledger? (A.) Yes.

By Mr Trayner—(Q.) Is it not in the cashier's ledger? (A.) This [No. 95] is the cashier's ledger; it contains what is right. (Q.) That is the book that Mr Stewart initialed? (A.) Yes. (Q.) It is right? (A.) Yes. (Q.) And there are no interlineations? (A.) No.

ROBERT MURDOCH.

By Mr Burnet—I was assistant cashier in the City of Glasgow Bank. I had nothing whatever to do with the foreign and colonial credits. Though it was not in my department, I came to know that large advances had been made to Smith, Fleming, & Co., Morton & Co., and other firms. I spoke of that to the manager, but not to anybody else, so far as I remember. (Q.) What was your object in speaking to him? (A.) I did not like that class of business; I thought there was too much of it. I spoke to him, but at a much later date, about whether there was security for the advances. That was within a few weeks of the suspension. I had spoken to him on the subject of these accounts shortly after his appointment as manager. (Q.) And you continued speaking to him from 1875 to 1878? (A.) Well; from 1876, at any rate. When I did speak to him about whether there was security immediately before the stoppage, he gave me to understand that the advances were all quite covered by securities. It was within my department to attend to the discount accounts of customers of the Bank. Henry Taylor & Sons had a discount account with the Bank. (Q.) In 1877 was their account considerably overdrawn? (A.) Discount could not be overdrawn. (Q.) Was their account current overdrawn? (A.) I should think so, but at this moment I cannot say. (Q.) Do you remember, in 1877, speaking to Mr Taylor or any member of his firm about the state of his account current? (A.) Yes, I spoke to him, principally about the discounts. I objected to the amount. This was sometime in the spring of 1877. I spoke to him about the state of his account. (Q.) What led you to do that? (A.) The extent of the discounts; they were increasing considerably. I knew about the state of his account current at that time. (Q.) Was it in a satisfactory or an unsatisfactory state? (A.) It was in an unsatisfactory state—the whole thing altogether. It was that which led me to complain to him.

By the Lord Justice-Clerk—(Q.) What state was it in? (A.) The account was considerably overdrawn, but the amount at this moment, I cannot tell.

By Mr Burnet—(Q.) But it was the amount of the overdraft that led you to speak to him? (A.) The two things put together. I do not know that any particular result followed upon my speaking to him. I did not find that my complaint had the effect which I wished. (Q.) What did you do in consequence? (A.) After a while (I do not remember when) I refused to take the bills, and sent them back. Shortly afterwards the bills were passed through, and I understand that Mr Taylor himself had come in and seen the manager himself on the subject, and got the bills discounted. (Q.) At all events, Mr Stronach authorised the discounting of the bills? (A.) Yes, he did.

By Mr Mackintosh—Messrs Taylor & Son had a discount account and an overdraft at the head office. The discount account consisted of bills bearing their endorsement. (Q.) Customers' bills? (A.) Apparently so. When customers of the Bank hand us bills and we discount them, we hand them a slip, and they may either pay the money in, or take it away. The bank advances the cash upon the credit of the customer and the other names upon the bills. It is quite common for mercantile firms in Glasgow to have large discount accounts. The extent of their discount account will to some degree depend upon the extent of their business. (Q.) What was the amount of the discount account of Henry Taylor & Son in 1877? (A.) At the time I spoke to him the amount then current was, I think, £110,000 or thereabouts. That was the total amount of the paper under discount. By the time the Bank stopped, that amount had been reduced to (as nearly as possible) £90,000. It was to Mr Taylor, junior, that I spoke in the first instance about these bills. My objection was that I had too many of them. (Q.) Was your objection to the credit of Messrs Taylor or of the persons who were the acceptors of the bills? (A.) It was to both; I did not want so much of that paper. (Q.) What paper? (A.) The paper then presented. (Q.) The paper of that particular acceptor? (A.) No; not altogether,—both the one and the other. (Q.) You did not like that acceptor's paper? (A.) No; I thought I had plenty of that paper. (Q.) You thought you had plenty of that acceptor's paper? (A.) Yes. Mr Taylor spoke to the manager, and the discount was granted. (Q.) Did that happen often enough with other customers? (A.) Occasionally. (Q.) The customer applied to you, and you objected, and the manager overruled your decision? (A.) Sometimes. (Q.) Had you anything to do with Mr Taylor's overdraft account? (A.) No; I do not think I had,—not with the granting of it. (Q.) You had not charge of it? (A.) No. The discount account was principally my department.

By Mr Burnet—(Q.) Do I understand you to say that you were dissatisfied with the bills, not only on account of the acceptor's name, but on account of the name of Henry Taylor & Son? (A.) Yes; I had quite enough of the whole of them.

Fifth Day.—Friday, 24th January 1879.

JAMES WENLEY.

By the Solicitor-General—I am manager of the Bank of Scotland in Glasgow. On the morning of Friday, 27th September last, I met Mr Davidson, treasurer of the Bank of Scotland, to arrange with him that I should call upon Mr Stronach. I was to refer Mr Stronach to the conversation which Mr Davidson had with him on 11th September, when Mr Davidson urged upon him the necessity of taking up a large amount of the acceptances of the City of Glasgow Bank as they fell due, and further, to state to him that in consequence of the rumours—— (Q.) Was there anything about the number being now greater than when that conversation took place? (A.) No; and with reference to that conversation to say that, in consequence of the rumours affecting the City of Glasgow Bank, which had prevailed on the two previous days, Mr Davidson thought that the necessity of taking up the acceptances of the Bank as they fell due was greater now than it had been at the interview to which I have referred. I called upon Mr Stronach at the Bank, and communicated the message to him. He received it in silence, and said nothing for, I should think, two or three minutes. (Q.) Who spoke first? (A.) I spoke first. (Q.) What did you say? (A.) The pause was painful, and I referred to the cruelty of setting afloat such reports as had been prevalent for the previous two days. (Q.) And which had driven your bank to take this step? (A.) And which had driven our bank to take this step. He said nothing, I think, for another minute or two, and then he remarked, in the possible event of the City of Glasgow Bank asking the other Banks for assistance, whether I thought that assistance would be given to them. I said I had no authority to speak on behalf of the other Scotch banks, but that I had no doubt the Bank of Scotland would be quite willing to give the City of Glasgow Bank any reasonable assistance upon two conditions,—1st, that they were shown to be in a sound state; and 2dly, that they gave security. Just about this time Mr Potter entered the room, and shortly afterwards Mr Salmond. I stated to both of them what had taken place,—what I had said to Mr Stronach, and they all objected to an examination into the Bank's affairs, on the ground of the risk of publicity. I said that I thought the object might be attained if some individual in whom we all had confidence examined the books, and said that he was satisfied. (Q.) Without revealing anything? (A.) Without revealing anything. I suggested that without giving any details, if such a person examined the Bank's books, and simply said he was satisfied as to the position of the Bank, that that might be enough. (Q.) What did they say to that? (A.) They did not assent to this suggestion. (Q.) Was anything said about how much would be needed, if they were to get assistance, to pull them through the difficulty? (A.) At first the amount named as likely to meet the case was from £200,000 to £300,000, but afterwards a larger sum was spoken of, and £500,000 was named as likely to meet the case. I asked Mr Stronach whether, in the event of their having such a sum as that, it would take all Morton's acceptances out of the way, and he answered, No. (Q.) Did Mr Potter say anything about that? (A.) No. (Q.) Was there anything else said before you parted company with them? (A.) Mr Potter said to me that he hoped that an examination of the Bank's affairs would be dispensed with. I immediately called on Mr Gairdner, of the Union Bank, and told him what had taken place. Mr Gairdner and I went to Edinburgh, and had a consultation with Mr Davidson, of the Bank of Scotland. Mr Fleming, of the Royal Bank, was unfortunately out of town in the afternoon, and could not be got. (Q.) As the result of your consultations, were you authorised to see Mr Potter? (A.) It had been arranged that Mr Potter was to call for me at the Bank of Scotland in Glasgow next morning, and hear the result. (Q.) I want to know what you conveyed to Mr Potter when he called upon you? (A.) I was authorised to say to Mr Potter that, with regard to an examination of the books, if each of the directors of the City of Glasgow Bank would give his own individual and personal assurance that the capital of the Bank was intact, we thought that possibly an examination of their affairs might be dispensed with. I told that to Mr Potter. He said that he himself could not give that assurance. (Q.) Did he say anything about the position of the Bank? (A.) He said he would not like to say anything with regard to the position of the Bank, that he could not answer for afterwards both to God and man. (Q.) Did he express any opinion about the position of the Bank? (A.) He said that things were in such a critical state that even on that day they might have to do something. I deprecated any hasty action on their part, being extremely desirous that no hasty step should be taken by the City of Glasgow Bank without the other Scotch banks being consulted. (Q.) Did he say anything about a meeting that had been called that day. (A.) He said that a meeting of the directors had been called that day at twelve o'clock in Mr Stewart's office. (Q.) Did you offer to go and see them all? (A.) He complained with a good deal of emotion of the whole responsibility being thrown upon him, and I offered to go to this meeting of the directors, and communicate to the whole of them the message I had brought. (Q.) But they did not send for you, I believe? (A.) They did not. Mr Potter called on me that day, but unfortunately I was out. I saw him afterwards at his own office.

By the Lord Justice-Clerk—This was on Saturday, 28th September.

By the Solicitor-General—I saw him about one o'clock. (Q.) And I think it was arranged that he and Mr Stronach should meet Mr Davidson, Mr Fleming, and Mr Gairdner in Edinburgh at the Bank of Scotland on the Monday? (A.) Just so. (Q.) Did he say anything at that meeting about Morton's acceptances? (A.) He said that the acceptances on account of Morton alone amounted to £1,200,000. I had a consultation with Mr Gairdner, Mr Davidson, and Mr Fleming in Edinburgh in the afternoon; and in consequence of that meeting I called on Mr Potter at his own house in the evening, and conveyed to him what had been arrived at at the meeting with Mr Fleming, Mr Gairdner, and Mr Davidson. I told Mr Potter that we thought that the sum of £500,000 which had been named was quite inadequate to meet the purpose in view, and I requested that he should on Monday bring with him the last detailed balance-sheet of the Bank, and also information as to the total amount of their acceptances. and state what acceptances were, in the ordinary course of business, for mercantile purposes, and what were for financing purposes. On Monday at twelve o'clock a meeting took place in Edinburgh. There were present—Mr Davidson, Mr Fleming of the Royal Bank, Mr Gairdner of the Union Bank, Mr Stronach, Mr Potter, and myself. At that meeting the state of the Bank was unfolded,—the large accounts of Smith, Fleming, & Co., James Nicol Fleming, Morton, and Innes Wright and Co., and also the large sum lent to the American railway, and other matters. It was arranged at a meeting of the Scotch banks that evening that Mr George Auldjo Jamieson should be asked to go and look into the books, and see if it was possible to do anything. He made a report.

By Mr Asher—At the meeting on 27th September I believe it was I who spoke first of a sum of £200,000 or £300,000. Mr Stronach replied to that remark, and spoke as if it would be sufficient. After Mr Potter and Mr Salmond came in, the sum of £500,000 was mentioned. Mr Stronach mentioned it as being amply sufficient to take the Bank out of its difficulties. Mr Potter asked him, "Are you quite sure that that sum will be sufficient?" and after some consideration, Mr Stronach said that he thought it would.

JAMES PAUL.

By the Lord Advocate—I was formerly a merchant in Glasgow. I retired from the firm of John Innes Wright & Co. in 1876. I had been a partner in that firm from March or April 1863. At that time the partners of the firm were John Innes Wright, William Scott, and myself. All three of us continued to be partners down to 1876. There were no other partners in the house during that period. While I was a partner there was a London house connected with the firm, not as partners, but as correspondents. The business of our firm, when I joined it in 1863, was that of East India merchants and commission merchants, shipping goods to the East India markets, and receiving consignments of cotton and other East India produce, which we realised in this country on behalf of clients in Bombay. Our business promised very fair for the first two or three years. We then began to lose money. I think at the close of 1865 or 1866, we were beginning to feel that we were losing money. Our first connection with the City of Glasgow Bank began, I think, about midsummer of 1866. Mr William Scott took charge of the financial department of our firm. I took a general supervision of the export department from this side as regards goods shipped by us, conducting correspondence relating thereto, and so forth. Mr Innes Wright, the senior partner, looked more immediately after the import department—consignments from abroad, and the realising of them. I think our first transaction with the Bank consisted in discounting a batch of mercantile bills. (Q.) I suppose you had a deposit and discount account in the ordinary form? (A.) Quite so; it amounts to that. From 1866 down to 1870, I am sorry to say, business matters did not improve with us. They got slightly worse. I think we were getting some assistance from the Bank previous to 1870, but I cannot condescend upon the particular time. (Q.) But about 1870 you began to need advances from the Bank? (A.) We began to get advances about that time. Mr William Scott negotiated these advances; it was his special department. I was occasionally asked specially by Mr Scott to go to the Bank about these advances, and I went at his instance. I think, in almost every case in which I was sent by Mr Scott, I got the money. Mr Alexander Stronach was manager at that time. I made no communication to him as to the state of my affairs, or the affairs of our firm on these occasions; I simply went with my message, as it were. On almost every occasion that I remember being sent to the Bank I got a note from Mr Scott to Mr Alexander Stronach relating to my mission. (Q.) And your mission was for money? (A.) Yes; and along with that I understood there was the usual cheque, as it were, for the amount, signed by the firm—Mr Scott. Sometimes I did not get the money at that particular visit, and had to go back. (Q.) I suppose you understood that it was an advance you were getting from the Bank? (A.) Clearly. (Q.) It was not a cheque, drawing your own money out of the Bank? (A.) Clearly. The largest sum I ever got on any of these occasions was, I think, £16,000. I got it in notes or cash slips—bank slips, as they are called; either notes or an equivalent. (Q.) And you have frequently got sums of £10,000 and £12,000? (A.) Yes. I cannot swear to the particular sum of £16,000, but the cheque will show what it was. Personally I did not communicate to Mr Stronach any impression that our firm was in difficulties at that time. Mr Stronach must have known it. Mr Scott and he had so many interviews that I always understood Mr Stronach knew it. I never required to say anything. Mr Stronach never asked me.

By the Lord Justice-Clerk—I think he could not fail to know it.

By the Lord Advocate—A balance-sheet of the firm was struck in 1866. After 1866, and down to the time I left the firm in 1876, there was no balance-sheet struck. The transactions with the Bank were always recorded by Mr Scott, whose special department it was, in the cash book; but up to a certain time—subsequent to 1871, I think—I found Mr Scott was keeping his cash on small slips or memoranda. After 1866 I never saw an account or balance of the affairs of the firm, or anything like an account of the state of the firm's liabilities. (Q.) But you knew that you were in difficulties? (A.) Clearly. (Q.) In deep water? (A.) In deep water. (Q.) What did you do with the money which you got from the Bank on those occasions? Did you apply it yourself? (A.) I always returned with the money and handed it to Mr Scott, who was the financial man—who had the conduct of the business. (Q.) Did you ever see any of the directors on these occasions? (A.) Never. (Q.) You have been speaking hitherto of Mr Alexander Stronach? (A.) Yes. (Q.) After he ceased to be manager, and his brother Robert Stronach took his place, did you pay visits to the Bank as before? (A.) Occasionally—much on the same footing. (Q.) And did you get the money from him on these occasions in the same way as you got it from Alexander Stronach previously? (A.) Yes, I got it,—always with a grudge, of course. (Q.) But you did get it? (A.) I think so; I might have been defeated in getting it once or twice, but I know I got money on several occasions.

By the Lord Justice-Clerk—(Q.) From Mr Robert Stronach? (A.) From Mr Robert Stronach.

By the Lord Advocate—(Q.) But unwillingly, and with a grudge? (A.) Mr Stronach naturally did not give the money without expostulating as to why we needed it, and so forth. (Q.) You were not giving the Bank security as against these advances? (A.) I did not give the Bank security. (Q.) Did you understand that your firm were giving any? (A.) I understood that they had got certain securities; the nature of them or the true value of them I could not condescend on; and all these securities were arranged for and sent by Mr Scott. (Q.) But you were quite cognisant that these advances were being got? (A.) Yes, I got some of them personally. (Q.) Was your partner Mr Innes Wright cognisant of these advances being got? (A.) I believe so. We kept no cash book or finance books. The books connected with my own department and with Mr Wright's department were all in perfect order up to the time I left the firm, but the finance books never were. (Q.) After 1870, or say after 1871, down to the time you ceased to be a partner, were you, or were you not, aware that the Bank was very heavily in advance to your firm? (A.) I was aware that the Bank must be in advance, but I had no earthly idea as to the extent of it. I frequently wished to know from Mr Scott, but never could ascertain what the amount was,—not even the probable amount. (Q.) On those occasions, taking 1871, and subsequently, when you went to Mr Alexander Stronach, and also to Mr Robert Stronach, in order to get money, did you ever allude to the necessity of your having to stop if you did not get it? (A.) Very likely I did. (Q.) But did you? Try to recollect that. (A.) Oh! I must have said so. (Q.) That if you did not get the advance you must stop? (A.) Yes. (Q.) I suppose that, having said so, it was the fact,—that if you had not got it, you must stop? (A.) Undoubtedly. (Q.) Did you ever consider or say anything about the effect that might have upon the Bank on these occasions? (A.) Never; I never could fancy that our indebtedness was of such a nature that it could materially affect the Bank. (Q.) From what you saw of the operations of your firm from 1870 down to 1876, was it your belief or understanding that you were getting into a better position pecuniarily, or into a worse? (A.) I was daily growing in the belief that we were getting into a worse position. I recollect Mr Innes Wright becoming a director of the Bank. (Q.) Did the fact of his becoming a director strike you at the time? (A.) Yes; it struck me at the time. (Q.) What occurred to you at the time in reference to it? (A.) That it was a somewhat irregular thing, Mr Wright being asked to be a director. (Q.) Did it not occur to you that there might be an irregularity in his consenting to be a director when asked? (A.) Yes. (Q.) You thought so? (A.) I thought so; Mr Wright, however, was asked to be a director long before that. (Q.) But he declined? (A.) He declined positively. This was in January 1871. (Q.) Had anything occurred since January 1871 that made it more proper for him to accept in 1875? (A.) Not that I know of. (Q.) Did you speak to Mr Wright on the subject in 1875, when he became a director? (A.) Mr Wright was my informant as to his having been asked to be a director. (Q.) Did he state whether he would accept it or not? (A.) No, he did not; evidently from the tenor of the conversation, it was under consideration by him. (Q.) Did he tell you who had asked him to be a director? (A.) He told me the first intimation he got on the subject,—the first approach on the subject,—was by Mr Robert Stronach. (Q.) Tell us what he said? (A.) And on a subsequent day, he had, I was told—by him, I think—a visit from Mr Salmond, following up the proposal. Mr Wright, evidently, had doubts about accepting it. (Q.) Did you express any opinion to him at the time, as to your view of his accepting it? (A.) I said, "How far is it right,—how far is it proper to accept a "directorship, Mr Wright, in the state of our account?" (Q.) What did he say to that? (A.) "I am alive to that, Mr Paul; Mr Stronach tells me that "that will be no difficulty; he will arrange all that." (Q.) Mr Robert Stronach? (A.) Mr Robert Stronach. (Q.) What was he to arrange, did you understand? (A.) That the indebtedness was to remain in abeyance, I suppose, and that the fact of our indebtedness would be made no disqualification. (Q.) Had Mr Wright any shares in the Bank at that time,—when he was applied to? (Q.) Not previously, that I know of. (Q.) Had he any money to buy them with, that you knew of? (A.) No. (Q.) In 1875, when Mr Wright became a director, had the character of your business remained the same as when you started the firm originally in 1863? (A.) Not quite, At the outset, it was purely a commission business, or nearly so. About 1870 or thereby the Suez canal and the telegraph to and from India came into operation, and consequent upon that, that description of commission business gradually subsided, and we assumed a position from that time onwards more as merchants,—along with such commission business as could be got. (Q.) Had it not become very much a finance business at that time,—in 1875? (A.) There was a good deal of finance, which was becoming more a feature in the business. Under the contract of copartnery each partner had a monthly allowance of £60. That was always paid by Mr Scott,—monthly. (Q.) Did you ever speak to Mr Wright about the position of your affairs? (A.) Mr Wright himself had frequent conversations about it, and more particularly about the disordered state of the books. He could not understand our position. Mr Wright knew more about the position of the firm than I did. (Q.) Did he not know that you were in difficulties? (A.) He knew we were in difficulties, but he had no earthly idea, I am pretty confident, about the extent of them,—consequent on Mr Scott's mode of doing business. (Q.) But he knew that you were in considerable difficulties? (A.) Quite so. (Q.) And that the Bank were under heavy advances? (A.) Quite so. (Q.) But he did not know the full amount? (A.) I think not. So far as I am concerhed, I did not; and I think Mr Wright could not have known either, for we had several conversations on the point. (Q.) From 1870 downwards, while you were a partner, were you ever doing anything but making losses? (A.) Well, it was the exception to make profit. Of course, there were individual operations that were profitable; but, on the whole, we were apparently going behind. (Q.) You knew that the result of your trading was that you were realising losses? (A.) Quite so. (Q.) And I suppose you knew then that the money you got to meet your liabilities must come from some other quarter than the profits upon your trade? (A.) Yes. (Q.) And that quarter was? (A.) The City of Glasgow Bank. Mr Wright succeeded James Nicol Fleming in the directorate. I was acquainted with Mr Fleming. There were business connections between him and his firm and ours. (Q.)

He was connected with various firms, I believe, under different names. With which of his firms did you trade? (A.) With James Nicol Fleming & Co., Calcutta. He was not a partner of Smith, Fleming, & Co.

By Mr Guthrie Smith—(Q.) Who provided the capital for the firm of Wright & Co. when the firm started? (A.) Mr Wright. To the best of my belief, we started with a capital of some £44,000, or £45,000, and Mr Wright supplemented it afterwards with some further payments, but I cannot give the particulars of these. The capital all came from him. According to the contract of copartnery, the allowance drawn by each partner was £60 per month. That always came through Mr Scott. I don't think Mr Wright ever exceeded that allowance. He lived in his own house, and very plainly indeed. Mr Scott had been a clerk in Mr Wright's employment. He was assumed as a partner on the same day as myself, in 1863. After 1863, each of us had a special department of the business to attend to. The whole of the finance business and the relations with the Bank were managed by Mr Scott. Mr Wright's department was the produce department. The whole of the books connected with it were properly kept down to the time when I left. (Q.) Was the borrowing of money from the Bank always done by Mr Scott? (A.) It was always negotiated by Mr Scott. (Q.) You had no knowledge of the extent of your indebtedness to the Bank? (A.) Never at any time. (Q.) You, I believe, frequently urged Mr Scott to give you particulars? (A.) Frequently, and Mr Wright also did the same thing. (Q.) But without effect? (A.) Without effect. It brought forth no actual result.

By the Dean of Faculty—(Q.) You have told us that after Mr Alexander Stronach ceased to be manager, you had called at the Bank and had seen Mr Robert Stronach. How often did you see him? (A.) That goes over a period of years; I could not tell you. I was at the Bank on an average once a week, at any rate, on some business or other. (Q.) He became manager in December 1875, and you ceased to be a partner of Innes Wright & Co. in 1876? (A.) Yes, on 19th March 1876. (Q.) Can you tell how often you saw Robert Stronach on these occasions when you called there asking for money? (A.) That is a very difficult question to answer. (Q.) More than twice? (A.) Oh! more than twice or thrice. (Q.) You stated that he expostulated with you when you made your request. What was the nature of his expostulation? (A.) Simply that he could not give the money; that he had made no arrangement with Mr Scott to give the money, and so forth. My message was done. (Q.) Did he ask for security? (A.) I cannot say. (Q.) Additional security? (A.) No. I always understood he was "nagging" at Mr Scott for securities. Whether he succeeded in getting any at the various times I could not state. I never was entrusted with any securities to give to Mr Stronach. (Q.) No; but did he speak to you in this way that he wanted more security before he would make an additional advance? (A.) Yes. (Q.) Did you carry that message back to Mr Scott? (A.) Yes. (Q.) And did you sometimes get additional security from Mr Scott to give him? (A.) No; if securities were given, they were given by Mr Scott, not by me. (Q.) Then you cannot tell me what the securities were which the Bank had against the indebtedness of John Innes Wright & Co.? (A.) Yes. The securities mainly consisted in shares in joint stock companies,—such as Glasgow Jute Company and Marbella Iron Ore Company. (Q.) Was the produce of imported goods sometimes assigned over to the Bank? (A.) No, not in my day. (Q.) Were bills drawn by your firm as against cargoes coming home in favour of the Bank? (A.) No, not in my day. (Q.) I understand you to say that you never knew the amount of your debt to the Bank? (A.) I never knew up till the hour I left the office what our indebtedness to the Bank was.

By the Lord Justice-Clerk—(Q.) You saw either Mr Alexander Stronach, when he was manager, or Mr Robert Stronach? (A.) Yes. (Q.) Was Mr

Robert Stronach in the management for the most part from 1874? (A.) Mr Robert Stronach did not take the management at the Bank, I think, until about January, or so, 1875. (Q.) But Alexander Stronach had ceased to act, had he not, before that? (A.) Yes. (Q.) Then before the formal appointment of Robert Stronach, whom did you see when you went to the Bank? (A.) Failing Mr Alexander Stronach, I next fell upon Mr Robert Stronach. I never saw a director or was brought into contact with a director. (Q.) You saw either one or other of the Stronachs? (A.) Quite so.

JOHN FLEMING.

By the Solicitor-General—I am a member of the firm of Smith, Fleming, and Co., carrying on business in Leadenhall Street, London. The firm is now in liquidation on our petition. It has been in existence since 1860. The partners were then Mr John Smith, myself, and Mr James Nicol Fleming. I have also had to do with the firms of William Nicol & Co. of Bombay, and Fleming & Co. of Kurrachee. I am a partner of these firms. The partners of Smith, Fleming, & Co. were all partners of those firms; but there were also other partners in them,—Mr Hamilton Maxwell and Mr Gilmore Hall,—who were not members of Smith, Fleming, & Co. (Q.) Since about 1865 have you had intimate business relations with Todd, Findlay, & Co., John Innes Wright & Co., and Potter, Wilson, & Co.? (A.) With Todd, Findlay, & Co., yes; less so with John Innes Wright & Co.; not at all at that date with Potter, Wilson, & Co. (Q.) When did you begin to have business relations with Potter, Wilson, & Co.? (A.) Subsequent to 1870; I cannot fix the date exactly. (Q.) When with James Morton & Co.? (A.) Shortly after 1865,—about 1866 or 1867. (Q.) And with Law, Brown, & Co. more recently? (A.) Yes; in 1875. (Q.) Previous to 1866, had you many transactions with the City of Glasgow Bank, or were they quite exceptional? (A.) There were very few, I think scarcely any, before that. (Q.) But since then your transactions have been frequent? (A.) They have. (Q.) Your brother James Nicol Fleming was a member of the directorate for a good many years? (A.) He was. (Q.) What was the whole of your indebtedness to the Bank at the stoppage in October? (A.) Something over £1,800,000,—between £1,800,000 and £1,900,000,—the exact figures I do not remember. (Q.) How much of that is on cash advances by the Bank? (A.) About one-half of it. I have not the figures with me. (Q.) How were the cash advances obtained,—I mean by what form of procedure? Were there special credits obtained from time to time? (A.) Some of these cash advances arose in this way, that originally bill credits were granted, and these bills were paid off by the Bank, and converted from the form of bills into that of cash advanced. (Q.) The Bank had to meet their own acceptances? (A.) They met their own acceptances. (Q.) And accordingly debited you with the cash as advanced by them? (A.) Yes. (Q.) Were there other sums advanced directly in cash? (A.) Yes, in some cases there were. (Q.) Which you were allowed to draw by cheque? (A.) Yes. (Q.) What security had the Bank for that sum, which we will take at one-half,—or call it £900,000,—in the meantime,—what security had the Bank for that? Or tell me first what was the whole amount of securities that the Bank had in its absolute control for the advances made to your firm? (A.) There was very little in the absolute control of the Bank. (Q.) What was the total amount that was in any way secured to them? (A.) The nominal value of the security was about £800,000 or £900,000. (Q.) As against £1,800,000 or £1,900,000? (A.) Yes. (Q.) When you say the nominal value, I suppose the realisable value would be a very great deal less than that? (A.) Well, the circumstances at present are adverse to the realisation of a good many of the securities. (Q.) Are there a great many of them worth nothing at all?

(A.) No. (Q.) You think they are all valuable? (A.) All more or less so. (Q.) Take it in 1876, what do you say would be the amount actually secured of the £1,900,000? (A.) I should not like to give a definite answer to that without looking over the securities. (Q.) Would it come up to one-half? (A.) I should say so. (Q.) About one-half? (A.) Yes. (Q.) In whose possession were the securities? (A.) Most of them in our own possession. Let me just modify that answer. Part of them also were in the possession of Todd, Findlay, & Co.,—a considerable proportion. (Q.) Was there any substantial part of those securities to which the Bank had a legal title at all? (A.) Not a large part. (Q.) I mean such a title as gave the Bank a right to use the security without the consent of others? (A.) There are a good many questions as to the right and title of the Bank to securities at present pending which have been raised since, and which I was ignorant of at the time. (Q.) But I want you to tell me how much they had, about which, in your view, no such question could be raised? (A.) Well, a number of questions which were quite new to me have been raised since my stoppage, and I find with regard to things which I believed to be theirs, the title to them is now questioned. (Q.) I suppose every question has been raised that can be raised within the last three months, but you can tell me how much of the securities no question has been raised about? (A.) A very small proportion. (Q.) Suppose the securities are all good to the Bank, how much are they worth now? (A.) It was estimated by my trustee that there would be from £500,000 to £600,000 worth now. (Q.) That is assuming all questions to be decided in favour of your assignee? (A.) That I understand. (Q.) Up to July 1870, had you any advances from the Bank which were not properly covered? (A.) None. (Q.) All the indebtedness has arisen since then? (A.) All the uncovered indebtedness. (Q.) How were your applications for advances generally made? (A.) By letter addressed to the manager. (Q.) In July 1870, did you see Mr Alexander Stronach, Mr Potter, and Mr Salmond about the state of your affairs? (A.) I saw Mr Alexander Stronach and Mr Potter. (Q.) And Mr Salmond? (A.) I believe Mr Salmond, but I am not quite so sure about him. (Q.) Was your brother present? (A.) My brother was present. (Q.) Where did you meet them? (A.) At the City of Glasgow Bank. (Q.) How many meetings had you with them at that time? (A.) I think, at intervals of a week or ten days, two meetings. (Q.) You say you are not so sure of Mr Salmond being present, but you think he was. You are not sure about the first meeting: was he present at the second meeting? (A.) My impression is that he was present at one or other of the meetings, but I am not prepared absolutely to swear that. (Q.) At those meetings what did you say to them with regard to the state of affairs—I mean did you say anything particular to them about the state of affairs? (A.) I told them that we were face to face with a very heavy loss through the difficulties which had arisen to our Liverpool agents, Nicol, Duckworth, & Co., and that it was necessary that we should stop. (Q.) What was said in answer to that? (A.) That it was unnecessary—that assistance would be provided. (Q.) By whom? (A.) By the Bank. (Q.) How did you stand with the Bank at that time? (A.) We had cash advances and credits at the moment to about £150,000, roughly—all covered. (Q.) Did you make it plain to them that you could not go on as you stood? (A.) I desired to do so; I believe I did. My brother took part in the meeting. He was of the same opinion, I believe. There was a good deal of discussion. The discussion was as to the means of rendering us assistance. (Q.) Who proposed plans for that? (A.) I cannot permit myself now to say who proposed them; various plans were proposed. (Q.) Did the proposals come from others at the meeting than from you? (A.) From others, not from me. One proposal, and the proposal which ultimately in a certain shape was carried out, was the immediate formation of a new Liverpool firm, which should accept bills to be discounted and used for our relief. I said that I did not consider that such a plan would be successful; I thought it would be fatal. I expressed myself pretty strongly upon that. I said it would bring discredit upon us, and that without the maintenance of our credit there was no chance of our retrieving our position and getting out of our difficulties. The proposal was pressed upon me. This was at the first interview. (Q.) Did you get rather hot—angry—upon the subject? (A.) I felt that it was trifling with a very big and difficult matter. (Q.) How much did you state to them was really the amount involved in the question of your failing or your being kept up? (A.) I don't exactly understand the question; the word "involved" means something outside of us.

By the Lord Justice-Clerk—We required over half a million of money to put us right.

By the Solicitor-General—I told them that. (Q.) When they pressed it upon you, how did you receive the pressure? (A.) The plan as proposed by them seemed to me to be quite ineffectual, and I said there was no use discussing it further. I then proceeded to leave the room. When I got out into the hall of the Bank, I was brought back again. It was Mr Potter who brought me back. (Q.) What happened when you got back? (A.) It was then promised that the Bank would assist, and if the proposed bills were not acceptable, if they were not negotiable, the Bank would discount these bills, so that we would not be forced into bankruptcy. I cannot say they said anything about what effect our stoppage would have if we did stop. (Q.) In short, did it come to this, that they undertook to pull you through if the plan proposed could not be effected as they suggested? (A.) That was what in effect was come to.

By the Lord Justice-Clerk—(Q.) Do you mean the bills drawn by the new company? (A.) Drawn on the new company. (Q.) That if these could not be discounted through the new company, the Bank would do it? (A.) Yes.

By the Solicitor-General—Was that carried out by credit being given to Brown & Co. to the extent of £300,000, and about £100,000 of securities belonging to your brother, which were held for you by the Bank, being transferred to them? (A.) Our firm in Liverpool, in accordance with that arrangement, entitled A. & A. G. Brown, was formed, and security for £300,000 was provided for them, of which about £100,000, belonging to my brother, and held by the Bank for me, was lent by the Bank. The handing over of securities to the Liverpool firm was not spoken of at the meeting I have mentioned; that was an arrangement of detail, settled afterwards. (Q.) When the acceptances of the Liverpool firm were got in order to raise money, did you find them acceptable? (A.) To a very, very limited extent. That was exactly what I had expected. I found the attempt to negotiate them injurious to our credit. That also was what I had expected. As the result, the Bank had to make the advances on the bills themselves. (Q.) Did the Bank get back the securities which had been sent to Brown & Co. (A.) Ultimately those which had not been realised and applied to the reduction of the credit were returned to the Bank. Let me say this, that, as regards James Nicol Fleming, any realisations that took place during the existence of the credit, were placed by the Bank to the credit of James Nicol Fleming, and not to our credit. By the end of 1870 the Bank had advanced to us, in consequence of this new arrangement, roundly, about half a million of money,—nearly so, I think. (Q.) To what extent was the Bank covered for that half million? (A.) I cannot speak off-hand,—I cannot positively say. (Q.) Would it be more than £200,000? (A.) Certainly; I should say it would be very nearly fully covered, but I speak just now very broadly—three-fourths probably. During the years since 1870, down to the stoppage of the Bank, I have kept the Bank informed of the state of our affairs from time to time. (Q.) Have you periodically submitted a balance-sheet to them of your affairs? (A.) I have submitted balance-sheets of our affairs in London, Bombay, and Kurrachee. Latterly I have submitted monthly statements of bills payable. That has been going on for several years; I cannot precisely say how long. From 1870 down to the present date I have been obliged, in the course of working the business, to support the firms of Todd & Findlay, and my brother's firm of James Nicol Fleming & Co., and also the firm of Fowlie, Richmond, and Co. I have kept the Bank informed that I was supporting these firms. (Q.) Were many of the credits specially applied for by you to support these firms? (A.) They were applied for to relieve the cash advances which we were under on account of these firms. (Q.) And applied for *nominatim* for that purpose? (A.) Certain of them were. (Q.) In regard to your affairs, have you seen Mr Potter frequently about them? (A.) I have seen him occasionally. (Q.) In consultation about them? (A.) Yes. I saw him at the Bank. (Q.) Has Mr Salmond made inquiry at you about your affairs? (A.) Not for some years. (Q.) How long is it since he ceased to make inquiry? (A.) I cannot precisely say. (Q.) But roughly? (A.) For the last three or four years. Previous to that, when in London, he used to call and ask generally about our affairs. (Q.) Did you inform him? (A.) Yes, I did. (Q.) How things stood? (A.) That is, generally. (Q.) Did you inform him that your debt and difficulty was largely increasing? (A.) No, I did not do so. He came to ask about our matters,—just how we were getting on. (Q.) Did you tell him the truth about them? (A.) I did.

By the Lord Justice-Clerk—(Q.) What did you say when you were asked about your affairs? (A.) Sometimes I told him—as was the fact—that perhaps things were looking better; sometimes it was that matters were rather bad.

By the Solicitor-General—(Q.) Did you gather from him whether he knew the amount of the advances of the Bank to you? (A.) No, there was no indication of any precise knowledge of that nature. (Q.) Was there an arrangement made in March 1875 in regard to your firm's affairs with the Bank? (A.) Yes, although not finally concluded. (Q.) But an arrangement was discussed and gone over? (A.) Yes. (Q.) And acted upon? (A.) It was subsequently acted upon. (Q.) What was the arrangement of March 1875? (A.) To give us relief, the rate of interest charged upon our cash account was to be reduced from 5 per cent. to 3½; the commission upon the credits which were granted to us for our accommodation was to be reduced from 2 per cent. to ½ per cent. per annum; and an arrangement to acquire £100,000 worth at par of the stock of the Canterbury Company, upon which we were to have an advance of £100,000 at 3½ per cent. The effect of this was that if this Canterbury stock yielded dividend in excess of 3½ per cent., that excess would go to the benefit of our account. These are the salient points of the arrangement. (Q.) Did you at that time lay before them a statement of your position? (A.) I did. (Q.) Whom did you give it to? (A.) I had been in correspondence with Mr Alexander Stronach for some time previously. [Shown No. 186.] That is a letter from me to Mr Robert Stronach, 12th April 1875. The first paragraph is:

> "Referring to the meeting I had with your directors on Thursday the 1st inst., "respecting the state of our account with the Bank, I now beg to detail the terms "of the agreement come to as I understood them."

(Q.) Who were present at the meeting you refer to in that letter? (A.) I am unable to recall. I saw that letter this morning, but I am unable to recall who were present on that occasion. The meeting was held in Glasgow, in the Bank's premises. (Q.) Was it a meeting of directors, though you cannot remember who were present? (A.) I cannot remember. I have seen that letter during the last few months in going through my correspondence. (Q.) But had you a meeting—though you cannot specify the individuals who were present—with several of the board upon this matter? (A.) Yes, I had.

By the Lord Justice-Clerk—(Q.) I understand the arrangement proposed was to give you relief in three ways—(1) in regard to the interest upon your bills, (2) in regard to the amount of the Bank's commission, and (3) a new advance? (A.) That is so. (Q.) In return for that was the Bank to receive any security or any advantage? (A.) The object was to make it possible for us to go on.

By the Solicitor-General—At this time, of course, we could not go on if we were not helped; but the load was almost unbearable. (Q.) Did you explain that to those who were at the meeting? (A.) It was well known—quite recognised. (Q.) Do you remember if Mr Potter was present at the meeting? (A.) I do not remember the details of that meeting at all; I cannot remember them. (Q.) Did you make any proposals for relieving your position; or who made them? (A.) I had some time previously appealed to Alexander Stronach to reduce the interest and to reduce the commission, but it was in the form of a suggestion or appeal, a considerable time previous to that. (Q.) But at the meeting were any suggestions made to you as to what should be done? (A.) I don't remember that. I remember there was a meeting, but I don't remember the details of it. (Q.) But referring to your letter, of which I read you the first paragraph, have you any doubt now that that is a perfectly correct statement of your understanding at the time of what had been agreed to? (A.) I feel quite certain that that is a correct statement. [Shown letters Nos. 185 to 188 from John Fleming to R. S. Stronach, dated 3d March, 12th April, 21st April, and 24th August 1875, the latter signed Smith, Fleming, & Co.] (Q.) Taking the four letters together, they embody in writing practically what came to be agreed to? (A.) Yes, they did. (Q.) As regards this period, did you ever come into contact with Mr James Morton in any of the discussions with the directors in regard to this matter? (A.) I don't remember James Morton having been ever present with any directors, but he was in the habit of seeing me in London. (Q.) In what capacity did you understand he came to you? (A.) He came as the confidant of Mr Alexander Stronach. (Q.) Has Mr Morton not been present along with you and Mr Potter when your affairs were discussed? (A.) I cannot be quite sure. He may have been, but I don't remember any particular occasion. (Q.) Try to recollect? (A.) I cannot, so that I could swear to it. (Q.) But was he a medium of communication between you and the Bank when he came to see you in London? (A.) Yes. (Q.) He conveyed messages from you, and brought messages to you? (A.) Yes. (Q.) As part of the arrangement for relieving your position, was Mr Morton to do anything? (A.) I did not know absolutely that he was to do anything. I believed that he was to provide some of the stock. (Q.) Out of his superfluity, I suppose? (A.) That was what I understood.

By the Lord Justice-Clerk—(Q.) You believed that—why? (A.) It was he who originally suggested the arrangement many months previously to its being made, and he spoke to it as a means of helping us—encouraging us to face a difficult struggle.

By the Solicitor-General—(Q.) You mean that he would provide a good handsome sum to help you? (A.) That he would provide the stock at par. (Q.) Why was he to provide the stock at par? (A.) The stock was supposed to be worth a great deal more than par, if not immediately, at all events prospectively. It was yielding a return much larger than the interest which we were to pay for the advance. (Q.) You understood yourself to be under the engagements to the Bank contained in these letters, and acted upon them? (A.) We did. (Q.) And you got the advantages which you were to get in consequence of entering into the engagement? (A.) We did.

By the Lord Justice-Clerk—(Q.) Can you tell me the amount of the indebtedness of your firm to the Bank at the date of this arrangement? (A.) About £1,300,000. I think the amount of credit was £562,000, and the cash advance £773,000.

N

By the Solicitor-General—(Q.) In August 1875 did you make a representation to Mr Robert Stronach about the impossibility of carrying out the arrangement? (A.) In consequence of difficulties which had arisen in connection with Collie's stoppage, I foresaw that we should be unable at the close of the year to carry out our engagements. (Q.) What did Mr Robert Stronach reply to you about that? (A.) I don't remember the exact reply. I remember being asked by Mr Robert Stronach to come to Glasgow, and to have a meeting with the directors in the month of July last year. By that time the amount of indebtedness had considerably increased. (Q.) How did you come to be able to carry on after Collie's failure till the meeting of July 1878? (A.) When we needed help we got it.

By the Lord Justice-Clerk—(Q.) From the Bank? (A.) From the Bank.

By the Solicitor-General—(Q.) And in consequence your indebtedness was always increasing, from that time onwards, down to the last? (A.) It was so. In July 1878 I was asking for an advance of £25,000. I went to Glasgow, and met Mr Robert Stronach, Mr Potter, and Mr Stewart. (Q.) Was your indebtedness to the Bank referred to at that meeting,—the amount of it? (A.) No. (Q.) Was it spoken of as being very large? (A.) The state of our account as being very unsatisfactory was spoken of. The amount was not discussed.

By the Lord Justice-Clerk—(Q.) What was said about the state of your account? (A.) It was alluded to as being very unsatisfactory. (Q.) Try to remember what was said? (A.) I cannot recall the exact expressions used, but it was spoken of as an unsatisfactory account, and that it was most unsatisfactory that the indebtedness had been increasing instead of diminishing; and I explained with reference to that, that the condition of trade for several years past had been deplorably bad.

By the Solicitor-General—(Q.) Was anything said about adding to the indebtedness by giving you more money? (A.) Very great reluctance to increase the debt was expressed. (Q.) How long were you with them? (A.) Probably three-quarters of an hour or half an hour; certainly within an hour. (Q.) Did you get the money? (A.) The credit I asked for was granted. (Q.) Did you state to them whether you could go on without the money? (A.) I said that I could not go on without that money. [Shown letters 185, 186, 187, 188.] Those are the letters I have seen. [Shown Nos. 189, letter, Smith, Fleming, & Co., John Fleming, R. M'Ilwraith, and W. Nicol, to R. S. Stronach; 190, 191A, 191B, three letters, John Fleming to R. S. Stronach, dated 27th August 1875, and 5th May and 26th November 1877; 285, letter, John Fleming to Lewis Potter, dated 6th March 1877; and 289, letter, John Fleming to James Morton, dated 2d August 1876.] I identify all these. [Shown No. 397.] That is a letter from Smith, Fleming, & Co. signed by me, dated 24th January 1876. [Shown No. 398, letter to R. S. Stronach, dated 20th December 1875.] That is a letter from my firm, signed by me. [Shown Nos. 402 to 421 inclusive, letters, Smith, Fleming, & Co. to R. S. Stronach, of various dates, between 1st September 1875 and 4th May 1878.] These are letters from Smith, Fleming, & Co. all signed by me. [Shown No. 444.] That is a letter from Smith, Fleming, & Co. signed by me. [Shown No. 191C.] That is a letter from Robert Stronach to myself.

By Mr Trayner—My meeting with the directors in July 1878 was on a Tuesday; I think it was on the 29th, but at all events it was on the last Tuesday of the month. I had never met Mr Stewart in my life before that meeting. He was not present at my meeting with the directors in March 1875. I never saw him in my life till the meeting at the end of July 1878. (Q.) At the meeting in July 1878 do you remember referring to some property of yours that was expected to be very productive and profitable? (A.) I brought down some specimens of gold which had been brought home in the beginning of the year from Wynard by an engineer—an expert—whom we had sent to India. (Q.) Specimens of gold found on a property belonging to you or your firm in India? (A.) Yes. (Q.) And from that you expected, I believe, to realise considerable and valuable results? (A.) What I said was, that it was the only ray of hope in our affairs. (Q.) But it was at that time a very brilliant ray in your mind? (A.) Well this much had occurred, that a few days previously a Californian of great experience, the agent of Messrs Rothschild, had seen these specimens, and had heard from my partner the circumstances under which they had been collected; and he said, that if the facts were as stated to him, there was probably something very great in it. (Q.) And you communicated these facts and these hopes to the meeting that was held in July 1878? (A.) I did. (Q.) As also, I think, your expectation that some arrangement might be made with reference to it between you and the Messrs Rothschild? (A.) My partner, Mr M'Ilwraith, had been in communication with the Messrs Rothschild concerning these matters, and he had a hope that they might, if satisfied of the genuineness of the matter, render assistance. (Q.) And you communicated that to the meeting in July 1878? (A.) I did.

By Mr Asher—I saw Mr Salmond occasionally in London. (Q.) Did he call to ask how business was getting on generally? (A.) Yes. (Q.) Not as an emissary of the Bank with reference to your account? (A.) No; he called in a friendly way, and made inquiries concerning the account. (Q.) Your conversations related to business in the country generally, did they not? (A.) The conversation generally passed into general topics. (Q.) Can you be more precise in regard to the number of years that have elapsed since you communicated with Mr Salmond in regard to your Bank matters? (A.) I cannot say more than that several years have elapsed. (Q.) When you went to the Bank in 1870, your indebtedness, you have said, was about £150,000, fully covered by security? (A.) Yes. (Q.) So that the reverses which came upon you then did not affect the Bank? (A.) That is so. (Q.) For what purpose did you go to the Bank? (A.) I was asked to go to the Bank before stopping. (Q.) Who asked you? (A.) My brother asked me. (Q.) He was a director of the Bank at the time? (A.) Yes. (Q.) That is Mr James Nicol Fleming? (A.) Yes. (Q.) Did he explain to you why he wished you to come to the Bank before stopping? (A.) No. He said before coming to a final decision he wished me to come to Glasgow and see the Bank manager. (Q.) What did you understand to be his purpose in requesting you to do that before stopping? (A.) In case the Bank might be willing to render assistance. (Q.) Did you go with the view of getting the Bank to make arrangements which would render your stoppage unnecessary? (A.) I went with the view of laying my matters before the Bank, and of getting assistance if they were willing to give it. (Q.) Did you think that if you got assistance, your matters would right themselves? (A.) I believed it was possible; our earnings during previous years had been large. (Q.) The sum you said you would require to put you right would be about £500,000? (A.) About that. (Q.) You were engaged in business to a very large extent, I believe. (A.) Yes. (Q.) What was the largest sum which your firm had earned as profit in your various businesses in any one year? (A.) Our profits during 1862 and 1863 were very large; they were hundreds of thousands in those days; but in the three years immediately preceding 1870 the average earnings of our three firms in London, Bombay, and Kurrachee had exceeded £90,000 per annum. (Q.) It was chiefly a commission business? (A.) Largely. (Q.) And these facts, I presume, would be explained to the Bank? (A.) Yes, certainly. (Q.) For the purpose of satisfying them that they would be safe to make advances to your firm? (A.) That there was a possibility of redeeming our position. (Q.) Your commission connection at that time was still intact? (A.) Yes. (Q.) So that if you could tide over your difficulty, you had no reason to doubt that a very valuable commission business would remain with your firms? (A.) That was what I believed. (Q.) And your brother, I presume—the director—was fully aware of these circumstances? (A.) Fully aware. Q.) Was Mr Alexander Stronach an intimate personal friend of yours? (A.) Not at all; not beyond business. (Q.) At no time? (A.) At no time. (Q.) You are John Fleming? (A.) Yes. (Q.) And your place of business is Leadenhall Street, London? (A.) It is. (Q.) You are the Mr Fleming, I suppose, who corresponded on behalf of your firm with Mr Alexander Stronach as representing the Bank? (A.) Yes. (Q.) Were you in the habit of exchanging letters with Mr Alexander Stronach, marked private, with reference to the Bank? (A.) Yes. (Q.) To your knowledge were burdens undertaken by Alexander Stronach for you on behalf of the Bank without the knowledge of his directors? (A.) I was not aware of it, excepting thus far, that I was aware from his correspondence that sometimes he had done things in anticipation of obtaining the assent of his directors. (Q.) Did you not know that the fact that he had made you advances without the knowledge of his directors was pressing heavily on his mind? (A.) Previously to 1875 some of the advances, I understood, were unknown to them. (Q.) At any time during Mr Alexander Stronach's management of the Bank did you not know that it was so? (A.) He represented to me that he had made advances without the knowledge of the directors, but required me to put matters into such a form that he might put them before the directors. (Q.) Did you not know that the fact that he had done so was pressing heavily on his mind? (A.) Yes, I am bound to say that I did. (Q.) When did that system begin which caused him that mental anxiety? (A.) That I cannot tell. It was only latterly that I knew that he had not fully disclosed all my affairs to the Bank. (Q.) I show you a print for the defenders. Be kind enough to look at the first letter in that print, dated 3d April 1872, addressed by Alexander Stronach to you, and marked private:—

" Private. 3d April 1872.

" My Dear Sir,—I am sorry to observe by your letter of yesterday that you think " you have reason to complain of my want of appreciation of your position gene- " rally, and that, if I had more sympathy with you under your burden, I would not " have hesitated in complying with your demands in the present case. I can only " appeal to the past as counterbalancing that statement, which, although you have " given expression to it, I cannot believe that you seriously entertain that opinion. " On the other hand, however, I fear that in looking so earnestly at your own posi- " tion and burdens, you are in some danger of forgetting mine. My position is, " and has throughout been an anomalous one, because, as you are aware, I could " not share the burden with my directors, and it has pressed upon me accordingly " with tremendous severity, without exciting much sympathy; at least very little " has been done in any way to lighten my burden. I have borne it, however, pati- " ently, and continue to do so uncomplainingly. The esteem and regard I have for " yourself and your brothers first induced me to undertake it, and now advises me " to continue, and although no other consideration on earth would induce me to " bear up under the severity of the pressure.

" I feel it is not quite considerate in you (however lucrative the result may appear " to be in prospect) to press on me so heavy an addition to existing burdens, and " on so very sudden a call, particularly at a time when I have *other very heavy* " calls. I think you must yourself admit the difficulty of my position in the matter, " and I trust that in any similar case you will either give me an opportunity of " judging whether I can give it or not, or present the proposal in such a shape as " I can get the board to share the responsibility of a transaction of such magni- " tude, however safe it may be.

" I have renewed the anticipated credits p. £30^{m}, and send them to-night, and " shall arrange a cash advance on special account p. £34^{m} further, for which please " send me *a cheque* to be paid into the first trust-account. I note that the latter " will be paid next month. I am sorry the drafts didn't mature before our balance. " —Yours very truly, " ALEXANDER STRONACH.

" John Fleming, Esq.,
" 71 Threadneedle Street, London."

What did you understand Mr Stronach to refer to when he mentioned the esteem and regard for you and your brothers inducing him to undertake a burden which no other consideration on earth would induce him to bear up under the pressure of? (A.) I consider that in writing that he was putting his own view of the case before me, because it was at his instigation that I went on. In the month of September 1870 I wished to stop, and pressed the stoppage, and he came up to London and reproached me for wavering in my intention of going on. (Q.) Did you repudiate the expression of esteem and regard for you and your brothers which he there indicated? (A.) No, I did not. (Q.) Did you reciprocate it? (A.) I should like to see what I wrote before, and what I wrote after, before I answer that question. (Q.) Have you any reason to doubt the truth of that statement, that he could not share the burden with his directors, and had to bear it himself? (A.) I understood that his directors did know, to a large extent, what was going on. (Q.) Did you challenge the accuracy of his statement? (A.) That I don't remember. I have not got my answer. Is it here? (Q.) Look at the letter printed at the foot of page 31, and at the top of page 32, dated 30th September 1873, and addressed by Alexander Stronach to you:—

"My Dear Sir,—I wrote you a few lines yesterday, enclosing Mr Aikman's notes "and memo., and shall be glad to have your reply thereto at your early conveni- "ence. Mr Paul, I presume, will now be due, when the financial statements will "also be got ready. Yours of yesterday I received this morning, and telegraphed "in reply, that as this was your mail day (which I suppose you had forgotten last "week in fixing Tuesday), to postpone our meeting till to-morrow at 11.15, and "which I hope will be suitable for you. At same time, I feel that my time here is "gliding past, and that we have made little or no progress in furtherance of the "main object which brought and keeps me here. We have much to talk over and "much to do in resolving on a proper basis in connection with your future busi- "ness arrangements; and I feel, as I daresay you do also, that we are up to this "time very much where we were when we met in Glasgow at the end of July or "beginning of August.

"I feel the distance between us is too great, as I feared it would be; and I think "I must therefore revert to my former proposal to get a house of call in the city "somewhere convenient and accessible, where we could meet daily, or every second "or third day, as our business required, until the whole was completed, and our "arrangements finally matured. I had letters recently from Mr Potter to inquire "what progress we had made, and I feel rather ashamed to answer him."

That was a proposal with a view to Mr Stronach and you meeting daily in the city of London, to confer in regard to your affairs; Mr Stronach was living at the south side of London at that time, I believe? (A.) He was living at Norwood. (Q.) And it had reference to your affairs? (A.) It was with reference to our affairs that he wished to have more intercourse with me. (Q.) He wished to have facilities for talking daily with you in regard to your affairs with the City of Glasgow Bank? (A.) Yes.

By the Lord Justice-Clerk—That is to say, when he says, "where we could "meet daily, as our business requires," he meant in reference to the affairs of your firm? (A.) Yes.

By Mr Asher—At page 148 there is a letter from you addressed to Mr R. S. Stronach:—

"Western Club, Glasgow, Thursday Evening.

"My Dear Sir,—Just a line to tell you that Salmond got hold of me here, and "asked me what was the meaning of my being in such close consultation with Mr "Potter to-day, and I thought the best thing to say was that he had been talking "of one of his sons joining us in Bombay.

"He rather closely questioned me on the subject, but I told him our conversa- "tion was quite general. I think it right to mention this in case he should allude "to the matter to you.—Yours very truly, "JOHN FLEMING."

Why did you think it right to mention that to Mr Robert Stronach? (A.) I never wrote such a letter to Mr Robert Stronach. (Q.) The principal is No.

296. [Shown No. 296.] (A.) This letter must have been written to Alexander Stronach, not to Robert Stronach. (Q.) Why did you think it right to mention the matter referred to in that letter to Mr Stronach, in case Mr Salmond should allude to it to him? (A.) I wished to let him know that Mr Salmond had questioned me about the matter. (Q.) Why did you wish to let him know that? (A.) I conceived that Mr Salmond was not fully informed about the matters that we were discussing,—that is, the full state of our account. (Q.) And it was to put Alexander Stronach on his guard in case Mr Salmond spoke to him on that subject; is that not so? (A.) Yes; that I had been discussing with Mr Potter and Mr Alexander Stronach, the question of the reconstruction of our firm, with reference to the state of our accounts. (Q.) Did you intend Mr Alexander Stronach to withhold from Mr Salmond knowledge as to the state of your account? (A.) No, I had no desire that he should withhold it. (Q.) Why put him on his guard? (A.) Simply that he might know that Salmond had been inquiring. (Q.) And might judge of the expediency of telling him or not? (A.) Truly so. (Q.) Look at the letter at foot of page 23 of the print. There is a letter there dated 14th June 1873, addressed by you to Alexander Stronach? (A.) There is only a little fragment of the letter here printed. (Q.) The excerpt is the postscript. The letter is dated 14th June 1873; the postscript is:—"I trust this will find you better. "I fear, however, it is ease of mind you need, and it is a terrible thought that it is "we who keep you on the rack." (A.) No doubt I had that feeling, but I should prefer that the whole letter was read. The whole letter will show that there was distress of mind on both sides. (Q.) Do you wish it read? (A.) I prefer that you should read the whole letter, though I don't know that it is material.

Witness read the letter as follows:—

"Hill Hall, Epping, 14th June 1873.

"My Dear Sir,—I have your letters of Thursday and yesterday. I attempted to "take up your memo. to-day, but a bursting head compelled me to give it up. I "came away at two o'clock. I hope to-morrow's quiet will enable me to take it up "and go through with it on Monday. With reference to your Thursday's note, "I welcome the idea of any arrangement by which you can become more "thoroughly and continuously informed as to our affairs. Indeed, it was in my "mind to propose something of the kind, but I could not see a way through the "difficulty of having some one in the office on behalf of the Bank without exposing "our situation and causing great danger. I am very grieved to hear of your state, "but quite understand it. If you come to the south near London, there should be "no great difficulty in frequently seeing you at your house without exciting com"ment, and it would not be absolutely necessary to have Bell or any other inter"mediate. I say this, not objecting to Bell, but am doubting whether James can "dispense with him in Glasgow, and whether it is quite polite, at the moment at "least, for James to open a separate establishment here. Findlay writes that of "the £28,000 said by Mair to be at credit of Todd, Findlay, & Co. in Glasgow, "£13,000 is credited merely by a cross entry, and of the balance, £9500 has been "returned in various ways, and £5000 paid to us.

"Will you have the kindness to return me the accounts I sent you from Mair, to "see how they bear out this.

"I quite agree with you that the Glasgow house of Findlay's should be closed. "The explanations I get seem always straight, but I don't get the money, which I "know has been made.

"I don't quite understand the suggestion that Mair should assume so much of "the burden. When he joined Todd, Findlay, & Co., it was under an express "agreement, which we guaranteed, that he should be kept clear of all liability in "respect of the debts of the concern before he joined.

"The letter you say is so clear, showing I was all right again, was written with "my head feeling as if it were bursting. It is this sort of feeling that comes on one "just now when I begin to think earnestly about anything, and it paralyses me. I "am quite well in body, and after my examination before the committee, which I "believe is to take place on Tuesday, I shall have but the one matter to attend to, "and hope I shall be out of it.—Yours very truly. "JOHN FLEMING.

"Alex. Stronach, Esq."

(Q.) Part of the body of that letter refers to a request by Mr Stronach? (A.) Yes. (Q.) The last paragraph on page 20 of the print for the defence forms part of the letter of 12th June 1873 that Mr Alexander Stronach wrote you, and which is acknowledged in the beginning of the letter you have just read? (A.) Yes. (Q.) I believe this is the statement in Mr Stronach's letter to which you refer in your reply:—

"My doctor seems determined that I shall go away for some time, and he says "that the neighbourhood of London would do as well as anywhere else. I am fully "alive to the non-desirability of coming to your office at all just now. But it has "occurred to me that as James has been desiring to open a London office, he could "transfer Bell up to an office near, and then our meetings there, or at my house, "would not be questioned, seeing the connection that subsists between. Besides I "am desirous to have his own matters with us also put into better shape, and "which, from his continued absence in Manchester, I cannot get done satisfactorily. "This much, however, between ourselves."

Now, returning to the P.S., you were aware that at that time Mr Stronach, to use your own words, was "kept on the rack," through the state of your affairs? (A.) No doubt of it. (Q.) And didn't you know that his mental anxiety on the subject was aggravated then by the knowledge that his directors did not know what had been done? (A.) I was not aware that his directors—at all events, I believe that some of his directors were aware of the state of matters. I was not aware that they were wholly ignorant. (Q.) At that time? (A.) At that time. (Q.) Just reflect for one moment. You were aware that Mr Alexander Stronach was merely manager? (A.) I was aware of that. (Q.) If he had been acting under the orders of his directors in what had happened, why should he be on the rack? (A.) Because our account was a very heavy account, and an increasing account. (Q.) If he had simply obeyed the orders of his directors, why should that put him on the rack? (A.) I should fancy that he took such an interest in the affairs of the Bank that he should be distressed about our account, a large account going bad. (Q.) If he had done it without the sanction of his directors, you have no doubt, I suppose, that he would be on the rack? (A.) If he had done it without the sanction of the directors, I have no doubt that would aggravate his distress of mind. (Q.) I think, if you will look at the immediately succeeding letter to which this is a reply, you will find that he had been acting without the sanction of his directors. In a letter to you of 13th June 1873, page 23 of the same print, one of the two acknowledged by you in the one from which the excerpt is made, he says in the third last paragraph—"So soon as the terms of our arrangements are "adjusted, and the whole scheme and securities are ready, I am desirous to "place it before the board, with the view of getting their sanction to it and my "own exoneration and relief accordingly." You must have known, therefore, when you wrote the excerpt of 14th June that your affairs had not been before the directors? (A.) That our complete affairs had not been put before the board —that I understood; but that they were partially before the board, I believe. (Q.) When you made the arrangement of 1875 with the Bank, did you expect to be able to carry it out? (A.) At the time I made it? (Q.) Yes. (A.) Yes. (Q.) And did you think that through the means of that arrangement you would be able to liquidate your debt to the Bank? (A.) I stated exactly what I expected to be able to do in my letter. (Q.) Did you state that if the Bank would assent to that arrangement, you had no doubt you would be able to liquidate your debt to them? (A.) I stated in that letter that I expected that in the course of fourteen years I should be able to pay off half-a-million out of our indebtedness of over £1,300,000. (Q.) I think one of the conditions of the agreement was that you should confine yourself to the extremely lucrative commission business which your firms had, and not enter on speculation at all? (A.) Yes. (Q.) The arrangement was made in April 1875? (A.) Yes. (Q.) Would you look at the letter on page 85 of the same print;

that is a letter from you on 24th July 1875 to Mr Robert Stronach, and I ask your attention to a portion of it, commencing at the third paragraph on that page. The arrangement there referred to is the arrangement of April preceding? (A.) Yes. (Q.) You there say:—

"I feel very confident that we can work the arrangement through. The experi-"ence of the past year's careful non-speculative business shows me that we can "depend upon an income which will enable us to carry through the arrangement "with the Bank, provided we are not hampered with embarrassments arising out "of old financial entanglements.

"I am anxious to start clear, and shrink from the idea of raising any part of the "money required for the first payment to the Bank by *floating* paper.

"The only modification I see in the arrangement is, that we be permitted to delay "the first payment in reduction of the debt to the Bank until June 1876.

"Although Morton has advised me not to write, I think it very much better "that I should tell you the truth as it appears to me, and I ask your kind advice.

"The object of the arrangement is to repay the debt to the Bank, and if a scramb-"ling effort to keep to the letter of the engagement, as present made, is cal-"culated to impair our credit, and so diminish our ability to earn money for "future payments, I submit it will be much better to postpone our first payments "for a few months.

"I will be guided by your kind advice.

"The arrangement is a most favourable one for us, and I have no fear about "being able to carry through our part of it, provided we get a fair start."

(Q.) Did that letter correctly express your state of mind at the time with regard to the arrangement with the Bank. (A.) It did. (Q.) And have you any doubt that you set out the considerations there stated to the Bank as the inducement to them to enter into that arrangement? (A.) Which letter do you mean? (Q.) The considerations referred to in that letter. (A.) Do you mean in the letter you have read? (Q.) Yes; that is written after the arrangement was made, you will observe. (A.) The arrangement had not been finally concluded until 24th August. (Q.) I observe that that letter is addressed to Mr Stronach, and is marked "confidential"? (A.) Yes. (Q.) Amongst the securities made over to the Bank, I think there were shares in in the Canterbury and Otago Company. Is that so? (A.) There were some shares belonging to myself which I made over to the Bank. (Q.) The written arrangement between you and the Bank contains the following article—— (A.) Is it the arrangement as finally understood, and which is dated 24th August 1875? (Q.) Yes. In that agreement there is an article in the following terms:—"We append a statement D showing the charges on our debts "and our probable income with its sources, by which it appears that we have "at present the prospect of an annual surplus of about £25,000 applicable "to the reduction of our debts." That statement was true? (A.) That statement was true. (Q.) In 1875 there was £100,000 advanced as part of the arrangement. Was that advance given against a security? (A.) Which £100,000 is that? (Q.) Part of the agreement of 1875? (A.) If you refer to the £100,000 advanced upon the security of Canterbury stock, we were debited with £100,000 by the City of Glasgow Bank in account with the City of Glasgow Bank, or the acquisition of a corresponding amount of Canterbury stock. (Q.) That was to be applied in the acquisition of that stock. (A.) Yes. (Q.) And at that time was that stock regarded as a highly lucrative investment? (A.) It was not paying well at the time, but prospectively it would be so. (Q.) That is what I mean,—it was an investment which prospectively would become highly remunerative? (A.) Yes. (Q.) And I suppose you explained that at the time when the advance was given? (A.) The proposal came from the other side, not from me. (Q.) As an additional security to the Bank? (A.) As an additional security to the Bank to help my account. (Q.) In short, it was regarded as an increase of the Bank's security to have £100,000 of that stock bought by you as in lieu of £100,000 of your account? (A.) Yes. And it was also expected that it would produce an income larger than the interest charged against me for advance. (Q.) And in that way it would lighten the burden of the accruing interest on your accounts? (A.) Yes.

By Mr Balfour—(Q.) You told us there had been a proposal for the reconstruction of your firm; was that about the end of 1874 or early in 1875? (A.) I think it was in the autumn of 1874. (Q.) Was the idea at that time to get in a young partner possessed of money? (A.) The idea was to get one or more partners in with money. (Q.) And was it proposed that Mr John Potter, the son of Mr Lewis Potter, should be assumed as such a partner? (A.) It was so suggested. (Q.) As a partner possessed of money? (A.) Yes. (Q.) Did you think, from the state of your business at that time, that if you got one or more partners possessed of money, you would be able to conduct the business to advantage and with success? (A.) I was of opinion that if we could get one or more partners possessed of money introduced into our business, and that our business should at the same time be purged of all finance, we had a prospect of doing well; but it was an essential part of the thing that there should be a purging of finance. (Q.) And I suppose you were ready to purge it of finance if you could get in a moneyed partner? (A.) No. I could not get a moneyed partner in without getting it first purged of finance. (Q.) But you wished first to purge it of finance, and then to get a moneyed partner in, and you believed all would be well? (A.) I believed so. (Q.) Did you at that time see the elements of a good London business in your transactions? (A.) Yes. (Q.) And had you particularly in view the advantage it would be to that London business of which you saw the good elements, if you got a moneyed partner? (A.) Yes. (Q.) And was it with reference to that proposal that you were talking to Mr Lewis Potter? (A.) It was. (Q.) I suppose that if his son was to come in with money, that money must have been got from Mr Potter, his father? (A.) I understood so. (Q.) That was the subject of your conversation? (A.) That was so. (Q.) And that was, of course, a matter which nobody else had anything to do with? (A.) No.

By Mr Mackintosh—(Q.) Do you know Mr Taylor? (A.) I have never seen Mr Taylor to my knowledge before to-day. (Q.) Had you any communication with him, directly or indirectly, with regard to your affairs? (A.) Never. (Q.) Or the affairs of the Bank? (A.) Never.

By Mr Robertson—(Q.) Looking back over the negotiations you had with the Bank with regard to your affairs, did you ever meet Mr Henry Inglis on Bank business? (A.) Never.

By the Dean of Faculty—My brother, James Nicol Fleming, left the firm of Smith, Fleming, & Co. in 1862. (Q.) You have been asked how much your firm made in the year 1870, of income, and you have told us £90,000 a year? (A.) Not in 1870. I said the average income for the three years preceding 1870 was over £90,000. It was very nearly £93,000. (Q.) And in 1875, the year preceding the arrangement that you came to with the Bank, how much were you making in your London house and in your foreign houses? (A.) I cannot say. In the year closing in 1875 we earned £28,000 of commission in London. (Q.) Of commissions in your London house alone? (A.) Yes, alone. (Q.) And the foreign houses were doing well also? (A.) Yes. (Q.) I suppose your house, Smith, Fleming, & Co., had the best commission agency business in London? (A.) Oh no, I don't say that. (Q.) But, at all events, a most excellent commission agency business? (A.) We had a good business. (Q.) After Alexander Stronach ceased to be manager, and the office was taken up by Robert, did you find him more strict to deal with than his brother had been? (A.) Yes. (Q.) You did not get advances so easily? (A.) No. (Q.) Would you look at page 60 of the print for the defence, and read the letter addressed by Robert Stronach to you, dated 22d January 1875? (A.) [Witness reads the following]:—

"Private. 22d January 1875.

"Dear Sir,—In answer to your private note of yesterday, and accompanying "official, applying for an extension of part of the Bombay Saw Mill Company's "credit, 31/38, for £30,000, to the extent of one-third, under the same terms and "conditions as before, I regret that this application did not reach me in time for "consideration at yesterday's board meeting; and as I cannot, on my own indivi- "dual responsibility, grant the extension your friends ask, it will, I fear, require to "remain over for another week. * * *

"In the meantime, please let me know if you have any advice that this *is* to be "done. It will be well for you to understand that all matters of this description "MUST go before the board in future.—Yours faithfully,

"R. S. STRONACH, Assist.-Manager.

"John Fleming, Esq."

(Q.) You see there that Robert Stronach says he won't do anything upon his own responsibility? (A.) Yes. (Q.) And that all this must go before the board? (A.) Yes. (Q.) In all your dealings with him, did you ever find that he made any advance upon his own responsibility? (A.) I am not aware that he ever did. (Q.) You have told us the amount of the indebtedness of your firm at the stoppage of the Bank, and the amount of the indebtedness at the date of the arrangement in August 1875, there being an increase between the two periods, between 1875 and 1878. Was a portion of that increase due to the accumulation of interest, and to the adding up of the payments that you ought to have made, but did not make, in the interim upon the old debt? (A.) To the accumulation of interest, and also to the addition of the £100,000 advanced upon Otago stock. (Q.) Just so; but you have explained to us in regard to that £100,000 that the security was given at the time in August 1875, and was then looked upon as perfectly sufficient to meet it? (A.) Yes.

By the Lord Justice-Clerk—(Q.) You have not quite answered the question whether the additional amount between 1875 and 1878 was caused mainly or largely or considerably by the accumulation of interest, and the payments which you were bound to make under the arrangement on the old debt? (A.) The payments that I was bound to make and did not make, would not add to my debt, but the accumulation of interest added to it, and there was also this £100,000 advanced, and there were also additional amounts which we had to receive to help us along. (Q.) What the Dean of Faculty wishes you to tell him, I suppose, is how much was due to the accumulation of interest and the £100,000,—what proportion of the difference? (A.) I cannot tell.

By the Dean of Faculty—(Q.) But it was a large sum? (A.) Yes, a sum probably of £100,000.

By the Lord Justice-Clerk—(Q.) That is to say, about £200,000 out of six? (A.) Out of five.

By the Dean of Faculty—(Q.) In the letter which Mr Asher read, of 24th July 1875, page 85 of the same print [see p. 200], third paragraph from the foot, you begin thus:—"The object of the arrangement is to repay the debt to the "Bank." That was the arrangement at that time? (A.) Yes. (Q.) And that was to be done by paying £25,000 a year? (A.) Yes. (Q.) Had you any doubt at that time, looking to your business, that you would have a surplus available for that purpose to that amount? (A.) I believed that we should have. (Q.) You did get advances from the Bank subsequent to that period? (A.) Yes. (Q.) Turn to page 103 of the same print: there is a letter there dated 4th May 1876, from your firm to Mr Stronach, in the following terms:

"With reference to credit No. 37/25 for £20,000, granted in favour of Messrs "Todd, Findlay, & Company, under our application of 1st September 1875, and "of which £10,000 only is now current, we would feel obliged by your accepting "the enclosed drafts for £5000 under same credit; and as security for the same "we engage to hold to your order the proceeds of 133 tons cutch, p. 'Mandalay,' "value £2600; 255 b. hides, do. £3200; and to keep you free from cash advance "in respect of such advance."

You got that advance, and you gave the security of the produce upon it? (A.) Yes. (Q.) Turn next to page 107 of the same print: there is an excerpt there from a letter by you to Mr Robert Stronach, dated 8th August 1876, in the following terms:—

"I can quite understand the disappointment felt at the absence of progress in "our affairs; but if the very general and extreme badness of trade be considered, "and the special difficulties we have had to contend with, through Collie's stoppage, "and the subsequent derangement of credit, I do not think there is any reason to "be dissatisfied with our position as compared with what it was twelve months ago, "nor to be discouraged as to the future."

(Q.) You entertained these hopes at that time? (A.) I did. (Q.) You did lose something by Collie's stoppage? (A.) Yes. (Q.) But still trade looked well for you at that time? (A.) I hoped there might be a revival of trade. (Q.) Look at page 112 of the same print: you got another advance from the Bank under the following letter of 17th October 1876, from your firm to Mr Robert Stronach:—

"We beg to apply for a credit to be operated under by Messrs W. Nicol & Com- "pany or Messrs Todd, Findlay, & Company, at six months' sight, to extent of "£25,000; and as security for same we engage to hold at your order the following "shipments, the proceeds of which to be applied to the retirement of your accept- "ances:—

"Balance of teak shipments to Mauritius,		£5400
"Do.	rice p. 'Cambay,'	2070
"Do.	do. p. 'Harriet M'Gilvray,'	1000
"Do.	do. p. 'Superbe Richesse,'	1400
"Do.	do. p. 'Rubino,'	1200
"Do.	do. p. 'Caterine Doge,'	1100
"11,870 B	do. p. 'Rangoon,'	5500
"1145 tons	do. p. 'Annati,'.	5800
"NK /10, 1 box pearls,.		2200
		"£25,670

"We further engage to keep you free from cash advance in respect of such "credit."

You got that advance and you gave the security? (A.) We did. (Q.) Let us pass on to page 125 of the same print. You have another letter there of the same kind, dated 10th April 1875:—

"Dear Sir,—We beg to apply for a credit in favour of Messrs W. Nicol & Com- "pany, Bombay, at 6 m/st., to extent of £15,000, and as security for the same we "engage to hold on your account the proceeds of——."

And then you give the proceeds of eight different ships to that extent? (A.) Yes. (Q.) Then on page 126, under date 5th May 1877, you write:

"I see no reason to modify the views I personally expressed to you; indeed, later "advices confirming the expectation of short shipments during the next six weeks "from India strengthen my belief in the certainty of a rise in the value of cotton."

You did entertain that belief and those hopes? (A.) Yes.

"Every day the situation is getting stronger. The stock from this time onward "will be daily lightened, and as these speculative transactions are settled, the cotton "passes into strong hands.

"I may mention also that I know that several of the large speculators who last "autumn were buyers, but turned round in January and became sellers, and have "continued so until lately, are now on the buying tack again."

(Q.) So that at that time trade was hopeful and good? (A.) In the matter of cotton there was an expectation that there would be a rise in the price of cotton. (Q.) Now, look at p. 127:—

"We beg leave to apply for a credit in favour of Messrs W. Nicol & Company, "to extent of £15,000 sterling, to be drawn under at six months' sight, and in re-"newal of credit No. 38/5 of a similar amount now current; and we engage to put "you in funds to retire the same at maturity."

That was a renewal of an old debt,—it was not a new transaction? (A.) No, that was not. (Q.) Look at p. 131:—

"Dear Sir,—We beg to apply for a credit in favour of Messrs W. Nicol & Com-"pany, Bombay, to extent of £8500, in renewal of No. 36/35 for a similar amount "now current, and on the security of 50 shares in the Bombay Saw Mills Company "(Limited), standing in the name of John Hunter, Esq., and 50 shares in the same "company registered in the name of James Morton, Esq.

"We engage to keep you free from cash advance in respect of all drafts accepted "under such credit.—We are, dear Sir, yours faithfully,

"SMITH, FLEMING, & COMPANY."

You gave these securities? (A.) They held these securities; that was a renewal of an old transaction. (Q.) And you got a renewal of it, and declared that the old securities should be applied to it? (A.) Yes. (Q.) Am I right in saying that in regard to all advances that were made upon new transactions subsequent to the arrangement of August 1875, you gave to the Bank securities of one kind or of another, generally produce and shipments then on their way? (A.) They were not all secured. (Q.) Was the greater part of them secured in that way? (A.) Yes. (Q.) Look at p. 132, letter of 27th September 1876, from Stronach to you:—

"While it is very gratifying to learn that you have been arranging most desirable "connections, which you anticipate will add considerably to your emoluments in "the future, it is to be regretted that you have been unable in some measure to "realise the expectations of the spring, and make a tangible reduction of your "debt to the Bank. The directors are of opinion that there is still a considerable "saving might be effected in the expenditure of the several drafts of your business "at home and abroad. Please look into this, and let me have your report soon. I "need not point out to you that even a saving of £5000 in this way would cover, at "the reduced rate of interest charged, about £150m."

(Q.) You had been arranging new connections? (A.) Yes, in Ceylon. (Q.) Opening up a new trade? (A.) At least adding to an existing trade. (Q.) Whereby you would get additional commissions to the £90,000 you had already got? (A.) Yes. (Q.) The Bank held from your firm as security property at Rangoon? (A.) Todd, Findlay, & Co. undertook to hold certain property for the Bank at Rangoon. (Q.) What were those properties valued at at the time when an advance was made as against them? (A.) I don't remember what figures were put down; but roughly, I believe, about £90,000. A portion of those properties, which stood in the books of Todd, Findlay, & Co. at 102,000 rupees, subject to a mortgage of £5000, was sold last week for 250,000 rupees; and if you deduct the mortgage, which is equal to about 65,000 rupees, that leaves a surplus of 90,000 rupees over the valuation in the books.

By the Lord Justice-Clerk—At the present rate of exchange that is not so much as £9000, but taking the rupee at 2s. it is £9000.

By the Dean of Faculty—We had property also at Kurrachee which was made the subject of security. (Q.) There is a railway now being made to Kurrachee? (A.) There is a railway now made; the Indus Valley line was completed this year. I fully expect that that will greatly increase the value of property there. (Q.) Then the sum at which the Kurrachee security was valued is not the real sum it will bring? (A.) Well, I am not sure about that; that is a very difficult question. At the present moment it would not realise what it is valued at. The railway has just been opened, and the expectation is that there will be a large increase of trade at Kurrachee, and that consequently all landed and house property will increase in value.

By the Solicitor-General—(Q.) Your attention has been called to some letters which were passing pretty early, the first being in April 1872. Look at page 5, letter from Alexander Stronach, 7th October 1872 :—

"I am being a little troubled just now with directors who have come on as a "committee on head office advance accounts, and who, having come across your "produce advance debit, wish more information than I can exactly give them. "They have seen the mode it works with us, but they are not at all pleased with its "size, and specially at the sudden large jump it has taken without their having "been consulted beforehand; and all the more that the securities, or many of them, "don't come into our hands at all, or are seen by us. I have detailed to them "that they are all regularly put up separately from your own securities in a box "which is held in trust for us in your safe, and, like your ticketed bills, for which "the account was first substituted, belongs to us exclusively against this balance. "Personally, I know it will be in perfect order, and it is because I believe it to be "so that I ask you now to detail the arrangements in connection with these securi- "ties, and how they are kept for us, and can easily be recognised as ours as distinct "from your own. All will come right doubtless by the end of November as stated, "when the reduction then expected takes place; but meanwhile you will require "to be more specific as to what you propose to put in during the next two weeks, "for these gentlemen's information."

Look at page 7, 10th January 1873, Alexander Stronach to you :—

"In these circumstances, I don't well see how I can substitute for these occa- "sional drafts a permanent increase to the Bombay credits, as you seem to point "at, the more especially as these latter drafts are already so largely in excess of "the authorised limit, and the directors who know of the matter are pressing to get "them reduced as soon as possible, instead of increasing them."

Now, look at page 18 :—

"Some of the directors have already gone over this memo., and I shall be glad to "have your views and criticisms, if you have any specially to offer, at your earliest "convenience."

Then on page 19 there is another letter by Alex. Stronach, 11th June 1873, in which he says :—

"I shall be glad how soon you can make it convenient to be in this city, in accor- "dance with your previous arrangements for coming north, as I should like to have "some further discussion on the subject matter of our recent interviews here, along "with Messrs Potter and Fleming, and the memo. which I enclosed for your care- "ful consideration yesterday, and remarks."

(Q.) Does that refer to a meeting that had been held with Mr Potter, Mr Fleming, and Alex. Stronach and you? (A.) It must be so. Look at next page, 12th June 1873 :—

"The impression has been growing very strongly upon me of late (and the same "idea has been mooted by Mr Potter without any communication with me), that "you and I should become more intimately acquainted with, or rather communica- "tive, as to what is doing from week to week, and that we should be more in con- "sultation on the *financial* position and prospects of the concern generally, seeing "that we have so deep an interest. I fancy I *could* be of essential service to both "parties if allowed, and certainly it would be much more satisfactory to the "directors (who must have the matter in charge now) that I were able to report "upon any application requiring to be made from my personal knowledge of the "circumstances."

Mr Balfour—Would you read the first half of the letter.
Solicitor-General—It is as follows :—

"I am sorry to hear, by yours of yesterday, that you are not feeling so well at "present. I have also myself been much knocked up of late, and had at last, in "something like desperation, to send for the doctor last night. This morning, "from the application he has given me, I feel rather better, but he will not hear of "my going out for some days, and insists on my going off at once for some months "rest. I fear that those heavy and unexpected demands you have been making on "us (and of which I had no indication when you were here, curiously enough), "although not perhaps the *cause*, have had their own effects in putting me in the "horrors for the last week or so, and I have no doubt have made me write you "morbidly on the subject. Now, however, that I know you are ill and unable to "write for a few days, I will wait patiently till you are able to write me fully, not "only as to the past, but also as to the future, and the prospects of greater ease, and "being able to recoup me. You know that I am wholly in the dark, and, in present "circumstances, apparently must always remain so as to what is coming, unless "some change in this respect can be effected."

And later on in the letter he says :—

"I am far from despairing as to the future, but it is clear that the change of policy "which you have lately introduced is the only sound one in present circumstances, "and the one only likely to lead you out of your difficulties ultimately."

Then look on page 22, 13th June 1873 :—

"Meantime, I speak for the memo. I enclosed to you the other day your calm "and earnest attention, as you will at once see it is based entirely upon what passed "at our meetings, at which Mr Potter and Mr J. N. F. (directors) were partly "present, and that all I have done in embodying the substance in this form of a "memo. was simply to amplify some of the details from the papers already in my "hands, so as to meet the circumstances and the facts."

Look at page 25, 8th July 1873 :—

"Referring to our interview yesterday, Mr Potter has been with me to-day, and "we have fully gone over the ground we traversed yesterday, making him aware of "all that passed between us. I have also discussed with him very fully the pro- "posed separation of the firms (in which he takes a deep interest), and after looking "carefully at the views you propounded as to the practical uselessness and inex- "pediency of such a change, we have failed, either of us, to see any valid objection "to the proposal itself, or how you can, by any other means, effect the same object, "and give the Bank an equally good security, which we believe that you are in "earnest in trying to provide for us. At the same time, we see strong and very "forcible reasons why you should meet our views in perfecting the securities to the "utmost of your power, notwithstanding that the mode proposed may soon be "repugnant to all your prejudices and feelings, which I scarcely believe it is."

And in the same letter :—

"On that subject, as well as on the nature of the business which is to be done "and what is to be avoided in the future, I have again read over your letter with "Mr Potter, and we are both of opinion that it would greatly strengthen our hands "in presenting your applications to the Board and getting them adopted, if you "would write us such a letter, signed by yourself and partners, which can be read "at the meeting, embodying very much what you have already written me on both "these subjects, and which you are in future resolved to abide by."

(Q.) These letters were all received by you from Alexander Stronach? (A.) I believe so.

By the Lord Justice-Clerk—(Q.) And you assumed the statements of fact in them to be correct, and acted upon them? (A.) I did.

By the Solicitor-General—(Q.) From 1873 downwards were you ever able to present any substantial change that had taken place in your affairs to the manager or directors of the Bank? (A.) Do you mean an improvement? (Q.) Yes? (A.) No. (Q.) Hopes always, but nothing more? (A.) Hopes, but nothing more. (Q.) And the only bright ray you have had for some years, I think, was the ray last year about the gold in this field? (A.) Yes. (Q.) Did the Bank at any time from 1873 downwards decline to give you any advance that you asked? (A.) Never; never finally declined. (Q.) Once, I think, it was temporarily declined, but granted at the following meeting? (A.) Yes. (Q.) On all other occasions was it granted at your first application? (A.) It was granted; I am not prepared to say on the first application, but certainly it was granted. (Q.) And without any additional security given from the time of the agreement? (A.) No, no. (Q.) What additional security was given from the agreement of 1875? (A.) There have been advances upon sundry securities—balances of shipments, and certain property. For instance, when the credit was given which formed the subject of the interview in July last year, there were securities specified against it. (Q.) So against some of them there were securities, and some not? (A.) Yes.

By the Lord Justice-Clerk—(Q.) What was the nature generally of the securities that were granted for the fresh advances after 1875? (A.) Generally shipments of produce, or portions of shipments, or debts due to us. (Q.) Can you tell us the proportion of unsecured advances from that date? (A.) I think the only specific uncovered advance was one of £65,000 originally, and from the commencement uncovered. (Q.) You think the rest of the advances were covered? (A.) At one time, when the produce of shipments was given in security, the proceeds were applied to payment of the Bank's acceptances.

JAMES MUIR.

By the Lord Advocate—I am an accountant in Glasgow, and a member of the Institute of Accountants and Actuaries there. After the 2d October 1878, I aided in an investigation into the books and accounts of the City of Glasgow Bank, and more recently I have been engaged by the Crown to make certain further investigations into these books. The whole of the books at the Bank were placed at my disposal for that purpose, and I examined them in Glasgow, within the premises of the Bank. I examined the balance-sheets printed and circulated among the shareholders for the years 1876, 1877, and 1878, along with the annual report. I also examined the books of the Bank as at the periods of the balances, for the purpose of ascertaining whether and how far these tallied with the books. I made out corrected balances of my own for each of these periods. I also compared these balance-sheets with the book entitled "City of Glasgow "Bank balance ledger, No. 3." That is a book containing the signatures of the directors, and it is No. 12 of the inventory. I also prepared states showing the difference between the entries contained in the balance-sheets as published and the books of the Bank. The credit and debit sides are differently stated in the balance ledger and in the published abstracts. (Q.) What is the difference? (A.) In the published balance-sheet the liabilities are on the left-hand side, and in the balance ledger they are upon the right-hand side; that is a matter of no moment, but it must be kept very strictly in view to avoid confusion. (Q.) Look at No. 28, being a scroll balance-sheet for 1876, and also at the published abstract as printed in the indictment, and state in detail the discrepancies. (A.) On the debtor or liability side, head 1. in the published sheet, "Deposits at the head-"office and branches, and balances at the credit of banking correspondents," is as published £8,364,056; in the bank ledger it is £9,370,273. In the published sheet it is therefore understated to the extent of £1,006,216. Taking the second item on the debtor side, the "Bank "notes in circulation" are properly stated on both sheets. Taking the third item, "Drafts outstanding, due, or with a currency not exceeding 21 "days, £326,853, 14s. 1d.;" and item four, "Drafts accepted by the Bank "and by its London agents on account of home and foreign constituents, "£988,520, 3s.," these are understated to the extent of £973,300 in the published sheet. The other items on the debtor side of the sheet are correctly stated. (Q.) Did you examine the books of the Bank with the view of tracing that deduction of £973,300? (A.) I did. (Q.) What did you find? (A.) I found an entry in the private cash-book on 4th June 1873. [Shown excerpt 2A from the City of Glasgow Bank cash book, private No. 6.] The entry that I found in the cash-book on the debtor side is "Foreign "and colonial credits No. 2, for the following credits to be retired as "they mature, and debited under the respective accounts to credit ac- "counts No. 2, against which securities are now held by the Bank, and in "process of realization and payment of proceeds, £973,300;" and on the other side the entry is, "Bills payable No. 2, for the following amounts under "acceptance at this date, to be retired by the Bank, under special arrange- "ments with the parties, of date 1st June 1873, against which certain securities "are now held by the Bank, and in process of realization and payment of the "proceeds, £973,300." (Q.) What arrangement, according to your view, was indicated by these entries? (A.) It would appear to me that if this entry were a true entry—— (Q.) Assume it to be so. (A.) Some arrangement must have been come to with certain parties who had obtained advances from the Bank, and who had lodged securities against these advances, the nature of the arrangement being that these securities were to be, and, in point of fact, were at that moment in process of realization, and that the bills with which the advances had been financed were to be paid off at their maturity by the proceeds of the realization.

By the Lord Justice-Clerk—(Q.) Are the debts enumerated which stood in that position? (A.) They are not; there are no details.

By the Lord Advocate—They are slumped on both sides. No details are given, either of the advances or of the supposed securities. (Q.) Did you find that that sum of £973,000, according to that arrangement, was kept up in the books down to the balance of 1878? (A.) It was. We found it there in October, at the time of the investigation. (Q.) What was the effect of it? (A.) The effect of it was, as used in the published balance-sheets, to make it appear not that the securities were to be realised, but that they had been realised, and that the bills to a corresponding amount were not to be paid off, but that they had actually been paid off.

By the Lord Justice-Clerk—It is not set forth twice in the balance-sheet. There is not a cross entry; it is deducted from both sides, so that it reduces the assets on the one side and the liabilities on the other.

By the Lord Advocate—In other words, is the effect of it in the balance-sheet not precisely the same as if these advances to the extent of £973,000 had been paid in cash? (A.) Exactly. (Q.) Upon the day the entry was made in 1873? (A.) And not only so, but that it was employed to retire the Bank's acceptances for an equal amount.

By the Lord Justice-Clerk—And therefore that they were not to be regarded as bills payable? (A.) Precisely. (Q.) And the amount was reduced to that extent? (A.) Exactly.

By the Lord Advocate—That was entered as an actual payment which was only an anticipated payment, and was not got during the five years afterwards? (A.) Yes; it seems as much an anticipation at October 1878, as it was in June 1873. (Q.) So far as the books go? (A.) So far as the books go.

By the Lord Justice-Clerk—Do you find any trace at all in the books of what that sum of £973,000 originated in? (A.) I did not find anything in the books, but I have seen a document which explains it. But I may say that it does not explain it to my satisfaction. I wish, my Lord, to impress it very strongly upon you, that no entry in a book can possibly take a bill payable off the circle, although some people seem to have thought differently. (Q.) Can you conceive any object in a trading company dealing in money as banks do, making an entry of that kind? (A.) Yes; it is obviously very important that the acceptances of the Bank should be made to appear in the balance-sheet as small as possible: a large amount of acceptances published in the balance-sheet would militate against the possibility of discounting the bills of the Bank in the broker's offices in London.

By the Lord Advocate—(Q.) Proceed with your examination of the other side of the abstract for 1876. (A.) On the credit side of the balance-sheet, as published at 7th June 1876, the first head is "Bills of exchange, local "and country bills, credit accounts, and other advances upon security," £8,787,804. That is understated in the published balance-sheet to the extent of £2,698,539. Then, "Cash on hand, that is to say, gold and "silver coin and notes of other banks at head office and branches," head III. of the published sheet, £862,812, is overstated £29,095. The next head—"Government stocks, exchequer bills, railway and other stocks and debentures, "and balances in hands of banking correspondents," were overstated to the extent of £753,211. (Q.) Could you ascertain what that consisted of? (A.) Yes; I have ascertained it. (Q.) In what way? (A.) By looking at No. 128 of the inventory, which is apparently the scroll of the balance-sheet. (Q.) Well, do not assume that in the meantime? (A.) It is overstated to that amount; but without looking at this scroll, it cannot be found to be so by the books. (Q.) Then, except for the existence of a scroll No. 128, the books of the Bank proper do not disclose whence came that over-statement? (A.) No. (Q.) But, in point of fact, if you had nothing but the books to go by, they simply show an over-statement of that amount, without anything to account as to where it came from? (A.) Quite so. (Q.) I suppose it is quite possible to conceal a good deal by making deductions on both sides of a balance-sheet, leaving the result the same as it originally stood? (A.) Yes. (Q.) In point of fact, I presume that the balance-sheet of a bank ought to show their whole outstanding liabilities and their whole outstanding assets? (A.) Undoubtedly. (Q.) Is it possible otherwise to form an accurate conception of the kind of trading they are engaged in, or what loss would result? (A.) Quite impossible. (Q.) To take six or eight millions off each side of this account would not alter the balance? (A.) Certainly not. (Q.) But it would alter the apparent character of the Bank's transactions? (A.) Entirely. (Q.) Now, turn to the next abstract balance-sheet for 1877. [See p. 29.] I ask you in the meantime to lay out of view these scroll sheets, and to confine yourself to a comparison between this abstract and the books of the Bank, beginning again with the liabilities. (A.) At 6th June 1877, the published sheet disclosed under head I. of liabilities, "Deposits at the head office and "branches, and balances at the credit of banking correspondents," £8,382,711, That was understated to the extent of £1,151,518. (Q.) With reference to that under-statement, leaving out of view those abstracts that I was speaking of, is there anything whatever to give a clue to the particular assets that had been deducted in making up this abstract? (A.) Yes, there is. (Q.) What is that? (A.) There are two books specially, one of which is called "Balances of deposit accounts," and the other "Balances of credit "accounts," which show the true balances of deposit and credit accounts which ought to have been entered in this balance-sheet. (Q.) That is perfectly true; but supposing the question were put to you, which part of their assets were deducted, is there any means of telling that from the books themselves? (A.) There is no means of comparing the books themselves with the published sheet, simply for the reason that there are no details in the published sheet. (Q.) Precisely so, and therefore you cannot, by looking at the published sheet, and then looking at the books of the Bank, tell whether the deduction was made from deposits or credits? (A.) No, or whatever may be, you cannot tell the precise nature of the debt which was omitted. (Q.) You may speculate as to why it was made, and how it was made, but there is no possibility of obtaining information as to that from the books? (A.) No, in consequence of the absence of details from the published balance-sheet. (Q.) Then what is the next item? (A.) The next item on the liabilities side is head II., "Bank notes in circulation in Scotland and the Isle of Man." That is understated to the extent of £76,110. The next item, "Drafts out-

" standing, due, or with a currency not exceeding 21 days, and drafts accepted " by the Bank and by its London agents on account of home and foreign " constituents," £1,350,335, as published is understated to the extent of £1,330,712, just about one-half. The other items on that side are perfectly correct as published, according to the books. (Q.) Then take the other side? (A.) The first item on the other side—" Bills of exchange, local and country " bills, credit accounts, and other advances upon security," £8,758,838—is understated to the extent of £3,227,154. Then "Cash on hand, gold and " silver coin, and notes of other banks at head office and branches," is understated to the extent of £30,000. Then "Government stocks, exchequer " bills, railway and other stocks and debentures, and balances in hands of " banking correspondents," £2,187,896, as published, is overstated to the extent of £751,775. (Q.) I suppose that from the books themselves you have no means of tracing that over-statement? I mean from comparing the books themselves with the published sheet, you have no means of finding the items? (A.) No; none whatever. (Q.) Now, assuming that the books are true, and that in publishing the result of the books there is a departure from them to the extent shown in this abstract, do you think it could be said that this abstract truly sets forth the condition of the Bank? (A.) Certainly not. (Q.) What do you think the effect would be of understating the third article on the debtor side by one-half—the bills payable—or by its own amount? (A.) What I have already said; it would make the bills which were offered to the London brokers for discount all the more marketable. (Q.) And I presume a good deal of the effect of such an under-statement might depend upon who were known to be the customers of the Bank? (A.) Undoubtedly. (Q.) Now, take the next abstract balance-sheet (p. 9 of the indictment, see p. 31) for the year 1878. (A.) On the liabilities side, head I., " Deposits at the " head office and branches, and balances at the credit of banking cor- " respondents," £8,102,001, is understated to the extent of £941,284. " The bank notes in circulation in Scotland and the Isle of Man," £710,252, as published, are understated to the extent of £89,031. "The " drafts outstanding, due, or with a currency not exceeding twenty-one " days, and drafts accepted by the Bank and by its London agents on " account of home and foreign constituents," £1,488,244, ought to be £2,881,252, leaving an under-statement on that head of £1,393,008, again nearly one-half. Then, on the other side, the first item of assets— " Bills of exchange, local and country bills, credit accounts, and other ad- " vances upon security," £8,484,466, is understated £3,520,913. The " Cash on hand," £845,963, is overstated to the extent of £219,522. The " Government stocks, &c." published at £2,296,839 are overstated to the extent of £926,764. (Q.) Do you say the same as to the impossibility of getting the details of these under the particular statements from the books? (A.) I do. (Q.) Now, will you take the balance accounts in the " Balance " ledger No. 3," or excerpt No. 12A. Take the year 1876. I wish you to contrast the entries in the balance ledger with the entries in the books, and state what, if any, discrepancies you find there? (A.) We will take this time the credit side of this document first, being the liability side. In the first place, there is " Bills payable" (five lines from the top on the right-hand side), £1,315,373. It ought to be £2,288,673; the difference is the £973,300. (Q.) Then the difference between the two entries tallies with the £973,300? (A.) Yes; and I find the true amount of the bills current in the " Bills pay- " able progressive ledger," No. 40 of the inventory. (Q.) But I mean to say that the entry in the balance ledger will tally with the entries in the books if you give effect to that as a liquidating arrangement? (A.) Yes. (Q.) If you treat unpaid debts to that extent as paid? (A.) Yes. (Q.) Is there any other? (A.) Yes. Four or five entries further down, deposit accounts are entered at £3233; that ought to be £455,444. (Q.) Will you look at No. 128. [See

Appendix II.] That is the scroll abstract of accounts for 1876? (A.) It appears to be so. (Q.) Is it not titled so? (A.) No; it does not say "scroll," it says "abstract," but it appears to be the scroll of the published abstract. I see it says "scroll" on the back; I was not aware of that. (Q.) That is a document written partly in black and partly in red ink? (A.) Yes. (Q.) Does that appear to you to have been the scroll from which the abstract was made up? (A.) It does. (Q.) From what does it so appear? (A.) I find that the slump totals under the various heads correspond with the slump totals under the various heads in the published sheet. (Q.) You see there an entry of "Drafts outstanding, "due, or with a currency," under head III.? (A.) Yes; it is "Drafts out- "standing, due, or with a currency, bills payable No. 1"—that is extended into a creditor column—£2,288,673. 17s. 1d. (Q.) That tallies with the books? (A.) Yes; and then, a little lower down, there is another entry, "Bills payable, No. 2," and there is a sum extended into a debtor column, £973,300, which sum is deducted from that I have just given. The difference, £1,315,373, is entered into a column called "Creditor balance," and that is the sum which is published in the balance-sheet. (Q.) So that if that be correct, that would explain the way in which the sum of £973,300 has been deducted and the balance-sheet made up? (A.) Yes. (Q.) Will you refer again to the balance ledger No. 3. Is the state of deposit accounts correctly given? (A.) No. The amount inserted in the balance ledger on the creditor side, on the left-hand side, is £3233. That ought to be £455,444. (Q.) Just explain how you come to that conclusion. (A.) I find that that is the amount of deposits at the head office by looking at the book, "Balances of deposit "accounts," which is No. 59 of inventory, and that book corresponds with the deposit ledger kept in the head office of the Bank. (Q.) That book shows in separate columns both the balances due to the Bank by overdrafts. and the balances due by the Bank to depositors? (A.) It does. (Q.) These are crossed? (A.) Yes, and the difference alone extended. (Q.) Do you think that is a correct operation? (A.) Not except in cases where the debtor and creditor are precisely the same? (Q.) Where there are cross accounts with the same person or firm? (A.) Yes, and representing the same interest. The same man may be representing different interests, and it would be most improper to cross such accounts. (Q.) In the scroll abstract how is that item dealt with? (A.) It appears in the books as two entries, one of £455,000, and the other of £452,211. (Q.) These are made to extinguish each other, and bring out the balance in the balance ledger? (A.) Yes, and £1346 is put in on the other side in the published sheet. (Q.) Which head would that fall under? (A.) Head 1, on the left-hand side of the published sheet. This balance ledger is not classified at all? (Q.) It appears in the book as two sums due by the Bank *to* depositors, and due *by* depositors to the Bank on overdraft? (A.) It does. (Q.) The difference only to the extent of £3000 odds is entered in the balance ledger? (A.) That is so. (Q.) In what account does this item appear in the scroll balance sheet? (A.) It appears on the other side altogether, £1346, 16s. 8d. (Q.) And that is the item which is given effect to in bringing out the total represented in the published sheet? (A.) That is so. (Q.) So that it appears in three different forms—first in the books; then a different sum in the balance ledger; and thirdly, a reduced sum in the scroll abstract? (A.) That is so; and that has arisen, I may explain, to some extent from certain entries having been made in the cash-book subsequently, apparently, to this scroll having been made up. (Q.) It may be accounted for from that? (A.) Yes, it is so; and the balance ledger is in conformity with the books after these entries have been made, but not the scroll. (Q.) There is nothing of the same kind to account for the change in the scroll? (A.) Nothing whatever. (Q.) In the "Balance ledger No. 3," come to "Credit accounts creditor balances." (A.) That is omitted altogether from the balance ledger. I find on looking at a book called "Balances of "credit accounts," No. 58 of the inventory, that there were such balances to the extent of £147,468. These are entirely omitted from the balance ledger. (Q.) Was that a correct omission? (A.) Certainly not.

By the Lord Justice-Clerk—What is that sum of £147,468? (A.) These are balances standing at the credit of what are called "Credit accounts." It is a little confusing. They are at the creditor of what are called the credit accounts,—a "credit account" being an account which generally has a balance at the debtor of it. A "Cash credit account" is the ordinary name for it.

By the Lord Advocate—(Q.) But upon these balances the Bank was the debtor? (A.) It was.

By the Lord Justice-Clerk—(Q.) They were balances due to customers upon their credit accounts? (A.) Yes. Instead of overdrawing their credit accounts, they, in fact, had deposited a little. (Q.) These are omitted altogether? (A.) Yes; they are altogether omitted; they are not in the balance ledger at all.

By the Lord Advocate—And, of course, they are not to be found at all in the scroll abstract? (A.) In the scroll abstract they are not to be found. (Q.) And accordingly they did not pass into the published abstract. (A.) They did not. (Q.) Is there any other discrepancy between the books and the balance ledger of that year? (A.) There is another "Adjusting account "of interest," the correct state of which I find from No. 144 of process; there is an omission there to the extent of £11,405. These are all the discrepancies I find between the books and the balance ledger.

By the Lord Justice-Clerk—(Q.) Are these accidental errors, or do you think they were systematically done? (A.) They were quite systematically done, but whether with an intention to defraud or not, I don't know. (Q.) But do they appear to have been accidental errors, or do they seem to have been systematically done? (A.) Quite systematically.

By the Lord Advocate—(Q.) Turn to the creditor side of the scroll abstract of accounts for 1878 [see Appendix II.], and point out how far it is, if it be, in disconformity with the books of the Bank? (A.) Being the scroll of the published sheet, it is disconform to the books of the Bank precisely to the same extent as the published sheet is. (Q.) It is just the same in result? (A.) The same in result as I have already given.

By the Lord Justice-Clerk—(Q.) That gives the key to these discrepancies, does it not? (A.) Yes, it gives the actual details, and enables me to say how the thing was done.

By the Lord Advocate—(Q.) Go now to the debtor side of the balance ledger, and contrast it first with the entries in the books of the Bank, and then tell me how far it coincides with the debtor side of the scroll abstract? (A.) The first item on the debtor side of the "Balance ledger No. 3" which is wrong is "Credit accounts No. 1, £1,981,934." That ought to be £2,129,403. It is understated £147,468, and it was the understated amount that went into the scroll abstract. The next item is "Foreign and colonial credits," £1,304,873, which ought to be £2,278,173,—understated by the £973,300; and it was the understated sum which was carried into the abstract. That is carried also into the scroll abstract of the published sheet. The next entry is "Deposit Account, debtor balances," being the indebtedness of the Bank to depositors at the head office, £452,211, which is entirely omitted from the balance ledger. It is also omitted in the scroll abstract. Then the "Adjust- "ing account of interest" is stated in the balance ledger at £19,696, which ought to be £31,101. It is understated £11,405. (Q.) Do these omissions appear to you to be accidental or intentional? (A.) I cannot say that they were accidental; they seem to me to be perfectly intentional. (Q.) Do you observe any transferences in the scroll abstract No. 128, which would account for the over-statement under the third head of what appears as assets in the published sheet, and what is there represented as Government stocks? (A.)

I find that deductions are made from head 1., which head is appropriated in the published sheet to the ordinary debts due to the Bank. I find the following entries deducted from that head, "S. F. & Co." (Smith, Fleming, and Co.), £200,875; "J. N. F." (James Nicol Fleming), £100,300; "J. M. "and Co." (James Morton & Co.), £450,600—together, £751,775. I find that brought down to head III, and there represented to be "Invest- "ments in Government and other stocks," and to precisely a similar amount. (Q.) That sum, made up of these three sums, deducted from their indebtedness, when added to "Government stocks and others" as really appearing in the books, makes up the sum stated in the abstract? (A.) It does. (Q.) Was that a correct statement? (A.) Certainly not. (Q.) Can you conceive any object or purpose in making such an addition? (A.) Yes. (Q.) What would the natural effect of it be? (A.) The natural effect of it would be to make the public have greater confidence in the Bank, as possessing a large amount of easily realisable securities. (Q.) Is there at that date a "Suspense account" in the books? (A.) There is. (Q.) Explain what a "Suspense account" means. (A.) It may mean a great many things; but in this case it means a lot of bad debts collected into an account. (Q.) How does that appear? (A.) It appears in the ledger of the Bank. These debts are collected under this account, apparently being in process of being wiped out at the rate of £10,000 a year, the whole sum to start with being £300,000. It would have taken thirty years to wipe that out. (Q.) The only operation upon these debts amounting to £300,000 was that the Bank were writing them off by degrees? (A.) By degrees—at the rate of £10,000 a year. (Q.) Is there any entry in the scroll? (A.) In the scroll there is only £50,000, which is under the head of "Bad and doubtful "debts." The reason why there is not £300,000 is that the entries in the private cash-book rearing up this "Suspense account" were made subsequently to the writing of the scroll, but prior to the making up of "Balance "ledger No. 3." (Q.) So that in point of fact the statement contained those? (A.) It did. (Q.) To the amount of £250,000? (A.) Yes; and represented as good debts to the extent of £300,000. (Q.) I thought you said that in the scroll £50,000 was taken off? (A.) That was so; £50,000 was included in the scroll, but the remaining £250,000 was included also in the scroll, under a different title. (Q.) They appeared as good in the scroll to the extent of £250,000, and as bad and doubtful to the extent of £50,000? (A.) But even this bad and doubtful sum was entered as a good debt in the published account. (Q.) It was carried into the summation of the assets? (A.) It was. (Q.) Now go to the balance account for 1877. Have you got the corresponding balance ledger for 1877? (A.) I have. (Q.) Give us the entries appearing in the ledger, beginning with the creditor side? (A.) On the creditor side I find, in "Balance ledger No. 3," under date 6th June 1877, "Bills payable," £1,707,748; that ought to be £2,681,048. The difference is the £973,300. The next item is "Deposit a/cs.," stated at £35,488. That ought to be £485,181.

By the Lord Justice-Clerk—That is done just in the same way as in the previous year.

By the Lord Advocate—Then I find from No. 58 of inventory, being a book entitled, "Balances of credit accounts," that at 6th June 1877 there were balances at the credit of those accounts to the extent of £220,683, entirely omitted from the "Balance ledger No. 3." Then there is a trifling sum of £59, 16s., being the "Credit accounts No. 2," which is also omitted. Then there is the "Adjusting account of interest" omitted to the extent of £11,008. That is all upon that side. On the other side, "Credit accounts "No. 1," are entered £1,806,987 in the balance ledger. They should be £2,027,670. The under-statement in the balance ledger is £220,683. Then there is the same trifling error of £59, 16s. Then from No. 59 of inventory

I find that "Deposit accounts" were due to the Bank at that time to the extent of £449,692. These are omitted. Then "Foreign and colonial "credits," stated in the balance ledger at £1,710,048, ought to be £2,683,348,—an under-statement of the old £973,300.

By the Lord Justice-Clerk—(Q.) That was in the balance ledger as well? (A.) Yes.

By the Lord Advocate—Then the "Adjusting account of interest" is in the balance ledger £19,858, and it ought to be £30,867—understated in the balance ledger £11,008. These are all the discrepancies. I have compared these with No. 127 and No. 131 [see Appendix II.]; there are two scroll abstracts for this year. (Q.) Are the discrepancies that occur between the books and the balance ledger carried into these drafts? (A.) They are. (Q.) Are they all reproduced there? (A.) They are. (Q.) Does the draft or abstract No. 127 give you any clue to the source from which these under-statements were taken? (A.) Both No. 127 and No. 131 must be taken together, and they do show that.

By the Lord Justice-Clerk—(Q.) Does it occur to you that the entry in the balance ledger was made after the balance-sheet had been prepared, or before? In other words, was the balance-sheet made from the ledger, or the ledger from the balance-sheet? (A.) The balance-sheet had evidently been made from the ledger,—undoubtedly. (Q.) What you mean is that the entry of £973,000 was given effect to in the balance ledger? (A.) Yes. (Q.) It must have been there before the balance-sheet was prepared? (A.) It appears as an open balance in the ledger, but instead of being allowed to remain at the amount in which it is in the ledger, when we come to the balance it is found deducted from another account, and the difference alone is given.

By the Lord Advocate—(Q.) In the abstract it appears that certain debts on open account are brought down under the head of "Government stock "and other stocks?" (A.) Yes.

By the Lord Justice-Clerk—(Q.) If the abstract of the balance-sheet had been correctly made from the balance ledger, that sum of £973,000 could never have appeared, as it is now? (A.) No, it would not.

By the Lord Advocate—(Q.) Would these sums have appeared as brought down? It it had been made from the balance ledger, would these sums have appeared as brought down under the head of Government stocks? (A.) Certainly not; there is no such entry in the books to substantiate it.

By the Lord Justice-Clerk—(Q.) I suppose whatever was the fact about these debts and the securities for them, they never should have come under that heading? (A.) Most undoubtedly not. The heading was entirely reserved for absolute investments. (Q.) These were permanent investments? (A.) Yes. (Q.) Over which the Bank had complete control? (A.) Yes, and which they had paid for with their own money. (Q.) And not security for outstanding debts? (A.) No.

By the Lord Advocate—(Q.) In the scroll abstract or draft for 1877, does the £973,300 appear as before? (A.) No, in neither 127 nor 131 does it appear. The amount of bills payable account, after having the £973,000 deducted, is carried into this scroll, but it has been scored out, as if some new idea had occurred to them—another way of doing it; and I find in No. 131 a pencil jotting which shows the new method that was adopted of falsifying the accounts. (Q.) Of something substituted for the £973,000? (A.) Yes. (Q.) What is substituted? (A.) I find, opposite the words "Bills payable," entered £2,683,348. That is wrong to the extent of £2300. Then from that is deducted "Cash lodged on D/A," £94,368, "Anticipations," £527,940; "S. F. & Co.," £552,704; and "J. N. F," £158,000—together, £1,333,012, 19s. 1d.; difference, £1,350,335, which was the sum stated in the published balance-sheet. (Q.) Is there any trace of these deductions to be found in the books? (A.) None. (Q.) Have you examined the balance ledger for 1878? (A.) I have. (Q.) Is it in conformity with the books? (A.) It is not. Taking first the creditor side, "Bills payable" are stated at £1,907,952. That ought to be £2,881,252. The difference is again the £973,300. Then "Deposit accounts" are stated at £33,959. The real liability in deposits then was £474,698. The balance-ledger is under-stated to the extent of £440,738. Then the "Credit accounts" are omitted altogether to the extent of £346,336, and a small sum of £119, 12s. The "Adjusting account of interest" is also omitted entirely, £9825. These are all the discrepancies on the credit side. Then on the debtor side, "Credit "accounts, No. 1" appear in the balance ledger at £2,009,752. That ought to be £2,356,088. It is understated in the balance ledger by £346,336. "Credit accounts, No. 2" are understated by the £119, 12s. Then "Deposit "accounts," £440,738, are entirely omitted from the balance ledger. Then "Foreign and colonial credits," £1,907,952, ought to be £2,881,252. The difference is the £973,300. The "Adjusting account of interest" appears in the balance ledger £27,405; this should be £37,230; under-statement, £9825.

By the Lord Justice-Clerk—(Q.) That is contrasting the balance ledger with the books? (A.) Yes, and these under-statements are also given effect to in the published sheet.

By the Lord Advocate—(Q.) Look at No. 124 of process [see Appendix II.]; that is the draft or scroll abstract for 1878? (A.) Yes. (Q.) Do the details there agree with the published abstract? (A.) They do. (Q.) The details there given show the method by which the alterations or the discrepancies as between the published balance-sheets and the books might be effected? (A.) That is so. (Q.) In fact all these scrolls that you have seen exhibit a method by which that end might be attained? (A.) That is so. (Q.) I suppose precisely the same results in the abstract might have been attained in a great variety of other ways? (A.) Yes.

By the Lord Justice-Clerk—Then as far as the errors in the balance ledger are concerned this is consistent with it? (A.) Yes. (Q.) But there are additional errors? (A.) There are additional errors—additional falsifications. In this case they could not possibly be errors. (Q.) But the balance ledger was erroneous in the particulars you have mentioned? (A.) Yes. (Q.) And this transcribes the errors, but adds some in addition? (A.) Yes, to a very large amount. (Q.) That is to say, those you have gone over already,—the transferences of those balances of Smith, Fleming, & Co., and the others down to "Goverment stocks?" (A.) Yes; and there is a very serious deduction, further than the £973,000, of £419,000 made from the "Bills payable," which is a most absurd and stupid entry. They say, "Amount of bills on the "circle, and against which an equal sum is at the credit of J. M. & Co. on "D/A., £419,708." That is made a deduction from the liabilities of the Bank. Now, if there was any "Sum at the credit of James Morton & Co.," it was also a liability; and they would seem therefore to reduce their liabilities by deducting other liabilities from them,—the most absurd and illogical thing I ever saw. (Q.) Is that the sum on the right-hand side, £419,000? (A.) Yes. (Q.) And what do you say that is? (A.) It is stated in this scroll, No. 134, to be "Amount of bills on the circle, and against which an equal "sum is at the credit of J. M. & Co. on D/A." Now *that* was a liability of the Bank's, and the bills payable were *also* a liability of the Bank, and yet they deducted the one from the other.

By the Lord Advocate—That is a very easy way of getting rid of liabilities? (A.) No doubt of it. (Q.) A man owes two sums of £1000 each, and he deducts the one from the other, and the result is he owes nothing! Is not that practically what was done? (A.) Apparently so. Besides which, I want to state that at that time there was no such "sum at the credit of James Mor-"ton & Co." They really owed the Bank £480,000.

By the Lord Justice-Clerk—(Q.) And whether that was true or false, that was not the way in which it should have been dealt with? (A.) Certainly not.

By the Lord Advocate—(Q.) There is also an addition of £200,000 to the gold held? (A.) Yes. (Q.) Which is ear-marked along with another sum of £480,000, and together making up £680,000? (A.) Yes, in branch 1. (Q.) Written off to cash account? (A.) Written off "Credit accounts No. 1." (Q.) And by that process converted into gold? (A.) Yes. I was asked to examine into the accounts of eight debtors to the Bank, viz.:—1, James Morton & Co., and the partners; 2, Smith, Fleming, & Co.; 3, James Nicol Fleming; 4, Potter, Wilson, & Co., and Mr Potter; 5, Matthew Buchanan and Co.; 6, John Innes Wright & Co., and the partners; 7, W. Glen Walker; 8, The Edinburgh Pastoral Association. These parties were indebted to the Bank in various forms. I was struck with the very large amount of their debts in the various forms, as compared with the debts of the ordinary customers of the Bank. (Q.) What were the forms of indebtedness? (A.) Cash credits, overdrawn deposits, bill credits, or foreign and colonial credits, as they were called, and discounts. (Q.) By cash credits, what do you mean? (A.) Hard cash lent by the Bank to them. (Q.) Either with or without security? (A.) Either with or without security. (Q.) What are "Overdrawn "deposits?" (A.) It is just another name for the same thing. (Q.) It is just a deposit account which happens to be overdrawn? (A.) Yes. (Q.) It is a current account to which the debtor may pay in,—a current account overdrawn at the time? (A.) Yes. (Q.) There were bills accepted on what are called "Open and marginal credits?" (A.) Yes; and which are styled in the ledger "Foreign and colonial credits." (Q.) But they were in both of these shapes? (A.) That is so. (Q.) State the total indebtedness of Morton and Co., and James Morton, to the Bank in the years from 1873 to 1878 inclusive? (A.) James Morton & Co.:—

1873,	£1,379,400
1874,	1,399,140
1875,	1,380,000
1876,	1,855,000
1877,	1,771,000
1878,	2,173,000

In the case of Smith, Fleming & Co., the corresponding figures are:—

1873,	£1,136,000
1874,	1,340,000
1875,	1,661,000
1876,	1,777,000
1877,	1,903,000
1878,	1,968,000

James Nicol Fleming:—

1873,	£738,000
1874,	861,000
1875,	1,005,000
1876,	1,136,000
1877,	1,188,000
1878,	1,238,000

Potter, Wilson, & Co., which includes Mr Lewis Potter:—

1873,	£78,000
1874,	109,000
1875,	76,000
1876,	75,700
1877,	64,000
1878,	108,000

Matthew, Buchanan, & Co.:—

1873	£31,000
1874	7000
1875	17,000
1876	7700
1877	17,000
1878	17,600

John Innes Wright & Co.:—

1873	£251,000
1874	368,000
1875	392,000
1876	431,000
1877	398,000
1878	485,000

Glen Walker & Co., which does not appear till 1875:—

1875	£4465
1876	3600
1877	30,000
1878	26,000

Edinburgh Pastoral Association, which apears first in the balance of 1877:—

1877	£30,000
1878	75,200

In 1873 the amount lent to the whole customers of the Bank on cash credit or overdrawn deposits, excluding foreign and colonial credits, which form another branch, was	£4,402,659
Of that there was lent to the eight firms before mentioned, excluding foreign and colonial credits, and to the manager, directors, and secretary, ...	1,339,348
Leaving the amount lent to ordinary customers, .	£3,063,311

1874. Total amount lent as before, ...	£4,723,608
Lent to eight firms before mentioned, and to manager, directors, and secretary, . . .	2,125,244
Leaving for ordinary customers, . . .	£2,598,363
Or little more than half.	

1875. Total amount lent, as before, ...	£4,649,526
Lent to eight firms before mentioned, and to manager, directors, and secretary, . . .	2,414,335
Leaving for ordinary customers, . . .	£2,235,190
Or less than one half of the whole.	

1876. Total amount lent, as before, ...	£5,507,857
Lent to eight firms before mentioned, and to manager, directors, and secretary, six-elevenths of the whole, ...	3,044,106
Leaving for ordinary customers, . . .	£2,463,751

1877.	Total amount lent, as before,	£5,436,835
	Lent to eight firms before mentioned, and to manager, directors, and secretary,	2,965,424
	Leaving for ordinary customers,	£2,471,411
	About the same proportion as the previous year.	
1878.	Total amount lent, as before,	£5,639,292
	Lent to eight firms before mentioned, and to manager, directors, and secretary, about three-fifths of the whole,	3,377,636
	Leaving for ordinary customers,	£2,261,656

I have made out similar details in regard to the foreign and colonial credits. These figures are taken as at the period of the balance for the year prior to that period. I have not taken the period subsequent to the balance of 1878.

	In 1873 the total amount lent by the Bank upon foreign and colonial credits—bill credits—that is to say, the Bank granted its acceptances to that extent,	£2,132,453
	Of that, the eight firms I have already mentioned got	2,111,697
	Leaving for general customers about	£20,000
1874.	Total amount lent as before,	£1,897,729
	Lent to the eight firms,	1,866,252
	Leaving for general customers,	£31,476
1875.	Total amount lent as before,	£2,124,880
	Lent to the eight firms,	2,106,536
	Leaving for general customers,	£18,344
1876.	Total amount lent as before,	£2,278,173
	Lent to the eight firms,	2,252,071
	Leaving for general customers about	£26,000
1877.	Total amount lent as before,	£2,683,346
	Lent to the eight firms,	2,589,148
	Leaving for ordinary customers,	£94,201
1878.	Total amount lent as before,	£2,881,252
	Lent to the eight firms,	2,848,839
	Leaving for ordinary customers about	£32,000

If you add to the foreign and colonial credits of these eight firms in 1878 the amount which I gave as lent to these firms and to the manager, directors, and secretary on cash credits and overdrawn deposits, it brings out a sum of upwards of £6,000,000. I was asked to examine and to give for 1876 the applications made for credits. So far as I can discover, there were (1) credits given upon applications which mentioned securities; (2) credits given upon applications which did not mention securities; and (3) credits given for which no application appeared either in letters of application or in the minutes. Of the £2,252,071 of "foreign and colonial credits" granted to the eight firms before mentioned in 1876, I find that £1,358,431 was granted upon letters of application mentioning securities, £359,500 upon letters which did not mention securities, and £534,140 without any writing at all. As regards 1877, of the £2,589,146 lent to these firms, £1,493,936 was under the first of these classes, £323,000 under the second class, and £772,210 under the third class. In 1878, of the £2,848,839 lent to these firms, £1,808,910 was under the first class, £156,000 under the second class, and £883,928 under the third class,—without any application letters at all.

By the Dean of Faculty—(Q.) That is, letters you did not see? (A.) Exactly; I neither found them, nor did I see any allusion to them in the minutes.

By the Lord Advocate—The debtor balance standing against Mr John Stewart at the balancing period was:

In 1873	£5,994
1874	10,040
1875	13,348
1876	12,198
1877	18,085
1878	8,956

Against Stewart, Pott, & Company, which begins in 1875:

1875	£12,877
1876	16,463
1877	17,674
1878	19,826

Henry Taylor & Son; in 1873 there was a balance at their credit of (if I recollect aright) £675, and the debtor balance against them was—

In 1874, ...	£17,673
1875, ...	35,945
1876, ...	38,829
1877, ...	55,295
1878, ...	72,266

Against John Innes Wright, whose balance begins in 1876:

1876, ...	£2797
1877, ...	2787
1878, ...	2771

That was being gradually diminished owing to the dividend on the Bank stock being credited to a larger extent than the interest which was debited.

Against John Innes Wright & Co.:

1875, ...	£217,707
1876, ...	254,211
1877, ...	239,496
1878, ...	334,783

As regards this firm, they had also credits of another description, but I find these had run off by 1875.

Against Henry Inglis:

1873,	£30,088
1874,	37,552
1875,	38,556
1876,	39,598
1877,	41,368
1878,	44,430

Against H. & A. Inglis:

1873,	£298
1874,	1799
1875,	3346
1876,	2931
1877,	6007
1878,	5455

By Mr Trayner—My reason for selecting the year 1873 as that with which to commence Mr Stewart's private account was that I had made an investigation of the books from the date when the £973,000 entry was made. I had no other reason. I cannot tell when Mr Stewart's private account commenced. I did not think it right or necessary for my purpose that I should ascertain that. I do not know when Mr Stewart became a director. I did not apply myself to find whether he had had advances before he became a director or not. I think Stewart, Pott, & Co.'s account began in 1875; the first balance I have is in that year. I cannot tell how that account commenced. I have dealt with the accounts entirely at the balancing periods. I do not know what sort of a business Stewart, Pott, & Co.'s was; I believe they had some connection with the wine trade. I was born in Glasgow. I am 39 years of age. I know Mr Stewart personally, but I never was in his office in my life, and I know nothing whatever about the nature or extent of his business.

By Mr Balfour—My evidence is given entirely as that of an accountant. At the request of the Crown, I made an examination of the books and documents of the Bank, and I deduce my results entirely from these. I had previously been engaged as the coadjutor of Mr Anderson, one of the liquidators. There are a very large number of books employed in the current business of the City of Glasgow Bank—so many, that I really could not approximate the number. It may be twenty, thirty, forty, or fifty. It is quite possible there are a great many more; the number is very, very large. There are a great many separate departments. I should think there must be sixty or eighty officials, including clerks, at the head office. In short, it was a very large establishment, with a very large number of books in use. In the course of our investigation we had the aid of the staff of the Bank which has remained on since the stoppage. We had also the aid of the staff of our own firm, which is a large one. We had such assistance as we desired from the clerks of Dr M'Grigor's firm, which is a very large legal firm. They were principally engaged in looking into securities and things of that kind. We had every possible facility for making an examination. With all these facilities, we found it a very laborious one, because we went into very great detail, counted every bill in the Bank, and looked at every balance of every separate account recorded in the books. Besides, a considerable amount of time was lost in getting the returns from the branches as to the state of the accounts there. There are about 133 branches, and we got the accounts from them also. The investigation with a view to making the report was conducted in the way I have mentioned. The evidence I have given to-day has been entirely from my own checking of the books, with very little assistance from clerks at all, because I thought it very important that I should not give evidence about what I had not personally seen. (Q.) You have used the expression repeatedly in the course of your evidence that certain sums in the published abstract were understated or overstated? (A.) That is so. (Q.) In so speaking of under-statement or over-statement, did you take as your standard the books of the Bank? (A.) I did. (Q.) And it means under or over certain entries in the books of the Bank? (A.) Yes, that is so. (Q.) You also said, I think, that you found what you regarded as errors in the balance ledger? (A.) Yes, under-statements. (Q.) In using that expression, have you regard still to the other books of the Bank? (A.) That is so.

By the Lord Justice-Clerk—(Q.) Under-statements and omissions? (A.) Yes.

By Mr Balfour—That is to say, things which you would have expected to be brought in from other books of the Bank? (A.) That is so. (Q.) This balance ledger purports to set out the results brought from a very large number of accounts in other books? (A.) Yes; the whole books of the Bank, credit and deposit ledgers, discount ledgers, and all the books of the Bank. (Q.) You would assume, I suppose, from looking at it, that the results of these different departments must have been given to some official who made up the balance ledger? (A.) Undoubtedly. That would naturally fall under the department of the accountant in such a Bank. It was his duty to make up the balance ledger. The entry of £973,000 was raised in June 1873, on the two sides of a book, the entries in which I have already read, and also on the two sides of the ledger. (Q.) But it was originally raised in the cash-book? (A.) The cash book entry was the subsidiary entry to what ultimately appeared in the ledger. (Q.) It was the first entry? (A.) Yes; that entry has remained in the private cash book and in the ledger ever since it was raised there in June 1873. (Q.) So, from 1873 down to the stoppage of the Bank, that was an entry appearing throughout the books of the Bank? (A.) It was so; but it was omitted from the balance ledger. (Q.) But it was in the books of the Bank? (A.) Yes. I have not seen all the weekly balances applicable to the head office, but I have generally glanced at them. I know the principle on which they are made up. The weekly balance applicable to 4th June 1873 (No. 13) was the first weekly balance after the entry of £973,000 was raised. On the right-hand side of the sheet, in the creditor column, I find an entry of £2,128,686, 11s. 9d. That is "Credit account, bills payable No. 1," as appearing in the other books. In the debtor column I find an entry of £973,000. What is carried out to the balance is the difference, being £1,155,386, 11s. 9d. (Q.) Has that been the principle upon which this sum has been dealt with ever since June 1873? (A.) I believe it has; in fact, I know it has. It has entered every weekly abstract balance since that time, and has been regularly deducted on each of these occasions, and the balance carried out. (Q.) Have you observed whether, in the balance ledger applicable to the different years, what has been entered under "Bills payable" has been the difference between what you say is the true amount and that sum? (A.) Exactly; in fact, this sum in the creditor column is the amount of the balance. That course has been uniformly followed since 1873. (Q.) Suppose that the principle upon which the directors checked the balance ledger was by the director watching the entries, and the accountant reading off the corresponding entries, what the accountant would read off and the director would see would be the difference? (A.) Simply. (Q.) And the directors so checking the balance ledger would have no cognisance of that fact? (A.) No, unless they had the sheet before them. (Q.) But assuming it was done as I have said, the directors would not see that entry, but would merely have the difference read out? (A.) Certainly. (Q.) Do you find that

—except in 1877, about which there was something special—in making out the scroll abstracts for the yearly balances, the £973,000 has been treated just as it was treated throughout the books of the Bank and the relative balance sheets? (A.) Precisely, the relative weekly abstracts. (Q.) Is it plain that from the first scroll of these abstracts that sum has been so treated in all those different years except 1877? (A.) I do not know whether these red-inked documents are the first scrolls or not. (Q.) But, from anything you have seen? (A.) Yes. (Q.) The earliest extant scrolls of these abstracts have this treated exactly as it is throughout the other books and papers of the Bank for those six years? (A.) So far as I have seen them. (Q.) Then it is plain, reading these documents, that, unless it be in 1877, there has not been any change in the mode of treating that, induced by after-suggestion? (A.) None whatever. (Q.) Are these entries simply passed into the ledger? (A.) They are so. (Q.) So that the ledger entries applicable to that will just be the same as these? (A.) Yes. (Q.) With no details? (A.) With no details. (Q.) Then the way in which it is entered in the weekly balance-sheet is in this form [showing]? (A.) Yes. (Q.) And it has been so fifty-two times every year since 1873? (A.) Precisely. (Q.) In each year from 1873, do you find that what is carried into the balance ledger is the total sum, what you think the true sum of bills, minus the £973,300? (A.) That is so. (Q.) In short, the figuring which is in the right-hand column is what is uniformly carried into the balance ledger in those years? (A.) The figuring which is in the right-hand column of this sheet [showing]. (Q.) Exactly; and in like manner in the abstract which ultimately becomes the published abstract, or the circulated abstract, is it treated in the same way? (A.) Except in 1877. (Q.) In the way in which the balance ledger is framed as regards the head office, does it bring into one the results of all the accounts as appearing in the balance of the week in which it occurs? (A.) Precisely. (Q.) Then as regards the branches, all that appears in the balance ledger is the total balance every year against the branch? (A.) Yes. (Q.) Whereas, as regards the branches in the abstract for publication, the transactions at the Bank are brought under the different headings? (A.) Yes, of the customers at the branch. (Q.) So that there is a different principle for that, and I suppose properly, in making up the balance of the two accounts? (A.) Quite properly. The details are contained in abstracts which are sent in. (Q.) You do not complain of that? (A.) Not at all. (Q) Then what I come to is this, if what the directors had before them was the balance ledger, and they only heard what was read off from it, they would not know of the £973,300? (A.) They would not. (Q.) Then I ask you again, are you perfectly satisfied, from your examination of the different scroll abstracts which you have seen, that the £973,300, except in 1877, has been treated just as it is in the books of the Bank, the original deduction? (A.) Just as it is in the weekly balance-sheets, but not as it is in the books of the Bank. (Q.) But as it is in the weekly balance-sheets? (A.) Yes. (Q. You don't find any change in the abstracts after the first scroll had been made up? (A.) I do not quite follow you. (Q.) What I mean is this, it appears to have been part of the original scheme? (A.) No doubt of it. (Q.) You next gave us some answers about the balances which you disapproved of. In particular, you pointed out what appears under the head "Debtor accounts;" that is, the balance of £1346, 16s. 6d. in the balance of 1876. That is the first you spoke of? (A.) Are you talking now of the balance ledger? (Q.) No; I am speaking of the scroll balance, No. 128A. Would you also look at No. 59A, excerpts from "Balances of deposit accounts." In the right-hand column of that paper, under 7th June 1876, does the sum of £1346, 16s 6d. appear as the difference between the debtor and creditor accounts? (A.) That is so. (Q.) Therefore that sum of £1346, 16s. 6d. is a balance, whether rightly or wrongly taken, still taken from the book of the Bank appropriate to these accounts? (A.) Undoubtedly. (Q.) Would you also look to the balance ledger for the same time, No. 12A. In the balance for June 1876 I observe under the head "Deposit accounts" £3233, being a different figure? (A.) That is so. (Q.) Going back again to No. 59A, do you find how that arises? (A.) Yes. (Q.) It has been done in this way. After apparently a summation bringing out £1346, 16s. 6d. has been made, there has been an additional sum brought in? (A.) Yes. There was an entry made in the cash book subsequently to this scroll being made up, as I have twice, I think, referred to. (Q.) And you think you can perfectly see how the sum of £4579, 16s. 10d. was entered? (A.) Yes. (Q.) Then the £3233 is the difference which appears in the balance ledger? (A.) Yes. (Q.) And whether the principle is right or wrong, that amount is a true entry brought from the book of the Bank applicable to such accounts? (A.) That is so. (Q.) Do you find that throughout the balance ledger the principle followed as regards "Deposit accounts" has been to bring the balance only between the total of the two sides? (A.) Yes, in the balance ledger. (Q.) Throughout? (A.) Throughout as regards "Credit accounts" and "Deposit accounts." (Q.) As regards both? (A.) As regards both. (Q.) Whether that is good or bad book-keeping, what has been done has been to bring true entries from the proper books and enter them here? (A.) To enter the mere differences. (Q.) I mean they are not fictitious entries? (A.) Certainly not. (Q.) The other two balances brought from their appropriate books, and entered in the balance ledger? (A.) That is so. (Q.) And that is the practice which, whether by good or bad book-keeping, has been pursued throughout? (A.) Yes. (Q.) How far do you find that practice to have been carried? (A.) As far back as I have gone, 1873. (Q.) You have not gone any further? (A.) I have not in that part of the investigation gone any further. (Q.) Then you do not find any book in which that practice has not been followed? (A.) No. (Q.) It was nothing new in 1876? (A.) Nothing new. (Q.) And the way in which the £973,000 was treated then was nothing new in 1876? (A.) It was not. (Q.) You said there were some things that you disapproved of in the balance ledger; did you find that these things existed in all the balance ledgers that you examined? (A.) From 1873. (Q.) And you examined no earlier? (A.) No. (Q.) So that whether they were right or wrong, that has been a scheme followed so far back as your examination goes? (A.) That is so. (Q.) There was no novelty in 1876 about these matters? (A.) No, not as to these special matters. (Q.) Then you gave an answer to the Lord Advocate about cross accounts. You said, I think, that where the same person had more accounts than one in the same interest, the crossing of accounts was quite proper? (A.) Yes. It is not a usual thing to be done, I believe, in a large establishment like a Bank, but it is quite legitimate. (Q.) It is quite proper? (A.) Perfectly proper. (Q.) You have nothing to say against it? (A.) Nothing whatever. (Q.) I suppose the accountant who was responsible for and in charge of these books would know better than you would do what were proper cross accounts? (A.) Well, I have asked him the question, and he was utterly unable to explain the entry to me. (Q.) But the accountant is the responsible official in charge of that class of work? (A.) Yes. (Q.) And he would be the natural person to know what were cross accounts? (A.) He would be the natural person to know. I don't know whether he would know better than I would do. (Q.) You gave some evidence with regard to the "Suspense account." The suspense account appears, I think, in 1876 as £300,000? (A.) Yes. (Q.) And then it gradually goes down £10,000 a year? (A.) Yes. (Q.) Did it appear to you from your examination of the books that the suspense account had been raised between the time of the scroll abstract being prepared, and the time of the balance ledger being prepared? (A.) It undoubtedly had. (Q.) That was clear? (A.) Quite clear to the extent of £250,000. (Q.) You told us how the £50,000 was treated? (A.) Yes. (Q.) That being so it would not surprise you that you found the suspense account in the balance ledger although you did not in the scroll abstract? (A.) No. (Q.) It would suggest that it had occurred to the officials that these accounts were proper to be in suspense in the interval between the two? (A.) Yes. (Q.) I suppose the idea of a "suspense account" is an account which contains debts which may or may not be good? (A.) "Suspense accounts" are of a very miscellaneous kind. A "suspense account" may mean a great many things; it is a very dangerous class of account. (Q.) But is not that the natural meaning of a "suspense account," an account that is neither clearly good nor clearly bad? (A.) No. (Q.) Is it not in "suspense?" (A.) That is so. (Q.) And in doubt? (A.) No, not necessarily. (Q.) But perhaps? (A.) Perhaps; but I should say that if the suspense account is being written off at a certain rate per annum, that clears up the doubt at once. (Q.) If an account was doubtful, and not improving, it would be proper to reduce it by degrees; if it was clearly bad, it should all go at once? (A.) Yes, it ought, and I say that £300,000 should have gone at once. (Q.) Because you think it was bad? (A.) Yes. (Q.) But if it was only doubtful, was not the proper way to treat it to reduce it by degrees? (A.) No. (Q.) Would you have kept it all up? (A.) I would have been disposed to have written it off, even although it had been doubtful. (Q.) Even if it was only doubtful and not bad, you would have been disposed to have written it off? (A.) If it had been so doubtful that I did not charge interest on it. (Q.) But is it not the case that if it were bad you would write it off, and if it were doubtful you would reduce it? (A.) If it was doubtful I don't know if I would reduce it. (Q.) But that is a matter which it was proper for the accountant to know? (A.) Yes, or for a person who knew the facts about the account. (Q.) That would depend on extraneous knowledge, which you have not? (A.) And which those who are in immediate contact with the account ought to have known thoroughly. They were the people who naturally ought to know. (Q.) The officials in charge? (A.) Yes. [Shown No. 131, see Appendix II.] There is a great deal of pencil figuring on that. (Q.) Do you also see traces of there having been previous pencil figuring which has been rubbed out? (A.) Not on this sheet, I think. (Q.) But at any rate, there is a great deal of pencil figuring, containing very elaborate calculations? (A.) That is so. (Q.) It would require an accountant of some skill to make calculations like these, would it not? (A.) It would. It caused me very great difficulty in tracing what they meant. (Q.) Even with your skill you found it difficult? (A.) Very difficult indeed. (Q.) So that you are quite satisfied that the man who was figuring with the pencil must have been an accountant of considerable skill? (A.) Well, I know who the accountant was, and I really must not commit myself to saying that he is an accountant of any skill. (Q.) But this is evidently the work of a skilled accountant, is it not? (A.) It is rather the work of a bungling person who seemed to be trying to get at a result. (Q.) But evidently an accountant? (A.) Undoubtedly. (Q.) And you see the kind of result that he got at? (A.) Yes. (Q.) You gave an opinion about a sum of £419,000. Did you find that, with respect to Mr Morton, there had been a system of issuing second sets of acceptances to retire the first? (A.) That was so. (Q.) Did you identify this entry of £419,000 with the dealings with the second sets of acceptances? (A.) I could not. I tried to do so, but I could find no details. (Q.) You merely, looking as an accountant, and without extraneous knowledge, cannot tell whether that may have been the discount money of the second set to retire the first or not? (A.) No, I cannot. (Q.) It may have been? (A.) It may. (Q.) Or it may not? (A.) Yes; but I see distinctly from the books that the unreduced amount of the bills payable was on the circle at that date. (Q.) No doubt that would be so during the days before the first set were retired and after the second were out? (A.) Both the first and second sets were current at the same time. (Q.) No doubt that would be so if the transaction was such as I have put to you? (A.) That would be the result.

By the Lord Justice-Clerk—(Q.) I suppose the system, whether it is a good one or not, implies drawing bills and putting them in the circle before the old ones are retired? (A.) Yes, and also that the bills would have to be given to Mr Morton to give him time to discount them, and get the proceeds into his hands before the first set became due. (Q.) So that the first set are current while the others are also current? (A.) Yes.

By Mr Balfour—(Q.) And you found that that also had been put into the deposit account? (A.) No; I did not. (Q.) I thought you said so? (A.) No; I said that Mr Morton at that time was owing the Bank £480,000 on overdrawn deposit and credit accounts. (Q.) Did you find that in any account? (A.) No; I could not trace that in any account. In order to trace that I would have had to know the particulars and the amounts of each of the several bills constituting the £419,000, but I did not know. (Q.) And therefore the books of the Bank did not enable you to say what that £419,000 was? (A.) They did not. (Q.) But you gave an opinion that that was a man really reducing his liabilities by taking one from another? (A.) Taking one liability from another, but simply from the wording of the sheet. (Q.) But suppose that the transaction was that it was discount money got in to take up the first set of bills, it was quite proper to treat them as they are treated here? (A.) Certainly not. (Q.) Why not? Both sets of bills appear in the aggregate of the bills? (A.) Yes. (Q.) So that if the aggregate stood as it was, it would have the bills for the same amounts in twice? (A.) No doubt it would, for both sets were in the hands of the public. (Q.) And no doubt the Bank were liable to the public for both sets; but if the Bank had got in discount money to take up the first set, was it not a perfectly proper deduction to make from the liabilities on bills? (A.) Certainly not. (Q.) Whether it was a proper deduction to make from the liability on bills it was a proper deduction to make, was it not, in ascertaining the Bank's aggregate liability? (A.) Certainly not. (Q.) You did not find the cash entering the deposit account? (A.) I could not for a single moment imagine that £419,000 was paid into the City of Glasgow Bank without being credited to some account. (Q.) It was not treated as cash in hand? (A.) It must have been in the cash chest at that moment. (Q.) But you do not find that sum of £419,000 carried in to reduce any other account? (A.) It must have been. If paid in by James Morton it must have been credited to James Morton. (Q.) Instead of saying what must have been, tell us what you found? (A.) I have told you that I have been unable to trace the money, because I could not tell the amount of the bills. (Q.) Did you find that £419,000 employed to reduce any account except the bill account? (A.) I did not specially find that sum. I could not trace the amounts that were got by the discounts of these bills. (Q.) Then your answer is that you did not? (A.) I did not; but, in any view, I would say that it was most improper to make that deduction from the bills. (Q.) You said that you found obligations with Potter, Wilson, & Co.'s name on them. Did you see that these obligations had been undertaken on behalf of the Bank by Potter, Wilson, & Co? (A.) I did not. (Q.) You don't know whether these were obligations undertaken by them with respect to the purchase of New Zealand properties? (A.) It was not on the face of them. The Bank had money invested in its own stock. This appears in the abstract under the first head. If it had been put under the third head, it should have appeared there under a separate line. It would have been very improper to represent it as "Government stock." (Q.) Do you read the third head as containing nothing but "Government stock?" (A.) No; I do not. It also says "Stocks of other companies," but you could hardly call the Bank's stock the stock of another company. (Q.) Still it was an investment; it was not a debt? (A.) Certainly not. (Q.) Nor was it security for an advance? (A.) No. (Q.) It was an asset of the Bank with nothing against it? (A.) Provided the Bank was solvent.

By Mr Asher.—(Q.) You know the balance account in the balance ledger which is docqueted once a year by the Bank directors? (A.) Yes. (Q.) Are you acquainted with three classes of books—the "Weekly balance book," the "Branches book," and the "Correspondents' balance book?" (A.) I have generally examined them. (Q.) Do the balance accounts in the balance ledger for 1876, 1877, and 1878 correctly record the balances in the three subsidiary balance books I have mentioned? (A.) The "Branches balance "book" contains the accounts made up on a different principle. (Q.) Does the balance account correctly record the balances for these three years in the three balance books? (A.) It correctly records them, but on a different principle as regards the branches. (Q.) Does the balance account in the balance ledger docqueted by the directors contain the names of the several branches? (A.) It does. (Q.) And opposite each branch there is the sum at the debit or the credit of that branch? (A.) Yes. (Q.) Is that sum, appearing in the balance account book opposite each branch docqueted by the directors, the same as the sum appearing in the branches balance book opposite that branch? (A.) I am not quite certain of the book you refer to, but if it is the branch abstract of balances, the sum that there appears is the indebtedness to the Bank of its depositors, or *vice versa.* (Q.) Do you find anything wrong in the balance account docqueted by the directors, in so far as they are entries with regard to the branches? (A.) Nothing whatever. (Q.) And in other respects the balances appearing in that docqueted account are correct as compared with the weekly balance book and the correspondents' balance book? (A.) That is so. (Q.) You find fault with the balance book with regard to deposits in respect there was not an entry in regard to deposits on both sides? (A.) Yes. (Q.) Do you find in the balance account which is docqueted by the directors any account entered on both sides? (A.) I would not anticipate finding an account entered on both sides. (Q.) I understood you to object to the balance of the deposits being entered in this balance account instead of the sum at the debit of deposit accounts on the one side, and at the credit of deposit accounts on the other? (A.) Yes. (Q.) Is that a fault? (A.) It is a fault unless the debtors and creditors are the same. (Q.) Is not the purpose of a balance account merely to show the balance on the whole deposits of the bank? (A.) No. (Q.) Do you find in this balance account any entry of an account on both sides? (A.) What I complain of is that it does not show the balance of the deposit accounts of the Bank. (Q.) But is the balance account not made up for the special purpose of showing the balance on the several accounts there mentioned? (A.) A balance account ought to be made up with the view of showing the debts and the liabilities of the Bank,—the one on the one side, and the other on the other. (Q.) The abstract of accounts is made up for that purpose? (A.) The balance book ought to be made up for that purpose also. (Q.) But is not the balance account intended to show the balance on the whole accounts in the Bank? (A.) It is intended to show that; but it does not show it. (Q.) You think it should show the amount at the credit of the deposit account on the one side, and at the debit of the deposit account on the other? (A.) Undoubtedly. (Q.) Then it would not show the balance of the deposit accounts? (A.) It would. (Q.) You would have to take the two entries on the two sides, and compare them, in order to find out the exact balance of the deposit accounts of the Bank, would you not? (A.) No. You would have to do that in order to find out the difference between overdrafts and deposits. (Q.) And to find out the exact balance on the deposits? (A.) Certainly not; the balance on deposit accounts is the balance without deducting the overdrafts. (Q.) Your view is that the balance is not the balance of deposits, but the balance of both sides? (A.) I say it is the balance of the deposits that should appear. (Q.) The published abstract is, of course, quite a different document from the balance account? (A.) That is so. (Q.) And it is not made up, I believe, from the balance account? (A.) It appears to be so to a large extent. (Q.) I mean the published abstract? (A.) That appears to be so to a large extent, except as regards the branches. (Q.) Don't you require to add what appears in the large number of books connected with the branches? (A.) No—two books. (Q.) Is not every item in the balance account varied by having incorporated with it the corresponding item from the branches? (A.) Certainly not. (Q.) Take the deposits; do you find the deposits in the balance account the same as the deposits in the printed abstract? (A.) Yes: I understand you are talking of the scroll abstract? (Q.) I am speaking now of the abstract which is published, the annual balance sheet of the Bank. (A.) They are amalgamated there. (Q.) And therefore, on looking at the two documents together, you find they are utterly different; the one is not made up from the other? (A.) No. (Q.) You cannot compare the one with the other without the aid of a large number of books? (A.) No; three or four books; not a large number. (Q.) But books which go to disclose the whole business of the agencies? (A.) That is so. (Q.) Are the totals of the two items necessarily different? (A.) They are. (Q.) So that, even to look at the summation of the balance account docqueted by the directors, you would not expect it to tally with the summation of the printed abstract? (A.) It does not. (Q.) And it should not do it? (A.) From the manner in which the books were kept, and as regards the branches, it should not do it.

By Mr Mackintosh—(Q.) Would you refer to your statement of the account of Taylor & Son with the Bank. What sum was at the debit of their account on 31st December 1876? (A.) I cannot tell. I directed my attention solely to the accounts at the balancing periods. I have not got the book here. (Q.) Can you tell whether it is or is not the fact that during 1877—between 1st January 1877 and 1st January 1878—Taylor & Son's overdraft was considerably diminished? (A.) No, I cannot tell. From my statements I only find that it was increased about £17,000 between the balance of 1877 and the balance of 1878. (Q.) But it is quite consistent with that, is it not, that it had been diminished in 1877? (A.) Yes, temporarily. (Q.) Is it quite consistent with the account as at 1st January 1878 having been considerably less overdrawn than it was at 1st January 1877? (A.) I am talking really about what I have not examined, but there is nothing inconsistent in it. (Q.) Is it not consistent with your knowledge than since 1st January 1878 there has been no operation upon the account at all in the way of drawing out? (A.) I cannot speak to 1st January 1878, as I have not specially examined it. (Q.) You have not got it with you? (A.) No. (Q.) Can you tell me whether it has fluctuated a good deal during its later period? (A.) I did not look into it. (Q.) Can you tell me whether it was squared up during its period? (A.) I cannot. (Q.) Did you not inquire into these matters? (A.) No. (Q.) Were you not asked to inquire into them? (A.) No. (Q.) Did you not think it material to inquire? (A.) I did not. I looked at the indebtedness of Mr Taylor when the crash came. I did not think it was material whether it was ever squared or not. (Q.) You stated the amount so as to make it appear to have continuously increased? (A.) Oh, no; I must not have any motive imputed to me. (Q.) But its result? (A.) Yes; the result was increased in the balance-sheet at the various balancing periods, for which I am not responsible. I did not enquire or examine the books to ascertain how long Messrs Taylor & Son had been customers of the Bank. I cannot tell whether Mr Taylor had got accommodation from the City Bank prior to his becoming a director, or, if so, to what extent. I was not asked to inquire into that; but I find that their overdrafts appear to have begun in

1874, because in 1873, as I said before, I think there was a little credit balance. I have not examined the account prior to 1871.

By Mr Smith—Mr Innes Wright's private account begins with his being debited with the sum of about £2,700. There has been no other operation upon that account, except the crediting of interest upon stock and debiting interest upon the account. That sum seems to have been the price of the shares purchased to give him a qualification as director. He has never drawn any dividend. The dividend is placed to his credit, and he is debited with interest; the result of which would have been that, if it had gone on long enough, Mr Innes Wright would have had his shares for nothing. (Q.) Would the shares, in your opinion, be a security for the advance? (A.) If the Bank was solvent.

Sixth Day.—Saturday, 25th January 1879.

JAMES MUIR *(resumed).*

By Mr Smith—(Q.) You stated that at 5th June 1875 the sum due by John Innes Wright & Co.—the debtor balance—was £217,707. Is that sum composed of the balances on credit accounts and deposit accounts brought together? (A.) It is. It includes the amount standing at the debit of Innes Wright & Co. on deposit account, amounting to £133,241. The amount standing on the same account at 5th June 1878 is £150,795. (Q.) What was the accruing interest in the interval between 2d June 1875 and 5th June 1878? (A.) I cannot tell you unless you show me the ledger. (Q.) Would it be over £20,000? (A.) It would. (Q.) So the result is that in the interval the sum paid in was greater than the sum drawn out? (A.) No, it could not be over £20,000. It could not be more than £5000 or £6000; but the ledger, which is in the inventory, will show it. (Q.) The sum at 5th June 1878 was how much? (A.) £150,000. I cannot tell, without looking at the ledger, how much of that was interest. I did not anticipate this line of examination. (Q.) Is it the case that the sum paid in in the interval between 1875 and 1878 was greater than the sum drawn out? (A.) I cannot tell; the ledger will show that. The amount due at 5th June 1878, in all, was £334,783. The difference between that and the £217,707 in 1875 is (roughly) £117,000. I cannot tell how much of that was interest; it will be seen from the ledger. The balance of £334,783 in 1878 includes two sums, the one of £32,233, and the other of £47,601. These two sums appear for the first time in that year. (Q.) Do you know what the £32,233 was? (A.) Yes, it has something to do with an account called "Wool lien "account." (Q.) That is the "Wool lien account?" (A.) Yes. (Q.) Was that an account which had been opened on behalf of Glen Walker & Co. (A.) Yes; it is so stated in the ledger, I think. That account is not closed. The £47,601 was the balance standing, at the balancing period of 1878, at the debit of Innes Wright & Co. for their short accountings upon the £100,000 of Glen Walker & Co.'s drafts substituted for those of Holmes, White, & Co. (Q.) Short accountings upon the discount account? (A.) Not that, but short accounting of proceeds of bills which had been given to them for the purpose of discounting. (Q.) Was that an overdraft? (A.) I would not like to characterise it. (Q.) It is not an overdraft? (A.) I must say I would use a much stronger expression than that if I were asked what it was. (Q.) If that sum of £32,000 odds was accounted for, and the £47,000 was out of the account, and the interest taken off, would the sum standing at the debit in 1878 be greater or less than it was in 1875? (A.) I have said I do not know the amount of the interest, so that I cannot answer the question. (Q.) But assuming that the interest was £33,000, would that be sufficient to account for the difference, with the other figures? (A.) Within £4000 of it. (Q.) Can you give me the details of the sum of total indebtedness that you make out against Innes Wright & Co. in 1875, £392,000? (A.) Yes. There is, first, cash credits and overdrawn deposits, £217,707; then there is William Scott's indebtedness, £121,801; then there are bills discounted by John Innes Wright & Co. with the Bank, £40,678; and there are acceptances by John Innes Wright & Co., discounted with the Bank by third parties, £12,324. I think you will find that makes up the sum. (Q.) As regards the charge for "bills discounted," £40,678, and "acceptances," £12,324, do you know if that sum was reduced in 1878? (A.) Yes; very materially reduced. (Q.) What does it stand at in 1878? (A.) In 1878, you may take it that the bills discounted by Innes Wright & Co. were then reduced to £24,500; William Scott's discounts were then £9198; and the acceptances of John Innes Wright & Co., discounted with the Bank by third parties, were £4304. (Q.) Mention has been made of the Edinburgh Pastoral Association, do you know who they were? (A.) I do not. I do not know who constituted the Association. It seemed to me to be very much an affair of the Bank's own. (Q.) Was it not simply the Bank? (A.) Well, it has all along struck me to be the City of Glasgow Bank.

By the Lord Advocate—(Q.) I omitted to ask you in what way interest receivable or received by the Bank is dealt with in the profit and loss account? (A.) It is credited to profit and loss, in a line called "Interest "received." (Q.) I show you No. 146, yearly balance-sheet at 5th June 1878; and I also refer you to No. 2A private cash book, No. 6. It is entered there also, is it not? (A.) That is so. (Q.) Just explain to us how it is dealt with? (A.) The interest received or receivable at the Bank on accounts of the debtors to the Bank was debited once every year. The resulting sum, or rather the resulting sums, are all added together, and credited to profit and loss account through the cash book to which you have referred; and I find it here [showing] £330,000 in this sheet as being one of the earnings of the Bank to that amount. (Q.) Refer to the cash book also, and see if the same entries pass through it? (A.) On the debtor side of the cash book of that date there is an entry "Profit and loss "account, balances transferred from the following accounts:—Interest re- "ceived," and figures that I have previously given, £330,849, 5s. 6d. Then there are several other items coming up to £398,743, and on the other side there is "Interest received, balance transferred to profit and loss," £338,549, 5s. 6d., and so on. (Q.) The sum of interest received there stated ought to represent the earnings of the Bank upon its debts for the year? (A.) That is so. (Q.) Does that sum of £330,000 include the interest upon those eight large debts that you spoke of? (A.) It does, every penny of it. (Q.) Which were not received; at least the books do not show that they were received, but the contrary? (A.) Quite so. (Q.) Does that occur in each of the three years? (A.) It does. I was very much struck, my Lord, with this, that the interest upon these eight accounts in 1878 amounts to £125,875, while the total amount of the clear balance, stated of profit for that year, is £125,094, being £780 less than the interest on these balances. (Q.) And which of course was not made if it was not got? (A.) No; assuredly not; besides which, in 1878, they carried to credit of profit and loss account the sum of £12,000, which had been added to the value of City of Glasgow Bank stock, beyond that they had paid for it in the market. (Q.) In 1877, what was the figure of interest that was so dealt with? (A.) Ir 1877, the interest upon these eight debtors was £128,900, and the available balance of profit for that year, appearing in the balance-sheet, was only £128, 5s. 11d., being less than the interest charged to the debtors by £487. Then in 1876, the amount charged to the debtors was £125,763, and the apparent available balance of profits was £125,762, a difference of about £1. You were examined on cross with regard to retiring one set of bills by another. Suppose there are a set of bills for £200,000 acceptances of the Bank, and that a fresh set for the same amount are issued to retire those, and the proceeds are received, is it a correct thing to treat the first set of bills as paid until that money has been actually applied in extinction of them, and the bills withdrawn from the circle? (A.) It is so utterly absurd that I can hardly conceive of anyone imagining that such a thing could possibly be done. (Q.) Until the money received by discount is actually applied in payment of the bill. There are two sets of liabilities floating against the Bank? (A.) Undoubtedly. (Q.) In regard to the scroll balance-sheets, you said that these looked like the work of an accountant; what do you mean by that precisely? (A.) They look like the work of a man who could say two and two make four, but that is about the extent of it. (Q.) Did you mean to suggest that none but an accountant could bring down these sums from the balance at the "Credit account" to the heading under "Stocks?" (A.) Certainly not; when I used the word accountant, I did not mean a professional accountant. (Q.) Did you intend to suggest that it required an accountant to convert £200,000 of that into surplus gold in the coffers of the Bank? (A.) Certainly not.

By the Lord Justice-Clerk—(Q.) Did you mean that you did not think it like the hand of a professional accountant? (A.) It simply looked like a man who understood arithmetic. (Q.) But was your impression, from the look of it, that it had been done by a professional accountant? (A.) I *knew* that it was the work of the accountant of the Bank. (Q.) It was not merely the work of a man who knew that two and two made four, but the calculations were, in fact, the work of the accountant of the Bank? (Q.) There is no question of that whatever. (Q.) I asked you yesterday if you could make me out a balance-sheet, as you think, on the lines of the balance abstract, it should have been made out? (A.) I have prepared some such statement, and my clerk is now copying it. (Q.) In the meantime, would you take the indictment, and turn to the statement of the errors on page 4. [See p. 27.] In the first place, have you been able to trace the system, rather than the principle, on which these statements proceeded? (A.) I have, and the statement which I have prepared will bring that out. (Q.) In regard to the amount of deposits at the head office, they are understated in the balance for 1876 to the extent of a million and some odds. Now, wherein does that mis-statement consist? (A.) There are deposit accounts omitted altogether, £455,444. (Q.) That is the balance due to customers which you told us of yesterday? (A.) Yes; then a debtor balance is made to appear where no such balance ought to be, amounting to £1346. That is a debtor balance appearing as if the customers owed the Bank that. (Q.) That depends upon the controversy between you and Mr Balfour about the balances being taken instead of both sides of the account? (A.) Quite so. These credit accounts are omitted altogether, £147,468. These are balances standing at the credit of parties who have paid in sums of money to the creditor side of their "credit accounts." They are just another name for a kind of deposit. They are omitted altogether. Then London and provincial and foreign correspondents are omitted, £14,216. (Q.) Where do you find that? (A.) In the balance ledger. Then adjusting account of interest is omitted, £11,405. I find that in the balance sheet of profit and loss, No. 144 of inventory. (Q.) But that is nowhere correctly entered? (A.) Not in the balance ledger. (Q.) In any of the books? (A.) It is correctly entered in the profit and loss balance-sheet. (Q.) Is there anything more? (A.) The true amount of branch liabilities appearing in the book called abstract of branch balances is £8,163,311. In the scroll the figures representing that are in red ink, and amount to £7,786,977. The difference understated is £376,334. I cannot tell what that under-statement consists of. That brings up the amount to the sum stated in the indictment. (Q.) Then the amount of "Drafts outstanding" is the £973,000 which we have heard so much about? (A.) Yes. (Q.) These figures make up the sum short in the first item; the second is the sum of £973,000. In regard to that, can you tell me when was the first appearance of that sum in any of the books of the Bank, except the private cash book? (A.) It never appeared anywhere till it appeared in the private cash book on 4th June 1873. (Q.) After that when did it first appear in the other books? (A.) It continuously appeared in the ledger of the Bank from that date till this date, an open balance appearing there ever after. (Q.) Did it anywhere appear as deducted from the head of the "Drafts outstanding" and the other things under that head? (A.) Not in any of the books of the Bank except the balance ledger, where it did appear so deducted. (Q.) Then, third, the "Bills of exchange" you say are understated to the extent of £2,698,000; where do you find that? (A.) In the first place credit accounts are understated to the extent of £147,468. (Q.) Does the balance which you have prepared show all these? (A.) It does.

[The witness handed the following documents to the Lord Justice-Clerk.]

1876.

Liabilities.	In Published Balance-Sheet.	In Bank's Books.	Under-stated in Published Sheet.	Overstated in Published Sheet.
HEAD I.	£	£	£	£
Deposit accounts,	Omitted.	455,444	455,444	
Credit do.	do.	147,468	147,468	
London, provincial, and foreign correspondents,	do.	14,216	14,216	
Adjusting account of interest,	do.	11,405	11,405	
Branch liabilities,	7,786,977	8,163,311	376,334	
Difference in "Deposit accounts," the published accounts showing a *Dr.* balance instead of the *Cr.* balance shown above, the amount of said *Dr.* balance being,	...	...	1,346	
Total under-statements in published sheet,	...	...	1,006,216	
HEAD III.				
Bills payable,	326,853	2,288,673	973,300	
Do.	988,520			
Total under-statements in published sheet,	...	...	973,300	

Assets.	In Published Balance-Sheet.	In Bank's Books.	Under-stated in Published Sheet.	Overstated in Published Sheet.
HEAD I.	£	£	£	£
Credit accounts No. I.,	1,981,934	2,129,403	147,468	
Deposit do. (overdrawn),	Omitted.	452,211	452,211	
Foreign and colonial credits,	1,304,873	2,278,173	973,300	
Suspense account,	50,000	300,000	250,000	
Amount deducted from Head I. in published sheet in order to be carried down to Head III.,	...	...	751,775	
Branch assets,	2,274,381	2,683,467	409,086	
Under-statements in published sheet,	...	...	2,983,841	
Past due bills,	248,500	174,393	...	74,106
Contingent account,	*Dr* 10,747	*Cr.* 2,507	...	13,254
Credit accounts No. 2,	143,087	100,296	...	42,791
Heritable property account should have been included under Head II. of published balance-sheet instead of Head I.,	...	...	...	119,541
Adjusting account of interest, viz.,	66,709	31,101	...	35,607
Over-statements in published sheet,	...	...	...	285,302
Deduct over-statements from under-statements,	...	...	285,302	
Difference, being nett under-statements in published balance-sheet,	...	...	2,698,539	
HEAD II.				
Heritable property a/c,	96,410	159,693	63,283	
Property a/c,				
Total under-statements in published sheet,	...	...	63,283	
HEAD III.				
Total gold and silver coin in hand,	862,812	833,717	...	29,095
Total over-statement in published sheet,	...	...	...	29,095
Government stocks, &c. :—				
Irvin & Co.'s debt,	11,995	...	...	11,995
Sums brought down from Head I.,	751,775	...	...	751,775
Sum in red ink in the scroll at foot of page,	3,656	...	...	3,656
Amount overstated,	...	...	...	767,427
London, provincial, and foreign correspondents,	32,171	46,388	14,216	
Amount understated,	...	...	14,216	
Deduct under-statements from over-statements,	...	...	...	14,216
Difference, being nett over-statement in published sheet,	...	...	...	753,211

1877.

Liabilities.	In Published Balance-Sheet.	In Bank's Books.	Under-stated in Published Sheet.	Over-stated in Published Sheet.
	£	£	£	£
HEAD I.				
Deposit accounts,	Omitted,	449,692	449,692	
Credit do.,	Do.	220,683	220,683	
Do. do. No. 2,	Do.	59	59	
Branch cross accounts deducted from liabilities in published sheet,	...	...	273,842	
Head office cross a/cs. do. do.,	...	...	207,240	
Total under-statements in published sheet,	...	...	1,151,518	
HEAD II.				
Circulation,	763,894	840,004	76,110	
Total under-statement in published sheet,	...	...	76,110	
HEAD III.				
Bills payable,	1,350,335	2,681,048	1,330,712	
Total under-statement in published sheet,	...	...	1,330,712	

Assets.	In Published Balance-Sheet.	In Bank's Books.	Under-stated in Balance-Sheet.	Over-stated in Balance-Sheet.
	£	£	£	£
HEAD I.				
Credit accounts,	1,806,987	2,027,670	220,683	
Deposit do.,	Omitted.	449,692	449,692	
Credit do. No. 2,	96,617	96,677	59	
Foreign and colonial credits,	1,352,636	2,683,348	1,330,712	
Remittances between branches and branches,	86,258	132,368	46,110	
Branch cross accounts deducted from assets in published sheet,	...	...	273,842	
Head office cross a/cs. do. do.,	...	...	207,240	
Amounts carried down to Head III.,	...	...	751,775	
Understated in published sheet,	...	...	3,280,116	
Heritable property a/c included under Head I. instead of Head II. to the amount of	...	...	...	52,961
Over-statement in published sheet,	...	...	...	52,961
Deduct over-statement from under-statement,	...	...	52,961	
Difference, being total under-statement in published sheet,	...	...	3,227,154	
HEAD II.				
Heritable property a/c.,	257,689	310,651	52,961	
Total under-statements in published sheet,	...	...	52,961	
HEAD III.				
Cash on hand,	891,018	921,018	30,000	
Total under-statement in published sheet,	...	...	30,000	
Brought down from Head I.,	...	...	...	750,775
Total over-statement in published sheet,	...	...	...	751,775

1878.

Liabilities.	In Published Balance-Sheet.	In Bank's Books.	Under-stated in Balance-Sheet.	Over-stated in Balance-Sheet.
HEAD I.	£	£	£	£
Deposit accounts,	Omitted.	440,738	440,738	
Credit do.,	...	346,336	346,336	
Do. do. No. 2,	...	119	119	
Cross accounts at branches, deducted from liabilities in published sheet,	...	...	154,090	
Total under-statements in published sheet,	...	...	941,284	
HEAD II.				
Bank notes in circulation,	710,252	799,283	89,031	
Total under-statements in published sheet,	...	...	89,031	
HEAD III.				
Bills payable,	1,488,244	2,881,252	1,393,008	
Total under-statements in published sheet,	...	..	1,393,008	

Assets.	In Published Balance-Sheet.	In Bank's Books.	Under-stated in Balance-Sheet.	Over-stated in Balance-Sheet.
HEAD I.	£	£	£	£
Credit accounts,	2,009,752	2,356,088	346,336	
Do. do. No. 2,	96,294	96,413	119	
Deposit accounts,	Omitted.	440,738	440,738	
Foreign and colonial credits,	1,488,244	2,881,252	1,393,008	
Carried to Head III., viz.:—				
To gold, £200,000 } To Government and other stocks, 926,764 }	...	...	1,126,764	
Cross accounts at branches deducted from Assets in published sheet,	...	...	154,090	
Remittances between branches and branches carried to Head III.,	...	108,553	108,553	
Total under-statements in published sheet,	...	...	3,569,609	
Less heritable property, should be included under Head II., but is put in under Head I. in published sheet,	...	...	48,696	
Nett under-statements in published sheet,	...	...	3,520,913	
HEAD II.				
Heritable property,	40,000	88,696	48,696	
Total under-statements in published sheet,	...	...	48,696	
HEAD III.				
Gold,	200,000 }			
Do.	338,500 }	338,500	...	200,000
Remittances between branches and branches, &c., brought from Head I.,	...	108,553	...	108,553
Overstated,	...	...	...	308,553
Head Office. Notes of other banks on hand—				
Tellers,	34,810	75,895	41,085	
Branches, Do. do.	29,081	77,627	47,946	
Understated,	...	...	89,031	
Deduct under from over,	...	...	...	89,031
Total over-statements,	...	...	...	219,522
Brought from Head I.,	...	...	...	480,614
				148,888
				297,262
Total over-statements,	...	...	...	926,764

(Q.) Among other things I wanted to know was what the result of the corrections would have been upon the statement to the shareholders of the position of the Bank? (A.) I have not yet made it up in that form, but I will be very glad to do so; I did not quite understand your object. (Q.) That was my object, because the allegation is that they made a false statement to the shareholders, and I want to know what would have been the true statement on the lines of this abstract. I can understand that you might go back on the books and make a totally different statement; but if they had stated the figures correctly in the abstract balance-sheet, what would have been the result presented to the shareholders? (A.) Perhaps I could answer the question in this way, by saying that the result of correcting the figures would have had no effect whatever upon the capital or the profit and loss, or upon the reserve fund, because what was deducted from one side was also deducted from the other. (Q.) Does that apply to the whole of them? (A.) To the whole of them. (Q.) That it would have had no effect at all? (A.) It would have had no effect on the capital as stated. (Q.) If you assume that the bad and doubtful debts are correctly estimated there, is that so? (A.) That is so; but the effect would have been to impress the mind of the public with the fact that the Bank had lent so much less money. (Q.) The effect on its credit would be entirely different, but the ultimate result on the profit and loss would be the same? (A.) Precisely the same. (Q.) I suppose the principal errors in this are the £973,000, which apparently has no foundation at all, and the £751,000, which is taken down from the credit accounts and inserted under investments? (A.) And also the gold, £200,000, and also the deduction of the £419,000, which, as I have said, is perfectly absurd. I cannot be too strong upon that.

WILLIAM GLEN WALKER.

By the Solicitor-General—I am a merchant and Australian sheep farmer, living in Surrey. I am principal partner of Glen Walker & Co., merchants, Melbourne. That is principally an agency for land and sheep farms. (Q.) There is a company called the Australian and New Zealand Land and Investment Trust (Limited), carrying on business in London. How was that company formed? (A.) That company was formed to amalgamate certain properties that belonged to the City of Glasgow Bank and myself. (Q.) That is to say, certain properties called the Edinburgh Pastoral Association? (A.) Properties that belonged to the Edinburgh Pastoral Association, that being another name for the Bank. (Q.) How long is it since the amalgamation was carried on? (A.) The company is still an inchoate company. I think it was registered in February last. A good many years ago, my firm had been acting as agents in Australia for Potter, Wilson, & Co. (Q.) And you were also at one time connected with the firm of Morton & Co.? (A.) Merely as their agent, at the same time that I was agent for Potter, Wilson, & Co. Mr Alexander Stronach was my brother-in-law; we married sisters. (Q.) Do you remember his speaking to you at one time about becoming a partner of Smith, Fleming, & Co.? (A.) Yes; that arrangement was once proposed. That was in 1873. I asked to see their position—how they stood. I found a very large balance-sheet, which was very difficult to understand; and I found an entry which was explained to me to mean that they were behind (if I remember aright) from £150,000 to £200,000—about £170,000, I think—but I speak from recollection, and have not had an opportunity of reviving my recollection. (Q.) During these negociations about your entering the firm of Smith, Fleming, & Co., had you a meeting with Alexander Stronach and two other people about it? (A.) Yes; the two others were Mr Potter and Mr Morton. The meeting took place in the Bank's office, Virginia Street. This was in 1873. (Q.) What was the nature of the conversation that took place at that meeting? (A.) The essence of the conversation simply meant that it would be very desirable, in the interest of the Bank, if I would join that firm. (Q.) Was anything said about the position of the Bank in regard to Smith, Fleming, & Co.'s deficit? (A.) I do not recollect it at that meeting, but there was subsequently. (Q.) Had you other meetings with Potter, Morton, and Alexander Stronach? (A.) I think I had; I certainly had with Alexander Stronach, and I think I had with the others, but I am not quite sure. (Q.) I believe, at the first meeting, Mr Taylor came in about the end of the meeting? (A.) He did not come in; he merely came to the door. He had no part whatever in the meeting. I did not know Mr Taylor then. (Q.) What was the object of the discussion at the meeting upon the part of the others towards you? What did they want? (A.) They wanted me to join the firm, and it was a question of terms. (Q.) What were you informed was the Bank's object in wishing you to become a partner? (A.) To have through me a better control over the business; they believed the business to be an excellent one. They wanted me to join on the basis of adopting that deficit, and they represented, and, I believe, honestly believed, that the good-will of the business was worth a great deal more than that deficit. (Q.) But you did not see your way to that at the time? (A.) The negotiation broke through, not altogether on that ground, but also because I wanted an undertaking from the Bank that it would carry Smith, Fleming, & Co. through, whatever the consequences might be. (Q.) When Robert Stronach became the manager of the Bank did he communicate with you about joining anybody as a partner? (A.) He suggested that I should join James Morton and Co. I came down from London and had an interview with him, Potter, and Morton, at the Bank, on that subject. (Q.) Who took the principal part in the conversation? (A.) Almost exclusively Mr Potter, myself, and Mr Morton. (Q.) Had you several conversations with them? (A.) I had several conversations,—I believe I had two or three conversations with them. I had a long conversation with Morton. (Q.) And with Potter had you several conversations? (A.) Yes, but only incidentally. (Q.) How long did this interview last at which Stronach, Potter, and Morton were present? (A.) Probably half an hour. (Q.) What did you say to them would be necessary before you could make up your mind on the subject? (A.) I wanted to know Morton's position, and I also wanted to know what policy would be adopted as regards Morton's large landed interests in New Zealand. (Q.) Did the value of the shares he possessed in these companies come up? (A.) Not at that meeting, but I was asked to meet Morton in the evening, and spend a night with him discussing these questions, and he then assured me that his position was this, that he was able to cover the Bank's account by the shares in the New Zealand companies with which he was connected at par. He told me—it was about the same time that Stronach became manager of the Bank, either a fortnight or so before or after; I cannot quite fix the date —he asserted that he had promised Mr Stronach to reduce his account by £400,000 as a means to induce him to become the manager, and he had also promised him to cover his account by stock at par.

By the Lord Justice-Clerk—This was about the time that Mr Robert Stronach became manager. I cannot fix the date.

By the Solicitor-General—(Q.) But going back to the meeting with Potter and Morton, do you remember anything being said about a premium on Morton's shares? (A.) Yes. (Q.) By whom? (A.) By Potter, but that premium simply meant par. (Q.) What was it he said? (A.) He asked if I would be prepared to join the firm on the basis of taking over Morton's shares at 60 per cent. premium; and that 60 per cent. is what I now mean by par. (Q.) Would you explain that to the Jury? (A.) It was in contemplation that the two companies in which Morton was largely interested should be amalgamated, and it was believed that the basis of the amalgamation would be the watering of that stock to the extent of 60 per cent. It was supposed that the stock was very much undervalued before. (Q.) Would you explain to the Jury the expression you used just now,—watering the stock? (A.) It simply meant a revaluation of the property. (Q.) Giving it a rosy effect? (A.) No, I don't say that; these properties we are now speaking of have been, and are, rapidly increasing in value. At the inception of these companies, the properties were valued at what was supposed to be the then existing price or value. At the new arrangement they had largely increased in value, and this watering the stock was required to give them what then was supposed to be the real value. (Q.) After Robert Stronach accepted the managership, had you and he conversations about Smith, Fleming, & Co.'s affairs? (A.) Very little indeed; I don't say we ever spoke about them. (Q.) I don't mean that you spoke much, but I want to know whether, from conversations with him, you learned anything about the amount in danger on James Nicol Fleming's account? (A.) I did not directly through Mr Stronach; I would not like to swear that I did from Mr Stronach, though I may have done so, but I certainly did from Mr John Hunter. (Q.) Did you, after hearing something from Mr Hunter, speak over the matter about J. Nicol Fleming's account with Potter and Hunter? (A.) It was quite understood between Potter and Hunter, and, I beiieve, by the others, as my relations with the Bank will show, that there was a deficit upon Nicol Fleming's account. I understood that deficit to be about £200,000. I believe that deficit was covered by promissory notes which Nicol Fleming or his firms had granted, and that these promissory notes again were represented by the good-will of his different businesses. (Q.) Was any proposal made for the purpose of overcoming that deficit? (A.) There was. (Q.) What was it? (A.) I was instructed to buy those properties you have already referred to as belonging to the so-called Edinburgh Pastoral Association. (Q.) For the purpose of endeavouring to cover possible losses through J. Nicol Fleming's account? (A.) For the purpose of covering those two deficits of which I have spoken. (Q.) Did you understand from Potter as to whether there was any hope of recouping the deficit with some such scheme? (A.) I understand from Potter that Nicol Fleming had not been a successful man, and that he did not like to rely upon the success of these businesses, and that he wanted additional security. [Shown No. 217, letter Glen Walker & Co. to Robert Stronach, dated 14th August 1876, as follows]:—

"Glasgow, 14th August, 1876.

"Pastoral Properties in Australia.

"R. Stronach, Esq.

"Dear Sir,—In continuation of conversations with yourself, and other gentlemen "connected with the Bank, I would now place in writing the suggestions which we "have been discussing towards increasing income, and recouping deficits by the "judicious acquirement of pastoral properties.

"More than one member of your board are connected with New South Wales "properties, which have on an average of many years, I am assured, paid a net "return upon present values exceeding 16 per cent. per annum.

"The purchase price usually is paid by partly a cash-deposit, and the balance "by bills, extending over several years. It is easy to finance against them in the "colony, and if 40 per cent. of the price was provided here, the remainder could be "arranged in the colony without further aid from this.

"If arranged in this way, finance probably would cost for interest an average of "6 per cent. per annum, and there would remain, on the basis of the experience "referred to as net profits, 10 per cent. per annum.

"The suggestion is, that the Bank grant credits to the extent of from £100^{m} to "£150^{m} towards the acquirement of pastoral interests in Australia.

"For example, if a value of £250^{m} was acquired, there should be a net profit of £25^{m} yearly, but £25^{m} yearly will, in fourteen years, repay £250^{m}, and 5 per cent.'

"interest, so that thus, by comparatively a very small outlay, a large amount can "be recouped.

"Mr Borron and myself will be glad to be interested in the project, and to manage "its detail, and finance can, in the Bank's option, be arranged either by cash ad- "vance or entirely by credit.—I am, &c.,

"W. GLEN WALKER."

(Q.) Now, was that letter written on the suggestion of any one? (A.) That letter was written as the result of a long negotiation, the principal parties to which were Mr Hunter, Mr Potter, and myself. (Q.) Was it written on the suggestion of any one? (A.) On the suggestion of some of us three, I cannot say which. (Q.) Was it your suggestion? (A.) It was intended to place on record that which we practically then had agreed to do. (Q.) Was it on your suggestion or on the suggestion of one of the other two? (A.) I cannot recollect. (Q.) But it was agreed between you that such a letter should be written? (A.) It was agreed between us that such a letter should be written. (Q.) Did you see Potter frequently at his own office on the subject before this letter was written? (A.) My principal negotiations were with Mr John Hunter. I sometimes called upon Mr Potter.

By the Lord Justice-Clerk—(Q.) And you embodied in that letter the result of your conference? (A.) That is so.

By the Solicitor-General—(Q.) And in consequence you or your firm bought properties for the Bank in Australia? (A.) I did. (Q.) And subsequently to that did you also purchase for them other properties in Australia from the Australian and New Zealand Land Company? (A.) I did. (Q.) Were these bought for the same purpose? (A.) Partly for the same purpose, but principally for another purpose. (Q.) What other purpose? (A.) That requires some explanation. The Bank were very largely interested indirectly in the New Zealand Company. (Q.) How? (A.) Through Morton's account, and I suppose through Fleming's account also. I suppose two-thirds of the whole belongings of the New Zealand and Australian Company, as I now know, practically belong to the Bank. At the time I knew of their large interest, but I did not know it was so large as I now know. (Q.) How did they practically belong to the Bank? (A.) I now find that these men are bankrupt, and that the assets of these men practically belong to the Bank. (Q.) As at that time? (A.) No. I say the assets of these firms, James Morton & Co. and Smith, Fleming, & Co., practically belong to the Bank, and these men are the owners of, I believe, from one-half to three-fourths of all the shares in that company. The Bank had discovered that these stations in Australia had been very badly managed—that a drunkard had been managing them for some years. They had learned that from their agents in Australia, and they wanted to get these properties into better management. That was the real reason of buying these properties. (Q.) And in order to cover their advances? (A.) Well, I have already said it was for two purposes, that being the principal purpose; but also incidentally for the same purpose as the other places were bought for—that is to say, to have properties paying a high rate of interest; the difference between the rate of interest current in this country and that higher rate of interest to be used to mortise these two deficits of about £150,000 and £200,000. (Q.) There were two objects: to recoup deficits and cover advances, the principal object being to recoup the deficits? (A.) The principal object, as I have said, with regard to one of them was so; and as regards the other, to get these properties into proper management. (Q.) As regards the price of the lands, of the first lot that you bought after the arrangement of August 1876, how was the price paid? (A.) Partly by money and partly by my promissory notes. (Q.) How much has the Bank paid? (A.) I really forget without referring to the accounts. In the inception of the transaction, I paid, I think, £30,000 or £40,000; but subsequently I have been converting leasehold into freehold property. A portion of that was leasehold property, and I have been converting it into freehold property; and I should fancy the advances have amounted altogether to about £130,000 or £140,000. (Q.) Were these moneys paid out by you—the £130,000 to £140,000,—for the Bank? (A.) Certainly. (Q.) And you got the money from the Bank? (A.) I got credits from the Bank, which I converted into money. (Q.) The advances that you made were simply as agent for the Bank? (A.) Certainly. (Q.) How was the rest provided? (A.) The rest was provided by my promissory notes. (Q.) They also being granted for the Bank? (A.) Certainly. (Q.) And for which they are liable? (A.) Certainly, I believe so. The liquidators say no. (Q.) Did you, in any way, throughout the whole proceedings, act for yourself, or did you act entirely as agent for the Bank? (A.) The directors intended, and I intended, that I should act as agent for the Bank.

By the Lord Justice-Clerk—(Q.) That seems to be a question? (A.) The question has been raised by the liquidators as to the purchase from the New Zealand Company being *ultra vires*. (Q.) But the character in which you understood you were acting was that of agent for the Bank? (A.) Certainly.

By the Solicitor-General—(Q.) You were to be remunerated for what you did? (A.) I was to charge a reasonable commission. (Q.) Which was? (A.) It would depend upon what I would charge it. (Q.) Was it never settled? (A.) Never settled. (Q.) Had you no interest except the commission? (A.) None whatever. I hoped to have, but I never have had. (Q.) How much were you in advance upon acceptances or promissory notes for account of these properties? (A.) I think at the present moment about £80,000 or £90,000. (Q.) Look at the letter No. 218, dated 14th August 1876, the same date as the other, and addressed also to Mr Stronach.

"Glasgow, 14th August, 1876.

" R. S. Stronach, Esq.

" Dear Sir,—It seems right that securities should be specially held by the Bank " as a basis for any drafts by my firm in substitution for others, and I suggest that " you place to a special account such securities as are required fairly to cover the " drafts about to be substituted, or to obtain any others for a like purpose.

" I should say that, personally, I am content without this; but I will require to " explain the transaction to partners, and then must justify it by explaining how the " Bank is covered by securities.—I am, &c. W. GLEN WALKER."

Just explain in your own words the purpose of that letter. (A.) This letter refers to a totally different transaction from what we have been speaking about, but it has some reference to the same transaction also. Mr John Hunter had at that time the management of the liquidation of Nicol Fleming's account. That account, I was informed, as I have stated, by Mr Hunter, showed an uncovered deficit, uncovered except by good-will, and I think a policy of insurance, he said, to the extent of a couple of hundred thousand pounds. At the same time, Nicol Fleming's name had been to some extent discredited; and Mr Hunter suggested that it would be very desirable if my firm's name could be substituted as drawers of drafts upon the Bank in substitution of £100,000 of Nicol Fleming's. I agreed to the arrangement conditionally upon securities being placed to cover those drafts for which I was becoming responsible; and an arrangement was made by which £100,000 of stock which belonged to Morton, over which the Bank held security, should be placed as a special security against these drafts when put in circulation. (Q.) How much of paper did you agree to allow your name to be used for? (A.) £100,000. (Q.) And were drafts signed by your partner Mr Brown, who was then in Glasgow? (A.) My partner signed blank drafts, and left them with the manager to be filled up in terms of that arrangement, and used as he wanted. (Q.) Was anybody present when the drafts were signed blank, and left with the manager except the manager and you? (A.) I cannot tell you that; but I was present when the manager and Mr Potter looked over the drafts. (Q.) Were these drafts of your firm used for that purpose? (A.) I understand they were subsequently. By the bye, I am wrong in saying I did understand they were; I have been shown a minute in which instead of being used to reduce Nicol Fleming's account, they were used in substitution of another account, but it was quite immaterial; it did not make any matter to me. I considered they had a perfect right to use them as they pleased. (Q.) As matter of fact, were they used for the purpose of retiring the Bank's acceptances to Holmes, White, & Co.? (A.) I know nothing more excepting that Mr Brown has shown me the minute you are now reading from. I was in Australia myself at the time. (Q.) There is a minute of the board of directors with regard to an application by John Innes Wright & Co. on 24th August 1876, for marginal credits to the extent of £100,000, to be drawn by Messrs Glen Walker & Co., Melbourne, against shipments of wool and other produce. Can you tell me anything about that? (A.) I arranged with Mr Scott, of Innes Wright & Co., that he should procure for my firm credits to be used in the ordinary course of business for granting advances upon wool, or for the purpose of sending produce to this country. He obtained from the Bank £100,000 of these credits, and he sent them to my firm; that was all. (Q.) How did that arrangement come to be proposed? (A.) I don't know that. (Q.) Had it anything to do with improving John Innes Wright & Co.'s position with the Bank? (A.) I did not know at the time if it was so. I believed Innes Wright & Co. to be a sound and solvent concern. (Q.) Was that arrangement acted upon? (A.) It was partly acted upon and partly not. I found that the credits were of no use to me, but I required some monies for the purposes of the Bank in connection with those land purchases that I had orders to buy, and I used a portion of the credits for that purpose, and I sent the bulk of them home. I used a few thousand pounds—I think £7000, if I remember right—in sending home produce; but I could draw from the colony on my own credit quite as well as using the Bank's credits, and consequently I returned them. [Shown No. 390, twenty-four blank drafts.] The blank drafts signed Glen Walker & Co. contained in that envelope, were signed by my partner, Mr Brown. (Q.) Were these part of the bills that were left blank at that time? (A.) That I cannot swear to, but they are similar. The arrangement was that if Mr Stronach wanted some more, he was to write to my partner for them.

By Mr Balfour—I have been a good deal in Australia, and I am pretty familiar with that colony, and its prospects and trade. As far back as twenty years ago I acted for Mr Potter's firm in Australia. (Q.) Potter, Wilson, and Co. trade with Australia as merchants, and also as commission agents? (A.) They were about the largest firm connected with Australia in those days. (Q.) And have they long been? (A.) I presume they are still. (Q.) And also as shipowners? (A.) They were in those days very large shipowners. (Q.) So that they had intimate relations with Australia—an intimate knowledge of it? (A.) Certainly. (Q.) And also with New Zealand? (A.) Certainly. (Q.) Did they also trade with New Zealand in a like capacity? (A.) They did. (Q.) Had you also a knowledge of New Zealand from having been in the adjoining colony? (A.) I have been in New Zealand, but I have not gone over the properties in which Mr Potter is interested, although I have made most minute inquiries about them. (Q.) But I suppose through having been in Australia, and your mercantile relations there, you were familiar with New Zealand and its prospects? (A.) Yes. (Q.) You mentioned that you had had a meeting with Mr Potter, and I think Mr Morton and Mr Alexander Stronach, and that the first matter you spoke of was, I think, Smith, Fleming, and Co.'s debt, and the proposal that you should join them? (A.) Yes. (Q.) On the occasion of these meetings was the business of Smith, Fleming, & Co. spoken of as one of great value? (A.) Undoubtedly it was. (Q.) Of great earning power? (A.) Undoubtedly. (Q.) What was the annual sum that was named as their profits? (A.) The commissions, not their profits, were talked of as £100,000 a year easily. (Q.) These were mere commissions? (A.) Yes. (Q.) And that is the safest of all kinds of business? (A.) There is no doubt about it. (Q.) Was it evident to you that Mr Potter, Mr Morton, and Mr Stronach believed that? (A.) Most certainly. (Q.) And regarded it as a business of great value? (A.) When the arrangement with me fell through, Mr Potter intended to put his own son into the business. (Q.) Was that Mr John Potter? (A.) I don't know. (Q.) But you know that after the arrangement with you fell through, Mr Potter intended to put his own son in? (A.) Yes. (Q.) It was desired at that time, was it not, to purge the business of Smith, Fleming, & Co. of finance, and reduce them to the safe business,—to the commission business? (A.) It was intended to purge the business of everything except commission business. (Q.) It was evidently the desire of these gentlemen to accomplish that? (A.) That is so. (Q.) And if that was accomplished, did they appear to be satisfied that it would be greatly for the advantage of the Bank? (A.) I think so. (Q.) You mentioned that it appeared from the statement shown to you that Smith, Fleming, and Co. were a good deal behind—in debt. Did you understand that their debt to the Bank was covered by securities, or was that not gone into? (A.) The question of their debt to the Bank never arose. (Q.) It was their total debt, was it? (A.) No, it was their deficit. (Q.) And that was what was spoken to in the communication with you? (A.) No, certainly not at the meeting with Mr Potter in the bank, but I had been with Mr Stronach in London, and in London we had gone narrowly into these questions. Subsequently this meeting took place, and it was assumed that I knew everything. (Q.) Then the question of the deficit was not gone into with Mr Potter and you, but had been gone into previously apart from Mr Potter with Mr Alexander Stronach in London? (A.) I believe that is the fact. (Q.) Now, although the deficit that was spoken of by Alexander Stronach and you was considerable, was it such as a very lucrative business like that might have been expected to wipe off in a short time? (A.) Certainly. If the business was paying £100,000 a year of commissions, £150,000 would very soon be wiped out. (Q.) The deficit was only a year and a half's income from the commissions? (A.) Yes. (Q.) The deficit was about £150,000, and you were led to suppose that they were earning about £100,000 of commissions? (A.) Yes. Mr John Fleming has stated to me within the last month that during the last year his commission account came to £50,000 on his foreign businesses alone. (Q.) And therefore I suppose you were not surprised that Mr Potter was willing to put his own son into a good thing like that? (A.) There is no doubt that Mr Potter at that time was perfectly sincere in his belief that it was a first-class business. (Q.) The next thing, I think, that you told us was about Mr Morton. Is Mr Morton a gentleman who is also well acquainted with the Australian and New Zealand colonies; has he commercial relations with them? (A.) He has had very old relations with these colonies, but I don't think he has ever been in the colonies. (Q.) But to your knowledge has he had for long intimate commercial relations with these colonies? (A.) Yes, undoubtedly. (Q.) And are you aware from your communications with him that he placed a very high value upon the land in these colonies and its prospects? (A.) I know that perfectly well. He is a very sanguine man, and always spoke in the most sanguine terms of these properties. (Q.) And as if he believed it? (A.) As if he believed it, most certainly. I believe he does believe it. (Q.) With regard to Morton and the shares he held, you used the expression "watering the stock of the two "companies." Was that done on the occasion of two companies which had formerly been separate being amalgamated? (A.) That was so. (Q.) And when these two companies were amalgamated, was the stock of each respectively put at the par value which was then believed to be its true value? (A.) I believe that was the intention. (Q.) And that is what you used the phrase of "watering" in respect to? (A.) The valuations were very much too low before, and they were put more nearly the correct value. (Q.) And was that a perfectly fitting and proper thing to be done when the reorganization was taking place, and the two being united? (A.) Perfectly. (Q.) And has subsequent experience proved that the valuations they made were not too high, but were fair? (A.) I can only answer that by saying that any valuation of colonial properties at the present moment would probably not exceed one-half or two-thirds of their intrinsic value; certainly not; and that these properties have recently been valued at more than these watered values. (Q.) Subsequent experience has proved that the values were not too high which were placed upon them at that time? (A.) Certainly not. (Q.) Did you believe that the proposal embodied in the letter of 14th August 1876 was a judicious one? (A.) I believed that if you can get over the difficulty, or if it was determined to get over the difficulty of the Bank adopting an expedient that was not banking business, no better expedient could have been devised. (Q.) Was that the kind of thing that a prudent man managing his own affairs, and wishing to do the best for himself, would naturally have gone into? (A.) A prudent man—certainly. (Q.) You said, with respect to the getting of the property into the hands of the Bank that there had been an unsatisfactory manager in charge? (A.) That was so. (Q.) And with a view to unshipping him, and putting a right man in his place, the next step was taken? (A.) The Bank at that time wanted to increase this kind of investment; they thought they had not quite enough, and I recommended them not to sell those properties which the company intended to sell, but to buy them from the company. I told them there were no better properties in Australia than these. (Q.) And when you gave them that advice you believed it to be sound? (A.) I know it is true. (Q.) If you had been acting in your own interests and affairs, would you just have done the thing that the Bank did there? (A.) Most certainly. (Q.) Was it the best way of getting the most value out of their securities? (A.) Most certainly—always assuming that they were prepared to spend some money upon them. (Q.) To lay out some present expenditure as a means of getting the most out of them? (A.) Exactly. (Q.) And was it with that view that the credits which you have described were raised and operated on? (A.) The part of the credits which I have spoken of as representing the £130,000 or £140,000 that have been spent, has been spent upon these properties. (Q.) Which are still held by the Bank, I think, or for them at all events? (A.) They ought to be, I say; the liquidators say no. (Q.) With respect to the next arrangement that was gone into under the letter of 14th August 1876, did it appear to you also that that was a thing that a prudent man managing his own affairs would have done for his own advantage? You said, "I suggest that you place to a "special account such securities." (A.) It was prudent for me to get the securities evidently. I think it was a prudent thing for the Bank to have done, seeing that they had the finance existing already. It was a prudent thing to put it in a name that was not discredited rather than in a name that was. (Q.) Does it come to this, that Nicol Fleming's name having sunk in credit rather, it was better to have them transferred to and worked in a better name? (A.) Exactly.

By Mr Smith—(Q.) Was the credit of £100,000 which was asked for on your behalf by Mr Scott, on 2d August, your first connection with Wright and Co.? (A.) I think it was. (Q.) And was that the only credit which you got for yourself from the Bank? (A.) I got one for £20,000. The one was for my firm, the other was for me as an individual. (Q.) You say part of the £100,000 was not used? (A.) I sent it back. (Q.) How much was used altogether? (A.) It is very difficult to speak accurately from memory. (Q.)

Was it only £57,000? (A.) My memory is that I sent back about £43,000. (Q.) That left £57,000 to be used in Australia? (A.) Yes. (Q.) According to your recollection, how was that employed? (A.) My recollection is that £25,000 and £17,000 were used on account of the Bank, speaking from memory; £7000 or £8000 were sent home in produce, £10,000 more was advanced upon a wool lien. (Q.) Was the £17,000 which was used for the Bank used in acquiring land for the Bank? (A.) It was expended upon improvements, purchasing land or making improvements upon the Bank's land. (Q.) Therefore of that the Bank got the benefit themselves? (A.) Altogether. (Q.) How was the £25,000 used? (A.) It was used in the same way, or in keeping up the Bank's properties. (Q.) Was there some employed also in the wool lien? (A.) I have said there was £10,000 of it; there was practically £35,000, but £25,000 of this wool lien were for the Bank. (Q.) If the Bank then are debiting Wright & Co. with anything of that wool lien, that is an error on the part of the Bank? (A.) No doubt it would be. (Q.) And there was about £7000 sent home in produce? (A.) So far as I remember. (Q.) Then the result of it all, I think, is that if that £7000 of shipment of produce was accounted for, the whole of this advance has been accounted for to the Bank; they got value for it? (A.) That I cannot tell you. I cannot answer that question. The arrangement was that I did not get these credits from the Bank. I got them from Innes Wright & Co. Innes Wright & Co. instructed me to send the proceeds in the shape of produce to Innes Wright and Co. I did so, and how they have accounted with the Bank I do not know. (Q.) That £7000 was sent in produce, but if that were accounted for, the rest is all accounted for? (A.) No; because I sent home produce representing the £35,000. (Q.) Which had been spent on the wool lien? (A.) Yes; I believe the wool lien turned out deficient. (Q.) Was there a loss on it? (A.) Not a loss exactly. £25,000 of it was invested upon a wool lien, of property belonging to the Bank. After this had been done, there was a very severe drought in Australia, and a very large number of the sheep perished in Australia; during that time ten millions of sheep died. About 50,000 of these sheep belonged to the Bank. The wool which ought to have been shorn from these sheep did not come forward, and consequently Innes Wright and Co. received less wool than the wool lien represented. (Q.) That was the Bank's wool? (A.) It was the Bank's wool.

By the Dean of Faculty—(Q.) When was the proposal that you should become a partner with Morton made to you? (A.) About the time that Robert Stronach became the manager. (Q.) Before he became the manager? (A.) I have been trying to recollect. I think it must have been before, but it was within a fortnight before or after. (Q.) Did you find that Robert Stronach was very reluctant to take the office of manager? (A.) He had been extremely reluctant. (Q.) You said something about a promise from Morton to reduce his debt by £400,000? (A.) Morton told me that it had been very difficult to get Stronach to accept the position, and one of his reasons was that Morton's account was a very large one, and because he had not his securities in proper order; and Morton, towards inducing him to accept the position, promised him that he would reduce his account by £400,000, and place securities, which he had elsewhere, with the Bank, so that his account should be fully covered at par. (Q.) It was after getting that promise from Morton that Stronach accepted the office? (A.) Undoubtedly so. (Q.) I am going to show you a letter, print page 107. (A.) I know this letter quite well. (Q.) 28th December 1875, by Mr Stronach to the directors. Did you know that Mr Stronach sent that letter to the directors? (A.) I was shown by Mr Stronach the draft of a letter something like this, and he subsequently told me that he had sent that letter to the board somewhat modified from what I had seen. (Q.) Can you tell me wherein the draft differs from the letter which we have here printed?

Mr Balfour objected to the question.

By the Dean of Faculty—(Q.) Was this letter which you call a draft letter copied out and sent in its original shape and in its original terms to the directors? (A.) I was not present at the board, and I can only speak as to what I saw. The draft which I did see contained the names of Morton and Fleming.

Mr Balfour objected.

By the Lord Justice-Clerk [to witness]—Don't tell us what the draft contained, but tell us what you saw done.

By the Dean of Faculty—(Q.) Do you know what Mr Stronach did with that letter?

By Mr Balfour—(Q.) From your own knowledge? (A.) Not from my own knowledge, because I was not present at the board.

By the Dean of Faculty—(Q.) What did he do with it so far as you saw? (A.) He informed me that he intended to deliver it.

By Mr Balfour—Never mind "informed."

By the Dean of Faculty—(Q.) What did he say he intended to do with that draft? (A.) To place it before the board. He said he would not accept the position of manager unless the board relieved him of the responsibility of these accounts. (Q.) Did he mention what the accounts were? (A.) Morton's and Fleming's——

Mr Balfour objected to this.

By the Dean of Faculty—(Q.) Mr Stronach wrote a draft of a letter—not this one—did he? (A.) He wrote the draft of a letter, and he wrote a letter other than this one. (Q.) That is to say, he copied over the draft that he had made, and turned it into a letter? (A.) Certainly. (Q.) Had that letter reference to the conditions upon which he was to accept the office of manager? (A.) Certainly; upon which he was willing to accept it. (Q.) Were you at the preparation of that letter? (A.) I was not present when the draft was written, but I was present when the letter was written, and I saw the letter.

By Lord Craighill—(Q.) Was this in the Bank? (A.) No; it was in his own house.

By the Dean of Faculty—(Q.) What did he do with the letter? (A.) Took it to the Bank I suppose. (Q.) What did he do with the letter after he had written and signed it? (A.) I saw him a day or two afterwards. (Q.) You were present when he wrote it; what did he do with it? Did he put it in his pocket and leave the house with it? (A.) I believe he did. (Q.) Then? (A.) I believe he did; I did not see him actually put it in his pocket, but he certainly took it to the Bank with him. (Q.) He carried it away with him, and he was going to the Bank—is it not so? (A.) Certainly. (Q.) Did you ever see that letter again? (A.) Yes. I did. (Q.) Where did you see it? (A.) I saw it in his house. (Q.) When? (A.) That night, I believe. (Q.) What was done with that letter? (A.) That I don't know. (Q.) Was it destroyed? (A.) That I don't know. (Q.) Did he tell you what he had done with the letter when he took it away with him and took it to the Bank that day?

Mr Balfour objected.

By the Dean of Faculty—(Q.) Well, he brought it back that night to his house? (A.) That is so. (Q.) Was the second letter written then? (A.) No, it was not. (Q.) When was the second letter written? (A.) That I cannot tell you. (Q.) Were you present at the writing of it? (A.) No, I was not. (Q.) Did you assist him in the preparation of it? (A.) No, I did not,—not this second letter. (Q.) Is the second letter in terms more modified than the first?

Mr Balfour objected.

By the Dean of Faculty—(Q.) The first letter is gone, is it not? (A.) The first letter was much more specific, and pointed to names, which this does not. (Q.) Do you know what became of the first letter? (A.) No, nor did

I see this second letter for a year or eighteen months afterwards. (Q.) Do you know if the first letter is destroyed? (A.) I have been told so, but I do not know it of my own knowledge. (Q.) Did Mr Stronach tell you anything as to its fate?

Mr Balfour objected.

By the Dean of Faculty—(Q.) Did he tell you what became of the first letter?

Mr Balfour objected.

By the Dean of Faculty—(Q.) What did he say?

Mr Balfour objected.

By the Dean of Faculty—(Q.) You transacted a good deal of business at this bank of various kinds personally before you went to Australia? (A.) Not a great deal of business; I had relations with the Bank, but not of a large character. (Q.) Did you transact business, on any occasion before you went to Australia, with the directors without the intervention of Mr Stronach? (A.) The only business connected with these matters in which I had any relations with the Bank before I went to Australia was the business that I have already testified to. (Q.) Did you come in contact with the directors before you went to Australia? (A.) I came in contact with Mr Potter only, I think. There are one or two of the minutes which refer to that time, from which it would appear that a committee of the board had made various arrangements with me. Now, that minute is all nonsense; there were no such negotiations. (Q.) What minute was that? (A.) Mr Taylor, Mr Stewart, and Mr Potter are represented as a committee. (Q.) What is the date of that? (A.) It is in 1876; it is the one in which they form themselves into a committee to arrange with me as to buying properties in Australia. (Q.) Is that the minute of 17th August 1876, referred to on page 109 [see p. 162]:—

"A letter from J. M. & Co., and two from W. Glen Walker, dated 16th and 14th " inst., in regard to the drawing of credits in lieu of those now drawn by Holmes, " White, & Company, and others, and one of the latter as to the acquisition of cer- " tain pastoral properties, were brought under the notice of the board; and, after " full consideration, the board came to the resolution that it was advisable to adopt " generally the suggestions contained in these letters, and they accordingly requested " the manager, associated with Messrs Potter, Stewart, and Taylor, to arrange with " Mr Walker as to all details."

(A.) That is the first, and there is a subsequent letter referring to the same subject. (Q.) Then there is a report by these gentlemen stating that "in " terms of the minute appointing us to arrange with Mr Walker in regard to " the acquisition of certain pastoral properties in Australia, we have to report " that we then authorised an investment to the value of £120,000 or " £130,000," and so on, what is wrong with that report? (A.) I say it is untrue. I say I never met—at least, to the best of my belief—either Mr Taylor or Mr Stewart on that subject. There are many other minutes with which I am connected that are untrue, or at least misleading. (Q.) But I suppose this is quite true, that you were authorised to invest to the value of from £120,000 to £130,000 as stated in this report? (A.) Yes, but not by Messrs Stewart and Taylor. I received instructions to buy these properties after a long negotiation with John Hunter; I saw Mr Potter once or twice, but it was principally John Hunter. I had scarcely any discussion with any one else on the subject. (Q.) But I suppose you have seen both Mr Stewart and Mr Taylor? (A.) I don't believe I did. I don't think I ever met these gentlemen. (Q.) With regard to Mr Stronach, was he a man of a yielding disposition, and one that would be easily influenced by men of a more decided character and positive views? (A.) Yes, he was the most credulous and facile man I ever met in my life. (Q.) However, did he seem anxious to do the best he could for the interests of this Bank? (A.) Undoubtedly. (Q.) Do you know whether the condition of some of these accounts was a source of affliction and misery to him? (A.) Latterly, there cannot be a doubt about it; but when he became manager, he expected they would come all right. (Q.) After he got that promise of the paying up by Morton of £400,000, he thought all the rest would come right? (A.) I think so. (Q.) Did you know that Smith, Fleming, & Co.'s account had been put on a more distinct footing in August 1875? (A.) I knew nothing of Smith, Fleming, & Co.'s account after I returned from Australia in August 1877. I was always led to believe that the account was keeping all right. I was in Australia until August 1877.

By Mr Balfour—(Q.) Let us understand about that first letter or draft; I wish to distinguish exactly what you saw from what was said to you or from your inferences about it? (A.) I said I did not actually see it put in his pocket.

By the Lord Justice-Clerk—(Q.) But your firm conviction is that he did take it away with him? (A.) Yes.

By Mr Balfour—(Q.) The last place you saw it was in his house? (A.) Yes. (Q.) And what he did was not matter of observation, but matter of inference or information? (A.) I was not in the Bank.

By the Solicitor-General—(Q.) I think you said that you saw the letter which was laid before the directors, about a year and a half afterwards? (A.) No; I saw a copy of it. Mr Stronach showed it to me in his house. (Q.) Would you tell me the names of the directors with whom you have met in regard to the purchase of these Australian properties? (A.) Do you mean since the purchases or before? (Q.) At any time? (A.) I met Mr Potter before their purchase; I believe I only met Mr Potter. After the purchases I think I met them all. (Q.) Do you mean after the purchase of them all? (A.) No, I mean all the directors. (Q.) But you did not see anybody but Mr Potter before the purchases? (A.) To the best of my belief I did not. (Q.) Do you mean before all the purchases or before the first of them? (A.) I mean before the first purchase. (Q.) With regard to that report of 19th October 1876, which reports an authorization by Mr Taylor, Mr Stewart, and Mr Potter, you say that you never met Mr Taylor or Mr Potter upon that subject? (A.) To the best of my belief I never did. I am surprised to see it here, because I think I did not know them to speak to till I came home from Australia. (Q.) Did you meet any committee of the directors upon the subject of purchase of Australian property? (A.) Subsequent to my first purchase I met a committee with reference to the second. (Q.) Who were the committee? (A.) Mr Stewart, Mr Taylor, and, if I remember right, Mr Salmond. (Q.) Was it not Mr Inglis? (A.) I beg your pardon; it was Mr Inglis instead of Mr Stewart. I saw Mr Stewart afterwards, but that committee consisted of Mr Inglis, Mr Taylor, and Mr Salmond. I met them two or three times. (Q.) You said you thought it was a prudent thing for the Bank to do to make those purchases in Australia? (A.) I did, considering all the circumstances. (Q.) Would you consider it would be a prudent thing for a Bank to make such purchases except for the purpose of recouping a deficit? (A.) I think exceptional difficulties require exceptional expedients. (Q.) That is not quite an answer to my question. Would it be a prudent thing except for the purpose of recouping a deficit? (A.) There might be other good reasons for doing so. (Q.) Of a similar kind? (A.) Or other kinds. (Q.) What other kind except for the purpose of meeting a loss already made? (A.) I know banks that build railways; it is quite common for banks to go into unusual transactions like this, though not a common thing for Scotch banks to do so.

JOHN HUNTER.

By the Lord Advocate—I am a merchant in Glasgow, and a partner of Buchanan, Wilson, & Co. I dealt at one time, from 1858, with the City of

Glasgow Bank. I was acquainted with the present manager, Robert Stronach, as well as with his predecessor, Alexander Stronach. (Q.) In the course of time you came to hold certain lands in Australia, or shares in hand in Australia, in trust for the City Bank? (A.) Yes. (Q.) Will you explain the origin of the transaction by which you came into their possession? (A.) The shares in my own name, or in my name along with others? (Q.) Well, both; which was first in point of time? (A.) The first in point of time are those in my name along with others in trust. The firm of Potter, Wilson, and Co., Morton & Co., and my own firm, were jointly interested in transactions in Australia and New Zealand. These properties were ultimately merged in the New Zealand and Australian Land Co. (Q.) These were held by Potter, Wilson, & Co., Morton & Co., and yourself? (A.) Yes. There was a guaranteed dividend secured when we made them over to the association. So long as that guarantee subsisted the shares were held by the three parties interested whom I have named. They were held in name of partners of the three firms. The three partners held them in trust, representing all the interests of the three firms. After the expiry of the guarantee, Potter, Wilson, & Co. and my own firm got their interests into their own possession. The interest of the third, Morton & Co., remained still invested in trustees. (Q.) I believe you were asked to give a letter stating that you held these in trust for the City Bank, or part of them? (A.) Yes. (Q.) Part of them were similarly secured to Overend & Gurney? (A.) Yes. (Q.) I suppose your understanding was that you held these to cover advances? (A.) I had no knowledge what they were held for. (Q.) What was the origin of your connection with Potter? (A.) I was connected with him in these New Zealand and Australian matters, but besides that we were partners together in a coal company. He was also one of the trustees in whom the shares were originally vested for joint behoof. I had nothing to do with the financing either of Potter, Wilson, & Co. or Morton & Co. At the request of the late Alexander Stronach I took over fifty shares of the Sawmill Company, Bombay, on account of Smith, Fleming, & Co. The object of that was not explained to me; I was merely asked to be allowed to put them into my name. (Q.) You were asked by the manager, Alexander Stronach, to permit them to be transferred to your name? (A.) Yes. (Q.) Were you in any other way connected with James Nicol Fleming, or Smith, Fleming, & Co.'s securities? (A.) I never had any connection with James Nicol Fleming's securities. (Q.) Prior to November 1874, did the manager of the Bank ever consult you or any person else with reference to advances to Morton & Co. and Smith, Fleming, & Co.? (A.) No. (Q.) Was it known outside the Bank that these firms had advances from the Bank? (A.) I think it was. Some time in 1874—early in the year, I think—Alexander Stronach asked me if I would, in confidence and as a friend, look into Nicol Fleming's matters, as he was not satisfied with the working of his account in the Bank. He did not say to me whether the account was bad or not. I at first told him I had no knowledge of the nature of Nicol Fleming's business, and did not feel competent to give a sufficient report, but that, if he really wished me to do so, and Fleming concurred, I had no objection to give him my opinion. Mr Fleming invited me; and I asked him to show me one or two of his Calcutta balance-sheets, the result of which was that I reported to Alexander Stronach that they were doing an unsatisfactory business, and that I did not think it could be made satisfactory in the way they were doing, and I recommended him to get rid of the account as soon as possible. (Q.) All the information the manager gave you was that the account was unsatisfactory. (A.) Yes. I don't remember the exact date when I made my report to Alexander Stronach, but I think it must have been in the spring or early summer of 1874. From my examination of Mr Fleming's balance-sheets on that occasion—which I assumed to be correct—so far as I examined them, which was for three years, he seemed to have been going backwards. (Q.) That is to say, as time went on he was getting worse? (A.) Well, the firm had made nothing for the three years of which I saw the balances. I had no knowledge whatever of Fleming's indebtedness at that time; I did not know that he owed anything. I had nothing to do except with the state of his business. Mr Fleming was a director of the Bank at that time. I made a communication to him also as to the unsatisfactory state of his balance-sheets, and at the same time I spoke to him about his position as a director.

By the Lord Justice-Clerk—This was in 1874.

By the Lord Advocate—I told him I considered it was not consistent with the position of his affairs that he should continue a director of the Bank. He did not view that as I did, and seemed rather disappointed at the prospect of his not continuing a director. I reported verbally to Alexander Stronach, in the Bank, when I advised him to get rid of this account. I don't remember that he made any particular remarks when I made that communication to him, but he did not seem to look upon the account as so bad as I made it out to be. (Q.) That is to say, he did not seem to think that Nicol Fleming was in quite so bad a state commercially as you reported? (A.) Yes. Nothing more that occurs to my memory passed on that occasion. Alexander Stronach was in failing health about that time. Subsequently, for a considerable period, he did not attend the Bank, but lived at his house near Biggar. I saw him there upon the subject of Nicol Fleming's account. I merely confirmed what I had said before. (Q.) Repeated it? (A.) Repeated it. He said then that he did not believe that it was so bad as I represented it to be. I said I only dealt with the figures I got from Nicol Fleming himself or his clerk, and could not make it better than I had represented. He did not say whether or not he had seen Nicol Fleming's balance-sheet. He said that if he were better he was quite sure he would make the account right in a year or two. That was the last occasion on which he looked at a statement of Nicol Fleming's account or went into it. I saw him again when he was rather seriously ill, when he repeated the same observation. I did not give him any details on that last occasion. I did so upon the previous occasion —I explained the grounds upon which I had come to my conclusion. On the occasion when he made the observation I have mentioned, when he was not so seriously ill, I spoke to him about Morton's account. (Q.) What led you to do so? (A.) Nothing, except the knowledge that Morton had a large account with the Bank, and I asked him how it was working. (Q.) How did you come to know it was a large account? (A.) It was very generally known, I think, in Glasgow, that it was a large account. (Q.) How did it come to be generally known? (A.) It was generally known he was discounting a large amount of City of Glasgow Bank bills. I think that was perfectly well known. Morton was a great deal about the Bank at that time. When I spoke to Alexander Stronach about Morton's account, he said it was working off all right; but on that occasion he asked me if I would speak to Mr Morton, and endeavour to get some additional security from him. I asked him to write such a letter as I could read to Morton, which he did. I read it to Morton, and the security he asked for, I believe, was given. Alexander Stronach ceased to take any active part in the management of the Bank, I believe, for a considerable time before his death. Mr Robert Stronach acted in his room during that time. (Q.) During that time, before Robert Stronach became manager himself, had you any conversation with him in regard to Nicol Fleming's account? (A.) I merely stated to him what I had stated to his brother. (Q.) Did you state to him all that you had stated to his brother? (A.) I think I did. (Q.) Did you speak to him about Nicol Fleming's continuance as a director? (A.) I don't quite remember whether I did or not. (Q.) Try to recollect that. You spoke about that to Alexander Stronach? (A.) No, I spoke about it to Nicol Fleming. (Q.) Did you not speak to

Alexander Stronach? (A.) I cannot remember whether it was to Alexander Stronach or Robert Stronach; I don't remember when Alexander Stronach left the Bank. (Q.) Whether it was Alexander Stronach or Robert Stronach, did he take the same view as Nicol Fleming himself about his continuing a director? (A.) No; whichever it was, he quite acquiesced in the view I took that he should not be a director. (Q.) He agreed that his position was inconsistent with his continuing a director? (A.) Yes.

By Lord Craighill—This was in the end of 1874.

By the Lord Advocate—I continued to press upon Robert Stronach the state of Fleming's affairs. I advised him, as I had done his brother, that the firm should be put into liquidation and wound up. His brother did not act upon that, but Robert Stronach immediately acted upon it, and the firm was put into liquidation in the end of 1874. I do not know whether he had become manager at that time, but he was acting as manager. James Nicol Fleming had a partner in Calcutta. That partnership was dissolved. That was the partnership that was liquidated. He started himself, along with another party, a new firm, on 1st January 1875. (Q.) After it was resolved to liquidate, were you consulted about the realisation? (A.) From time to time I was consulted as to the realisation. (Q.) You became cognizant of what was done? (A.) Well, I never saw Nicol Fleming's books. I merely gave advice as to the realisation when I was consulted by his clerks. (Q.) A list of the securities was furnished to you, was it not? (A.) Yes. (Q.) And you gave instructions for the realisation? (A.) Yes. (Q.) By what time was the realisation practically concluded? (A.) There were some assets in India that were a long time after 1st January 1875 before they were concluded. It must have been some time in 1876—the end of 1876, I should think. (Q.) Or 1877? (A.) Or 1877. (Q.) There was an exception, however, in the realisation in the case of certain Australian land shares? (A.) Yes. So far as I am aware there are certain securities not realised yet—a part of the New Zealand shares. (Q.) Was the liquidation satisfactory in point of results? (A.) No. (Q.) Did it leave a large balance unsecured? (A.) Yes. (Q.) Were the times bad for realising that particular security, or how did that arise? (A.) I don't know that it was altogether on account of the times. There were not very many securities to realise. (Q.) Did you communicate information to any of the directors of the Bank, other than Mr Stronach, in regard to Fleming's liquidation,—I mean, upon either of these points, the state of Nicol Fleming's business which led you to recommend liquidation; in regard to the fact of liquidation; or the unsatisfactory results of the liquidation? Had you any communication with any other director than Mr Stronach upon that point? (A.) I think I must have named it to Mr Potter; and, although the amount was never named, subsequently, to my knowledge, it became known to Mr Taylor and Mr Stewart; but I don't think, never in my presence, did they know the amount. (Q.) Just repeat that, so that the jury can hear it. (A.) I think I mentioned it to Mr Potter, and subsequently, to my knowledge, Mr Taylor and Mr Stewart became aware that there was a balance upon the account, but the extent of it, I am not aware that they ever knew, any of them. (Q.) Nothing passed in your presence which could suggest that they knew the extent of unsatisfactoriness? (A.) No. (Q.) When was it that you came to know that Mr Stewart and Mr Taylor did know something about the fact of there being a balance? You say "afterwards." I want you to fix the period a little more. (A.) It must have been in 1876 I think. (Q.) Was it not in 1877, after the liquidation, or was it whilst it was in progress? (A.) It was whilst it was in progress. (Q.) What was the extent of your communication with Mr Potter upon the subject? (A.) Simply that there was a large, uncovered balance. I don't know that I ever told him the exact amount. (Q.) Simply that there was a large uncovered balance upon that account? (A.) Yes. (Q.) How did you come to give that information to Mr Potter? Did you meet him casually, or upon the business of the Bank? (A.) No. I was in the habit of meeting him frequently; we were connected in business. (Q.) Then it was casually mentioned? (A.) Casually mentioned. (Q.) When were these communications with Mr Potter that you have just referred to now? Were they during the liquidation in 1876? (A.) No; I think it must have been in 1875. (Q.) You became aware of the acquisition of certain lands in New Zealand? (A.) Yes. (Q.) That was about eighteen months or two years ago? (A.) Yes, about two years ago. (Q.) At that period, when that transaction was being carried through, or after it, had you any further communication with the directors or any of them in regard to the state of Nicol Fleming's account? (A.) It was on that occasion that I understood that Mr Taylor and Mr Stewart became aware of the state of the account. (Q.) That was the occasion that you previously informed us of about their general knowledge? (A.) Yes. (Q.) Did you meet them on business at that time? (A.) I was invited to meet them. (Q.) For the purpose of giving information upon that point? (A.) For giving my opinion as to the value of Australian and New Zealand property. (Q.) You were at that time, and had been previously, a director of the New Zealand and Australian Land Co., Limited? (A.) Yes. (Q.) And you were conversant with that species of property? (A.) Yes. (Q.) Were you given to understand at that time that the Bank had in contemplation to acquire lands there? (A.) I understood so. (Q.) You were given to understand that? (A.) I was given to understand that. (Q.) And were you given to understand what purpose they had in view in buying land? (A.) I don't know that I ever heard of the purpose they had, but I understood it was for Nicol Fleming's account—to cover it. I understood it was for the purpose of making Nicol Fleming's account right, to cover whatever discrepancy existed upon it. (Q.) That is to say, by making a profit on the Australian land, they would cover any loss upon his account? (A.) Yes. (Q.) Were you not given to understand, by two of the directors, that it was for that purpose? (A.) I quite understood it was for that purpose. (Q.) Who gave you to understand that? (A.) I don't know that it was ever in so many words said it was for that, but I considered it was the fact of my looking into Nicol Fleming's accounts that led to my being consulted. (Q.) With whom had you communication about it chiefly? (A.) Mr Stronach and Mr Potter, and Mr Taylor and Mr Stewart occasionally. (Q.) With whom chiefly? (A.) There was not much difference as to that. (Q.) With all four? (A.) With all four. (Q.) Did you see them together or separately? (A.) I saw them together from time to time, but at long intervals. I had very few meetings with them altogether. (Q.) Where did these meetings take place? (A.) In the Bank. (Q.) Had you not a meeting with Mr Graham at Potter, Wilson, & Co.'s office? (A.) Yes. (Q.) What is Mr Graham? (A.) Mr Graham is a member of the firm of Graham & Co. of Poverty Bay, New Zealand. (Q.) Were you told how the Bank were to work the investment they proposed to make in New Zealand and Australia, the purchase through Mr Graham. (A.) I understood it was to be drawn in drafts of Graham & Co. from New Zealand to a certain extent, and Potter, Wilson, & Co. were to manage the rest of it. (Q.) Did any of the directors in these conversations which you had with them refer to the large returns that were expected from these investments? (A.) I don't remember whether they referred to that or not, but it was quite understood that they expected large returns. (Q.) When you say it was quite understood, do you mean that nobody said a thing about it, or that it was obvious from what they did say that they assumed that would be the case? (A.) No. I mean that I may have said to them that there would be large returns from Australia and New Zealand properties if they were properly purchased. (Q.) You were asked to advise whether there would be large returns or not? (A.) Yes. (Q.) And you said if properly purchased, it was your opinion that there would be? (A.) Yes.

(Q.) Was nothing said by the directors? Was no hope or expectation expressed that these large returns would be sufficient to extinguish Mr Nicol Fleming's debt? (A.) Yes, that was said. (Q.) By whom? Was that hope not expressed by one or other of them in presence of the whole gentlemen you have named? (A.) I cannot remember whether it was or not in presence of the whole; but I have no doubt that it was mentioned.

By the Lord Justice-Clerk—(Q.) Was it by one of them or by you? (A.) I think it would be by me.

By the Lord Advocate—(Q.) Did they acquiesce in your view? (A.) Yes. (Q.) From what passed on these occasions when you were discussing this matter, would it not have been plain to any third person who was there, that the purpose of making these investments was to wipe out that liability? (A.) I don't know if any stranger had been present that that would have been apparent, but it was apparent to me, because I understood how matters stood. (Q.) Then probably you were advising the Bank before? (A.) Yes. (Q.) Mr Stronach? (A.) Yes. (Q.) Did you meet the directors along with Mr Graham in Potter's office? (A.) No. (Q.) Had you been previous to this consulted about other pastoral properties, as they are called, in Australia? (A.) Yes; I was consulted about those which were purchased through Glen Walker. (Q.) Which, if any, of the directors did you meet with regard to that matter? (A.) The same as in the case of the other—Mr Potter, Mr Taylor, Mr Stewart, and the manager. (Q.) What did you understand as to the purpose for which these acquisitions were made? (A.) I quite understood that it was in connection with Nicol Fleming's matter. I knew that they did make a purchase at that time. I frequently met Mr Glen Walker on the subject. (Q.) Who is entitled to the credit of the name "Edinburgh "Pastoral Association?" (A.) I really don't know who originated that name. I don't know what was the object in giving it that name. I did not think of it at the time. In 1874 I was asked by Alexander Stronach to go to Bombay in connection with William Nicol & Co.'s affairs. He said he would like if I would go out and look into their matters, as they were interested in Smith, Fleming, & Co.; that they were all right, but he believed that there was great extravagance going on, and he wished me to go out to try if I could put it right. (Q.) Would you repeat that answer so that the jury may hear it? (A.) He asked me if I would go out to look into William Nicol & Co.'s matters, as the Bank were interested in Smith, Fleming, & Co.; that there was nothing wrong with them, but he thought there was great extravagance going on, and he wished me to go out and put it right. I declined to go, and I heard nothing more of the matter.

By the Lord Justice-Clerk—(Q.) Who made that offer? (A.) Mr Alexander Stronach.

By the Lord Advocate—(Q.) Do you recollect of being applied to in February 1875 by Mr Robert Stronach in connection with some stock which he wished to be held in the name of third parties? (A.) Yes; not in 1875. It was in 1877. (Q.) The date is not material, but you recollect of it? (A.) I do recollect. (Q.) What was the proposal? (A.) He told me that he wished to take in some stock, and he would be obliged if I would allow him to put it in my name for a short time. I consented. There was a transfer sent to me which I executed. I afterwards waited upon Mr Stronach before the annual balance, and requested him to take my name out of the books, as I did not wish it to go forth to the public. That was before the annual meeting in July 1877. He agreed to do so. I examined the list of shareholders which was issued afterwards—the published list of shareholders—and found that my name was not there. I did not examine the register of shareholders in the Bank. I never got notice after that to attend meetings or anything of that kind. I have discovered now that my name is on the stock ledger for that stock, and has been so all along. I had no intention whatever then of becoming a shareholder of the Bank. (Q.) Would you have become a shareholder at that time? (A.) Well, I don't know. At that time I would not have become a shareholder in any bank. (Q.) I mean in 1877? (A.) Yes; I would not have become a shareholder in any bank at that time, because my funds were otherwise taken up. (Q.) Would your knowledge of Nicol Fleming's account have affected you? [Objection taken and question withdrawn.] I don't remember whether I read the balance-sheet of 1878. The stock of the Australian and New Zealand Land Company has never been quoted on the Exchange. (Q.) Are the shares depreciated at present? (A.) I cannot say, because there have been no sales. (Q.) I suppose you regard the intrinsic value as being as good as ever? (A.) I do. (Q.) Is it an investment that is easily realised? (A.) The land is easily enough realised, but the shares are not so easily realised, because they are not upon the Stock Exchange.

By Mr Balfour—(Q.) Do I understand that your communications with Mr Alexander Stronach about 1874 were as his private friend with regard to the matters you have explained? (A.) Yes. (Q.) You had his confidence with regard to these matters, which I need not say you respected. (A.) Yes. (Q.) You also were asked with regard to the accounts of Mr Morton and Mr Nicol Fleming. Were you satisfied that Mr Alexander Stronach believed that Morton's account would come out all right? (A.) He said so to me on more than one occasion, quite emphatically, and that it gave him no concern. (Q.) You believed him that that account was not a cause of anxiety to him? (A.) I believed him. (Q.) With regard to Mr Nicol Fleming's account, you have also given us some answers. I think you did not like some of the operations in which Mr Nicol Fleming was engaged? (A.) No, I did not. I advised him that the nature of his transactions was such that I did not think the firm could be successful. (Q.) And you communicated that view, which you arrived at by an examination of the books, to Mr Alexander Stronach? (A.) By an examination of Mr Nicol Fleming's balance-sheets,—not the books. (Q.) You were still in these communications acting as the confidential friend of Mr Alexander Stronach? (A.) Yes. (Q.) You were advising him confidentially? (A.) Yes. (Q.) Did you find that Mr Nicol Fleming had a lucrative commission business? (A.) Yes. (Q.) And that if he stopped speculative business and confined himself to commission business, he might do well? (A.) He might do well. He had a good commission business. (Q.) Then in the result you advised that Nicol Fleming should be put into liquidation, which I think was done at Robert Stronach's instance about the beginning of 1875? (A.) Yes. (Q.) Was there a new firm constituted as part of that arrangement? (A.) There was. (Q.) It was to take up the commission business which was regarded as good and sound? (A.) Yes. I made out that it was worth about £20,000 a year, so far as I could judge, and the result of the first year's operations of the new firm seemed to confirm that. (Q.) That was clear profit from commissions alone? (A.) Yes. (Q.) Was it part of the arrangement under which the liquidation was agreed to and a new firm constituted that any sum should be paid annually to the Bank? (A.) There was an arrangement by which Mr Nicol Fleming was to give the whole of his profits from that new firm and from a firm in Manchester with which he was connected towards the payment of his debt to the Bank. At the same time he insured his life for £100,000, and I believe he assigned the policies. I had no knowledge of that, but I believe they were assigned. He also made over additional shares in the New Zealand Company. (Q.) What was the amount that was expected to be annually paid to the Bank in redemption of the debt if that arrangement was faithfully carried out by Nicol Fleming? (A.) So far as I remember I think it was expected that there would be sufficient to pay interest upon the balance due to the Bank, and over a period of years that the principal would be redeemed. (Q.) And have you any reason to doubt that if Mr Nicol Fleming had kept clear of speculative business and stuck to his commission business that result would have been realised? (A.) I think it was very likely to be realised. (Q.) But he did not afterwards keep clear; he resumed speculation? (A.) Yes. After the first year he himself went out to India and went into speculative transactions. (Q.) He went into some shipping transactions? (A.) Yes. (Q.) And in consequence of his not having done what he promised, the expectations were not realised? (A.) No. (Q.) You were also asked with regard to the New Zealand Land Company's shares. I think you have been in the colonies, and have yourself gone over the ground belonging to the Company? (A.) I have. I did so in 1869 and 1870,—both the Australian and the New Zealand land. I am a large holder in that company; Mr Potter is also a large holder in it. (Q.) You need not give names; but are there many others of the best known commercial men and bankers in the country holders in it? (A.) There are. (Q.) Are you still satisfied that these shares have a very large intrinsic value? (A.) I am. I think there is a good prospective value in them. (Q.) From your communications with Mr Morton, did you form any opinion as to what he thought of these prospects? (A.) He had a very high opinion of them. (Q.) And did you believe an honest opinion on his part? (A.) Perfectly honest on his part. (Q.) Whether it was a too sanguine opinion may be a matter as to which people may differ? (A.) Yes. (Q.) Was Mr Morton a man who had great force of character and power of impressing his views upon others? (A.) Yes; he had great force of character. (Q.) From your knowledge of the value of land in the colonies, did you think that the purchases gone into through Glen Walker and Potter, Wilson, & Co. would likely accomplish the ends which you have explained they were intended to achieve? (A.) Yes; I think they would, if judiciously managed and kept for a few years. (Q.) You think they would have accomplished what they were intended to do? (A.) Yes, to reduce Nicol Fleming's account. I believe the value of these lands has risen, notwithstanding the prevalent depression of trade over the world. I am acquainted with Mr Lewis Potter. I have known him for a great many years—over twenty years. He and I were fellow directors of the New Zealand Land Company. We were also partners in the Hamilton Coal Company. I have had occasion to see a good deal of Mr Potter in business. (Q.) What opinion have you formed with regard to his business qualities? I mean what kind of departments of a business has he made his own, and what does he leave to others? So far as my experience of Mr Potter goes, he never would go into details, but took a broad view of matters, and where he had confidence, he was perfectly satisfied to take for granted a great deal that was put before him. (Q.) Have you found that to be the case in those companies that you have been concerned with him in? (A.) Yes. (Q.) As regards general experience and judgment he was able and sound? (A.) Yes. (Q.) But rather keeping off details? (A.) Yes. (Q.) Is he a man who goes into books or any detail? (A.) No. (Q.) Is that a kind of thing which he leaves to the officials of the companies that he is connected with, so far as you have seen? (A.) Yes. (Q.) Is he much of a bookeeper at all, do you think? (A.) I don't think he is. (Q.) Have you always found him honest and upright and honourable in his dealings? (A.) Invariably. (Q.) And is that the repute that he has always enjoyed? (A.) So far as I know it is.

By the Dean of Faculty—I have known Mr Robert Stronach for nearly twenty years. I think. (Q.) Before his brother's illness, what position did he hold in the Bank? (A.) I am not quite sure. I think it was joint manager, but I am not quite sure as to that. (Q.) Before his brother's illness was he not a clerk in the Bank, an assistant? (A.) I did not know him when he was a clerk in the Bank. I may be wrong as to the length of time I have known him, but he was in a position in the Bank then. (Q.) What kind of disposition is he of? Is he a man of a yielding disposition; would he give up his own opinion to a person of more decided views? (A.) Yes, I think he would be influenced by people of more decided views. (Q.) Was the gradation of rank of the officers in the Bank, first the manager, then the cashier, then the accountant? (A.) I cannot answer that; I don't know. (Q.) Did Robert Stronach hold a subordinate position in the Bank before his brother's illness? (A.) Yes; but I don't know exactly what it was.

By the Lord Advocate—(Q.) I suppose you don't know where Mr Nicol Fleming got money to speculate with—whether he got it from the Bank, or from any other source? (A.) No; I don't know that. (Q.) But you know that he did speculate unprofitably? (A.) Yes. (Q.) And you think he ought not to have done it? You think he ought not to have engaged in that speculation at all? (A.) I think so. (Q.) You say he had a very good commission business? (A.) Yes. (Q.) Had he a very bad other business? (A.) Yes. (Q.) He had a big good business, but a bigger bad one? (A.) Undoubtedly; but the bad one could be stopped at any time; it was mere speculation. (Q.) It could be wound up? (A.) Yes; he had simply to cease the operations. (Q.) But in point of fact it was not stopped? (A.) It was. Mr Robert Stronach stopped it. (Q.) Do you think that there would have been a reasonable prospect of making a large profit on these Australian lands or shares except by holding them for some years to come—I mean some years from the date of the investment? (A.) They would require to be held for some years to come to make a large profit. (Q.) They could not in any view be regarded as an immediately realisable security? (A.) They were immediately realisable, but not to realise a large profit. (Q.) They were not realisable for the purpose for which the investment was made? (A.) No. (Q.) Did you ever meet with Mr Potter on business which required him to go into details of books? (A.) Yes. (Q.) And he never did so? (A.) He never did so. (Q.) Was he an intelligent man of business? (A.) Yes. (Q.) Did he understand what a deficit was upon a large account due to him? (A.) I have no doubt he did. (Q.) And I suppose he was capable of looking after the question whether he held security for it or not? (A.) I should think so.

ROBERT YOUNG.

By the Solicitor-General—I am a shipbroker in Glasgow. I first became a shareholder of the Bank in 1869. I acquired £2000 of stock. In August 1873 there was a new issue, and I took £400 additional, for which I paid £800,—a premium of 100 per cent. In 1874 I bought an additional £100, for which I paid £137 premium. My whole holding is £2500. My original purchase was suggested to me by Mr Alexander Stronach. I bought it from White & Saction, bill-brokers, London, who I afterwards found held it in trust for the Bank. Shortly after getting the stock in 1869, I met Mr Potter. He said he was glad to see that I had become a shareholder of the City Bank, that it was an excellent investment, and that I should never have cause to regret it. He then said that the directors were glad to get the names of good parties who would continue to hold the stock. I regularly got the reports issued to the shareholders, and I read them carefully. The dividends paid were in 1869, and first half of 1870, 8 per cent. August 1870, 9 per cent. February and August 1871, and February 1872, 9 per cent. August 1872 and February 1873, 10 per cent. August 1873 and down to February 1877, 11 per cent. August 1877 down to August 1878, 12 per cent. I first heard of the stoppage of the Bank on the morning of Wednesday 2d October, from one of my children reading the newspapers. I was very much surprised. I was first present at a meeting of the shareholders in July 1877. Mr Inglis presided. On that occasion he spoke of a secret that he might tell us from the Bank parlour, which had been so far talked of by the directors, although it was not yet assuming actual shape, and that was to issue a quarter of a million of new stock at a premium, and that it would likely be brought before them again at a future time. (Q.) Was any allusion made to the previous fresh issue of stock in 1873? (A.) As being a success. I was asked to move a vote of thanks to the chairman, which I did, and I took occasion to object to the proposed new issue of capital. I have had to pay £12,500 in respect of the call which has been made by the liquidators. I knew nothing of the position of Morton's debts to the Bank, or that the Bank was purchasing large quantities of land in Australia, or shares in railways. If I had known that I certainly would not have approved of it, and I would not have remained a shareholder.

CHARLES COWAN.

By Mr Pearson—I live at Murrayfield, near Edinburgh. I hold £3600 stock of the City of Glasgow Bank. I acquired it at various times from 1868 downwards. In 1873 I took an allocation of additional stock then given off,—100 shares, at 100 per cent. premium. I retained the shares which I purchased, in the belief that the Bank was in a prosperous condition. I don't remember reading the report of 1873 in particular, though I have no doubt I did read it. Reports and balance-sheets were sent to me in ordinary course. I was in the habit of perusing them. They seemed to me to be satisfactory, particularly the last report of 1878. (Q.) Was there anything about it that seemed to you particularly satisfactory? (A.) Entirely satisfactory, if it had only been true. (Q.) A dividend of 12 per cent? (A.) Yes. It was on reliance on the statements made in these balance-sheets and reports that I remained a shareholder.

A. F. SOMERVILLE.

By Mr Burnet—I am a papermaker at Lasswade. I am a shareholder in the City of Glasgow Bank. I hold 110 shares—£11,000 of stock. It cost me £24,000 at any rate. I first became a shareholder about 26 years ago. I was made an Edinburgh director about 1871. Mr Inglis was on the Edinburgh board when I joined it. He was also one of the Glasgow board at the time. I did not know anything about the Bank purchasing property in New Zealand or Australia. (Q.) Mr Inglis never mentioned anything of that kind to you? (A.) No, I think not. I met him regularly once a week at the Edinburgh meetings. (Q.) Did you know whether the Bank were in the habit of purchasing their own stock to a considerable extent? (A.) No. About the end of January 1877 I asked Mr Usher to join the Edinburgh board. He agreed at first, but afterwards withdrew on account of some rumours which he had heard. In consequence of what Mr Usher said to me, I went to the Bank office in Glasgow and saw Mr Stronach and Mr Potter. I spoke to them about Mr Usher's objections. I told Mr Stronach that one reason why Mr Usher objected to join the board was that he had heard they had made a loss through a person named Binning, and that he had also heard reports that the directors had been getting advances. I said for these two reasons he would not join the board. I had told Mr Usher that I thought his information was wrong,—as I believed it to be at the time,—but that I would go to Glasgow and examine into the matter, and report to him (Mr Usher) the result. Mr Stronach at once acknowledged Binning's debt, but said it was all written off, and that the position of the Bank was not affected in the very smallest at that time. (Q.) What was said about the advances to the directors? (A.) I put the question to Mr Potter, and he said it was not the case, and that so far as he was concerned he had never got a sixpence of advance, and he appealed to Mr Stronach that he was correct in saying so, and Mr Stronach said he was quite right. (Q.) Your question had reference to advances to all the directors? (A.) Yes, not all; it was some Mr Usher said. (Q.) But it was not Mr Potter alone? (A.) No.

By the Lord Justice-Clerk—(Q.) The information you had got from Mr Usher was that some of the directors had been getting advances? (A.) Yes. (Q.) And Mr Potter said that, so far as he knew, that was not the case? (A.) Yes.

By Mr Burnet—(Q.) And Mr Stronach confirmed it? (A.) Yes. I returned to Edinburgh perfectly satisfied that the statements made to me in Glasgow were true, and I told Mr Usher so, but he would not join. (Q.) Had you ever any conversation at the meetings of the Edinburgh board with Mr Inglis about Nicol Fleming's responsibilities to the Bank? (A.) Yes; we spoke of that, and Mr Inglis, I think, stated to me that they had ample security for the account, that it was being lessened, and that in the course of time it would be all right. I cannot give the exact date of that. During the whole time I sat at the board with Mr Inglis, from 1871 to 1878, he never indicated to me that the Bank was in difficulties; the very opposite.

By Mr Robertson—The duties of the Edinburgh board were to attend to overdrafts or cash credits, and give an opinion upon any point that the manager, Mr Bain, might think it his duty to bring before us. Our duties were confined to the branch at Edinburgh. We had no concern with the general affairs of the Bank. I am aware of the declaration subscribed by the directors under the Bank's contract, to the effect: "We pledge ourselves not "only to do so," that is, to perform the duties of the office, "but also to observe "strict secrecy with regard to the transactions of the company with their "customers, and the state of the accounts of individuals, and, in general, "with relation to the business of the Bank." That applies to communications both to partners of the Bank and to the outside public. (Q.) There was nothing in the position or duties of the Edinburgh directors which entitled them to more communications from the general board of directors than the other partners? (A.) No. Mr Bain held the position of Edinburgh manager during the whole period of my directorate. We did not charge ourselves with the duty of checking or ascertaining the position of any of the accounts of customers. (Q.) Did you do more in fulfilling the duties of director than merly to attend to such business as the manager laid before you? (A.) No. (Q.) And you considered that to be sufficient fulfilment of your duties? (A.) Yes. It was arranged when the Edinburgh board of direction was formed, that the Edinburgh directors' accounts should be under the jurisdiction of the Glasgow board, and not of the Edinburgh one. (Q.) When you went to Glasgow on the occasion you have mentioned, did you yourself investigate into the affairs of the Bank so far as you could in one day? (A.) I went for a special object, and that object being attained I did nothing else. I had no documents put before me. I contented myself with the statements there made. I have met Mr Inglis regularly during the period of our joint direction. I have never found him deficient in candour or fair dealing. As regards the performance of his duties as a director towards myself, my opinion is that he was highly honourable in every respect. I could not conceive that Mr Inglis would do anything—that was the opinion I always formed of him—unbecoming a gentleman; and that is my opinion at the present moment, and after all that has happened.

By the Dean of Faculty—When I went to Glasgow I made no special inquiry about advances to Nicol Fleming. His name was never spoken of. (Q.) Was it not about advances to him that you made special inquiry? (A.) No; I went through for the special purpose of getting information on the two points mentioned. There was no other business talked of. I was not told then that Nicol Fleming had got advances. I cannot say when I was told that. I heard he had got some advances. Mr Inglis mentioned that, but said that it was all right, as I said before. No directors' names were mentioned at that interview between Mr Potter, Mr Stronach, and me. I put no question about who they were.

JOHN GILLESPIE.

By the Solicitor-General—I am a Writer to the Signet in Edinburgh. I have been a director on the Edinburgh board of the City of Glasgow Bank since 1862. I continued in office until the stoppage of the Bank. The other directors were Mr Inglis, Mr Somerville, and Mr Craig. Mr Bain, who was the manager of the Edinburgh branch, attended our meetings as such. The business brought before the board referred exclusively to the business of the Bank in Edinburgh and the immediate neighbourhood, and the looking into the books of the Hanover Street business from time to time. The business in our branch showed a steady increase in profit. I am satisfied it was a safe and profitable banking business. Our balance-sheets were transmitted to Glasgow half-yearly, for the making up of the general balance of the Bank. I think we were twice consulted about the fixing of the dividend,—in 1876 and once before that. We had nothing to do with the making up of the report to the shareholders. I don't think any change was made on the dividend in 1876: I think it is about ten years since the arrangement was made of having a member of the Edinburgh board and a member of the Glasgow board in one person. I think that was arranged on a suggestion of my own, that we might have an opportunity of getting such information as we wished as to the general progress of matters connected with the Bank. Mr Inglis was accordingly appointed a member of the Glasgow Board: he was the only one of our number who ever sat in Glasgow. At our board meetings, I and the other directors present spoke now and then to Mr Inglis about matters connected with the general business of the Bank. (Q.) Do you remember inquiries being made at Mr Inglis about any particular accounts of firms in Glasgow or London? (A.) I do not recollect any inquiries being made particularly. Certain accounts were now and then named,—James Nicol Fleming, and Smith, Fleming, & Co.—James Nicol Fleming notably. (Q.) What did Mr Inglis tell you about the advances to Nicol Fleming? (A.) The general impression conveyed to us was that his advances were covered by sufficient securities of various kinds. At our weekly meetings it was my custom to read out the exchanges from the clearing-house returns and the bills of the week, and latterly these exchanges were very much against us. That caused us some little anxiety, and we used to ask information how that occurred, and why it was so constantly on our side. That was spoken about much more frequently than Nicol Fleming's account. We were told by Mr Inglis that it was of paramount importance to maintain large reserves in London, and that it was owing to that that these exchanges were so much against us; and specially, I recollect, we were told on one occasion that there was a large shipping account kept in Glasgow, that large wages were paid in Glasgow, the price of the ships being paid in London, and that accounted so far for these exchanges being adverse to us in Scotland. (Q.) May I take it, generally, that any explanations made here at the Edinburgh board regarding the general business were made by Mr Inglis? (A.) They must have been, because no other one had any knowledge. We heard about American securities, chiefly in connection with difficulties before the stoppage of 1857. Mr Inglis told us that these were improving very much, and though not immediately realisable, they were now yielding a fair return, and would probably by and by be got out without loss. I recollect 6 per cent. being at one time named as the return, but I cannot tell upon what security. On the day before the stoppage of the Bank occurred, the Tuesday—that being the day of our board meeting,—there was a general feeling of anxiety, I cannot tell very well how, and I remarked that we still retained the confidence of the public, because our shares maintained their price in the market, unless, I said, the Bank are buying them in. I asked Mr Inglis if they were doing so, and he gave me to understand they were not. In the course of making new arrangements for bringing one of my sons into the business, my partner, Mr Paterson, and I, in the last week of July, or the first week of August 1878, purchased each £500 stock in the Bank, at, I think, £236, or within a pound of that. The purchase was made through Mr Bain, and the transfer was signed by Mr Tod of Peebles. Before that I held £2000 stock, part of which I held from 1859. Besides the information I got from Mr Inglis, I was in the habit now and then of speaking to Mr Bain about the state of matters generally, and getting certain information from him such as he had. I had no means of getting information except from Mr Inglis or Mr Bain. I cannot tell whether Mr Bain had any direct knowledge of the state of the Bank in Glasgow.

By the Lord Justice-Clerk—(Q.) Had you any anxiety to get further information about the Glasgow proceedings? (A.) Now and then, in the course of the period we sat there, we had; and on one occasion Mr Somerville went to Glasgow to make inquiry, and on his return he told us he was satisfied, or at least I understood he was satisfied.

By Mr Robertson—My inquiries were not intended to elicit specific information from Mr Inglis as to the accounts I mentioned; it was general conversation with regard to their position. I was quite aware it was the duty of the directors to observe strict secrecy with regard to the transactions of the Bank with its customers and the state of accounts of individuals; but I was not aware any obligation to that effect was signed. (Q.) But you would not have desired or expected Mr Inglis to communicate to you particular information regarding accounts which were in a critical position? (A.) I don't know; I think the purpose of his double appointment was to keep us pretty much informed on the same questions as the Glasgow directors. I am not aware there was any special appointment of him as holding the double office. The information he gave us was in general terms; we never heard anything of figures. (Q.) At this distance of time can you charge your memory with more than the result upon your mind that there was no reason for alarm? (A.) No, I cannot. The subjects for the deliberation of the board were brought before us by the manager, who had a note of any matters he wanted to bring before us, and, after these were disposed of, it was my custom to read the bills, exchanges, and variations on deposits and cash accounts during the week. Then, once a month, we were in the habit of counting the cash. (Q.) But as to accounts, it is the case that the manager took the initiative in selecting such accounts as required the attention of the board? (A.) Certainly. I have asked questions about certain accounts without my attention being called to them. but that was not the practice. If anything had attracted my attention, I should certainly have brought it before my colleagues or Mr Bain. It was very rarely that anything of that kind occurred.

By the Solicitor-General—So far as I knew, we had no debtors owing large sums about which I was not sure whether they would be paid. (Q.) If you had heard of such, you would have made very careful inquiry? (A.) I hope I would. (Q.) If you had heard of such a thing as an arrangement being required to recoup a deficit, you would have looked very carefully into it? (A.) Well, I ought to have done so.

Seventh Day.—Monday, 27th January 1879.

ROBERT CRAIG.

By Mr Pearson—I am a papermaker living at Craigesk House, near Edinburgh. I have been a member of the Edinburgh board of directors of the City of Glasgow Bank since about 1863. I think Mr Bain, the manager, asked me to become a director. I purchased stock to qualify. I had not been a shareholder previously. I continued in the directorate till the stoppage of the Bank. The business of the Edinburgh board was to attend to local business. We had no connection with the business in Glasgow. I don't remember our being consulted by the Glasgow board about any matters. We reported the Edinburgh business from time to time to Glasgow. I don't recollect the circumstances under which Mr Inglis became a member of the Glasgow board. I think he was asked by the Glasgow board to join them. I never heard anything from Mr Inglis calculated to shake my faith in the stability of the Bank. I continued to purchase stock from time to time. I think my last purchase was made in 1876. I continued to hold the stock, and at the date of the stoppage I held upwards of £20.000 stock. The first call that has been made upon me is for upwards of £100,000. I purchased and continued to hold the stock in the belief that the Bank was in a prosperous state. The annual reports and balance-sheets were furnished to me from time to time. It was in reliance on the statements in these that I continued to believe the Bank was in a state of prosperity. I was chairman of the meeting of shareholders at Glasgow on 22d October 1878. At that meeting a resolution was passed for voluntary liquidation. No. 102 is the minute of the meeting, with my signature as chairman appended to it.

ADAM CURROR.

By Mr Burnet—I am a shareholder in the City Bank. I held £2460 stock at the time of the stoppage of the Bank. I became a shareholder first in 1863. I acquired other shares in 1864. All I got afterwards was given by the Bank. The printed annual reports and balance-sheets were sent to me from time to time. I remember getting those for the last three years. I read them carefully. (Q.) What did you rely upon in continuing to remain a shareholder of the Bank? (A.) I considered that the reports they gave were quite correct, and I thought very highly of them; I trusted entirely to them. If true, they were satisfactory to my mind.

JAMES RITCHIE.

By Mr Pearson—I am a stationer in Edinburgh, and a shareholder in the City of Glasgow Bank. I bought some shares in 1869. I subsequently purchased stock at various times. I applied for an allocation of stock in 1873, and got one share (£100 stock) at the price of £200. In January 1877 I bought four shares. I have regularly received and perused the reports and balance-sheets. It was purely in reliance on these that I purchased and held the stock. I considered them, if true, to be satisfactory.

Rev. JOHN PULSFORD.

By Mr Burnet—I became a shareholder in the City of Glasgow Bank in 1874. I made different purchases of stock in subsequent years, and at the time of the stoppage of the Bank I held £1700. I received and read the reports and balance-sheets. I was induced, in the first place, by Mr Somerville, one of the Edinburgh directors, in whom I had entire confidence, to become a shareholder; and, having entered on his recommendation, I bought in from time to time, being assured that the Bank was sound and prosperous, that the capital was growing, and the dividend would in all probability grow too. I saw also that the report declared a dividend of 12 per cent. with a reserve of £450,000, and I was consequently induced to pay £240 for the stock. The following are the dates of my purchases:—December 1874, £300; in the same month, £200; July 1875, £200; November 1876, £500; November 1877, £300; August 1878, £200.

JAMES RUSSELL.

By Mr Pearson—I am in partnership with my brother William as a merchant in Glasgow. I was offered new stock in the Bank in the allocation of July 1873, in respect of £500 which I had previously held, and I took one share at that date. In 1877 I became aware of the increased dividend that the Bank had paid of 12 per cent. In consequence of that I bought £300 of stock at £236 per £100. It was the published balance-sheet of 1877 that induced me to make that purchase.

ROBERT DICK.

By Mr Pearson—I am a coalmaster near Glasgow. I am the holder of eleven shares in the City of Glasgow Bank, which have been acquired by me at various dates—from 1863 downwards. The last purchase I made was eight shares in July 1877. I relied, in making that purchase, on the published report and balance-sheet of 1877, which had been issued by the directors a few weeks before.

PETER HUME.

By Mr Burnet—I am a warehouseman in Glasgow. I am a shareholder in the City of Glasgow Bank. I first acquired stock in July 1877. I had not been a shareholder before. I bought three shares then at £241. I was induced to buy them from seeing the published report by the directors, which was a favourable one. I unfortunately believed it to be true.

EDWARD M'CALLUM.

By Mr Burnet—I am a licentiate of the College of Physicians and Surgeons. I am a shareholder in the City Bank. I purchased £200 of stock in 1877. I held at that time some stock, which I had purchased before. The reports and balance-sheets were regularly sent to me. It was in reliance upon them that I bought that additional stock in 1877. I was also a depositor in the Bank. I paid my money into it in the same way, believing it to be a sound concern.

ALEXANDER FERGUSON.

By the Solicitor-General—I am the treasurer of the Caledonian Railway Company. On 19th July last year I purchased through James Watson and Smith £500 of City of Glasgow Bank stock. The seller who was disclosed to me appears to be Maggie Walker, of Fernbank, Kilbirnie. In September last I heard unfavourable rumours about the Bank, and I gave orders for selling. I sold the stock through Watson & Smith to a Mr Sutherland. I understood he acted for the Bank. Before the transfer was ready for presentation to be registered, the Bank failed, and I have been held liable for calls on the stock. I am not now in litigation with the liquidators. My case has been decided against me. I have been found liable by a judgment of the Court as the proprietor of these shares. I never held stock in the City of Glasgow Bank before July of last year. I was induced to make the purchase by seeing in the papers the directors' report to the shareholders, which showed the Bank to be in a flourishing state.

WILLIAM HOWE.

By Mr Pearson—I am cashier to warehousemen in Glasgow. I hold five shares of the City of Glasgow Bank. I bought them in the beginning of August last. I did so in reliance on the last annual report and balance-sheet published in July 1878. I perused it. I noticed that the dividend was 12 per cent. I regarded as particularly satisfactory the directors' recommendation in the report that the loss of £8000 in gold by a robbery from the Bank of Mona should be written off. It was all written off. I thought that showed that the Bank must be in a satisfactory state.

JAMES DRUMMOND.

By Mr Burnet—I am a retired spirit merchant. In September last I purchased £1000 stock of the City of Glasgow Bank. My mother and two sisters were shareholders previously, and so I came to see the balance sheets and reports. I was led to make the purchase by the statements in these reports and balance sheets. I know Mr Stewart. I had business dealings with him. I told him that I had purchased the stock, in September, after I had made the purchase. He said it would be a good thing for me some day. On 30th September, the day before the stoppage, I heard some unfavourable rumours about the Bank. I went to Mr Stewart and asked to see him. I told him that he was aware that my mother and two sisters, as well as myself, were shareholders, and that if anything were going wrong with the Bank it would affect us very seriously. I said, "You are the chairman; you are behind the scenes, and you can tell me if there is anything wrong or not." Mr Stewart said there were rumours about everybody going to fail, and he said, "I will go and see about these rumours." He went away, leaving me standing in the office. (Q.) He left you there without giving you any satisfaction? (A.) Yes. This took place in Mr Stewart's private office. I was also a depositor in the Bank. I had £2700 deposited in it from 24th May, and I increased my deposit at the time I bought my shares. In doing so I trusted to the credit of the Bank.

By Lord Craighill—I did not wait after he had gone; I went away.

By Mr Burnet—My mother and sisters were also depositors as well as shareholders.

ROBERT THOMSON.

By Mr Pearson—I am a tobacco manufacturer, of the firm of Thomson and Porteous, Edinburgh. I live at Portobello. We had a deposit account with the Hunter Square branch of the City of Glasgow Bank for some years. At the stoppage our deposit would be over £7000 I think—partly on current account and partly on deposit receipt. In making and continuing these deposits, I relied on the Bank being in good credit, and in a flourishing condition.

JAMES HAMILTON.

By Mr Pearson—I am a partner of Hamilton & Inches, jewellers, Edinburgh. (Q.) You have had an account with the Hunter Square branch of the

City of Glasgow Bank for many years past? (A.) Yes. At the stoppage the deposit was £1000, and the open account about £1300. It had been deposited for some years, from time to time. I believed the Bank to be in good credit, and in a flourishing condition.

ALEXANDER WATSON.

By Mr Pearson—I am a partner of the firm of Mossman & Watson, provision merchants, Edinburgh. (Q.) You have had an account with the Grassmarket branch of the City of Glasgow Bank for many years. At the stoppage the amount due by the Bank on that account was £2326. Of that, £1000 was on deposit receipt, and the rest on current account. I have applied for payment of it, but it has not been paid. I continued to deal with the Bank to the last, in the belief that it was in good credit.

HENRY CHRISTIE.

By Mr Burnet—I am a tobacco manufacturer in Edinburgh. I was a shareholder in the City of Glasgow Bank. I held eleven shares. I acquired the first of them in 1868. I saw the annual reports and balance sheets. I read them carefully. I was perfectly satisfied with them. It was this which induced me to become and to continue a shareholder, along with the circumstance that the stock always stood well in the market.

JOHN RITCHIE.

By Mr Burnet—I live in Pollokshaws. I am a dairyman. On 1st October last I deposited £120 in the City of Glasgow Bank there. That was my first transaction with the Bank. It stopped next day. The £120 was a legacy which I had got.

JOHN WILKINSON.

By Mr Burnet—I am a joiner in Glasgow. I had eighteen shares in the City Bank. The reports and balance-sheets were sent to me regularly, and I read them. I was satisfied with them. It was entirely in reliance on them that I continued to hold the shares. (Q.) And I believe you are now a ruined man? (A.) For aught I see, I am. I was also a depositor in the Bank. In depositing my money I trusted to the Bank's reputation.

DAVID LIGET.

By Mr Pearson—I am a cloth merchant in Barrhead. I am a holder of £2000 stock in the City of Glasgow Bank. I acquired that stock by purchase at various times. My last purchase was in 1876—£600. I bought that a very short time after the issue of the annual report that year, at £225 per share. I had previously been a shareholder for many years, and been in the habit of receiving the annual reports and balance-sheets, which I read. It was in reliance on these that I continued my confidence in the Bank. I have frequently attended the annual meetings of shareholders. I was at the annual meeting in 1878, and at the request of Mr Leresche I seconded the re-election of Mr Stewart as a director.

JAMES BECKET.

By Mr Pearson—I am a calico printer in Glasgow. I have held stock in the City of Glasgow Bank since 1862. At the date of the suspension I held

£1500 of stock. I had a considerable amount allotted to me at the issue of new stock in 1873, at £200 per cent. I have continued to hold a portion of that ever since. I generally looked over the published reports and balance-sheets. I considered them very satisfactory. It was in reliance on these that I continued to hold stock. I have regularly attended the meetings of shareholders for several years past. In 1875, at the request of Mr Stronach, I seconded the motion for the election of Mr Innes Wright as a director. I had previously known Mr Wright as a Glasgow merchant.

ALEXANDER SUTHERLAND.

By the Solicitor-General—I am sole partner of the firm of Reid & Co., stockbrokers, Glasgow. I have done business as a stockbroker for the City of Glasgow Bank. (Q.) What instructions had you, and from whom, about the purchase and sale of stock? (A.) The instructions for the most part, I think, were from the manager of the Bank. (Q.) And for the less part? (A.) All the instructions came from the manager. My firm has acted for the Bank for about thirty years. I have myself acted for it for about twenty years. The manager, when I first began to act for it, was Mr Salmond, then Mr Alexander Stronach, and then Mr Robert Stronach. Mr Salmond ceased to be manager shortly after the Bank opened again after the stoppage in 1857. I have frequently bought stock for the Bank. I have done so during the whole period, I think. I bought stock for the Bank in 1876, 1877, and 1878. (Q.) When you bought stock for the Bank, how did you let them know that you had bought it? (A.) By sending them the contract note in the same way as to any other client. (Q.) Then if you had bought for the Bank, did you in regular course get the funds from them for the day of settlement as stated in the contract note? (A.) Yes. (Q.) In any case, where you purchased on the instructions of the manager during 1875, 1876, 1877 or 1878, was the name of the Bank disclosed as being the purchaser? (A.) No, in no case. (Q.) How was it arranged that the name of the Bank should not appear? (A.) I simply got names from the manager in the same way as I got them from any other client. (Q.) The Bank sent you the names into which the transfers were to be made out? (A.) Yes. I was once or twice made a transferee myself. The transfers were sometimes made out in name of Thomas Matthew in trust. [Shown Nos. 458 and 456.] No. 458 is a bundle of seven sheets, being a transcript from my firm's ledger. The ledger itself is No. 456. These detail the purchases and sales made through my firm on the instructions of the Bank commencing 10th February 1875. Between 28th September and 2d October, I negotiated the purchase of over £10,000 worth of stock for the Bank, just before the Bank stopped. (Q.) How much stock stands in the registers in name of Thomas Matthew? (A.) I cannot give you that. (Q.) Look at the sheets (No. 462), and see if I give you the figures correctly. For 1875 was the amount £9314? (A.) The document that I have got is simply a copy of our register, and the summation is not made in it. (Q.) Well, I will take it generally. Were the purchases of much larger amount than the sales in name of Thomas Matthew? (A.) So far as passing through our books they were. (Q.) On some occasions, were the purchases in one year approaching to £10,000, and no sale at all? (A.) There may have been that amount of stock transferred. In those cases where I was made a transferee myself, I did not get any certificate showing me to be the holder of the stock, nor did I receive any dividends. [Shown Nos. 463, 464, 465, 466, and 467.] The first four of these are letters or memoranda received by me from Mr Robert Stronach. The date of the memorandum No. 463 is about 12th May 1875. It says—"I can take £800 "of the Bank stock at £233. Please let me know the result.—Sincerely "yours, R. S. Stronach." The second, No. 464, which is written on the outside of an envelope, is dated about 20th May 1876, and is as follows:—"Sorry to get such a tremendous amount of stock. Don't take more. Who "is the selling broker?—R. S. S." The third, No. 465, is a letter dated 10th November 1876 in the following terms:—"My dear sir,—In the hurry when "I saw you this forenoon, I omitted to ask you to write to Mr Bell, Edinburgh, and ask why he was pressing the sale of the stock so much, and unduly "throwing down the price to £223. Perhaps you could ascertain the names "of the sellers. Kindly let me know before the close as to amount of stock "in the market, &c.—Yours sincerely, R. S. Stronach." The fourth document, No. 466, is a letter dated 2d August 1877 from Mr Stronach, in the following terms:—"My dear Sir,—I have your note of to-day's date, and "will let you have the £400 stock for the several parties noted,—Yours "sincerely, R. S. Stronach." No. 467 is a bundle of four receipts for moneys realised by me on the sale of stock, and signed "for R. S. Stronach, John "Wardrop." The dates are 4th October 1875, 5th October 1875, 5th November 1877, and 22d July 1878. I think these were all my transactions by way of sale for the Bank during those years.

By the Dean of Faculty—I am aware that by the contract of copartnery of the Bank the directors had full power to purchase for behalf of the company any of the shares of the capital stock which might be offered for sale. I understood it was under that article of the contract that I so acted as directed by Mr Stronach.

WILLIAM DREW.

By Mr Burnett—I am a stockbroker in Glasgow. I have purchased stock of the City of Glasgow Bank, for the Bank, by orders of Mr Stronach. During the last three or four years I have purchased about £6000 or £7000 stock a year in that way. I have sold very little stock for the Bank. When I purchased I got various names from the Bank as the name of the transferee. The name of Thomas Matthew was used frequently, and sometimes my own name. When my name was used I was simply holding in trust for the Bank. The Bank supplied cash to pay the price. On 27th September last,—a few days before the stoppage of the Bank,—I made a purchase of £800 stock, under the instructions of Mr Stronach, at, I think, £236. That transaction has not been carried out, because the Bank stopped before settlement, and that stock has been left on my hands.

JAMES SMITH.

By Mr Pearson—I am a partner of Messrs James Watson & Smith, stockbrokers in Glasgow. My firm bought stock of the City of Glasgow Bank, for the Bank, in 1875, and also in 1878. We completed in all five transactions. These transactions were carried out by the instructions of Mr Robert Stronach, communicated to me verbally. On 28th September 1878, on Mr Stronach's instructions, I purchased £2020 stock, part at £236, part at £237, and part at £238. The price of the stock rose that day from £236 to £238. These purchases have not been carried out in consequence of the stoppage of the Bank. The other transactions which I have carried out on Mr Stronach's instructions are as follow:—In 1875 I purchased £1231 stock at a cost of £2823, and £900 stock, costing £2068; in all, £4892. Then there was nothing more till February 1878, when I bought £500 stock at £239, costing £1207; in April, £1841 stock, at £237, costing £4408; and May 29, £1400 stock, at £237½, costing £3360; total, £8976. The price of those stocks was paid to me in the usual way; by a cash slip handed over the counter by the teller.

By the Dean of Faculty—Besides these transactions, I bought and sold stock of other companies for the Bank: Chathams, Great Eastern, Caledonian, Metropolitan, East London, North British, Metropolitan District Preference, and so on. In the case of purchases they were paid for and taken by the Bank; but in the case of sales the Bank held them. It was generally from the stock clerk or transfer clerk that I got the name of the transferee for of the Bank's own stock.

JOHN WILSON.

By the Solicitor-General—I am a member of the firm of Honeyman and Wilson, wholesale grocers in Edinburgh. At the time of the Bank failure I was treasurer for the City of Edinburgh. I first became a shareholder of the Bank about 1862 or 1863. My last purchase was made from the Bank in 1872. I hold 19 shares at present. I regularly received the balance-sheet and report every year. I examined them with care, comparing the one sheet always with the other. I observed that the reserve fund was increasing every year. The dividends rose steadily from 7 to 12 per cent. I sold some of my stock once or twice. This had nothing to do with the reports; but because I happened to require the money in my business. I have not sold any since 1872 or 1873. I was also a depositor. At the stoppage I had between £5000 and £6000 deposited. This was for my firm,—for the carrying on of our business. I had also a small open account of my own,—a few hundreds.

DUGALD BELL.

By the Lord Advocate—I am a book-keeper. Till lately I resided in London. I am now in Glasgow. I was secretary of the Australian Land and Investment Trust, Limited, till lately. I ceased to hold the office in December. I was at one time clerk to James Nicol Fleming. I entered his employment when he opened his office in Glasgow, in February 1863. I remained in his employment till the end of 1877. I was in Calcutta for about a couple of years. (Q.) But till April 1875, when you went to India on account of Mr Fleming, you were continuously in Glasgow, as a clerk in his office? (A.) That is so. (Q.) Were you acquainted with Mr Fleming when you became his clerk. (A.) No, I had only heard of him. (Q.) Did Mr Fleming, shortly after you entered his employment, open an account with the City of Glasgow Bank? (A.) Yes. He took me to the Bank and introduced me to Mr Alexander Stronach, the then manager, so that I might be known as his (Mr Fleming's) agent, and operate on his account. (Q.) Mr Fleming's business was not successful I believe eventually? (A.) It was not. I recollect Mr John Hunter, merchant, Glasgow, inquiring into Mr Fleming's affairs. This was early in 1874. I never saw any report by him. No one communicated to me the result of his inquiry. (Q.) What followed on his inquiry, to your knowledge? (A.) I understood that Mr Fleming's affairs were put in liquidation, and I was sent out to Calcutta shortly afterwards.

By the Lord Justice-Clerk—(Q.) Was that in 1874 or 1875? (A.) 1875.

By the Lord Advocate—(Q.) Mr Fleming traded under the firm of Nicol Fleming & Co.? (A.) In Glasgow it was simply James Nicol Fleming? (Q.) What were his other firms? (A.) In 1868 I think the firm of J. Nicol Fleming & Co. was started in Calcutta. [Shown book No. 370.] That is J. Nicol Fleming's private ledger; it was kept by me down to 1877. It is all in my handwriting down to the end of 1877. (Q.) It was opened at the time that he started that second firm in Calcutta in 1868? (A.) About that time. (Q.) What is the state of Mr Fleming's capital account as stated in that ledger, when it begins on 31st January 1868? (A.) It begins on 1st February 1867. (Q.) At 1st February 1867, what was the state of it? (A.) On this point I am in the hands of the Court. I wish to state that, although I have no knowledge of Mr Fleming's movements or intentions, yet I suppose it is quite probable that he may yet come forward to speak for himself, and perhaps that should be kept in view in any questions that may be asked me. I am quite prepared to go into it if the Court shall so rule.

The Lord Justice-Clerk—I think you are bound to disclose any knowledge that you may have.

By the Lord Advocate—In February 1867 the balance at the credit of Mr Fleming's capital account was £48,239. (Q.) Had there been a gain or loss upon capital account from the time you joined him down to that date? (A.) There had been a loss in round numbers of about £212,000 from 1863. (Q.) So that at the time you joined there must have been about £260,000 of capital? (A.) Yes. (Q.) Of which about £212,000 had been lost in 1867? (A.) Yes. The balancing period in the book was 31st January. At 31st January 1868 the balance to the credit was reduced to £25,818. It remained very nearly the same at the balancing periods of 1869 and 1870. At 31st January 1871 the balance was at the debtor of capital account to the extent of £7716. (Q.) That is to say, the capital was all lost that he had begun with, and a debt of the amount you have mentioned was left instead? (A.) Yes. At the balancing period in 1872 that debit balance was increased, and it then amounted to £35,383. At the balancing period in 1873 the debit balance was still increasing; it then amounted to £84.420. In 1874 the balance, still on the same side, was £104,300. In 1875 the balance was £213,588, still to the debit. (Q.) What was that last increase of upwards of £100,000 owing to? (A.) It was owing to a number of old accounts having been closed in that year before I left for Calcutta, and the debits carried to profit and loss. (Q.) How much was the amount carried from profit and loss that year against capital in closing these accounts? (A.) £86,131. Some of those accounts had been open for a considerable time, in the hope of making something out of them. There was always something expected to come in from them, but nothing came, and so they were closed and carried to the debit of the capital account. I went out to India in April 1875. (Q.) When did you bring up these balances in the book afterwards? (A.) After I returned in 1876. In January 1876 the balance is £248,905 to the debit. In 1877 it is £322,366, and by the end of 1877 it is £365,143. (Q.) So that in that business he had lost £365,143 *plus* the £48,000 you told us of that stood at the credit during these years, from 1868? (A.) Yes. (Q.) Therefore, between 1868 and the end of 1877 he had lost £413,383? (A.) Yes. (Q.) Does that represent the whole of Mr Fleming's tradings and losses during that period? (A.) No, it does not. (Q.) It was just one branch of them? (A.) Just one branch. (Q.) On whose instructions did you proceed to Calcutta in 1875, and how long did you remain there? (A.) Mr Fleming spoke to me first about going, and afterwards Mr John Hunter and the manager, Mr Robert Stronach, spoke to me. (Q.) You understood the estate, or part of it, was in liquidation then? (A.) Yes, I understood the old firm of J. Nicol Fleming & Co. had gone into liquidation. (Q.) For whose behoof? (A.) For behoof of the Bank. (Q.) And I suppose it was because of the Bank's interest in the liquidation that Mr Stronach, the manager, and Mr Hunter came to you? (A.) I understood so. (Q.) You understood so at the time? (A.) Yes. (Q.) What was your object, or what were your duties to be in Calcutta when you went out in 1875? (A.) I was to realise the assets of the old firm as speedily as I could without sacrificing them, and remit home the proceeds. (Q.) To whom were you to remit the proceeds? (A.) To Mr Hunter. (Q.) How long were you out there? (A.) About a year. (Q.) Did you find the duty of realising an easy or a difficult one? (A.) Well, I found matters had been going behind, and that there was very little to realise. (Q.) In fact, you found assets, but you found debts too? (A.) I found large debts. (Q.) Bad ones? (A.) Yes.

(Q.) There were some coals, were there not? (A.) That was the principal asset; a large claim we had upon a native firm for coals. Nothing came of that so far as I know. We could not get anything out of it. (Q.) Did you realise anything really to send home in that year? (A.) No. After paying some of the debts of the firm, there was really nothing to send home. (Q.) Were you a good deal down at the premises of the City Bank before you went out to Calcutta? (A.) Yes; I was frequently down at the Bank. (Q.) In relation to this matter of the liquidation? (A.) In relation to Mr Fleming's business generally. (Q.) Including the liquidation? (A.) Yes. (Q.) Were you not there almost daily for a time? (A.) I daresay I was, for some time before I went to Calcutta. (Q.) What individuals did you come in contact with on these occasions when you were at the City of Glasgow Bank? (A.) Very seldom any one else than the manager. (Q.) That is to say, generally you saw Robert Stronach? (A.) Yes. (Q.) Whom did you see besides Robert Stronach upon these matters; I do not mean simply that you saw them, but who did you meet or converse with on the subject of James Nicol Fleming or his liquidation? (A.) I saw Mr Hunter frequently before going out, of course. (Q.) Anybody else? (A.) Mr Potter spoke to me about it also. (Q.) Was Mr Robert Stronach the manager at that time? (A.) No, I think not. I think he was assistant manager only. I think his brother was absent, and he was acting as manager, I understood. (Q.) Did you see Mr Potter at his own office in Gordon Street about it? (A.) His office was then in Great Clyde Street, I think. I saw him there twice, I think. He removed to Gordon Street while I was away. (Q.) When you saw Mr Potter at his office, did you see him alone on any occasion? (A.) Yes. Mr Hunter came in upon one occasion. (Q.) What was the object of your conferences with Mr Potter? (A.) Mr Potter impressed upon me the necessity of doing all I could to send home remittances—to realise the assets and send home remittances. I went to see Mr Potter by arrangement, at the suggestion of Mr Hunter. Mr Hunter suggested that I should go to see Mr Potter about my going out to Calcutta. (Q.) For what purpose? (A.) He did not say for what purpose. He just suggested that I should see Mr Potter, and I did so. Mr Potter inculcated upon me the necessity of realisation and sending home remittances to be put to Mr Fleming's credit and to reduce his debt. (Q.) Did he seem anxious that as much as possible should be realised? (A.) Yes, he impressed that upon me very clearly. (Q.) That you must do your very best to get money out of the realisation? (A.) Yes. [Shown No. 31A, excerpt from credit accounts Nos. 3 and 4.] I observe the balance of £487,906 carried over to the debit of James Nicol Fleming. I should say that is a balance due in respect of cash advances, as at June 1876. I have no doubt it was the balance carried over after my realisations in Calcutta.

By the Lord Justice-Clerk—It was the balance at his debit after all realisations up to that time.

By the Lord Advocate—I saw that account in the ledger with Mr Morison. When I went down to see it I became aware it was transferred to the private book, from which No. 31A is an excerpt.

By the Lord Justice-Clerk—The date of the balance is 7th June 1876.

By the Lord Advocate—I did not understand the reason for so transferring the account at the time. I understood that the effect of that entry would be to take it out of the cheque box. I knew Mr Fleming had other indebtedness than represented by that balance, but I knew the details of that balance better than I knew the details of any other. (Q.) Were there any business relations during the time you were in Fleming's office between James Nicol Fleming and Co., started in 1868, and the firm of John Innes Wright & Co.? (A.) Yes. These continued during our liquidation. There were certain credits that had been granted by the Bank to James Nicol Fleming & Co., which were continued during the liquidation. These were drawn upon by bills from Calcutta. The acceptances were by the Bank. They were discounted by various parties—some by James Morton & Co., others by Innes Wright & Co., and others I discounted myself at different banks. These bills were sent to this country from abroad. They were all sent for acceptance. Their currency was six months after acceptance.

By the Lord Justice-Clerk—These bills began shortly after the Calcutta house was opened, or perhaps about the year 1870. (Q.) Were they carried on to a larger extent during the liquidation? (A.) Not to a larger extent; they were decreasing. (Q.) They were mere renewals? (A.) Yes, they were renewals.

By Mr Smith—I knew Mr Wright. I formed a good opinion of him. His partner was Mr Scott. (Q.) Was it Mr Scott who conducted the affairs of the firm? (A.) Yes. It was Mr Scott chiefly whom I saw in regard to the matters about which I called. What brought me in contact with the firm was chiefly the discounting of bills,—I handing the bills to them for discount, and they handing me the proceeds.

By Mr Balfour—When Mr Potter impressed on me the propriety of realising what I could, I understood it was with the view of reducing Nicol Fleming's debt to the Bank. It was quite plain that Mr Potter was desirous to do his best for the Bank.

By the Dean of Faculty—The liquidation of the Calcutta firm began in January 1875. The liquidation in Glasgow had been going on for some time previously. By liquidation I mean turning the securities which the Bank held into money, and applying that to the reduction of J. Nicol Fleming's debt. I don't think that process of liquidation is finished yet. The realisation account goes on after June 1876, over 1877 and 1878. I obtained various sums of money from property belonging to Mr Fleming, and dividends. He had New Zealand and Australian Company stock. I do not know if it is sold. My accounts during 1877 contain entries of the dividends I drew from that stock and elsewhere.

By the Lord Advocate—(Q.) Did you meet Mr Innes Wright about the discount of these bills as well as Mr Scott? (A.) Occasionally; chiefly when Mr Scott was from home.

JOHN INGLIS.

By the Solicitor-General—I am a clerk, formerly in the employment of Potter, Wilson, & Co. I was with them for about fifteen years, up till the stoppage of the Bank. I was bookkeeper. There was a great number of bills between Potter, Wilson, & Co. and James Morton & Co. They were accommodation bills principally. (Q.) And for a good many years had there been anything but accommodation bills between them? (A.) For a good many years there had been nothing but that. (Q.) Were any of the bills ever paid during the time that you were there? (A.) Rarely; but sometimes they were. (Q.) Did you ever know Morton pay a bill? (A.) No; I never knew Morton pay a bill in his life. (Q.) The whole time? (A.) Scarcely ever. (Q.) Where were all these bills discounted? (A.) A large number of them were discounted by Mr Morton. They were our acceptances to James Morton & Co. (Q.) Was there a large number of bills discounted with the City Bank? (A.) No. (Q.) What bank did you get any of these bills discounted at? (A.) We discounted very few of them. They were our acceptances to James Morton & Co., who discounted them, I think, principally in London. (Q.) Were Potter, Wilson, & Co. correspondents of Holmes, White, & Co., of Melbourne? (A.) They were. (Q.) During the time you were with them did drafts for large amounts come home to Potter, Wilson, and Co. from Holmes, White, & Co. (A.) Yes. (Q.) Drawn in favour of James Morton & Co. and Potter, Wilson, & Co.? (A.) Yes. (Q.) On whom? (A.) The City of Glasgow Bank. (Q.) Who got the proceeds? (A.) In cases in which I had to do with the discounting, the City of Glasgow Bank got the proceeds. (Q.) Do you know what happened in cases that you had not to do with? (A.) No. (Q.) Have you heard Mr Lewis Potter saying anything about these credits? (A.) Will you explain. (Q.) About the year 1870 what were the relations between Potter, Wilson, & Co., and Morton and Co. and the Bank, so far as you knew? (A.) I scarcely understand the question. (Q.) You had an account in your ledger at that time called the City of Glasgow discount account? (A.) Yes, I opened that account. (Q.) When you discounted Holmes, White, & Co.'s bills, what was done with the proceeds? (A.) When I discounted Holmes, White, & Co.'s bills, I credited the City of Glasgow discount account with the amount, and I debited that account with the proceeds of the discount, which squared the transaction. (Q.) Who in your firm took the management of all these affairs? (A.) Mr Lewis Potter. (Q.) Had he blank forms? (A.) He had. (Q.) From Holmes, White, & Co? (A.) From Holmes, White, & Co. (Q.) Signed by them? (A.) Signed by them. (Q.) Were these used as required by filling them up as bills drawn by Holmes, White, & Co.? (A.) That is so. (Q.) What was on the bills written out when Mr Potter got them? What was added in to what was printed? (A.) The amount, the date, the currency, and the place,—Melbourne. (Q.) Was all that put on in Glasgow? (A.) It was all put on in Glasgow. (Q.) Nothing but the signature was not put on in Mr Potter's office? (A.) Nothing but the signature and the lithographed form. (Q.) As regards the putting of the dates on these bills, were they put on of the date on which the date was written? (A.) No. They were put on as at a mail date. (Q.) You mean a date which would correspond with their having made a journey from Melbourne? (A.) Yes. [Shown Nos. 372 to 389. Eighteen books, each containing fifty blank drafts (unstamped), by Holmes, White, & Co. on the Bank, of which fifty had been used, and the counter-foils alone remained.] (Q.) Are these books of bills signed by Holmes, White, and Co.? (A.) Yes. (Q.) Blank, ready for use? (A.) Yes. (Q.) Where were these kept? (A.) Mr Lewis Potter kept them. (Q.) In his own private possession? (A.) Yes. (Q.) When they were to be handed out for use, what was done? (A.) James Morton & Co. applied by a memorandum for certain credits. There was a memorandum book kept by me. I looked and compared these, anticipating certain bills,—a bill due on such a date, perhaps eight days forward,—I checked this by Mr Potter's orders, to see that on no account was Morton to be allowed to anticipate. I then explained that it was correct to Mr Potter, who handed out the drafts, and they were filled up and handed to James Morton & Co. (Q.) Who were they filled up by? (A.) Sometimes by me, and sometimes by other clerks. (Q.) Do you remember in March 1877 of any communication coming from Holmes, White, & Co. about the protracted use of these bills? (A.) I cannot speak as to the date; it must have been prior to that. (Q.) They objected to their name being so freely used? (A.) A number of years prior to that they did. (Q.) But did they particularly object in the beginning of 1877? (A.) Not that I am aware of. (Q.) They had been objecting prior to that? (A.) Yes. (Q.) Who told you that? (A.) I saw it in their letter. (Q.) Did Mr Potter speak to you about it? (A.) Mr Potter at all times was very averse to these bills being given out by us at all. (Q.) Did he speak to you about Holmes, White, & Co. objecting to so many bills being issued? (A.) He did not.

By the Lord Justice-Clerk—(Q.) Why did he give them out? (A.) I cannot say that. (Q.) What do you mean by objecting? (A.) He gave them out with the greatest reluctance. (Q.) How did he show that; was he under obligation to give them out? (A.) Not that I am aware of.

By the Solicitor-General—(Q.) Were you told anything by Potter about an arrangement that was made in 1877 for substituting a new credit? (A.) Yes.

Mr Potter called me into his room in Gordon Street, I think early in January 1877, and told me that it had been arranged that a portion of credit 24/6, presently financed by James Morton & Co., was to be transferred to another credit to be financed under the name of Glen Walker & Co.—that I was to take charge of it—that it was to be apart from our firm—and that I was to call upon the manager of the Bank, Mr Stronach. (Q.) Was anything said as to who was to have the management of that? (A.) The bills were to be drawn under Glen Walker & Co.'s credits in favour of Innes Wright & Co., who were to account to the Bank. I superintended the operation of that account for about ten months.

By the Lord Justice-Clerk—(Q.) You say they were to be drawn in favour of Innes Wright & Co. on the Bank? (A.) Yes.

By the Solicitor-General—(Q.) Had Mr Potter blank forms for these bills? (A.) Yes, in the same way as the others. (Q.) Did Innes Wright & Co. fall short in accounting for the proceeds of these bills? (A.) They did. Mr Potter spoke to me about that, and also Mr Stronach, frequently. (Q.) And ultimately was the discounting of bills to Innes Wright & Co. stopped? (A.) It was stopped. (Q.) Who got the financing after that? (A.) I think it was Mr Morton. With regard to these shortcomings by Innes Wright & Co., I frequently saw William Scott about them, almost constantly. I also saw Mr Wright in Mr Scott's absence, and complained about it several times. (Q.) Was he quite aware of these shortcomings when you spoke to him? (A.) He seemed to be quite aware.

By Mr Smith—The bills were handed to Wright & Co. as bill discounters. The business was practically managed by Mr Scott. He rendered accounts to me, which I examined, and then submitted them to the manager of the Bank. (Q.) Up to November 1877, what was the shortcoming as shown in these accounts? (A.) I am merely speaking from recollection, but there was a letter which I received from Mr Scott, in which he promised to make me a payment of £38,000 during that week. (Q.) Was he to be allowed to have a margin to any extent? (A.) At first he was not, but it was always told me by the manager that he would be allowed a margin of £15,000 to enable him to finance such a large amount. (Q.) When you saw Mr Wright on the subject, did he say anything about Mr Scott managing it? (A.) I met him as a partner of the firm, and I spoke to him concerning a subject which they were both cognisant of. (Q.) But did he say anything about Mr Scott having charge of the business? (A.) He did. He said that Mr Scott took the entire charge of all these matters.

By Mr Balfour—Potter, Wilson, & Co. carried on a very large business both as shipowners and as commission merchants. They had intimate relations with the New Zealand and Australian colonies. They were the agents in this country for Holmes, White, & Co., during all the time to which my evidence applies. The bills drawn under the credits that I have spoken to applicable to Holmes, White. & Co., were sent home with Holmes, White, and Co.'s name upon them, as drawers, to Potter, Wilson, & Co., to be used as occasion required, and they remained to be used by Potter, Wilson, & Co., as the agents of Holmes, White, & Co. (Q.) When the time came for using these bills, did Mr Potter fill up the date so as to have the same effect as if it had been dated before coming from the colony? (A.) Yes. (Q.) Did it make the least difference whether these bills drawn in the colony were sent home with authority to Mr Potter to fill up that date, or whether the date was written in the colony? (A.) No; it made no difference in my estimation. (Q.) Then, were these bills treated by Potter, Wilson, & Co., in accordance with the mandate or authority which they had from their constituents, Holmes, White, & Co.? (A.) They were. (Q.) Did Potter, Wilson, & Co., get any sort of benefit by them? (A.) None. (Q.) Were they merely executing their agency in the ordinary way of business? (A.) Precisely. (Q.) Not for their own benefit? (A.) No. (Q.) Was there anything in the least irregular in that? They were executing it in the ordinary way, you have told us? (A.) I would not care to pass an opinion upon that. (Q.) Does your evidence apply to the whole of the credits you have spoken to in which Holmes, White, and Co. were interested? (A.) Yes. (Q.) The City Bank were the acceptors of the bills drawn under these credits? (A.) They were. (Q.) And the money was applied for its proper purposes? (A.) Yes. (Q.) And before Mr Potter gave out any bill, was the application always initialed by the proper officer of the Bank? (A.) It was invariably; he would not give them out without. (Q.) Then you spoke about certain bills to which Morton was a party, or in which Morton was interested; I believe you called them accommodation bills? (A.) Yes. They were entirely for Morton's accommodation. Potter, Wilson, and Co., got no benefit from them. They were the acceptors for Morton's accommodation, but for that alone. (Q.) You spoke about a credit which was transferred from being worked by Morton to be worked by Glen Walker and Co.; was that the credit known as 24/6? (A.) Yes. (Q.) Do you know that the Bank held securities against that credit? (A.) I was informed so, both by the late manager and his brother, and also by Mr Potter. That credit was entirely for Morton's benefit. I cannot say why it was transferred to Glen Walker & Co.; I was not informed of the reason. I was simply told that the securities for that £100,000 were transferred from 24/6 to 38/47. (Q.) You also mentioned the transaction with Innes Wright & Co. when they failed to account for the money they had raised by discount, the £48,000. When they so failed to account for that money, was Mr Potter displeased? (A.) Very much so. (Q.) And he expressed his displeasure at that impropriety? (A.) Yes. (Q.) What did he do in consequence of that? (A.) He told me frequently to call for Mr Scott, and urge upon him the propriety of making payments. (Q.) To pay up that £48,000? (A.) It was not always £48,000; it fluctuated. (Q.) But to pay up the balance which Scott was short of the sum he had got by discount. (A.) Yes.

By the Lord Justice-Clerk—(Q.) That was a defalcation on Scott's part? (A.) Yes.

By Mr Balfour—(Q.) And which Mr Potter did his best to recover? (A.) Yes; both Mr Potter and Mr Stronach. (Q.) Were there other credits which Potter, Wilson, & Co. worked? (A.) Yes. (Q.) Were they worked for behoof of the Bank? (A.) Yes. (Q.) And that alone? (A.) And that alone, with one exception,—our own credit. (Q.) What was the one exception? (A.) We had a credit. Speaking from recollection, I think we had an advance of about £9000. (Q.) How long was that ago? (A.) Just at the time of the stoppage of Potter, Wilson, & Co. 40/11 was the credit, I think. (Q.) Was that the only credit in which Potter, Wilson, & Co. had any personal interest? (A.) It was the only credit in which we had any interest. There was one credit for £10,000, a wool credit; I cannot say whether the £5000 that was running at the time of my leaving is still in existence or not. (Q.) Then these are different credits from any you have spoken to? (A.) Yes. (Q.) Were these credits covered by securities in the regular way? (A.) All that we had, with the exception of this wool credit and the £9000, were amply covered by securities. (Q.) So that, in the credits you were examined about by the Solicitor-General, did Mr Potter get any sort of benefit from any one of them? (A.) No. The regular banking business of Potter, Wilson, and Co.'s firm was done with the British Linen Company, and also with the National Bank, both of Glasgow. These banks always gave Potter, Wilson, and Co. any banking facilities that they required for their business. We never found any difficulty about that. I always looked upon these as our regular bankers.

By the Lord Justice-Clerk—Their transactions with both of these banks were to a large amount.

JOHN WARDROP.

By the Solicitor-General—I was lately transfer clerk in the City of Glasgow Bank at Glasgow. I held that situation for four years. (Q.) What was the procedure in purchases of stock for the Bank; did the broker send you in a contract note? (A.) He sent it to the manager. The broker who had bought the stock for the Bank then, on the name day of the Stock Exchange, called at the Bank for the name of the purchaser. The Bank supplied that name. After that a letter came in from the seller's broker giving the particulars. That letter would come to Mr Leresche, and he would hand it to me, if it came in during the week before the Thursday. I would hand the whole letters to Mr Leresche, with a list of the transfers to be laid before the board. None of the directors took charge of the transfer business, so far as I know. (Q.) Who were buying for the Bank, and coming to the Bank to get the names of purchasers to hold for the Bank? (A.) Mr Drew, Mr Sutherland, and Watson and Smith. As a rule, since I went there, the name of the purchaser generally given was Thomas Matthew. When the names were given it was my duty to get the parties to sign the transfers. I usually got the name signed by the person given out by the Bank as the purchaser. I never had any difficulty in getting their signature; they signed without remark. (Q.) These persons were entered in the ledger as holding in trust? (A.) Thomas Matthew was; I don't exactly know the heading in the ledger. It would not appear in the stock ledger that that stock was held in trust for the Bank. It was entered just as "in trust," during the time I kept the stock ledger. (Q.) Did the stock thus purchased for the Bank enter the balances of the Bank? (A.) I gave a note to the accountant of these amounts of stock on the balance day of each year. I don't know what he did with it. Mr John Innes Wright became a partner of the concern by purchasing stock in 1875, when he became a director. The first stage of the transfer to him was gone into on the day he was elected. There was a transfer of £1200 stock to him, the first stage of which was entered upon about one hour before the meeting. I don't think John Innes Wright held any stock previously to that. The amount of stock held by the Bank in 1876 was £140,751; Mr Drew, £2970; Thomas Matthew, £9216; William Scott, £1300; John Innes Wright, £2681; total, £156,962. Total in 1877, £185,721; in 1878, £202,312. In January 1878, Mr Stewart sold £5000 stock. The Bank purchased it. Mr Stronach gave me instructions about the transfer. Latterly the dividends upon all stock held by Drew, Matthew, and others, in trust for the Bank, were credited to an account headed "City of Glasgow Bank stock account." They were not paid over to any one. That applies to the last three half-years.

By Mr Trayner—The proceeds of the stock held by Mr Stewart were paid in to the credit of Mr Stewart's account. No money was paid to him; it was paid in to his credit in the account he had then running with the Bank.

By Mr Smith—The qualification for a director is the holding of £900 stock. I think £1200 stock was found for Mr Wright to qualify him for a seat at the board. Mr Wright held £2681 stock for the Bank. I think the transfer of that stock was made shortly after he became a director in 1875. I don't know through whom his consent was asked. I don't know if a clerk was sent from the Bank to ask his consent. I don't think there is any other director who holds stock in trust for the company. Mr Wright still holds that stock.

By Mr Asher—Mr Salmond holds £2200 stock. Prior to 1873, he held £1800, and in 1873 he took £400 of new stock. Since then he has held £2200 down to the close. He holds also £360, as trustee for a Mr Thomson. With regard to the purchases of stock for the Bank, it was with Mr

Stronach that I communicated. None of the directors ever spoke to me on the subject. None of them ever asked to see the stock ledger or the transfer ledger. So far as I recollect, Mr Salmond has the largest holding of stock amongst the directors. I don't think he ever sold a share all the time he was connected with the Bank.

By Mr Mackintosh—Mr Taylor at the date of the stoppage held £1800 stock; his son and partner, Mr Henry Taylor, £500; and his brother and former partner, Mr Patrick Taylor, £500. I cannot say whether Mr Taylor was an original shareholder of the Bank, or whether he accepted an allotment of new stock in 1864. I am aware he got £300 new stock alloted to him in 1873. The same year he bought £120 to make his holding even. Neither Mr Taylor nor any of his family ever sold a share since they became connected with the Bank.

By Mr Darling—Mr Stronach holds £900 stock. Ot that he acquired £800 in August 1876. Previously he had held only £100.

JAMES HUTTON.

By the Lord-Advocate—I am a chartered accountant in Glasgow. I have had submitted to me the balance abstracts published by the directors to the shareholders of the City Bank for June 1876, 1877, and 1878. I have also had access to all the books of the Bank, and I have examined these so far as is necessary for ascertaining how far the published abstracts coincide with the entries in the books. [Shown published abstract as at 7th June 1876.] This document is headed City of Glasgow Bank, Abstract Balance-Sheet as at 7th June 1876. On the assets side, there is, first, "Bills of exchange, local and country bills, credit accounts, and other advances upon security," £8,787,804, 17s. 9d. These assets were understated to the extent of £2,698,539, 0s. 4d. The correct amount, according to the books of the Bank, is £11,486,343, 18s. 1d. With regard to the details of that under-statement, I find from the scroll abstract of accounts that the bad debts are only stated at £50,000, while in the books of the Bank they appear at £300,000. I further find that the credit accounts, amounting to £147,468, 16s. 11d., are entirely omitted from the abstract of the Bank. I further find that the deposit account balances, amounting to £452,211, 5s. 6d., are entirely omitted from the abstract of the Bank. The sources from which I have got that information are the scroll abstracts for the year 1876, and from the general ledger. I find that foreign and colonial credits are understated,—entirely omitted,—to the extent of £973,300. They appear in the abstract at £1,304,873, 17s. 1d.; and the true amount was £2,278,173, 17s. 1d. I find that there has been transferred from this first branch of the assets to the third branch of the assets, a sum of £751,775, consisting of three items, marked with the initials S. F. & Co., £200,875; J. N. F., £100,300; J. M. & Co., £450,600; in all, £751,775. The practical effect upon the statement of assets of bringing down that amount from head I. to head III., is to convert what might be considered a doubtful asset into what would be considered by the shareholders and the public an asset that was very assured,—that is to say, to convert an asset that might be doubtful—an asset that might not have been paid at all, into an asset that is beyond doubt—assured, in the nature of a Government stock or other stock—a good investment held by the Bank. The next item in error is an item deducted as cross accounts—£373,334, 5s. 3d. The next item is £32,751, 17s. 11d.—the balances on remittances outstanding between branches and branches and the head office. (Q.) I understand you are taking your information as to these from the scroll abstract and the books? (A.) Yes. (Q.) And assuming the scroll abstract as the basis of the abstract published? (A.) Yes. The gross of what I have just read out amounts to £2,983,841, 5s. 7d., but there are several over-statements in the abstract balance-sheet. Past due bills appear in the scroll abstract at £248,500, 13s. 6d., and they appear in the books at £174,393, being a difference of £74,106. The contingent account has a credit balance of £2507, while in the books there was a debit balance of £10,747, a further error of £13,254. Credit accounts No. 2 appear in the scroll at £143,087, 18s. 7d., while in the completed balance-sheet from the ledger it only amounted to £100,296, 5s. 2d., being a difference of £42,791. Heritable property appears in the first branch of the abstract, but should have appeared in the second—119,541. Adjusting account of interest, £35,607, 13s. 8d. That, it appeared, was only the difference between the interest due by the Bank and the interest due to the Bank. These gross over-statements amount to £285,302, 5s. 3d., and deducted from the previous omissions, amounting to £298,384, 5s. 7d., it shows an under-statement on the first branch of the balance of £2,698,539. Second branch—heritable property, advances on heritable property, &c., appear in the books at £319,949, 5s., and in the abstract at £256,650, 10s. 1d., giving a difference of £63,283, 15s. Under the third head, "Cash in hand, gold and silver coin and notes of other banks at head office and branches," £862,812, 4s. 4d., there is a deduction from this head of £29,095. Government stocks, exchequer bills, railway and other stocks, £2,218,868, 13s. 7d.; there is the transfer I have already referred to of £751,775. There is an omission of the remittances outstanding between branches and branches of £3356, 16s. 11d.; there is an item due by Irvin & Co. of £11,991, 9s. 9d., which, before the balance closed, had been wiped off to suspense account, and these deductions amount to £753,211, 2s. 6d., accounting for the difference of £792,306, 2s. 6d., which, deducted from the former sum mentioned, leaves a balance of £197,516, 12s. 10d.,—the difference between the assets as published and the assets that were disclosed in the books of the Bank. (Q.) They are understated to that extent? (A.) Yes. The amount in the balance-sheet is £12,126,151, 5s. 9d., and the true amount is £14,105,667, 18s. 7d. The result is that about two million is taken off each side of the account, and with under and over statements upon both sides of it. There is under-statement of certain items, over-statement of certain others, and a general deduction. Coming to the liabilities, the first branch is—"Deposits at head office and branches, and balance at credit of banking correspondents," £8,364,056, 18s. 5d. That is understated to the extent of £1,006,216, 12s. 10d., arising in the following way:—I find that the deposit account balances have been entirely omitted, amounting to £455,444, 5s. 10d. I find that deposit accounts credited are deducted in error in the abstract, £1346, 16s. 6d. Credit account balances have been entirely omitted, £147,468, 16s. 11d. Balance due to London and Provincial Banks, £14,216, 15s. 2d.; that has been omitted. Adjusting account of interest due by the Bank, £11,405, 13s. 2d. has been omitted entirely. (Q.) You are giving us what makes up that total of £1,006,000? (A.) Yes. I find that cross accounts have been deducted in error amounting to £376,334, 5s. 3d.,—making in all, £1,006,216, under the first branch. There is nothing wrong under the second branch,—"Bank notes in circulation in Scotland and the Isle of Man." Third branch—"Drafts outstanding, due, or with currency not exceeding twenty-one days," &c., £1,315,373, 17s. 1d., are overstated to the extent of £973,300. I find no explanation at all in the books of that £973,300. These two sums amount together to £1,979,516, 12s. 10d., which are the total under-statements of the liabilities of the Bank at this balance. There is stated as at profit and loss in the balance-sheet, £136,365, 10s. 3d. (Q.) Have you any observations to make upon that item? (A.) In the first place, of that sum there was drawn forward from the previous balance the sum of £10,602, 16s. 2d., leaving as the revenue of the year, £125,762, 14s. 1d. I get that from the profit and loss account in the books of the Bank, showing the earnings derived from the use of capital. I made up a memorandum of interest chargeable to the eight largest debtors of the Bank. The amount of the interest is £125,763, 12s. 8d., being about 18s. 7d. under what the sum declared as dividend was that year. (Q.) Did it appear from the books of the Bank that this interest had been paid upon the accounts? (A.) No. They were added to the debts of the parties. (Q.) In the profit and loss account, which showed the trade profits of the Bank for the year, were they entered as profits received? (A.) They first came in under a general entry in that way as interest received, but it really was a general entry of interest added to the debts of the various parties, and transferred to the credit of profit and loss account. (Q.) So that, in point of fact, the divisible profit and loss would be payable out of capital? (A.) It seems so. (Q.) Leaving a claim against these parties for the profit supposed to have been made? (A.) Undoubtedly—added to their debts. (Q.) Is the interest upon the accounts of these firms dealt with in precisely the same way in the profit and loss account and in the balance-sheets in the next two years? (A.) In precisely the same way all through. (Q.) It is distributed amongst the shareholders as if it were money earned and in hand? (A.) It is indeed. (Q.) Although it only subsisted as a debt against these men? (A.) It only subsisted as a debt—increasing the liability. (Q.) Are the alterations made on the balance-sheets of subsequent years much the same as in 1876? (A.) They are all entirely on the same lines, with the aggravation at the ultimate balance of heavier sums transferred in the same way. (Q.) And for the first time in that balance-sheet there is a conversion—if you follow the scroll abstract—of balances on credit account into gold in the Bank coffers? (A.) Yes, to the amount of £200,000. (Q.) What was the reserve fund in 1876? (A.) The amount of the reserve fund in the balance-sheet published to the shareholders was £450,000. That was raised from time to time by any surplus that may have been at the credit of profit and loss transferred annually to the fund called Reserve Fund; but I am prepared to submit to you that it is an entirely fictitious entry of the amount now stated in the balance-sheet for 1876 at £450,000. (Q.) On what ground do you come to that conclusion? (A.) On the ground that there has been transferred to interest account sums of interest on assets that were yielding no return at all, and a sum equivalent to the amount said to be at the credit of this account. (Q.) You are still speaking of 1876? (A.) Yes. In the balance ledger for 1876 there is at the credit of what they call a railway and debenture account a large sum, and of that there is a sum of £351,330 of interest debited to it that had really never been earned, but simply charged upon this account. In 1862, there has been charged to this railway and debenture account a sum of £16,046, 0s. 6d.; in 1863, £20,551, 10s. 10d.; in 1864, £22,492, 5s. 3d.

By the Lord Justice-Clerk—(Q.) Are these sums carried to the reserve fund which in reality had no existence at all? (A.) Not directly to the reserve fund, but they are interest charged on these inoperative accounts; and, in process of time, transferred to profit and loss account, and then from profit and loss account to the reserve fund.

By the Lord Advocate—(Q.) There having been no receipts during the period? (A.) None. (Q.) What is the total of them? (A.) For the last three years there are receipts:—for 1871, £45,762, 15s. 11d., when there was earned £16,009, 12s. 1d.; for 1872, £46,325, 18s. 10d., when there was earned £17,280, 14s. 11d. (Q.) When you say earned, what precisely do you mean? (A.) The natural dividend accruing upon this stock. In 1873, £47,820, 2s. 8d., when there was earned £16,744, 17s. The gross receipts from 1862 to 1873 only amount to £50,090, 18s. 10d., while the gross debits to interest account amount to £401,421, 0s. 10d., leaving a nett overcharge of £351,330, 2s. (Q.) Do you mean that, in point of fact, they credit themselves as if they had £400,000 coming from that source? (A.) That is so. (Q.) Whilst in point of fact only £50,000 came from it? (A.) That is so. The next item is that the Bank held stock of their own, and from time to time revalued their own stock, and this revalue they transferred in the same way to interest account, then to profit and loss account, and ultimately to reserve fund. In 1864, they revalued the stock, and transferred £15,858. (Q.) You need not give the details? (A.) Well, between 1864 and 1875 the gross is £128,854, 7s. 1d.; and, added to the interest on the railway debenture account, the gross sum is £480,184, 9s. 1d., entirely absorbing the reserve fund. (Q.) Look at the published balance-sheet for 1877, and beginning with assets, head No. 1, tell me what over or under-statement, if any, there were? (A.) For the balance-sheet of 1877 the under-statements amount to £3,227,154, 12s. 8d. (Q.) That is the total under-statement of what? (A.) Of the assets under the first branch.—£3,227,154, 12s. 8d., the balance-sheet disclosing £8,758,838, 17s. 8d., while the true amount was £11,985,993, 10s. 4d. Then head II. of the assets in the balance-sheet is understated to the extent of £52,961, 19s. 10d. Head III., under the gold, was understated to the extent of £30,000, and the credit accounts still have a transfer from branch I. to branch III. of the three items formerly referred to, amounting to £751,775. (Q.) Done just as in the previous year? (A.) Yes, making the gross under-statement of the year to be £2,558,341, 12s. 6d. (Q.) About half a million more under-statement than the year before? (A.) That is so. (Q.) The actual amount of their transactions was increasing by half a million, but it is brought down to about the same level? (A.) Yes. Then the liabilities were understated to the extent of £1,151,518, 13s. 5d. (Q.) That is the first head? (A.) Yes; the balance-sheet disclosing £8,382,711, 12s. 10d, while the true amount was £9,534,230, 6s. 3d. From the second branch there is deducted £76,110,—understated to that extent; and from the third branch there is a sum of £1,330,712, 19s. 1d., making the difference between the published abstract and the true. The liabilities in the published abstract are £12,095,442, 6s. 5d., while the true amount was £14,653,783, 18s. 11d. (Q.) How about profit and loss in this year? (A.) The profit and loss disclosed at the credit in the published balance-sheet was £148,501, 12s. 6d., but of this there was brought forward from last year £19,990, 10s. 3d., leaving as the natural revenue of the year £128,511, 2s. 3d., and the interest on the same eight chief debtors amounts to £128,998, 19s. 9d., being more by £487, 17s. 6d. than the dividend declared. (Q.) Is the reserve fund in 1877 brought out in the same way as you have explained? (A.) It was entirely absorbed in 1876, and, of course, continues to be so until now. Then in 1878, the first branch of the assets is understated to the extent of £3,520,913, 11s. 8d.; the balance-sheet disclosing £8,484,466, 9s. 2d., while the true sum is £12,005,380, 0s. 10d. The second branch has an under-statement of the heritable property amounting to £48,698, 7s. 6d. The third branch this year has a transfer from the credit accounts of £200,000 as reserve gold, and the former entries of £751,000 now appear as £926,764, the gross difference being £1,146,286, 5s. 10d., and the difference between the true and the published assets being, the balance-sheet disclosed, £11,892,593, 11s. 8d., while the true sum is £14,315,917, 5s. 1d. (Q.) The two sides of the account were larger really in this than in any of the two previous years? (A.) Yes; the transactions were all larger. (Q.) Whereas, in point of fact, they are shown on the whole to have been the same, or nearly £300,000 less? (A.) Yes. Then on the liabilities side in 1878, the liabilities under the first branch are understated to the extent of £941,284, 13s. 5d. The balance sheet discloses £8,102,001, 0s. 4d., while the true sum is £9,043,285, 13s. 9d., errors in the same line as those I have read out from the first balance sheet. Under the second branch there is deducted notes in error, amounting to £89,031. Under the third branch there is omitted entirely the difference between the true and the published amount of bills payable, £1,393,008, the actual amount being £2,881,252, 18s. 6d., while the abstract only discloses

£1,488,244, 18s. 6d., giving the difference referred to of £1,393,008. The profit and loss for this year instructs that there was a credit entry of £142,095, 12s. 10d., whereof there had been transferred from last year's account £17,001, 12s., leaving only, as the natural revenue of the year, £125,094, 0s. 4d.; and the interest upon the eight large debts, already referred, to for the year amount to £125,875, 9s., being an excess of the dividend declared of £781, 8s. 8d. (Q.) Is that an ordinary mode of dealing with a profit or loss account? (A.) Quite an ordinary mode. (Q.) To enter in it interests not received? (A.) Quite a usual circumstance. (Q.) Was it a correct entry in this case? (A.) I think it was, if it had been paid. (Q.) But that is just what I wanted to know. I asked you if it was a correct entry to insert in a profit and loss account that which had not been paid? (A.) At this particular balance I should have said it was a correct entry; but, looking to the fact that for the previous years the interest had not been paid, it was not a correct entry. But for any one year by itself, it is quite a correct entry to transfer to interest account the interest upon any debt. (Q.) But not in a case where the interest is standing out unpaid from year to year, and simply made an addition to the debt? (A.) I should say not, where it has been continued from year to year unpaid.

By Mr Balfour—(Q.) I suppose you merely examined these books and the abstracts as an accountant does, and not having that knowledge extrinsic of the books which the officials of the Bank might have? (A.) I certainly did it as an accountant, but I got all the knowledge that the officials could give me. (Q.) But at all events, you did it merely taking the books of the Bank on the one part, and the abstracts on the other? (A.) Entirely so. (Q.) About this manner in which interest was treated, I understand you to say that if it had not been that the accounts had not been producing interest in previous years, you would have thought it was quite right to charge interest upon them, and to bring that into profit and loss? (A.) Yes; but of course I have the knowledge here that they were not paying the interest, and they were not paying the principal, but both principal and interest were being accumulated to an enormous amount. (Q.) In other words, you formed the opinion that these were bad or doubtful debts? (A.) I certainly did. (Q.) And it is upon the view that these were bad or doubtful debts that you think interest was wrongly charged upon them? (A.) Entirely so. (Q.) Apart from that view, and but for that view, what was done would have been quite right? (A.) I should say so. If the debt was to be paid, and the interest was to be paid, it was all in order. (Q.) And I suppose, in the books of the Bank, the interest was carried from profit and loss in the way you have described? (A.) It is so. (Q.) Being the usual way? (A.) The usual way. (Q.) So that, with regard to the manner of treating the interest, there is not a disconformity between the abstract and the books of the Bank? (A.) Not in the very least. On the contrary, they agree. (Q.) And if the abstract had not treated the interest in the way you have described, it would have departed in that matter from the books of the Bank? (A.) No doubt it would. (Q.) You said something about the American debentures, that arrears of interest were charged upon these? (A.) Yes; all through the years that I deponed to. (Q.) Did you find from the books of the Bank that these debentures had begun to pay interest latterly? (A.) Yes, I see that now. I saw it for the last three years. They have been producing a very fair return, but they are not producing the return by one-half that is charged in the books of the Bank against them. (Q.) That may be, but they have begun now to produce a return; and whether the whole may be paid or not is a matter, I suppose, beyond your knowledge? (A.) I could not say.

By Mr Mackintosh—I know Mr Taylor. I have known him for a very long time—for upwards of fifteen years. I have been in the way of meeting him very frequently in business. (Q.) What opinion do you hold as to his character? (A.) Do you mean in the light of the present case, or prior to the present case? (Q.) I mean as a man of integrity? (A.) Well, I think a very great deal of Mr Taylor. I always considered him to be a very honourable and a very upright gentleman, and it was a very great pleasure to me to meet Mr Taylor at any time.

By the Dean of Faculty—(Q.) Has there been any interest charged upon these American bonds except the £40,000 that was remitted home from America in payment of the interest? (A.) Yes. (Q.) During the last three years? (A.) No, not during the last three years; but there were a number of years when there was no interest got at all, and it was charged then. (Q.) But there has been nothing charged during the last three years except what was actually got? (A.) Oh, no. There is a regular charge in the books of the Bank for interest. (Q.) But not in excess of what was got? (A.) It is in excess of what was got. (Q.) During the last three years? (A.) During the last three years it is in excess of what was got. (Q.) Just explain that to me. There was 7 per cent. of a return obtained. Is there anything else charged? (A.) I am not aware that there was 7 per cent. obtained. (Q.) Is there anything more than 7 per cent. charged? (A.) I will read each item for the last three years. In 1871 there is charged in the books of the Bank, and credited to interest account—— (Q.) I am not speaking of 1871. I am speaking of the last three years, and I ask you to keep to them? (A.) I never made a single reference to the interest of this account since 1873. I only quoted to the Lord Advocate up to 1873, because since 1873 they have been drawing a very fair return. (Q.) And there is nothing more charged in the books than what they drew? (A.) Nothing since 1873.

By the Lord Advocate—(Q.) What you said was not that during the years 1876, 1877, and 1878, there was not a dividend due upon that stock from America? (A.) No; I did not quote anything in these years. (Q.) I understood not; but what you stated as to the three years, as earnings that ought not fairly to have been entered in the books, was the interest upon this large account, amounting to about £125,000? (A.) Yes; in almost every year. (Q.) You stated that you thought that ought not to have been brought into profit and loss, because it was not in course of being received by the Bank? (A.) Certainly not; but that neither the debt nor the interest has been paid for some years.

By the Lord Justice-Clerk—(Q.) How, in your opinion, ought they to have dealt with the principal and interest? (A.) I think there was nothing to hinder them from adding interest to the debt that was due; but I think they should not have transferred that to a divisible account, and paid it away when they knew that they were not getting in the money. In course of time their coffers would have been empty. (Q.) Would you have carried it to bad and doubtful debts, or to a suspense account? (A.) I would have carried it to "Suspense account, No. 2" in the special circumstances of the case.

The Lord Advocate stated that this closed the evidence for the Crown, and intimated that he confined the charges against the panels to the first three charges in the indictment.

EVIDENCE FOR MR STEWART.

ALEXANDER MOORE.

By Mr MacLean—I am a chartered accountant in Glasgow, and a partner of the firm of Moore & Brown, accountants and stockbrokers there. I know Mr Stewart. I first became acquainted with him about twelve years ago. I was employed at that time professionally to adjust accounts—family accounts—in which his brother and he were interested. These accounts had been kept by one of his brothers, Mr Robert Stewart, and I was called in to adjust matters between them. Mr Stewart, up to 1874, was the leading partner in the firm of John Stewart & Co. That was a very old-standing firm in the wine trade, and one which has done a very considerable business for many years. (Q.) Were you called in at any time to deal with the accounts of that firm? (A.) I was called in, in the year 1872-3, to adjust the partnership accounts on a dissolution. The partners up to that time were Mr Stewart, his brother, and Mr Stewart's own son. The dissolution of the firm was carried through in the year 1874-5. Since that date the firm, which is now Stewart, Pott, & Company, has consisted of Mr Stewart and his son. Upon a dissolution, Mr Robert Stewart took over a portion of the business, the distillery portion, into his own hands. Since the dissolution I have audited the balance sheets of the new firm yearly. Under the old firm of John Stewart and Co., I think the bookkeeping department was principally under the supervision of Mr Robert Stewart. For the firm of Stewart, Pott, & Co. I have merely audited the balance sheets since the dissolution. I have done so for the satisfaction of the partners, but chiefly, I think, from Mr John Stewart's want of knowledge of bookkeeping. (Q.) Is he deficient in his knowledge of bookkeeping? (A.) He has often expressed himself so in my hearing. (Q.) Had you any reason to doubt that? (A.) I believe he is deficient altogether in the knowledge of figures and accounting. (Q.) Apart from that, did he show a desire that everything should be correct and properly stated? (A.) He was always extremely anxious that everything should be right. (Q.) You have had occasion, in consequence of the employment you have spoken of, to meet with him often? (A.) Very often. (Q.) What opinion have you formed of him? (A.) That he was a highly honourable man. (Q.) Upon the stoppage of the Bank Mr Stewart and his firm, as we know, were indebted in certain sums of money to the Bank? (A.) They were. (Q.) He had a personal account, and his firm had the firm's account, in the City of Glasgow Bank? (A.) Yes. (Q.) Has Mr Stewart assigned to you investments of considerable value to meet the claim? (A.) Immediately on the stoppage of the Bank, he assigned to me investments to the amount of his liability to the Bank as a debtor, and his firm's debt as well. (Q.) So that upon these overdrafts the Bank will not lose one shilling? (A.) I cannot say as to that. They are not realised yet. (Q.) But so far as appears? (A.) The amount was equivalent, so far as appeared, to the debt. (Q.) Mr Stewart remains a shareholder. Deducting what he has assigned to you in satisfaction of the overdrafts, what property remains to Mr Stewart to meet the calls which will be made upon him as a shareholder? (A.) I may say that Mr Stewart executed a trust assignation in my favour. Taking his investments in the New Zealand Land Company at their par value, I estimate that Mr Stewart's assets exceeded his liabilities by £85,000 at that date. (Q.) And is it consistent with your knowledge that Mr Stewart has been, during all the years that you have known him, a comparatively rich man, and with his means steadily increasing? (A.) I examined as to his means in the year 1871, and the result then was made about the same as it was at October, when the Bank stopped, £85,000. (Q.) Then he has been worth about £85,000 during all the time he has been a director of the City of Glasgow Bank? (A.) Yes.

By the Lord Justice-Clerk.—(Q.) Did I understand the £85,000 to be over and above the securities assigned to you for the advance from the Bank? (A.) No; the total value of his assets over his whole liabilities. (Q.) How much is the balance for which you had securities assigned? (A.) £44,000.

By Mr MacLean.—(Q.) And over and above that he has a fortune of £85,000? (A.) No.

By the Lord Justice-Clerk—(Q.) No; £45,000. His fortune, I understand, was £85,000 altogether? (A.) Yes. (Q.) But he owed £45,000 odd to the Bank? (A.) Yes; for which he assigned security. (Q.) And his fortune is the balance? (A.) Yes.

By Mr MacLean—(Q.) Let us understand about this—is it after making provision for the payment of the overdrafts that the balance of £85,000 remains? (A.) It is.

By the Lord Justice-Clerk—(Q.) You said the reverse just now. I asked you whether out of the £85,000 the amount due to the Bank must come? (A.) After paying the Bank, there is £85,000 remaining. (Q.) You have got securities for the amount of the Bank's debt, and over and above that there is a fortune of £85,000. Is that so? (A.) The Bank is secured out of a certain portion of these assets. (Q.) Will you answer my question. You have got securities to the extent of the Bank's debt, and Mr Stewart has over and above, when the Bank is paid, £85,000? (A.) Yes.

By Mr MacLean—(Q.) Then it follows, from what you have just said, that his fortune in 1871, which you stated at £85,000, had been increased by the £44,000? (A.) Not at all. Mr Stewart's total assets in October last amounted to £120,000; his total liabilities amounted to £34,000.

By the Lord Justice-Clerk—(Q.) How much did he owe to the Bank? (A.) Of these assets he assigned to the Bank £44,000 odds, in security of his personal debt and of his firm's debt.

By Mr MacLean—(Q.) As an individual, and as representing the company, the amount owing to the Bank was what? (A.) It was £44,000 altogether. (Q.) Now go back and give us the assets and liabilities as at 1871. (A.) In 1871, Mr Stewart's total assets amounted to £91,000, and his personal liability to the Bank at that time was £5300. Mr Stewart had opened his account with the City of Glasgow Bank a very long time back. I don't know how long. [Shown Bank book.] I see from that book that the account was opened on 23d July 1868, with a sum placed to his credit of £5600. The account of Stewart, Pott, & Co. with the City of Glasgow Bank was opened in June 1874. They had previously dealt with the Commercial. The account there was closed by a payment to the Commercial of £18,008. The average value of the stock in trade of Stewart, Pott, & Co. was about £10,000, and their outstanding debts £20,000. Their sales, on the average of the last three years, have exceeded £60,000.

By the Lord Advocate—(Q.) You say there was £34,000 of indebtedness against £120,000 of assets. Was any part of that £34,000 bank debt? (A.) Yes. (Q.) To what extent? (A.) £11,000, which is the balance of his private account. (Q.) After deducting that £34,000 of liabilities, that left about £85,000? (A.) Yes. New Zealand land shares are what is assigned in security of the debt which he owed to the Bank, and the debt which his firm owed to the Bank. (Q.) Covering the debt which is included in the £34,000? (A.) Yes.

By the Lord Justice-Clerk—The whole amount of Mr Stewart's indebtedness as an individual is £34,000 odds. The debts of the firm are about £45,000, in addition to the £34,000. I do not take the assets of the firm into calculation in the £120,000; I take Mr Stewart's capital into account.

JAMES HAY STEWART.

By Mr Trayner—I am joint-manager of the Commercial Bank at its head office in Glasgow, and have been so since February 1865. I know Mr John Stewart. I knew his firm of John Stewart & Co. It had an account in our Bank, which was closed in 1874. That account had been in the Bank from February 1840. Throughout the whole period of my acquaintance with that account, it was a most satisfactory account to the Bank. (Q.) Was it an account which in 1874 your Bank would have been very glad to have retained? (A.) Yes; I rather think we regretted the fact of its leaving us. At that date there was an overdraft of above £18,000. That overdraft was not one to cause us any uneasiness in the least, looking to the persons with whom we were dealing, and to their business. We had no security for it, except the credit and responsibility of the partners of the firm.

WILLIAM M'KINNON.

By Mr Trayner—I am a chartered accountant in Glasgow. I was one of the liquidators of the Western Bank, and I was asked to be one of the liquidators of the City of Glasgow Bank, but I declined. I have looked at the books of the City of Glasgow Bank, with the view of giving certain information. I have seen the balance ledger which is signed and docqueted by the directors. It is annually docqueted. I have looked at the accounts for 1876, 1877, and 1878 respectively. (Q.) Are these accounts, docqueted for these respective years in the balance ledger, correct according to the entries in the Bank's books? (A.) They are quite conform to the books of the Bank. (Q.) And, as a balance, are they framed upon correct principles? (A.) Yes; I believe them to be so.

By the Lord-Advocate—(Q.) I suppose, when you say that, you mean that they correctly give effect to the entries in the books of the Bank? (A.) Precisely. (Q.) You are not indicating any opinion as to the correctness of the entries in the books in the Bank? (A.) No; I am giving an opinion upon the balances that appear in the balance ledger. (Q.) But it reflects what is in the books? (A.) Quite. I have not found any entry of £973,000 in the balance ledger. I have seen it in the cash book of 1873.

By the Lord Justice Clerk—It is quite traceable. It is very difficult to say what it is. (Q.) But you say you can trace it? (A.) Yes; I can trace it in the books quite well. It represents a credit entry. It represents in the books a credit entry as regards bills payable for £973,000. (Q.) On what debts? (A.) On bills payable to the Bank, and also on foreign and colonial credits. (Q.) Is it so dealt with in the abstract of the balance? (A.) The weekly abstract. (Q.) The abstract balance, and in the weekly abstract; how is it dealt with there? (A.) It is dealt with there as a debit and a credit. (Q.) That is to say, it is taken out altogether? (A.) The effect is to take it out of both sides. (Q.) Then what do you gather from that fact was the nature of this sum of £973,000? (A.) The effect of it is to decrease the foreign and colonial credits. (Q.) But what do you gather was the nature of the transaction out of which it arose—are the bills retired? (A.) No; it is a decrease of the bills payable. I cannot tell why it was put there. I cannot find anything in the books to account for its being there. When a debt is irrecoverably bad, it should be written off altogether; that is to say, when the directors come to be satisfied that it is hopeless. (Q.) Where the manager or directors of a bank are not satisfied that a debt is hopeless, and hope it may be paid, but where there is no incoming for two or three years, what is the proper way of dealing with it? (A.) I should say that suspense would be the proper way to deal with it. (Q.) A suspense account? (A.) Yes. (Q.) You would not carry the interest on such debts to profit and loss in the first instance? (A.) No;

unless there was some very good reason for so treating it. (Q.) But on the whole, the proper way would be not to write it off altogether? (A.) No. (Q.) But to put it into suspense? (A.) Yes.

EVIDENCE FOR MR POTTER.

CUNNINGHAM SMITH.

By Mr Balfour—I am a merchant in Glasgow. I am a son of the late William Smith of Carbeth-Guthrie (who was at one time Lord Provost of Glasgow), and nephew of the late Mr James Smith of Jordanhill. I am a partner of Potter, Wilson, & Co., merchants, Glasgow. Mr Lewis Potter is the senior partner. I joined the firm in 1853, and have continued to be Mr Lewis Potter's partner ever since. The business we have carried on has been principally a commission business. It has been very extensive and very lucrative. (Q.) What was Mr Lewis Potter's share of the profit of that business of late years? (A.) £5000 or £6000 a year. (Q.) From that business alone? (A.) Yes. He was also a partner of the separate business of Lewis Potter & Co., owners or agents for a line of steamers trading between Dublin and Liverpool. I believe that also was an extensive and lucrative business. I have been told that Mr Lewis Potter's average income from that business was £3000, but I have no means of knowing. I know that he is possessed of a valuable landed estate—Udston. I do not know the return from it. I am aware that, besides its land rent, it is a valuable mineral estate. It is in the neighbourhood of Hamilton. There is a very valuable coal-field opening up there now. (Q.) As to Mr Potter's business qualities—what departments of the business has he directed his attention to, and what has he left to other's? (A.) Latterly, he left the details of the business very much to myself and to his son. (Q.) And in what respects has he taken part in the business? (A.) For some years he has taken very little part in the business. He has been gradually withdrawing from an active share in the business. (Q.) And has he avoided going into details? (A.) Very much. (Q.) As regards figures—was that a matter that he concerned himself with, or did he leave that to the subordinates? (A.) Always to the subordinates. (Q.) As regards his style of living and expenditure—was he very moderate with reference to his means? (A.) Very moderate indeed. (Q.) With what banks were your firm's account or accounts kept? (A.) The British Linen Company, the National Bank of Scotland, and the City of Glasgow Bank. (Q.) How long has the firm kept an account with the British Linen? (A.) Ever since I joined it, and, I believe, ever since it was commenced. (Q.) Did they keep an account there from 1846? (A.) I believe so. (Q.) Down to the present time? (A.) Yes. (Q.) Was there any particular reason why an account was kept with the British Linen? (A.) I fancy because Mr Patrick Brodie, agent of the Bank in Glasgow, was a brother-in-law of Mr Wilson, the original partner of Potter, Wilson, & Co. (Q.) How long has the firm kept an account with the National Bank? (A.) When I joined there was an account kept for the Clyde and Australian Shipping Company, of which Potter, Wilson, & Co. were the agents. After that company was dissolved, we were requested by the Bank to continue our account on our own account. (Q.) Were some of the partners of the Clyde and Australian Shipping Co. interested in the National Bank? (A.) Yes. (Q.) And that led to its being kept there? (A.) Yes. (Q.) And it has been continued ever since? (A.) Yes. (Q.) When did it begin to be kept at the National Bank? (A.) Before 1853; how long before

I cannot tell. I recollect Mr Potter becoming a director of the City of Glasgow Bank. After that, as before, the accounts with the British Linen and National Banks continued to be kept. (Q.) Did the requirements of your business, or any requirements of Mr Potter's, as far as you know, make the City Bank of importance to your firm? (A.) Not at all. (Q.) You did not need anything of it? (A.) No. (Q.) After he became a director of the City Bank, did the officials express a desire to have a share of his business or of the business of the firm? (A.) I believe so. (Q.) And was there an account opened there also? (A.) Yes. (Q.) Kept first at the West End City branch? (A.) When I first joined. (Q.) And afterwards transferred to the head office? (A.) Yes. (Q.) Was that a drawing account or a discount account? (A.) The West End was entirely a drawing account, so far as I recollect. (Q.) After the Bank asked and got a share of the business, had your firm sometimes credits from them? (A.) Sometimes. (Q.) Had you credits of the same kind from the British Linen? (A.) At one time. (Q.) Was anything that you had in the way of credits given in the ordinary way of banking business? (A.) Yes. (Q.) Is that a lucrative branch of a bank's business? (A.) I believe so. (Q.) Are you aware that there were certain accounts standing unsettled between Mr Potter, or the firm of Potter, Wilson, & Co. and Morton & Co.? (A.) Yes. They were under reference for many years. An award has been pronounced very lately by Mr Hunter. (Q.) Upon those accounts was your firm a considerable creditor of Morton's? (A.) Yes. (Q.) Did you ever have a conversation with Mr Potter from which you could form an opinion as to whether he was uneasy as to Morton or his credit? (A.) Yes. Mr Potter seemed to believe that Morton's share in the New Zealand and Australian Land Co. would more than cover all his liabilities. (Q.) Did he appear to be at all uneasy about getting all his debt paid? (A.) No, I think not,—in time. I knew that Mr Potter himself was a large shareholder in that Land Co., and a director. (Q.) So that he had the means of forming an opinion as to the value of its shares? (A.) Yes.

By the Lord Justice-Clerk—I do not know to what extent he was a shareholder in that company.

By Mr Balfour—(Q.) From your intercourse with Mr Potter, can you say whether he thought highly of the present value and future prospects of the stock of that company? (A.) Yes. (Q.) Did the business relations which his firm had with the colonies give him good opportunities of knowledge on that subject? (A.) Very good. (Q.) In certain business transactions on the part of your firm, did you sometimes have occasion to get guarantees? (A.) Yes. (Q.) And have you sometimes had guarantees from the City of Glasgow Bank? (A.) We had. (Q.) Was your object in getting guarantees to have the caution of some person or body which was regarded as safe? (A.) Exactly. (Q.) And were these taken as being so? (A.) Yes. (Q.) From your connections with Mr Potter in regard to these, could you form an opinion as to his view of the worth of the guarantee of the City of Glasgow Bank? (A.) He seemed to consider that it was quite safe. (Q.) Then whenever he got the guarantee of the City Bank, he felt that he was quite safe? (A.) Yes. (Q.) You have had 25 years' experience of Mr Potter. Have you always found him an honourable, upright, and straightforward man in his dealings? (A.) Quite so. (Q.) Not a man who would be guilty of any impropriety or fraud? (A.) Certainly not.

By the Lord Advocate—(Q.) Had you any knowledge of the internal management of the City of Glasgow Bank? (A.) None whatever. I should think Mr Potter was a director of it nearly the whole time of our business connection, but I am not quite sure when he joined. (Q.) Did he, or did he not, take an interest in the management of the Bank? (A.) He attended the meetings regularly; I know no more. (Q.) You know nothing of his connection with the Bank except the fact that he went to the meetings? (A.) Nothing. (Q.)

That is all you know? (A.) That is all I know. (Q.) Did your firm have any transactions which might be called financing on account of the City Bank? (A.) Yes. (Q.) Did Mr Potter know of it? (A.) Yes. (Q.) Did he take any interest in that? (A.) Yes. (Q.) Much? (A.) He knew of it; it was done with his knowledge. (Q.) Who, on behalf of your firm, transacted in regard to these matters with the Bank? Was it you or Mr Potter? (A.) I did principally. (Q.) With whom did you transact? (A.) With the Bank. (Q.) Can you not name anybody? (A.) I scarcely ever had any—with Mr Stronach, if with any one; but merely with the officials of the Bank as officials. (Q.) But who arranged the matter between your firm and the Bank? (A.) The matter was arranged first by Mr Potter. I took charge of the details after it was arranged. (Q.) You said Mr Potter did not know much about details? (A.) I took all the details; he arranged the matter first. (Q.) Had he knowledge sufficient for that? (A.) I should think so; but he never interfered with the details. (Q.) But he had quite sufficient knowledge to arrange the transaction beforehand? (A.) He arranged the transaction beforehand. (Q.) Do you think he understood the transaction which he arranged? (A.) Certainly. (Q.) But you did not think him capable of going into the details of it; do you mean to say that? (A.) I did not mean to say that; I say he did not actually do so. (Q.) But do you mean to convey the impression that Mr Potter, though capable of arranging a transaction, was unable to understand the details of it? (A.) No; I simply said that he practically did not attend to the details of it. (Q.) What was the character of those financing transactions of which you conducted the details? (A.) The City of Glasgow Bank bought certain shares in the New Zealand and Australian Land Company from Potter, Wilson, & Co., and Holmes, White, & Co. (Q.) And it was to enable the Bank to meet their acceptances against these shares that you financed for them? (A.) Yes. (Q.) Tell us how that financing was carried out in detail? (A.) The City of Glasgow Bank accepted drafts by Holmes, White, & Co. of Melbourne, in Potter, Wilson, & Co.'s favour; the bills were discounted by Potter, Wilson, & Co. (Q.) Where did these bills come from? (A.) From Melbourne. (Q.) Who signed them there? (A.) Holmes, White, & Co. (Q.) As drawers? (A.) As drawers. (Q.) And then they were sent home? (A.) Yes. (Q.) What became of them when they came home signed by Holmes, White, & Co.,—where were they put? (A.) They were discounted.. (Q.) Where were they kept after they came home? (A.) They were kept by Potter, Wilson, & Co. (Q.) Where were they kept? (A.) In their office. (Q.) Who kept them? (A.) I kept them. (Q.) How many came home at a time? (A.) Fifty or a hundred. (Q.) Did not Mr Potter keep these himself? (A.) Sometimes—partly; they were kept in the office. (Q.) Had you a bundle apiece? (A.) No. (Q.) What did you do with them? (A.) After they were accepted by the Bank, they were discounted, and the proceeds paid into the Bank. (Q.) What was done before they were presented to the Bank for acceptance? (A.) I don't understand you.

By the Lord Justice-Clerk—(Q.) They were filled up? (A.) They were filled up.

By the Lord Advocate—(Q.) Was there a date put in? (A.) Certainly. (Q.) By whom? (A.) One of our clerks. (Q.) Under whose directions? (A.) Under my direction. (Q.) What date did you make him put in? (A.) The date the mail left Melbourne. (Q.) The date about two months before? (A.) Yes. (Q.) And then they were presented to the Bank for acceptance, and then you discounted them? (A.) Yes. (Q.) What did you get for all that trouble? (A.) Nothing. (Q.) Had you no commission upon it? (A.) None. (Q.) What was the object—there must have been some object—in dating these bills a month or two back, so as to make it appear that they had been drawn in Melbourne? Why did you do that? (A.) To save trouble; the bills came home in batches of that kind, and we filled them up as if they had come from Melbourne by that mail, which they would have done otherwise. (Q.) Suppose you had filled in the date when the bill was presented to the Bank, what would have been the consequence? (A.) I cannot say. (Q.) Do you say that seriously? (A.) I don't understand you. (Q.) I am sorry for it, sir. Would you have had difficulty in discounting them if you had not put in a mail date prior to—— (A.) Probably. (Q.) Did you not anticipate that you would have had difficulty, sir? (A.) I never thought of a difficulty; it never struck me. (Q.) Why did you not put in the real date? (A.) Because it was the natural date at which the bills should have come forward. (Q.) Did you not wish to conceal that the bills were really filled up in this country? (A.) Yes. (Q.) Why did you wish to conceal that? Was it for no reason; and if it was for a reason, be so good as to state it? Why did you wish to conceal it? (A.) I can hardly explain it, it seems to be so natural. The bills were filled up at the date at which they ought to have come from Melbourne, to save the troubie of having them sent out and back again every mail. (Q.) But what would have gone wrong if he had known that they had not gone out to Melbourne, for that was the thing that you wanted to conceal?

Mr Balfour—That was the Lord Advocate's expression.

The Lord Advocate—The witness assented to it.

The Lord Justice-Clerk—(Q.) Was that what you meant to say? (A.) That we did not wish it to be known. (Q.) That the bills came blank, and you filled them up? (A.) Yes.

By the Lord Advocate—(Q.) What was there which might have followed, if it had been known, which led you to desire that it should not be known? (A.) Possibly there might have been difficulty in discounting them. (Q.) Why? (A.) Because the bankers might have thought that they were finance bills. (Q.) They were finance bills? (A.) They were finance bills as far as the City of Glasgow Bank was concerned. (Q.) And you did not wish any suspicion of that fact to get abroad? (A.) No. (Q.) Now, I ask whether you do not know the fact that these bills were filled up in your office, and dated at your office, in case the clerks at the Bank should see it done, or know that it was done? (A.) No, I do not. (Q.) You don't know that? (A.) I do not know that. (Q.) In point of fact, they were filled up at your office? (A.) Yes. (Q.) And not at the Bank? (A.) Not at the Bank. (Q.) Land was purchased by the Bank in or near Poverty Bay? (A.) Yes. (Q.) And that land was taken in the names of the individual partners of your firm? (A.) Yes. (Q.) Was that purchase made truly on behalf of the Bank? (A.) Yes. (Q.) And did you finance to purchase money there too? (A.) Yes.

By Mr Balfour—Were your firm of Potter, Wilson, & Co. the agents in this country for Holmes, White, & Co.? (A.) They were. (Q.) And were those bills sent home by Holmes, White, & Co. to your firm as their agents? (A.) Yes. (Q.) And was what you did done as their agents? (A.) Yes. (Q.) With their authority? (A.) With their authority. (Q.) Did it in the least matter whether a bill sent home to be treated as you treated these had the date filled up in blank, and was then put out, or whether it was allowed to remain in Melbourne, and the date written on there, and then sent home? (A.) Certainly not. (Q.) Did it matter in the slightest degree to any human being? (A.) Not in the slightest degree.

Mr Balfour—I can give your Lordship the information which you asked as to the amount of the Land Company stock in the individual name of Mr Lewis Potter. It was, of ordinary stock, £37,608, and of A preference stock (4 per cent.), £25,073. Then there is some held by him and Hunter and Morton in trust.

By the Lord Justice-Clerk—(On the suggestion of the Lord Advocate.)—(Q.) Is your firm sequestrated? (A.) It is.

By Mr Balfour—[Shown list of proprietors in the Land Company.] I have seen this list. (Q.) It includes the names of a number of the best mercantile men and bankers, does it not? (A.) Yes. (Q.) Mention some of them? (A.) Colonel Hamilton, Mr Campbell of Camis Eskan, Mr Davidson of the Bank of Scotland, Mr Ducroz of London, Mr Robert Ewing, the late Mr Alexander Ewing, Mr Gourlay, and many other names that I know.

By the Lord Advocate—(Q.) How many shares does Colonel Campbell hold? (A.) ordinary stock, £2783; four per cent. preference, £1856. (Q.) And Mr James Morton? (A.) I know nothing of this, except from what has been handed to me. James Morton and James Nicol Fleming, merchants, Glasgow, are put down at £23,825. (Q.) And there are a good many City Bank names,—Matthew and Hunter? (A.) Yes. (Q.) James Nicol Fleming? (A.) Yes. (Q.) And Mr Potter? (A.) Yes.

By Mr Balfour—(Q.) Mr Davidson of the Bank of Scotland is there? (A.) Yes; he seems to be there. (Q.) For how much? (A.) £3340 ordinary stock, and £2227 preference. (Q.) And Mr Henry Davidson, his brother, also? (A.) Yes, £11,805. (Q.) Mr Gairdner of the Union Bank, and others? (A.) Yes.

[List put in.]

JOHN ALEXANDER POTTER.

By Mr Balfour.—I am a son of Mr Lewis Potter, and a partner of Potter, Wilson, & Co. Both Potter, Wilson, & Co., and Lewis Potter & Co., have been very long established firms, and successful. (Q.) What were your father's profits from Lewis Potter & Co.? (A.) From £2500 to £3000 a year, I believe. (Q.) So that he had about £8000 a year from his business? (A.) Yes. (Q.) Is he proprietor of the lands of Udston, Greenfield, and Burnbank, near Hamilton? (A.) Yes; previous to his sequestration. He bought Udston in 1853, Greenfield in 1857, and Burnbank in 1859. They cost a little under £40,000 altogether. There has been a very great rise in their value since he bought them. Minerals have been discovered in them, and are being worked. The properties were valued lately at £120,000. My father has been receiving a return of about £8000 a year from his land, including mineral, and, I should say, about £2000 from other investments. He was a man with an income of from £17,000 to £18,000 a year at the time the Bank stopped. His expenditure never exceeded £3000 a year, which included the expenditure of those members of his family whom he supported. He is a brother-in-law of Mr Bain, who was the manager of the Edinburgh branch; Mr Bain is married to his sister. Mr Bain has been a shareholder of the Bank for some time, and to the extent, I believe, of £1200 stock. A sister of Mr Potter, Mrs Davidson, was also a shareholder, at the time of the stoppage, to the amount of £1450 stock. To both of these persons the stoppage has been ruin.

By the Lord Advocate—(Q.) When did your father acquire his shares in the City Bank? (A.) I understand he had some before the stoppage of the Bank in 1857. (Q.) And then he had some when he became a director? (A.) I think he had his director's qualification at that time, because he was made a director shortly after the resuscitation of the Bank in 1857.

[Evidence closed, with the exception of that of Mr J. Wyllie Guild, to be taken to-morrow.]

EVIDENCE FOR MR TAYLOR.

HENRY TAYLOR.

By Mr Mackintosh.—I am a son of Mr William Taylor, and a partner with him in the firm of Henry Taylor & Sons, grain merchants. The firm was formed in 1835. The partners at that time were my grandfather, Henry Taylor; my uncle, Henry Taylor; and my father, William Taylor. I went into the business in 1861, and I was assumed a partner on 1st January 1868. The partners at that time were my father and my uncle, Patrick Taylor; my other uncle and my grandfather having previously died. Patrick Taylor retired on 1st January 1873, and since then my father and I have been the sole partners. Our business has been a large one. During the last five years the average turn-over of the firm would be about £650,000 per annum. Our business consists in importing grain from abroad, and selling it to our customers. Our books have always been regularly kept from the time I first entered the business. They have been regularly balanced at 31st December. Bad debts have invariably been written off, and for doubtful ones provision was made. We have had no speculative transactions in connection with our business; we have confined ourselves to the legitimate business of buying and selling. We have never had any accommodation bills at all. (Q.) When did your firm become customers of the City of Glasgow Bank? (A.) We have had an account with the City of Glasgow Bank ever since the formation of the Bank. When I went into the business in 1861 we had a regular account current, and a No. 2 account, which was the acceptances of the City Bank or the London Joint-Stock Bank, to our foreign correspondents. Our ordinary current account was kept in the Argyle Street (West End) branch. That account has continued to be kept there ever since till the stoppage of the Bank. Considerable sums have frequently been at our credit there. Account No. 2 has been in operation, during the last twenty years, to a greater or less account. In 1869, another account, No. 3, was opened. That was an account on which we subsequently obtained over-drafts. It continued in operation until the beginning of 1878. Prior to my father becoming a director of the Bank, we had occasionally and repeatedly obtained large advances from it. (Q.) How much? (A.) Sometimes we would have £50,000 or £60,000 of unsecured indebtedness to the Bank. (Q.) How long might that unsecured indebtedness last? (A.) For several months frequently. (Q.) The Bank, having accepted drafts on your account, gave you up the documents? (A.) Yes. (Q.) And that was under No. 2 account? (A.) Yes. We had also had advances on No. 3 account previous to 1871. At 31st December 1876, there was a balance at the debit of No. 3 account of £73,850, including interest. There was paid into the credit of that account, during 1877, £19,000 odds, and there was drawn out £14,000, so that the debit was reduced by £5000. In 1878 nothing was drawn out of that account at all. The account frequently fluctuated from time to time. It was squared off more than once. We had a discount account with the City of Glasgow Bank, and also a discount account with one of the other Scotch banks in Glasgow. In February 1878 we had £110,000 of bills discounted with that other bank, and, at the stoppage of the City of Glasgow Bank, we had £75,000 of bills discounted there. In the spring of 1877 we had bills discounted with the City of Glasgow Bank, to the amount of about £110,000. At the time of the stoppage of the Bank that had been reduced to about £90,000. (Q.) I believe some of the officials of the Bank had suggested it had better be curtailed? (A.) Yes; we were asked by Mr Stronach and Mr Murdoch, on one or two occasions, to reduce our discount account.

The reason they gave was just that they wished all their discount accounts reduced. We accordingly reduced our account to the amount I have stated. My father joined the board of the City of Glasgow Bank in 1871. At that time there was standing at his credit in the books of our firm £22,085. His private estate over and above amounted to £10,100,—valuing his securities at market prices. I can give the details if required. There was stock on the Glasgow and South-Western Railway, and some heritable property, and other assets. He was worth, at that time, about £32,000. That was exclusive of my own assets, and the assets of my uncle Patrick. The business of the firm continued very profitable down to 1874. In 1874 we made heavy losses. These losses were not of an amount sufficient to exhaust our means; we had always a large surplus of assets over liabilities. (Q.) And in 1876 and 1877 did you make considerable profits? (A.) Yes; we made good profits during those years. (Q.) At 1st January 1878, what would be your father's total means? What was the balance at his debit in the firm's books,—was it £5507? (A.) Yes. There was at the debit of partners altogether £11,900 odds. The private estates of the partners amounted to £22,000. I have details of that, if necessary. (Q.) For instance, there is Langbank, your father's estate; that was sold lately for £6500? (A.) Yes. It was bonded to the extent of £4000. There was also stock of the Glasgow and South-Western Railway of the value, at market price, of £2600 odds. There were shares in the Glasgow Corn Exchange then worth £300. There was a life policy with the Scottish Amicable Society of old date, the surrender value of which was then £400 odds. Then there was a share in a certain ship, for which my father paid £1000, and it was worth fully that it 1878. Then there was City of Glasgow Bank stock worth £5000, taking it at its market value. There were also Scottish Imperial Insurance Company's shares, worth about £1700; and shares of the Glasgow Storage Company (Limited), £2000—that is a very good concern. There were some shares of the State Line Shipping Company in liquidation, and also some shares of the new company as well. We valued the shares of the old company at £1 each, which was about £500, my father having paid a great deal more for them; and he paid for the new shares £5000, and these were valued at their cost price. Over and above these, there was furniture, &c. The total of his estate was £20,000, and there was £2000 of my own, made up of City Bank stock and my own dwelling-house. (Q.) So there was £22,000, from which the balance at the debit of the capital fell to be deducted, leaving a surplus of £10,000, according to the books? (A.) Yes. In addition to that, there was a sum of £6000 put aside in suspense account. The reason for that was, that in the end of February, before our balance had been finally adjusted, there were some bad debts that seemed likely to be made in Belfast, and, as we could not at that time exactly ascertain what the amount of these might be, we put £6000 to suspense account to meet any contingences that might arise. Our firm possessed a large property in Hope Street, Glasgow, for which they paid £40,000, and they expended £14,000 additional upon it. That was bought in 1874. It was valued in our books at £54,000, cost price. Property in that part of Glasgow rose very materially in value between 1874 and 1878, and in the beginning of 1878 we considered that property worth £16,000 more than the sum at which it stood in our books. That fell to be added to the sum I have mentioned; and, taking in the profit upon that property, the total balance in favour of my father and me would be about £32,000. Our firm lost largely, through customers becoming insolvent, directly after the stoppage of the Bank. (Q.) How did it happen that you came first to obtain this overdraft from the City of Glasgow Bank? (A.) In 1874, or towards the beginning of 1875, there was a change in the mode of conducting the American business, in which we were largely engaged. Up to that time the drafts of our American correspondents were invariably passed upon us free,—that is to say, the documents were sent to ourselves direct, and the drafts were drawn at sixty days' sight; but owing to the commercial panic in America the system was changed, and all documents were attached to the drafts, and required to be paid for before we could get possession of any of the goods at all. (Q.) In fact, you had to pay cash instead of getting credit? (A.) Yes. It was in connection with that change of circumstances that we got our overdraft. The advances from the Bank were got in the usual way. Either I or my father arranged them; but I generally got them,—either ourselves or our cashier. In the beginning of January 1878, we had a large stock of grain in hand,—not less, I think, than from £50,000 to £60,000 worth. It was entirely unburdened. Mr Stronach knew that we held grain largely. (Q.) Had you any debts to speak of except your debt to the Bank? (A.) Almost nothing at all. (Q.) Your stock was free, and your assets generally were free? (A.) Yes. My father was an original shareholder of the City of Glasgow Bank. He held at first, I think, £1080 stock. He accepted an allotment of £300 stock additional in 1866, for which he paid £390. In 1873 he accepted a further allotment of £300 stock, for which he paid £600; and in order to square his holding, he purchased £120 stock, for which he paid £232, which altogether made up £1800 stock. He continued to hold that till the Bank stopped. He never sold a Bank share. I purchased £500 stock in 1873, for which I paid £1000. I did so on my father's recommendation. My uncle Patrick at the same time bought £500 stock, for which he paid £1000. He and I have continued to hold our stock until now. Mr Stronach was aware we had the Hope Street property. He knew of our expenditure upon it. He never asked to have a formal conveyance of it to the Bank. If we had, we would not have objected to grant a formal conveyance. My father handed to Mr Stronach all the scrip in his possession, Glasgow and South Western and other scrip. My father has for a number of years past been much occupied with public matters in Glasgow. At the date of the stoppage of the Bank, he was a director of the Scottish Imperial Insurance Company, and of the State Line Steam Shipping Company; he was chairman of the Glasgow Storage Company; a director of the Glasgow Corn Exchange; a trustee of the Clyde Navigation; a member of the Glasgow School Board; chairman of the High School Committee; and a member of the Mearns School Board. He had previously been preceptor of Hutcheson's Hospital for some years, and a magistrate of Glasgow. He was also a director of several charitable and benevolent institutions. His time was very largely occupied in connection with these offices. I should think that for the last fifteen or sixteen years he must have spent not less than four or five hours every day on these matters.

PETER CLOUSTON.

By Mr Mackintosh—I reside in 1 Park Terrace, Glasgow. I am a deputy-lieutenant for the county of Lanark. I was Lord Provost of Glasgow for three years, from 1860 to 1863. I have now retired from business. I was formerly an insurance broker and underwriter. I have known Mr Taylor for a very long period—I should say thirty to forty years. I knew him when he was a very young man in business. I have known him all his life. I had considerable business dealings with him at one time when I was attending to business, and I have also met him in public business. He entered the council in 1861, and he worked so assiduously during the year, and seemed to be such an acceptable town councillor, and I had such confidence in him, that I asked him to enter the magistracy as one of the river bailies in 1862, when he had been only twelve months in the council. He went progressively up, and ultimately became preceptor of Hutcheson's Hospital. I was, however, out of the council by that time. (Q.) Is this preceptorship a high and honourable office? (A.) It is one of the most enviable offices in connection with the town council. I think I have had an ample opportunity of forming an opinion as to Mr Taylor's character. My opinion of him has all along been that as a business man or as a public man, he was a man of thorough integrity and probity. (Q.) Is he in your opinion a man capable of wilful falsehood in any shape or form? (A.) I never could have conceived it. (Q.) Is that your opinion still? (A.) Still. I still trust Mr Taylor as I have trusted him in the past, and hope that he will be restored to society. Mr Taylor's firm was of very high standing in the trade, and of reputed means. They did a large business, and it was understood to be a lucrative business for a long time, although latterly I have heard that he has sustained very heavy losses.

GEORGE WILSON CLARK.

By Mr Mackintosh—I am a merchant in Glasgow. I am a shareholder in the City of Glasgow Bank. I hold £2500 of stock. I am acquainted with Mr Taylor. I have known him for thirty-seven years. I have frequently met him in business and otherwise. I have had many full opportunities of judging of his character. I have always considered him a highly honourable man. (Q.) Is he a man capable, in your opinion, of falsifying a balance-sheet or anything of that sort? (A.) It is the last thing I could suppose him to be guilty of doing. He and his firm have always occupied a high position in Glasgow. Before the stoppage of the Bank his firm had the best of credit. We trusted them ourselves occasionally. Mr Taylor was reputed to be a man of means.

Eighth Day.—Tuesday, 28th January 1879.

EVIDENCE FOR MR TAYLOR (resumed).

ROBERT TOD.

By Mr Omond—I am a grain merchant and miller at the Leith Flour Mills, and also in Glasgow. I know Mr Taylor, the accused. I have known him for upwards of twenty-five years. I have very frequently done business with him,—a large business. I have been in the habit of going to Glasgow two or three times a week for twenty-five years. During that time I have had frequent and very large transactions with the firm of Taylor & Sons. They did a large business: about as large as any firm in the corn trade, I should think. I had ample opportunities of forming an opinion as to Mr Taylor's qualities. I have uniformly found him upright, honourable, and straightforward in all his dealings. I should think him quite incapable of doing anything like a dishonourable action. His firm was in very good credit in the trade in Glasgow—no firm more so, I should think, in the corn trade. (Q.) Did you think Mr Taylor was a man of a confiding and trusting character? (A.) Yes, remarkably so; he was a very trustful man,—the most so I ever met in business; and I have seen him suffer large losses in consequence of that.

REV. FREDERICK LOCKHART ROBERTSON.

By Mr Mackintosh—I am minister of St Andrew's Church, Glasgow. I hold £1400 stock in the City of Glasgow Bank. I took part in the meeting of shareholders at which the investigation committee's report was presented. I came to Glasgow, I think, in 1872. I have known Mr Taylor intimately since

I came to Glasgow. I have frequently met him on public business, especially in connection with Hutcheson's Hospital, and also in private. (Q.) What opinion have you formed of his character? (A.) I considered him an honest and upright man. (Q.) Is that your opinion still? (A.) Yes, I still consider him an honest and upright man, but I am not so sure about his being so competent as I once thought. (Q.) Do you think he is a man capable of falsifying a balance-sheet? (A.) Well, no; whatever Mr Taylor's faults may be, and I, as well as others, have suffered from his faults, I do not believe for a moment that he would soil his soul by so dishonourable an act.

EVIDENCE FOR MR WRIGHT.

PATRICK PLAYFAIR.

By Mr Smith—I reside at Woodside Terrace, Glasgow. I was a merchant in Glasgow, but retired from business about four years ago. I hold the office of Lord Dean of Guild of Glasgow. I have known Mr Wright and his family for upwards of forty years. I esteem him very highly in his character. (Q.) As a man of integrity? (A.) Yes. (Q.) Do you think he would be a party to making false statements knowingly? (A.) I don't think he would. (Q.) Is he of a trusting and confiding character? (A.) I think he is decidedly so, very confiding to others, especially parties who might take advantage of him. He is a quiet unobtrusive man, and has always lived in a plain manner.

MICHAEL CONNAL.

By Mr Smith—I am a member of the firm of William Connal & Co., merchants, Glasgow. We are largely engaged in the sugar trade. I am chairman of the School Board of Glasgow. I have known Mr Wright for upwards of fifty years. My opinion of him is, that he is a man of singular simplicity of character, and, I think, an honest man. (Q.) A man of honour? (A.) A man of honour. (Q.) But of a trusting character? (A.) Of a confiding character. He has always lived in a remarkably quiet unobtrusive way. (Q.) Do you think he was likely to be a party to making a falsified statement? (A.) I don't think he would be a party to the issuing of a false statement, knowing it to be false.

EVIDENCE FOR MR INGLIS.

LAUDERDALE MAITLAND.

By Mr Robertson—I am proprietor of Eccles, in Dumfriesshire. I have been acquainted with Mr Henry Inglis very nearly since we were boys. I am his oldest acquaintance. I lived in Edinburgh till 1843. Since then I have lived in Dumfriesshire. I have been in the habit of coming frequently to Edinburgh, and on these occasions I have lived very much in Mr Inglis' house. Mr Inglis has practised the law as a Writer to the Signet since 1828. He passed in that year. His firm for many years has been H. & A. Inglis. I am aware of the character of the business carried on by that firm—a very high-class conveyancing business. Mr Inglis occasionally went to his property at Torsonce. I have been with him there. He occasionally went in the end of the week, and stayed there on the Sunday. Beyond that, he constantly resided in Edinburgh. He is a man of very great cultivation and literary taste. He took very much interest in his property in Midlothian. (Q.) Have you ever, during your life-long acquaintance with Mr Inglis, seen any cause to doubt his perfect honour and integrity? (A.) Never. I have perfect reliance on everything he did. (Q.) Was he a man of scrupulous honour? (A.) Scrupulous honour.

EVIDENCE FOR MR STRONACH.

JOHN COWAN.

By Mr Darling—I am a Writer to the Signet in Edinburgh, and one of the trustees under the ante-nuptial marriage-contract of Mr and Mrs Robert Stronach. I am also agent for the trust. They were married in July 1871, and have three children surviving, the eldest of whom is about seven years of age. The trustees under the marriage-contract hold nothing but what was Mrs Stronach's own money before her marriage. I have a pass-book with the City of Glasgow Bank in the name of Mr and Mrs Stronach, to be operated upon by either. I have examined the entries there; and, with the exception of four sums of small amount, I have found them to correspond exactly with the remittances made by me to Mrs Stronach for the last six years. The pass-book begins in 1872, and comes down to the stoppage of the Bank. The account is balanced as at 22d October 1878, and there is at its credit then £712, 12s. 3d. I have received a letter from the liquidators, dated 9th December 1878, certifying that that is the amount at the credit of the account. The last cheque passed upon that account was on 25th September 1878, for £40.

WILLIAM BORLAND.

By Mr Darling—I am agent in Glasgow for Mr Robert Stronach. In that capacity I paid for him the first instalment of the first call on the City of Glasgow Bank stock which he held. I have produced in this process the receipt for it. It is No. 2 of the inventory of productions. (Q.) What was the amount of the call? (A.) The amount was £2250, and it was paid on 23d December 1878 by a cheque of my firm. (Q.) Can you say, from the inquiries you have made, what was about the amount of Mr Stronach's means at that time? (A.) So far as I could form an opinion—I did not go into it exhaustively—but they seemed to amount to about £12,000.

SAMUEL RALEIGH.

By Mr Darling—I am manager of the Scottish Widows' Fund. I was one of the liquidators of the Western Bank. I know Mr Robert Stronach. I have known him since 1871, when he married the daughter of an old friend, in whom I am much interested. I have seen a great deal of him since, and I have heard a great deal of him too. I have had ample opportunities of forming an estimate of his character. I consider him in every way a good man, strictly conscientious and upright, and kind and unselfish in a high degree. (Q.) Did you always find him conscientious in his dealings? (A.) Yes, in so far as I had business transactions with him, which were not many; but I knew about his transactions. (Q.) Would you be more ready to believe in his committing errors of judgment than of moral intention? (A.) Certainly. I think he might err in judgment, but not in moral purpose or intention. (Q.) And after all that has passed, what is your opinion of him now? (A.) I would still confide in his moral integrity and good intention.

EVIDENCE FOR MR SALMOND.

RICHARD HUGHES EVANS.

By Mr Asher—I am secretary of the Netherlands Indian Steam Navigation Company, whose business premises are at Austin Friars, London. I know Mr Robert Salmond very well indeed. I have known him for many years. He is a director of the Netherlands Steam Navigation Company. He has been so since, I think, 1864. There is a book kept in connection with that company called the Directors' Attendance Book. The directors enter their names in that book on the dates when they are present at meetings. I have that book here. I find from it that Mr Salmond was present at meetings on 6th, 9th, and 12th June 1876. He is not entered as present at any meetings in July of that year. In 1877 Mr Salmond was present on 5th, 7th, 8th, 11th, and 13th June, and on 9th and 11th July. In 1878 he was present on 28th and 31st May, and again on 7th and 13th June; not afterwards in June or July. I have known Mr Salmond since he joined the Company as a director in 1864, and I consider I have had a good opportunity of forming an estimate of his character from my intercourse with him both in business and otherwise. My opinion of Mr Salmond's character is, that he is a most honourable, upright, straightforward man.

MICHAEL CONNAL.

By Mr Asher—I was formerly a merchant in London and in Glasgow. I have now retired, and reside in London. I have been acquainted with Mr Robert Salmond for more than twenty years. I have known him very intimately. In the summer of 1876 I went to Homburg, in Germany, for the purpose of drinking the waters there. I arrived at Homburg on 16th June 1876, and I resided at the Hotel de Russie. When I arrived I found Mr Salmond there; I met him there on that day. He was there for the purpose of drinking the waters also. I remained at Homburg for what is called the usual cure, three weeks, and I left on 6th July. Mr Salmond was there during the whole time; I was in his company every day. He was to leave on the afternoon of the same day, 6th July, but a little later than I did. From my long acquaintance with Mr Salmond I have had a good opportunity of forming an estimate of his character. I have the highest opinion of Mr Salmond's character, and I have always had. In my opinion, he is a man who is utterly incapable of falsifying books or balance-sheets.

ALLAN SANDILANDS.

By Mr Goudy—I am manager of the Palace Hotel, Buxton, in Derbyshire. I know Mr Robert Salmond. There is a visitors' book kept at the Palace Hotel, in which are entered the names of all visitors. I have got that book here for 1878. On 20th June of that year Mr Robert Salmond is entered as staying in the hotel; his own signature appears in the book at that date. He continued to stay in the hotel, at that time, until 5th July. He was at the hotel every day. He was taking the waters at Buxton while he was there.

RICHARD RAIMES.

By Mr Asher—I am the senior partner of the firm of Raimes, Blanchard, and Co., of Leith. I reside at Bonnington Park. I am acquainted with Mr Robert Salmond. I have known him for about forty-seven years. I had frequent banking transactions with him when he was agent for the Western Bank on the South Bridge and afterwards. I have had a good opportunity of forming an estimate of his character, both from my business intercourse with him and also as a private friend. In both ways, I think I can answer very satisfactorily for Mr Salmond as an honourable, just man. I have ever found him so. (Q.) Is he capable, in your opinion, of falsifying books or balance-sheets, or committing fraud? (A.) I daresay he is capable, but I doubt that his principles would be so much against it that he would never dare to think of such a thing. (Q.) Is that your opinion still? (A.) That is my impression at present.

DAVID COWAN.

By Mr Asher—I am a chartered accountant in Glasgow. I have looked at certain books of the City of Glasgow Bank as at 5th June 1861, which was the last balance under the management of Mr Salmond. I examined the monthly balance of deposit accounts, and the monthly balance of credit accounts, and found that the name of Smith, Fleming, & Co. does not appear there at all. Their account did not exist at that date, neither did the account of Nicol Fleming & Co. or Innes Wright & Co. There is an account in name of James Morton & Co. at that date, on which was a debit balance of £4535, 2s. 10d.

Mr ASHER put in execution of citation against Henry Hall, manager of the Burlington Hotel, London; and stated that although it had been intimated by telegraph that Mr Hall had left London the previous evening, he had not yet appeared in Court. The facts which Mr Hall was intended to prove were, that Mr Salmond's name appeared in the bed-book of the Burlington Hotel as having slept there on the following dates:—Every night from 5th to 11th June inclusive, 1876; every night from 3d to 13th June inclusive, 1877; and from 6th to 13th July inclusive, 1877; and every night from 25th May to 19th June inclusive, 1878.

The LORD ADVOCATE agreed to give an admission of these facts.

[Evidence closed.]

ADDRESSES TO JURY.

THE LORD ADVOCATE.

May it please your Lordships, Gentlemen of the Jury,—You have listened to evidence in this case in very great detail; and the time has now come when, with the aid of addresses for the Crown, whom I represent, and also for the panels at the bar, you must make up your minds, with the further assistance of the Bench, as to the true result of that evidence upon the guilt or innocence of the prisoners. The charge which is brought against them in the libel before you is, I need not say, a very serious one. The only points which you have to consider are the first three in this indictment, in relation to balance-sheets published in the years 1876, 1877, and 1878. But before saying a word as to the particulars of the charge, I desire to say to you once for all, that even in this Court it is impossible to disguise the fact, that the unfortunate state of the City of Glasgow Bank has been for months past the subject of private conversation and of public comment throughout the length and breadth of the land; and I say so, for this reason, in order that I may call your attention to the object of this prosecution at the instance of the Crown. It is to lay before you that which those who conversed about it, and wrote about it, have not been thoroughly conversant with,—the real facts of the case; and I shall ask you, and I trust you will make it your honest endeavour in considering the facts of this case, to dismiss entirely from your minds what may have been said, or written, or printed out of doors, that is in the least degree calculated to prejudice in your estimation the prisoners at the bar, and to endeavour to come to a dispassionate judgment upon the facts, and nothing but the facts, which have now been for the first time put in evidence before you.

Gentlemen, the charge is based upon the fact that certain abstracts were published from year to year purporting to represent the true state of affairs of the Bank, and that the abstracts so published were in point of fact not true, but false; and, in the second place, that the falsehood of these abstracts was not mere matter of chance or accident, but the result of intention or design, to conceal from the shareholders and from the public the true state of affairs of the Bank. In each of these years you will find, gentlemen, that there is a double charge—there is an alternative charge,—and I had better explain to you precisely the effect of that. There is a charge, in the first instance, against each and all of the panels of having been art and part in fabricating these balance-sheets with the intention of deceiving, concealing, and misrepresenting the true state of the Bank's affairs. If they had merely prepared a false balance-sheet, and had done nothing with it but laid it aside or put it in the fire, that would not have constituted a crime according to the law of Scotland, because it would merely have been a guilty intention abandoned on second thoughts. The whole gravamen of the charge is, that having prepared it with that purpose, the purpose was put into execution by issuing that false and fabricated balance-sheet to the shareholders of the Bank. But then, under the second alternative, it is not necessary, in order to constitute the guilt of the accused, that they should have been parties to the fabrication of the balance-sheet. It is quite sufficient to constitute the alternative offence if, knowing that it was a false balance-sheet, and that it had been fabricated or prepared for the purpose of concealing the true state of the Bank, they lent their names and authority to the issuing of it to the shareholders and the public, with, of course, the same intention to deceive.

Now, gentlemen, I think it would be as well, in the course of the observations which I have to address to you, to consider, in the first place, whether there was falsification of all or of any of these balance-sheets; and, in the second place, to consider whether that was intentional and with a design to conceal and misrepresent the true state of the Bank. I cannot deal with that second question without some inquiry into the state of the Bank, and that involves, perhaps, a still more important question for you to consider—whether, assuming the state of the Bank, it was known to the directors and to each of them. And lastly, if you are satisfied that the balance-sheet was prepared falsely,—that the Bank was in a condition requiring, in their opinion, misrepresentation, and if they did issue these abstracts with the view of misrepresenting the position of the Bank, then you have to consider which of these persons at the bar you are to hold guilty of the crime. Now, in regard to the published balance-sheets, the abstracts which you have upon pages 3, 6, and 9 of the indictment [see pp. 27, 29, and 31], I do not think it can for one moment be doubted, in the face of the evidence you have heard, that they are false and fabricated. I am not going into details upon this matter; I shall have a word to say upon it by-and-by. But just let me call your attention to the balance-sheet of 1876, and point out to you the general character of the alterations that were made in order to lay a false state of affairs before the shareholders, because it humbly appears to me that the very character of those alterations is exceedingly suggestive of the object and purpose for which they were made. In the first place, the general result of these is to reduce both sides of the account, and, speaking in round figures, the result of the alterations in each of the years in question is to reduce the assets of the Bank by a couple of millions or upwards, and to reduce the liabilities of the Bank by a couple of millions or upwards. A question or two was put in the course of the evidence, which seemed rather to suggest that some reliance was to be placed, on the part of the accused, upon the fact that the manipulation of both sides of the balance-sheet resulted in the same figures standing at balance, as capital, reserve fund, and profit and loss. That is no test whatever of the truth or falsity of a balance-sheet. The purpose of such a balance-sheet or abstract, is to disclose honestly to the shareholders and the public the amount of business the Bank is doing, their turnover, the extent of their transactions; and it must be obvious to you that they might have altered the balance-sheet by six or eight millions more, by taking that sum off both sides, with precisely the same result of leaving those figures standing at balance as information to the public. But would that have been a right or proper thing to do—to suggest that the Bank was carrying on a business of precisely half the extent with precisely half the amount of money got upon deposit with which they were intrusted? It is a question for you, and I rather think that when you come to examine into details, you will find that the general purpose of representing that the Bank was doing a much smaller trade than it really was doing in money, was coupled with this, that it was also intended and calculated to represent that they were doing a much better and a much sounder trade than they actually had. Because they diminished the amount of their liabilities by cutting off large sums—in this case we are always dealing with large sums, nothing short of hundreds of thousands and millions—on both sides of the account; and thus they put out of sight an enormous quantity of bill transactions which might give a clue to the public, who knew, in a general way, the amount of the dealings of some whom I shall call the leading customers of the Bank—the gentlemen who absorbed a great deal of its capital from 1870 onwards, and who, at the time the Bank stopped, had had advanced to them about three-fifths of the whole money the Bank had lent. That was one object gained: but in order to keep the two sides of the account square, they had to diminish the assets—that is to say, what they held in the shape of debts due to them, and in the shape of investments and other securities. And how is that side of the account dealt with? Of course, at first it looks a very fair thing to reduce assets; but this is done in order to preserve the balance on the two sides of the account, and then this feature is very skilfully introduced—if you look at the top of the left hand page, Article 1, on the credit side [see p. 31],—they frame their abstract so as to reduce bills of exchange and so forth, and that kind of stock-in-trade is reduced in 1878 by about three millions, which is more than the deduction from the other side of the account; but then they compensate for that by turning credit accounts,—outstanding sums due them by customers,—a portion of them, into Government stock, Exchequer bills, railway and other stocks, debentures and balances in the hands of foreign correspondents. In other words, while they diminish their assets upon the credit side of the account, they perform this further operation on the credit side of the account, that they take off some from an inferior class of assets, and add these to assets of a better class, thereby leading any one who examined the balance-sheet to believe that the Bank had £700,000 or £800,000 more of good investments than they in reality held, and about two millions less of floating bills and credit accounts, which they might or might not recover. And I need hardly suggest to you, who are conversant with mercantile affairs, that assets in the shape of outsanding securities and balances due by firms of large dealings, like Smith, Fleming, & Co., James Nicol Fleming & Co., Morton & Co., and Innes Wright & Co., are not on the whole such good assets or reliable assets as Government stocks and balances in the hands of correspondents. So much for these two sides. But that is not quite all. They have a reserve fund every year of £450,000, and that seems to have been a sort of stock reserve fund that is carried along. Well, it was explained to you by the gentlemen who have examined the books of the Bank how that fund was raised. There were sums credited which they had not got—in other words, they professed to have received interest which they had not got. They got a lower rate of interest or none at all, and what they had not got they carried into profit and loss account, and finally into a reserve fund,—consisting of what they never had got, and what, according to all human probability, they had not the slightest chance of ever getting. Then the next profit and loss in the balance-sheet for 1876 is £136,000. These items are made up and dealt with in precisely the same way throughout all the three years and the three balances, with which we are dealing. Now, how was that profit and loss account got up? I am certain you will accept the statements made in regard to it, because, being quite distinctly and plainly stated and explained to you by the accountants who appeared as witnesses for the Crown, not one single word was put in cross-examination by any one of my numerous friends who represent the panels at the bar tending to shake or discredit the statements which they made. They said—"That which you are dividing as profit and loss "year by year was really never earned at all." You must know very well that the profit and loss account for a year amounts to the earnings for the year; and it would not be a matter of imputation against any banker who was making up a balance-sheet, that, in stating his account of profit and loss, he should include in it interest which was regularly paid, although it had not come to hand. There is nothing whatever wrong in that. If their income was coming in steadily each year, they had quite a right to regard it as earnings and income, and to distribute it. But that is not what was done here. They bring into this account interest upon outstanding and unpaid balances. The principal was not paid, the interest was not paid, and they were speculating in Australian stock to recoup their deficit upon these transactions; and in that state of matters they all speak hopefully as to the ultimate profit to be obtained from that source. But how about the immediate distribution? And they actually go on dividing and paying dividends, rising from 11 per cent. in the year 1876, to 12 per cent. in 1877 and 1878; whereas, if they had struck off the sum of £125,000 odds, calculated as interest due on those debtor balances, there would not have been a sixpence to divide. If there had been any reasonable ground for so putting it, that might have been some justification; but it humbly appears to me that it was just as unjustifiable as it would be in any man who had £50,000 lent to a debtor who was unable to repay him, to go on spending interest which he had not got, and which there was very little probability he would ever get, as his yearly income. The result is perfectly plain. That money was divided among the shareholders. That money was not in the Bank. It stood in the books as due upon those book balances which they were speculating to recoup; and therefore they paid it away out of some other asset; and therefore, when they were paying away those dividends, they were simply eating into the capital of the Bank, and paying the shareholders dividend out of their own stock, if, indeed, there was any stock to pay it out of at all, which is very doubtful.

Now, gentlemen, there are in process, and these have been adverted to in the evidence, some very remarkable documents, which, I understand, you will be allowed to examine for yourselves at a future stage of this case. I refer to what are called the scroll abstracts for the years 1876-77-78. [See Appendix.] Let me tell you that you must not be misled into the view that these things constitute the crime which the Crown says the panels have committed. The crime which the Crown alleges has been committed is that these abstract balances in the indictment before you, being false, were given to the public as true, with the view of misrepresenting the state of the Bank. There is no charge founded upon these scroll abstracts, but they are very important links of evidence in the present case. They show the hand of the fabricator; they are the key to his work. You can reduce these balance-sheets in the way they have done, with similar results, in millions of different ways, by taking figures of a certain kind away here, and putting figures of a certain kind on there, But this is one way of attaining the end to be attained, to reduce the two sides of the balance-sheet, to magnify the character of the assets by giving them a character which they had not, and to conceal the amount and character of the liabilities by striking them off wholesale,—a practice carried so far that in 1878 the credit account on bills outstanding and due was represented to the extent of £200,000, as solid gold in reserve in the coffers of the Bank. It was only that year that it occurred. That is the end to be attained; and these scroll abstracts will show you one way of doing it, and they show very probably, indeed, almost certainly, the way in which it was done. But it has no more connection with the charge which is before us than the very common case which occurs in forgery, where you find A's name at a bill written by B, in order to represent A's. The bill passes into currency, and when A refuses to pay it because it is forged, you find a sheet of paper in the handwriting of B, the forger, with all sorts of signatures of A written upon it, so as to make the forger sufficiently expert to commit the final act. There is just the same kind of connection here. You can trace the mind and intent of the forger in the one case, because he is trying to acquire sufficient expertness to enable him to fabricate the signature of another. And in this case, in the same way, you can see the steps by which the ultimate results which are embodied in those balances have been attained,—by a process of calculation, making the two false ends fit in—a process which is very easily performed when you come to deal with figures. If that is so—and I think, upon the face of these balance-sheets, if I have correctly represented them, and I shall be in your judgment if I have not done so,—the next question is, what was the purpose of doing it? It could hardly be accidental. Mistakes will often occur in matters of figures, but a mistake that goes two millions wrong, or four millions, taking the two sides of the transactions, and yet brings out a consistent and even sum total on both sides, is not one of the kind of freaks generally played by fortune or chance. I am going to take just now the effect of the untrue balances. I shall ask your attention by-and-by to the persons who are responsible for it. It is impossible to dissociate the one thing from the other; and in dealing with its truth or falsehood, when we come to the state of the Bank, it will be very necessary for you, in the narrative which I shall be compelled to submit to you in order to make the case intelligible, to keep in view who are the parties that appear upon the scene, and what is their connection with it, and what their amount of knowledge of the state of the Bank. The charge in the libel before you is, that the balances were fabricated in order to conceal the true state of the Bank's affairs. Of course that is a meaningless and idle proposition, unless it be the fact that the Bank's affairs are thereby concealed, or that they stood in need of concealment. You might have alterations upon a balance-sheet, and it might turn out upon an examination of the affairs of the Bank that the Bank was on the whole better than the balance-sheet showed. That would be to a jury conclusive evidence that there was no intention to misrepresent; but I am afraid that you will hardly be able to come to that lenient conclusion on the facts of the present case. Because what was the state of the Bank? And, in considering that, I must desire you to keep in mind—it is quite right and proper that you should—and discriminate to the best of your ability between that which we now know of the state of the Bank, and that which the prisoners at the bar did know, or must be presumed to have known, during these transactions for the years 1875, 1876, 1877, and 1878, that are embodied in the balance-sheets published as at the first Wednesday of June in the last three years. Because undoubtedly we know, or may know, in an investigation like this, a great deal more than any director knew during that period; and it may be that according to the evidence there are directors who knew nothing at all about it. I must make some observations upon the state of the Bank at the time of its stoppage, because there is some reflex light thrown by it upon the actual state during the period in question; but I beg you to keep in view, in fairness to the panels, as well as for the ends of justice—on the part of the Crown I ask you to keep in view that that is not the question as against the panels; the question as against them is—the state of the Bank now being ascertained to be so and so—what did they know, whilst the Bank was carrying on business, as to the results which are stated in those abstract balance-sheets? We know now that in July 1876-77-78—for that is the date of the annual meetings at which those abstracts were published—this Bank was represented by those placed in the conduct of its affairs as a solvent and prosperous concern, able to pay 11 or 12 per cent. dividend to its shareholders, and with brilliant prospects for the future. These prospects, according to the representation of the balance-sheet never were fairer, never more prosperous, than as at the balance of 5th June 1878; and we know that in four months from that date the Bank was bankrupt, and its losses were roughly estimated by a professional gentleman who looked into its affairs at millions sterling—I need hardly tell you the amount. You heard the evidence of Mr Jamieson, who made an investigation on behalf of the other banks, who refused their aid, and refused it—it is not by any means unimportant to know—the moment they saw the enormous amount of the dealings of the Bank with certain firms, to whose transactions I shall have to refer you more particularly. I quite admit that the failure and stoppage of the Bank, on the 2d of October, might well be a surprise to the directors; but it does not in the slightest degree follow that they were ignorant of the position of the Bank, or the position of its accounts, or ignorant of the fact that these balance-sheets were entirely false and fabricated. It is a strange thing that when they first begged assistance, and when Mr Wenley was in communication with them, they were exceedingly unwilling to have any examination of the books,—exceedingly unwilling. Necessity drove them ultimately to show their whole hand; it would not hide. But they declined at first even to let a neutral man in a confidential position make an inquiry in the interest of both parties; and he was merely to state the result without giving the figures from the books or exposing any secret, or telling with whom they were dealing. When the directors found that enquiry had come to be inevitable, and Mr Wenley was taking his leave, Mr Potter expressed, in marked terms, the hope that an examination of the books would be dispensed with, and that the banks would give assistance without it. In one point of view, if the state of the Bank was known, it is not surprising that they should be unwilling that the books should be gone into, because the books would have exposed the position of matters, and at that date,—I don't want to take all the firms; but I shall take three—the worst of them—viz., Morton & Co., Smith, Fleming, & Co., and James Nicol Fleming,—at that moment the advances from the Bank were to the following extents:—Morton & Co., £2,173,000; Smith, Fleming, and Co., £1,968,000; and James Nicol Fleming, who has been liquidating for several years,—that is to say, paying off his debts,—at least, that is the general meaning of the word,—had the modest sum of £1,238,000; making for these three firms the respectable total of indebtedness to the Bank of £5,317,000, and that was a state of matters that had been growing gradually —it was nothing new. In 1875,—that is, before the period of dealings of the present directors began; because the board has remained constituted as at present since the accession of Mr Wright, who came in the place of Mr James Nicol Fleming, and Mr Stronach, who became manager in place of his brother in December 1875,—when the board, as constituted at the date of the stoppage, began its operations, the state of these accounts was as follows:—Morton & Co. had £1,380,000; Smith, Fleming, & Co. had £1,661,000; James Nicol Fleming had £1,005,000,—in all, £4,046,000, so that the increase of their indebtedness between the time of the directors entering on office and the stoppage of the Bank, or in three years, amounted to £1,333,000. It may have been, that to a person who knew these figures, the stoppage of the Bank could hardly be a surprise; on the other hand, it might be a surprise, and yet these directors might have had quite sufficient knowledge of the state of the Bank to have made it an entirely wrong and criminal thing for them to sanction the issue of such a balance-sheet as any one of these three. They may have believed that Australian land would so richly repay the investments that they had made in it as to recoup their deficits; but even on the very best of the evidence that we have had upon this point, either in cross-examination by the panel's counsel, or in chief from their own witnesses, it only comes to this, that it was a matter in the future. It was a matter of hope and expectation; it was not a case of holding security, and ample security, against a present debt. The failure of the Bank may have surprised them, because they may have hoped, by more speculations of that sort, by getting another £500,000 to invest here or there, to be able, some day or other, to put these accounts into what they were trying to do—a state of order. But the mistake, and worse than mistake, committed throughout all those years of management—and you will see who were responsible for it, and in the knowledge of it—was this, that they treated these as good assets, assuming that there were good securities against them, whereas they knew at all events—whether they knew the full amount in £ s. d. is not a material thing—that there were deficits so serious and so extensive, that to enable the Bank to recoup them, they were obliged to enter into transactions which they themselves recorded on the face of their own minutes as not being legitimate banking transactions.

Now, gentlemen, I shall proceed to inquire as to the history of these three accounts, and I shall take them because they are quite sufficient of themselves to account for the insolvency of the Bank, and I shall just ask you to follow me through some details in order to see whether it be the fact that the directors of the Bank did not know of them. Now, if they did know of them, they knew the cause of the rottenness of the Bank; because it can hardly be suggested for one moment that all that enormous deficit, which became apparent whenever there was an impartial investigation—aye, and a very hurried one, in the month of October 1878—it can hardly be suggested that all that enormous loss of millions occurred between 5th June 1878 and the 2d October of that year. I have not heard such a suggestion, and I can hardly think that you will be asked to believe that it occurred in four months, when the facts clearly show that it was not so. And I think they also clearly show that the directors knew very well about these accounts—knew that they were very bad accounts—knew that, instead of reducing these bad accounts, they were going on increasing more and more. It may be that they were flinging good money after bad, in the hope of recouping themselves in the end; but they knew they were sending that money after the bad in the hope of getting it back; and they must have known that these accounts, so enormous as they were in extent, must have seriously affected the state of the Bank. At least it is for you to judge whether it would have been possible for any man knowing their extent, not to know at the same time that they placed the Bank in a position, if not of ruin, at least of the most imminent peril. It is all very well to say, and I have no doubt it will be said, that these gentlemen did not attend to details of business—that they managed large transactions, but did not go into details, and, therefore, must not be judged hardly about their knowledge of results, and about what you discover from the books of the Bank. Why, Mr Jamieson only made a rough estimate after he had been four hours at work; and it took the investigators, with the aid of a large staff of clerks, a fortnight to work it out. But what were they doing? They were unravelling the transactions for years back, which these gentlemen during these years were carrying on with their open eyes, from board day to board day, in the management of the Bank. It is one thing to spend so many hours in investigating the acts of a body of directors from what is recorded in their minutes and ledgers, and quite another thing to be one of the body of directors from day to day, and from week to week carrying on these transactions—refusing advances to-day and giving them to-morrow. All that an accountant can do is to try to discover from the books what the directors have been about; and, therefore, it will never do to say to you, who have a general knowledge of business, that a body of directors are to be held as justified in giving persons enormously indebted to the Bank, board day after board day, more credits and more money, until the advances comes up to millions, and then turn round and say, "We really are very simple, quiet, "honest, fellows; we did not look into details; two millions are gone, but how "were we to know?" Well, gentlemen, keep this other fact in view, in justice to a certain portion of the servants of the Bank. The City Bank was not all bad management. On the contrary, there was one portion of its affairs that was exceedingly well managed—I refer to the business of the Bank conducted at its branches in Scotland. You have it in evidence from the inspector of branches, Mr Miller, against whose evidence there is no suggestion, because it is founded upon the most explicit facts—that for years past the average actual earnings of the branches of the Bank were £70,000 per annum. That was made after writing off about £10,000 a year for bad debts. But there was another cause of the prosperity of the branches. It was very well explained by more than one witness. In dealing with advances at the branches, the manager (Mr Miller says) was very strict about getting security. He was very strict about parting with a penny in the way of loan at the branches until it was covered by money's worth; and the result of it is, as I have stated to you, that the earnings or legitimate profits of the Bank at its branches in

Scotland, during many years of its trading before its stoppage, were enough to pay a dividend of 7 per cent. on its paid-up capital of one million. So that if the company had traded through its branches alone, and instead of dealing with Morton & Co., Smith, Fleming, & Co., and Nicol Fleming, had simply deposited the money they had in Glasgow with another bank, and had got deposit receipt rates upon it, they would have saved their capital and their money, and would have been able to pay a dividend of 7 per cent. to their shareholders. But that illustrates and very strongly brings out this point, that if the management at the branches was good, the management at the head office, which is responsible for all the enormous losses of the Bank, was as bad as that of the branches was good. We shall see whether there was the same strictness there in parting with money. I have not the least doubt of the perfect accuracy of Mr Miller's statement that the manager, Mr Stronach, was exceedingly strict in getting proper security from a poor fellow in the country who wanted to get a little money in advance; and if they had only applied the same rule to some of those so-called capitalists, who indulged in those firm names I have repeated so often, it would have been a great deal better for the Bank.

Now, gentlemen, to return to those advances, and to the period to which I will direct your attention—namely, the period of the present management. In the evidence of John Fleming, there was a good deal to suggest that Alexander Stronach did not always, in giving him advances, take the Bank directors into his confidence, and that specially applies to John Fleming's evidence about the transactions of the years 1870 and 1874. That is quite possible. But we have no question here about Alexander Stronach. The case I put to you is this, that whatever Alexander Stronach may have done, his successor, Robert Stronach, the prisoner at the bar, did not, in that respect, follow his example. On the contrary, I think you will find that he was aware of the nature of those accounts and their danger—that he was so impressed with the character of those accounts, and the deadly peril to the existence of the Bank that their continued indebtedness involved, that, like a sensible man, and acting the part of an honest man, he brought that fact clearly before the directors before he would accept office, and accepted office only upon this condition—that the directors would act with him and keep him right, and help him with these accounts. The directors accepted upon that condition, and I venture to say this, that it will require on the part of the directors, other than the manager, some much plainer testimony than any evidence in this case affords that they departed from that arrangement—that Robert Stronach, instead of enforcing fulfilment of the sole condition upon which he accepted office, took the whole responsibility of these accounts upon himself, and managed them at his own hand, concealed them from the directors, so that these gentlemen, only having heard the note of warning in 1875, entirely forgot it, and lapsed into a state of belief that there was nothing wrong with these accounts at all. The thing is hardly credible, that when a manager comes forward and says, "I "will try to help you out of this ugly position into which the Banks affairs "have got, provided you will apply yourselves to giving me efficient aid in "dealing with these accounts," he should all at once have resiled from that position, and declined their aid, and taken the whole responsibility upon himself, and that they should have forgotten all about it, or been ignorant of it. I venture to say, that after the plain terms in which that was brought before them, it would have been the grossest breach of duty on the part of each and all of those gentlemen if they had not given the manager the assistance he desired; still more a breach of duty if, knowing the danger of those accounts, and knowing how they affected the position of the Bank, they stood by for three years, knowing that there was a mine beneath them that might explode at any moment, without being at the trouble to inquire how those accounts were going on. Gentlemen, that this was brought before them, and most distinctly brought before them, very plainly appears from the letter of the manager, and I must ask you to permit me to read it :—

"City of Glasgow Bank, 28th Dec. 1875.

"GENTLEMEN,—In thanking you for the offer of the management of this Bank, "which you have kindly made to me, I beg to state my willingness to accept it. "But, before undertaking this responsibility, I deem it prudent to ask the board to "minute its approval of the policy which has been pursued of supporting several "accounts of an unsatisfactory character since my brother discontinued personally "to manage the Bank; and, further, to appoint a committee to investigate and "place on record what may have been the exact position of these accounts, and "the advances generally when my brother ceased to be manager; and also to act "and guide me in any important detail therewith connected, as I am in no wise "responsible up to this date for the state of certain advances, which I need not "here particularise.

"You will, I hope, admit the reasonableness of the precaution which this request "involves; and I feel you will the more readily do this when you consider that "whilst we are all hopeful that these advances may eventuate without loss, yet the "working out of them must of necessity be a work of some time. And when you "also consider that there may be changes in the board during this time, and I "should have to explain to new directors what you know regarding my connection "with the inception of these advances."

Gentlemen, that was a communication surely calculated to make the directors consider seriously their position, whatever may have been their knowledge of there being unsatisfactory accounts before. It gave them distinct warning; it gave them this warning, that although the accounts might eventuate without loss, that was a matter which only time could decide. And he says that he did not need to particularise them. I don't think you will have any difficulty in making up your minds as to the meaning of that word—saying, in other words, as plain as language could put it, "I won't recapitulate these "accounts here, because you know them well enough." I need not tell you this, that if the directors had not known what these accounts were that were indicated in that letter, it was the gravest matter of duty to the Bank that they should instantly require an explanation, and ask what are those accounts referred to in that statement—what are those accounts which may eventuate without loss, but, of course, may eventuate in loss—what are those accounts which will take a long time to realise before we know whether there will be loss or not? But it was obviously quite unnecessary for them to make any such inquiry, and, accordingly, they made none, but took the matter into their full consideration. Accordingly, Mr Leresche, at p. 75, G. [See p. 145.]

LORD JUSTICE-CLERK—Don't you think you had better take the minute along with the letter?

LORD ADVOCATE—I am going to take it along with the letter. Mr Leresche's account of what took place at the meeting on the 30th December 1875 is :—"There were present Messrs Taylor, Potter, Stewart, Salmond, Inglis, "and Wright. Mr Alexander Stronach having retired, that was the whole "board at the time. On that occasion the burning of notes was again "adjourned, and I again left the room; but I cannot say whether I left the "agenda book behind me or not. The board had a long deliberation that "day. I should say it must have been two hours." Your Lordship in the chair put a question to Mr Leresche, "Are you speaking from recollection "alone?" and his reply was, "I remember it because the 30th was the occasion "when the letter of the manager was read accepting the appointment." Then he is recalled after the whole of the directors, with the exception of Mr Stronach, had considered the matter. Mr Leresche is recalled,—because he was not permitted to be present at important deliberations upon these matters. They had a very singular way in that Bank of dealing with their secretary. The manager conducts his private correspondence, not through the secretary of the Bank, who ought to be trusted officially in such a case, but through a private clerk, who communicates directly with the manager, and conceals a lot of information in regard to these matters that would otherwise in the course of bank management have gone to the secretary. And I must do him (the manager) the credit to say that the directors pursued precisely the same course in regard to Mr Leresche, because as soon as an important question like this came up—you will see one or two instances of it by-and-by —again the secretary of the Bank gets the hint that his room would be rather more desirable than his company. Out he walks, and the directors deliberate; and then they write up their own result of the deliberations that take place in the absence of the secretary, and hand it over to Mr Leresche in order that it may be engrossed in the minutes. There was a book called the agenda book that was prepared by Mr Leresche for the meeting. He noted down the business that he knew of that was to come before the meeting, and then the chairman, or some other component member of the meeting, wrote opposite that piece of business the way in which it had been disposed of. On this occasion, at the end of the two hours, the doors of the council chamber are opened, and Mr Leresche is called in, and the result of their deliberations upon the manager's most important letter is handed to Mr Leresche in the form of a resolution, on a slip. It is in the handwriting of two of the directors —the first part of it is in Mr Taylor's, and the last part of it is in Mr Inglis', handwriting; and that was embodied by Mr Leresche in the minute of the meeting of the directors. I must ask you to attend to its terms. This is the result of their deliberations. Mind that Stronach was not there. They cannot say it was Stronach this time. I have no doubt they will say it was Stronach on some other occasions, but they cannot say it was he this time, because he was not there. The result of their deliberation was embodied in this document, which was under the hand of two of themselves—Mr Taylor, the chairman of the board, and Mr Henry Inglis. The minute, which is just a copy of the resolution, is as follows [see p. 145]:—"A letter was read from Mr Robert "Summers Stronach, of date 28th December 1875, accepting the office of "manager of the Bank, and the same having been considered and approved "of, is ordered to be recorded in the minute-book; and all the members of "the board of directors a committee to comply with his request." And then they add—" The directors wish also to record, on their own behalf, the fact "that the matters alluded to in the letter in question were not at any time "brought before them by the late manager." Does not that resolution assume, from beginning to end of it, that all these gentlemen knew the matters alluded to—knew the unsatisfactory nature of these accounts? They consider this letter, and approve of it; and the only thing they take exception to is a statement to the effect—or rather they guard themselves against a statement—that these matters had been brought before them by the former manager. With the exception of that single point they accept the letter. They do not for a moment dispute their knowledge of the matters to which the letter refers; and in order that these accounts may be considered with the aid of all, instead of remitting the subject to a small committee, they appoint the whole body of the directors to act as a committee with Mr Stronach. Therefore, I think it quite impossible for any one to suggest that these directors had no knowledge at that time of the accounts—no knowledge as to what was the character of those accounts, or to deny the desire of Mr Stronach to be aided with them. Now, in what follows, gentlemen, I am sorry to say we are left to evidence from the records of the directors themselves. It is most important in this case to know what was the state of the Bank, what was the knowledge of the state of the Bank, and one of the most important questions is how far, after they had come to that resolution to aid Mr Stronach, the directors continued to have knowledge of these accounts. I shall go over what took place in the interval between that letter and the last balance-sheet and the stoppage of the Bank, as shortly as I can consistently with bringing the details before you, because it humbly appears to me that this is a very vital part of the case, because, as I have said before, without a knowledge that the state of the Bank required misrepresentation and concealment, I could hardly ask you to return a verdict of guilty against any one of the accused. I think, however, that a consideration of the different steps that took place after the date of that appeal made to them by the manager will show very clearly that they did continue in the knowledge of these accounts. You already have known that these grew enormously, and you will see how they grew. Take Morton & Co. for instance. Morton stands at £1,380,000 in 1875; in 1876 (which was just the year after this point had been brought up by the manager, he mounts up to £1,885.000; in 1877 he is reduced a little bit —to £1,771,000; and then in the year 1878 he is up a long way—to £2,173,000; or, in round numbers, he had got £900,000 more of the Bank money than he had in 1875. Now I don't think there will be any attempt in this case to suggest to you that these gentlemen covered their indebtedness to the Bank—that either Mr Morton or any one of them did so. There is no suggestion of it. You might as well suggest that there ought to be no liquidators, and no calls, because there is no deficit, and the Bank is really a healthy concern, if they would only realise their Australian land and shares. But you have a curious insight into what was known about that in the book kept by Morris, the private secretary, who superseded the most important part of Mr Leresche's functions,—the private securities book, in which there was kept a note of the special securities held against cash credit advances and bills, and which was brought to a kind of balance in 1877. It was spoken to by Morris. There were three big accounts in it,—Nicol Fleming's, Smith, Fleming, & Co.'s, and Morton & Co.'s. That certainly was a very wonderful illustration of the kind of business which the Bank was doing with these people at that time. There were securities stated by Mr Nicol Fleming equal to the amount of his indebtedness, which was very large. But when you come to look at the securities, they consisted, as they did in every case, to a large extent of this—£200,000 or £300,000 as the stock of the firm indebted; and that was dealt with as a special security available to the Bank. But the idea of taking a man's stock, with which you permit him to trade, as a special security, is a most extraordinary fallacy, and that must have been known to these men. You take the security of a man's stock in case of his failure to pay; but suppose he fails and loses his stock-in-trade, the security is also lost with the stock-in-trade. Then, again, they insure his life for £100,000; but unless they intended to poison him in the Bank parlour and realise in that way, I don't see how they were entitled to set that down as a cover to the extent of £100,000. And then there was what I have no doubt was done in perfect good faith, but it just exposes the inadequacy of the whole thing; it was explained by Morris that there was a quantity of shares at par value of £62, 10s., and by a calculation which he made he found out that if he added 400 per cent. to the value of these shares, he brought up the total to between £700,000 or £800,000, and covered Mr Fleming's indebtedness. It was only in that way that Fleming's indebtedness was covered. But even in that book there was not the slightest attempt to represent Morton's advances as covered, and, accordingly, his securities, which include £65,000 of insurance, bring out a deficit of £840,000 upon his account, even supposing his capital was realised as well as his life policy. That word "deficit" has a considerable deal of meaning in this case. This much must be said of Mr Morton that, although he had enormous dealings with the Bank, he is a gentleman who keeps very much in the dark, and the way in which the Bank dealt with him was not calculated to relieve his on-goings from that obscurity. He is found in connection with all concerns and things. When you are going to make a Pastoral Association by way of a little bank speculation in Australia, when you are going to buy shares or going to Poverty Bay or elsewhere with a view to recoup the losses of the Bank, Mr Morton is always in the neighbourhood, and is a large holder; but I am sorry to say he is a large debtor to the Bank himself. Morton's account does not appear much, but it does appear, and it was treated with very great secrecy by the directors. You have in the minute of 11th January 1877—"It was proposed and agreed that the Bank should accept "drafts by Glen Walker & Co. to the extent of £100,000 to retire a like "amount drawn by Holmes, White, & Co., Melbourne, on account of "James Morton & Co. The securities at present held against Holmes, "White, & Co.'s draft to be placed as security against the drafts of Glen "Walker & Co. Letter to be obtained from Jas. Morton & Co. to this "effect, and no drafts to be accepted until this letter is in possession of "the Bank." There were present at the meeting—Mr Inglis in the chair, Mr Potter, Mr Salmond, Mr Stewart, Mr Wright, Mr Talyor, and Mr Stronach. Then on the 18th of the same month—"With reference to the "minute of 11th January authorising the Bank to accept the drafts of Glen "Walker & Co. to the extent of £100,000, so as to replace a like amount "drawn by Holmes, White, & Co., it was considered that the letter of Messrs "James Morton & Co., dated 16th August 1876, and referred to in Bank's "minute of 17th August 1876, was sufficient authority to the Bank to adopt "the securities which were held against Holmes, White, & Co.'s drafts as "applicable to the new arrangement." The letter referred to is a letter on page 32 of the smaller print of documents, to the following effect:—

"In consideration of your arranging with Messrs Glen Walker & Co., of Mel-"bourne, or any other firm, for the drawing of credits to take place of a like amount "at present discounted by us, we hereby authorise you to transfer to a separate "account in security for same a proportionate amount of the securities held by you "on our account—it being understood that our account is to be credited with the "amount of the credits given out during this arrangement, and advising us of same.
"JAS. MORTON. Jas. Morton & Co."

Now, gentlemen, that account was under the consideration of the Bank, and I must ask you to attend to what Mr Leresche, in his evidence, says—"In the agenda book, under date 11th January 1877, there were present—"Mr Inglis (chairman), Messrs Potter, Salmond, Stewart, Wright, Taylor, and "the manager. The ordinary business of that meeting was closed by a letter "from Mr Bain, and the initials of Mr Inglis are after that piece of business. "The board remained in deliberation after that for a considerable time—a "long time. I was called in, and a draft resolution was handed to me to be "entered in the book. I cannot recollect in whose handwriting it was—pro-"bably it was in that of Mr Inglis. (Q.) It was not preserved? (A.) I have "no knowledge of it. On the left hand side in the agenda book is an entry, "'Morton's account,' in the handwriting of Mr Inglis. It was put in as a "separate piece of business from what had been made up by me for the use "of the meeting. Morton's account was never spoken of in my presence." Mr Leresche makes up the list of subjects to come before the board for discussion on that day. Mr Inglis initials that as chairman, and then proceeds to enter in the agenda book that new piece of business to which I refer, which he enters under the title of "Morton's account." Out goes the secretary as usual, and they consider that in private, and then he is called in, and the terms of the minute which I have read to you are given to him as adjusted. Then on 18th January you have the letter I have already read. Shortly after that date, there follows another very important minute. The date of it is 15th November 1877. The directors present were Mr Stewart (chairman), Mr Potter, Mr Salmond, Mr Inglis, Mr Innes Wright, Mr Taylor, and Mr Robert Stronach. At that meeting the manager was requested to lay before the board at their next meeting a vidimus of the securities held by the Bank in connection with the Australian and New Zealand advances, and then there is this part of the minute to which I must ask your particular attention:—"It was "resolved that a committee of the whole board should sit periodically to con- "sider the position of the various accounts of the Bank. The committee of "inquiry above mentioned will meet not later than four months from this "date." Now, gentlemen, there, upon those matters coming before them, this resolution is come to, that a committee of the whole house shall sit upon the position of the various accounts of the Bank. Can there be any doubt or hesitation as to what those accounts of the Bank were that a committee of the whole directors were to consider? It was what they had pledged themselves to do in favour of their manager by the minute of December when they accepted his letter. It plainly refers to the same matter; but there is a very singular addition here. The committee of inquiry, as entered in the minute, "will meet not later than four months from this date." Now, on this occasion, I think you will find from Mr Leresche's statement—that the desire of the manager was, when he brought this matter before them, that the board should sit at once and consider these accounts. That did not seem very palatable to some of them, and one of them makes a motion not unlike in form to what occurs elsewhere. When the opponents of a disagreeable and distasteful measure object strongly to it in either House of Parliament, it is customary to move that it be read that day six months or three months; and here the motion of one of the directors is very much equivalent to that—that those accounts be considered that day four months. Mr Leresche says, that at this meeting on 15th November 1877, there were present Mr Stewart (chairman), Mr Potter, Mr Salmond, Mr Inglis, Mr Wright, Mr Taylor, and the manager—the whole of them again. "I was absent," he says, "from the "meeting during the latter part of it, when they were deliberating on the New "Zealand matters. Afterwards I was called in and recorded the deli- "verance." (Q.) After you had engrossed the board's deliverance about the New Zealand and Australian advances, did the manager say anything "in your hearing to the directors? (A.) Yes. (Q.) Did you hear what "passed? (A.) He said that he wished that a committee of the whole board "should sit periodically to consider the various accounts of the Bank. (Q.) "Did you hear what passed on that suggestion? (A.) Yes, it was agreed to, "and I then entered this resolution:—'It was resolved that a committee of "'the whole board should sit periodically to consider the accounts of the "'Bank.' A conversation then arose as to whether the manager wished this "to be done at once, and a suggestion was made that it should begin six "months afterwards. (Q.) Who said that? (A.) I cannot remember who "said it. (Q.) Was it Mr Stronach or some one else? (A.) It would not be "Mr Stronach; it would be one of the directors; and afterwards it was sug- "gested, so far as I can recollect, by Mr Taylor, that it should be four "months. (Q.) What was to be done in four months? (A.) The looking into "those securities. (Q.) The sitting of this committee? (A.) Yes." And accordingly it was minuted that this should not take place for four months. In the agenda book it is entered in what appears to be Mr Taylor's handwriting, that "It was resolved that a committee of the whole board should sit "periodically to consider the position of the various accounts of the Bank. "This is not to take place for four months." Now, it is perfectly plain that the manager again on this occasion brings these accounts before the board, and he is met by this, "in six months," then "in four months," then "not later "than four months." Now, gentlemen, is it possible to say that those men had not Morton's account in view,—that they were not prepared when called upon then to fulfil the undertaking they had given to their manager in the end of 1875, to the effect that they would lend their aid to look after these accounts? Is it not clear that the manager then thought things were not straight with these accounts, and that they ought to be looked into; and is it not equally plain that the directors must have known that, and must have known it even although they desired to put it aside as not a very convenient and pleasant thing? It must have interfered with dreams of 12 or 14 per cent. dividend, and probably that was not a pleasant consideration; but the thing was there, and pressed upon them; and I ask whether, in the face of that, you are to assume that in that long discussion the manager's desire for aid was the merest sham and quibble, and that these gentlemen knew nothing of his real desire to have those matters investigated with their assistance; and investigated why? Because, according to the fact, these accounts which were unsatisfactory—the chance of putting them right merely a hope, a scintilla of hope, in December 1875,—were getting a great deal worse at the date when he made that request in 1877. Then, again, we have no trace of a meeting of that committee. In fact, it seems to have been to a considerable extent shelved by that adroit movement. But again, on 14th March 1878, you have the matter up. It is brought before them again; and upon that occasion "it "was agreed that Messrs Stewart, Potter, and Salmond be appointed a com-"mittee, along with the manager, to examine the accounts at the head office "weekly, and to deal in particular with the account of James Morton & Co." That is their own record of a meeting where there were present Messrs Stewart, Salmond, Wright, Taylor, Potter, and Stronach,—all except Mr Inglis. But that comes up again at the next meeting, when Mr Inglis is present, for this appears—"In regard to the committee appointed at the last "meeting as to Morton's account, consisting of the foregoing gentlemen, "along with Mr Salmond, Mr Stewart further reported Mr Morton's engage-"ment to realise as quickly as possible, consistent with prudence, his 4 per "cent. preference stock of the New Zealand and Australian Land Company "held in security by the Bank,"—and at that meeting there were present Mr Stewart, Mr Salmond, Mr Taylor, and Mr Inglis, the last of whom had not been at the previous meeting.

Now, gentlemen, are we to assume—and you will be asked to assume—that these gentlemen were ignorant of Morton's account and its state. No matter what the manager warnings; no matter his repeated request that they would fulfil their pledge; no matter that a committee is appointed—they knew nothing about it,—the manager or some inferior official of the Bank is responsible for all that, and for the state of Morton's account. That you will hear that argued, I have not the slightest doubt. It is very difficult to get into their board-room when Mr Leresche was shut out; but surely you are not going to hold that what passed in the board-room, and the minutes made and written in the hands of directors at the board, are to be treated as a mere mockery and a delusion,—that such things never took place,—that the account was not discussed,—that their deliberations were a farce,—and that nothing earthly was done about Morton or disclosed about his position. Un less you are prepared to accept that,—to accept a suggestion coming from counsel as an answer to a deliberately recorded resolution at the time, you will, I venture to say, have great difficulty in coming to the conclusion—if it is possible for you to come to it—that these gentlemen were not one and all aware of Morton's increasing indebtedness, and aware that the huge account to which their attention was called in 1875 was growing like a snowball from year to year under their management. And it was not Morton's account only. Any one of them was big enough to frighten a prudent man—but just take Smith, Fleming, and Co.'s; and it is very curious in itself,—a very curious specimen of the career of a mercantile man, wo makes a large fortune, and loses a large fortune, and gets pulled through by the Bank, leaving the Bank and himself both a great deal the worse of the operation. In 1870, Mr John Fleming told you his agents, Duckworth & Co., failed, and the result of Duckworth's failure was that he became embarrassed, and finding he could not go on, he at that time came to Glasgow to see if arrangements could be made with the City Bank. There seems to have been faith everywhere in the City Bank, but I do not know that any one had more implicit confidence in the City Bank than those impecunious gentlemen who were constantly drawing upon its funds, and to use language that appears elsewhere, "absorbed"—a word very characteristic of the fact—the greater part of the Bank's capital. They had implicit faith in the Bank, and their faith was justified. He comes down to the Bank. He owed them then £150,000, and he says—I have no doubt he believed it, whether it was precisely the fact or not; we need not take him too strictly to task—he believed it was well covered. Well, let it be so. But it is quite obvious that £150,000 did not altogether disclose the extent of Mr John Fleming's, or rather the state of his firm's, indebtedness at that period, because the modest sum which he names as absolutely necessary to pull him through in the crisis of his fortunes in the beginning of 1870 was £500,000 cash. Well, it is said, "You "may do this in various ways," but he says, "Oh no, I object to the way "proposed by the Bank; I won't hear of a new firm in Liverpool drawing "upon me!; it would destroy my credit." Accordingly he objected; and the Liverpool firm did not prove successful after all, and he said (I have no doubt with perfect truth), "If you do not give me £500,000, what I will do is, I'll "come down; I will fail, and go into the *Gazette*." That seems to have been a very alarming threat; why it should have been it is not very easy to see. But it seems to have given great alarm to some of the directors of the Bank, because when Mr Fleming was leaving the room, Mr Potter rushed after him and brought him back. They would not let him come down, and the result was, that he was as handsomely treated then as at subsequent periods. He got his £500,000 from the Bank to pull him through—at least something like it, because at the end of that year the Bank was in advance £500,000. It is right to say that Mr Fleming thought they were covered to the extent of three-fourths of that debt. Here is a man on the verge of bankruptcy, who must come down if the Bank will not give him £500,000, and to keep him up the Bank are in advance to him at the end of that year to the extent of £125,000 of balances uncovered. That seems to have been the whole advantage the Bank got out of the transaction—that whereas they were covered at the first, they were uncovered to the extent of £125,000 at the end of the year. And that was the beginning, so far as Smith, Fleming, & Co. were concerned, of that deficit which the Bank were straining every nerve to recoup at a later period of their history. Because, unfortunately, John Fleming's difficulties did not end there. They recurred in 1875, if indeed he was ever free from them. He never seems to have repaid the Bank; but in 1875, in the beginning of the year, he is in difficulties again, and he has been trading pretty largely on his credit with the Bank; because when these difficulties, as he was pleased to call them, overtook him in the beginning of 1875, the state of his account with the Bank stood thus: he had got upon bill credits £562,000, and he had got in cash advances £773,000, making in all, £1,355,000. And then, being in difficulties, he proposes, and there is made an arrangement. Now, gentlemen, I think you will find that at this stage the arrangement and the position of Smith, Fleming, & Co. were known to the directors. The arrangement was made—it is called the arrangement of March 1875 in the evidence before you, and it was embodied in a letter by Smith, Fleming, & Co., part of which I shall read, written by Mr John Fleming on the 12th April 1875, but it was not adhered to, for this reason, that Collie's failure, of which you may have heard, took place shortly afterwards, and once more Mr Fleming was overtaken by difficulties, and consequently the arrangement of March was modified in August of that year. That failure affected the credit and cash of Smith, Fleming, & Co., and the result was, that a new arrangement had to be made. The fact of this arrangement is, however, let me say, by no means so important as this other fact, that the Bank and certain of the directors, at least who are sitting at the bar, knew quite well about these things. Mr John Fleming in his evidence undoubtedly told you that he was obtaining advances from Stronach, which were not known to the directors; and notwithstanding the air of moral dignity with which Mr Fleming emitted his disposition before you, I do not think it was a very straight action on his part to help to keep those facts from the directors. He obviously did so; because when one of the directors, Mr Salmond, called and asked questions, he gave him at least an evasive, if not an untrue reply, and then he wrote a warning note to Mr Stronach, in case Mr Stronach should give a true and therefore a different reply, and involve him with the directors. It was not straight sailing by any means, and I do think it can be said that until 1875 these matters were really divulged to the directors; but he stated with equal emphasis—and the correspondence to which he was referred by Mr Stronach's counsel in cross-examination entirely bore out the statement—he stated, I say, that that was not the case when Mr Robert Stronach came to be manager, and that one of the first acts of Stronach in January 1876, after he became manager of the Bank, was to inform him (Mr John Fleming) distinctly in writing, that he would not personally give him any advances without the knowledge and sanction of his board. And so far as Mr Fleming knew and understood, he never from that date till the Bank closed its doors got a sixpence from Mr Stronach individually without the knowledge of the directors.

But now about the letter of arrangement—which, of course, was Stronach again, according to one view of this case, but we shall see about that. As to the arrangement of March 1875, Mr Fleming wrote to Mr Stronach on the 12th April, in the following terms:—

"Referring to the meeting I had with your directors and yourself on Thursday, "1st inst., respecting the state of our account with the Bank, I now beg to detail "the terms of the agreement come to as I understood them:—1. Smith, Fleming, "and Co. as a firm, and the partners as individuals, pledge themselves to abstain "absolutely from all speculative operations, unless specially sanctioned by the "Bank. 2. They are to hold all property belonging to the firm as per annexed "statement, as security or cover to the Bank for its various advances to them: but "inasmuch as it is of the greatest importance that the credit of the firm should not "be injured, but be carefully maintained, no public transfer of the property is "meanwhile to be made. The realisation of the property is to be left in S., F., and "Co.'s hands, who undertake faithfully to account for and pay over to the Bank, "the whole proceeds of all property realised. 3. The Bank's charge for commission "for all credits issued for S., F., & Co.'s accommodation, as per list herewith, shall "be at the rate of ½ per cent. per annum, and this arrangement is to be retro-"spective as from 1st January 1875. 4. The Bank's charge for interest on all cash "advances to S., F., & Co. shall be at the rate of 3½ per cent. per annum, as from "1st January 1875. A statement of the balances of various accounts as on 31st "March last is appended. 5. The Bank shall advance the sum of £100,000, at "the rate of 3½ per cent. per annum, for the acquisition of £100,000 of the stock of "the Canterbury and Otago Company, £7800 of which is to be provided by me, "credit for the equivalent of £7800 being given to Smith, Fleming, & Co. in "account with the Bank as at 1st January 1875. 6. The £100,000 of stock as "above shall be held by trustees in trust for the following purposes:—(1) To pay "interest, at the rate of 3½ per cent. per annum, to the Bank for the £100,000 "advanced for the purchase of the stock; (2) to pay the whole of the surplus "income arising from the stock, after meeting the charge for interest as above, to "the credit of S., F., & Co.'s account with the Bank, and to continue doing so until "all S., F., & Co.'s debts to the Bank have been liquidated; (3) nothing was agreed "as to the ultimate disposition of the stock upon the final liquidation of all S., F., "and Co.'s obligations to the Bank, but I venture to suggest that in that event the "trustees be directed to retransfer the stock at cost price (viz., par) to the parties "who furnish it, or their assignees or heirs."

That letter, which states the arrangement, has appended to it a statement of his indebtedness to the Bank, which is stated at the figures I gave you—namely, bill credit to the amount of £562,000 odds, and cash advances to the extent of £771,000 odds. And here you have a sort of indication, beginning even then, of the kind of way which the Bank take to recoup these losses. Such a balance is due, and here is how they try to make it up. It is a very generous course of procedure, but a very singular one. Your debtor owes you a balance which he cannot pay up, and you say to him, "Very well, "you owe me £100,000, and are not able to pay it. That is perfectly true. "But here I have got another £100,000 in my pocket, and I will lend it to "you; and you will go and buy stock and shares in New Zealand, which will "yield 8 per cent. That will enable you to pay me back 3½ per cent. on the "old debt, and you will pay in the balance of the 8 per cent. towards "liquidation." But then you don't even settle who is to get the balance of the capital over £100,000, if it should turn out well. The chance of gain is left in the most generous manner to your debtor instead of making a profitable investment for yourself—a very handsome way of doing, but surely suggestive of this, that there was something very far wrong with a balance requiring to be recouped by such a mode of speculation on the part of the Bank. Well, after the Collie disaster, a new arrangement is made, and the chief feature of that arrangement, which your Lordship will find at page 11, is the way in which they deal with the realisation of the security which is to be bought with the new loan of the Bank? The letter says (p. 12)—"In the event,"—they had not quite settled how the surplus was to be dealt with if those shares were realised; but in this letter of August the conditions are made more tight in favour of the Bank, for this reason, that their debtor had become so much worse by reason of Collie's failure, being involved in it, and, accordingly, it is stipulated in this letter—"in the event of a sale, to apply the proceeds first in liquidation of the afore-"said advance of £100,000, the whole of the surplus over and above the "said advance being paid to the credit of our account with the Bank. The "Bank shall have the power to direct the trustees to realise the stock at such "times, and on such terms, as they (the Bank) may think proper. It is never-"theless understood and agreed, that the Bank shall not exercise its power to "sell or order a sale of the stock until the expiry of five years from this date, "when the Bank shall have the power and option to dispose of the stock for "the sum of £300,000, or to continue to hold it for two years longer, in "which case the interest to be charged upon the advance shall be at the rate "of 5 per cent, instead of 3½ per cent." Now, there is a remarkable circumstance with respect to that letter, at least so far as regards one of the prisoners at the bar, to whom I shall specially refer before closing—I mean Mr Potter—because Mr Potter undoubtedly does appear throughout all these transactions of the Bank more prominently than any other director. And not only so, but he comes upon the stage at critical periods, and, I think, himself gives impulse to very decisive action. He disappears as fast as he appears, but not till he has set the machine in motion. In this instance you have a very singular illustration of it. I don't know whether he means to say that he knew nothing about these accounts. I don't know whether the evidence of yesterday, relating to his general incapacity for or neglect of details, is to be held as excusing him from the knowledge of the indebtedness to the Bank. But here he is in 1875 obviously a party to this arrangement, because upon the first of these letters is an important alteration, evidently made to adjust it in terms of the second. Both Mr Stronach and he were parties to it. Mr Morris speaks to that. He is shown the letter of April, and is asked, do you see certain marks on the document—in whose handwriting are these? He says—"Some "in Mr Stronach's." Then he is referred to another addition—"Five years "to hold securities, then sell as required; £25 when due." This is just the substance of the alteration made upon the agreement of March by the subsequent agreement of August. Mr Morris is asked—"In whose handwriting "is that addition? (A.) Mr Potter's. (Q.) On the next page there is "another alteration in Mr Potter's handwriting? (A.) Yes; life policies." He is dealing with that arrangement, and that arrangement depends for its substance upon the advances which had been made at that date, amounting to £1,300,000 odds. Can it be suggested that with that information,—when Mr Potter is told that amongst other accounts, Smith, Fleming, & Co.'s is a source of such anxiety to Mr Robert Stronach, that he cannot accept the responsibility of becoming manager, unless he has the aid of the directors in attending to that account—can it be said that Mr Potter did not fully understand the effect of the appeal that was made to him by Mr Stronach? It is a wearisome task, and one I need not try to pursue, to trace from that date, the agreement of 1875, down to the final consummation, the stoppage of the Bank, the course of this account. It is very graphically described by John Fleming himself, who knew perfectly well the whole details of it. He says he remembers being asked by Robert Stronach to go to Glasgow, to meet with the directors in July of last year. "By that time the amount of indebted-"ness had considerably increased. (Q.) How did you come to be able to "carry on, after Collie's failure, till the meeting of July 1878? (A.) When "we needed help we got it." Then his Lordship in the chair put the question, "From the Bank? (A.) From the Bank." That account went on from bad to worse. The result of it was, as Mr Fleming very fairly said, that, talking in round numbers,—because gentlemen like Mr Fleming deal with large figures, and don't content themselves with merely £5000, or anything like that,—at the date of the stoppage he was owing from £1,800,000 to £1,900,000. "(Q.) What were your securities? (A.) About £450,000, if the "Bank gets all, which it may not do, as there is a dispute about them." And that is the result of it,—a result which it was pretty plain to see, because this is a gentleman who was always liquidating and trying to pay; and what is called, or seems to have been called, in the books of the Bank, and according to the management of the Bank, "liquidation," is the most extraordinary proceeding that I ever heard of as contrasted with what is popularly understood by liquidation. The usual process in liquidating an account is to sell off the securities and ascertain the balance; but in the case of Mr John Fleming there was nothing to sell. Liquidation, if you go to the root of the word, means "melting," and the idea is that you are to melt down the man's means and pay off his liabilities. But in this case there were two liquidations going on. They were melting down his securities when they could, but the Bank funds were melting just as fast, because what came from the Bank and went to Fleming flowed a great deal faster, and in much larger quantities, than anything that ever came from Fleming to the Bank. As showing how they were dealing, and how true the statement of Mr Fleming is that the directors, and not Mr Stronach, or rather both together, sanctioned his advances after 1875, let me refer to another minute, because it shows how they dealt with Smith, Fleming, & Co., and it shows the lamentable straits to which the fostering of these enormous credits on the part of one or two houses had placed the Bank, when it came face to face with a legitimate mercantile transaction. I refer to the minute of the directors' meeting of 11th May 1876, at which there were present—Mr Taylor (in the chair), Mr Potter, Mr Salmond, Mr Stewart, Mr Innes Wright, and Mr Stronach:—"A letter was read from Messrs Smith, Fleming, & Co., "dated London, May 4, 1876, applying for an open letter of credit for "£10,000 in favour of Messrs W. Nicol & Co., Bombay, to be drawn at 6 "mos/st. against the security of goods and produce detailed in said letter. "The application was agreed to on the usual terms and conditions. A letter "was read from Messrs Smith, Fleming, & Co., dated London, 4th May 1876, "for an open letter of credit for £5000 in favour of Messrs Todd, Findlay, "and Co., Rangoon, to be drawn at 6 mos/st. against produce as detailed in "said letter. The application was agreed to on the usual terms and con-

"ditions. A letter was read from Messrs Smith, Fleming, & Co., dated London, "20th December 1875, intimating that owing to the failures that occurred "during the last crisis"—Mr John was always getting into a crisis—"and to "general derangement of credit consequent thereon, they are unable to fulfil "their engagements to the Bank, entered into in March 1875, without some "temporary assistance being granted, and asking that a special credit be "opened in their favour to the extent of £45,000, to enable them to do so, "and undertaking to liquidate"—liquidation again—"the new credit in the "course of the year 1876. After explanation by the manager, it was agreed "to grant the credit by accepting the drafts of Messrs W. Nicol & Co., "Bombay, to be drawn at 6 mos/st. to the extent of the credit asked, the "proceeds of the said drafts to be applied in payment of (1) the interest "amounting to "£25,033, 12s. 10d., due at 31st December last, on the "Bank's cash advances to Messrs Smith, Fleming, & Co.; and (2) the special "cash advances, amounting to £20,000, made to them during the months of "October and November last, it being understood, at the same time, that this "temporary arrangement is not to interfere with or supersede the arrangement "of March 1875." Did the gentlemen who stipulated that that was not to supersede the arrangement of March 1875 not know what the arrangement of March 1876 was? Did they not consider it when they expressly stipulated that it was not to be superseded, and especially when they were considering it with the view of doing what they did with their eyes open, which was simply to give the Bank name and liability to the extent of £45,000, to enable John Fleming to pay his debt to the Bank—a sort of transaction again of the most singular character—to keep up his credit. It is just the same as if your debtor came to you and said, "I undertook to pay you £45,000 to-day, 28th "January 1879; I undertook to do that last November, but I cannot do it. "I cannot meet my obligation; give me £45,000 to pay you." And you give it to him, and he pays his debt, and the thing is satisfactorily squared off. Could that deceive any man sitting at the board, even men who don't go into details, and who only deal in large and general transactions? If they choose to go into that agreement of 1875, the sums were big enough to satisfy a mind more ambitious of large transactions than even Mr Potter's appears to have been. Then, as a contrast to that, we have instances showing what was the real effect,—that they were strict at the branches, and sometimes at the head office too. They had no money except for Smith, Fleming, & Co. "A "letter was read from J. C. Cunninghame, applying, on behalf of Merry and "Cunninghame, for an overdraft of £150,000 on the security of his estate "of Foyers and the St Vincent Street property belonging to the firm, and "intimating, at the same time, that it was the intention of the firm to transfer "their working account to this Bank and its branches." But £150,000 upon good heritable security in Scotland was far too big a transaction for the City of Glasgow Bank. "The directors, after mature consideration, while feeling "gratified that the proposal should have been made to them, felt "that the transaction was too extensive to be entertained as a fixed loan." Then, again, as to this arrangement, and as showing the knowledge of all, there is a minute, and an important one. On 10th May 1877, there is an application by Mr John Fleming. There are plenty of applications by him through the minutes, but I need not weary you with them all:—"10th May 1877.—Present, Mr Stewart (in the chair), Mr Potter, Mr "Salmond, Mr Wright, Mr Taylor, and Mr Stronach,"—all present except Mr Inglis. "The application by Mr John Fleming for letters of credit for "£20,000, to be used in connection with cotton purchases, which was before "the board at their last meeting, was again brought up, and an explanatory "letter from Mr Fleming, dated London, 5th May 1877, having been read, "the application was granted—this being special, but not to exceed six "months; and this not to interfere further with the terms of the original "agreement, dated 24th August 1875." Again we have the agreement before them; recognising the agreement, they say it is not to be departed from, and yet I fancy the suggestion will be made—unless I mistake the line of the examination pursued in the course of the evidence in this case—the suggestion will be seriously made to you, that these simple gentlemen knew nothing whatever about the arrangement, or about Smith, Fleming, and Co.'s debts. Then, again, in the minute of 1st August you have embodied the result of Mr John Fleming's visit to Glasgow, as he told you. On that day their business largely consisted again of Smith, Fleming, & Co.'s credits. They asked for a renewal of £18,500 against shipments of shellac. The persons present were Mr Salmond (in the chair), Mr Stewart, Mr Potter, Mr Inglis, Mr Wright, and Mr Stronach. Letters were read from Smith, Fleming, & Co., dated London, 24th July, applying for £15,000 credit in favour of W. Nicol and Co., Bombay, and £10,000 credit for the same firm, all of which were granted on the usual terms. "In regard to these various applications of "Smith, Fleming, & Co., the manager reported that he had requested a "meeting with Mr John Fleming, who came to the Bank on Tuesday last, "30th July, and had an interview with him and Mr Stewart and Mr Potter. "Very full explanations were given by Mr Fleming, and the directors on the "whole thought it proper to agree to the advances." Mr Taylor was absent from the meeting, but Mr Stewart was there, and he does not challenge the statement and report of the manager. And if you will allow me to refer to the account of the meeting given by Mr Fleming, I think there are two important considerations that may be derived from it—viz., that this account was represented to be, and considered at that meeting to be, in a very unsatisfactory state, and that the cause of its being unsatisfactory was that the indebtedness of Smith, Fleming, & Co. was being constantly added to. "In "July 1878," Mr John Fleming says—"I was asking for an advance of "£25,000. I went to Glasgow, and met Mr Robert Stronach, Mr Potter, "and Mr Stewart. (Q.) Was your indebtedness to the Bank referred to at "that meeting—the amount of it? (A.) No. (Q.) Was it spoken of as being "very large? (A.) The state of our account as being very unsatisfactory was "spoken of; the amount was not discussed." Then he is examined by his Lordship in the chair. "What was said about the amount of your account? "(A.) It was alluded to as being very unsatisfactory. I cannot recall the "exact expressions used, but it was spoken of as an unsatisfactory account, "and that it was most unsatisfactory that the indebtedness had been increasing instead of diminishing, and I explained, with reference to that, that the "condition of trade for several years past had been deplorably bad." Well, that may be so. Bad trade may have accounted for the want of money on the part of Smith, Fleming, & Co., but it does not account for the fact that these accounts, being in the view of the directors unsatisfactory, should have had their indebtedness added to? And if the directors had any knowledge of these balance-sheets, how did they come to deal with a bad account, which was being added to, as an account that was paying interest divisible among the shareholders? Now, gentlemen, that is another of these accounts; but Mr Nicol Fleming's was not a whit better. The sums were hardly so large, but, on the whole, his credit was even worse than that of Smith, Fleming, & Co. This account of Mr James Nicol Fleming, or James Nicol Fleming & Co.—because it assumes two shapes in the course of these transactions with the Bank—is an important account, for this reason, that it seems more immediately to have led to the attempt to recoup deficits by means of investments in Australian and New Zealand land shares. Mr Nicol Fleming's final indebtedness to the Bank was £1,238,000, having grown to those dimensions from £1,005,000 in 1875, and it attained that growth and magnitude, notwithstanding the fact that, during that period, Mr Fleming was practically, from first to last, if you accept the statements made as true, in liquidation. In other words, he was recognised as a bad debt, requiring to be paid off, but only likely to be paid off if the realisation of his assets went on slowly. Now you heard no further back than yesterday the evidence of Mr Dugald Bell, his clerk, who managed one part of his transactions in Glasgow. What Mr Bell knew did not represent the whole of his indebtedness, but I think his evidence discloses very clearly the very rapid way in which Mr Nicol Fleming, from 1868 onwards, was going down hill. He had started about 1863 in his Glasgow business with something like £260,000 of capital, and in 1868 the capital at his credit was £48,239, so that he had lost in the interval about £212.000. On the 31st January 1868 the balance at his credit was reduced to £25,818. It remained very nearly the same down to 1870, but at 31st January 1871 the balance was turned, and began with a debit of £7716. In other words, he not only lost all his capital of £260,000, but £7000 more. In 1872 the loss on capital account was £35,000; in 1873, £84,000; in 1874, £104,000; and in 1875, £213,000 upon that account alone; and I think you will not be surprised when you find that he went practically into what is called liquidation. There was another witness (Mr Hunter) who spoke upon this matter. He was consulted about the liquidation, but Mr Bell, the clerk, was selected to liquidate in Calcutta on behalf of the Bank, so that he went out for both interests. Any man who knew the result of that liquidation in Calcutta must have known how hopeless this balance of Nicol Fleming's had become. Just take Mr Bell's account of it. He was asked, "What were your duties to be in Calcutta when you went out in 1875?" and he answered, "I was to realise the assets of the old firm as speedily as I "could without sacrificing them, and remit home the proceeds. (Q.) To "whom were you to remit the proceeds? (A.) To Mr Hunter. (Q.) How "long were you out there? (A.) About a year. (Q.) Did you find the duty "of realising an easy or a difficult one? (A.) Well, I found matters had been "going behind, and that there was very little to realise. (Q.) In fact, you "found assets, but you found debts too? (A.) I found large debts. (Q.) "Bad ones? (A.) Yes. (Q.) There were some coals, were there not? (A.) "That was the principal asset; a large claim we had upon a native firm for "coals. Nothing came of that so far as I know. We could not get anything "out of it. (Q.) Did you realise anything really to send home in that year? "(A.) No. After paying some of the debts of the firm, there was really "nothing to send home." And that gentleman, before he went, was in communication with the Bank, and in communication with Mr Potter about this realisation. The counsel for Mr Potter elicited from the witness this statement, that "when Mr Potter impressed upon me the propriety of realising "what I could, I understood it was with the view of reducing Nicol Fleming's "debt to the Bank. It was quite plain that Mr Potter was desirous to do his "best for the Bank." I do not doubt for one moment that Mr Potter was desirous that by that liquidation Nicol Fleming's debt to the Bank should be reduced; but that surely infers knowledge on the part of Mr Potter that there was a debt to be reduced, and the more startling the amount of that debt the greater the necessity that there should be a good realisation. It is an ample explanation of his desire for a good liquidation that there was a big debt, and it is absurd to speak of his desire that it should realise a great deal if Mr Potter was not aware that there was a debt, and was not aware of its magnitude and importance. But did Mr Potter fail to inform himself of the result of the liquidation? Can you take it that he ever knew, or had reason to suppose for one moment, that the liquidation of those coals or anything else,—which came to nothing, as Mr Bell told you,—satisfied in any way that large debt he was so anxious to meet? There is nothing to suggest that. On the contrary, there is the clearest evidence offered by those witnesses who came in contact with him, and by the way in which that debt is dealt with in the minutes of the directors, to show that there was knowledge again on their part of the amount of the indebtedness. Then, in the same way, Mr Hunter supervised the liquidation on behalf of the Bank, and he formed a bad impression of the debt, and recommended liquidation. Whatever might be the knowledge derived from his report, he gave a very bad account of it, and recommended a liquidation, which practically ended in nothing, meaning by that, that they failed to reduce the debt, and that the realisation of assets in India turned out to be a simple farce. But what is perhaps the most important part of this is, that the directors seem to have been, about the end of that liquidation, or even whilst it was going on, thoroughly aware not only of the extent of these accounts—unsatisfactory accounts—to which the manager on taking office had called their attention, but had obviously come to know this, that upon these accounts there was a very serious deficit, and that unless some other means than those which had been taken up to that time were resorted to, the end would be certain loss to the Bank. They became aware of the deficit, and they resorted to means to meet it.

Now, were those means, let us consider, of a kind sufficient to warrant them, or to warrant anybody, in treating these as good debts that would bear interest—in treating these as debts covered by securities, so that they might fairly bring them down as assets held by the company, and not as debts without security against them? Very far from it. The fact of their resorting to unusual, and, in ordinary circumstances, illegitimate speculation—that is their view, gentlemen, not mine only,—for the purpose of recouping or satisfying these debts, plainly shows a knowledge of the deficit, and the intention, if possible, to meet it. But how was it intended to meet it? By investing either directly or indirectly in land—not with the expectation even of immediate payment, but in the hope that, some day or other, when Australian or New Zealand property increased in value, the return from it, or the proceeds of it, would enable them to meet their obligations. With all those deficits staring them in the face, what was the plain duty of the directors to do—which course were they to take with that knowledge before them—which was the only honest and fair course to take as regards the shareholders and the public?—to treat these as debts covered by securities at that time, so well secured that the interest they were yearly adding to them was to be regarded as recoverable and divisable profit; or, on the other hand, to set them aside in a suspense account as debts which might one day be recovered and repaid, but debts which could not be recovered and repaid until a number of years had passed, and a good realisation, which was a matter of speculation, had rendered them able to meet these accounts? Well, they applied to Mr Glen Walker, and Mr Hunter was also employed on the subject, and he saw a number of gentlemen in connection with it, amongst others, Mr Stronach, Mr Potter, Mr Taylor, and Mr Stewart. I take Mr Hunter's statement upon this point:—" (Q.) Were you given to understand what purpose they had in " view in buying land? (A.) I don't know that I ever heard of the purpose " they had, but I understood it was for Nicol Fleming's account—to cover it. " I understood it was for the purpose of making Nicol Fleming's account " right, to cover whatever discrepancy existed upon it. (Q.) That is to say, " by making a profit on the Australian land, they would cover any loss upon " his account? (A.) Yes. (Q.) Were you not given to understand, by two " of the directors, that it was for that purpose? (A.) I quite understood it " was for that purpose. (Q.) Who gave you to understand that? (A.) I don't " know that it was ever in so many words said it was for that, but I considered " it was the fact of my looking into Nicol Fleming's accounts that led to my " being consulted. (Q.) With whom had you communication about it chiefly? " (A.) Mr Stronach and Mr Potter, and Mr Taylor and Mr Stewart oc- " casionally." The result of these communications was an arrangement, embodied in a letter by Mr Glen Walker, who addressed the manager upon 14th August 1876 in these terms:—

"DEAR SIR,—In continuation of conversation with yourself and other gentlemen "connected with the Bank, I would now place in writing the suggestions which "we have been discussing towards increasing income and recouping deficits by "the judicious acquirement of pastoral properties. More than one member of "your board are connected with New South Wales properties, which have on an "average of many years, I am assured, paid a net return upon present values ex- "ceeding 16 per cent. per annum. The purchase price usually is paid by partly a "cash deposit, and the balance by bills extending over several years. It is easy "to finance against them in the colony; and if 40 per cent. of the price was pro- "vided here, the remainder could be arranged in the colony without further aid from "this.

"If arranged in this way, finance probably would cost for interest an average of "6 per cent. per annum, and there would remain on the basis of the experience "referred to as net profits 10 per cent. per annum. The suggestion is that the "Bank grant credits to the extent of from £100,000 to £150,000 towards the ac- "quirement of pastoral interests in Australia.

"For example, if a value of £250,000 was acquired there should be a net profit "of £25,000 yearly, but £25,000 yearly will in fourteen years repay £250,000 and "5 per cent. interest, so that thus, by comparatively a very small outlay, a large "amount can be recouped.

"Mr Borron and myself will be glad to be interested in the project, and to "manage its detail; and finance can, in the Bank's option, be arranged either by "cash advance or entirely by credit."

Then that letter, which is of date the 14th August, came before the board upon 17th August 1876, and this is how it was dealt with:—"A letter from "Messrs James Morton & Co., and two letters from Mr W. Glen Walker, "dated respectively Glasgow, the 16th and 14th inst., with regard to the "drawing of credits in lieu of those now drawn by Messrs Holmes, White, & "Co., and others, and one of the latter, as to the acquisition of certain pastoral "properties, were brought under the consideration of the board, and, after "full consideration, the board came to the conclusion that it was advisable "to adopt generally the suggestions contained in these letters; and they "accordingly requested the manager, associated with Messrs Potter, "Stewart, and Taylor, to arrange with Mr Walker as to all details. "While arriving at this resolution, the board were fully sensible of "the undesirableness of such investments as the purchases proposed in "the letters; but having in view the position of certain old accounts, "and looking to the whole circumstances, and particularly to the fact that the "contemplated arrangements for the working of the credits are large part of "tranactions in existence for many years, and previously brought under the "consideration of the board by the present manager, the board deemed it "expedient to come to their present decision,—as referred to in the minute of "30th December 1875." Now, the persons present at that meeting were Mr Stewart (in the chair), Mr Wright, Mr Taylor, Mr Potter, and Mr Stronach. In connection with this it is important to observe, that though Mr Inglis was not present, he not only saw that minute, but made an alteration upon it in his own handwriting, putting in the words "previously brought under con- "sideration of the board by the present manager." Mr Salmond was present at the meeting when it was read. Mr Leresche, being shown a draft re- solution in the handwriting of Robert Stronach, says,—"My recollection is, "that I was called down some days after the meeting of the 17th, into the "manager's room, and I was handed this draft resolution. I was asked to "bring my agenda book down, and enter therein as under the date of the 17th. "So far as I recollect, Mr Taylor and Mr Inglis were present when Mr "Stronach handed it to me, and my memory is confirmed by the fact that "there are in Mr Taylor's handwriting the words, 'read and agreed to,' "and in Mr Inglis' handwriting, 'insert in minutes, deliverance of board.' "(Q.) So you have no doubt that those two gentlemen were the two who "were present. (A.) That is the impression I have at present. The words "at the side of the memorandum 'as referred to in the minute of 30th "'December 1875,' and 'as referred to,' are in my handwriting. The "whole body of it is in the handwriting of Mr Stronach, except two lines "which come in, 'and previously brought under consideration of the board "'by the present manager,' which are in the handwriting of Mr Inglis. So then, when about to recoup the deficit by Australian loans, it is done for the purpose of recouping it upon those very accounts which are again in the hands of the board, and which, as recorded by them, had been brought under their consideration by the manager in 1875, when he took office.

Gentlemen, I do not need to say much more upon this matter of investment in land. It is for you to judge, not so much whether it was a legitimate investment,—that is not the question that is before you just now,—you are not here asked to say whether the management of the board was prudent or reckless, was right or wrong,—you are here to ascertain what were the facts connected with that management—what was the knowledge of the panels at the bar in regard to it—did they know the state of the Bank arising from these accounts, or did they not?—that is the question for you,—not what was the cause of the Bank getting into that condition; through whose weakness or leniency towards debtors,—that is not the question; the question is, did they know the state of the Bank?—the next question being, if they knew it, what did they know of the issuing of those false abstracts to the shareholders? Now, whatever may be said on the part of one of those gentlemen—I refer to Mr Salmond—as an inference to be drawn from the circumstances that he was absent about the period when that annual balance was prepared and published, I say nothing at present, but I think it will be very obvious to you that nothing which may be said upon that point can in the least degree touch or affect his knowledge of the state of these accounts, because throughout the whole of those proceedings, he is a party along with the other directors, and shares with them the knowledge which they obviously possess; and although he does not admit it in his declaration, the words that he there uses go very far to suggest that if he did not know it at all, he was shutting his eyes to the fact. The statement he makes about it—and you will bear in mind that he was an old bank manager, and tolerably well understood the way to govern the affairs of a bank—in as follows:—"I first come to know that the Bank was "not in an easy condition some three or four years ago"—just when Mr Stronach told him—"but I thought nothing of it, believing that it would all "come right in a short time;" and here he states what I do not dispute—

"The real cause of the unsatisfactory state of the Bank, was the absorption of "the capital by the foresaid advances; and though I did not know the amount of "the advances, I was satisfied that the accounts must have been in a very unsatis-"factory state to require such absorption. I suspected or inferred that there was "something wrong with these advances, without knowing what it was.

"Declares further—As regards what took place at the weekly meetings, I explain "that the advances made to the parties before mentioned came up in the ordinary "way, but were not specially stated. They came up just in the ordinary general "way, the same as advances to other customers."

But they were dealt with very differently; for whilst the other customers got theirs on the usual and proper terms, those other firms got theirs on very different ones. But you can hardly take from Mr Salmond the statement that he knew these accounts were unsatisfactory because they had absorbed the capital of the Bank, and yet that he did not know that it was a wrong thing; or at least a thing involving the Bank in danger, to continue giving those firms further advances, instead of seeing that the accounts were placed on a satisfactory footing. Upon the matter of these Australian advances, you have a report by Mr Taylor, Mr Stewart, and Mr Potter, and another by Mr Inglis, Mr Taylor, and Mr Salmond, which show clearly that they were employed in this matter, and were presumably conversant with it. The first is dated 19th October 1876, and is as follows:—

"In terms of the minute of the board of directors, of date 17th August 1876, appointing us to arrange with Mr Walker with regard to the acquisition of certain pastoral properties in Australia, we have to report, that we then authorised an investment to the value of £120,000 to £130,000, and have granted letters of credit in favour of Messrs Glen Walker & Co., Melbourne, for £45,000 for the first payment, the balance to be financed by them, and the property, as acquired, to be held in trust by Messrs Borron & Co., and by them registered in such names as the Bank may instruct. (Signed) WM. TAYLOR, J. STEWART, and LEWIS POTTER."

The next is dated 24th October 1877—another transaction of precisely the same class for recouping the deficit:—

"The committee appointed by the board, to communicate with Mr Glen Walker as to the purchase from the Australian and New Zealand Land Company of their Queensland properties, have had various meetings with Mr Walker, and beg to report that they have confidence in his knowledge and discretion, and recommend the directors to authorise him to acquire the properties in question, at the price of about £150,000, on the best terms which he can accomplish, looking to his own memorandum, marked H. I., 24th October, and to the letter from Mr Mackay, similarly marked and dated. (Signed) HENRY INGLIS, WM. TAYLOR, and ROB. SALMOND."

Now, these appear to me conclusively to show this, as the result of the examination of these accounts, that their character, their unsatisfactory character, was disclosed to the directors by Mr Stronach when he took office in the end of 1875,—so unsatisfactory, that Mr Stronach would not undertake the position of manager unless he was to be relieved of the load of responsibility which a struggle to put such accounts into shape would necessarily involve; that they knew it; that they agreed to help him; that they went on dealing with those accounts from month to month, and from year to year; dealing with those accounts which were becoming more unsatisfactory than ever, even liquidation producing nothing, but always giving more and more; and yet I presume that, in the face of these facts recorded in their minutes and correspondence, the directors would fain turn round now and say, "Entirely the manager's doing. Some of us don't understand the details of business; none of us knew these details; we were innocent of that knowledge which might have led us to suspect that something was seriously wrong with the Bank." Gentlemen, that is a matter for you. If you can accept that explanation as a fair and true explanation, it would give a very different complexion to this case. I can hardly conceive that you can arrive at that result—that you will take it off the hands of gentlemen who have undertaken to aid the manager in regard to these accounts, who deal with these accounts, who continue to treat with these customers, that they knew nothing of the character of the debt; that they knew nothing of the increasing loss and risk to the Bank; and that they did not know, and had nothing to suggest to them that it was not a legitimate thing to treat those bad and uncovered accounts as solid assets, and to deal with those profits in the air, which never came to them, and consisted of nothing but an entry in the books as actual earnings, to be paid over to the deluded shareholders in the shape of 12 or 13 per cent. dividend.

I had hardly intended to meddle with any except these accounts; but there is one other account which I cannot fail to notice, because it comes very near to one of the panels—I mean Mr Innes Wright. Mr James Nicol Fleming was a director in 1875, and when Mr Hunter began to look into Mr James Nicol Fleming's affairs, he came to the conclusion, which I think any honest man would have arrived at, that a person who was getting advances to the tune of hundreds of thousands of pounds from the Bank, and who was constantly wanting more, was not just the sort of person who ought to sit as a member of the board of directors. He was too good a customer of the Bank—from his own point of view, not the Bank's—to be really in the position of a director, especially after he had come to occupy in reality the position of a director who could not pay. Mr Nicol Fleming did not quite see it in that light. I suppose he thought his account would probably be better if he remained a director to look after it. But at length he goes, and, having got rid of a member of the board placed in that ambiguous and very painful position towards the Bank and its shareholders, they made a new acquisition, in the shape of Mr Innes Wright, to supply his place. Mr Innes Wright was asked to become a director. He says so, and it does not appear to be contradicted anywhere in the evidence. I do not know what made the presence of Mr Innes Wright at the board of directors such a desirable thing in the interests of the Bank. I have gone over the evidence in this case most carefully, and I have utterly failed to find any qualification that Mr Innes Wright had for becoming a director of the board at that time, except these three—he was not a shareholder, he had not a penny to buy a share with, and his firm, of which he was the leading partner, was owing the Bank about £334,000 sterling. These were his qualifications. How and why he became a member of the board is a matter of speculation. He knew something, at all events, about the indebtedness of one firm to the Bank, and I think you will agree with me in holding that he became equally acquainted with the indebtedness of these other firms. His admission to the board was managed in a very snug and comfortable way, apparently with general consent. This is what he says about it:—" I had not the necessary " qualification of stock when I was elected a director. I stated this to the " manager, but I obtained the qualification a few days afterwards. I also " urged the condition of my firm's account as a reason against my having any " connection with the board. Stronach was apparently anxious that I should " be a director, and Mr Salmond also urged me to consent. The request to " be a director came to me quite unexpectedly, and I am not aware what " reason induced them to make the request." The question arises here, what on earth induced him to accede to the request when it was made? " The " stock necessary for my qualification was acquired for me by the Bank. No " cash passed, but I gave a cheque for the amount, and that cheque stands " against my account with the Bank to the present day." He knew the state of his firm; but just let me give it to you, because it is in more correct language than mine would be, from the narrative given by Mr Paul, who was a partner of the firm, but whose functions seemed to come to an end because the character of the firm changed from an exporting business to a sort of financing business, in which he had little to do, and he retired from the firm in 1876. This is the account which he gives of that flourishing concern, the senior member of which became a director:—" (Q.) Did he tell you who " asked him to become a director? (A.) He told me the first intimation he " got on the subject, the first approach on the subject, was by Mr Robert " Stronach, the manager. (Q.) Tell us what he said? (A.) And on a sub- " sequent day he had, I was told,—by him, I think,—a visit from Mr Salmond, " following up the proposal. Mr Wright evidently had doubts about accepting " it. (Q.) Did you express any opinion at the time as to your view of his " accepting? (A.) I said how far is it right, how far is it proper, to accept a " directorship, Mr Wright, in the state of our account? (Q.) What did he " say to that? (A.) He said, 'I am alive to that, but Mr Stronach tells me " 'that will be no difficulty, he will arrange all that.' (Q.) What was he to " arrange, did you understand? (A.) The indebtedness was to remain in " abeyance, I suppose, and that the fact of our indebtedness would be made " no disqualification." Now, as to the state of the firm, he says:—"(Q.) From

"1870 downwards, while you were a partner, were you ever doing anything "but making losses? (A.) Well, it was the exception to make profit. Of "course there were individual operations that were profitable; but, on the "whole, we were apparently going behind. (Q.) You knew the result of "your trading was that you were realising loss? (A.) Quite so. (Q.) And "I suppose you knew then that the money you got to meet your liabilities "must have come from some other quarter than the profits upon your trade? "(A.) Quite so. (Q.) And that quarter was?"—the old answer—"(A.) The "City of Glasgow Bank." Now, what did these gentlemen want to have this independent shareholder as a director for; to aid them at the board in putting these accounts right? And what did that debtor want at the board in the way of legitimate management of the concerns of the shareholders? It is an ugly feature in the board of direction. That he was tolerated, would be bad enough; that he was required, is worse still; and that he went, is bad enough too. I don't think you could expect much reduction of accounts by a man who did not want to reduce his own, who wanted to put his own account into that pleasant state that was described by his partner as in abeyance. What is abeyance? That the Bank is not to be paid till it meets their convenience, if it should ever be convenient for them to pay—that is the plain English or Scotch of it, whichever you like. And in the meantime these accounts which were elsewhere heard of in the course of evidence as dormant—a very good expression, too, because they simply slept on without either being paid or bearing any fruit—remained unpaid. And if you want a picture, there is the state of the Bank. I should like very much to know what inference can be drawn as to those who really thought that such a man, in that position, would be a useful aid in performing the task which the directors had undertaken to their manager in December 1875. What was the honesty of the intention as regarded his account—ay, and as regarded those other accounts, because I think it matter of considerable doubt whether they were to be separately treated? But, gentlemen, it is matter of no small comfort to me that these are questions with which you must deal, and not I. It is my duty to lay these considerations before you, and to ask you to consider, upon the whole matter of these recorded transactions—and these accounts as I have given them to you from their proceedings and minutes from first to last, whether there was, on the part of all or any of those directors, a knowledge of the state of the Bank which came to light so late as October 1878? Their own books show that they had looked into the matter,—that they had suspicions. If they really and truly knew that things were wrong, they were not entitled to shut their eyes and not look. A man may, through negligence or carelessness of habit, or from want of intellectual perception, fail to see a thing, and he could not be held criminally liable for such failure; but, on the other hand, I venture to tell you, that shutting your eyes against what you know to be a fact, not because you do not know it, but because you do not want to see it, and do your duty by it, infers criminal intention just as surely as if you kept your eyes open, and discredited or refused to recognise the fact.

Now, gentlemen, if the state of the Bank was, as I have represented, generally known—not in precise details, but the actual fact in general terms, known to those gentlemen—I put the question to you next, are those abstracts before you, which are as I pointed out to you, in essential particulars false, calculated or not calculated to conceal and misrepresent the true state of the Bank? If so, if you have actual misrepresentation, you have a motive for misrepresentation, because there was something to conceal. Do you think, if the truth had been made known as to the real state of matters; that they had never got a penny of these accounts; that their reserve account was made up of unpaid and hopelessly lost interest; if they had told the truth as to the actual amount of the better class of assets they had, and disclosed the enormous amount of bad assets they had in the shape of finance paper,—if they had not concealed these facts, would not things have taken a different course? Mr Cunningham Smith yesterday was very unwilling to admit that there was any distinction in the market, or according to public view, between legitimate transactions in the shape of bills coming from Australia and drawn against produce, and bills kept in a bundle in a safe in Mr Potter's or his partner's room, and brought out and ante-dated a month or two, to make it appear that they were actually drawn by an Australian house upon their correspondents or the Bank in Glasgow. But he partly admitted it, though he unfortunately seemed to labour somewhat under a defect in his moral vision, which did not enable him thoroughly to appreciate the distinction. But then, if that had come out, would it not have been known, and did they not wish to conceal, that the Bank were financing at their own hand through Mr Morton, Mr Potter, and others? In other words, they were using bills to pay their debts, while all the time they were liable under these bills, and it was not an unuseful thing to cut off the enormous amount of indebtedness upon such bills, because you must bear in mind that a bill is a liability as well as an asset. If A owes for a £1000 and pays you, you are £1000 the richer; but if A gives you his bill, and you discount it with your name upon it, and you get your £1000 in the meantime, it does not follow you are much the richer man, because if A does not meet that bill you will have to do it; and accordingly, under an asset of that kind, there always lurks a liability. If the other names on the bill are good, you get the money; but if they are bad, you pay the money yourself.

Well then, gentlemen, I repeat that there is a distinct connection between the state of the Bank and those misrepresentations or falsifications that are introduced into the balance-sheet. I have not the slightest hesitation in asking you as a jury to hold this, that whoever may have been the person or persons who executed those fabrications, who falsified the balance-sheet, and issued it in that false and fabricated state to the public, knew the state of the Bank, and did it because he wished that state to be concealed. What earthly purpose could there be, if the Bank were not in that state, in misrepresenting one single item in this balance-sheet as taken from those books? If the Bank were really and truly doing a business so good that it had earnings sufficient to pay a dividend of 12 per cent. on its capital, if its capital was intact, if it had a reserve fund of £450,000, and, moreover, ample assets, and good assets, to meet all its obligations, why on earth should that state of matters have been concealed—what earthly reason not to disclose the whole assets and the whole obligations? But it was not so, and I do not say that you will ever get at the true balance-sheet by making corrections on the errors so plain on the face of this. The whole thing was intended as falsification,—falsification in order to make things better than they really were—and better than they even appeared in their books by any fair interpretation—simply to still those rumours that might arise when accounts like Morton's and others were talked about outside the Bank, or the finance paper was discovered, or anything arose which would disclose the character of the investments they were going into, and which are so carefully concealed upon the face of this abstract. There is not a word about heritable property in Australia here,—not a syllable. They know how to describe heritable property when they find it in Scotland, but they cannot find a name to cover heritable property in Poverty Bay or in Australia, except by calling it Government stock or balances in the hands of foreign correspondents; and it is for you, gentlemen, to say why. I am not saying one word about individuals at this moment, but it is impossible to dissever the preparation of this false balance-sheet, made up within the walls of the Bank, from a knowledge on the part of him who made it up, of the true state of the Bank, and a desire and the purpose, by publishing it in all its falsity, to conceal and misrepresent

—to draw a red herring across the track of those persons outside who might otherwise have got a clue to the utterly rotten condition of the Bank.

Well, then, who did it, and who are responsible for it, is the serious question which, if you agree with me, so far as I have gone in the facts of the case, it is next your duty to face. And I here repeat that, in order to a conviction of any one of the panels upon the charges which this indictment contains, it is not necessary that he should have had an active hand in the preparation of that false abstract. It is not necessary that he should either have guided the pen, or directed the calculations of the man who made up the scroll abstracts, and transferred them from that to the published balance-sheets. It is not necessary, in order to convict a panel of the alternative offence charged, that he should have known every particular item of the arithmetical mode by which these results were attained, so as to make the sheet balance. It is enough if he knew and was aware that the balance-sheet was not a true but a false balance-sheet—if he knew and was aware that, being false and untrue, it was given out to the public for the purpose, not of honestly informing the shareholders and the public, but of misleading them as to the true character of the Bank's position and assets, and trading. On this part of the case I cannot help saying to you that it is wholly a jury question. You cannot expect from the Crown evidence of all that transpired within the walls of the Bank, all that took place at the councils of these directors, because necessarily these operations are conducted in secret. The deliberations of the board are conducted in secret—in the present case with a privacy unusual in boards; because whenever you touch upon the tender and diseased parts of the Bank's trading, there is no secretary there—the directors only. Whenever these things come up, bear in mind, the door opens, and out goes Mr Leresche, and the door closes whilst the deliberation goes on, and until it is finished. You cannot therefore expect in this case direct testimony. The little shred that would have been left is cut away by the act of the directors themselves, and they cannot be heard to complain of the want of it. Their act has made direct testimony impossible, and that being so, you will judge them upon what they have done and recorded. And you are at perfect liberty, in the whole circumstances of the case, to determine, so long as you do it honestly, according to your conscientious belief, whether each or any of them was, or was not, connected with this crime, either as an active participant in the preparation of these falsified balances, or as an assenting party to their being issued to the public for the purpose of deceit. It is impossible to disguise that between certain of the panels who sit at the bar there is this great distinction—Messrs Potter and Stronach occupy the one class, and the remainder of the directors the other, for this simple reason, that so far as the fabrication of those balance-sheets is concerned, the evidence against them is quite different. It is most distinctly deponed to by the witness Morison, the accountant of the Bank, who prepared these false abstracts—I fear I cannot say unknowingly—but bear this in mind, that although Morison must at least have strongly suspected, if he was not fully aware of, their falsity, yet he had not the information in his possession which could either have induced him to fabricate them himself, or have enabled him to know where the shoe pinched, and what it was that the false representations should hide. He had not the securities book; he had no access to the cheque-box; he had to take the statements of Mr Potter or Mr Stronach for the fact that there were securities standing against this or that, or that these were such utterly good securities that they might even be treated as gold. There are one or two passages of Mr Morison's evidence which I should like to bring to your recollection upon this very matter of the preparation of those scrolls and balance-sheets. Take the balance-sheet of 1876, for I ought to explain that whilst Mr Morison distinctly says that Mr Potter was there in 1876, and advised and directed the scheme of falsification, that scheme was followed implicitly, with a small variation in regard to the £973,000 in the years 1877 and 1878. The evidence runs:—" (Q.) How long were Mr Potter and you engaged in " revising that balance-sheet, resulting in the red figures being put on? (A.) " Perhaps an hour or two. On the left hand side of No. 128 there are entries " S., F., & Co. (Smith, Fleming, & Co.), £200,875; J. N. F. (James Nicol " Fleming), £100,300; and J. M. & Co. (James Morton & Co.), £450,600. " These were credit accounts, entered in that part of the abstract which con- " tains advances on credit. (Q.) But you bring them down and insert them " among what? (A.) Government stocks, railway stocks and debentures, and " other securities. (Q.) In the abstract of 1876 there is an entry under assets, " 'Government stocks, Exchequer bills, railway, and other stocks and deben- " 'tures, and balances in the hands of banking correspondents.' Was the " effect of that to represent debt due on credit account by those firms, to the " amount of £751,000, as either a Government stock or security? (A.) Yes. " (Q.) By whose instigation were these sums brought down? (A.) Mr Potter's. " (Q.) Was it by his directions it was done? (A.) Yes. (Q.) Did he assign " any reason or justification for it? (A.) That the Bank held certain stocks " against the debt of £751,000." *By the Lord Justice-Clerk*—" (Q.) And " therefore treating them as good assets? (A.) Yes." *Examination continued*—" (Q.) Did Mr Potter seem to understand the different items they " were considering? (A.) Apparently so. (Q.) Did he appear to be quite " conversant with them? (A.) Quite conversant." Now, gentlemen, it may be suggested—it is just possible that it may—that Mr Morison, the accountant of the Bank, did all that out of his own head; and for what purpose? I can hardly conceive such a suggestion seriously made as that a man in his position, with the limited knowledge in which he was kept in regard to the affairs and trading of the Bank, should set to work for some purpose or other to falsify the accounts, as if he had been really able to divine the state of the Bank. That is something perfectly incredible. But if not, were Mr Potter and Mr Stronach not there? If they were, you have evidence upon which you are entitled to rely—if you think it reliable—directly connecting them with the fabrication; and, if so, I think you will have little doubt as to the result of the evidence in this case, so far as these two gentlemen are concerned. So far as the other panels are concerned, you must keep in view that they had that knowledge of the affairs of the Bank, according to the assumption of my argument—and you will judge how far it is well founded—which certainly should have made any man of ordinary knowledge and common-sense aware that that was not a true abstract which was issued to the shareholders. I do not say that the mere fact of suspicion that it was untrue is enough to entitle you to convict them of that alternative charge. But if they knew that the balance-sheet had been altered so as to make it false, and if they also knew that the purpose of doing so was to conceal the state of the Bank, and allow that to go forth to the shareholders, I tell you—under correction of his Lordship—that they are guilty of that alternative charge. It is for you to consider the case of each one of these five prisoners separately and apart, to consider what they jointly knew, and to consider the extent and means of knowledge which they separately had, and to come to an independent conclusion in each case. If you can arrive at the result that they had the knowledge I have suggested, I ask you, because I am entitled to it, for a verdict against them upon the alternative charge. I ask it on behalf of the Crown, and in the name of justice. But equally in the name of justice, if you are honestly unable to arrive at that conclusion, you will give the prisoners the benefit of the doubt, and a verdict which at least will have the effect of dismissing them from the bar. Gentlemen, I have only one word to say in conclusion, and I regret that that word should have been forced upon me by the enormous mass we have had in the present case of evidence of character. I don't ask you to lay aside for one moment the fact that these were gentlemen of position and of high repute. They are entitled to any fair presumption arising from their having such repute; but to press that evidence to the length to which it has been pressed by witness after witness in that box, is the most preposterous thing I ever heard in a court of justice. If it be true that not one of them is capable of committing such an offence, nobody did it—a very singular result. Evidence of character in connection with certain offences is a valuable ingredient in determining the guilt or innocence of the accused; but I tell you, in a charge of this sort, evidence of character—although it is not to be laid aside—means that you are not to treat them as if they were men of bad character; it amounts to no more. I tell you that an offence such as this is impossible except to a man of good character. If a man has not a good repute—if a man has a bad repute—you will never find him in the position of a director of a great bank, entrusted with millions by the public, or in a position to work that wreck upon any institution which has befallen the City of Glasgow Bank.

MR TRAYNER'S ADDRESS FOR MR STEWART.

May it please your Lordships, Gentlemen of the Jury,—I attend you in this case on behalf of the prisoner Mr Stewart, and I rise to address you on his behalf with a feeling of anxiety, which I have never perhaps experienced in the course of a somewhat lengthened practice. I have not approached any case with more anxiety as to its result, nor with a deeper feeling of the responsibility imposed upon me as a counsel, than I feel at this moment, when I rise to address you. Why is it so? Do I apprehend an adverse result from the evidence? Has Mr Stewart's character been such as to lead you to convict him of the offence charged? No, gentlemen, these are not the causes of my anxiety, but I feel that you cannot have come into that box without being deeply prejudiced against Mr Stewart, and against every member of the directors' board of the City of Glasgow Bank. That Bank closed its doors in the beginning of October last, and from the time it closed until the time you were enclosed where you are, the public clamour has been unceasing, not for justice upon the directors, but for vengeance upon the men who had lost five millions of pounds. The public clamour has been raised, not merely, as the Lord Advocate told you, in private conversation, swelling out into public chatter; but we have the press painting, in its deepest colours, the distress of the persons who have suffered in the ruin of this Bank, and some of them pointing, and pointing with emphasis, to this as the only possible result and remedy for the disaster—that the directors should be punished, and punished most severely. Gentlemen, I am not so much astonished that the newspapers did this. It was a matter of great public moment, attracting almost unique attention; but I am astonished, and I am grieved to see that the press was not the only exponent of public opinion, or the only director of public thought, that lent itself to the hue and cry which was raised for vengeance, as I have said, and not for justice. Gentlemen, you know, as I do, from the public prints, that the pulpit has been degraded into a platform for semi-political and semi-social discussion. It has been used by men to whom it was committed for a higher and nobler purpose to hound on the public feeling against these unhappy men; and clergymen have stood up in the pulpit and preached against the directors as men who have been guilty of crimes which cannot be painted in colours too deep or too black. Gentlemen, I would that those ministers had taken a lesson from the great Master they profess to serve, and had not allowed themselves, with passion and prejudice behind them, perhaps within them, to be pushed into a position utterly unworthy of their high office. Do you remember how public clamour, sometimes unreasonable, but always powerful, once raised its cry for immediate vengeance and execution of sentence upon one of whose guilt there was no question? She had been taken in the very act, and public clamour demanded that she should be executed, and executed at once; but the great Master to whom they appealed, was not moved by that public clamour and that senseless cry, for He stood by calmly and unprejudiced by the public cry, to deal with the matter which was brought before Him, as I would His servants had done here. There was guilt—unmistakable, convicted guilt,—but he was not the first to throw a stone at her. Would he have treated the directors as these ministers have done—all unheard, no investigation, no defence offered, or explanation given? And yet His servants, occupying His place, and professing to teach His principles and follow His practice, forget themselves so far that, whereas He was slow to inflict punishment where guilt was certain, they cry out for punishment and vengeance where guilt is not brought home, and where no defence has been heard.

Gentlemen, these are the things that make me anxious when I address you—not the merits of the case,—because I cannot help feeling that when you came into that box, you must of necessity have been prejudiced against the men you were to try. Has there been nothing to fan that prejudice even in the case we have had before us? What does the indictment charge these men with? It charges these men with three acts of fabricating balance-sheets, uttering these balance-sheets in the knowledge that they were false, uttering them for the purpose and with the intention of defrauding the public, and with the result that the public were defrauded and deceived. It proceeds further to charge three of them individually with having embezzled the Bank's money committed to their care, using it for purposes for which it had never been intended it should be used, and it concludes with no less than ten several acts of theft which it is said these gentlemen, each and all, or one or other of them, committed. Was there no propriety in the observation that the press and the pulpit should have been slow to condemn men who had not been heard upon their defence? The Lord Advocate, in the exercise of his duty, a public duty incumbent upon him, thought it right in the indictment to set forth the different charges to which I have now referred, but the result of the investigation has been that he, who has been investigating these matters for months with all the assistance that the Crown and the Crown Office can afford him, has been led in the course of the inquiry, and at the end of day after day's proof in this Court before you, to abandon more than one-half of that indictment. All the theft has gone; all the embezzlement has gone; and gone from your consideration as if, to use the Lord Advocate's own expression, these charges never had existed, and these men sit here charged with fabricating and issuing a false balance-sheet, and that alone. But does that not point to the propriety of what I have said—that before people, either in one position or another, cry out for the condemnation or punishment of men whom they think to be guilty, they should not merely make themselves well acquainted with the charge itself, but should wait until they have heard all that can be said legitimately, and as forcibly as possible, in defence of the men so charged. But gentlemen, if I have been oppressed with anxiety when I commenced the case, I hope the result of the investigation will be to relieve me of a great deal of that anxiety, especially on account of the gentleman on whose behalf I am addressing you. You had your prejudices—I cannot think otherwise—when you came into that box, but you have attended to the evidence, and you have heard as the result of it, that the Lord Advocate had to give up all the charges of theft and all the charges of embezzlement. I proceed to ask you now to consider with me whether the Lord Advocate has proved the three remaining charges against the prisoner whom I represent. And, gentlemen, let me say at the outset, that if I make any observations in the course of the argument which apply more especially to the causes of the other panels, do not for a moment let it be supposed from anything that I say that I am here to charge any of them, or even suggest that they are guilty of a crime of which I profess to be innocent myself. As a member of the board of the City of Glasgow Bank, Mr Stewart undoubtedly had serious responsibilities. He had his duties to perform, and the question you have to consider is how those duties were performed. He is not here, nor am I here for him, to say one word about the other prisoners at the bar, for they will be well defended by the gentlemen who have their cases entrusted to them. Before I proceed to notice in some detail, but as shortly as I possibly can, the particular features and points in this case which require some little argument, and perhaps some little explanation, I desire to ask your attention, in the first place, to the observations which fell from the Lord Advocate shortly before he resumed his seat. He said you cannot have direct testimony in each case, and that the directors must not complain of that, for they had themselves deprived him of the possibility of putting before you such testimony. Gentlemen, I do not care how it has been done—I do not admit the Lord Advocate's proposition, or that the directors did it—but I don't care how it has been done, why it has been done, or by whom it has been done. You are not entitled—the Lord Advocate's opinion notwithstanding—to convict the prisoners at the bar, or any of them, except upon direct testimony to your satisfaction that they are guilty of the crime laid against them. I am here to say that, while you are entitled to make reasonable inferences from the evidence, you are not entitled to take anything as evidence of the guilt of these men except what may not only fairly, but in the reasonable use of language, be described as direct testimony of their guilt. I was astonished to hear the Lord Advocate dwell—for he came over it more than once—upon the somewhat trivial circumstances of Mr Leresche having been requested to leave the directors' board-room before the close of the meeting. Have none of you confidential clerks with whom you trust all your business, into whose hands you will trust all your money, but whom you do not think it right to consult when your special customers or clients are with you? Is every gentlemen in this city who has a confidential clerk or private secretary sitting beside him to be suspected of doing something wrong or nasty, because, when a client comes into his office, he asks that private secretary to step into another room? Why, how absurd it is! The Lord Advocate surely had other things in this case sufficiently strong for his purpose, as he put it, without dragging into his service a triviality like this! We don't know anything about Leresche, except that he was the secretary of the Bank. We do know that when he came into that office, according to his own statement—which I don't impugn—he was requested by Mr Alexander Stronach to confine himself to his own department, because the previous secretary had been rather prying, and had displeased the directors. Mr Leresche properly enough, as far as I know, confined himself to his department; and he went to the board meetings with his agenda book in his hand, and told the directors what business they had to transact; and when that business had been considered, or when they desired to consult in secret, they requested him to retire until the matter was settled. How, in the name of wonder, can that be said to be any indication on the part of the prisoners that they were doing something they did not want to be known? The very next thing the Lord Advocate made a complaint of was, that when the consultation had been held, and when the directors had resolved upon that on which they desired to consult when they made Mr Leresche leave the chamber,—when that was done, the result was given to Mr Leresche to put into the minute book. I don't suppose that Mr Leresche was very anxious to hear the pros and cons of the debate that led to the resolution, and I don't think it would have instructed or amused the Lord Advocate, or helped him in the prosecution, to have been able to go over the pros and cons to-day. But it is of the last importance for you to keep in mind—the Lord Advocate naturally did not press it upon your attention—it was no part of the Lord Advocate's case, and did not have the importance to his mind that it has to mine—that there was no consultation and no occasion spoken to by Mr Leresche or anybody else, of which, when the meeting was over, the import and purpose of the meeting was not recorded in the minute book. If the directors on these different occasions were doing that which they knew to be dishonest, if they were doing that which they even thought to be doubtful or wrong, they never would have recorded in the minute book at all. However foolish, reckless, and careless these directors may have been—or use any other term to designate their conduct you think fit, except criminal—if their conduct had been criminal they never would have entered these things in the minute book; and if anything short of criminal—if foolish, reckless, careless, sinful if you like—but if anything short of criminal, it is no matter to you what their proceedings were at all. Gentlemen, you were asked under this indictment, as originally presented to you, to convict Mr Stewart of being a swindler and a thief. Mr Stewart is a man who has lived a long, a useful, and an honoured life. The Lord Advocate thinks that is not of much moment, and he protested with a heat which I have seldom seen a public prosecutor show, that it was a matter for denunciation by the public prosecutor in the present case that witnesses had been called as to the character of the men who are at the bar. Why not? If the Lord Advocate thinks it right to call this man a thief and a swindler, am I not right to bring a man who knows him better than the Lord Advocate does to prove that he is wrong? I never heard such an objection in my life. He says no man but a man of good character could have been a director of a bank, and, therefore, the presumption is in the directors' favour, and then he starts with that special circumstance as being against the man. It will not do for the Lord Advocate to blow hot and cold in the same breath in this matter. But I am not, so far as Mr Stewart is concerned, open to the remarks the Lord Advocate made about witnesses called as to character. I did not put witness after witness into the box to prove character. The very first witness for the Crown, except the formal witnesses who spoke to the declarations, was the one witness I asked to speak to the character and personal worth of Mr Stewart. and who was that witness I asked to justify Mr Stewart's character? Dr M'Grigor of Glasgow,—a man in universal esteem, and there is no man in the profession to which Dr M'Grigor belongs who holds a place of higher esteem, or who deserves a place of higher esteem, than he. A man of culture and education; a man of strong and clear observing powers; and a man as purely and essentially honourable as ever breathed the breath of life—what is his opinion of Mr Stewart? "He has known him "a long time; he is essentially honourable. (Q.) Would he have fabricated "a balance-sheet? (A.) No. (Q.) Did he know of the Bank's affairs, according to your opinion? (A.) No. (Q.) He professed ignorance of them? "(A.) He did. (Q.) Did you believe him? (A.) I did believe him." Gentlemen, I might have brought you twenty men from Glasgow, and, probably, twenty men from Edinburgh, to prove the very same thing about Mr Stewart; but to get one witness like Dr M'Grigor is worth more than the whole of them put together. I leave Mr Stewart's character upon that basis. I say, in the face of the prosecution, that, notwithstanding all they have attempted to prove, or have proved, Mr Stewart is here unassailable as an honourable, honest man; and I shall fail in the duty I have undertaken if I do not show to you, before I resume my seat, that the estimate which Dr M'Grigor had of Mr Stewart was the right one, and the one you will ultimately adopt. What more than this honourable character did Mr Stewart risk here? For remember, if Mr Stewart was lending himself to fabricate and utter false documents—to commit a crime of this kind—he was perilling everything that man holds dear. He was perilling his liberty; he was perilling his fortune; he was perilling that which is dearer than fortune—the good name he had always held. Well, you have heard what his good name was; what was his social repute in Glasgow? What was he in point of means? A man is said, in Scotland at least, to be very careful in anything that touches his pocket. Let us test Mr Stewart, even by that low criterion; let us see what he had at stake. He joined the Bank in 1871—a man possessed of a fortune of £80,000. He remained in this Bank until 1878, and was then worth £122,000, and you are asked to believe that a man, until then (and he had grown old) honest and upright, a man entitled to be called essentially honourable, suddenly becomes a criminal, and consorts for three years with other directors of the Bank in fabricating and falsifying their accounts, and issuing these false and fabricated accounts to the public for the purpose of defrauding them. He does all this,—he risks his good name, and he risks his whole fortune,—because every man in that Bank has been rendered bankrupt,—he risks his whole fortune; in the name of God, for what? I listened to the Lord Advocate's speech to hear upon what ground or authority he was going to attribute corrupt motive or bad purpose to this man. Take it as reasonable, common sense men—does a man risk his name, his character, his position, and his whole fortune, without something to be gained by it? If he puts his all upon the cast of such a die as that, it must be a great stake the man is playing for. I ask again, what was Mr Stewart, or any of his co-directors for that matter, to gain? Were they making to themselves large fortunes? Were they speculating? Were they even gaining pecuniary advantage by ready advances of money? That was the kind of case put upon the indictment, and that is the kind of case the Lord Advocate has had to abandon. The idea that Mr Stewart came into that Bank, or remained in that Bank, or did a wrong thing in that Bank, for the purpose of getting advances to himself or his firm, was as preposterous an idea as ever a Lord Advocate or a Lord Advocate's assistant suggested. When Mr Stewart joined the Bank in 1871, he had had an account with the Commercial Bank of Scotland for something like forty years before. What was the state of that account? You had the manager of the Commercial Bank put into that box to tell you the state of it; and he left the box without a single question being put to him in cross. Therefore I take it you will accept as absolutely correct both his statement and the fair inference to be drawn from everything that gentleman told you. What was the result of his evidence? That in 1874 Mr Stewart's account was not only one of the most satisfactory in the Bank, but one which they were very sorry to lose, and it was then overdrawn to the extent of £18,000, without one shred of security, except the credit of the man who was the drawer. Now, there is a man esteemed as essentially honourable, possessed of a fortune of £80,000, with ample credit at his banker's, and with all the advantages pertaining to a social position which no man can better pretend to than Mr Stewart,—he has all these things to peril, and nothing to gain. Having gone thus far, I think I am entitled to say that the presumption in starting is in favour of Mr Stewart. There is nothing to suggest to you that up to the time he became a director of the Bank, or up to the time the first balance-sheet was fabricated in 1875, Mr Stewart was not essentially an honourable, upright, and honest man. What came, then, to change his character? What inducement was held out to him to be other than he had been—what was he to gain by deceiving and defrauding the public? Can you see the purpose? Have you been able to unravel from the case for the prosecution anything that will suggest to you the benefit Mr Stewart was to receive? If you have done so, you have been much more attentive and acute than I have been. I have listened attentively to the case from beginning to end, and to the Lord Advocate's speech from beginning to end, to find the suggestion of a benefit, and I have failed to find anything of the kind.

Now then, gentlemen, what is the question which you are here to try? The Lord Advocate's speech was a very able and a very powerful one. It must be so, being his. No one can present his case in stronger or better terms; but it occurred to me that that speech would have been much better if delivered in another part of the building—if the Lord Advocate had been discussing with me the liability of Mr Stewart for the debts of the Bank, or for damages at the instance of the liquidators, in respect that the shareholders had been misled by Mr Stewart. I should then have understood the entire applicability of every word he said; but I fail to see the connection or application of one half of what the Lord Advocate said to a question which merely raises this issue—Was Mr Stewart's conduct criminal, or was it not? Many things will give rise to an obligation on the part of Mr Stewart or his brother directors to make good the losses of the Bank—to make good to the whole extent of their fortunes the losses which their negligence or bad management may have originated; but there may be the most reckless management, the worst management that ever was known or conceived of, without there being any criminality whatever, and what you have to determine is whether there was crime, not bad management. So the Lord Advocate told you, and so far I agree with him. Let us look now at what it is with which these prisoners are charged. They are charged that, "on one or more days in the month of "June 1876, in or near the head office of the City of Glasgow Bank, you did, "all and each or one or more of you, wickedly and feloniously, with intent to "defraud the members of the said Company and the public, and for the pur-"pose of concealing and misrepresenting the true state of the affairs of the "said Company, concoct and fabricate, or cause or procure to be concocted "and fabricated, a false and fictitious abstract balance-sheet or statement of "affairs, purporting to represent the true condition of the Bank's affairs in "the following or similar terms." Then comes the balance-sheet of 1876, and the indictment goes on, "which abstract balance-sheet or statement of "affairs was false and fictitious, and was known by you to be so in the follow-"ing particulars, or part thereof." Then they are charged that, "on the 5th "July 1876, in or near the Chamber of Commerce, Glasgow, you did, all and "each or one or other of you, wickedly and feloniously, and with intent to "defraud, use and utter the said false and fabricated abstract balance-sheet "or statement of affairs as true, by then and there reporting the same to "the members of the Company, along with a report on the Bank's affairs, "in which you did, wickedly and feloniously, and falsely and fraudulently, "represent and pretend that said Company was in a sound and prosperous "condition," and so on. Now, gentlemen, the Lord Advocate says the question which you are to try is twofold—first, whether or not the directors did concoct or fabricate this false balance-sheet; and secondly, it being concocted as alleged, by whom it was uttered in the knowledge that it was false, and for the purpose of defrauding the Company and the public. His Lordship seemed to distinguish, in the end of his address, between the prisoners as divided into two classes, and he pointed unmistakably—for he used their names—to two of their number as the persons against whom he charged the crime of concocting and fabricating; and then he said that the other prisoners were in a different class—that their offence, as I understood him, rather came to this, that they uttered the document referred to in the knowledge that it was false and fraudulent, and for the purpose of defrauding. Now, gentlemen, you observe the elements which the Lord Advocate must prove to make out this charge. First, the balance-sheet must be false; secondly, it must be false in the knowledge of the directors; thirdly, it must be uttered by them in the knowledge that it is false; and fourthly, it must be so uttered, with the intention to defraud.

The first question is, then, Is the balance-sheet false? Gentlemen, if I were to pretend to discuss with you the question of the balance-sheet, I would not be Mr Stewart's representative. Mr Stewart did not understand the balance-sheet in 1878, when it was presented to him and he saw it; and although he has heard evidence addressed to the question of that balance-sheet for the last eight days he does not understand it yet. Therefore, observations on that subject by me would be observations of my own, and not the observations of Mr Stewart. Gentlemen, I am going to relieve you, so far as I am concerned, from any discussion of the question whether or not the balance-sheet was true. I shall assume, for the purpose of the argument, that it was not. The Lord Advocate may make it as false as he will; I shall assume it to be false, for I knew nothing of its falsity. Upon the subject of whether it was false, or whether the alterations in it were justifiable, you will have argument from other gentlemen who are to follow; but for Mr Stewart the defence is simply this, that, be it false or not, he knew nothing about it. There are three charges in the indictment, relating respectively to the years 1876, 1877, and 1878, and you heard the evidence of Mr Morison in regard to the manner in which these documents had been prepared, and I desire to say a word in case my silence on the subject should be misinterpreted,—not because of anything the Lord Advocate said in reference to it, because I think the Lord Advocate—I was going to say with generosity, but certainly with fairness—did not press upon your consideration a circumstance relative to Mr Stewart which does not tell against any of the other directors except Mr Potter and Mr Stronach. In 1876, the balance-sheet is not brought home to the knowledge of any director except Mr Potter and Mr Stronach. In 1877, the same observation applies. In 1878, you undoubtedly have the balance-sheet of that year laid before Mr Stewart. I am not anxious to shirk the consideration of that subject, and let me take from the Crown the evidence in regard to what took place on that occasion. The evidence is Mr Morison's:—"A clean copy of that abstract was made by instructions of Mr Stronach after "it was red inked." [Balance-sheet with red ink and pencil markings exhibited to the jury.] I do not say that these alterations are not quite justifiable. Upon that I have nothing to say. But, then, when you have seen this balance-sheet in its altered condition, you see how very unlikely it was to attract Mr Stewart's attention when it was presented, or rather how much less likely it was to attract attention when presented in the shape of a clean copy. Now, that is the document which was shown to Mr Stewart. Mr Morison says, that after he had made the one with the red ink alterations he got instructions from Mr Stronach to make a clean copy. He says:—"After it was "made, Mr Stewart, Mr Potter, and the manager met in the manager's room "and went over it. I was present, but I did not go over it with them. I "was in the room. I do not think the annual abstract issued to the share-"holders had been printed at that time. (Q.) Did these three gentlemen "not compare the clean document with the abstract? (A.) They compared "the clean document with the abstract published in the previous year's re-"port." Then, just one other sentence from the same witness:—"When the "clean copy without the red ink marks was submitted to the manager, Mr "Stewart, and Mr Potter, I was in the room to give any information wanted. "(Q.) Were you asked to give information about anything? (A.) The only "information I was asked for was to compare the 1877 report with the 1878 "one. (Q.) Which report? (A.) I mean the annual balance-sheet. I was "asked to do so, I presume, in order to compare the different sums, the one "year with the other. (Q.) Simply for the purpose, I suppose, of stating "what was the difference in the trading of the Bank between those two years? "(A.) I was not asked to explain any entry in this account; merely to com-"pare results." And then he said the time occupied was not an hour. Now, in the first place, that document shown to Mr Stewart contains on the face of it nothing whatever to attract the attention of a man who was even a better bookkeeper than Mr Stewart was. He was not there for the purpose of testing the balance-sheet; it was not his business to make up or test the balance-sheet. Whatever is the duty of a director—and I shall have a word to say upon that by-and-bye—it was not the duty of the directors unquestionably to make up the balance-sheet for the year. Well, then, as regards 1878, I do not believe you will be disposed to think—the Lord Advocate evidently was not disposed to think—that the mere fact that Mr Stewart was in the room, and looked at this clean copy which had been made, was in itself any indication that he was in the guilty knowledge that this was the result of manipulation, and had been cooked. Gentlemen, I must say this for Mr Stewart, that if the account of which this is the clean copy was manipulated and false, it is quite obvious that he was not a party to the falsification. He was not allowed to see the balance-sheet till all the traces of the red ink marks and the alterations had been removed. He is not called in to consider whether any alteration should be made or not; and so far from being called in to consider whether those alterations were right or prudent in the circumstances of the Bank, he is excluded, then and at every other time, from the consideration of a balance-sheet when that balance-sheet was undergoing preparation. The Lord Advocate said that it is not in this abstract that the offence consists: the offence consists, according to his Lordship, in the abstract which was published to the world. Well, I look at the abstract published to the world: I look at this which was the abstract of the affairs of the Bank shown to Mr Stewart, and I compare them, and you will compare them for yourselves. They are identical, and if the balance that was presented to Mr Stewart by the manager and Mr Potter was a true balance-sheet, then the abstract published to the world was true. If it was not a true balance-sheet, Mr Stewart was deceived, and not deceiving. It will not prove that Mr Stewart was in the guilty knowledge that this was a cooked and manipulated balance-sheet to say that he was present at the meeting when it was gone over and looked at. On the contrary, you must infer that he regarded it as true and honest, because he was a party to the publication of the report which went forth to the public in 1878. I could quite understand, if the published abstract had been in any material respect different from the figures shown in the balance-sheet, that it might have been said, "Mr Stewart, how could you publish that when you had seen this?" But you cannot presume that there was anything wrong with what was published to the world so far as Mr Stewart was concerned, so long as you find that the only means of knowledge which Mr Stewart had was entirely consistent with the results and the figures published to the company and to the public. I come now to a question, gentlemen, which is of some importance. The balance-sheet which you see before you, and which was subsequently epitomised and issued to the public, is said to have been manipulated and cooked. Now, what was Mr Stewart's duty, or the duty of any director, in regard to that? The balance-sheet, observe, so far as laid before the directors at all, is the work of the functionaries charged with that particular duty. It is not a director's duty to make up a balance-sheet, or to keep any of the books of the Bank; but when that balance-sheet is laid before him, is there any duty upon Mr Stewart, or any director of any Bank, to test its accuracy by looking into the Bank books? Upon that matter I cannot do better than read to you what has been said by a very high authority, as to the duty of a bank director in reference thereto. In 1861 there was a very important trial in this court, in an action at the instance of a reverend gentleman named Dobie against Sir William Johnston and Mr George Eliza Russell of this city, Mr Dobie being a member or shareholder in the Edinburgh and Glasgow Bank, and the other two gentlemen I have named being directors of that Bank. Mr Dobie had purchased certain shares on the faith, undoubtedly, of the representations made to the public in the published balance-sheets of the Bank, and he raised an action against these two directors for recovery of the loss he had sustained,—for, as you know, that Bank also failed,—in consequence, as he averred, of the false and fraudulent misrepresentations the directors had made in balance-sheets which they issued to the world. And it was undoubtedly proved abundantly in that case that the balance-sheet was wrong; that it contained false statements and undoubted misrepresentations. After a lengthened trial, the jury found that the balance-sheet was wrong, although they found it had not been proved that the defenders issued it fraudulently or in the knowledge of its falsehood. What I want you to notice is the fact that undoubtedly there was falsehood in it, that it misrepresented the state of the Bank, and induced one of the public to buy shares, which he undoubtedly never would have bought if these representations had not been made. In that case it came to be a question, among other things, how far the directors were responsible for the false statements which appeared in the balance-sheets. The Judge who presided at the trial was the present head of the Court (then Lord Justice-Clerk), and, among other things, his Lordship, in charging the jury, said this, in reference to the duty of directors:—

"You must keep in view that the directors are generally selected from a class of " the community who have business of their own to attend to. Happy is the joint-" stock company that can get a good director who is retired from business, and yet " is fond of work. He is a most valuable man; but such men are not to be had " every day, and therefore, generally speaking, as a class, you must take it that " directors of a joint-stock company, and of a joint-stock bank, like all other joint-" stock companies, are selected from among men who have business of their own " to attend to; and therefore, it is only a limited portion of their time, of course, " that they can be expected to devote to the business of the Bank."

And then his Lordship goes on further to make this observation:—

"Then, gentlemen, it must be equally obvious to you that parties situated as they " are, and undertaking that kind of duty which I have now been describing, cannot " be expected to make themselves familiar with the books of the Bank—in the first " place, because that would be impracticable, consistently with the ordinary work " of the Bank day by day. If you had the directors constantly reading the books of " the Bank, I don't know how the books of the Bank are to be kept, unless, indeed, " you are to ask the directors to read them overnight,—those books that are used " during the day. It is quite impossible to suppose that they are to enter into an " examination of the details of the books, and therefore they must take results from " the books, and not details."

Then his Lordship goes on further, and asks a question to which I ask your attention, because it touches very closely indeed upon the case which the Lord Advocate has presented to-day in the case against the present panels. He says:—

"Supposing that a bank has an old debt of this kind—such as the Edinburgh " and Glasgow Bank had—in a state of suspense, unproductive at the time, but " with securities more or less valuable, which may be realised to a greater or less " extent hereafter, and unsecured portions of the accounts, and other accounts un-" secured altogether, the value of which depends on the ultimate solvency and " credit of the debtors in the accounts,—how far are the directors to be expected to " investigate into the probable recoveries to be hereafter made under these accounts, " particularly if they are debts of the origin of which they have no personal know-" ledge, having been incurred, and, indeed, become partly desperate, before they " acceded to the management? That is a very delicate question. I am not pre-" pared to say, gentlemen, how far it is or is not the duty of directors to look into " these matters and satisfy themselves, by their own personal consideration and " opinion, of the probable solvency of these debtors, and of the value of their securi-" ties. But one thing appears to me perfectly clear, that at least it is not so " obviously and certainly a part of the duty of a bank director to do that, that the " neglect of that duty should be visited upon him as a clear and plain violation of " his duty under the contract. I cannot see my way to that."

And, accordingly, his Lordship said that to entitle the pursuer even in a civil trial to damages against the two defenders on account of misrepresentation, the pursuer must prove, and the jury must find, that the statements were made by the defenders "in the knowledge of their falsehood, or in the belief "of their falsehood, or, at least, without belief in the truth, and that they were "made for the purpose of deceit—fradulently." Gentlemen, these words are weighty words, and if they were words of weight and importance in a civil case, involving merely a question of damages, of how much greater importance are they to be regarded in a case like this, involving criminality? If it was not so clearly the duty of a director to look up those old accounts and investigate securities—if the neglect of that would not involve him in damages in a civil action—how can it be said that it is to infer on his part a criminal responsibility for which he is to answer at the bar of this Court? Still further, there was a later case which arose in the liquidation of the Western Bank, and in which one or two judges of great eminence expressed themselves in language almost similar. I refer to the case of Adie *v.* the Western Bank, reported in III. Macpherson. From the evidence it appeared that the pursuer had been a partner of the Western Bank since 1848, and that he had received the annual report from the directors. He made the purchases, knowing that the Bank was the seller, upon the faith of these reports and the representation of its manager at Coatbridge, and on the faith of the Bank being in a position to pay a dividend at the rate of 8 per cent.; and the report in May 1855 contained a false statement of the position of the Bank, large debts being included in the assets, which the books and documents showed to be bad.

The LORD JUSTICE-CLERK—Don't you think that, after the passage you have read, a reference to this case and a statement of your proposition will be sufficient.

Mr TRAYNER—Perhaps it will be sufficient.

The LORD JUSTICE-CLERK—I don't want to interrupt you, however.

Mr TRAYNER—The observations are so apt that, with your Lordship's leave, I should like to read to the jury just a sentence or two. There was nothing in that false statement in the report and balance-sheet of the Western Bank which, according to the statement of the Lord Advocate, is not to be found existing in the present case. The assets were misrepresented, the debts were misrepresented, and altogether there could be scarcely anything nearer a parallel than what was proved in Adie's case to that which is stated by the Lord Advocate to have occurred here. In that case the Lord President, charging the jury, said:—"It is not incumbent on the directors personally to "go through the books to test their accuracy or the results brought out from "them. It is not to be expected or supposed that the directors had done so, "and their report is not to be taken as importing or implying that they did "so. They are entitled to rely on the information furnished to them by the "officials to whom the details of the business is committed, and in whom "confidence is placed. That affords reasonable ground for believing in the "truth of the results and the inference reasonably deduced from them, and if "it should unfortunately turn out that the information so furnished to the "directors was false, by reason of the negligence or fault of those whose duty "it was to furnish correct information, the directors who honestly received it, "and thus were deceived by it, cannot be held to have practised any fraud "on the shareholders or the public." I do not detain you by reading further from the report of that case, because that expression of opinion by the Lord President, in charging the jury, was excepted to by counsel, and the matter underwent discussion in the First Division of the Court of Session, and the judges of that division, and particularly Lord Curriehill, concurred in the view which the Lord President had stated—that it is no part of the duty of directors to look into the books of the Bank, to ascertain whether the balance-sheet or abstract report is correct or not. They are to apply for information to the particular officials charged with the duty of making up the accounts, and when they get it, they are entitled to rely on that as true. If it unfortunately be untrue, then they are not responsible for any untruth that goes forth to the world arising from the negligence or fault of those charged with the duty of giving information. There was also a recent case before the Master of the Rolls in which the same principle was enunciated, —that the duty of directors is not to look into the books of the company, and that they are not to be held as knowing the contents. If that be the duty of directors, I ask—What is the fault of Mr Stewart? This balance-sheet is put before him, and he says—"Well, I see it brings out a profit of "so much per annum, and I see it is absolutely conform to this which is "published to the world." Is he to look into that account to check its accuracy? How many items does that cover? The first entry is "Local bills." Well, to satisfy himself of the figures brought out there (£766,878) involves an investigation into a number of bills which might take him a month merely to count,—it may be so,—or it may be that the bills are few in number, and of large amount. But all he has to do is to ask the accountant of the Bank to be *honest* and truthful in making up the ledger, and to put before him and his brethren in the direction the results of the Bank's books. And what is most remarkable in this case is, that if Mr Stewart and his brother directors had gone to the books to test the accuracy of the balance-sheet, they would have found nothing wrong. The balance ledger which they docquet is exactly conform to the other entries in the books from which these results are taken. Mr Muir, the Crown's first witness on the matter of accounting, said it was not the case that the balance ledger was in conformity with the other books of the Bank; but, upon his subsequent explanations, I think it was brought out that the balance-sheet was practically, and in effect, conform to the rest of the entries in the books, and that there was no disconformity or fault to be found in the books themselves. Whether Mr Muir's evidence came to that or not, I really do not very much care, because it was sworn to by M'Kinnon, on behalf of the defenders, and by Mr Morison, ou behalf of the Crown. Therefore, in the first place, you have that balance-sheet without anything on its face calculated to excite suspicion or draw attention to its particular terms, laid before Mr Stewart simply for the purpose of comparing the figures with the previous year's report. In reference to that balance-sheet, there is nothing to bring home guilty knowledge to Mr Stewart's mind. There was nothing shown to Mr Stewart which was not shown to everybody else, apart from Mr Potter and Mr Stronach, who prepared it. All that was laid before the directors at their meeting was the abstract which went out to the world; and again I say, if you compare that abstract with the balance-sheet shown to Mr Stewart, the two tally exactly; and again I say, that there is a total absence of proof, on the part of the Crown, of anything to bring home to Mr Stewart the guilty knowledge that that was a false and fabricated statement. Well, then, the Lord Advocate says you may not have direct testimony that Mr Stewart and the other directors knew it was false, but you are entitled to infer, from what you do know and have seen, that a guilty knowledge was there. I think that is putting the proposition a little too broadly; but still I won't quarrel with it. Take Mr Stewart—his character and his position, and the other circumstances I have alluded to—take these altogether, and take this balance-sheet, and what was done with it, and say whether you can fairly infer that there was guilty knowledge. The Lord Advocate asks—"Where did the "profit come from? If you knew there were so many bad accounts, how "could you say there was any profit to divide?" Why, gentlemen, I do not think that is a matter upon which you are likely to infer guilty knowledge on the part of Mr Stewart. The branches were yielding £70,000 alone. To pay 12 per cent. on the capital needed £120,000. Well, the branches were paying 7 per cent. alone, and laying past over and above that £10,000 every year to meet bad debts and possible loss. There was an excellent business; and surely the City Bank, at its head office, was making something. It was not all Nicol Fleming, or Smith, Fleming, & Co. The Bank had a large and lucrative connection; and the very best evidence of the fact that the business of the Bank was worth taking up was this, that both at its head offices and branches every other Bank in Scotland was anxious to take up the goodwill of its business. It was not all Nicol Fleming, or Smith, Fleming, & Co., though there has been a good deal too much of that, I confess; but every bit of it is consistent with the idea of something else than criminality; and so long as you can account for anything on a different basis than the basis of criminality, you are not to convict the prisoners. I am not going into detail upon these accounts, though I must of necessity advert to one or two of them. What was the case, so far as Mr Stewart was concerned, with Nicol Fleming and Co.? Just look for a moment at the minutes of the directors in regard to Nicol Fleming's account. You will remember that Mr Stewart became a director in 1871, and Nicol Fleming's account had undoubtedly been long in existence before that time. In 1870, as the Lord Advocate explained, he came to this Bank trying to get further accommodation, and there was nothing more heard about Fleming again till 1873; but Mr Stewart had nothing to do with the matter, and he (Fleming) saw no Mr Stewart then. There was an attempt in 1875 to recoup a probable deficit on Fleming's account by an investment in land in New Zealand; but Mr John Fleming said that he never saw or knew Mr Stewart in connection with the Bank until the month of July 1878, a month after the whole events charged in this indictment are said to have taken place. But let us see how this account of Smith, Fleming, & Co. was dealt with. In 1875 there was a committee appointed, consisting of Messrs Potter and Salmond, to look into these accounts; and I find in the minute of 1st June 1876 that the committee upon that account reported that they had seen it put into shape. Now, from that time down to the end of the Bank's affairs I do not find, except upon one occasion, that Mr Stewart had anything to do with Fleming's account.

The LORD JUSTICE-CLERK—To which accounts are you referring?

Mr TRAYNER—To Smith, Fleming, & Company's account and Nicol Fleming's. There is no doubt whatever, and I do not pretend to deny,—the Lord Advocate seemed to think we would, though I do not know why,—that Smith, Fleming, & Co.'s account and Nicol Fleming's account were in an unsatisfactory condition. One does not like to say anything unpleasant, or to say anything reflecting upon a man who is not here to answer for himself; but there is no doubt whatever that this account took its origin in the time of a man who is no longer here to answer for what he did. The account went on. Smith, Fleming, and Co. and Nicol Fleming & Co. were most extensive merchants. They had an enormous business, and it rather startled one to hear that in more than one year these firms had made £93,000 a year on Commission business alone. One can very well understand that men carrying on a business like that would not only be in need of advances, but men that would be eagerly sought after by any Bank. They did harm to their own interests, and ultimately to the interests of others; but, gentlemen, when you come to it all, is it not just this, that the directors of the Bank, in giving them advances without getting proper security, just committed an act of reckless and foolish mismanagement? But when you are asked, in respect of that and the state of their accounts, to find that they were criminally responsible because of a false balance-sheet, I confess it takes some time and difficulty to find out the connection between the one proposition and the other. It seems to me that the Lord Advocate puts his case in this way. This is a false and fraudulent balance-sheet, and it was a false and fraudulent balance-sheet within your knowledge, because you (the accused) knew that Smith, Fleming, & Co.'s accounts were overdrawn; because you knew that Nicol Fleming's account was overdrawn, and other accounts were overdrawn; and in that balance-sheet you did not sufficiently take into account that these balances were unsecured, and were not only now unproductive, but might never be recovered; and, therefore, as you have lost so much money (for the Lord Advocate treats it all as positive loss), you could not possibly have had the funds that you represent yourself to have had, and could not have paid the dividends you professed to pay. Now, it is all very well in the result to say that, but it is a totally different thing to say that it was criminal in the directors not to have gone through that sort of calculation, and a totally different thing to say, that when this balance-sheet was issued to the public, every one of these gentlemen, or any one of them, knew that they were issuing a false statement, a fraudulent lie—a lie for the purpose of deceiving others, and a lie which could not in the very least tend to their own profit or advantage. Now, gentlemen, there is one thing to be noticed. In 1870 there was, if I recollect aright, about half a million of money due by this firm. In 1875 there was an arrangement made by which it was to be paid off at the rate of £20,000 a year; the result of which arrangement undoubtedly was expected to be that in fourteen years Nicol Fleming's account, and Smith, Fleming, & Co.'s account, would be wiped off, interest and all. But to show you that Mr Stewart was not the able business man, or regarded as the able business man which some people would now represent him to be, I think I may refer to one of the minutes, and to an observation made upon it by Mr Glen Walker, one of the witnesses for the Crown, which shows how true it is that while Mr Stewart was a director of the Bank, he was not, in point of fact, a man, if a may say so, who should ever have been in that position. Just look at the minute of 17th August 1876, where this matter of Glen Walker's having come up, it was thought advisable generally to adopt the suggestions contained in the letter, and the directors accordingly requested the manager, associated with Messrs Potter, Stewart, and Taylor, to arrange with Mr Walker, and to go into details. And then, after that, you have this in the minute of 19th October 1876:—"In connection with the resolution come to at the "meeting of 17th August last, Messrs Potter, Stewart, and Taylor handed in "their report, which was read as follows:—In terms of the minute of the "board of directors of 17th August 1876, appointing us to arrange with Mr "Glen Walker as to the acquisition of certain pastoral properties in Australia, "we have to report that we then authorised an investment to the value of "£120,000 to £130,000," and so on. Now, Mr Walker's observations upon that is that it is nonsense. He never met Mr Stewart about the thing at all; and it just comes to this, that Mr Stewart was put upon that committee, that he was never asked to attend the committee, and that he never paid any attention to those questions. He was not in a position to help those financing men; it was not in his way. His name was put on the committee, and he may have gone to a meeting or he may not; but if he had gone he would have been of no use to them, and of no assistance in furthering the arrangement. And that is exactly what was thought of Mr Stewart. Mr Glen Walker laughed, and said that minute was all nonsense,—he had never seen anything of Mr Stewart in the matter; and probably Mr Glen Walker, who is one of those gentlemen accustomed to deal in a very offhand way with a great deal of money, would not have been bothered with a simple man like Mr Stewart, because he was not capable of entering into the minutiæ and particulars of a large transaction of this kind. In short, to use a very homely phrase, at that board Mr Stewart may have been an ornamental man, but essentially he was of little use. He was not qualified to go into these accounts—he was not qualified to check the balance-sheet. If he has been guilty of doing anything at all, it is of being in a position and undertaking duties he was not able to perform; but criminality is as far from him as it is from one of us.

Gentlemen, it would only weary you and occupy time to go into all the questions of the different accounts to which the Lord Advocate has alluded.

There is only one of them further, as bearing upon Mr Stewart's case, which I should like to say a word about. You remember that when one of the clerks in the Bank brought the attention of the manager and the directors of the Bank to the fact, that Mr Innes Wright's partner (Mr Scott) was not accounting for the discounts which he ought to have accounted for, it was arranged that Mr Stewart and Mr Potter should go and see Mr Scott on the subject. They met Mr Scott, and Mr Stewart told him that his conduct could only be designated by one name. Mr Stewart was indignant, honestly and fairly indignant, at Mr Scott's conduct, and he showed it both by his manner and by his language on that occasion. Does not that show you that the only time in which Mr Stewart ever came face to face with a proper defalcation—what he knew was a defalcation—he at once resented it as an honest man would have done? And just as certainly as he insisted upon an arrangement being made by which Mr Scott should hand over the money which he had improperly retained—just as certainly would Mr Stewart have insisted upon an arrangement with Fleming & Co., and everybody else, if he had known that things had gone the length to which we are now told they had gone. Can you say that Mr Stewart has acted criminally here? What can lead you to that conclusion? Has anything in the whole course of his actings indicated criminal intention or criminal purpose? Has anything been brought home to him, which would warrant you in branding him with the name either of thief, swindler, or liar? Do you believe that he ever put his pen "to a page that registered a lie?" Do you believe he told a lie, verbally or in writing, to the public? If he did, was it not very inconsistent with the whole of the rest of that man's conduct. He had hitherto, as far as we have seen, acted uprightly and honestly with all men; and while he may have been foolish, reckless, or ignorant in the fulfilment of his duties in the Bank parlour, you cannot say he ever acted dishonestly or falsely. It is from very small things that one gathers at times more assistance than from large things in estimating a man's character. A witness was brought by the Crown, I suppose to prove their case against Mr Stewart—a retired spirit merchant, Mr Drummond, with whom Mr Stewart had had dealings long before. He went to Mr Stewart in September last, and told him that he was going to buy a share in the City of Glasgow Bank. Mr Stewart replied that it would be a capital thing for him some day. Do you think that Mr Stewart met Mr Drummond face to face and told him the purchase of the share was a good thing for him, when he yet knew the Bank was about to close its doors? What on earth was his motive for deceiving poor Drummond? Do you believe Dr M'Grigor when he tells you that Mr Stewart appeared astounded at the information he got from him? Do you believe that Mr Stewart was sincere when he rushed past Dr M'Grigor at the Bank door wringing his hands, and declaring he was a broken-hearted man? I believe Dr M'Grigor. Have you any reason to doubt him? But if Dr M'Grigor's evidence is worth listening to, the result of it is to prove that the revelations brought to light in the report which Dr M'Grigor and Mr Anderson issued were new to Mr Stewart. And not only by the evidence of Dr M'Grigor is that made plain, but Mr Jamieson, one of the liquidators, tells you that a day or two before the stoppage of the Bank, he went through to Glasgow to see whether any arrangement could be made by which the Bank might be carried on, and that when he told Mr Stewart the result of his investigation, Mr Stewart was distressed by the information, and seemed to be greatly put about. In the course of this case there was an argument, before you were empannelled, with regard to the relevancy of the indictment, and, in pronouncing judgment upon that question, the Lord Justice-Clerk said, that in order to entitle the prosecutor to succeed in the charge he had made, he must prove, as against the directors, "some element of bad faith, some corrupt motive, some "guilty knowledge, some fraudulent intention." Where is the guilty motive?

If there was a motive at all when the disastrous state of the Bank became known—and it became known too late to help it—the motive was to keep everybody straight, to prevent the utter ruin which would follow on the Bank's doors being closed; and it was then there was an effort made to keep the Bank going by appealing to the other banks for assistance. Corrupt motive in Mr Stewart's case there was none. I say emphatically there was none; and I have listened to the Lord Advocate to find wherein he imputed corrupt motive to Mr Stewart. Guilty knowledge certainly was not brought home to him; and the suggestion that he is guilty of the crime laid to him is just about as much brought home to him as it is brought home to you. I am not going to detain you at any further length in reference to this case. You cannot convict Mr Stewart unless you are satisfied that he issued the balance-sheet of the Bank in the guilty knowledge of its being false. What does that involve? That this man, from 1876—for he is charged with this as much as with the act of 1877 and 1878—knew the Bank was in a rotten and tottering state, and might any day come down, and yet he left his fortune at its risk. He knew that Bank to be in a rotten state, hopelessly insolvent, and not paying anything, and yet he continued in its direction and allowed himself to be re-elected in the month of June 1878, when, if he had had guilty knowledge, and had aught of intelligence above the veriest idiot, he would have hurried from the board and saved everything he could. That was not the case with any one of them. Foolish they may have been,—reckless they may have been,—bad managers to the last extent they may have been,—but, gentlemen, I think you will search this proof in vain for guilty knowledge, and without guilty knowledge there is no crime. I have said all I purpose saying to you on behalf of Mr Stewart. The Lord Advocate asked you very pertinently, just as he concluded his address, If this document is false and fraudulent, who did it? That is for you to answer. Permit me to say it is not proved that Mr Stewart did it. The Lord Advocate did not put that to you. The Lord Advocate did not suggest to you that Mr Stewart had anything to do with the concocting or fabricating of that balance-sheet, if concocted or fabricated it be. If it be concocted, did Mr Stewart utter it in the knowledge that it was false? It was contrary to all his character and to all his interest to do so. Why, if he had been a guilty man, he would have acted very differently for himself than he has done. And, gentlemen, all I ask from you is a patient consideration of the evidence which has been led. I do not doubt that you will give this. Now that you have been in the box so long, and have listened to the evidence so carefully as you have done—when you have seen that that which the Lord Advocate has charged and tried to prove has had to be given up—all these things will go to show you that the prejudice which you may have felt before you came here against the directors must be laid aside. If you will put it aside—if you will endeavour to do so, as I don't doubt that you will do—I am entirely hopeful. It is your high prerogative to stand between public clamour and injustice. You are placed here to do your duty not only to the public, but to these unhappy men. They have been reduced in fortune; do not make them bankrupt in character. Do not find them guilty of criminal intent until it has been made clear to you that, upon the evidence, it is impossible to come to any other conclusion; and unless you are satisfied that Mr Stewart has been guilty of criminal intent to defraud some one and to benefit himself—that he knew these falsehoods were in the balance-sheets, and that he issued them for the purpose of deceiving the public, when he had no motive to deceive the public, and no personal object in view. Unless you can assert all these things as the result of the evidence, you must not find him guilty. Therefore, gentlemen, I ask you to proceed upon the evidence, and if you proceed upon the evidence in the case, you will acquit Mr Stewart. I leave the case in your hands confident of that result, because the evidence does not bear upon the face of it, or upon careful search through it, anything to warrant a verdict of guilty against Mr Stewart. If you return an adverse verdict against Mr Stewart, it will be, not because he is guilty, but because I have failed to show you that which it was my duty to show upon the evidence —his innocence.

Ninth Day.—Wednesday, 29th January 1879.

MR BALFOUR'S ADDRESS FOR MR POTTER.

May it please your Lordships, Gentlemen of the Jury,—I appear for Mr Potter, whose name stands second on this indictment, and I think it will be entirely unnecessary, in presenting his case to you, to repeat the observations which both my learned friends, the Lord Advocate and Mr Trayner, made yesterday at the outset of their speeches. You will recollect that both of them dwelt, and very properly dwelt, upon the exceedingly serious nature of the charge preferred against Mr Potter and the others, and they both cautioned you very strongly to beware that there should be no influence exerted upon your minds in reaching the result at which you may arrive, except that which is founded on the evidence led in this Court, and on such comments and arguments as may be addressed to you upon it. That having been done, gentlemen, I feel it to be perfectly unnecessary to repeat it once more. I think the caution was required, because, beyond all doubt and question, the duty which you have to discharge in this case is very different from that which commonly falls to the lot of juries, being infinitely more onerous and greatly more responsible. In the ordinary case, a jury know nothing at all about the matter they have to try, until they are empannelled, and there is no fear of any extraneous knowledge, or supposed knowledge or influence, acting on their minds. Unhappily that is not so in this case, as you are well aware, because the City of Glasgow Bank has for four months past been the engrossing topic of conversation, and the subject of many articles in the press; and undoubtedly the failure of that Bank, with its disastrous consequences all over the country, has produced a depth and a strength of feeling which I daresay some of you may find it difficult to resist. It was not altogether unnatural, when regard is had to the consequences of that stoppage and that failure, that there should have arisen in the public mind a certain feeling of indignation against those persons who were in the administration of the Bank's affairs, and who, therefore, might be supposed to be responsible for the disaster. But, gentlemen, that is a feeling which, while it may be perfectly intelligible in the outside public, ought to have no weight and no influence with you here; and I merely say again what the Lord Advocate said at the outset, that all considerations of that kind you must endeavour to do your best to discharge from your minds. I do not say that the effort will be altogether easy to you at first; but I am perfectly sure that you will make the effort, honestly and faithfully, and I doubt not that you will make it successfully. I therefore don't think it necessary to say anything more by way of preface, and I shall now proceed to state to you, as shortly as I can, though I fear it must be in some detail, the case for Mr Potter; feeling quite certain that when I ask to that statement your calm and dispassionate, as well as your careful, attention, I shall not prefer my request in vain.

Now, gentlemen, you have already heard more than once, that in this indictment, as it was originally presented, there were three separate and distinct charges made. The first was the charge of falsifying the balance-sheets, or alternatively of issuing them in the knowledge that they were false; the second was the charge of getting overdrafts or accommodation without security by directors; and the third was the charge of theft and embezzlement of certain bills. The third of these charges has now been abandoned, and you have to treat it, as the Lord Advocate said, as if it had never been made. The second of these charges—I mean the one of getting accommodation or loans of money through holding the position of a director—never was made against Mr Potter from the first. I ask your attention to that, gentlemen, for reasons which, by-and-by, you will readily see, if you have not seen them already, as I daresay you have; because I think it will come to have a most important bearing on the result at which you shall arrive upon the only charge made against Mr Potter. Meantime I trust you will bear in mind that it never was asserted by the Crown from the first that he used his position as a director to obtain one single sixpence of advantage to himself, and no such assertion could have been made, because if it had, it would have been entirely baseless. So that, gentlemen, your attention is confined, as regards Mr Potter, simply to the first charge—that is, the charge of falsifying the balance-sheets, or issuing these balance-sheets, knowing them to be false. Now you will at once see, indeed I think it has been already quite sufficiently explained to you—so that I need not go into it again—that the essence of that charge is the guilty mind and intention of the person against whom it is made. The questions which were put, and I think perfectly fairly and well put, by the Lord Advocate upon that matter were these: he first put the question—Were these balance-sheets or abstracts in point of fact false? Whatever answer might be returned to that question would, of course, go a very short way in this inquiry, and the Lord Advocate again quite correctly said that the second question is the vital one—Were the sheets false in the knowledge of the persons accused, and did they issue them for the purpose of perpetrating the frauds alleged? If you look to the indictment, which I shall not trouble you by reading again, you will see that the allegation is not only that the balance-sheets were falsified, but that the falsification was with intent to defraud the members of the company and the public. So that what is really the controversy between us, and what you will require to fix your attention upon, is the question whether these balance-sheets were falsified (in the sense explained) by Mr Potter, or whether, if they were not actually falsified by him, he was a party to issuing them to the public, or to the shareholders, in the knowledge that they were false, and for the purpose of committing a fraud. Now, from that statement, gentlemen, you will at once see that the guilty mind and the guilty intention, coupled with the guilty knowledge, are the essentials of the crime. Gentlemen, I don't care to go, and I don't require to go, into the question whether these balance-sheets and abstracts were false, in this sense, that they were not entirely correct from a book-keeping point of view. I am perfectly willing to assume, for the purposes of argument, that a skilled accountant might have made up these balance-sheets or abstracts upon a different principle. You had it stated by accountants, and the reasons commend themselves I think to one's judgment, that for the purpose of getting a complete view of the Bank's affairs presented, you should have before you all the assets on one side, and all the liabilities on the other, under the appropriate heads, and that it is not enough, according to strict views of accounting, that balances only as distinguished from the total items should be brought into the sheet. I am perfectly willing to assume that to be so, and to take the argument upon the assumption that if the books of this Bank had been put into the hands of such a gentleman as Mr Muir, or any other accountant of high skill, he would have thought that the proper way was to state the whole assets on the one side and the whole liabilities upon the other, and not in any case, except where there were cross accounts between the same debtor and the same creditor, to bring in balances only. Therefore, gentlemen, I don't go into that matter at all; but what I shall ask your attention to, and where I do join issue with the Lord Advocate, is upon the second question, that is whether, assuming these sheets or abstracts to be erroneous in the particulars which he alleges, they were either fabricated by Mr Potter, or sent out by him in the knowledge that they were false. Now, gentlemen, upon that point I most absolutely and entirely deny that the Lord Advocate has proved a case which would entitle you to convict Mr Potter; and I also deny that Mr Potter did those things in fact. Now, gentlemen, before proceeding to examine the evidence bearing upon that point (for I merely mentioned the others to clear the ground of them) I would ask you to keep steadily before you what the definition of the offence charged is, as I have just given it, and as it has been given by others before—not only what it involves, but what it excludes. Whenever you reach the conclusion that the guilty intention and the fradulent purpose are of the essence of the charge, it is plain from the very statement of it that the Crown will not prevail in proving the case upon such a charge, merely by establishing such things as neglect of checking books, trusting too much to subordinates, not looking into books, and the like, seeing that, as you heard Mr Trayner read from the charge of the Lord President in the case of Dobie, it is no part of the business of a director to do things of that kind. But even if it were a part of the duty of director to do such work. omission of duty—neglect of duty, which might be followed by civil consequences or civil damages, would be perfectly unavailing to make good a criminal charge such as that which you have to try. In the second place, it would be idle to support such a charge by merely pointing to the existence of what I may call errors of book-keeping, or mistakes in the theory of book-keeping; that is to say, such things as bringing in balances and the like instead of bringing in totals, which, for the purposes of this question, I am willing to assume should have been done. And, in the third place, gentlemen, the definition of the offence very plainly excludes errors or mistakes of judgment; such as taking too sanguine a view either of debts or of the possibility of recovery. It excludes all those things which do not possess the quality of guilty mind and guilty intention; and I think, under that head, I may fairly say that it excludes even the idea of what might in a sense be irregularities or improprieties, being sufficient to make the crime which is here charged.

Gentlemen, I have made these few remarks, merely for the purpose of asking you to keep them in view when you come to examine the facts which are established in this case, because, I think, when you make a careful and dispassionate examination of the evidence, you will see that that guilty mind and guilty purpose the Crown has utterly and absolutely failed to prove.

I must say, gentlemen, that in listening, as I did, carefully and attentively to the Lord Advocate's address, I was a little surprised at the kind of reasoning by which he attempted to sustain such a grave charge. One would naturally have expected that a charge like the present would be supported by some very direct and cogent, and explicit evidence; but what the Lord Advocate said was this, in substance,—he said, I cannot give you any direct evidence on the matter. He did not attempt to explain how these sheets were made up, or what was done by the directors in the course of making them up. He did not go into that at all. I shall go into it, gentlemen; but he did not. The kind of reasoning upon which he sought to reach his conclusion was this: he said, I cannot go into that Bank parlour,—what was done there I cannot tell, but I shall ask you to examine the history of this Bank, as it appears on the recorded minutes and upon the recorded letters, and from these I shall ask you to draw these conclusions, that the Bank was in an unsound condition,—that it was unsound in the knowledge of the directors, including Mr Potter; that that unsoundness and the knowledge of it gave a motive for concealment; that these balance-sheets, in fact, concealed that unsound condition; and that, therefore, you must infer the guilty knowledge. Now, gentlemen, I think you will agree with me that that is not a very satisfactory course of logic, by which to reach such a conclusion, because it is perfectly plain, as I think I shall show you, that even if it had been the fact that this Bank was in such a position in the knowledge of the directors as the Lord Advocate represents, that would not in the least lead you to the conclusion that they made or issued these balance-sheets for the purpose alleged. But, gentlemen, I submit to you,—and I hope you will assent to the proposition,—that instead of beginning at that end,—which is, I submit, the wrong end, for it is not commencing at the beginning, but commencing at the end,—the proper way to ascertain whether the directors, and Mr Potter in particular, made and falsified these balance-sheets, is to put yourselves in their place according to the evidence, from the time when the sheets began to be made up, to see what was done in the course of making up the sheets, to observe what information they had before them when they made up the sheets, and then to say whether the matters charged on the fourth page of the indictment as to 1876 under the seven heads [see p. 28],—because the Lord Advocate has abandoned the eighth,—whether the matters charged, stated thus particularly and categorically, were within the knowledge of the directors, or could be within the knowledge of the directors, when they made up these sheets. I must say, gentlemen, I think that when the Lord Advocate had put in an indictment particulars and figures,—when he had made not a mere general charge of concealing the state of the Bank's affairs, but had given the figures wherein he said these sheets were erroneous, one would naturally have expected to hear him say something about how the directors had, or how they could have had, the knowledge that these figures were wrong; but that was a department upon which he did not enter at all. Now, gentlemen, while I shall follow him in the course he took, so as to see what his reasoning comes to, what I shall ask you to do is to put yourselves in the place of these directors, and enquire what they had before them when they made up these sheets or passed these sheets, and whether the information which they had before them fixed them with a knowledge of the things which the Lord Advocate says were wrong; or whether, on the contrary, the evidence as to how these sheets were made up—apart from the one of 1876, to which I shall speak separately—does not plainly exclude the notion that they could have had that knowledge.

Now, gentlemen, the Lord Advocate dealt with the case of Mr Potter under three heads. He first stated the case against him in common with all the directors; that is to say, he dealt with the case of the directors as a body, and to that the greater part of his address was directed. He did not single Mr Potter out until towards the close of his address, until he took up his second point, and he then said, even supposing you should not think that there was on the part of the directors generally a knowledge of the falsity of the sheets, Mr Potter was brought into contact with the making up of the abstract of 1876, and therefore as to it, at all events, he was guilty. And in the third place, he dealt shortly with the question of what was called the clean sheet, in the course of the evidence, for the year 1878. Now, gentlemen, I shall deal with each and all of these heads; I shall not shrink from one of them. I will go through the evidence applicable to each; I will consider them in their order; and I undertake to demonstrate to you that the conclusion which the Lord Advocate asked you to draw is not borne out by the evidence, but that the evidence shows affirmatively that the directors had not the knowledge that the sheets were false. You will have the goodness to keep in view that I am now going to deal with that part of the case in which Mr Potter stands on the same footing with the other directors. I beg you, however, to understand, gentlemen, that I am not going to shrink from dealing with the separate case applicable to 1876. That I shall deal with amply; but I ask you in the first place to take the case as it was taken by the Lord Advocate, and see what there is against Mr Potter, in so far as he is on common ground with the other directors, to fix him with that knowledge which the Lord Advocate says is guilty knowledge, and that intention which the Lord Advocate says is guilty intention.

Now, gentlemen, I think the fair and proper way of examining that point is to see exactly what the course of making up these sheets was, and what the directors had before them when they put them through their hands. That, I think, is a better and a fairer way of judging than by going to the minutes and drawing an inference from them; because you are there dealing with evidence of the actual facts, and are not in the region of inference at all. What then was the course of making up these abstracts which are complained of as false? That, gentlemen, is a matter which we don't require to draw inferences about, because we have it precisely proved. The Lord Advocate says we are not able to go into that Bank parlour to see what was done there. Gentlemen, in this matter we are able to go into that Bank parlour, because we can accompany Mr Morison, the accountant, who tells us the exact course that was followed in the preparation and presenting of these abstracts. And therefore, gentlemen, you are not here relegated to surmises as to what passed in some secret chamber; you have positive and direct evidence of what was done in the transaction of the ordinary business of the Bank. I shall summarise very shortly to you the result of the evidence, because I don't know whether you may have entirely followed it as it came from successive witnesses and at intervals of time, in the middle of evidence relating to other matters. But this, gentlemen, I think you will agree, when you cast your minds back to what was said, is a fair and correct statement of the result of the evidence upon that matter. The books of the Bank are in the charge of Mr Morison, the accountant, unless perhaps some special books which are in the charge of the manager, and I think some in the charge of Mr Morris. That is the books at the head office. The books at the branches are of course in the charge of the agents at the branches; and Mr Miller, the inspector of branches, with his officials, makes up sheets applicable to these. On the occasion of each balance, Mr Morison, the accountant, makes out from the books in his possession, and which the directors—I cannot say exactly had no business to see, but had no duty to see, and didn't in fact see,—from these he prepares certain documents which were described to you I think thus: he makes up in the course of each week a weekly balance of the affairs of the branches; there comes from the branches a weekly balance applicable to the branches, and there is superinduced upon that a statement of the business of correspondents; that is, banks in London and other places. Well, the first document that is made up with a view to the balance is the balance ledger; and that is the document which is placed before the directors, and which is signed by the directors as correct. That balance ledger is made up entirely by Mr Morison, the accountant, and I pray your special attention to this, that it has not been said or suggested from the beginning to the end of this case that any director ever proposed a single alteration upon that balance ledger. The importance of that, gentlemen, you will see immediately; but I pray your special attention to the fact—that the balance ledger is the work of Mr Morison, and the work of Mr Morison alone. Well then, when that balance ledger is made up, it is taken into the Bank parlour where the directors are assembled, and here we follow Mr Morison into their deliberations. He told us what they do. Mr Morison, of course, does not take along with him all the hundred books of the Bank. That would be absurd. He takes the sheets which he himself has made up as professing to show the correct results of these books, and while a director has before him the balance ledger,—while one or more of the directors run their eyes down the balance ledger, Mr Morison reads from the documents which he holds in his hands the items which the directors are asked to compare with the books, being the results which Mr Morison has drawn from the books, and that is the comparison, and the only comparison, made in the preparation of the balance ledger. Now, gentlemen, you will at once see what is the result of that statement. Nobody says that that is a wrong way of making up the balance ledger; but even if it was a wrong way, it would be a neglect and not a fraud. Nobody says that the directors should check the balance ledger against all the books of the Bank, but even if that was their duty to do so, their not doing so would be merely a neglect, and not a fraud. You have it therefore that the way in which that business is done,—and nobody says it is not rightly and sufficiently done,—is for the directors to listen to what Mr Morison reads off,—for something must be trusted to the officials,—and then to see whether the sums which he reads agree with what they have before their eyes. Now, gentlemen, I will let you see—because, as business men, I think it is right you should see—what the course of this matter is, what kind of thing this balance ledger is, and what sort of entries are brought into it. I hold in my hand the sheets of that ledger applicable to the year 1878—for one year is as good as another—and these four sheets together constitute the balance ledger for the year 1878. You will observe that it is prepared upon the plan of putting into the debtor side a very large number as entries, and into the creditor side also a very large number of entries—some of them I will ask your attention to,—and then follow the entries as to the branches. These four branches [pointing them out to the jury upon the sheet] happen to be debtors, and others were creditors, and the rest of the sheet is concerned entirely with balances from branches.

The LORD JUSTICE-CLERK—What number is that?

Mr BALFOUR—No. 12A. Excerpts from balance ledger No. 3. There is the docquet, and the only docquet which the directors sign; and, as Mr Morison explained, the way in which the sheet is checked is by their running their eye down that column, while he reads off from his weekly state. Now, that is the course of it, and I ask you to notice the way in which the different entries are made in that sheet. I may take the first three. The first entry on the creditor side is the stock account, which is the capital; the next is upwards of seven millions of notes; the next is the reserve fund, which you have heard of, amounting to £450,000; the next is the balance at the credit of profit and loss—that is, the profits divisible for the year; and then you go on with the bills payable, and a number of other things.

The LORD JUSTICE-CLERK—Mr Balfour, give a couple of copies of it to the jury, and they will be able to follow you more precisely.

Mr BALFOUR—Here is a set, gentlemen. [Handing them to the jury.] Now, that is the document, and the only document which meets the eye of the directors, and the directors check that, as I have explained, by following the reading of Mr Morison. Now, gentlemen, you will immediately see the importance of that.

A JURYMAN—Is that the abstract of the balance-sheet?

Mr BALFOUR—This is the balance ledger. This is what goes before the directors.

The LORD JUSTICE-CLERK—Mr Balfour, you had better take one year, so that we may see exactly what you are speaking to.

Mr BALFOUR—Well, I take the year 1878, gentlemen. It is all the same. I would again ask you to note this, that the balance ledger is entirely the work of Mr Morison, and no human being, from beginning to end of this trial, has suggested that anybody else had anything to do with it. Now, I shall immediately show you what is and what is not in it, because, I think, I shall be able to demonstrate to you that a very large number of the things which are said to be fraudulent errors in, or fraudulent alterations of, the ultimate balance-sheet, exist in that balance ledger before the abstract is made up at all, and that it is out of the question to attribute, and that no one has attempted to attribute, any complicity in the making of these errors as they occur in the balance ledger to any director. To pursue the history of that document for a moment, what is done with it? It is prepared for the information of the directors, and of them alone. Nobody else is to see it. It is not to go to the public, and it does not go to the public. And therefore, gentlemen, you will at once perceive that even if the directors had been seeking to commit a fraud, or to make a falsification, they had no interest to falsify that document, because nobody was to see it except themselves. If they had attempted to falsify the balance ledger, this would only have been to deceive themselves, and not to deceive anybody else. But, gentlemen, it is necessary, for the purpose of informing the shareholders of the state of the Bank, that an abstract should be prepared. That abstract is prepared, as was explained by Mr Morison, from the weekly sheets applicable to the week of the year in which the balance occurs, with regard both to the head office and the branches. It necessarily summarises the entries, as you will see from the indictment, because the abstract is quoted in the indictment. You see it is quite a different sort of thing from the balance ledger, because it summarises under separate heads a very large number of those entries which appear separately in the balance ledger.

Now, gentlemen, with that explanatory statement, I shall now ask you to carry your minds backwards to the evidence of those witnesses who tell us wherein the alterations which are said to be falsifications consist; and I think I shall demonstrate to you not only that the evidence does not prove the directors to have had to do with these alterations, but that it proves they had not. Mr Muir, who was the leading accountant examined on the part of the Crown, said there were errors in the balance ledger. The one I have noted them from is that of 1876. He said there were four heads of errors in that balance ledger. Well, I shall show that these flow into the abstract, and that, therefore, the directors could not possibly have had anything to do with them. He said there is first the deduction of the £973,300 from bills payable, of which you have heard so much; in the second place, that, into the head of deposit accounts, a balance is brought instead of the total amounts of the two sides of the account; in the third place, there is the sum of £147,668 entirely omitted, being the amount of balances at the credit of credit accounts; and, in the fourth place, there is £11,405 omitted from the adjusting account of interest. Your Lordship will find the references to that on pages 148, 150, and 151 of his evidence. [See pp. 210, 211, and 212.] Now, gentlemen, these are four things which are said and proved to exist in the balance ledger, which was the work of Mr Morison alone, and which the directors had nothing to do with at all, except to check what he read off.

And as so great importance has been attached to that sum of £973,000, of which you have heard so much, and will hear more, I shall show you how that does not appear in the balance ledger any more than in the abstract, and I will also show you what Mr Morison read off to the directors at the meeting at which they were assembled. He read off, gentlemen, from a document which was the weekly state of the business of the Bank, and there [showing to the jury] is an example of it, where the total amount of the bills payable is put in that column, where the £973,000 is in that column, and where the balance is brought out in that column.

The LORD JUSTICE-CLERK—Where is that? Is it in 1876?

Mr BALFOUR—No. 130A, for the year 1876.

The LORD JUSTICE-CLERK—That is the weekly balance.

Mr BALFOUR—Yes; that is what he read.

The LORD JUSTICE-CLERK—Now kindly read out yourself the thing that he read.

Mr BALFOUR—What he read was the balance of £1,315,373. That is a figure as to which, gentlemen, you have heard a good deal. Now, you have that in the balance-sheet of 1876. I show you what Mr Morison says he read out. I show you what the director passing his finger down the sheet would see. He would see exactly what Mr Morison read out, and he would see nothing else. And, therefore, the director checking that balance-sheet, would not see or know anything about that entry of £973,000. And gentlemen, I will just take, as another instance, the next of those things which Mr Muir says is an error in the balance ledger. I take the balance of the deposit accounts, which is £3233, and which it is said should be £455,000. Well, gentlemen, that again is a balance. It is not a falsification at all. It is a balance, and there it is [showing to jury] in the balance ledger—put in by Mr Morison, presented to the directors there; and when Mr Morison read out what he chose to read out, and did read out, the director would find nothing in the sheet except what Mr Morison read. That, gentlemen, is the second thing in regard to which it is said that these sheets are false and fraudulent, because forsooth, instead of the totals of the deposit accounts being brought in, there was only a balance brought in. And yet that was done in the only document shown to or laid before the directors—was done from 1873, and so far as we see, as long as there were balance-sheets of this Bank. Now, gentlemen, I say that, in regard to each of these entries, I have demonstrated to you that there was no fraud on the part of the directors,—no knowledge on the part of the directors that there was anything wrong; and I must say that when I disclosed that upon the cross-examination of the witnesses, I should have expected, and I think I was entitled to expect, that the Lord Advocate should state his views upon it; because it was made perfectly plain in the cross-examination that I was going to take that point, but I have heard no answer to it, and shall hear none now.

The next alleged error, gentlemen, is £147,463, which is an omission. Mr Muir says that entry does not come into the balance ledger at all. Well, gentlemen, of course, if it does not come into the balance ledger, the director running down his finger would not see it in the balance ledger, because it was not there. And, therefore, how it can be said that it was in any sense an improper omission by the director, when the omission was made by Morison who prepared the sheet; and when the directors could not see it, because it was not there, and would not hear it read out, because Morison did not read it out, I leave to your judgment to decide. I make the same remark in regard to the adjusting account of interest, £11,405. That was not put in by Morison either. I don't care whether these were good or bad pieces of book-keeping; they were what the responsible officer of the Bank, charged with the duty, placed before these directors, and what they had no means of finding out to be wrong.

These, gentlemen, are the four heads, and you will see their importance immediately, when we come to the abstract,—these are four things, in which the balance ledger had exactly the same errors, if they were errors, as the abstract had. They were not the work of the directors, they had no knowledge of them, and they could have none.

Now, gentlemen, what is the next thing about which any complaint can be made against the balance ledger? In the latter part of the case, the Crown counsel changed the whole front of their case, when they had to depart from the eighth charge,—the bad and irrecoverable debts. They did not put a question to Mr Muir on the first day about profit and loss and the reserve fund; but on the second day, when they brought him back, they examined him about it, and they examined Mr Hutton about it; and now they make the complaint, and I think it is the only one on which the Lord Advocate stated an argument,—about keeping up a reserve fund of £450,000, and entering profits when they say there was no reserve fund and no profits. But was that a novelty in the abstracts? Was it something put into the abstracts by the directors, or any of them? Not at all. These were things which appeared not only in the balance ledger, but in every book that the Bank kept, and in every weekly state that the Bank made out. You will see it in the weekly state. There is a head for it, and it regularly appears. [Shows it to the jury.] There is the stock account, capital £1,000,000; there is the reserve fund, £450,000; here are the profits which are entered as applicable to the week of the year in which the balance is struck; all appear there, and all appear in the balance ledger. Mr Morison read them all off, and they all agreed with the books; and therefore, I ask you, gentlemen, with respect to these, as well as with respect to the other entries, how was it possible that the Lord Advocate could represent that it was a fraud on the part of the directors to allow these entries to appear in the published abstracts when they exist in the books? They were read from the books by the responsible official; where then is the blame of the directors in regard to them? You will at once see that when the Crown reaches this part of its case, it drifts into utter inconsistency. The first five heads of the charge in the indictment are complaints of disconformity between the abstract and the books; and you may recollect that the question the Lord Advocate put in the whole first day's examination was—Is there a disconformity in these respects between the balance ledger or the abstract and the books?

At that time, gentlemen, and down to this time, for the first five entries in his particulars in the indictment, the books are the standard of truth, and a departure from the books is a falsification, a falsehood, and a lie. But whenever he gets into heads six and seven—which I think formed the gravamen of his charge at the end, about the reserve fund and the profits—he has to take a different ground altogether, because the reserve fund and the profits exist in the books, and if they had not been carried into the balance ledger and into the abstract, there would have been a disconformity to the books in not so carrying them in. And therefore, gentlemen, I put it to you that when, instead of wandering about among minutes and drawing unreliable inferences from them, you follow these men into the Bank parlour, and see what they did, you get it demonstrated that, as regards all these six items which I have now dealt with, they had no means of knowing that there was anything other than it ought to be; they simply got the results from the responsible officials of the Bank, whose duty it was to record the results, to bring them into the balance documents, and read them out to the directors. I will deal afterwards with the question whether the directors were wrong in allowing these entries to be kept up in the books. I will not omit to deal with that, because the Lord Advocate's case had to come to that in the end; but I am now asking you to consider whether it is a correct representation to say that there was any falsification of any one of these six things which either appeared in the balance ledger, or did not appear in the balance ledger, which was to meet no eye but the eye of the directors themselves, which they had from their responsible officials,—information read off by them, and which there could be no possible reason for their seeking to falsify, because they could deceive nobody but themselves if they did so.

But, gentlemen, there are other errors which are said to be new in the abstracts, and let us see about them; I mean errors which were not in the balance ledger, but which appear in the abstracts for the first time; and I ask you there again to consider with me, when we have regard to the way in which these documents were made up, whether it is established that the directors could have cognisance of these. I am still asking you to keep apart the question of the 1876 abstract as applicable to Mr Potter. I will deal with that as I promised; but I am asking you, setting that aside, to see whether the directors had any means of detecting the other omissions or alterations in the sheet. Now, I think the only additional one which is said to have existed in the sheet of 1876—for that is the first sheet I am dealing with—

is the £751,775 that Mr Muir refers to on pages 252 and 253. [See pp. 212, 213.] By "additional" I mean the only one which does not occur in the balance ledger, or which is not omitted in the balance ledger,—in short, the only thing which is new in the abstract which went to the directors and the public. Now, gentlemen, suppose for a moment that the directors were not at the making up of that, but suppose the course explained by Mr Morison was followed—that the abstract was prepared and submitted to them—I ask, what was there to show that £751,000, which is entered under the head of Government stocks, was not truly Government stocks held by the Bank? There is the head of Government stocks [showing it to jury]; the amount against it is two million odds, and I ask you, gentlemen, how could any director looking at that head see that £751,000 of it was not Government stocks, but something else? It is impossible, gentlemen. You see, gentlemen, that they could not. If it had been the duty of the directors to call up all the stocks; to disbelieve the official who presented that sheet to them, and to say "show " us stocks for £2,218,868"—if it had been their duty to summon up all these stocks from the vaults of the Bank, to count and check them against the sums entered in the abstract, and to find that they were £751,000 short, then I can understand how it might be said that the directors were or should have been cognisant of the error. But that was not done, and nobody says that it was the duty of the directors to do it. They would have been turning themselves into auditors, and stopping the business of the Bank,—I suppose it would have taken a week or a fortnight,—and nobody says they should have done that, or that they did it. Therefore, when you have regard to the nature of these different errors—and I have taken every error in these sheets that the accountant has given for 1876, and the same remark is applicable to the other years—I say it is perfectly impossible that the directors could have cognisance of any one of them, unless they were at the making of the scroll abstract, which is another matter altogether.

Now, gentlemen, that disposes of every one of the things which is said to be wrong in the balance-sheet of 1876; I mean, disposes of it so far as regards the question of the directors' knowledge that there was something wrong, and of their guilty intention. As I said at the outset, the directors must trust something to officials. You heard what the Lord President said about their having no business, or at all events, duty to go through the books. I say that applies here, and I think, gentlemen, that to enquire what was actually done in making up the balance-sheet is a much fairer way of enabling you to answer the question, whether the directors issued it knowing it to be false, than by keeping away from the history of how it was made up, going through minutes for three or four years, and asking you to jump to the conclusion that it was all a fraud. I have taken you from beginning to end of the progress of the making up of these sheets, and I have shown you, I hope, that the charge against the directors on that point is unfounded.

Well then, gentlemen, I don't know that I need go through the other balance-sheets for the purpose of showing that the same things happened with respect to them. The particulars would be a little different, but the histoiy and the result would be the same in the case of all of them. The great bulk of the things which are said to be errors appear for the first time, or are omitted for the first time, in the balance ledger—the work of Mr Morison — which he brought and presented as accurate, and which the directors had no means of checking, except listening to what he read out.

But I may say a word here on the matter of profit and loss, which does appear in each of the abstracts, and which in the end, I think, the Lord Advocate chiefly relied upon. I have pointed out already that in that matter of profit and loss the balance-sheets agree not only with the books, where these accounts stood, but with the weekly sheets and with every other document of the Bank. This being so, gentlemen, the charge which the Lord Advocate would be compelled to alter his libel into would be a wholly different one from what he has made. What is complained of is the fabricating and issuing of false balance-sheets—that is, balance-sheets disconform to the books. But in regard to this matter of profit and loss, his complaint, if he has a complaint, ought to be that these accounts were kept up in the books of the Bank—were allowed to remain in the books of the Bank; that the directors did not put them out of the books, or direct that they should be put out of the books. That is a wholly different kind of charge from any presented under this indictment. It is not the theory nor the scheme of this indictment. And just observe how that is said to be an error. The reason why it is said that it was wrong to keep up the reserve fund, and to state a sum to the credit of profit and loss, and to divide it, is this—that there is a large number of old accounts, the number, I think, on which the Lord Advocate relied was about eight—which were said to have been in a doubtful or dangerous condition, on which interest had not been paid for years, and interest on which it is therefore said should not have been carried to the credit of profit and loss. Now, gentlemen, I am bound to say that, as that is the only reasoning by which this charge is supported, it looks most uncommonly like coming in again with the particular which the Lord Advocate dropped out of the indictment, I mean particular No. 8, in which he complained that bad and irrecoverable debts exceeding a million had been kept up and treated as available assets. Gentlemen, it is just by keeping up these debts, and treating them as available assets, that the interest and reserve fund are brought out, and there is no other complaint against them. And, therefore, to come back upon this and seek to rear up a charge in respect of that manner of calculating and carrying forward interest upon these accounts, is just proving the article which the Lord Advocate was constrained to abandon, because he had given no proper notice of the accounts, which he meant to prove to have been bad and irrecoverable, when interest was charged upon them.

But I don't care to dwell upon a technicality, gentlemen. I will take the substance of the thing, and deal with the case, assuming the eighth particular still to be in the indictment, and that the Lord Advocate had been allowed to go into the inquiry if these debts were bad and irrecoverable. Why was it a fraud—for that is the charge—why was it a fraud to calculate interest on these debts, and bring them into profit and loss? I can quite understand that if a debt is bad, that is to say, in a mercantile sense, if it is irrecoverable, you should score it out altogether, and not charge any interest on it; but if a debt is good, then I am not aware of any reason why you should not charge interest upon it; and if interest is growing upon it—whether it is paid or not—if it is good, it is an asset of the Bank, and I know of no reason why it should not be carried to profit and loss and divided. If the debt is doubtful, then you get into a question of judgment, which may be right or wrong, and which possibly no two men would agree about. But I am not aware of any reason why a debt that is only doubtful, but not bad, should not have interest charged upon it in the books of the Bank. Is it to be said, that a Bank or an individual, when he has a doubtful debt, is to acquit his debtor of interest? Not at all. But if he is not to acquit his debtor of interest, why should he not enter it into his books? And if the interest has been entered in the books by the responsible officials of the Bank, and brought by these responsible officials to the credit of profit and loss account in the books of the Bank, I ask you, gentlemen, as men of common-sense and fair dealing, is a director to be said to be fraudulent, because, when he had the result of these books put before him, with that reserve account standing there, and having stood there for many years back—is that man guilty of fabricating a false balance-sheet because he did not say—"Draw your pen through all that?" for it comes to that, gentlemen. I ask you to put yourselves in the place of these directors. It is not by looking back now in the light of the loss of five millions that you are to deal with this question. You are bound, in fairness and justice to these men, to put yourselves in their place when they had these balance-sheets before them, and ask what you would have done with these sheets when they were placed before you. I put it to you, gentlemen, can you say that if these balance-sheets had been laid before you,—abstracts or stock ledger, weekly states,—every book in the bank containing that reserve fund, and containing those interests treated as profits,—you would have been guilty of a fraud, because you did not order all that to be struck out? It may have been an error of judgment,—but these men are not being tried for errors of judgment. I don't admit,—on the contrary I deny, that it was an error of judgment, because I shall show you when I come to follow the Lord Advocate through his correspondence and his minutes, that the directors did not believe these debts to be desperate or hopeless; they believed that they would be recovered. And, therefore, this attempt to fix on them a falsehood and a fraud because they kept up that reserve fund, and that divisible profit derived from interest growing upon those accounts, fails just as much as every one of the other charges made against these directors fails. Why, gentlemen, just consider for a moment what it would have implied to go through the operation of pronouncing all these debts to be bad or doubtful. Mr Hutton, the second accountant for the Crown, who spoke to this matter of interest, which Mr Muir only did when called back on the second day—Mr Hutton, when asked about this, said he did not think there would have been anything to complain of in the way the reserve fund and the profit and loss were treated if it had not been that no interest had been paid on these accounts for years. Therefore, the only way in which the accountants for the Crown can support this item of the charge is not by bringing in any fabrications of 1876, or any faults or omissions of 1876; it is by looking back to the previous state of these accounts, and by that only can they attempt to establish that this was an error. Mr Hutton said there would not have been much to complain of, but for the way in which these accounts have been standing inoperative for some years. Now, as one of the examples, you will recollect Mr Hutton spoke of the American railway debentures. Well, gentlemen, a debenture is simply an acknowledgment of debt; interest grows upon it, and interest is due on it, whether the person or company owing it is able to pay or not. It grows on that debt just as much as any other debt. In the case of these debentures, we have a very good illustration of the argument I am now submitting to you, because we find that in 1873 they did begin to pay interest, and they have paid interest ever since. They began to pay interest in 1873; and I say that is just an instance from which it appears that the directors were not wrong in continuing to charge interest on such accounts. I daresay some of you may have been connected with railway companies which have not paid interest on their debentures for years, and then began after all that time to pay interest again. And the idea of saying that when you were making up your own books, or the books of a firm in which you were a partner, or the books of a bank, if you happened to be an official, and, still more, if you were a director, only looking over the books,—it was a fraud not to draw your pen through that, would be something very like an outrage on common sense.

I am not going through the balance-sheets of 1877 and 1878. I have taken, as a sample, the sheet of 1876, and the sample agrees with the bulk, because every observation I have made to you about the sheet for 1876 is equally applicable to the sheets for the other years; and I think you will agree with me that when you come to close quarters with the question it changes its appearance very much. It is not by holding aloof from the figures that this question is to be solved. I ask you to come to close quarters with the figures, and when you do, I think you see that the charge is utterly baseless—I mean the charge preferred against the directors as a body, of either fabricating these sheets, or issuing them in the knowledge that they were fabricated and false. Now, gentlemen, I don't intend to detain you farther upon the general question of the evidence bearing upon the preparation of these documents as affecting the directors as a body.

But I now come, gentlemen, to what the Lord Advocate dealt with very shortly,—in a few minutes towards the end of his speech, although it is undoubtedly an important part of the case,—I mean the incident of 1876 which is said to affect Mr Potter; and I will ask your special attention to that. You know what I mean. The charge there made is that Mr Potter met the manager, Mr Stronach, and Mr Morison, in June or July 1876, and directed a number of alterations to be made upon what Mr Morison says he prepared as a true abstract, for the purpose of turning that abstract into a false abstract. Now, gentlemen, I shall ask your very careful attention to the evidence bearing upon that charge. because it depends entirely upon the testimony of one witness, unsupported by any corroboration, and, as I think I shall show you, altogether unworthy of credit. But there is one witness undoubtedly who, if he is accurate and speaks the truth, does attempt to fix a charge upon Mr Potter of falsifying the balance-sheet. I shall submit to you, gentlemen. that when you recall to your minds—perhaps it is fresh in your minds —at all events when you recall to your minds the appearance of Mr Morison and what he said, you must be convinced that it would be utterly unsafe and dangerous—ay, and unjust—to hold that witness to have proved this very grave charge against Mr Potter. No human being on earth, except Mr Morison, makes any such charge, or corroborates any such charge; and one witness is quite insufficient to prove a fact, unless he is in some way corroborated. Mr Morison is one witness; he is uncorroborated; he has contradicted himself as often as it was possible for a man to contradict himself; and I think you will be agreed that the account he gives of himself, and of what he was a party to on his own showing, is such that if his evidence had been consistent and accurate, instead of inconsistent and inaccurate, it would not have been trustworthy. It would not have been evidence which, even in a question of £10, you would have been safe to rely on, far less in a case affecting the character, the credit, and, it may be, the life of my aged client Mr Potter. Now, gentlemen, I shall ask you to recall, in the first place, what Mr Morison said in regard to the alleged alterations. I shall further ask your attention, in the second place, to the consideration of whether, apart from the inaccuracies and inconsistencies in what he said, you could feel safe in believing Mr Morison,—whether he is a man you could believe; and then, even assuming what Mr Morison said to be accurate and true, I shall ask you, in the third place, to consider whether it proves a fraud by Mr Potter.

Mr Morison, gentlemen, was examined on parts of three different days. I think he first appeared on Tuesday afternoon; he came back again on Wednesday, and he was recalled by his Lordship on the Thursday. Upon each of these occasions he gave an entirely different and inconsistent account of what was done at the meeting in question. I will give you chapter and verse for that immediately. He gave accounts which cannot possibly stand together. At one time he said that Mr Potter had directed one alteration, at another time he said he had directed another alteration, and all his accounts were perfectly inconsistent with each other. I have noted from the evidence, and I shall give you a note of what he said upon the different items referring to that matter. The only thing that he was consistent about—the only thing he said twice,—was that Mr Potter directed the bringing down of the £751,000 of securities under the head of stocks. That I admit, gentlemen, he consistently said that Mr Potter had directed. But then, gentlemen, he gave two inconsistent accounts with respect to the £973,300. He said, in the first place, that he got no instructions from Mr Potter or the manager to deduct that, because it had been deducted in the books and in the balance ledger; and so it had. On two days he said that; but on the third day he said the opposite, asserting that Mr Potter had directed that also to be done. Now that I can demonstrate from the books is simply untrue. Well, the third alleged alteration related to the sum of £147,668 which I showed you,—he said on one of the occasions that he had been told to leave that out. That, gentlemen, I shall show you cannot be the case, because I have proved to you already that he had left it out of the balance ledger. In the third place, there was the sum of £29,000 of notes in transit from the offices. On his first day's examination he did not enumerate that as one of the things he was told to touch at all; but on another occasion he said that he had been ordered to enter it, and if he had been so ordered, he would have been ordered quite rightly, as I shall show you. Now these four things are what he said on the Wednesday. What he said on the Thursday was this, —when he was recalled by his Lordship, who, plainly seeing how utterly irreconcilable all the rest of his evidence was, put to him categorically the question [see p. 155]—"Mr Morison, enumerate to us the things you were told to alter; "begin at the beginning and tell us them all." And if it could be suggested that there was any confusion or mistake on the part of Mr Morison on the two previous days when he was under examination by counsel, I think you will agree that when he had two nights to sleep and to think over his evidence, and was then at last examined by his Lordship, asking him to begin at the beginning, and tell us them all, he had no excuse for being under any mistake. Well, on that last occasion his enumeration of the alterations was this:— There was first the £751,000; there was second, the sum of £30,000 deducted from heritable property, of which we had never heard a word on any of the previous days, and which nobody has ever heard of since; and there was the old £973,000 again; and then he brought in that £29,000 of notes.

Now, gentlemen, I should be sorry to do injustice to Mr Morison or to any other witness, and, therefore, as this is a matter of the most vital importance to Mr Potter, I shall, with his Lordship's permission, refer to the evidence, and show that everything I have now said to you as to these three irreconcilable accounts is entirely correct.

The LORD JUSTICE-CLERK—I was going to ask you to do so. I think it is quite right that you should do it.

Mr BALFOUR—It is of the most vital importance for the interests of Mr Potter and the justice of the case. He is first asked about this matter on page 89 of the evidence from the shorthand writer's notes, printed from day to day. At page 89 D he is asked about the bringing down of the £751,000 from credit accounts [see p. 114]. I shall show you on the abstract No. 128A how that was done [see Appendix].

The LORD JUSTICE-CLERK—You had better show that to the jury.

Mr BALFOUR—There are copies of it ready for the jury.

The LORD JUSTICE-CLERK—They had better have three or four copies.

Mr BALFOUR—[Showing it to the jury.] There is the head in which the total amount of the deductions made occurs; here are the three entries you have heard about—Smith, Fleming, & Co., Morton & Co., and J. Nicol Fleming. [Copies of No. 128A were now handed to the jury.] The three sums of these three accounts are taken from here [showing to the left on 128A], and carried down under the head of Government and other stocks. These three sums make the £751,775, and they appear in that sheet under Government stocks. Now, that is the only thing in which Mr Morison is consistent, and I will read to you what he says about it. On page 89 D [see top of p. 114] he is asked, "By whose instigation were these sums "brought down?" and he says, it was by Mr Potter's. Then he was asked in regard to the credit accounts. At the foot of page 89 [see p. 114] the Lord Advocate asked him about bringing in the balance of the deposit accounts instead of bringing in the sums, but he does not say that he got any orders about these; and he could not have got any orders, because he had brought only the balance into his balance ledger. Well, this sum of £973,000 is the next that he deals with, and I will read to you the account which he gives about that. On page 90 B [see p. 114] he is asked, "Why was the "sum of £973,300 deducted from the foreign and colonial credits? (A.) Be- "cause there was a credit account to that extent. (Q.) Did you get instruc- "tions from anybody to deduct it? (A.) No; it was in the ledger. (Q.) "Why did you put it in the ledger?" and then he gives the account which you have heard, that in June 1873 Alexander Stronach, the late manager of the Bank, raised that account for the first time in the cash book, and made the deduction from the bills payable. Now, whether this entry is accurate or inaccurate is no concern of mine; but he made this entry, "against which "securities are now held by the Bank, and in process of realisation and pay- "ment of the proceeds." Now, gentlemen, from the year 1873 it has been kept up, and treated exactly in the same way as it is in that balance. And there you will notice Mr Morison quite distinctly says he got no instructions to treat it so at all. Well, on page 113 [see p. 128], he was asked again about it—"(Q.) "In preparing your balance-sheet for your abstract or scroll balance for each "year, did you give effect to that without anybody's instructions?" and he answers, "Yes." So that he has twice said perfectly distinctly that he did that at his own hand. He says the same thing at page 114 F G [see foot of p. 128], but I don't know that I need trouble you with it. Here is what he says there. I put the question to him, "Can you say that before you had the meeting with "Mr Potter and the manager in 1876 you had given effect to the entry of "£973,300 as usual, just as it had been for the three years then past? (A.) "Yes. (Q.) So they had nothing whatever to do with the mode of treating "the £973,300? (A.) No. (Q.) Neither in 1876 nor at any time? (Q.) No." So that three times over he told the truth about that, as we can see perfectly, for it runs through all the sheets. But then on page 135 [see p. 141], for some reason best known to himself, he gave a different account of it. The account which he gave there was under examination by his Lordship. It was not the examination of any counsel, but his Lordship put some questions to him as to the figures, and I ask you, gentlemen, to notice this, because it is very important. His Lordship put this short question to him—"How did you get the figures? "Did Mr Potter or the manager come with figures ready in their heads to you, "or how did you get your figures?" and then with respect to bills payable, from which this deduction is made, what he said was in substance this—That they sent for information, that he got details as to bills payable, and then was told to make this deduction. He was asked, "Where was it made?" and he says, "First in the private cash book." Then his Lordship puts this question [see p. 141]—"You said you were told to get the detail of bills payable, and "you understood the reason why they wanted the details to be that they might "make some deduction from them; you also said that when you came back "with the information, they directed you to deduct £973,000—is that right?" and his answer is, "That is right." So that the story he told this time was diametrically the opposite both of what he had three times said before, and of the truth; because it was untrue that he went and got information at that meeting about bills payable, and made the deduction in consequence of that information. Now, what do you make of that, gentlemen?

I come next to the £147,000 entry, and what Morison says about that is at page 92 D [see foot of p. 115]. He says—"I cannot tell why that sum was left "out. I left it out of the statement in consequence of instructions given to me "by Mr Potter and the manager. I have no recollection whether they gave me "any reason for leaving it out." Now, gentlemen, it was with special reference to this statement that I was at pains to show you that the sum of £147,000 was left out of the balance ledger; and it was left out of the balance ledger by himself before he tendered that balance ledger to the directors at all. He does not say that any director—either Mr Potter or anybody else—had anything to do with the omission in the balance ledger, and yet Mr Muir proved that it was left out of the balance ledger, just as it was left out of the abstract.

The LORD JUSTICE-CLERK—Was Mr Morison asked why it was left out of the balance ledger?

Mr BALFOUR—No, my Lord. Mr Muir was examined after him, and we did not know at that time that any point was to be made of it, otherwise we should have put the question. But it was only from Mr Muir that we got the fact that it was not in the balance ledger. If we had known that Mr Muir was going to say that, we should have put the question to Mr Morison about it. I therefore submit to you, gentlemen, that with respect to that £147,000 his statement is plainly untrue, because we know that it was left by himself out of the balance ledger, and if he had not left it out of his scroll, he would have made his scroll different from his balance ledger.

That, gentlemen, is his Tuesday's account and his Wednesday's account, and then comes his Thursday's, and this I pray you to note. I will read the question that was put by his Lordship to give Mr Morison a third chance. His Lordship puts it thus, at page 160 [see p. 155]—" On your first " examination we were led to understand that the document, No. 128, " of which we have a lithograph [see Appendix 128A], was the original " abstract of accounts which you first submitted to the manager and " Mr Potter—that is to say, without the red ink markings, and that the " red ink markings denoted the alterations which you were instructed to " make. Yesterday you corrected that, and you told us that this abstract, " so far as it appears in black ink, was not the thing which you submitted to the " manager, but was another copy made after your interview with the manager; " is that not so?" He answers, " Yes." Then his Lordship puts a question I ask your special attention to. " Now, then, tell me exactly what the figures " are on No. 128—go over them *seriatim*—which you were instructed to " alter, and which appear as altered on the document as it now stands." Now, gentlemen, I put it to you whether any question could give a witness clearer notice. or a better chance than that. Begin at the beginning of the alterations, and go on to the end of them. Well, then, he first enumerates these three sums, amounting together to the £751,000, and I admit that he was consistent about that. Then the next sum he refers to is that the new amount of £30,000, which we never heard of before, and have never heard of since, and what it is to this hour I don't know. His Lordship asks—" What was the " next alteration which the directors directed you to make on this sheet, still " dealing with the debit side? (A.) Under the heading of heritable property " account there is a sum of £30,000 deducted." His Lordship asks—" You " were directed to do that? (A.) Yes. (Q.) Is that in red ink or black ink? " (A.) Black ink. (Q.) Then that must have been done after the meeting? " (A.) Yes. (Q.) Is there not before that a sum of £430,000 struck out? " (A.) No." That was evidently a question relating to the deposit account, as to which he had given a different story before. So, gentlemen, you see that for the first time he makes mention of this £30,000. What it was, what the effect of the deduction would have been, he does not tell us. You find there is such a sum [pointing it out to the jury] in his black ink figuring; but what it is he does not tell us, and what its effect was he does not tell. But he mentions it for the first time. Now, on the two previous days, he had been asked and had enumerated the alterations without saying a word about that £30,000. Then, again, his Lordship, pursuing the enumeration of the alterations, asks the question—" Well, what next? What is the next deduction you " were told to make? (A.) Under the heading of foreign and colonial " credits there is a sum of £973,300 deducted from bills payable." Further, his Lordship says—" And that, you told us, reduced the apparent amount of "bills payable?" And his answer is—"For foreign and colonial credits in "the meantime. (Q.) By nearly a million of money? (A.) Yes; with the "explanation that that £973,000 entry was in the general ledger."

Now, what can you make of that? I have shown you that he had twice before said, what was perfectly true, that it was not a deduction made by order of the directors at all. Nobody told him to make it, but he brought it in from the books, and it had been in the books from 1873. He twice told you (on pages 135 and 160) [see pp. 141 and 155], contrary to the fact, "that he was told "to take it down by the directors." Now, I think it is almost wasting time over a witness who speaks in that way—even in point of accuracy. I shall have another observation to make about him by-and-by. Then his Lordship asks—"Is there anything else material in that state which you were directed to alter by the directors?" And he says, there is the same £30,000 that was deducted from the heritable property account which he had before mentioned. His Lordship asks—"Anything else?" and the reply is, "There is a sum of "£29,095 added to the amount of notes of other banks on hand. (Q.) Are "those the material alterations which you were told to make? (A.) Then "there are the £200,875, £100,300, and £450,600 brought down that I "spoke of before," making up the £751,000. Here you have in this ultimate examination two new things brought into the field for the first time, viz., the £30,000 and the £29,000 of notes. Now, in the first place, gentlemen, it does not appear that the directors knew anything at all about that, but if they had told him to bring that down they would have done quite right; and he says so, because he explains what these notes were, in another part of his evidence. The entry of these notes, you will observe, is one of the things which we are charged with in the indictment as a crime. He explains it at page 123 G [see p. 134]. I don't detain you by reading it, but I will accurately state the import of it. As you know, in the course of business, banks come to be possessed of the notes of each other, and they exchange those notes from time to time, and get back an equivalent amount of their own notes. In like manner, in conducting the business between the head office and the branches, it sometimes becomes necessary to send notes from the one to the other, and on page 123 what Mr Morison explains about the £29,000 of notes is, that these notes were in transit from the branches to the head office at the time when the balance was struck. They had not reached the head office at that time, and so they could not appear in the original amount of notes, but they were on the road from the branches, and I need not say to you, gentlemen, that whether a note is at the head office, or at a branch, or in the hands of a messenger in transit between the one and the other, it is equally in the hands of the bank; it is, therefore, a proper deduction, and it would have been an improper thing not to deduct it. And, therefore, I don't care whether Mr Potter ordered that deduction or not—I say it is utterly false that he did order it—but I say that if he did order it, he did quite right. And so says Mr Morison. Yet the Crown positively comes to you still with that charge remaining unwithdrawn in the indictment. Well, that is the sum of £29,000 of notes, and I make the same remarks as to the £89,000. At 111 G, and 112 A [see p. 127], he gives an account of the sums of notes which are deducted in the balance-sheet of 1876, which appear like alterations on the balance-sheet of 1878; and he explains that these were notes which were changed with other banks between the close of business on the Wednesday, which was the balance day for the year, and the beginning of business on Thursday; and he says he thought it was perfectly right, even in respect to those exchanged notes, to deduct them, because they were in before the Bank began business next day. Then I asked the question, did you put in this at your own hand? and he said, yes. Well, then, if he put in at his own hand the £89,000 of notes, which were exchanged, why should he not have put in at his own hand those £29,000 of notes, which were much more clearly a proper deduction, because they were not exchanged, but were in the hands of the Bank at the time when the balance was struck, although they had not come back to the head office?

Now that is Mr Morison in point of accuracy, and if you should think that a witness who gives as many accounts as that—perfectly bewildering and totally inconsistent accounts—could be safely relied on as accurate in the smallest transaction of ordinary civil business, I should be very much surprised; and I should be still more surprised if you relied on his accuracy in a question such as we have to try here.

But I have something more to say about Mr Morison. Take Mr Morison's account as it was given, suppose it to be true,—which I utterly deny,—that Mr Potter did make all or any of those alterations for the improper purpose which Mr Morison imputes to him, what would you think of Mr Morison allowing himself to be made the hand to execute such an act? Mr Morison was not the servant of Mr Potter; Mr Morison was the servant of the Bank—the responsible official of the Bank, and he owed a duty to the Bank and to its shareholders. Well, gentlemen, if what he says was true—that Mr Potter directed those things for the purpose of falsifying the balance-sheets, then Mr Morison made himself participant in that fraud. His is the only hand you will see on any one of those sheets. And therefore, if I put it to you, gentlemen, that Mr Morison is a person of such a moral character as regards honesty that you could not trust a word he says, I give you no worse account of him than he gave of himself; because I say that a man who would be participant in such a thing is a man who would be unfaithful to his duty; and if a man would be unfaithful to his duty and make these alterations, even on the order of another, he would not scruple to do it himself; nor would he scruple, when Mr Potter and the other directors are sitting at that bar with their mouths shut, to throw the blame off himself and on to their shoulders. I should not, without good cause, make such an allegation or suggestion against a man; but I call himself as a witness to prove it. And therefore, I am in your judgment whether it would be safe to trust either Mr Morison's accuracy or his veracity in a question of this kind. The Lord Advocate in his address said it was possible that the suggestion which I am now making to you would be made. It was possible. I disclosed it perfectly plain in my cross-examination of Mr Morison. I indicated it to the Lord Advocate, the Lord Advocate took the indication, and he knew it would be made; so that you will judge whether you would be safe to find upon that point against Mr Potter.

But then the Lord Advocate says, what interest had Mr Morison to do these things? Well, gentlemen, I answer that by putting another question—What interest had Mr Potter to do these things? Because the one fact that shines out conspicuous through the whole of this case—as I shall have occasion to show you a little more in detail afterwards—is, that if these frauds were committed by Mr Potter, there is not a suggestion of any motive which could actuate him to commit them, except to ruin himself and every one connected with him, which the failure of the Bank has done. Therefore, so far as I have gone, you must see how utterly unsafe it would be to rely on Mr Morison in that matter. But it does not stop there, because you will recollect the appearance he presented when he was examined about the red ink alterations. I may recall the picture to your minds. At first he distinctly conveyed the impression, which he had no doubt previously conveyed to the law officers of the Crown, who of course examined him on carefully prepared precognitions, that all the red ink alterations were made on the order of Mr Potter and the manager. And so he at first said. But on the second day he gave a wholly different account—just as different as any two accounts which he gave of anything he spoke to during the whole three days he was in the witness-box. But you will observe that the £751,000 don't appear in red ink at all. The £30,000 does not appear in red ink, and many of the other things don't appear in red ink. I put the question to him, how it was possible—if the black ink was the basis of the balance-sheet and the red ink was the alteration—how that could be, and how it happened that most of the red ink alterations related to the branches; and then there began a scene of vacillation and inconsistency such as is rarely witnessed in a court of justice. He said this was not the first sheet, but he could not tell what had become of the first sheet. He then made this most extraordinary statement, that the first sheet had been all black—branches and all—that he altered it partly in black ink and partly in pencil; and that the red ink appeared for the first time as giving the result of that for the information of himself! This paper which was to go before no human being after it was altered, but was merely to be abstracted further so as to assume the shape in which it was laid before the shareholders, he told us was in black ink, but the red ink alterations were for his own information! Now, gentlemen, I put it to you whether, in that state of the evidence, it would be in the slightest degree safe to rely upon a single thing in that man's evidence?

But, gentlemen, my third remark upon Mr Morison's evidence is this. I have already indicated that there is one thing that he is consistent about, and that is, that Mr Potter directed the £751,000 to be brought down. Now, suppose you should come to be of opinion, contrary to what I have been suggesting to you, that that alteration was directed by Mr Potter and the manager, the question then would be, is that a fraud? Gentlemen, I submit that very clearly it is not. It may not have been correct bookkeeping. I should rather say that it was not correct bookkeeping; because I quite agree with the suggestion that was made, that if the entry represented bills payable, although ordinary securities or possibly even stocks were held against them, it should not have been allowed to remain under the head where we find it. But if stocks were held against the bills, Mr Morison's own view is that there was no harm in the entry. He was asked about it, and justified it; and I shall put it for your consideration—whether it was right or wrong to bring down that sum as Mr Morison did, or to direct it to be brought down, if the manager or Mr Potter directed that to be done, was that a fraud? Mr Morison does not think so. He says it would depend on whether there were stocks held. Now, is not that just one of the things which a director of a bank must take from his officials; and if Mr Morison thinks that is a thing which was not wrong, I mean wrong in morals, it would be at the worst only an irregularity or a mistake, and not a wilful errcr or a falsification at all.

And therefore, gentlemen, I ask you to reject altogether, as utterly untrustworthy and unsafe, the whole of Mr Morison's evidence from beginning to end, for reasons which I have now, perhaps at too great detail, stated to you, but which I hope will carry conviction to your minds.

That, gentlemen, is the second point attempted to be made against Mr Potter,—falsifying the sheet of 1876. The scrolls of 1877 and 1878 Mr Potter admittedly had nothing earthly to do with. Here again, however, Mr Morison is inconsistent as before; and although this inconsistency is rather a point which my learned friend the Dean of Faculty, who represents Mr Stronach, ought to deal with, I will just mention it in passing, because it affects Mr Morison's general credibility. In one part of Mr Morison's evidence, he said that he carried on the same system in 1877 and 1878, as had been inaugurated at the meeting in 1876; but in two other parts of his evidence he said exactly the opposite. He said he framed his abstracts correctly from the books for 1877 and 1878, that he did not carry on these alterations at his own hand, but framed them correctly, and that he was afterwards asked to alter them by Mr Stronach. I will give you the reference to that, because it has an important bearing.

The LORD JUSTICE-CLERK—I rather think he said he did not carry them into the books.

Mr BALFOUR—Oh! they never were carried into the books.

The LORD JUSTICE-CLERK—I think that was what he intended to say,—not that he did not carry them into the second balance.

Mr BALFOUR—I thought the gravamen of the charge was that they never appeared in the books. But I shall read the two passages I had marked. Here is what he first says, and I pray you to observe, gentlemen, that it is in answer to his Lordship, and therefore it cannot be represented that he was confused in any way by the examination. At page 94 D E [see p. 117], his Lordship, referring to the sheet of 1877, asked, "Did you prepare it according to the "alterations of the year before?" and the answer is, "I prepared it in the "usual way,—the correct way." Then he is asked, "So the same alterations "would require to be made again? (A.) Yes. (Q.) And they were made? "(A.) Yes." Now, if there is any doubt as to what that means, gentlemen, I will ask you to attend to another sentence on the next page. He is questioned about the balance-sheet of 1878, and he says he prepared it with a view to the annual abstract as in previous years. Then he says, "The abstract I "prepared as the basis of No. 124. was correctly made up from my own "abstract and that furnished by Mr Miller, and was in conformity with the "books. Alterations were made upon that abstract for 1878. They were "made by the directions of the manager, Mr Robert Stronach." And in answer to his Lordship he further says—"I made them. There was no other "person concerned in it. These alterations were almost on the same lines "as before" [see p. 117]. Therefore, gentlemen, he did not carry forward these alterations, according to his own account.

The LORD JUSTICE-CLERK—You are quite right.

Mr BALFOUR—He says in another place that he did not. Gentlemen, I am unwilling to weary you with more of his inconsistencies, but I have shown that in that part of his evidence he says he did not carry these into next year. You will see that the importance of that is very great, because it utterly dissociates Mr Potter from any complicity, actual or possible, with any alterations in these later sheets. But I should like, gentlemen, as giving you some light upon Mr Morison's evidence, to ask you to look for a minute at the appearance of his scroll abstract for 1877 [see Appendix]. I think that scroll tells a very significant tale to the eye.

The LORD JUSTICE-CLERK—That is No. 127/A.

Mr BALFOUR—Yes. I think it tells an instructive tale. It entirely bears out our theory of the case,—that all this was Mr Morison's own work. [Shows it to the jury.] You see, gentlemen, the black ink, red ink, and pencillings. Now I put some questions, which, perhaps at the time you might not see the bearing of, but I think you will see it now, as to whether it was not perfectly plain that Mr Morison was here laboriously figuring out some scheme of his own. Look at the amount of pencilling; that is not the work of a man just told to bring down a particular item from one place to another. That was easily done, and would not have altered the result at all. But there is a sheet covered with pencillings, in the hand from beginning to end of Mr Morison, just as the black ink and the red ink is all in Mr Morison's hand, and I say that tells a tale which cannot be mistaken—that it is Morison's work,—he is trying to make a symmetrical balance-sheet which shall be pleasing to his accountant's eye; working it out on his own theory and upon his own lines. I leave to your judgment, gentlemen, whether that is not so.

There is one observation that I should like to make upon his abstract of 1878, because, I think, it also tells a most important tale with regard to Morison. I ask you to look at it for a moment. This [showing it to the jury] is the abstract of 1878 [see Appendix], and you will observe that it contains a great deal of black ink and a deal of red ink, and it also contains some figuring by Mr Morison. Now look at the deletions there, and see the effect of them.

The LORD JUSTICE-CLERK—Which deletions are you referring to?

Mr Balfour—The deletions in red ink.

The Lord Justice-Clerk—On the right hand?

Mr Balfour—All of them. I was going to make a general observation upon them. Mr Morison started upon a theory which would have been perfectly intelligible. He started at first with a theory that everything that was in black ink had been there originally, and that everything in red ink was alterations. All that, gentlemen, is perfectly intelligible, if it had been so. If he had put in red ink afterwards, it was quite intelligible that he should score out the black. But then there were some difficulties suggested to Mr Morison in the way of that theory. I called his attention to this—"What "about your additions? for your additions include black ink. There is the "black ink which had the red ink upon it." He then went to this new story, that that was not his original abstract at all, but that was the result of what, for anything he could tell, might have been half-a-dozen previous abstracts.

The Lord Justice-Clerk—Do you say the black ink additions include the red ink alterations?

Mr Balfour—They do in this case [showing]. I only put the one to Mr Morison,—the £14,000 odds. Mr Morison was then driven out of his theory that these red ink alterations were made on the basis of the black, because the summations would not agree; and then, as a last resort, after other difficulties in the way of his first story had been suggested, he told this most amazing and incredible tale, that after the successive meetings with Mr Stronach, for Mr Potter had nothing to do with this,—he positively prepared this sheet as a *fac-simile* of the result. A *fac-simile* of the result, gentlemen! Who on earth would do such a thing, writing part of it in red ink, and making it perfect as the lithographer's art could make it—so perfect that he deleted part of it: and for whom? For nobody! Gentlemen, if it were not of such vital importance to my client, I would not waste your time with it; it is simply adding another to that catalogue of inaccuracies, or something worse, of which I think you will agree Mr Morison has been convicted. Therefore, I pass from Mr Morison, and I say that the charge relative to the abstract of 1876 is not only unproved, but entirely discredited. Now there only remains one point more which is said to be special in the case of Mr Potter, and in this he is said to be associated with Mr Stewart; I mean in having seen the clean abstract of the balance-sheet of 1878. It is not said that Mr Potter, or anybody else, saw these previous or scroll abstracts for that year. Mr Morison did say that he showed to Mr Potter and Mr Stewart the result brought out in that form. He admitted that it would not be easy upon that [showing] to trace these results, and I quite agree with him. It is very difficult. But there is one entry upon that abstract which I would like to ask your particular attention to, because, you may recollect, I put some questions about it. I put that specially, because it is one of the particular heads relied upon by the Crown as regards 1878. I refer to the deduction of £419,708. Now I ask you to allow me a word of explanation about that. You may recollect that Mr Muir made light of it, as a most absurd entry.

The Lord Justice-Clerk—Can you give me the figures out of which that arises?

Mr Balfour—No, they don't appear. It is a deduction from bills payable, but the figures out of which it arises don't appear. The way in which that is entered, gentlemen, I will show you, and then leave it, and you will see if there is anything to put a director on his guard there. Here [showing] is the £419,000, and here against it is "amount of bills on the circle, and against "which an equal amount is lodged in cash." Now that statement, of course, was one on which any director seeing it was entitled to rely, coming as it did from the responsible officials of the Bank; and I put it to you, whether there was anything in it to excite the least suspicion. I think, on the contrary that with that statement it would have been incorrect not to make the deduction. I will just recall to your recollection the explanation which I got of it from Mr Morison himself, who made it. The explanation was simply this, that Mr Morton, of whom you have heard a good deal, had large amounts of bills running; he was not able to pay these in cash; and with a view to taking up these bills, a second set was drawn for the same amount, to be discounted by Mr Morton, and to have the discount money applied to take up the first set. It is perfectly true, and I quite agree in what Mr Muir and some of the other witnesses said,—that both of these sets of bills, as long as they were in the hands of the public, were bills inferring liability on the part of the Bank. That is true. But both of these sets of bills would not get into the hands of the public; the second set would not get into the hands of the public unless they had been discounted; and what were they to be discounted for? They were to be discounted, as Mr Morison told us, to take up the first set. Consequently, unless Morton committed a fraud—which nobody says he did—he was bound to pay that discount money into the Bank, to be ready to retire the first set at maturity. But that is exactly what this entry says—"amount "of bills on the circle against which an equal amount is lodged in cash." And Mr Morison says—and here I agree with him—that if that statement was true, and that amount was lodged in cash, and had not gone into any other account in the Bank,—and Mr Muir agrees it did not go into any other account in the Bank, for he could not find it—if that money was not applied to reduce any other account in the Bank, or to go to the credit of any other account in the Bank, but was lying separated and appropriated to that purpose—then, gentlemen, not only was there nothing wrong in deducting it, but it would have been wrong not to deduct it, because although it was perfectly true that there were two sets of bills out for these three days in the circle, these sets of bills were for the same sum, and there was the money that the second had produced lying to take up the first. And no man has been put in the box to say that that statement by responsible officers of the Bank was untrue. And, therefore, I put it to you in regard to that sum, as in regard to all the other sums, that there was nothing whatever to show the directors that these balance-sheets were wrong in any one particular. I am not going further into this matter. I might treat in the same way other items if your time permitted, but I do not intend to do so. I have taken these as convenient examples, and I think you will agree with me that the fair result of the evidence is,—the Lord Advocate did not go into one bit of this—that putting yourselves in the place of the directors at the time, following them in what you know they did, and not drawing suspicions against them from their minutes, but going into their council chamber, from which the Lord Advocate says he was excluded, though Mr Morison took you there, and seeing how the abstracts were made up, not only that the Crown has failed to prove affirmatively that there were any fraudulent knowledge on the part of the directors, but I have proved that there was none.

I shall now, gentlemen, deal shortly with the view that was presented by the Lord Advocate, on which he asked you to draw an inference contrary to all the evidence that I have now brought before you. What the Lord Advocate says in substance is this: he says, as I cannot go into this secret chamber, I shall read the minutes, and I shall draw inferences from what these contain as to the knowledge which the directors had of the condition of the Bank, and from that I shall infer a motive for falsifying the balance-sheets, and from that I shall make the farther inference that they did falsify the balance-sheets, or issued them knowing them to be false. The Lord Advocate made a remark, which I thought a very just one, at the outset of his speech, when he stated that you were not to try these directors upon the knowledge which you have now, or in the light of subsequent events, but that you must try them upon the knowledge, and only upon the knowledge, which you see they had at the time. I am not quite sure that the Lord Advocate applied that excellent maxim consistently throughout, because within a few minutes after he had laid it down, he stated that five millions were proved to have been lost in October 1878, and then he said, was it possible that that could have been done since the balance-sheet of 1878, and yet that the directors could not have known it. That was very like a bit of reasoning back from subsequent knowledge—an application of that late wisdom which is very wise after the fact; but I merely mention that in passing. No doubt it was a mere slip, and I do not complain of it. But I do ask you to consider this part of the case, not in the same light as the Lord Advocate did, not in the light of what the catastrophe showed—this catastrophe which came like a shot upon the whole of these directors—but in the light of what we see they knew at the time. Now, this part of the Lord Advocate's case, although he necessarily and quite properly went into it in much detail, I think I may deal with shortly; and I think I correctly and fairly represent it, when I say that the alleged knowledge of the unsound condition of the Bank was founded upon what the directors are said to have known in regard to three accounts—the account of Smith, Fleming, & Co., the account of James Nicol Fleming, and the account of James Morton. The Lord Advocate said there were over five millions owing on these accounts at the crisis; that there were four millions owing on them in 1875, and that the directors had such knowledge, therefore, as made it plain that they could not believe these balance-sheets to be correct. Now, gentlemen, the proper way of dealing with that question is not to look at the amounts only that are standing against these names from time to time in the books, or at the disastrous result, but to endeavour to ascertain, if you can, what was the honest belief in the minds of the directors at the time as to how these accounts would turn out. That is the fair question. The directors may have been too sanguine. The result would seem to show that they were. How much that failure of forecast was due to the disastrous depression which has weighed like a load of lead upon the world for some years past, you will probably know better than I do, but at all events much is due to that beyond all doubt; and what I shall ask you to do is to follow me very shortly in an examination, not of inferences from minutes, but of what we know from the testimony of living men examined by the Crown, as to what the opinion of the directors was, and what the opinion of the Messrs Stronach was, in regard to the prospects of these accounts. And I may here say, with respect to one part of the Lord Advocate's speech, that he entirely misapprehended the ground I was to take for Mr Potter when he supposed that I was going to represent Mr Potter as a man not fit to understand business, and not fit to understand or know the state of an account. I made no such representation, and I never intended to make it. But I do represent, and you will judge whether the representation is not a fair representation, that Mr Potter, at the time over which this inquiry extends, was not a man who went into the details of accounts. That assertion I do make, and I make it on the evidence of Mr Cunningham Smith, his partner, and of his son, and of Mr Hunter, the persons who know him best. I suppose it is a thing not unfamiliar in your experience that a man, when he has got to seventy years of age—which was the age of Mr Potter in 1876—he is seventy-two now—and has been at the head of great businesses and large firms for forty or fifty years, does avoid details. He does that in his own business, and he does that in other people's business. He leaves details to younger men—men who are more conversant with details, better figurers and better accountants; at all events, whether they are better or not, his time for that sort of thing is past. What you expect to get from a man of that age is his ripe experience, his broad and general views, and not that he should sit down at a desk like an office boy, figuring away at accounts and states. I don't dispute that Mr Potter had a certain amount of knowledge in regard to these accounts from 1870 onwards. I think he had only an imperfect knowledge down to 1875, but after 1875 I don't dispute that he knew generally the state of these accounts. What that knowledge amounted to, and what it implied, I shall immediately show; but it is no part of my case to deny that he had a certain amount of knowledge of their position.

Now, gentlemen, I shall make a few observations on each of these three accounts, and bring under your notice very shortly what I think cannot fail to satisfy you that the entravagant and exaggerated inferences drawn by the Lord Advocate from the minutes were not in accordance with the honest belief of Mr Potter and the other directors at the time.

I will take first the account of Smith, Fleming, &. Co. That is one of the three accounts, and it is the one that the Lord Advocate dealt with first. Now, gentlemen, Smith, Fleming, & Co.'s account we know of from the year 1870; it was proved in evidence, that in the year 1870 there was a meeting between Mr Stronach, Mr Potter, and Mr John Fleming—whom you saw—in regard to that account. The reference to that is in John Fleming's evidence, page 217 G [see p. 190]. The Lord Advocate gave you. and quite correctly gave you, yesterday, the substance of that interview, and I don't trouble you by repeating it. But the state of John Fleming's affairs at that time was this. He was at that time indebted to the Bank in £150,000, fully secured. The account, therefore, at that time, gentlemen, was not a bad account. As far as the Bank was concerned, it was fully secured. Mr John Fleming had got embarrassed in other ways—I suppose indebted to people who were not fully secured; and, apparently, there was a desire to save this very lucrative business,—a desire which the Bank appears to have shared. Well, at that time, Mr John Fleming had a most lucrative business. He had from commissions alone,—from a safe commission business—a return of upwards of £90,000 a year. His losses had been through reckless speculation. Everybody was desirous to save that lucrative business for him, and for any who might be associated with him, to get him out of his difficulties, and rid him of his speculations. Well, apparently it was proposed that that should be done, and he got accommodation from the Bank. The Lord Advocate said quite correctly that by the end of the year it appeared that he had got advances to the amount of about £500,000, covered to the extent of about three-fourths. So that, by the end of the year 1870, his unsecured advances was about £125,000,—not a year and a half's income from his safe commission business. Well, that was not a state of matters fitted to alarm anybody very much; and no more it did. What does appear then and after to have given anxiety to those connected with the Bank was the speculative tendency of these Messrs Fleming. If they could only have been kept out of speculation, they had a magnificent business, of enormous earning power, and all would have been well. But the next step in this history is not so satisfactory, either from the point of view of Mr John Fleming or of Alexander Stronach. But it entirely exculpates the directors. It appears that between 1870 and 1874, Alexander Stronach, the late manager, had got into the way of giving advances to John Fleming without the knowledge or authority of his directors; and you will no doubt recollect my friend Mr Asher putting to John Fleming a very pathetic letter, written on the 3d April 1872, in which Alexander Stronach writes in very piteous terms to Mr John Fleming, imploring him to do something to reduce the amount, speaking of the burden which he cannot share with his directors being too much for him to bear, and saying that nothing on the earth would have induced him to undertake that burden but "the esteem and regard I have for you and your brother,"—John Fleming and James. So that at that time, gentlemen, there was undoubtedly concealment from the directors; and, therefore, I say that you cannot impute anything to them with respect to the state of the accounts at that time, even if these accounts were alarming, of which I see no evidence. But the next stage in the history of these accounts is of great significance. That is the state of them in 1873 and 1874, and I shall recall to your recollection evidence of much greater value in regard to the estimation in which these accounts were held by the directors at the time,—which is the question here,—than anything you can gather from reading dead and dry minutes. You had two men examined by the Crown,—Mr Glen Walker and Mr Hunter,—who were on intimate and confidential terms both with Alexander Stronach and John Fleming, and you may recollect that it was proved by Mr Glen Walker—your Lordship will find the evidence on pages 284 and 289 of the proof [see p. 235],—that Alexander Stronach, who was a brother-in-law of Glen Walker, wanted Glen Walker in 1873 to go into partnership with John Fleming to keep him straight, to keep him out of speculation,—and to keep him to his commission business. Mr Glen Walker, in the passages I have referred to, says that a state was put before him at that time, showing the condition of Fleming's affairs, and that it showed he was behind (to use Mr Glen Walker's expression) to the extent of about £150,000 or £200,000,—he thinks about £170,000. Now, gentlemen, that was not very alarming in the case of a man who had a safe commission business of £90,000 a year. I think you will agree that the difference between his liabilities and his assets was nothing very startling. It was not above two years' earnings. Can you believe that either Alexander Stronach or anybody else thought that account was dangerous then? If so, gentlemen, you must believe that Alexander Stronach wished to bring about the ruin of his own brother-in-law, for what he wanted and suggested was, that Mr Glen Walker should go into partnership with John Fleming. But as affecting my client, Mr Potter, the next step in this history is of much more significance and importance, because apparently when Glen Walker was not quite willing to undertake that responsibility, the next proposal was that Mr John Potter, the son of Mr Potter, should go into partnership with this Mr Fleming. That appears to have been proposed about the year 1874. You will recollect that there was a letter read about an interview in the Western Club with regard to that matter, and I put some questions to Mr John Fleming about it, and got full explanations of the whole affair. It was simply this,—Mr Potter seems to have shared the belief, which Alexander Stronach evidently had, that if Mr John Fleming could only be relieved of his present difficulties, and kept straight, he had a splendid business, which it would be an enormous pity for himself and everybody else that he should lose. It was proposed that, with the view of getting him out of his difficulties, he should take in one or more moneyed partners,—to use Mr John Fleming's expression,—and the proposal was—and Mr Potter was in negotiation about the proposal—that his son John Potter should be that moneyed partner. Now, John Potter had no money of his own. He was to get the money from his father. And so, gentlemen, I appeal to those two acts,—to the act of Alexander Stronach in 1873, proposing that his brother-in-law should go into partnership with John Fleming; and the act of Mr Potter in 1874, proposing that his son should go into the like partnership, as entirely fatal to the idea that either Alexander Stronach or Mr Potter then regarded these accounts as desperate or bad. If you are to believe that the business of Smith, Fleming, and Co. was in their knowledge the gulf of indebtedness which the Lord Advocate has represented it to have been, that proposal amounted to this, that Mr Potter wanted to throw his own money, ay, and his own son, into that gulf. I put it to you, gentlemen, whether that is credible. But that is not the solitary instance of the Crown's theory requiring the supposition that people must have acted in the most irrational and unnatural way. I shall show you immediately that if that theory is well founded, Mr Potter must have wished to ruin himself and everybody connected with him. I make the same remark as to the proposal to go into partnership with John Fleming, that unless Mr Potter had been a perfect fool he would never have proposed such a thing; and the Lord Advocate did not suggest, and I do not suggest, that he was or is a fool. Well, I appeal to that real and living evidence of the state of opinion of Mr Potter as to that matter in 1874. The next step in the history is, that in April 1875 an arrangement was made, which I need not trouble you by going into, because the Lord Advocate read it to you—for clearing Smith, Fleming, & Co. of their difficulties. By that time the debt to the Bank was considerable, and this scheme of relief was proposed. An advance of £100,000 was to be made, a relief of interest was to be given, and there was to be a diminution in the rate of commission charged by the Bank. Fleming was to get that £100,000, which he was to invest in New Zealand shares or land; he was to pay 3½ per cent., and the difference between that and what he got from his shares was to go to recoup the debt. Now, gentlemen, those who knew about that transaction believed that it was a feasible one—that all would be well. And what motive there could be to make an arrangement of that kind, if the account was regarded as hopeless, you will have the advantage of me if you can understand or divine. But Collie's failure came on after that, and there were difficulties about the arrangement being carried out, and the last step in the history of this account was the purchase of the New Zealand land in August 1876, to recoup the debt. Now, gentlemen, the Lord Advocate has commented upon that very severely. Whatever may be said of it as a banking transaction—and the observation that it is not banking is very fair; but gentlemen, even if it was what might be called bad banking, what connection had that with the knowledge of the account being hopeless? And if it had been hopeless, why should the transaction have been gone into at all? There is no doubt it was an anxious account, though by no means a hopeless one, and therefore the directors endeavoured to do what many men endeavour to do—to meet an exceptional emergency with an exceptional remedy. It may be that it was stepping a little out of banking: it may be that you may call it an expedient, but it was an expedient required by the emergency, and which everybody connected with it thought would succeed. And if it had been carried out, and if the Bank had not come down, there is no reason to suppose that it might not have succeeded. Now that is the short history of Smith, Fleming, & Co.'s account, and I put it to you, gentlemen, if you want to arrive at the state of mind of Mr Potter and the other directors, whether it is not a safer way to ascertain that state of mind by the kind of examination that I have now gone into, of what these men were doing from time to time from 1870 onwards, than by pointing to the big sums standing against these firms in the books of the Bank. Whether a debt is large or small depends to a great extent on who is your debtor, and on his power of earning money. If he is a man capable of earning £90,000 a year, then a sum which would otherwise startle one would not be alarming.

I shall now, gentlemen, give you a like summary of Mr Nicol Fleming's account, because there the inference is altogether unwarranted, that although it was an anxious one, it was either hopeless or desperate. I think I need not trouble you by beginning with Mr Nicol Fleming's account earlier than 1874. We see that Mr Nicol Fleming was a gentleman whose fortunes had been very varying. In 1862 and 1863 his profits had been hundreds of thousands a year, in Mr John Fleming's own words. There had been great losses after that, but nevertheless he was, even down to 1874 or 1875, in possession of a commission business worth not less than from £20,000 to £25,000 a year, and if he too could have been kept out of speculation, all would have been well. In 1874 Alexander Stronach appears to have been anxious about his account. Probably this was because he was rather keeping things from his directors; but his state of mind about this matter you learn from Mr Hunter, who was his confidential friend. What Mr Hunter says is at pages 303 and 304 [see p. 247]. I will not trouble you by reading it, but I will tell you the substance of it. Mr Hunter is a gentleman who seems to possess the confidence of very many, persons, and to have time to consider difficult questions, and his advice was and is prized. He was the confidential friend of Alexander Stronach, and Alexander Stronach asked him, as his confidential friend, to look into James Nicol Fleming's affairs. The report which Hunter gave was that they were not satisfactory. That seemed to be rather a surprise to Alexander Stronach, because Mr Hunter said Mr Stronach did not appear to think so badly of them as his report showed. That he says quite distinctly at page 304 [see top of p. 248]. However, the result was that Mr Hunter advised that James Nicol Fleming's firm should be put into liquidation; and although that was not done immediately in 1874, it was done when Mr Robert Stronach came into the practical management of the Bank in 1875. That liquidation, as you may recollect, inferred an arrangement which, if carried out, would have recouped the deficit due to the Bank at the rate of £25,000 a year, which would have very soon brought it down to a moderate figure. Nicol Fleming, however, could not be kept out of speculation. He did not keep his promises; he went to India, and lost money on shipping, and more debts arose. In consequence, there was a purchase of land gone into to recoup that deficit, in the same way as to recoup the other deficit, and I repeat with respect to that what I have said with respect to the other. Now that is an epitome of the evidence which we have as to J. Nicol Fleming's account, and I think you will see that there was nothing in regard to that account more than in regard to the other to lead to the supposition that these directors, even if they had known all that Mr Stronach knew about that account, regarded it as either bad or irrecoverable, or more than anxious, and possibly attended with danger.

The case of Morton is very similar. It appears from page 285 [see p. 236] that Alexander Stronach had proposed to Glen Walker, his brother-in-law, to join Morton; because Alexander Stronach's great difficulty seems to have been to keep this man out of speculation; and Mr Hunter, at page 305 [see p. 248], also speaks to the interviews which he was having with Stronach, as his confidential friend, and says that Stronach told him that Morton's account was working off all right,—that he believed Morton would come out all right; and Mr Hunter has no reason to doubt that the belief thus expressed by Stronach was true. Alexander Stronach knew more at this time about Morton's account than the directors did. Robert Stronach made Morton promise that he would reduce his account by £400,000 before he would become manager; and although the account grew, yet between 1876 and 1877 it was reduced by £80,000 from what it had been in the previous year.

Now there is just one other matter which the Lord Advocate relies upon on this point, and that is the minute of December 1875, when Robert Stronach's letter was addressed to the directors before he would take office. Robert Stronach asked that the board should "minute its approval of the "policy which has been pursued of supporting several accounts of an unsatis- "factory character, since my brother discontinued personally to manage the "Bank, and further, to appoint a committee to investigate and place on "record what may be found to have been the exact position of these accounts, "and the advances generally when my brother ceased to be manager, and "also to act and guide me in any important detail therewith connected, as I "am in nowise responsible up to this date for the state of certain advances "which I need not here particularise. You will, I hope, admit the reason- "ableness of the precaution which this request involves, and I feel you will "the more readily do this when you consider that whilst we are all hopeful "that these advances may eventuate without loss, yet the working out of "them must of necessity be a work of some time, and when you also "consider that there may be changes in the board during this time, and I "should have to explain to new directors what you know regarding my "connection with the inception of those advances." That is approved of, and a committee appointed to comply with the manager's request. And then they minute this:—"The directors wish also to record, on their own behalf, "the fact that the matters alluded to in the letter in question were not at any "time brought before them by the late manager." Now, the Lord Advocate founded very much upon that letter, and he seemed to think that it in some way or another fixed the directors with a knowledge and an opinion which would necessarily lead to their being found guilty under this indictment. But that letter and that minute are not in the least inconsistent with what I have submitted to you as to the real state of knowledge and opinion of these directors. It is true that down to 1874 or 1875 Alexander Stronach had been keeping something from them, and I don't think anybody doubts that the statement which the directors minuted was correct, when they said that the matters alluded to in the letter were not at any time brought before them by the late manager. Although they knew something about them, they did not know the whole. But when they came to know more about them in 1875, where is there any evidence that they thought they were either bad or hopeless? Mr Robert Stronach records the very opposite, because he said they all hoped they would eventuate without loss; and I say that was the hope these men had,—that these accounts would eventuate without loss. And I put it to you, whether what these directors did, even in buying land in New Zealand, when they suddenly found themselves confronted with the difficulty which they had been got into without their knowledge,—even if that was irregular or bad banking, was it not more the part of courageous men doing the best they could for the other shareholders, as they would have done in their own affairs, to try and weather the vessel out of the storm, rather than to surrender or lie down at their posts? I say you cannot infer guilty knowledge from what those men did. They were bold, I admit, but it was a boldness for no bad purpose; their endeavour was to get out of the difficulty which they had been got into, without their knowledge, by Alexander Stronach. And I should be very much surprised, gentlemen, if you judge harshly men who were at that time doing their best, and not sparing any pains to do it, even if they have erred in judgment, even if they have erred in rashness—I say I should be very much surprised if from that you were to draw the conclusion that they were guilty of dishonesty and fraud.

The Lord Advocate made one special observation in regard to Mr Potter, and I shall meet it without the smallest difficulty. He said Mr Potter was always appearing on the scene and disappearing again. He spoke as if Mr Potter had been some evil genius who appeared, wrought some mischief, and then disappeared into the darkness. But, gentlemen, I ask you to consider for what purpose, and to what effect, did Mr Potter appear on any one of the occasions to which the Lord Advocate either could or did point? Did Mr Potter at any time, in any of these minutes, appear except for the purpose of doing his best for the Bank? Mr Potter never from beginning to end appeared to subserve any end of his own or of his friends, so far as we can see. I was certainly surprised to hear the Lord Advocate so speak of those appearances of Mr Potter, when he was drawing, to some extent, out of his own business, —aged man as he was,—and going about the Bank, not as a bookkeeper or clerk, not entering into figures, but asking in a broad and general way how things were getting on. If that man, with the intimate knowledge of the New Zealand and Australian colonies which he had from his forty or fifty years' trade with them, was giving the benefit of his opinions and advice in regard to the best way of getting the Bank out of its difficulties, and the wisdom of going into what, if you like, you may call speculations in land in

Australia,—I say that is not matter for which you could blame him, still less hold him criminally liable.

Now, gentlemen, I don't know that I need say anything more. I think I have dealt with all the points referred to by the Lord Advocate, as well as with those he did not go into, as to the actual facts about the preparation of these sheets; and I have only one or two words more to say on the part of Mr Potter before sitting down. If you should think, gentlemen, that there was some doubt about the case,—if you should think that I had not succeeded, not only in showing the case to be unproved against him, but in demonstrating that the case utterly fails against him, I would then ask you to consider this,—what motive or inducement had Mr Potter to perpetrate the frauds with which he is charged? In any question of crime, gentlemen, it is of the utmost importance to see whether a man has a motive to do the thing that he is said to have done. In crimes of violence, or sudden passion, or fatal impulse, it is always important to see whether there is a motive. Sometimes it is difficult to trace the motive in cases of that kind; but where you have a crime like that charged here, which is in the nature of a commercial fraud, you necessarily will have a motive, you necessarily will have foresight, you necessarily will have reasoning, and scheming to gain some end. I never heard of a man who was guilty of deliberate and persistent commercial fraud without having or thinking he had something to gain by it. The very object of such frauds is gain. Now, I ask you what suggestion is there of any such motive on the part of Mr Potter? I showed you at the outset, that from the beginning to the end of this indictment the Crown made no charge against Mr Potter of having overdrawn his account, or taken a penny of benefit from his position as a Bank director. Well, what was Mr Potter's financial position,—what was his position otherwise at this time? He was a man, as you had proved to you, at the head of two large businesses,—that of Potter, Wilson, & Co., from which he was deriving an income of £5000 a year. His partner told us so. He was also the head of the great shipping firm of Lewis Potter & Son, from which he was deriving an income of about £3000 a year. So that he was making £8000 a year from his two businesses. He had also valuable lands worth £120,000, from which he was getting a profit, including the minerals, of about £10,000 a year. So that whatever else may be said about Mr Potter, he was not a needy speculator, or a man who wanted money either of the City of Glasgow Bank or any other bank. He had an income of £17,000 or £18,000 a year. The City of Glasgow Bank were not even his bankers. His bankers, for many years—certainly from 1853,—had been the British Linen, apparently because one of his partners had been a friend of Mr Brodie, the manager; and he had another account with the National Bank, because he was associated with an Australian Company, which was in some way friendly to that bank; and it was from those two banks that any accommodation he needed, if he needed any, which I don't know that he ever did, was got; and it was only when the City of Glasgow Bank begged for a share of his business, that they got it. But I maintain to you, without fear of contradiction, that not only has there been a failure to prove, but there has been no attempt to prove that Mr Potter had the slightest end or object to gain either by his connection with the Bank, or anything he did in regard to it. You had it also proved to you that Mr Bain, the manager of the branch in Edinburgh, was his brother-in-law—a gentleman who is very likely known to some of you, and whom we heard Mr John Gillespie and others speak of in the highest terms. His sister was Mrs Davidson. Both were shareholders of the Bank, and Mr Potter was a shareholder himself. What he is accused of in this indictment is fabricating and publishing false balance-sheets to defraud the shareholders, including his brother-in-law, his sister, and himself. If, gentlemen, by shadowy and slender inferences drawn from a perusal of these minutes, which the Lord Advocate went through yesterday, instead of looking the solid facts in the face, examining how the balance-sheets were made up, inquiring into the knowledge which the directors had, seeing what they thought and whether they were too sanguine or not about these accounts,—in the absence of all motive, you reach the conclusion that Mr Potter is guilty of all or any of the crimes charged against him, I think it will be matter for very great surprise.

I am not, gentlemen, going to make any appeal to your feelings on the part of Mr Potter. From beginning to end I have gone through this matter as a matter of business, speaking to you as business men, because I can confidently appeal to the facts in these documents and sheets, and I don't require to make any appeal to your feelings. But, gentlemen, I think it would be impossible for you or for any one else to witness without emotion the spectacle of a man seventy-two years of age, after his laborious, his successful, and his honoured life, brought to sit there upon a charge of this kind; and I am sure that you will not, without much clearer reason than anything we have heard, find him guilty of that crime. I don't appeal to your feelings, but I do appeal to your reason and your sense of justice in this matter. I have gone through the facts, facing them from beginning to end, and I say that treating this, not as a matter of feeling, but as a matter of judgment, and of what is the fair inference and the fair conclusion to be drawn from the evidence, that conclusion is for innocence, and not for guilt; and, therefore, I ask you for a verdict of acquittal.

MR ASHER'S ADDRESS FOR MR SALMOND.

May it please your Lordships, Gentlemen of the Jury,—It is now my duty to address you on behalf of Mr Robert Salmond, whose name stands third in the indictment, and whose defence has been entrusted to my care. This protracted and important trial is now rapidly drawing to a close. The time is not far off when it will become your duty, on consideration of the evidence which you have heard, to return a verdict which will either acquit the unfortunate gentlemen who are now seated at the bar, or will pronounce their doom. The unwearying patience and steadfast attention which you have invariably displayed through the eight long days you have now sat there is, I am sure, an earnest of the judgment, the temper, the firmness, and the courage with which you will proceed to discharge your last important duty as jurors in this case. And, gentlemen, I cannot refrain from saying that qualities such as these were never more needed by any jury who have sat here to try a case, for the circumstances under which this case is presented to you are in many respects unique. They press heavily on the accused, and they cannot fail to embarrass you. We have now for several years in this country been passing through a commercial crisis of unexampled duration and severity. Trade has been paralysed, labour unemployed, credit impaired, large fortunes have crumbled to nothing, and universal distress has prevailed throughout the land. It is in the midst of that period of adversity, and as a part of it, that the City of Glasgow Bank stopped payment, and when men's minds were naturally strained, it was only what was to be expected that that additional monetary catastrophe should produce widespread feeling throughout the community. Facts were misrepresented, the wildest theories prevailed, no rumours were too extravagant for acceptance by the general credulity. Gentlemen, you will not be surprised that in circumstances like these, drawn as you have been by the accident of the ballot-box, from the midst of that external excitement to sit in judgment upon these men, we should one and all be unable to approach the facts of this case without a word of warning in regard to the prejudice out of doors against the accused, which is a fact, and which, therefore, it is our duty to recognise. But, gentlemen, I have a further reason for referring to the circumstances I have mentioned, and it is this. We have suffered from them already. These gentlemen sitting there have already gone through the long period of three months' imprisonment, in breach of the law, against their legal rights, because of an unthinking popular clamour, and have suffered in that manner to an extent which no verdict of yours ever can repair. It is not surprising, therefore, that we should recognise as a fact, and by our observations endeavour to displace, that prejudice which has attacked and overwhelmed the accused, even in high quarters, inflicting an injury which, as I have said, nothing ever can repair. It is the right of every citizen of this country to be presumed to be innocent until he is proved to be guilty; and it is his further right,—his statutory right,—to be liberated on bail unless he is charged with an offence of such gravity that the law will not allow him that privilege. Gentlemen, the only charge which you are now asked to consider is not of that aggravated character. Any man charged merely with that which now remains of this indictment, has by statute law the right to demand liberation on bail; yet it is a fact that the accused have throughout been denied that right; and why? because there were preferred and maintained against them, charges so aggravated as not to be bailable by law, but which, after this trial began, were abandoned without an attempt to prove them. I can attribute that result to nothing but this, that the public clamour was too strong even for those who were guiding the conduct of this case for the Crown. The public prosecutor bowed before the storm, when it would have been more manly to have stood up and protected the accused against it. Gentlemen, that is my apology for saying to you, be on your guard. I cannot tell you to delete from your minds all that you have heard before you took your seats in that box. It were in vain to do so. It were to ask you to effect the impossible. The human will has no power to erase that which is impressed on the tablets of the memory. The mere effort to do so would but more firmly fix that which it seeks to expunge. But I can appeal to you as men full of honour, as I am sure you are; as men full of fairness, as I am convinced and believe you to be; I can appeal to you to struggle manfully against all antecedent prejudice, all preconceived impression which may have been in your minds against the accused before you entered these walls, and to try these men upon the evidence you have heard, as, if your places were reversed, you would expect them to deal with you.

Gentlemen, as this charge was originally presented, it had a formidable look. I have rarely seen a document, either in its bulk or in its contents, more calculated to strike terror into an accused, than the indictment before you. It is a long indictment, extending over as many as thirty-six pages, detailing crime upon crime laid at the door of these men; but by a single sentence from the public prosecutor, it has been brought down to eleven pages, and the eleven pages containing the charges which are in their nature of the least aggravated hue. Why has that been done? I will tell you why. Because these charges were in their inception unfounded, and there never was any evidence against the accused upon them. Do you think that, having kept these men in prison for three months upon the allegation that they were guilty, not of one theft merely, but of theft upon theft,—ten separate charges of theft of such an aggravated type that the law even denied them the ordinary privilege of bail; do you think these charges would have been abandoned without adducing one single witness in support of them, had it not been that the allegation was one which, from beginning to end, was without foundation, —one which, I venture to say, never should have been made. But I have another complaint to make. I say that these charges should have been expunged at the earliest moment they were discovered to be an error. We appeared at this bar prepared to stand our trial, prepared to face that long indictment from beginning to end, and prepared, I hope, to satisfy you that it was unfounded from beginning to end,—anxious to have an opportunity of dispelling the clouds of criticism and prejudice which had been darkening the air around us. We have had no opportunity of doing so with respect to the most serious charges in the indictment, and we are therefore entitled to say that of them we are not guilty. I am further entitled to say that, having been withdrawn before a single witness was produced in support of them, they should have been withdrawn at the outset of the case, and not have been left dangling under your eyes for the long period of seven days. Doubtless each day, as you looked from the indictment to the accused, you thought, "There " stand men charged with having committed not one theft, but ten successive " thefts," and who can tell the extent to which your anticipations as to the evidence expected upon those grievous charges may have influenced your minds when considering that which was being proved in regard to the minor charges? I say, therefore, that at the earliest moment in this case, when it was discovered by those conducting the prosecution that they had no case in fact to support these charges, they should have stood up like men, and said, "We have made a mistake, and we withdraw them," and should not have allowed them to remain as part of the charge under your eyes from day to day. I believe you will overcome any impression these things may have produced; but that will be due to you, and not to those who have conducted the prosecution. It would have been much more in accordance with precedent and with usage if, at the earliest possible moment, when it was discovered there was no evidence in the Crown proof to support these charges, they had been instantaneously withdrawn. In that feature this case is without precedent, and, gentlemen, in the interests of liberty and of justice and of law, I hope it will remain a solitary example, and that it never will become the usage of the criminal law of this land to violate statute and civil right in order to bring any criminal, however great, to justice.

Gentlemen, as I have said, this charge has become contracted to a marvellous degree, but enough still remains; and I am very far from saying that anything which I have said as to the injury to which the accused have been subjected should withdraw you from the important duty you have to discharge in considering what remains on its own merits. I would desire, in the first place, to ask your attention to what the charge is, because until you thoroughly comprehend it, it is impossible for you to say whether the prisoners at the bar are guilty or not. Gentlemen, it has been repeated throughout this trial again and again, and is undoubtedly a great public misfortune, that so far as has been hitherto ascertained, a large deficit will accrue on the accounts of the City of Glasgow Bank. Gentlemen, I admit it is inseparable from this inquiry that that fact should appear from time to time; but do not for a moment suppose that that is the charge which the directors are here to answer, because what I am here to deal with on behalf of Mr Salmond, my client, has nothing whatever to do with that. You will, of course, have laid out of view the last item in the schedule, upon page 4 of the indictment [see p. 28],—that part which relates to bad and irrecoverable debts, it having been withdrawn by the Crown. You will also exclude from your minds all reference to the loss of the capital of the City of Glasgow Bank. There is not one single syllable in the indictment, as it is now before you, which says that the capital of the Bank is lost,—that it is not a trading concern at the present moment; far less does it put, as a charge for which the directors are here being tried, the loss of the capital of the Bank at all. They are here to answer that which is perfectly plain and intelligible, and, if true, is a very vile offence, and it is this,—the fabrication and falsification of a balance-sheet of the books of the Bank for the purpose of deception. That charge we are prepared to answer; but do not for a moment be misled by imagining—be you as satisfied as men can be that the capital of the Bank has been lost by recklessness and bad management,—that that has one particle of connection with the criminal offence which is here charged, which is the deliberate statement of a falsehood in the knowledge that it was false, for the purpose of defrauding, and with the effect of producing fraud. Then, it is also said that the directors wickedly and feloniously, and with intent to defraud, concocted and fabricated these abstract balances; and you will observe from your indictment that the particulars in which this falsification is said to have consisted, are enumerated with great precision. You will, as I have already requested, have deleted the eighth article of that schedule, and, having done so, I will direct your attention to the nature of the charge that remains, with reference to the seven items still standing; and, with regard to these, I should request you to divide them into two classes, because I think it is very plain that there is a principle for their distinction, which must go far to bring home to your minds the precise nature of the charge I am here to answer. Gentlemen, the first five of these items stand markedly distinguished from six and seven. There is this vital distinction between them,—there is an allegation of falsehood with regard to them all; but with regard to one to five inclusive, it is an allegation of falsehood as to a fact, while with regard to six and seven it is an allegation of falsehood in the sense of an error of opinion, and I am sure you will not fail to appreciate the marked difference between these two things. If I say of a man that, knowing a specific fact, for example, that he was at a given place on a given date, and that he denied that fact in the perfect knowledge of the untruth of the denial and for the purpose of fraud, I make a charge against him which is intelligible and distinct. On the other hand, if I say of a man, in regard to a matter on which various views may be entertained in perfect honesty and sincerity, that in putting forward and upholding one of these various views, he has stated that which is false, it may be so—his opinion may be wrong, and therefore it may false,—but you cannot fail to see that falsehood in regard to that opinion is a very different thing from a falsehood with regard to a fact, the knowledge of the contrary of which was in the man's own mind. There is a further marked distinction between these two classes of charges. In charges from one to five the falsehood consists of this—It is falsehood through making an abstract issued to the public directly in conflict with the authentic record of the facts contained in the books of the Bank. I understand perfectly that that is a charge of fraud. If it is said to a director, "Look at your own books; turn them up, there you "find recorded certain figures; and look from these to this abstract presented "to the public; compare the two, and there is a direct conflict between "them;" then I accept that as a definition of a falsehood and a lie; but if I am told, on the other hand, to look at a particular account, the amount of which is large—the debtor is a man of a speculative turn, with an enormous business, his profits ranging from several hundred thousand pounds one year down to ninety thousand the next,—and if it is said that in expressing the opinion that the large balance due on that account will be paid, I am telling a falsehood and a lie; my answer is that it is an abuse of terms to say that. I may be too sanguine, and I may be relying upon that on which I should not rely as justifying that opinion; but to place the statement of that opinion in the same list with a direct representation that two millions in the books of the Bank is the same as one million in the abstract—to say there is no difference between these misrepresentations,—is to forget the meaning of words, to confound fact with opinion, between which two categories it is absolutely essential that you should have a sharp and clear distinction in your minds if you are to do justice in this case.

Gentlemen, with regard to the first five items, as I have said, they are charges of falsification of the books of the Bank in the printed abstract, for the purpose of deceiving the shareholders and the public. I shall not waste time, so far as my client is concerned, by addressing myself to the question whether that is proved or not. If you are of opinion that, in these several particulars, the abstract given to the public is false as compared with the books, then I adopt every word which has been said for the prosecution as to the gross impropriety of that act; and nothing would induce me to stand up here and in your presence for one moment to defend it. That is not my defence,—not for one moment. If it is proved that this falsification took place, my defence is that my client is as innocent of that, ay, and as ignorant of that, as any of you were when you went into that box. I have a separate case in regard to the last two items of the schedule, and I shall come to that afterwards; but with regard to that which constitutes the gravamen of this charge, I must ask you, in fairness to my client, whose case you must individualise and single out from the others, to follow me while I deal with the evidence and see whether the Crown has a shadow of proof against him in respect of knowledge of these falsifications. Gentlemen, the balance-sheet which has been selected as a type of the rest—and in a case of such magnitude there is a great convenience in taking types—is that of 1876. There is a manifest advantage in choosing that, because, whatever may be the credibility of witnesses, the evidence is all one way in regard to this, that that is the first occasion upon which there was any ground for the suggestion that the printed abstract did not tally with the books of the Bank. Now, you heard Mr Morison give his evidence in regard to that matter. It is no part of my case to displace one single word of what has been said by my learned friend Mr Balfour with regard to Mr Morison's evidence as bearing upon Mr Potter's case, but assuming every word Mr Morison uttered to be true—and I shall do so for the purpose of my case—the issue I put to you is whether, on that assumption, the Crown has connected Mr Salmond with the falsification of the published abstract balance-sheet. If you turn to page 3 of the indictment [see p. 27], you will observe that the abstract in question is an abstract balance-sheet as at 7th June 1876. Now, that means that the books of the Bank were balanced as at that date, and that abstract necessarily is prepared at a date subsequent to the 7th of June, which is the date of the balance incorporated in it. It is quite impossible that any man could have done anything in the way of falsification prior to that date, for the very simple reason that the document embraces accounts brought down to that date, and is necessarily therefore prepared subsequent to that date. Now, an abstract or statement is prepared apparently by the accountant, and a good deal of detail is gone through, resulting in the production of this abstract from the books of the Bank for the purpose of putting it before the public. Now, what is there in this case to connect Mr Salmond with a knowledge of the falsification of the abstract to which Mr Morison spoke? I do not admit the falsification; I do not dispute it; I have no interest to do either; but for the purposes of this question, I assume that every word that was said by Mr Morison as to the concoction of that abstract and the alteration of the figures in it is true; and assuming that, I ask, can you by any legitimate process draw the inference that Mr Salmond, either at the time, or before, or subsequently, had anything whatever to do with that? Why, gentlemen, it was begun at a date subsequent to the 7th of June; it was completed; it was put before the public; it was submitted to the general meeting of shareholders on 5th July 1876. The whole thing was begun and finished, was past and gone, during a period when Mr Salmond was not in Glasgow at all; and how my learned friend the Lord Advocate, in the face of the evidence led as to where Mr Salmond was at the time, could find it consistent with his duty to press the charge against Mr Salmond, I confess, passes my comprehension. I could understand evidence as to the whereabouts of a man at the time a particular thing was done being impugned; I could understand comments made upon its credibility, but where it is not disputed by the Crown that he was not near the *locus* when the crime is said to have been committed, I put to you, as men of fairness, whether this charge should not have vanished with that large residuum of the case which would not stand the light of day, and which disappeared by withdrawal before a witness was brought into Court to support it.

Gentlemen, you will remember the evidence with regard to Mr Salmond on this matter, and I shall shortly recall it to your recollection. Mr Salmond is a director of the Netherlands Steam Navigation Co. (Limited), whose place of business is in London; and it appears from the evidence of the secretary of that company that Mr Salmond was in London, and attended meetings of that company upon the 6th, 9th, and 12th of June. There can be no mistake about these dates. The secretary did not speak from recollection. He had his minute-book there, and turned it up and verified what he had said. There is Mr Salmond's signature; there he signs his name as a director. It further appears that on the 15th of June he was at Homburg. He goes on the 12th of June from London to Homburg, where he is joined by Mr Connal, a retired merchant. Mr Connal, who was examined here, remained with him in the Hotel de Russie there until 6th July 1876, when he returned to Glasgow. Gentlemen, that evidence, I should say, would be enough, not having been impugned to any extent by the Crown; but it is confirmed in the most direct manner by the minutes of the City of Glasgow Bank, which contain a record of the directors present at the various meetings; and the secretary, Mr Leresche, speaking from his agenda book, in which the names of the directors present were inserted by the chairman, depones, that at none of the meetings between the dates I have mentioned was Mr Salmond present; and those were the meetings at which all the business connected with the annual balance-sheet was conducted. Gentlemen, I am anxious you should not forget this. Would you be so good as note upon page 3 of the indictment, what I submit is proved upon uncontroverted evidence, that from 6th June to 6th July Mr Salmond was not within the city of Glasgow? And would you take along with you the fact, proved by Mr Leresche, that the annual general meeting of the City of Glasgow Bank that year, at which the published abstract was submitted, was held on the 5th of July? What warrant, then, is there for saying, on the evidence before you, that the falsification of that abstract, if it was falsified, was a thing with which he had anything to do? Is it to be said that you are to spin some wild theories in your minds as to secret negotiations passing between Mr Salmond and the Bank in regard to that? That is too untenable a supposition to require to be displaced. It is very plain indeed that if that falsification was done at all, it was done in secret and in private,—not disclosed to many who were much nearer home than Mr Salmond, and not likely to have been communicated to a man away from the scene of the operation altogether.

Gentlemen, I trust I have now satisfied you that, with regard to the fabrication of the balance-sheet of June 1876, the direct participation of Mr Salmond in that is a physical impossibility. That is, of course, the important balance-sheet in this question, because, as I said, that was the first occasion on which it is suggested that any falsification took place; and it is not suggested that in any of the subsequent years the person whose hand put the false figures there was in communication with any director whatever in regard to what he was about. It is therefore a matter of comparatively little moment to bring under your notice Mr Salmond's position with reference to the subsequent years, because if that which occurred in 1876, without his knowledge or participation, was merely formally repeated in 1877 and 1878, all the presumptions and probabilities are against any knowledge on the part of one who must have been ignorant in 1876. But as this matter has been mentioned, and the facts are not the same, it is right to point out in a single word what Mr Salmond's position is with regard to absence or presence in these subsequent years. During 1877, the evidence which was led yesterday establishes that he was at meetings of the same company in London on the 5th, 7th, 8th, 11th, and 13th of June, and again on the 9th and 11th of July, and it is quite true that there is an interval between these two sets of meetings, during which Mr Salmond was in Glasgow, and present at meetings on the business of the Bank. But when we come to 1878, he is again obliged, through ill-health, to be absent at that season of the year, and the evidence establishes that from 24th May to 5th July 1878 he was out of Scotland. He was in London engaged in business, and attending meetings of the company I have mentioned in the end of May and on 7th and 13th June, and he was thereafter at Buxton from 19th June to 5th July, without having at any time returned to Scotland from the time he left Glasgow on 24th May. So that, with regard to those three years, you have the fact established, that in two of them he was absent during the whole time the business was being done connected with the annual balance; and as to the intermediate year, he was absent during the most important period, viz., up to 13th June, which was the exact time Mr Morison said he was engaged preparing the balance-sheets, and when any tampering with the figures would take place. Therefore, I put it to you, that not only is it not proved against Mr Salmond that he had anything to do with falsification of the balance-sheets, but it is absolutely disproved by evidence of the clearest kind.

That leads me, in the next place, to consider whether Mr Salmond was in any way connected indirectly with these false balance-sheets. Is he, before he left or after he returned, in any way brought face to face with the knowledge that there was vitiation in his absence in regard to those balance-sheets? His name appears along with those of the other directors signing the annual balances for each of these three years; and what does that imply? It implies neither more nor less than this, with regard to the years he was absent, that finding his brother directors' names there when he returned, he, without any inquiry whatever, and as a matter of form, appended his signature. In regard to the year he was present, what does it imply? It implies simply this, that he had compared with the accountant the balances in the balance-ledger with those stated in the three subsidiary balance books; and nobody has suggested that there is any discrepancy between them. It is said, that having taken in his hand this balance-sheet which was issued to the public, a mere examination of its figures should have brought to his mind the knowledge that there was falsification of the abstract. That has been suggested no doubt in general terms, but I should have liked to have heard it explained,—which is the item in that abstract which a director, with merely a general knowledge of the business of the Bank, could not have looked at it without having brought to his mind the knowledge that it was more or less than what the books of the Bank showed? If he had placed it side by side with the balance-sheet which he himself had docqueted, he certainly never could have found it out, because it was explained by the accountant for the Crown that there is an utter dissimilarity—an utter and intentional dissimilarity—between the balance-sheet docqueted by the directors and the abstract put before the public; and for this simple reason, that the two documents were constructed on totally different principles, and for totally distinct purposes. The balance in the balance ledger is a mere epitome of the whole balances, debtor and creditor, in the books of the Bank. The whole accounts in the head office are there gathered together under their respective heads, debtor and creditor, according as the balance may be, and each agency also is treated as a separate customer. But when the abstract to be laid before the public is prepared, that balance-sheet is analysed, the whole of the accounts at the head office are taken, the whole of the branches are taken, and the accounts in the head office and branches which belong to the same class are put together, and massed into one for the purpose of showing under one sum the total amount at the debit or credit of each class of accounts throughout the whole of the business of the Bank, head office and branches included. Therefore, it is a mathematical impossibility that any man, by looking at the balance book he docqueted, could discover a discrepancy, either in details or sums total, between it and the abstract put before the public, or could have it for one moment suggested to his mind that there was anything wrong about the abstract shown to the public. I have no doubt Mr Salmond read the abstract issued to the public, as every other director of the Bank did, but unless he had been in the position of having clear in his mind the whole bookkeeping details of the Bank throughout the whole range of its business, which the greatest gymnast in figures in Great Britain could not do, it would have been impossible to have verified the accuracy or inaccuracy of that abstract, merely by the perusal of that which appeared on it. Therefore, with regard to the charge of falsification of that abstract, I wash my hands of it altogether, both on the ground of absence at the time it was prepared and issued, and because not a single duty which devolved on Mr Salmond in connection with his position as director was calculated for one moment to suggest to his mind that any error or inaccuracy had taken place in regard to these documents.

But, gentlemen, it is said, notwithstanding what I have stated to you, that there is still a case against my client, which is this,—he is one of the directors, and that is enough for the Crown. Being a director, regardless of the specialities of his case which clear him conclusively from all crime,—being in this unfortunate brotherhood, you are asked to convict him. On what grounds? Because, forsooth, he had knowledge that there were large accounts in the books of the Bank. Now, gentlemen, I must ask your attention again in regard to the particular portion of this indictment upon which a conviction on that ground is asked. It certainly is not in respect of the alleged falsification in the first five heads of the various schedules in the indictment. That, as I pointed out, belongs to a clear, distinct, and intelligible category of the libel. But the conviction is asked on a strained construction of the sixth and seventh articles of this schedule. Gentlemen, that construction I shall submit, under the direction of his Lordship, is unwarrantable. But don't misunderstand me, gentlemen; it is my duty to bring the point of form before you, but I am by no means seeking to escape from the facts; and I shall certainly, lest the point of form should be ruled against me, deal with the facts before I am done. But amidst the mass of confusion that constitutes this indictment, it is important to see what is the specific charge brought against the accused in articles six and seven. It is said that it was illegitimate to enter the amount of profit in the abstract of the Bank's affairs, because the accounts which yielded the interest going to make it up were bad and irrecoverable debts? If that is the suggestion, then my answer to it is, that the Lord Advocate, in making that suggestion, would be justifying the charge made in the course of the trial, that there was an attempt being made to bring in by a side wind what was excluded upon a direct challenge. If it is necessary to the Lord Advocate's case to make out that certain accounts, the interest on which was included in profit and loss, were bad debts, then the plea upon which we got rid of article eight strikes equally against that also. Why was article eight struck out? Not as matter of decision by the Court, but because the Crown recognised the force of the objection, and withdrew the charge, and why? Because the unfairness of not telling us what debts were said to be bad and doubtful was so transparent, that the judgment of the Court was not asked. Are we to be misled by the shadow of a concession, and is the substance of the thing still here? Are we still to be tried for the loss of capital and interest upon bad debts, the names of which have not been given to us, and which the Crown has not been allowed to enter upon plainly and distinctly as a head of charge? I dispute altogether the right of the Crown to say to us—In fairness we can't charge you with having kept up in your books accounts which were bad, and we therefore withdraw that part of the case; but in the same breath we will charge you under another head with having credited interest on these accounts, which you should not have credited, because these accounts were bad. It was as essential for us to have notice of the particular accounts, in order to defend ourselves on the matter of interest as on the head of capital. We ask, therefore, the judgment of the Court on the sixth and seventh articles of the schedule. We contended that they must follow article eight, being open to the same objection, and I understood they were merely allowed to remain, because they were said in the indictment to be items of falsification of the balance-sheet, and it might quite well have appeared on the evidence that the balance-sheet was false, in respect that there was no profit appearing on the books, and that there was no reserve fund in the books, and these two heads, interest and reserve fund, would in that case have belonged to the same category as those which preceded them. But are they to be allowed to stand for the purpose of allowing it to be proved that certain debts are bad and doubtful, which the Crown departed from as a substantive charge, but which they seek to use against us in the matter of interest? I am entitled to assume, for the purposes of this case, that in the withdrawal of that eighth charge the Crown says to those directors, "You did not commit any crime in "regard to the capital of bad and doubtful debts." But, gentlemen, if that is the position of the Crown—if it is admitted that there are no bad and doubtful debts recorded in the books which ought to have been written off—is it suggested that these accounts standing on the books should not have interest debited to them from time to time? I ask you as men of common sense, would it be consistent with the duty of the Bank to retain in their books the names of debtors owing these large sums, and yet not charge them interest for the outstanding advances? The thing is nonsense. If the capital is standing—and the capital is standing, by concession, upon the withdrawal of article eight—then it is nonsense to suggest that it was a crime to charge interest on that capital. It is true that late in the day a suggestion was put forward, which was an attempt to thread the way of the prosecution by dexterous means through these difficult paths; and it was this. Be it that the accounts were right in the books of the Bank, be it that you were right in charging interest, you should have carried it to suspense account, and not to profit and loss. Gentlemen, has it really come to this, that this stupendous prosecution, this long category of crime, levelled at the heads of these unfortunate men, has positively collapsed into this, that a certain amount of interest, legitimately charged to subsisting accounts in the books of the Bank, was by an error of judgment carried to profit and loss account instead of to suspense account, to see if it would ultimately be good? Just keep in view that that, according to this latest suggestion upon the part of the Crown, is the sum and substance of this remaining charge; and I ask you to consider it for the purpose of contrasting it with the charges which precede it, the iniquity of which I admit. Where you have the books of the Bank showing sums of capital, or debts, or of bills discounted, and those sums not faithfully reproduced in the abstract to the shareholders, I say, if that is proved, it is a crime, and should be punished; but I do set my face against a man being brought here and charged with crime because he may have erred in his judgment, if error it was, in a mere matter of bookkeeping—whether a certain item of interest, admittedly properly debited in the proper book of the Bank, and falling to be dealt with in some way, should go to that folio of the ledger at the top of which there stood profit and loss, or to suspense account. And what had the directors to do with that? Were the directors to go and examine every detail of the books of the Bank, ponder every account to see whether the particular amount of interest debited to it at the time, as a matter of course, was to be written to suspense account or profit and loss account. At the meeting at which the matter of profit and loss and dividend was dealt with, what took place was this:—The books having been balanced, they were compared with the subsidiary books; they were all correct; upon that balance book the item stood, "Profit for the year" so and so, and the question was asked—How will you deal with it? That, and that only, was the function they had to perform at those meetings; and yet you are asked to say that each and all of them should have constituted himself an auditor of the Bank, and gone and ransacked its repositories,—and after they had done that they could not have fulfilled the task, for it involved a knowledge of the details of the business, of the solvency or insolvency of every customer of the Bank,—that they should have taken that balance on profit and loss account, and parcelled it out into various accounts with reference to the supposed solvency or insolvency of the various parties. I never heard anything so extravagant suggested as being within the range of a director's duty. What he had to consider was, there being presented to him by the authorised officials a balance-sheet showing a certain amount of profit, what was the manner in which it ought to be dealt with? And therefore, gentlemen, subject to the direction of his Lordship, I put it to you, that all that remains charged in this indictment with reference to that matter of profit and loss is an error in judgment, by the ordinary officials of the Bank, in putting to the profit and loss account a sum which, with the knowledge we now have, they might have more appropriately put to suspense account. And how stands the reserve fund? Is it suggested that there was any falsification of the books there? Not at all. There it stands in the books of the Bank, and has stood for a long time; and how is it displaced? Why, we have Mr Hutton, a witness for the Crown, produced towards the end of the evidence, for the purpose of endeavouring to explain away this fund. He said it consisted in part of interest on an American debenture, which years ago was put into the interest account as annually accruing, although not regularly paid. Now, is it to be said that there was a falsification of the books in 1876, because that which was taking place in 1863 or 1864 or 1865—that was about the date, I think—implied an error in judgment on the part of the officials of the Bank, in supposing that the interest would become payable at an earlier date than was actually the case? During the years 1876, 1877, and 1878, the period charged in the indictment, that debenture was regularly bearing interest, and there is not £1 credited in respect of it during that period which it has not yielded. The charge, therefore, as to the reserve fund truly dwindles into this, that at some previous period there was an expectation that that debenture would yield interest yearly which was not realised, and that, therefore, there was an error committed in crediting it so soon. Now, gentlemen, if you follow me through the somewhat complicated detail which is involved in the explanation of these charges, I am certain you are with me. If there are any of you, and I trust there are many, who are accustomed to deal with figures, and able to grapple with such matters, it is to you I appeal. I ask those of you who are most apt in figures to guide the rest, and if you will apply your minds to those details in the manner which I have presented them to you, you will be satisfied of the shadowiness and the unsoundness of the charge founded upon them.

But, says the public prosecutor with regard to my client, "You are an old "manager of the Bank, and you are an old director." Gentlemen, that is true, and I accept the responsibility and justify my client's actions with reference to these positions. I did not understand exactly what use was to be made of the fact that Mr Salmond was at one time manager of the Bank. It was brought out on every occasion that it could be mentioned. I always expected something was to come which would show the relevancy of that.

But the Crown's case was closed without anything of the kind, and I can only interpret the repeated reference to that fact by supposing that it was dwelt upon for the purpose of creating some prejudice against Mr Salmond. I hope you will not allow it to have any such effect upon your minds, gentlemen, especially looking to the evidence which we had yesterday from the accountant, Mr Cowan, by whom it was proved that at the month of June 1861, the last balance under the management of Mr Salmond, there did not appear in the books as a customer of the Bank either the name of Mr Nicol Fleming, or Smith, Fleming, & Co., or Wright & Co. Morton's account, it is true, appears there, but merely with the moderate balance of £4000 at its debit. And therefore, gentlemen, what the fact that Mr Salmond was manager of this Bank prior to 1861 has to do with these charges of fraud in 1876, 1877, and 1878, I confess, passes my comprehension. But, it is said, he knew of these accounts, and knowledge was enough. The Lord Advocate seemed to think some great defence was to be submitted, by which we were to represent to you an entire ignorance of everything. Gentlemen, that is not my defence. The Lord Advocate took the somewhat unusual course of reading a passage from the declaration of my client, Mr Salmond, for the purpose, I presume, of convicting him out of his own mouth. Gentlemen, I am glad that that course was adopted. It is one of the misfortunes of a prisoner, of a person who is accused, that he is taken before the authorities, unassisted, and unrepresented by any other person, and is given what is called an opportunity of clearing himself, but with this quality adhering to his statements,—that they may be evidence against him, but can do himself no good. I should not, therefore, have been entitled to refer to his declaration as being to any extent evidence in favour of Mr Salmond; but as it has been quoted as evidence against him, I am entitled to say, as I do, that the passage which the Lord Advocate read puts, as distinctly as words can put it, the measure and extent of Mr Salmond's knowledge witn regard to this matter, and is full of a frankness and a fairness inconsistent with the idea of guilt. Kept hours and hours waiting in the sheriff's chambers in Glasgow to emit the declaration, he was brought in and confronted suddenly with the law officers, and charged with this long list of crimes; but even then he had the presence of mind to remember that the truth was the best defence, He says—"I came to know that the Bank was not in an easy position some "three or four years ago, but I thought nothing of it, believing it would all "come right in a short time. The real cause of the unsatisfactory state of the "Bank was the absorption of the capital by the foresaid advances, and "although I did not know the amount of those advances, I was satisfied that "the accounts must have been in an unsatisfactory state to require such "absorption." I take it that that accurately describes the extent of Mr Salmond's knowledge. Is it a crime that his knowledge was not more distinct than that? Why, if Mr Salmond had been the Bank manager still, I could have understood it being said that it was his duty to make himself acquainted with all the details and figures in the Bank, and that if he had not done so, knowledge must be presumed against him. But why did Mr Salmond resign the position of manager? Simply for this reason, that, having become old in the service of the Bank, with years advancing, strength failing, and mental energy waning, he felt that he could no longer undertake the heavy responsibility and burden. Is it suggested that, throwing off that burden and the remuneration incident to it, there still remained this heavier burden, that he had to supervise those who filled his place, to track them in every detail of their duty, and look into every figure of the Bank's multifarious business? The suggestion is ridiculous. There is not a bank director in Britain who discharges his duty—be his honour or his integrity what it may,—if it involves doing that which you are asked to believe it was a crime on the part of these gentlemen to neglect. Gentlemen, Mr Salmond having retired from the Bank, went to reside in the country. It is proved that he has had no house in Glasgow for many years. He came from Ayrshire weekly, when at home and able to do so, to attend the weekly meetings of the directors, and remained as long in the Bank as was necessary for transacting the business which was put before him. That business simply consisted of disposing, item by item, of the various points noted in the agenda book prepared by Mr Leresche, and in confining his attention, as I ask you to believe he did, to that which was so put before him, I venture to say he was simply doing what every bank director does. And yet you are asked to believe that he had a minute acquaintance with all the details of these various accounts, the value of the various securities held by the Bank in connection with each, the progress which the debtors in these accounts were making in their various stupendous businesses towards liquidation of that which was due. Such a proposition is altogether out of the question. Mr Salmond resides in the country. His occasional attendances at the Bank, and the limited nature of the business put before him, were precisely of the character to produce the amount of knowledge which he himself describes in his declaration—a consciousness that there were accounts in the Bank which might involve anxiety, but a want of such knowledge of the details of these accounts, either as regards amount or security, as would have justified him in taking direct action in regard to any of them. It is not surprising that a man who has lived a long and laborious life, and has reached the age of seventy-four, should have lost that vigour of body and of mind which is necessary to deal with affairs of stupendous magnitude like these. Is it said it was his own fault that he was there? Who put him there? He was put there by the choice of the shareholders of the Bank. Did the shareholders expect that a man of his advanced years was capable of interfering and grappling with the details involved in clearing up an institution, the precise position and ultimate result of which are still to a great extent in darkness even after all the eight days' trial we have had? The thing is absurd. It could never have been expected of him, and therefore it never was his duty, and in failing to do it you cannot arrive at the conclusion that he did that which was wrong. I do find evidence of a desire on his part to do what was right, and to get at the facts, when he was not quite so old as he is now. There was a time in the history of this Bank when, beyond all doubt, things were happening which ought not to have happened, but for which the directors were not responsible. If there is a fact in the case clear to demonstration, it is this, that these accounts in their origin were not the work of the directors, but of the then manager, now deceased, without the knowledge of the directors. A letter has been referred to as passing between Mr Alexander Stronach and Mr Fleming. I don't detain you with reading its terms; but it is impossible to read it—no ingenuity could put any other construction upon it—without seeing this, that Alexander Stronach, out of his friendship to the Messrs Fleming, made them advances which he should not have made without the knowledge of the directors. I believe he paid the penalty of that, for his health gave way under the burden very shortly afterwards. But there is a letter which you may remember I brought under the notice of the witness Mr Fleming, which will account well and satisfactorily for a measure of knowledge short of that which is complete on the part of Mr Salmond. That letter was written by Mr John Fleming, who was examined before you, and addressed to Alexander Stronach. It says—

> "My dear Sir,—Just a line to tell you that Salmond got hold of me here, and "asked what was the meaning of my being in such close consultation with Potter "to-day; and I thought the best thing to say was that he had been talking of one of "his sons joining us in Bombay. He rather closely questioned me on the subject; "but I told him our conversation was quite general. I think it right to mention this "in case he should allude to the matter to you."

That lets in a flood of light upon the relation subsisting between the late manager of this Bank and the debtors on these accounts on the one hand, and the directors on the other, at that time. What was the meaning of that letter to Alexander Stronach? It is a letter which certainly reflects little credit on the writer, but I should be sorry to characterise it in language it does not warrant. I prefer therefore to use the language of the writer himself. I asked him why he wrote it, and he said, "I wrote it to put Mr Alexander "Stronach on his guard in case Mr Salmond should ask him to give informa- "tion as to the state of my account." Is it to be held that directors in that position—met with tactics like that—are to be responsible for a want of knowledge as to particular accounts, although deliberately misled by their own officials? That was years ago, when Mr Salmond must, according to the laws of nature, have been gifted with more capacity of mind and of body than he has now. But it is said, late though it be, old though he be, worn out though he may be, there was a letter put before him in 1875, which at least brought to his mind a knowledge of these facts. That is the letter written by Mr Robert Stronach when he was appointed manager. I admit my client was present at the meeting at which that letter was read. I admit it would have been an act of prudence and expediency, in consequence of that letter, to have done more than appears to have been done. But are you to say that, because this director, living in the country, attending merely at the regular meetings, and doing what was put before him, did not, of his own action, originate an investigation into the affairs of the debtors on these large accounts—because he did not take the initiative and summon committees, and exercise a direct control as to details—nay, I presume, go to India and make an examination into Smith, Fleming, & Co.'s affairs,—because he did not do all that, are you to say that he is to be held to have had guilty knowledge, knowledge of the actual sums at the debit of these accounts, and to what extent they shall be ultimately irrecoverable, and because of that knowledge to be sentenced as a criminal? Gentlemen, I am sure, as men of sense, you will accept no such extravagant view. It is out of the question to say that the mere failure to set in motion all the organisation which would have been required to clear up the position of these large accounts in 1875; that the inability of my client, physically or mentally, to enter upon such a task, is now to be imputed to him as a crime. Of guilty motive to defraud the shareholders he assuredly was free, and the result has been absolute ruin to himself.

Gentlemen, I fear I have detained you too long, but I trust to your indulgence, considering the magnitude of the issues which are involved. It is impossible to disguise the seriousness of these issues with regard to a person at the advanced age of my client, and I ask you to bear in mind, notwithstanding what the Lord Advocate has said, that his long life, which is now drawing to a close, has been spent in such a way as to secure to him the esteem and regard of all with whom he was associated. I ask you to bear in mind that he was a shareholder of the Bank to an extent which, if the prediction of the Crown proves true, involves ruin to himself; that he held these shares throughout, never selling a single one, and taking an additional allotment in 1873, which, if he had the knowledge imputed to him, demonstrates his insanity; and that he has throughout the later years of his life, in respect of failing vigour, been necessarily absent from the Bank to an extent which distinguishes his case in the most marked degree from that of all the others who now sit in the dock beside him. You cannot, as men of sense, take these circumstances into view, and give them their due weight, without coming to the conclusion that whatever may be the result of this trial with regard to others, so far as he at least is concerned, you should, in justice and fairness, give him a verdict which will leave him to spend the brief remainder of his days not in the squalor of a prison, but in the society of his friends, and, gentlemen, which will do more than that—which will dismiss him from this bar with his character unstained and his honour unsullied.

MR MACKINTOSH'S ADDRESS FOR MR TAYLOR.

May it please your Lordship, Gentlemen of the Jury,—I attend you on behalf of the panel Taylor, and I confess that I rise to do so under a sense of some embarrassment. I cannot but feel, after the course which this case has taken, and after the addresses to which you have listened from my learned friends, that any observations from me may appear superfluous. But this case is so anxious a case, and it involves so many elements of prejudice and confusion, that I must, even at the risk of repetition, ask you to give me your attention for a little, while I state to you the view I take of the evidence as it affects Mr Taylor, whom I represent. The case against the prisoners is now confined to the charge of falsifying the balance-sheets, and I do not require to say anything in regard to the charges which have been withdrawn. It must now be assumed that these charges are unfounded, and were unfounded from the first; and I think it is unfortunate that, being unfounded, they were preferred, or, when preferred, that they were not sooner withdrawn. I cannot but regret that this Court and the public have not had an opportunity of judging as to the grounds on which these charges, and in particular the charge of theft, which involved such serious consequences to these panels, were preferred. But it is not necessary to discuss these questions here. It is enough to say that these charges, as the Lord Advocate quite candidly put it, must now be dealt with as if they had never been in this indictment. The sole question you have to consider in reference to my client and others is this, whether they are proved to have been parties to the falsification of those balance-sheets; and next, whether they issued these balance-sheets in the knowledge that they were falsified.

Gentlemen, the balance-sheets in question begin in 1876, and I think I may take the balance-sheet of that year as a specimen of the whole, because the questions arising on all three are the same. And I daresay you will be satisfied that, if the balance-sheet for 1876 was falsified behind Mr Taylor's back, it is not probable that the balance-sheets for 1877 and 1878 were falsified before his face. And, therefore, the question being as to the circumstances in which the balance-sheet of 1876 were prepared and issued. I would, in the first instance, ask your attention to Mr Taylor's position at the time he was elected, and to the history of his connection with the directorate. Gentlemen, Mr Taylor joined the board of the City of Glasgow Bank in 1871, and you have heard what his position was at that time. He was a merchant in Glasgow, the head of a leading firm, and a wealthy man. You have heard what his character was, and you will judge whether he was a man likely to be taken into the confidence of persons engaged in questionable transactions. He was obviously selected as a man of probity and repute. Almost as soon as he joined the board, he was put upon the committee of the branches, the best and best managed department of the Bank's business. He continued upon that committee to the end; and so little was he mixed up in what I call the inner circle of the Bank's operations, that John Fleming did not even know him by sight, and Glen Walker did not know him to speak to till August 1877. In short, whatever the merits of Mr Taylor may have been, I do not think he can claim the merit of having been a very active director of this Bank. The truth was, I suppose, that he had too many other occupations, because, as his son told us, he not only had his own business to attend to, but he was also giving up an average of four hours a day to public business. Now, gentlemen, that being the position of Mr Taylor when the balance-sheet of 1876 was issued, the question which you have to consider is, whether you are prepared to affirm that Mr Taylor was a party to, or was cognisant of, those manipulations upon the balance-sheet which made it disconform to the books of the Bank. In other words, the question is, whether you are prepared to affirm that Mr Taylor was a party to, or was cognisant of, those operations and alterations upon the scroll balance-sheet, to which Mr Morison spoke, and the effect of which Mr Muir explained. Now, gentlemen, upon that question I take it there can be no possible controversy. There has not been a shadow of evidence adduced to connect Mr Taylor with the falsification of that balance-sheet. He is not brought into connection in any way with that scroll which Mr Morison prepared, and which Mr Morison went over with the manager and another of the directors. On the contrary, Mr Morison distinctly stated that all that was before the body of directors, including Mr Taylor, in connection with this or the other balance-sheets, were two documents—first, the balance ledger, which they signed and docqueted, and, secondly, the abstract balance-sheet, which was issued to the shareholders. I am not going to repeat, gentlemen, the argument upon the effect and character of those documents which you had this morning from Mr Balfour. I think his explanations must have made it clear to you how these documents stood, and what the process was by which the directors checked the balance ledger, and what the process was by which the abstract balance came to be issued. It is enough to repeat that, so far as the balance ledger is concerned, the document which the directors signed is not impugned as being disconform to the books of the Bank; and that, so far as the abstract issued to the shareholders is concerned, it is not suggested, and cannot be suggested, that on the face of it it discloses to a director reading it the suspicion that the figures had been manipulated, and that the totals did not represent the totals in the books of the Bank or the balance ledger. They would have required, in order to check the abstract issued to the shareholders, an analysis of the books of the Bank, an analysis of the balance ledger. It would have required arithmetical operations extending over a long period of time to ascertain whether the totals in the abstract were or were not correct. The directors had the abstract put before them by the responsible officials of the Bank. They had no suspicions there was anything wrong with it. They trusted, as they were entitled to trust, to the arithmetic of their officials. Having docqueted the balance ledger, their function might be regarded as done, and they then allowed the abstract balance-sheet to be issued to the shareholders, as any board of directors in Great Britain would have done, relying upon it being a faithful abstract of the books of the Bank; and therefore, gentlemen, the result is that Mr Taylor believed, and had no reason to doubt, that the balance-sheet issued to the public was in conformity with the books of the Bank. If I have carried you thus far, gentlemen, I venture to think I carry you a great way; I venture to think I carry you the whole way; because, that being so, the next question which arises is, whether this is not enough. It must be enough, unless you are prepared to affirm one or other of two propositions—either, first, that it was Mr Taylor's duty personally to investigate or audit the books of the Bank, so as to see whether they were correct or not; or, secondly, that Mr Taylor is proved to have had brought under his notice that the books of the Bank were falsified or manipulated. It being once established that Mr Taylor believed the balance-sheet to be in conformity with the books of the Bank, you cannot refuse to acquit him, unless, as I say, you are prepared to affirm one or other of these propositions. Now, gentlemen, the first of these propositions is extravagant. I don't think anybody has been found to suggest that it is the duty of directors to turn themselves into auditors, and ascertain on what principles the book-keepers and accountants whom they employ keep their various books. I don't think anybody has suggested that it is the duty of directors to check every cross entry in the books of the Bank, and satisfy themselves that each cross entry is a correct entry. I do not think it has ever been suggested that it is the duty of a director to go over every item of profit and loss, in the profit and loss accounts of the Bank, and satisfy himself that there is not there an item which ought properly to be carried to the suspense account or some other account. In all these matters the directors of an institution like this trust, and are entitled to trust, to these responsible officials who have skill in these matters, and who are employed to keep the books on correct principles, and whose results the directors are entitled to accept. And therefore, gentlemen, the question comes really to be reduced to this—is it proved to you that it was brought under Mr Taylor's notice that those books of the Bank were in any respect falsified or manipulated?

Now, gentlemen, I am not going to discuss the question whether or not, in point of fact, the books of the Bank were correctly kept. Charges have been made against the bookkeeping. Some of these charges are based, as I venture to think, upon far-fetched theories, but others are made which *prima facie* at least, seem difficult to meet. But this much is certain, that if there is anything wrong with those books, there is not a vestige of evidence to show that that was ever brought before the board of directors, or ever came to the knowledge of Mr Taylor. I begin with the first item—the first point upon which it was contended that the books of the Bank were wrong—I refer to the entry of £973,000, of which we have heard so much. It is quite true, gentlemen, that that entry appears in the books of the Bank, and so far as that entry is concerned the balance-sheet is in conformity with the books, and the question is, whether the entry in the books was a right one. I am not going to discuss that; I do not think I need repeat what Mr Balfour so clearly pointed out and explained this morning, that the existence of that entry in the books of the Bank never came under the notice of any one of the directors. The entry was made in a private cash book. I do not suppose directors are in the habit of investigating the private cash books of their accountant, and besides, there is not a suggestion that any of the directors did so. The entry is made in that book. It appears in the weekly balance-sheet which is brought before the directors for comparison with the balance ledger; but although it appears in the weekly balance-sheet, it does not appear in the balance ledger, and the weekly balance-sheet containing that entry is not checked by the directors; it is held by the accountant in his hand, and in reading off, for the purpose of checking, he does not read off the deduction on the one side and the addition on the other of the £973,000. He reads off, as you will see from the balance ledger itself, the result on the one side, after deduction of the £973,000, and on the other after its addition. Therefore it is vain to suggest that as regards my client—and the others were in the same position—there is any knowledge brought home to him in regard to this alleged questionable entry. The next point upon which the books, as I understand the Lord Advocate's argument, are said to be erroneous, is the matter of the reserve fund. And here I feel that I should weaken my case if I attempted to add anything to the admirable argument to which you have just listened on that point by Mr Asher. Let me just say this, however. The reserve fund is not attempted to be cut down, and cannot, under this indictment, be attempted to be cut down, on the ground that there were bad and irrecoverable debts in the books of the Bank to the amount of £450,000. The reserve fund is attempted to be cut down in this way, that if you go back to the years between 1861 and 1873, when this reserve fund was reared up in the books of the Bank, you will, it is said, find that this was reared up by transferring to profit and loss, and thereafter to this reserve fund, certain sums of interest on certain American debentures which were not received, but which were year by year falling into arrear. Gentlemen, having had no notice of that matter from the Crown, we cannot say whether, upon the books of the Bank, the accountant's evidence is or is not justified; but I am quite willing to take it as true. But observe what it comes to. Be it that the reserve was, during those years, reared up in that way; be it that an examination of the books between 1861 and 1873 would have disclosed the entries to which objection is now taken; was it the duty of Mr Taylor, who entered the management in 1871, to go back, in the year 1876, and audit and examine all books of the Bank for years before he became a director, in order to trace the manner in which this reserve fund was reared up? Surely, gentlemen, that proposition is about as extravagant as some others which we have heard in the course of this trial. But then, gentlemen, there is a third point, and that is the last, in which the books are said to be incorrect, or to be incorrectly kept, and that is in regard to the profit and loss account. Now here, again, I entirely adopt the argument of my friend Mr Asher, but let me add this: The suggestion is that it was improper to debit profit and loss with interest upon accounts which were not actually paying interest at the time, and the accountants appeared to assume that eight accounts in the name of certain large customers were in that position. Gentlemen, although that had been so, it would by no means follow that the theory of the accountants as to the proper mode of bookkeeping in this matter was correct; it would, further, by no means follow that even if the accountants were correct, the directors had brought under their notice the circumstance that these particular interests had been improperly debited to the profit and loss account. But what I have to point out is this, that the accountants are incorrect, at least to a large extent, in point of fact. I don't know why these eight accounts were selected. Some of them certainly are not, or were not at the date of the stoppage, of the nature of bad or doubtful accounts. But taking them as they stand, if you refer back to Mr Muir's evidence (see page 216), I think it will be found that at least five of these accounts were at this time bearing interest, and that interest was actually being paid upon them. I find, for example, taking the largest account—that of Mr James Morton—that in the year 1875, the year before this balance-sheet was prepared, he had not only paid up the whole interest accruing for the year upon his account, but had in addition to that diminished the principal of his account by the sum of £19,000 odds. I find that in 1874 the sum at his debit was £1,399,000, and I find that he paid interest upon that, and reduced the principal sum in the next year to £1,380,000. Then in the year 1877, the same thing happened, but to a larger extent; Mr Morton paid the interest for that year on the account, and reduced the principal sum by £84,000. Can it be said, therefore, that, as regards this account, it was improper or irregular to carry the interest thus paid into profit and loss—always assuming, as we are entitled for the purposes of this case to assume, that these accounts were assumed by the directors to be not immediately, but ultimately, recoverable. Taking another account—Potter, Wilson, and Co.'s account—I find that in the years here in question, 1875, 1876, and 1877, they paid regularly the interest upon their account, and not only paid interest upon their account, but made large payments towards capital. I find that in 1875 the amount at their debit was £76,700. In 1876, after debiting interest, it appears to be £75,000. Then in 1877, interest being again debited, the account is reduced to £64,000. That is Potter, Wilson, and Co.'s account. Then, take Buchanan & Co. I find that in 1876—the year we were dealing with, or the year immediately after that we are dealing with—interest was paid, and the account was reduced to the extent of £10,000. Then, coming to Glen Walker & Co.'s account, I find that in the year 1876 their account was reduced—the principal sum, that is—by £800, the interest being debited as before; and then, when I come to the eighth of the accounts to which the accountant referred, and upon which his whole calculations proceeded, I find that that eighth account is the account of the Edinburgh Pastoral Association, a concern whose business consisted in holding land in New Zealand, land yielding from year to year a return, and which was therefore undoubtedly in the position of yielding income, although sums were being advanced by the Bank from time to time for the purchase of other properties, with the result of increasing the total debit for the year 1877-

78. And, therefore, the Crown case,—which I cannot help thinking is very much of an afterthought, for it was brought out by the second of the two accountants, or at all events not by Mr Muir,—this part of the case, afterthought or not, fails at the very outset; it fails upon the facts. And what, gentlemen, is left? We reach this result, that Mr Taylor is not fixed with knowledge that the balance-sheet is disconform to the books; and, next, that neither is he fixed with the knowledge that the books are in any way falsified or fabricated. Then what is left upon which you can convict him on this charge? He believes the balance-sheet to be conform to the books; he believes the books to be conform to the facts. What more would you have? "but," says the Lord Advocate, "Mr Taylor was a director; Mr Taylor "knew the state of the affairs of the Bank. At least, he knew of the existence "of these large accounts; he therefore had a motive to falsify this balance-"sheet, and from the existence of that motive I shall infer the fact." That is an inference which I venture to think you will hesitate to accept. It is very much as if the Lord Advocate had put his case in this form, "The person who falsified this balance-sheet knew the affairs of the "Bank; you knew the affairs of the Bank; therefore you are one of "the persons who falsified the balance-sheet." I must say that kind of reasoning is what in one's early days one was accustomed to denote by a certain name. It strikes one not only as fallacious, but as very plainly sophistical. It is simply nonsense, even if you assume the premise from which the reasoning starts, viz., that Mr Taylor had the knowledge ascribed to him of the affairs of the Bank, and of the position of these accounts. But, gentlemen, how does this matter stand? I am not going to maintain to you that Mr Taylor knew nothing of these old accounts. I quite admit that from the beginning of 1876,—at all events from about that time—he had a general knowledge that certain accounts in this Bank were not in a satisfactory state—nay, more, that by the end of 1876, at all events, he came to know that Nicol Fleming had at his debit a considerable unsecured balance. But what I put to you is that there is no evidence that Mr Taylor knew the extent of the indebtedness of these various firms on the one hand, or, what is equally material, the amount and value of the securities held against that indebtedness on the other. To ascertain these facts would have required an examination which took the investigators into the affairs of this Bank sixteen days to accomplish. It is not proved that any book bringing the whole matter into a focus was ever submitted to the directors or to Mr Taylor. If he wanted to ascertain how each particular account stood, and how the securities for each particular account stood, he would have had to go through a number of books, through a number of accounts in each of these books; he would have had to make not only calculations but also valuations in order to inform himself; and you will judge whether that is what a director was likely to have done, or what any director could reasonably be expected to do.

But, gentlemen, it is said that certain minutes to which the Lord Advocate referred bring home to the directors, including Mr Taylor, a knowledge not merely that certain accounts were unsatisfactory, but a knowledge of the amount of the indebtedness on these accounts. As I read the minutes, I find no foundation for such an assertion. As regards Mr Taylor, there are only three minutes in which he is referred to at all. The first minute is at the time when Mr Robert Stronach was appointed. That minute recognises that information had been communicated to the board as to certain accounts being unsatisfactory, and the board resolved that a committee should be formed, consisting of the whole board, for the purpose of putting on record what the state of those accounts was a year previously, when Mr Robert Stronach entered on the active management of the Bank. Gentlemen, whatever the cause was, one thing is certain,—that committee never acted. No statement as to the position of these accounts was ever put on record. And, gentlemen, I think I can suggest an explanation why this committee did not act. A committee had previously been appointed on 18th February 1875, in consequence of the dissolution of the firm of Nicol Fleming & Company, to inquire into the position of the accounts of Smith, Fleming, and Company and Nicol Fleming & Company. Sometime after Robert Stronach's appointment to the managership—on 1st June 1876—that committee, of which Mr Taylor was not a member, reported that these accounts had been put into a satisfactory position. I take it that Mr Taylor was quite justified in accepting the report of that committee, but you will judge. But then it is said it is true that there was another committee appointed on 15th November 1877, when the whole board was formed into a committee to inquire into and consider the position of the various accounts of the Bank. It does not appear that this committee had special reference to any particular account; it was to consider the position of the various accounts of the Bank. But, gentlemen, it would not be possible at once to have these accounts put in shape, and it seems to have been proposed by some director that the investigation should be commenced six months afterwards; but Mr Taylor proposed that it should be commenced four months afterwards; the resolution that was ultimately come to being, that the inquiry should begin not later than four months afterwards. Well, gentlemen, the four months passed, and what do you find?

The LORD JUSTICE-CLERK—What did you say the dates of the minutes were?

Mr MACKINTOSH—There is the minute of November 15th, 1877, and the minute of 14th March 1878. Under the first minute of November 15th, 1877, it was resolved—"That a committee of the whole board should sit "periodically to consider the position of the various accounts of the Bank. "The Committee of Inquiry above mentioned will meet not later than four "months from this date." Counting four months from 15th November brings you down to March, when this resolution was passed—"In "connection with the minute of 15th November last, it was agreed "that Messrs Stewart, Potter, and Salmond be appointed a committee, "along with the Manager, to examine the advance accounts at the "head office weekly, and to deal in particular with the account of "Messrs James Morton & Co." I take it that all that this committee did, as appears from the next page of the minute, was to press Mr Morton to grant additional securities, and that he undertook to do. But that, I think, explains pretty well how, although on the face of the minutes Mr Taylor twice appears to come in contact with the books of the Bank, and with these accounts, yet he does not, in point of fact, come in contact with them until you come to the New Zealand purchase in the end of the year 1876; and that New Zealand purchase merely brings to his knowledge this—that J. Nicol Fleming's account has at its debit a balance not satisfactorily secured of about £200,000. And that, gentlemen, I put to you, is the effect of the evidence as to the extent of Mr Taylor's knowledge in regard to these accounts, and I say that not without book, because I think you will probably be satisfied that Mr Glen Walker, the brother-in-law of Alexander Stronach, and the confidential friend of the manager, Mr Robert Stronach, was likely to be as well informed as to the position of Mr Fleming's account as Mr Taylor was; and what was Mr Glen Walker's information as to the unsecured balance of the debit of that account? You will find in the evidence that at the time these New Zealand purchases were made, having the full confidence of the directors and Manager, he was in the belief that the extent of Mr Nicol Fleming's deficit—that is to say, the extent of the indebtedness not covered by securities—was about £200,000. That was also Mr Hunter's belief. You will judge whether individual directors of the Bank were at all likely to be better informed. But all this evidence about the condition and extent of Mr Taylor's knowledge as to the position of these accounts is altogether immaterial, except as bearing on the question whether he falsified or was a party to the falsification of these balances. The Lord Advocate suggests that the presumption is, that any person who knew about these accounts must have known there was falsification. You will judge of that upon the reasons I have endeavoured to submit to you.

And now, gentlemen, I do not know that I have much to add. There is just one part of the case to which I must refer, and that is the evidence as to Mr Taylor's character. The Lord Advocate was pleased to denounce the evidence as to character as preposterous. I venture to think that you will be of a different opinion, and that you will consider that in no kind of question is evidence of character more important than in this. Gentlemen, men don't fall from virtue like Vulcan from heaven—in a day. It takes a long course of demoralisation to convert an honourable and upright gentleman into a trickster and a knave. And I take it that that process of demoralisation cannot go on without its effects being apparent in the man's daily life. I submit to you. therefore, that the evidence of character which you have in this case is all-material. And if it is material at all, I think you will agree that seldom in a court of justice has such testimony to character been given as Mr Taylor received from Mr Peter Clouston, Mr Thomson, Mr Clark, and the Rev. Mr Robertson. It is not often that you witness the spectacle of men ruined by another's neglect coming forward to express their firm belief that, although they have suffered through that neglect, it was neglect, and nothing more. I know that in dealing with the question whether Mr Taylor is or is not proved to have been a party to this falsification, you will give that evidence of character its full weight. I have said that this is an anxious case. I feel it to be a painfully anxious case. To a gentleman in Mr Taylor's position we know what an adverse verdict means. I feel that to him this is truly a matter of life and death. I know that if he leaves this bar branded by your verdict as guilty of this crime, time to him can bring no solace, and life can retain no charm. But I decline in this case to appeal to your feelings, or to demand your sympathy. Such appeals may be useful in the balance of a doubtful case; but here I am content to ask for simple justice. I ask you to be dispassionate; I ask you to dismiss from your minds all prejudice; I ask you to discard all vague surmises and all far-fetched suspicions; I ask you to judge upon the evidence; and, if you do so, I have no fears of the result.

MR ROBERTSON'S ADDRESS FOR MR INGLIS.

May it please your Lordships, Gentlemen of the Jury,—I address you on behalf of Mr Henry Inglis. So much has been said, and so well, by the learned gentlemen who have preceded me in to-day's speeches, that I feel it entirely unnecessary to follow them, as I should do ineffectively, and at a disadvantage, into those numerous points in this case, which form the common ground of defence of most of the directors. Certainly, it would be unnecessary that I should remind you of the nature of the case which the Crown has to make out against the prisoners, of the nature of the case as disclosed upon the indictment, and as indicated by the speech of the prosecutor; unnecessary, moreover, to remind you of the facts which form the common ground of defence of at least five of the persons at the bar. The fact that they are charged with publishing a false balance-sheet, of which not one of them is proved to have had a hand in the preparation; unnecessary to refer to the fact that during the course of years which you have been asked to travel over, not one of them has been brought into contact with any one of the books which form the source of information from which that balance-sheet was prepared. Therefore, gentlemen, it is my intention, as these subjects have been so well and exhaustively discussed, to confine myself rigidly to the facts in the case which specially affect the case of Mr Henry Inglis. And I feel quite confident that, late as is the hour, and wearied as you must be, you will aid me in the effort to keep your attention to that issue—an issue which in your kindness you will remember is as momentous to Mr Inglis as if he alone sat at the bar.

You know, gentlemen, that each one of these men comes here from scenes most unlike that in which, unfortunately, we are met. Each has his own hopes and fears; each has the consciousness of guilt or innocence; and each makes his appeal to you upon a common ground, that ground which each possesses as his own sacred defence—the ground of your justice.

There are, however, two topics upon which I shall venture to dwell for a single moment, these topics having been, notwithstanding, already alluded to by some of my friends. I don't think it would be seemly, and it certainly would be inconsistent with the habit of mind—and the good nature and friendliness of the man for whom I appear,—if I were to leave to the counsel for the prosecution a monopoly of professions of sympathy for the shareholders of the City of Glasgow Bank. Gentlemen, my entire sincerity on that subject cannot be doubted. If by remissness, for which he must ever blame himself, Mr Inglis has contributed to the ruin of the Bank, upon whom has the ruin first fallen? Upon these men and their children. If Mr Inglis has lost other men's money, has he not lost all his own? And, gentlemen, I am sure you will not leave out of account the months of anxiety and of disgrace which have been spent before he could be brought to the bar, whence I hope he will attain his triumphant acquittal.

The other topic is one which I would very much rather not refer to. Mr Asher has, with a courage and propriety which I think deserves the praise, at all events, of all his brethren, challenged the conduct of the Crown regarding the omitted charge of theft. I feel specially called upon to speak upon that subject; and for this reason: I was thrown into prison on the charge of theft. I was brought before the magistrate on a charge of theft; and when Mr Inglis was asked what he had to say to that charge, he made answer to the magistrate, and made answer to the Lord Advocate, with a fervour and indignation which the Lord Advocate's own conduct in the case completely justifies. Gentlemen, it would be presumptuous in me, were this an occasion of mere public discussion, to censure or question the conduct of the eminent men in whose hands, to the great advantage of the country, the administration of the department of justice is at present confided. It would be foreign to my disposition and prepossessions. But I will say this, that I should fail in my duty if, standing in my place as counsel for this man, whose liberties have been invaded by the proceedings to which Mr Asher has referred, I did not protest against and denounce them.

Now, gentlemen, there is one point which I desire to clear up in the case against Mr Inglis before proceeding further. You are aware that one of the vestiges of these abandoned charges still remains in the evidence. We were brought here to answer not merely the charge of theft, but to answer, in the case of several of the directors, the charge of having embezzled the money of the shareholders by taking unwarrantable advances for ourselves. You remember that was in the indictment when the case was opened; it is out of the indictment now. But there is a fact to which the Lord Advocate did not refer, and I am quite sure he did not refer to it from good and generous reasons, but to which I feel bound in justice to my client to allude. In the course of Mr Muir's evidence it was proved incidentally, and I cannot help thinking it must have been intended to bear on the abandoned charge of overdrafts, that when the Bank stopped Mr Inglis was due a certain sum of money upon an overdrawn account. Now, I am in the judgment of his Lordship, who will direct you upon this as upon all other subjects in the case, whether that fact of the advance to Mr Inglis on an overdrawn account is not one of those facts which are out of the case, although incidentally they were proved in the course of Mr Muir's evidence. And I will tell you why I insist upon that. I was brought here to answer a charge of overdrawing my account, and was ready to meet it, and would have satisfied you upon it; but that part of the case being withdrawn from your consideration, I should have been wrong if I had wearied the Court and troubled you with evidence bearing upon my private affairs; and for this reason, that the Lord Advocate, by withdrawing the charge against me that I violated my duty in overdrawing the account, concedes that what I did was perfectly right, and within the legitimate exercise of my duties as director. Gentlemen, the idea of bringing forward that as a point against me, would at once appear to you to be vain and absurd, when you remember that Mr Inglis was a man of landed estate,—a man carrying on a most lucrative business in Edinburgh; and really, if every question about some thousand pounds being overdrawn, with estates like that behind, were to be raised, you would be engaged in controversies over men's private affairs which have nothing earthly to do with the department of criminal law.

Having referred to that, as I think it was right I should do,—and you will see the propriety of it as the case advances—I ask your attention now to the evidence affecting Mr Inglis. And, gentlemen, to deal with the subject to which Mr Mackintosh last alluded, I might say a great deal about the presumptions arising from the position and character of a man such as Henry Inglis. I might do that, but I think it is better, far better, that every man should be tried upon common ground; and although I might tell you of friends who will never believe in his guilt, and of a generous character which precludes its possibility, I prefer to go to you, fifteen of my countrymen, upon the general facts of the case. I am quite sure that I shall never fail in securing a favourable answer to a case which is presented on the footing of facing every difficulty which the Crown put against me, and, as I hope I shall be able briefly to do, giving them a conclusive answer.

Gentlemen, the case which is made against Mr Inglis, as explained by the Lord Advocate, is this. The Lord Advocate has not professed or contended that in the preparation of the balance-sheet, of which complaint is here made, Mr Inglis had any hand whatever. But from the reference which the Lord Advocate made to the alternative charge, on which he seeks your verdict, his case, as I apprehend it, is this. Certain persons, whom you will identify in the course of these proceedings, made up balance-sheets which, in certain essential particulars, were false. Mr Inglis was not engaged in that concoction, or the preparation of these balance-sheets—that is conceded. But it is said Mr Inglis is guilty for this reason: because, when he saw that balance-sheet, he must have known that the particulars set out in it were different from the true state of the facts, and, in that knowledge that the document contained falsehoods, he yet was a party to issuing it to the shareholders. I think you will agree with me that that is a fair statement of the case against me; at all events, it is stating the case against me at the outside, and in short terms. And with that case I shall deal. And let me say I must confess I was a little surprised at the method by which the Lord Advocate, following up the case into the minutest details of the evidence, laid evidence on the completeness of his evidence, that certain documents, minutes of the meetings, in which the critical affairs of the Bank were discussed, were in the handwriting of Mr Inglis. He treated, or affected to treat, that as a question upon which there was controversy, and by a skilful device, which is very familiar in these Courts, emphasising the importance of that point, he leaves you to suppose that his opponent would be equally astute in trying to get out of that conclusion. When I come to the details of the evidence, I shall show that the Lord Advocate need not have given himself any anxiety on that point. Mr Inglis is not a criminal—if he is a criminal—who requires to be trapped by devices of that kind. Wherever the Lord Advocate says the document is in Mr Inglis' handwriting, I say it is so. And I shall show you bit by bit—and fortunately there are few items in this matter, but they are very important—that wherever the Lord Advocate has done that, he has, in the prevailing obscurity of these transactions, just revealed the righteousness of Mr Inglis' case and conduct.

Gentlemen, let me say that it is with reference to some of these facts that I intend to trespass for a few minutes on your indulgence.

But there is one general observation, indicated as it was in the observations of my learned friend Mr Balfour, but certainly worthy of repetition, to which I ask your attention. In my case, in the case of Mr Inglis, more distinctly probably than in any other, the evidence of the Crown may be summed up in one word: it is the minute book. Now, gentlemen, I must say that I think there is very great force and very great common-sense in the observations Mr Balfour made upon that mode of evidence. This minute book is a series of scrappy records of multifarious transactions by seven or eight men meeting together. It contains no dividing asunder of the several parts which are played by the persons who are there present. Everything is put in a lump. The directors do this, or the directors do that; and, gentlemen, you are in as much ignorance, after reading that minute book, of each particular act which was done by each particular person as if you had never seen the minute book at all. And I think it is of vital importance in this case, as the first step in dealing with one individual of the accused, to ascertain a few facts about himself. And I shall give you these. In the first place, keep this steadily in view. We are admitted sometimes behind the scenes of the City of Glasgow Bank's affairs; and without saying anything which can militate against any one of the prisoners at the bar, I think you will agree with me in this, that no important step in the transactions which you are now investigating was ever taken for the first time at a board meeting; but that, on the contrary, all arrangements which led to anything affecting the questions now before you were concluded before the board ever had it under consideration. I shall give you chapter and verse for that as to one or two of the transactions; but I make this preliminary observation to explain the reason why I mention the next few facts. Here we are on solid ground, perfectly clear of any controversial matter. It is quite certain that Mr Henry Inglis was resident in Edinburgh during the whole of the period in question. The other gentlemen, with the exception of Mr Asher's client, are actually resident within the city of Glasgow; and without saying anything against these gentlemen, I think you will be satisfied of this, that they were all very much on the spot, always at hand, and ready for consultation, if consultation with them was desired.

You are very well aware also that it accords with the policy of a banking establishment, whether it is sound or unsound, that they should invoke the presence at the board of a person representing another or external interest, and Mr Inglis' part in these proceedings has been confined to that part which you would naturally expect from the bare fact of his residence. I put to you this question, is there in the evidence from beginning to end any suggestion, far less any proof, that Mr Inglis ever consulted or deliberated upon any of these questions now before your consideration, except at the board of direction? There is one exception which I shall mention, and that is the purchase of Australian land; and how he became connected with that you will hear immediately. But in the meantime you have this fact to begin with, and there is no doubt about it: you have here a professional man, unconnected with commerce, practising the law in Edinburgh, busy with the professional firm I have mentioned, and which you all know to be a firm of the highest standing—industriously engaged in carrying on business in this city. Therefore, gentlemen, if it be the fact that he was behind the scenes to this extraordinary extent, that he was meeting with all those people—and you have no evidence of it—all I can say is, that it is extremely surprising. But there is more than that. The other members of the board of direction, I think, were almost without exception merchants and in trade, and of some of them it is perfectly fair to observe, that they were mixed up at that moment in a kind of speculation and a character of business which it seems the City of Glasgow Bank cultivated too much. But Mr Inglis did not carry into that board of direction a single item of knowledge which could qualify him to control any of the proceedings to which I have referred. He was not a commercial man; not a lawyer conversant with commerce; not a resident in the town—these are the facts I ask you to take along with you when you come to ascertain his position in these proceedings.

I come now at once to that which I think is the turning point of the case—the meeting of the 28th December 1875. I fix on this date because, beyond all question, the Lord Advocate will not obtain a conviction from you of any one of the directors whose counsel is now addressing you, or who have preceded me, unless he establishes upon Mr Stronach's letter that they were put in possession of information which demonstrated that the Bank was rotten from beginning to end. The letter which was addressed by Mr Stronach to the board of direction, and which was read at the meeting of 30th December 1875, has been so often quoted that I do not require to do more than remind you of the facts. In that letter, Mr Robert Stronach, while accepting the office of manager, refuses to do so unless it is placed on record that the directors approve of the policy which had been followed by his brother in regard to certain accounts. Now, what do the directors do on receiving that letter? They do this. The minutes bear that a letter was read from Mr Robert Stronach accepting the office of manager to the Bank, "and the same having "been considered and approved of, is ordered to be recorded in the minute "book, and appoint all the members of the board of directors a committee to "comply with these articles. The directors wish also to record, on their own "behalf, the fact that the matters alluded to in the letter in question were "not at any time brought before them by the late manager." Now, the Lord Advocate has proved about that minute so far that it was in the handwriting of one of the members of the board; but the importance is in what follows. He has proved also that when this minute was prepared there was added, and by Mr Inglis, the following words:—"The directors wish also to record, on "their own behalf, the fact that the matters in question were not at any time "brought before them by the late manager." Now, the Lord Advocate reads that as bringing home to me knowledge. I ask, knowledge of what? But I found on it now as its being his own volunteered protest of his ignorance, and his protest also of this that he was free of responsibility for the accounts then in question. And from this point I propose to go back a little in order to ascertain what had been the history of the accounts, so far as Mr Inglis is concerned. I wish to refer to two accounts, and to two only, because these alone affect my case. I refer to the accounts of James Morton, and Smith, Fleming, & Co. Now, gentlemen, take this one fact along with you about these accounts—in 1875, when this protest of Mr Inglis was placed on the minute book, what was the state of the Bank as regards the two-thirds of the total deficiency which was said to be held by a few firms? Taking it in round figures, at that time Morton had £1,300,000, and Smith, Fleming, & Co. had £1,600,000. Now, gentlemen, have this steadily in view throughout the case. Up to the date of which I speak, it is certain that during Mr Alexander Stronach's administration, he did that with his own hand, and what is more, you have in that significant minute framed by Mr Inglis, the reminder of all concerned, that that was the first time they knew anything about those accounts. Gentlemen, I put it to you as men of sense, whether the Bank at that date was not irretrievably committed to the two houses. And I shall ask you to go back, and to follow me into the facts we know about these two houses, and how they were connected with those two houses.

Take, gentlemen, the case of the Flemings. It is an observation of very great significance that whenever you have a man in the box who can tell you what every man in the City of Glasgow Bank was doing, then it appears that Mr Inglis was not participating in these deliberations. It is only when we get into the obscurity of the minute book that anything which can be said to approach this is found. The Lord Advocate holding it up as if the whole thing were a prosecution for debt, where I should be liable even if it were proved constructively, says, "I turn up your own minute book, and I find this "in your own hand." I say that you must have not merely collective responsibility, but personal responsibility, in the matter of crime. You have here, as a matter of conscience, to fasten upon me personal knowledge of any item which goes to make Mr Inglis guilty in publishing this balance-sheet; and here I say that in these transactions of Smith, Fleming, & Co., Mr John Fleming is quite distinct, that everything of importance was settled long before 1875. The evidence on which I here found is at pp. 217 to 219 (see p. 190). I don't read that evidence now, but I give his Lordship that reference. Let me remind you, however, as it is some time since the evidence was given, of the import of these negotiations and of a few of the facts.

The LORD JUSTICE-CLERK—I am anxious to understand what you say about this. What page do you refer to?

Mr ROBERTSON—Page 217 (see p. 190): "(Q.) In July 1870 did you see Mr "Alexander Stronach, Mr Potter, and Mr Salmond about the state of your "affairs? (A.) I saw Mr Alexander Stronach and Mr Potter. (Q.) And Mr Sal- "mond? (A.) I believe Mr Salmond, but I am not so sure about him. (Q.) "Was your brother present? (A.) My brother was present." Mr Fleming said that he met the gentlemen in question at the City of Glasgow Bank. To state my point, then, in a single sentence, what I say is this, that you have here from the mouth of a credible witness for the Crown, who came to tell you the truth on the subject, an account of these negotiations which resulted in showing that the Bank were bound to keep the firm of Smith, Fleming, & Co. on its feet, although the Bank, or the gentlemen whom Mr Fleming had named, were told that without some extraordinary assistance, without pledging the credit of the Bank to the firm, it must come down. I take another passage in John Fleming's evidence relating to a subsequent period, the agreement of March 1875. That you will find on page 221 F (see p. 192). Without going into details, it was an agreement by which the Bank were still further pledged to maintain the credit of the firm of Smith, Fleming, & Co. There is a letter which was written by Mr John Fleming to Mr Robert Stronach, in April 1875, and the first paragraph of it says—"Dear Sir,—Referring to the meeting I had with "your directors on Thursday, 1st inst., respecting the state of our account "with the Bank, I now beg to detail the terms of the agreement come to, "as I understood them." Mr Fleming was asked who were present at the meeting therein referred to, and he replied, "I am unable to recall." On that I pause, to make the observation that, when Mr Fleming refers to the meeting which he had with "your directors," he does not refer to a meeting of the board at all. That is evidenced by the fact that no meeting of the directors was held on that day. He refers to "your directors" in the sense of those of the directors with whom he had a meeting. He is asked, as I said, "Who were present at the meeting you refer to in that letter?" and he answered, "I am unable to recall." But, fortunately, he is able to recall the name of one person who was not present at any meeting he had on the whole of the negotiations on this subject, because at page 235 B (see p. 201) you will find he is asked this, "Looking back over the negotiations you had with the

"Bank with regard to your affairs, did you ever meet Mr Henry Inglis on Bank "business?" The answer is, "Never." I have mentioned those facts bearing upon the position of Smith, Fleming & Co., in order that you may see with what good reason Mr Inglis appended the addition to the minute in December. To show you still further that the concerns of this firm was in the hands of other persons than Mr Inglis, I would refer to the committee appointed on the 18th of February 1875 with reference to new arrangements in regard to these firms owing to a dissolution. I refer to these things in order to bring down to date, the 30th December 1875, Mr Inglis' position in regard to the firms of Smith, Fleming, & Co., and James Nicol Fleming. You see from my narrative, and I canvass examination of the evidence in this case to show whether I am right or wrong, that on the date the letter was read from Mr Stronach, saying, "Take warning, you are responsible," Mr Inglis was right when he gave his answer, that he never heard of them till then.

I take the case of Morton & Co.; and there, again, I don't think it is necessary to enter into details. You will find that they negotiated with the Bank in 1873 for the same purpose, and pretty nearly with the same result, as Smith, Fleming, & Co. Morton wanted support and got it. I have looked over the record of the proceedings of the Bank, so far as Morton & Co. are concerned, and I find that Mr Inglis never touched affairs which directly or indirectly related to that firm until the Australian lands were purchased. And, gentlemen, I affirm, therefore, free from any apprehension of my statement being impugned, that at this time Mr Inglis was not cognisant of the affairs of the Bank relating to these accounts. What information did he get by the communication in December 1875? or what was he likely to get? He is a man who goes to the Bank once a week, while others were there every day. He was a man who could not bring to the unravelling of accounts, such as those in question, the skill and experience of any of those persons who had entered on such adventures. Then I put it to you, as men of sense, whether it is likely—and more than likelihood is needed here—whether it is likely that any information was conveyed to Mr Inglis which could prove that Smith, Fleming, & Co. were in a rotten state. I adopt, and do not need to follow, my learned friend's argument on that, which shows that the position of Smith, Fleming, & Co. in 1875 was not hopeless at all. So far from that, if the times had been better and commerce had proved more elastic, no extraordinary measures would have been required to bring them right again.

Gentlemen, I ask you to remember this. You have seen in the witness box Mr Glen Walker and Mr John Fleming. You have not seen Mr Morton. I must say I think the Crown should have allowed us the privilege of hearing his account of these proceedings. As I said before, whenever you can put witnesses in the box who can tell what share each person had in those transactions, everything is clear. But Mr Morton was not produced to say what A, B, and C told him, and to whom he made his proposals. I am not aware that Mr James Morton has followed Mr James Nicol Fleming to other climes, and I must say we had a right to expect that, where the Crown are perilling their case, and perilling our liberties on the question what is our knowledge of Morton's affairs, Morton himself should have been produced to tell the truth.

But, gentlemen, I pass to consider what was done after the year 1875. Certainly, if we have reason to complain of a deficiency of evidence in this part of the case, we have the advantage of being able to draw from the appearance and the mode of calculation adopted by men of enterprise like Mr Glen Walker and Mr Fleming, some conclusion as to the stories which would be told to inquiring directors. I venture to say that all the probabilities in this case would be upset, and every fact which we know regarding these men would be set at defiance, if you did not believe that these gentlemen would be well able, and that Mr Morton, with his delusive tongue, would be still better able, to show before that body of directors, or such of them as happened to have no other sources of knowledge, facts that would demonstrate the complete stability of the concern. And, gentlemen, it would not have been fiction, because there were elements of hope, and elements of substantial advantage, in those firms, which in more hopeful times would have freed the Bank of its present ruin.

But it did not so prove; and now I want to ask your attention to the operations which resulted in the arrangement with Smith, Fleming, & Co., and Morton & Co. Here, again, I have to thank the Lord Advocate for the industry with which his subordinates have traced out my handwriting. I have to thank him for this reason, that there is a minute of considerable importance with regard to the purchase of Australian lands, as to which there is a very instructive piece of evidence on page 145 of the proof.

Before I refer to that, however, allow me to resume, in a single word, the history of the Australian lands. Their purchase, and the knowledge we have of the necessity of their purchase, is pressed against us in this way. It is said that was not a speculation within the ordinary compass of banking operations; and that is quite true. But it is said, further, that the special and only reason for that anomalous step being adopted was this—that we were satisfied that some measure of extreme risk was necessary to recoup the losses upon the overdrawn accounts of Smith, Fleming, & Co., and Morton & Co. Gentlemen, that is no doubt the case, and it is no doubt the case also that the Bank took that step for the reason which the Lord Advocate has assigned. Here, again, the minute in question is that of 17th August 1876, and it records a letter from Morton & Co. relating to the transactions of Glen Walker & Co.; and the board came to the conclusion that it was advisable to adopt generally the suggestions contained in those letters; and they accordingly requested the manager, associated with certain directors, of whom Mr Inglis is not one, to arrange with Mr Walker as to all details; and then follows:—

> "While arriving at this resolution, the board were fully sensible of the undesir-
> "ableness of such investments as the purchase proposed in the letters; but having
> "in view the position of certain old accounts, and looking at the whole circum-
> "stances, particularly to the fact that the contemplated arrangements for the
> "working of the credits are largely part of transactions in existence for many years,
> "and previously brought under consideration of the board by the present manager,
> "the board deem it expedient to come to their present decision."

And there the minute ended; and Mr Inglis added these words, and added them in a way which, I think, completes the connection and integrity of his actings in the matter,—he put in the words, "As referred to in minute of 30th "December 1875." Now, I pray you to observe upon that minute this—Eight months had elapsed since Mr Robert Stronach had been appointed manager,—eight months during which the board of direction were necessarily engaged in trying to put things right. Is it likely, if Mr Inglis had obtained information which convicted him and brought home to him a full knowledge that those accounts were desperate,—is it likely that he would, with his own hand, have written down words which would point out his condemnation? I take it, gentlemen, that the explanation of that addition is this, that Mr Inglis connected this, and rightly connected it, with a policy for which he, for one, was not responsible, because he was ignorant of it; and that he had no more information when the Australian lands were purchased than he had at 30th December 1875.

And here I ask you to have regard to the ordinary springs and motives of human conduct, and I put it to you, as men of sense, whether those minutes, and the part which Mr Inglis takes in their preparation, are not demonstration of the conscience which could write those words without guilt. You will have anticipated to some extent the question which I now put with emphasis. I want to ask you what the Lord Advocate means—and this is a question you must answer—What is it that the Lord Advocate wishes you to say, when he bids you affirm that Mr Inglis was aware of the state of those accounts? That he was aware of the existence of those accounts is most true; that he was aware also that they were unsatisfactory accounts, I think is matter of certain inference; but, gentlemen, we are reading all this at a time when the severe importance of those accounts is now brought to the front. We are not reading them in the light of four years ago; and I ask you whether there is anything in those facts which are proved out of the minute book, to show that Mr Inglis was then aware of anything more than this—that those accounts with large, enterprising, at one time prosperous firms, were accounts which required close looking after? Now, it is all disclosed for your information; you can go back over those four years; you can say—If this had been stopped in 1875, the Bank would have been open and flourishing; but I appeal to you in fairness, whether there is anything in the evidence before you, to bring into that lurid light, in December 1875 and August 1876, the transactions which are in question? And, gentlemen, again I would remind you that it is your duty here, as throughout the inquiry, not to rest content with the applause which I think you would not obtain from a discerning public if you sent all these men in a body to prison, merely to show your indignation at this commercial disaster. You are strong, but justice is stronger; and I make certain of this, that you will rise to the dignity of your position, that you will remember that each one of those men is to be tried as if he alone were at the bar; that you will remember that the investigation in which you are engaged is not a demonstration of public indignation against commercial disaster or commercial dishonesty, but that you are meting out to each of the men at the bar a criminal sentence which he can only deserve if he has been guilty of crime.

Now, there is another question to which I think I should advert. I am sure there has passed through your minds—the thought is indeed irresistible—some such inquiry as this: if we had been there in 1875, and by that letter read to us been put on our guard, what should we have done? Gentlemen, what was done was this—and you will remember that Mr Mackintosh mentioned this fact, but I mention it in order to keep it fresh in your recollection—a resolution come to in 1877, that a committee of the whole board should sit on those accounts, was superseded when the time came by a resolution that certain other gentlemen—not Mr Inglis—should conduct investigations for the board. That took place after the crisis of 1875; but at the very time of that crisis two members of the board, Mr Potter and another, had taken upon themselves this investigation into the affairs of Smith, Fleming, & Co., and Nicol Fleming, and therefore, in 1875, just as in 1877, when a similar committee was appointed, the board might resolve formally to sit as a committee and investigate into those accounts; but from the necessities of the case, and from what I think was the propriety of the case, the actual investigations were made by gentlemen skilled in commerce, and who were specially versed in the affairs then in dispute. You know who these men were. I am not here to say a word which can militate in your view against any of the accused at the bar; but I may here ask you, as judges of the question against Mr Inglis, to have this in view, that if probability be treated as a guide in this matter, it is not Mr Inglis, absent and unacquainted with commercial affairs, who would be charged with the inquiry; and all he would be allowed to receive, or be entitled to receive, from his colleagues, was merely the results of their investigation.

There is one other subject to which I ought to refer, although the Lord Advocate, with characteristic fairness, made nothing of it against me. Passages in the evidence sometimes occur, and take hold of the minds of members of the jury, even although counsel on the other side do not regard them as pressing in favour of his case. It was suggested in the course of the evidence that Mr Inglis held a position of peculiar duty, a position which laid upon him the duty of outspokenness and communication with the members of the Edinburgh board of directors. You heard the members of the Edinburgh board of directors examined upon that subject; and I am in your recollection whether it is not the case that Mr Somerville—of whom I speak with the respect due to a man who has lost all his money, and is not embittered by it—told you that the Glasgow board of direction were under a pledge of secrecy to their partners in regard to the affairs of the Bank. Now, I do not say for a moment that such a pledge of secrecy implied, that if a man knew that the Bank was rotten he was to lock that up in his own bosom and say nothing about it. I don't suggest that for a moment. I think his duty was to wash his hands of it and come out of it. But you will observe this, if I am right and have carried your conviction along with me as to Mr Inglis' position at the board, he never had information which it would have been anything but the height of disloyalty and impropriety to communicate to any person, even were he an Edinburgh director. And I will tell you why. If anything was certain about these firms it was this—that theirs being to some extent a speculative business, that business depended for its very life on credit and reputation; and if Mr Inglis had said to Mr John Gillespie or Mr Somerville, or any other member of the Edinburgh board of direction, "Well, I must say Smith, Fleming, & Co.'s account is not a safe one," don't you see that what he would have done would have sufficed to bring down the Bank? I beg of you to consider whether you will send a man to prison or penal servitude because with a reserve, which a generous and prudent man, I think, was bound to observe, he kept his counsel, and did not sound a note of warning. You will, I think, applaud his conduct and commend it. You will condemn it if the case be this—that, knowing that things were rotten and at an end, he suppressed that fact, and told untruths. I am in your judgment whether the best evidence after all, in reference to the effect of these communications made by Mr Inglis to his coadjutors in Edinburgh, is not to be got from Mr Somerville himself. I did not bring witnesses as to character on behalf of Mr Inglis, because I did not, I think, require it. I do not think that a citizen of Edinburgh requires that, though it was quite right and proper that the others should bring their friends from Glasgow to tell you something about them. I did not ask certificates of character, but at the end of the examination of Mr Somerville by the Crown, when they had endeavoured to get something out of him in the way of a misrepresentation or a blind by Mr Inglis as to the affairs of the Bank to the Edinburgh direction, used against the safety of his own brethren, I thought it right to ask what Mr Inglis said about those accounts, and the import of the evidence was, that Mr Inglis said that Smith, Fleming, & Co.'s affairs would all come right. And Mr Somerville winds up with this, and this is the impression produced on the mind of the man to whom the statements were made:—"As regards "the performance of his duties as a director towards myself, my opinion is "that he was highly honourable in every respect. I could not conceive that "Mr Inglis would do anything—that was the opinion I always formed of him "—unbecoming the character of a gentleman. That is my opinion of Mr "Inglis at the present moment, after all that has happened."

Gentlemen, that is the conclusion of a man who has been ruined by this disaster; it is the conclusion of the man to whom these statements were made; and it is the conclusion which I ask you on this branch of the case to adopt.

When Mr Inglis was brought before the magistrate he was asked explanations regarding his connection with the Glasgow Bank, and he said this—it expresses so well and with such propriety, and, I must do him the justice to say, with such reserve, and, at the same time, such frankness, his own position in this case, that I will venture to read his words to you—"My crime, if crime "it be, was the possession of the most entire confidence in every statement "and in every figure which was laid before me." Guilty of that; of a remissness, the consequences of which have been so stupendous that it must cast a shadow upon the remainder of his life. Guilty of that; but of falsehood, of fraud, of any crime contained in that indictment, of sin against honour, or offence against the law, not guilty.

MR J. GUTHRIE SMITH'S ADDRESS FOR MR WRIGHT.

May it please your Lordships, Gentlemen of the Jury.—I have now to state the case for Mr John Innes Wright, who was invited to join the board so recently as 1875.

He was then well advanced in years, and for a considerable period had surrendered the active management of his business to younger men—Mr Paul and Mr Scott. The Lord Advocate laid emphasis on the fact that he had none of the qualifications for a director. He was not a shareholder. He had no experience in the business of the Bank. That is true. It is also true that at that time his firm was considerably in debt to the Bank, although, as I shall afterwards show you, he was not aware of the precise amount. Gentlemen, I could have wished, knowing what has since occurred, if, for Mr Wright's own sake, he had refused the offer which was made to him in 1875, and showed the same firmness as he did in 1871 when a similar offer was made to him. But, gentlemen, we are not to expect in the feebleness of age the vigour of early years, and if this is but an example of his easy and accommodating spirit, it quite accords with the character which he received from the Dean of Guild of Glasgow and Mr Connal. But if, in your opinion, there is anything in the circumstances in which he accepted office open to censure, I pray you to remember that between mere imprudence and deliberate fraud there is the widest possible distinction, and if I should show you, as I hope to be able to do, that he took no improper advantage of his position as a director, then I think you will gladly inquire into the facts of the case to see whether there be not some important differences between his case and those of the other directors.

Gentlemen, Mr Wright's case is that when he entered the Bank in 1875 he was in entire ignorance of its position, and that he remained in that ignorance all through till it suspended payment in 1878. My first point is that, when he entered the Bank in 1875, he was in entire ignorance of its position. I shall first ask you whether the evidence shows that that is true, or rather, whether there is anything in the case by which the contrary is established. At this time it is proved that the men who had the best opportunities of judging—Mr Leresche and Mr Turnbull, the former down to 1878, and the latter down to the beginning of the year when they began to meddle with the gold—had no suspicion of the position of the Bank. Mr Murdoch, the secretary, and Mr Miller, the assistant-cashier, knew only that the branches were worth about £70,000 a year. If the officials inside the Bank, having the best means of information, believed it to be a solid and stable concern, which it appeared to be, I presume that outsiders in the position of Mr Wright would not be better informed. He had nothing to guide him but the reports of previous years, and the large dividends which had been declared. Everything appeared satisfactory. The Bank was doing a large business, and competing successfully for public confidence along with the other banks of the kingdom, and if, in those circumstances, he was induced to join this concern, it must have been in the belief that it was a solvent establishment. On no other footing would he have consented, immediately after he became a director, to receive as trustee for the Bank £2681 of its stock. If he had reason to believe that there was anything the matter with the Bank, he would have done no such thing. These circumstances, that he involved himself at all in these obligations, are conclusive to my mind that in 1875, when Mr Wright became a director and accepted a seat at the board, he really had no suspicion that there was anything the matter with the Bank. If that is a legitimate deduction from the evidence in the case, I think it is also established that Mr Wright at this time was equally ignorant of the past management of the Bank. He had no conception of the existence of those large accounts. He knew nothing of Smith, Fleming, & Co., James Nicol Fleming, or Mr Morton's account. Mr Morris, when examined, was asked (see p. 175): (Q.) At "the end of 1875, had there been incurred by Smith, Fleming, and Co., "nine-tenths of that debt which they were owing to the Bank when it "stopped? (A.) I should think so. The greater portion of James Nicol "Fleming's debt was incurred before 1876. I don't think there was any "advance made to him from the beginning of 1876 onwards, except in con-"nection with the Australian and New Zealand properties." So that I think, if Mr Wright can be acquitted of any knowledge of the position of the Bank in 1875 when he joined it, the inference is also irresistible that he was equally ignorant of any of those accounts, or of the character of the management which had for some years prevailed, and for which he is, of course, in no ways responsible.

Gentlemen, I come now to a point on which some evidence was led, and to a question which seems to me to have a very material interest as regards the charge in the indictment. The question I ask you to consider is, whether it is proved that in entering this board Mr Wright had any personal ends to serve. I propose to show you from the evidence led that it is abundantly established that Mr Wright had no personal ends to serve whatever. I think that this is a point of some importance, because it was made a matter of charge in the indictment as originally framed, and as sent to the jury, that Mr Wright took advantage of his position as a director for the purposes of appropriating fraudulently the moneys belonging to the Bank. That charge having been completely destroyed by the evidence, was withdrawn by the Lord Advocate at the end of the day.

I propose now to remind you of the facts and the figures brought out in the evidence led, in order to prove, as I think I shall be able to do, how entirely innocent Mr Wright was of this particular charge, and how completely, so far as he is concerned, such a charge is altogether without foundation. Gentlemen, there are three accounts in the Bank's books relating to the firm of Innes Wright & Co. and its partners—there is the account of Mr Wright himself, there is the account of his partner Mr Scott, and there is the account of Wright & Co. I begin with Mr Wright's own account, and there are no operations on that account save one, that by which, in July 1875, he was entered as debtor for the stock which was given him in order to constitute his qualification as a director. There is no entry of any advance to him personally before that date, and there is no entry of any advance to him personally after that date. On the one side the interest is charged on the price of the stock, and on the other side he is credited with the dividends upon it. These dividends Mr Wright never touched. It was entirely a nominal qualification he held, and he took no advantage personally of his position to acquire any of the Bank's money for his own personal use. Indeed, had he done so, it would have been inconsistent with all we have heard of his character. He was engaged in no personal speculations, and he lived in a quiet unobtrusive way, never exceeding the allowance which was drawn by him as a partner of the firm. And, in particular, he lived utterly unacquainted with the manner in which his partner, Mr Scott, had for some time been conducting himself; for while it is proved that the sum standing at the debit of the firm and his partner amounted to £393,000, of that sum £121,000 was due by Mr Scott. It was due by Mr Scott personally as distinct from the firm. And do you suppose for one moment that if Mr Wright had possessed the slightest idea that his partner was already a debtor to the Bank on his own personal account to the extent of £121,000, that he would have allowed him to remain in partnership with him? That single fact explains, in a large measure, the relationship that subsisted between them, and is fully confirmed by the important testimony which Mr Paul gave us as to the position of the firm. Mr Paul, who was a partner, retired in 1876. His evidence will explain how the matter stood. Mr Paul stated that he and Mr Scott were taken into partnership in the year 1863. The whole capital of the firm was advanced by Mr Wright, and it amounted, in the first instance, to about £45,000, which was subsequently supplemented. Each partner was assigned his proper department—Mr Wright himself attended to the import department, Mr Paul attended to the export department, and Mr Scott managed the finance business of the firm. The whole finance department of the business was entrusted to Mr Scott, and none of his partners apparently took anything to do with it. Now, this being the position of the matter, Mr Paul was asked whether he had any idea of the amount of the debt which the firm was owing to the Bank, and his answer was in these words—"I was aware that the Bank "must be advancing, but I had no earthly idea as to the extent of it. I "frequently wished to know from Mr Scott, but never could ascertain what "the amount was—not even the probable amount." And then he goes on further—"I never could fancy that our indebtedness was of such a nature "that it could materially affect the Bank;" and then later on he says that Mr Wright's position was the same. He says that Mr Wright "knew we were in "difficulties; but he had no earthly idea, I am pretty confident, about the "extent of them consequent on Mr Scott's mode of doing business." And he says also—"So far as I am concerned, I did not know; and I do not "think Mr Wright could have known either, for we had several conversations "on the point;" and he explains how both of them frequently asked questions at Mr Scott, and were unable to get information. I suppose you will not doubt that this evidence, which was given by Mr Paul, of the position of matters down to 1876 is to be believed; and it just comes to this, that Mr Paul's state of mind may be taken as a correct reflex of the state of mind of Mr Wright also; that both of them knew that there was a debt due to the Bank by the firm, but that neither of them had any idea that it was of such an extent as materially to affect the position of the Bank. Both of them knew there was a debt, but both were ignorant as to the amount of it, and it was in that state of mind that Mr Wright consented to accept office.

Now, gentlemen, the next and material question is, whether it is true, upon the evidence and the productions, that Mr Wright, being on the board, took advantage of his position in order to obtain money from the Bank. I think I have already shown you that he himself got nothing, and I am now going to show you that his firm got nothing except moneys which can be properly accounted for, and which came entirely through Mr Scott. Gentlemen, I have already told you that, according to Mr Muir's evidence, the account of the partners of this firm altogether, including Mr Scott's £120,000, was £393,000 in 1875; and in June 1878 the sum due was £485,000—showing a rise of £90,000. But in this rise of £90,000, you will bear in mind we have both principal and interest. The account amounts to close on £400.000 in 1875, which would represent at 5 per cent.—you can make the calculation yourselves—to about £20.000 of interest accruing on that balance, so that for the three years together it would be about £60,000, leaving £30,000 on the account of all the partners as the excess. But it will be a fairer test to see whether the account was materially increased by overdrafts or advances; and I will ask your attention to some other figures which were given by Mr Muir with respect to the account proper of the firm. Now, gentlemen, Mr Muir's statement on the subject is that the credits and the overdrafts, including the £120,000, and some other bills discounted, and so on, came in 1875 to £217,707, and that in 1878 this sum was £334,000, showing a rise between 1875 and 1878 of about £117,000. Now, gentlemen, I ask you to attend for a moment while I endeavour to explain from Mr Muir's evidence how that arose. In the first place, I take credit for the interest which was always running, as you will observe, upon this balance of £217,000, and which again at 5 per cent. would give close upon £11,000 a year, or in three years about £33,000. I thus put down £33,000 for interest; and then, gentlemen, you will remember that in 1878 there were placed to the debit of Wright & Co. two sums—the one of £32,000 and the other of £46,000, as to which I desire to make some explanations. Gentlemen, the debit of £32,000 arose through the transactions of Mr Glen Walker under the letter which is dated 2d August 1876. That letter was written in the name of Innes Wright & Co. by Mr William Scott.

The LORD JUSTICE-CLERK—That is, the matter of the marginal credits, is it not?

Mr GUTHRIE SMITH—Yes, my Lord. I wish to remind you, gentlemen, of the terms of that letter, and shall read it to you. It runs as follows:—

"R. S. Stronach, Esq. Glasgow, 2d August 1876.

"Dear Sir,—Referring to the letter addressed to you by the writer on 12th "ultimo, we now beg to apply for marginal credits, as undernoted, for one hun- "dred thousand pounds (£100,000), to be drawn by Messrs Glen Walker & Com- "pany of Melbourne, the partners of which are William Glen Walker, William "Geddes Borron, and Ferdinand Spiro. In security for same, we engage to hold "for or lodge with you the documents for wool and other produce sent to us by "Messrs G. W. & Co. as received (stipulating that the same represents an excess "of 20 per cent. over the amounts drawn), or we shall pay you cash to the amount "of your acceptances. We beg to enclose copy of letter received from W. G. "Walker, Esq., requesting the credits now applied for, and who purposes leaving "this for Melbourne in a few weeks, for the purpose of giving the business his per- "sonal attention.—We remain, &c.

"JOHN INNES WRIGHT & CO.

"Marginal credits at 4 or 6 m/s d, payable in London. In force for one year. In twenty bills for £5000 each, and in triplicate."

Now, gentlemen, you will see that that letter is written by Mr William Scott, in the name of Innes Wright & Co., on behalf of Glen Walker & Co. It was a perfectly legitimate and proper banking transaction on the face of it —the substance of it being that this credit of £100,000 was to be used by Glen Walker in the purchase of wool and other produce from Sydney, and being sent home to this country, the proceeds were to be paid into the Bank when realised by Mr Scott on behalf of Innes Wright & Co. Such was the transaction; but, gentlemen, Mr Glen Walker explained that after he proceeded to operate upon this credit, he found that it was necessary to apply a large part of it in discharge of obligations incurred on behalf of the Bank itself. He is asked (p. 357, letter F, see p. 240)—"Was that arrangement acted upon?" His answer is—"It was partly acted upon and partly not. I found that the "credits were of no use to me; but I required some money for the purpose "of the Bank in connection with those land purchases which I had orders to "buy, and I used a portion of the credits for that purpose, and I sent the "bulk of them home. I used a few thousand pounds—I think £7000, if I "remember right—in sending home produce; but I could draw from the "colony on my own credit quite as well as using the Bank's credits, and "consequently I returned them." So you see, gentlemen, that Mr Glen,

Walker, the recipient of these drafts, himself explained that no part of this credit was applied to the purpose originally contemplated, except to the extent of £7000 in the purchase of produce. That produce was bought and sent, not to the Glasgow firm at all, but to the London firm of Wright & Co., for the purpose of realisation, and was in course of realisation when the Bank stopped. I don't think that is said in the evidence, but such is the fact. Then as to how the rest of that credit was applied. Mr Walker says that of the £100,000, £40,000 were sent back, and £3000 were not presented for acceptance, leaving £57,000 as the amount of the credit which the Bank had given. Of this £57,000, £17,000 he explains was expended by him in purchasing and improving land which was held for the Bank; and, consequently, Wright & Co. got none of that, and cannot be accountable for that. That reduces the sum of £57,000 down to £40,000. Then Mr Morris stated that £25,000 was paid into the Bank—that £25,000 having been obtained by Wright & Co. upon a wool lien credit for £35,000, which had been shipped by Mr Glen Walker from Australia. And thus you see, gentlemen, that instead of being debited with this £32,000, we are really not indebted on that sum at all—at all events, not beyond the £7000 representing the produce which was consigned to our London house, and which was in course of realisation at the time the Bank failed. The reason of the difference of the £25,000 produced and paid in by Wright & Co., and the £35,000 spent by Glen Walker for wool, was explained by Mr Walker as due to wool being short from the effects of the severe drought in Australia, which killed off so many millions of sheep.

The LORD JUSTICE-CLERK—Is there any balance remaining over all that?

Mr GUTHRIE SMITH—None but the £7000 of produce which was in course of realisation. We could not have paid the money in until the goods were realised.

I come to the next item, the item of £46,000, which was entered also to our debit in the year 1878, and which arose in this way. This £100,000 is explained by Mr Morris.

The LORD JUSTICE-CLERK—Is this Scott's defalcation.

Mr GUTHRIE SMITH—Yes, my Lord.

The LORD JUSTICE-CLERK—That was brought out very clearly.

Mr GUTHRIE SMITH—It was, my Lord. This £100,000 of bills, drawn by Glen Walker & Co. and accepted by the Bank, were handed over to Wright & Co., or rather William Scott, for the purpose of being discounted. Of course they were given to Wright & Co. simply in the position of bill-brokers, and it became the duty of William Scott to send them to his brother in London for the purpose of being discounted. They were so sent and so discounted, and there was a defalcation on the part of William Scott, which is now stated at the sum of £46,000. I am not here to justify that defalcation; far from it. I think it is a serious matter for Mr Scott; but I think that, from the beginning to the end of the evidence, there is not a single item of proof that Mr Wright had anything to do with that matter at all. He may be civilly responsible for his partner Scott, but surely you will not hold him criminally liable for the acts of his partner, done without his knowledge or concurrence? This is made manifest, not only by Mr Morris' evidence, but also by the evidence of Mr Inglis, who says that he called upon Mr Scott for a settlement. He had an interview, in his absence, with Mr Wright, who uniformly stated that these matters were all managed by Mr Scott. That is confirmed by Mr Paul, and may be taken as a fact in the case—that with these matters Mr Wright had no concern whatever, and was not responsible for this defalcation.

The LORD JUSTICE-CLERK—As I understand it, this was not for the benefit of Wright & Co. at all. Scott acted as an attorney or the hand of the Bank in discounting the Bank's own bills.

Mr Guthrie Smith—That is so, and that being the real position of the matter, in ascertaining the relations between Mr Wright and the Bank I think I am entitled to say that it was wrong to place to his debit this large sum of £46,000. I have accounted for the £32,000, the wool lien credit, and if you add to that sum the sum of £33,000 of interest, you will see that all through from 1875 down to 1878, the accounts of Mr Wright and Wright and Co., so far from increasing, were really in course of being diminished.

I think I have now demonstrated that he entered the Bank in ignorance of its position, and to serve no purpose of his own. The result shows it. He got no benefit from the Bank, and he needed no benefit from it.

The next question with which I have to deal, is whether, being in the Bank, having gone into the Bank in ignorance of its position, anything occurred at the board to lead him to suspect it was an insolvent concern. The Lord Advocate asked you how did he come to be there at all? and the theory his Lordship suggested was this:—There being a vacancy, and the Bank having got into that insolvent state, it was necessary to avoid inquiry. There was a vacancy in the directorate, and Mr Wright was elected as a person not likely to insist upon inquiry, and therefore was offered the seat. If it had been shown that Mr Wright was a party to this arrangement, there might have been something in the theory of the Lord Advocate; but, according to his Lordship's own showing—Mr Wright having no knowledge that this was the object—he never succeeded in getting any information as to the position in which the Bank stood. Let me direct your attention, gentlemen, to the abstract of the accounts of 1876. Can you find from the beginning to the end of it anything to show that Mr Wright knew the position of the Bank during the first year that he entered it from July 1875? I pass over the first meetings of the board held during the autumn of that year—there were only four or five altogether. The first thing which the Lord Advocate founded upon as bringing knowledge home to us all, was the letter dated 28th December 1875, which was written by Mr Robert Stronach to the directors when he was appointed to the office of manager. That letter is certainly worthy of your consideration; but you will remember that it is so expressed as not necessarily to give any information to Mr Wright, who was an entire stranger to the administration. It speaks of certain accounts which were of an unsatisfactory character, which had been operated upon since his brother discontinued personally to manage the Bank. Therefore the effect of the letter upon a stranger was to tell him, that since November 1874 there had been certain operations which were not quite satisfactory, but "we are all hopeful," said the writer, "the advances may eventuate without loss." Now plainly, gentlemen, a stranger hearing that letter for the first time would naturally say—This is a matter which was entered on by my colleagues before I became a member of the board; I don't know anything of it; I must leave it to them. More particularly when you find that, at a meeting a fortnight before this, a report was presented to the assembled board, and the half-yearly trial balance-sheet at the head office and branches, made up to December, was submitted, showing a net profit to the amount of £76,393, 13s. 4d., or a little over 15½ per cent. per annum on the paid-up capital. Gentlemen, that trial balance-sheet is presented and laid on the table of the board, made up by the proper officer of the Bank—an officer whom a director was entitled, nay, bound, to trust; because it is no part of a director's duty to go and count the money in the till or examine the books. He is merely a member of an advising board. The affairs are managed by its paid officials, and the directors are there to control them; but it would be impossible to get directors to manage those great institutions unless on the condition that they were to place due reliance on the public and paid officials. So when this balance is presented to Mr Wright and the other directors on 16th December 1875, showing that the Bank was then doing a business of about £150,000 a year of profit, allowing a profit of 15¼ per cent., do you not see that, reading that letter that followed in December, he would naturally conclude that the accounts there referred to, though unsatisfactory, were not of the serious kind which afterwards they turned out to be. Therefore, naturally, Mr Wright left these matters to the determination of his colleagues, who had been in office since 1870. But, then, the Lord Advocate says that if this letter did not supply full information, it was enough, at all events, to arouse suspicion. Gentlemen, in this case, as has been frequently observed before, the mere circumstance that that letter was calculated to arouse suspicion, and that there was a failure to show requisite alacrity to make investigation, is not enough to convict these gentlemen—at all events, to convict Mr Wright. Negligence, imprudence, will never warrant a jury in convicting a man of deliberate fraud. The question is knowledge; and my observation upon that letter is this, that it was not of itself sufficient to inform Mr Wright of the accounts in question, nor indeed to suggest to him that anything else should be done than that the letter should be left to the determination of his colleagues, who had been in the board from 1870. Perhaps one man in five hundred, not knowing what has since happened, would have insisted on some inquiry being made; but because Mr Wright did not show the same diligence in that matter, that is no reason why a verdict of fraud should be returned.

Now, the Lord Advocate went on to say that if this letter were not enough, there were other documents brought up sufficient to inform the directors as to the position of these three accounts of which you have heard so much—Morton & Co.'s, Smith, Fleming, & Co.'s, and J. N. Fleming's. As to the whole of these accounts, the first important entry, subsequent to the time when Mr Wright joined, is in June 1876, and is in these terms:—" The committee " appointed, February 18, 1875, to look into the accounts of Smith, Flem- " ing, & Co., and J. N. Fleming & Co., reported that they had seen that " these accounts had been put into shape." Mr Leresche explained in his evidence (p. 212, letter E) that it was not till January 1876 that Morton's account was mentioned at all, and it was then remitted to a committee. It appears it was again mentioned in January 1877, and then Morton does not appear again, as far as the minute book is concerned, until 14th March 1878, when the report of a committee previously appointed was given in. Now, that is the case as regards Morton's account. Then as regards Smith, Fleming, & Co.'s account, and J. Nicol Fleming's account, it appears that although these were the subjects of investigation by the committee appointed on 18th February 1875, before Mr Wright joined at all, that committee did not report till 1st June 1876; and thus it appears that, although these accounts were before committees of the board, Mr Wright, not being a member of these committees, had no means of judging of their nature and extent. In fact, the existence of these committees was enough to withdraw them from his consideration. On any occasion on which Morton's name was mentioned it was in connection with other matters, as, for instance, the one as to which Mr Leresche stated in his evidence (p. 247):—" A letter from James Morton " and Co., and two letters from Mr W. Glen Walker, dated respectively " Glasgow, the 16th and 14th instant, in regard to the drawing of credits in " lieu of those now drawn by Messrs Holmes, White, & Co., and others, and " one of the latter as to the acquisition of certain pastoral properties, were " brought under the notice of the board, and after full consideration, the " board came to the resolution that it was advisable to adopt generally the " suggestions contained in these letters."

Now, gentlemen, that is all that happened before the report was issued in June 1876. As to Morton, throughout that year there is no mention at all. As to Smith, Fleming, & Co., all that was before the board is this report in June, immediately before the report is issued to the shareholders in June, from the committee appointed on 18th February 1875, that the accounts had been put into shape; and I ask you whether, from these documents, you are at liberty to assume that Mr Wright was duly informed of the state of those accounts. Is it not more likely and more consistent with the truth that he, coming into that board as a stranger, these being matters which had been entered on before he became a member at all, he remained in utter ignorance of the position of those accounts, and of the extent of the indebtedness of the Bank? If that is so, can you really affirm, upon that evidence, that this abstract of 1876 was issued in the knowledge of all the mistakes, all the inaccuracies founded on by the Crown? Why, one of them is this, that they understate the assets by the sum of £973,700. That sum had been hidden away in the private cash book, No. 6, in 1873. How could Mr Wright have found out anything of that £973,000? Assuming, as I am doing for the sake of argument—what of course is not admitted,—that it was an improper transaction so to deal with that £973,000 in 1873, how can you convict Mr Wright, who had recently joined the board, of any knowledge of that matter; and how, therefore, can you say that he can be responsible for issuing that report with a fraudulent knowledge of that fact? And so with the other accounts referred to.

Now, gentlemen, if this is so as regards 1876, I think there is nothing in the evidence to show that Mr Wright's mind was ever better informed as to the position of matters either in 1877 or 1878. I have searched all through this minute book and all through the evidence for any scrap of evidence which could be said to be of a criminatory kind, but I can find none. There are committees appointed to expiscate particular matters, but Mr Wright is not a member. Mr Hunter holds consultations with some members of the board, but never with Mr Wright. Mr Morton and he seem to be entire strangers. No one is brought forward to say that Mr Wright ever gave false information, or any information at all as to the state of the Bank. There is nothing that I can see, from beginning to end, connecting Mr Wright in any way with the administration beyond this, that he attended directors' meetings; and you are asked to say, upon the most shadowy evidence, that being in the board-room, and having a seat at the board, he had there the means of acquiring information which he failed to use.

Gentlemen, in a serious charge of this kind, that, in my humble opinion, is not sufficient. It is insufficient to convict him of guilty knowledge at all. I think, if you will recollect the account which Mr Jamieson gave you of the meeting with Mr Wright and Mr Stewart on the 28th September 1878, you will not be astonished to find that these two gentlemen were as much surprised as any one at the position of matters. The ignorance they were then in of the disaster that was about to occur may have been due to a great extent to their remissness and their own negligence of duty, but it was not due to any fraud. It certainly cannot be alleged against Mr Wright that there was any intention to commit the serious crime that is here led to his charge. All through life his character has been entirely without reproach; and therefore, gentlemen, without fatiguing you further at this late hour, I confidently submit that, so far as Mr Wright is concerned, the evidence wholly fails.

The LORD JUSTICE-CLERK (addressing the jury) said—We shall meet to-morrow at half-past ten; but I think it right to tell you that, after hearing the Dean of Faculty, we propose to adjourn till Friday morning, in order that you may come fresh to the consideration of the case, and also in order that I may have, what I much need, a little time to methodise the voluminous evidence and the elaborate pleadings which you have heard in this case.

Tenth Day.—Thursday, January 30, 1879.

THE DEAN OF FACULTY'S ADDRESS FOR MR STRONACH.

My Lords, Gentlemen of the Jury,—I have the misfortune here to address you in the last place; and I suffer from the great disadvantage of speaking to men whose minds are already preoccupied, and whose attention has been strained by this long and somewhat wearisome investigation. In asking you to give me your attention for a little longer, I do so upon this ground—I promise to condense my observations into as short a compass as the nature of the subject will permit of; and I will endeavour to aid you in arriving at a comprehension of these complicated accounts. Furthermore, I have a duty here to discharge in behalf of the gentleman for whom I appear, the late manager of this Bank. And I think you will consider yourselves somewhat indebted to me if I aid you in the discharge of the duties which the law and constitution of the country have imposed upon you, in arriving at a satisfactory conclusion upon this evidence.

There were, as this indictment was first presented to us, three charges—First, the fabrication, which is a Latin word for making—the making of false balance-sheets, and the issuing or uttering of them with intent to defraud, whereby the public were defrauded. That is the first branch of the charge. The second charge was that certain of the accused were guilty of embezzlement; and the third charge was that they were all guilty of theft. We came here, gentlemen, to meet all these charges. We came here under the load of obloquy which necessarily lies upon every one whom a person occupying the high position which the public prosecutor must necessarily bear, when he charges them with such grievous offences as these. And the trial went on, and day after day passed, and witness after witness was examined, but the two main charges—those of embezzlement and theft—were heard nothing of; until at last, on the fifth day, we were told that these were withdrawn—withdrawn when they had served their purpose. Withdrawn they cannot be, gentlemen, without a verdict. The Lord Advocate has submitted them to the knowledge of an assize, and you must pronounce your verdict upon those charges which he says he has withdrawn. That verdict, of course, must be not guilty upon the second and third charges. But I complain most grievously of this. I complain most grievously that, by the exhibition of such charges as these against the prisoners at the bar, they not merely have been subjected to the needless misery of three months' imprisonment, but they have suffered this greatest of all inconveniences and disadvantages and misfortunes—that by their imprisonment they have been rendered incapable of giving to their counsel and their advisers that assistance in the understanding of these accounts, in order to meet the charge that has been persisted in, which would have been valuable for them now. We, who were strangers to these accounts, have been obliged to grope in the dark. Had these men been at liberty, we would have had their assistance in getting up this case. We have had no advantage of that sort—no aid whatever. If a doubt occurred, we had to send a long distance to a prison to clear it up. We had to put questions to prisoners who had no books to refer to. We come here with our hands tied, not knowing really and truly what was the case to be made against us—not knowing, until we heard from the accountants for the Crown, what were the figures which made up the misstatements of which they accuse us. Gentlemen, I say I think I have good ground of complaint here; and if we have failed in satisfying you as to the entire innocence of these men of all intent to defraud in what they did, I beg you will make allowance for the disadvantages under which we labour, in having been thus kept in the dark by this needless imprisonment of the accused.

I will endeavour to explain the case as distinctly and clearly as I can. I will face the case for the Crown by taking one of their charges. I will take it to pieces; I will take each head of it, and I will show you that what was done here may have been upon a bad system, but that it was a system consistently carried out during the time for which we have its history. Nothing new was inaugurated by the accused at the bar, and there was certainly no intention to defraud.

But, gentlemen, before I deal with the part of the case which has already been so admirably dealt with by my friend Mr Balfour, and whose observations upon that point I mean merely to supplement,—before dealing with that part of the case which raises general questions, I must say a word on behalf of the person for whom I appear—Mr Stronach. He was manager of the bank, and, along with the other gentlemen at the bar, he is now charged with a criminal offence. I must say, at the outset, that a more melancholy scene than this I have never witnessed, even in this Court. I have seen many sad scenes here, but a more melancholy scene than that now before us I have never witnessed—of men who had stood on a pedestal among their fellows, men who had been merchant princes, men who had engaged in enterprises worthy of the best days of the English commercial world, men against whom the wheel of fortune, in one or two cases, has turned—these men are now accused, for no end of their own, of knowingly falsifying a balance-sheet. Remember, gentlemen, that the key-note of all this investigation is this—you have it in the first page of the indictment in great big print—"with intent to defraud." It is of no consequence in the world that this sheet be proved perfectly false or untrue. Unless you go further, and hold it to be proved as matter of positive evidence that there was intent to defraud, there is no crime, and you cannot convict on this indictment. I beg you to bear that in mind in listening to the explanation I am going to give to you upon the specific charges which the Crown has stated, with this view, that if the explanation I give is one consistent with entire innocence, although proceeding upon a bad system, then that charge of intent to defraud is not proved.

Well, Mr Stronach is here put at the bar, along with these other men, as manager. He was a man whose history has been traced by little incidental narratives that we have got from the witnesses. His brother had been manager of the Bank. Apparently he seems to have been a man of great energy and great ability. He had conducted the business of the Bank from the period of Mr Salmond's resignation down to the year 1875. His brother Robert was at that time a clerk in the Bank. He states in his declaration that he is 50 years of age, married, and has three children. Robert was a clerk in the Bank when his brother's illness came on—an illness which we see by his letters was brought on by the painful, restless anxieties, consequent upon the condition of two or three accounts. He complains in his letters of want of sleep, of incapacity of attention. Although desirous of doing all he can on behalf of this institution, he breaks entirely down, and retires. Robert is asked to take his place. Well, the brother at that time occupies a subordinate position as a clerk. He is not cashier, accountant, or anything; and apparently not from love of office, but from fraternal affection, he is induced to become, during 1875, assistant-manager. And then he becomes acquainted with the position of certain of the accounts, and more especially with these great accounts which have been so often referred to. In the month of December 1875, Alexander, his brother, resigns, and Robert is offered the place of manager. Well, now, what is it he does? We have the account of his hesitation, of his reluctance, of his repugnance, one would say, to this offer told us by Mr Walker, with whom he consulted at the time. Mr Walker tells us that he had the very greatest repugnance to the office, that he did not see his way to accept an office that could produce endless anxieties and impose intolerable burdens; but at last, through the entreaties of some, and the remonstrances of others, he is induced to do it—first getting a promise from Morton that he will reduce his account by the payment of £400,000. That would reduce one of the largest accounts, and take away one of the greatest difficulties in his path. But then, he is not certain, after all; and he writes a letter to the directors in answer to their offer. There were two letters written. The first letter we do not know the contents of. The second letter we have preserved, and find in the minute book of the directors. And in that second letter, which has been so often read to you, he says, you will remember,—Before I accept this office, I request your particular attention to certain accounts which are of an unsatisfactory nature. I wish you to say whether or not you approve of the policy which ended in the contraction of these accounts. I want an explanation on this subject, as I cannot proceed to the acceptance of the office unless there be some clear understanding come to between us as to my responsibilty in regard to these things. That, gentlemen, is the paraphrase I put upon that "as to my responsibilities in regard to these "accounts." Now, this is laid before the directors, and it came upon them with surprise. They have recorded in their minutes that the matters to which Mr Stronach called their attention were matters entirely novel to them. They had not been brought before them by the late manager. Gentlemen, that is a statement which, being put upon record then and there, and which, having all the minutes before us, we can believe. It does not appear from any of the prior minutes that these things had been brought before the directors prior to this period of December 1875, in such a way as to arouse their attention, or to cause them to reflect, or to lead them to take positive and instant action in order to obtain relief. They say, "We did not know anything about these matters." Well, gentlemen, they approve of the letter of Mr Stronach, and they accept him upon the conditions which he has expressed, and which conditions are these—I cannot be responsible for these old accounts of Morton & Co., Smith, Fleming, & Co., J. Nicol Fleming, and Innes Wright & Co.; I am not to have anything to do with them; I will do my best to get you out of the difficulties that surround you; but, so far as I am concerned, remember this, that I had nothing to do with the policy under which they were contracted. I had nothing to do with that policy, or the action to be taken with regard to these men. That is approved of. A committee is appointed to help Mr Stronach. Now, gentlemen, what follows reminds me just of one of those cases where a man is trying to disengage himself from embarrassments from which he has no power to obtain relief. A man gets entangled in a wheel of machinery, and he is hurried on and on, and he cannot wriggle himself out of it. Robert Stronach, during the year 1876, we see, had to endure, as his daily portion, ceaseless anxieties. He was constantly bringing the matter up before the directors, and the directors—unhappy men, who were the heirs to this most doleful inheritance of bad accounts—had trouble enough themselves.

Now, I shall show you immediately what was done in consequence of these remonstrances of Mr Stronach—what they tried to do. And this I will only say, on behalf of these directors, that it is easy for people now to say—people who see no difficulties whatever in very trying circumstances, when the circumstances are such as they never had experience of—it is easy for people now to say what these directors should have done—put a match to the whole concern and blown it up in the year 1876. It is very easy to say that now. It might have been better, on the whole, than to attempt to carry on this concern, which was so deeply involved by these advances to the four debtors. They did their best, these directors; but what I am anxious about at present, gentlemen, is to show you how persistent Mr Stronach was in keeping before the directors the conditions on which he accepted office; and how also—I am bound to say that on behalf of these directors—how they did their best to aid him as far as they possibly could. On the 22d June 1876—that is, about six months after his appointment—there is a meeting of directors, at which "It was resolved to appoint Messrs Taylor and Potter a committee to examine "into certain old accounts of the Bank, and to assist the manager in arranging "these under one general heading, with full powers." Mr Leresche informs us that that committee was obtained in consequence of the entreaties and remonstrances of Mr Stronach. This is what Mr Leresche says:—(see p. 146) "(Q.) Do you remember the manager saying anything while you were present "on that occasion to the effect that he wished those old accounts looked into? "(A.) I do remember now. I would write this in probably just at the time "when I was at the meeting. I do not recollect anything more that took "place on that occasion. The manager was desirous that certain old accounts "of the Bank should be looked into. (Q.) It was on the suggestion of the "manager that the committee was appointed? (A.) Yes. (Q.) Was any 'specification given of the accounts referred to, or were they spoken of in "that general way? (A.) Just in a general way." They did not require any further specification of them. These unhappy gentlemen knew perfectly well what accounts they were, and they required no specification of them. That is in the month of June 1876. Whether that committee met or not we do not know. Mr Leresche could not tell us, because, as "the secretary, it was "no part of his duty to attend the committee meetings." But once more, these old accounts are referred to in that minute of the 17th August 1876 (pages 115 and 116), which was in reference to the acquisition of pastural properties in Australia. The board ordered these properties to be purchased, and they say, "While arriving at this resolution, the board were fully sensible "of the undesirableness of such investments as the purchases proposed in the "letters; but having in view the position of certain old accounts, and looking "to the whole circumstances, and particularly to the fact that the contem- "plated arrangements for the working of the credits are largely part of transac- "tions in existence for many years, and previously brought under considera- "tion of the board by the present manager, the board deemed it expedient "to come to their present decision, as referred to in minute of 30th Decem- "ber 1875."

Lord CRAIGHILL—What is the date of that minute?

The DEAN OF FACULTY—17th August 1876. You see he is at them in August. August, September, October, and November pass on. Once more, on the 15th November 1877 (p. 131), Mr Stronach comes before the directors. It was then resolved that "a committee of the whole board should sit "periodically to consider the position of the various accounts of the Bank. "The Committee of Inquiry above mentioned will meet not later than four "months from this date." Now, I think the Lord Advocate was unfair to the directors in his comment upon that minute. As it appears in the agenda book, it would seem as if Mr Taylor, one of the directors, had recommended that this committee should meet not sooner than four months from that date. If the agenda book can be so read, that is a blunder of Mr Leresche's in taking it down; and the Lord Advocate, in assimilating it to the practice of a place with which he is familiar—that a bill be read a second time this day six months—seemed to insinuate that the directors intended to give the go-by altogether to the entreaties of Mr Stronach that they should take up these old accounts. This minute, however, puts the matter right. This is the thing revised by the board. It is, "not later than four months,"—apparently, I suppose, on this ground—to give time to have the whole accounts in such a condition that the board could consider them; and perhaps to give time for the return of certain dividends or investments, or the produce of cargoes then on the way. We don't know the reason for this postponement. No doubt it had a reason. I suggest that as a probable reason. But the importance of the matter to me is this—that this never ceases to be a subject upon which the attention of the board is requested by the manager. That is on the 15th November. Mr Leresche says [p. 85 E.], that he (Mr Stronach) wished that a committee of the whole board should sit periodically to consider the various accounts of the bank. Then there is the question, "Did you hear what passed on that suggestion?" and the reply is, "Yes. It was agreed to, and "I then entered this resolution;" and then he tells us how the matter was agreed to. What was to be done in those four months?—those securities were to be looked into. Well then, once more, on the 14th March 1878, "it "was agreed that Messrs Stewart, Potter, and Salmond be appointed a com-"mittee, along with the manager, to examine the advance accounts at the "head office weekly, and to deal in particular with account of James Morton "and Co." That is in March 1878. We are now approaching the beginning of the end. That committee meets apparently, but the whole concern is now involved in hopeless entanglement. Various desperate efforts are made to keep the ship from sinking, but all in vain. The times are bad. Trade is depressed. People are failing all round. Famines in foreign countries deprives their best customers of *their* best customers. Ready money cannot be got; the investments of the bank are locked up in unrealisable property, which at some future time, not far distant, may pay off every penny of the debt of this Bank. Well, then, down to March 1878, we see this first,—that Mr Stronach consistently kept before his employers, his masters, the condition upon which he accepted office—the condition, namely, that they were to look into these accounts—the condition that there should be, if possible, a restriction of those accounts; and the directors recognised their duty in this respect, for they met and appointed committees. No minutes have been preserved of those meetings, and some of them seem to have met without any practical effect; nothing can be known of them; but they knew their duty. Mr Stronach, during the whole of this period,—What does he do? Was he taking it upon himself to advance money to anybody? Was he responsible for one single sixpence of the debt due by the four firms to whom I have referred? Now, keep this in view. It applies not merely to Mr Stronach, but to a number of these men at the bar. Every penny of Morton's debt—the great debt to this Bank, upwards of two millions—was incurred years and years before. A great part of Smith, Fleming, & Co.'s debt—upwards of one million, or nine-tenths of it,—John Fleming tells us, and Mr Morison or the accountant, or some other person, confirmed it, was incurred years and years before. Not one penny was advanced to Smith, Fleming, & Co. from 1st January 1876 down to the close of the Bank in October 1878, except upon the security of cargoes on the way. Don't you remember the ships, the names of which I read out to you from the letters of Smith and Fleming asking for advances? Not one single penny was advanced to them except upon the security of the produce contained in vessels on the way, or to retire some old liability upon which the Bank were already debtors. Nicol Fleming stood in the same position. Nicol Fleming's case was treated by Robert Stronach in a very clear and distinct way, showing that there was to be no doubt about his matters. Robert Stronach, as soon as he enters upon the business of manager, employs Mr Hunter, who seems to have the respect and esteem of all Glasgow, and from the way in which he gave his evidence, he seems to deserve it. Mr Hunter was asked, as a personal friend of Robert Stronach, to look into this man Nicol Fleming's account, and the first thing he tells Robert Stronach is, "That is a bad account. Have nothing to do with him. The speculations "into which he is entering in India are such that I could not advise you that "he is a person to whom advances ought to be made." And, accordingly, Robert so acted. The moment he got the advice, Nicol Fleming is put under liquidation, which is still going on, and there is still a quantity of property of Nicol Fleming's to be realised.

But this conduct on the part of Mr Stronach, of not merely asking the directors to meet, but asking them by some means or other to get rid of this intolerable burden, by compelling those men to restrict their adventures and to realise some of their property, if they had any, as something towards the liquidation of their debt, this conduct of his was strictly carried out in his own dealings when he had to deal with people who asked money from him. For example, even when he was assistant-manager, he indicated the path he was going to tread by the following letter, written on the 22d January 1875, and addressed to Mr John Fleming (p. 60 of panel's print):—

"In answer to your private note of yesterday, and accompanying official, apply-" ing for an extension of part of the Bombay Saw Mill Company's credit, 31/38, for " £30,000, to the extent of one-third, under the same terms and conditions as be-" fore, I regret that this application did not reach me in time for consideration at " yesterday's board meeting."

Now, this is the sentence to which I particularly want your attention :—

"And as I cannot, on my own individual responsibility, grant the extension your " friends ask, it will, I fear, require to remain over for another week. In the mean-" time, please let me know if you have any advice that this *is* to be done. It will " be well for you to understand that all matters of this description MUST—

and MUST is double underlined—

" MUST go before the board in future."

Now that letter, as to the footing upon which all applications for money are to be treated, was not merely to be applied to Smith, Fleming, & Co. ; it was applied to every one of those debtors who were in arrears. Mr Paul, a member of the firm of Innes Wright & Co., told us the history of that unfortunate concern, in which Mr Wright, one of the accused at the bar, puts in the whole capital that was to carry it on, and in which the financing business is worked by a man of the name of Scott, his partner, and in which Mr Paul takes one portion of the business—the working portion—but knows nothing of the finance. He was, however, made the go-between between Stronach, the manager, and Scott, the partner, when the latter wanted money. When Scott could not face the manager himself he sent Mr Paul, and he found Mr Stronach on all these occasions very reluctant to deal with him, and "whenever," said Mr Paul, "I got any money from him it was with " a grudge, and with demands for additional security, and only after great " delay."

Therefore, gentlemen, the remark which the Lord Advocate made the other day,—one of the very few unfair remarks he made in a very fair speech,—to this effect, "Oh! Mr Stronach was very strict with a poor fellow away in the " country who needed accommodation at some of the branch banks, with re-" gard to any of these great people in Glasgow he was quite the reverse. " Money flowed out in an uninterrupted current in their favour, though some " poor fellow away in the country was treated very differently,"—gentlemen, that insinuation, that sneer is undeserved. It is difficult to answer a sneer, but I do say that it is totally undeserved so far as can be judged from the evidence. Mr Paul and Mr Fleming, the only two men brought into direct contact with Mr Stronach, tells you how difficult it was to obtain money from him, and that it was only after repeated promises—promises which very often the event belied—and only on additional security, that he gave him anything. It was only then that they got it. The promises were good and were believed; and it was only then that Innes Wright & Co. got additional advantages. I am dwelling upon this in order to show you how very little of individual action in regard to the contraction of these great debts, upon which the Lord Advocate dwelt so much, can be traced to Mr Stronach. I have shown you from the very first that he protested, and he goes on protesting—begs for action on the part of his masters, which he himself could not take. He is their servant, and must do their bidding. But he never ceases to lay the matter before them, and they never refuse to hear him. They do what they can in the different circumstances in which they are placed. They appoint committees to investigate; but, alas! investigation only showed how deplorable was the condition to which the Bank had come in some respects unless the property of these debtors turned out as they themselves expected.

In the year 1877 the Bank entered into a number of investments which have been denounced by the Crown--I cannot understand why they were imported into this case, unless for the purpose of aiding the charge of fraud —viz., the purchases of property in New Zealand and Australia. Gentlemen, this may or may not have been good banking. I believe the business of a bank consists, not in lending out money on heritable security, or in buying houses, or in investing it in other kind of property where the return, though certain, is small, and where the capital cannot be got immediately. A banker's business is to lend upon bills. He lends upon bills, chiefly upon personal credit, he himself trusting to his own knowledge of the circumstances of his customers. But banks must often invest in other properties than in discounting bills on the credit of the people with whom they deal, and they invest in heritable property; and if the return on heritable property is more than the interest which is paid to their depositors, of course they make a profit, and that is part of the source from which dividend is paid.

Now, there was an investment made in the year 1877 by the Bank in Australian and New Zealand property, and that property is still theirs, and it is a property the value of which we have heard nothing from the Crown. They have not put any person into the box to show that it was worthless, and would never make any return. But their has been evidence laid before you by four or five witnesses that that investment will in time, and if trade revives, be an investment which will double the money paid for it—triple it according to Mr Glen Walker, or, at least, double it according to Mr Hunter.

But, gentlemen, I refer simply to this investment which the Crown has dwelt upon only for the reason that Mr Stronach had nothing in the world to do with it. That was an investment resolved upon by the board for reasons that seemed good to them. The reason may have been to endeavour on their part to recoup or get repayment of an old debt due to them, or it may have been for the purpose of investing surplus capital that they had no other means of dealing with. But be it the one or the other, the investments were made by the directors, who took this mode of making it. On the 26th of July 1877, Mr Stronach received a letter signed by "Henry Inglis, chairman," in the following terms :—

"Dear Sir,—As authorised by the meeting of directors held of this date, you will " be so good as instruct Messrs Potter and Stewart, two of our number, to purchase " freehold land in New Zealand on behalf of this Bank to the extent of £50,000."

Then on the 6th September 1877—

" It was considered advisable to authorise the committee to invest a further " sum of £150,000 in property in New Zealand or Australia. This investment, " in addition to the sums already authorised, will now, therefore, amount to about " £400,000, and this, in addition to the interest of about £100,000 already held, " completes an investment to about £500,000."

That is a meeting at which Mr Stronach was not present, and, as I said in the case of the first meeting, the instructions take the shape of a letter addressed to the manager by the chairman of directors.

Gentlemen, I am not saying that that investment was a bad investment. I could not say so consistently with the evidence. I say it was a good investment. I look to that as a source from which the unhappy shareholders of this unfortunate Bank may yet get a return for those calls that they are now making payment of. I believe that that property in new Zealand, of which men competent to speak, like Mr Walker and Mr Hunter, gave such glowing prospects, will double in value. I have not laid before you evidence upon that point, contenting myself with what incidentally came out. And my reason for not laying before you express evidence on that point is that it would have been evidence of opinion—evidence in anticipation of good times. There are three millions of money belonging to this Bank sunk in these properties in New Zealand and Australia. Double that value—triple, one witness says,—will be got for it—nine millions in all, leaving six millions of surplus, after paying every farthing of the advances that were made to Morton and Nicol Fleming, and in the purchases by the Bank themselves. I say that that was one of the best, most politic, soundest, and most judicious acts that these directors did at the time they did it; and so far from incurring condemnation and censure, it shows that they were men who, in the difficult circumstances in which they were placed, acted for the best.

My concern with this matter is simply to show you how I was nothing more than a servant, doing my best on behalf of this institution, doing my best by humble entreaty and persistent effort to get my masters to take action in this matter. I am not saying that they did not. Far be it from me to pour obloquy upon their heads, or bring against them any accusation at all. They were brethren in misfortune; but from the first to the last, from what we find in these recorded minutes, and from what we find in the action of Stronach in dealing with those customers who demanded new advances of money, his position was this—I won't give you a penny more until you give me additional security.

Now, it is exceedingly hard, gentlemen, that, after two and a-half years of a life which could not have been happy, during which the day's labours must have been followed by sleepless nights—no doubt it must have weighed down many of these men, no doubt they were not comfortable under it—it is very hard, I say, that after all, when no human effort could avail to save the coming doom, they should, while really attempting to save the concern, and to save the shareholders, be accused of a crime, that they should be accused of intent to defraud, and that they should be placed here at the bar of a criminal court. If they are guilty, it must be upon some technical ground that brings them within the sweep of the criminal law. It must be on a ground that is reconcilable to one's moral sense. It cannot be upon any ground that is acceptable to our judgment. They may be technically responsible; and men have been punished upon technical grounds.

But let us consider for a moment if there are any grounds in this case—any reasonable grounds—upon which you can arrive at the conclusion, not that these balance-sheets which are complained of are erroneous or false, but that they were made false and erroneous with the intention of defrauding.

That brings me to the second part of the observations I was going to make, and in regard to this I am going to deal with figures. I will endeavour to make it as plain as I possibly can, but as the object is one of the deepest importance, I have to ask your indulgence and your patience while I go over each one of these heads that you have in page 4 of this indictment (see p. 28.) I will take up each one of these, and I beg of you to listen to the explanation I have to make upon it.

Before I do so, however, I have something to say as to the authorship of these balance-sheets against which these specific charges are made. The gentlemen at the bar are accused of fabricating, which is simply a Latin word for making—making a false balance-sheet. Now, you have got the balance-sheets before you. We have got the balance-sheet, gentlemen, and we have got the abstract of accounts from which the balance-sheets were framed; and the first thing we find is this, that although there is a good deal of figuring and a good deal of writing on those balance-sheets and abstracts, there is not the scrape of a pen of any one of the men at the bar on these balance-sheets. The whole of the balance-sheet and the whole of this abstract is in the handwriting of Mr Morison, the accountant. Therefore, *prima facie*, the responsibility for these documents is a responsibility that one would attach to the man who evidently had written it out. You saw Mr Morison in the box, and he informed us of this—that he prepared the balance-sheets of 1876, of 1877, and of 1878. Of the balance-sheet of 1876 he had a very distinct recollection—a minute recollection. Of the preparation of the balance-sheet of 1877 he had no recollection. It was an entire blank—faded away into oblivion altogether. But of the balance-sheet of 1878, what does he say. He remembers all about it quite clearly. Now I must say it did excite my suspicion when I heard that man tell us in regard to the balance-sheet of 1877 that he could recollect nothing about it; that he could not comprehend for a moment what was the meaning of it. He remembered 1876, and then he remembered 1878. Well, it was curious he had forgot the intermediate year; but I found out the reason, and I shall tell you immediately what it was. There was discovered in the Bank a document which left unmistakable traces of Morison's action, and of its authorship, that he did not like; and, accordingly, that part of the examination of 1877 was treated most gingerly by the Crown—no questions put. He was allowed quietly, in his own mind as he thought, to retire from this Court, by simply saying, "I don't recollect any-" thing about it." But about the year 1876 he was quite distinct, and about that year he tells us that he made it up under the direction of Mr Potter and Mr Stronach. And he did give us a most extraordinary account of the mode in which the document was prepared. The Crown had come into the Court —and I was prepared to hear evidence to that effect—had come into the Court with a precognition, given by him, to the effect that he, Mr Morison, had taken in the correct thing in black ink to Potter and Stronach, and that he had retired from their presence with alterations made by them in red ink —the alterations being false, and made with a view to deceive. That was the story that came out in his first examination; he laid it off glibly to the Lord Advocate. Now, this did look uncommonly black. The right thing taken in, and the bad thing coming out after the interview with those fearful villains—Potter and Stronach. What a risk they ran! But the examination continues, and the first thing we find is this: He is compelled to admit at last that the red ink was upon the sheet when he took it in to Messrs Potter and Stronach,—put upon it by himself before ever he saw them; and then he is compelled to admit that the summation which is in black ink includes the red ink figures and the black too. The whole charge that he brought against these two men fell away. Here is a man paltering with the truth.

The Lord Justice-Clerk—On which of them is the summation in black ink?

The Dean of Faculty—That for 1878.

Now, gentlemen, we have here thus to deal with a man who gave such evidence upon such an important point as this—a point which had a most powerful and dramatic effect upon every one, even upon us, hardened as we are in regard to these matters. This charge then disappeared, and we began to look at the man—at this witness who was dealing in such charges, and bringing such charges against Mr Morton, Mr Potter, and Mr Stronach. You heard yesterday from Mr Balfour how incorrect this gentleman was—how slender was his attachment to truth in a great many particulars; nay, how strong was his attachment to error, if I may use a mild phrase, in regard to a number of things. I will not go over that again. But to show you how little the statements of this man can be relied upon, I must ask your particular attention to the balance-sheet or abstract for the year 1877, which is one of the most extraordinary documents I have ever looked at.

Now, gentlemen, in the sheet which I am looking at, which is No. 127 (see Appendix)—

The LORD JUSTICE-CLERK—I should be very glad if you could explain a little about this document—what the real effect of these writings is.

The DEAN OF FACULTY—Yes, my Lord. Every figure in pencil, in red ink and black ink, in the sheet, is Morison's, and the whole of the writing, except what is in print, is his too. Now, it is exceedingly interesting to study and trace the workings of a man's mind. One can do it perfectly well here the moment the key has been obtained. It is like unravelling writing in cypher, where, if you have got the key, it all comes out. Now, Morison was the accountant of this Bank, and it was his duty to prepare the balance-sheet and the abstract; and the first thing he requires to do is to get a note from all the officials—how much gold from Mr Turnbull; from the other clerks the result of their books; from Mr Miller, the inspector of branches, the particulars about them—and having collected his information, he sets to work to make up this abstract. He had, amongst other things, to set forth the amount of the City Bank notes in circulation. This is required by the law in the case of all chartered banks. In all chartered banks the amount of notes in circulation requires to be ascertained; but for the purpose also of this balance-sheet, it required to be obtained by him. Now, the true amount of the bank notes in circulation was £840,004. The true amount is brought out down here. [Shows.] But it did not suit him to put that in. What he does is this: The amount published is not £840,000, but £763,000—the amount in the printed abstract—so that there is a difference between the fact and what is stated in the abstract of £76,110. We are all agreed that that was the real amount of notes in circulation at that time.

The LORD JUSTICE-CLERK—I don't quite follow that, Mr Dean. I see £840,000, and then in red ink £714,000.

The DEAN OF FACULTY—If you look away to the right hand of the sheet, at the bottom, you have the figures £840,004.

The LORD JUSTICE-CLERK—That is under the word Circulation?

The DEAN OF FACULTY—No, it is still further away.

The LORD JUSTICE-CLERK—What was done with it?

The DEAN OF FACULTY—I am just going to trace that. I am just coming to that. Now, two inches further up, in the same column, he puts down £860,355, and underneath that he puts the correct sum of £840,000. He then takes the one from the other. He is experimenting all this time. The £860,355 was the circulation of the previous year. That was the meaning of it. He wants to see how it would look, deducting the one from the other, and brings out £20,355 less. But he is not satisfied with that. The next thing he does—

The LORD JUSTICE-CLERK—What do you say the £860,355 was?

The DEAN OF FACULTY—The circulation for the previous year.

Mr BALFOUR—There are the words "last year."

The DEAN OF FACULTY—Yes; your Lordship will see that from the indictment. Well, now, he is not pleased with that experiment, which brings out the balance of £20,000. The next thing he does is this: he thinks he will compare the years 1874, 1875, and 1876 together, and see how that will do; and you find in the middle of the right-hand page, under "Circulation," various figures which he has put down—£898,490 for 1874, £892,776 for 1875, £860,355 for 1876, and £840,004 for 1877. After he has got this circulation, he carries out in red ink what he tells us was the difference between the circulation of the Saturday and the circulation of the previous Wednesday. That is what he does; and then, after getting that, he deducts £714,000, which was the amount of the Wednesday's circulation, from the £840,000, and brings out £126,000. He seems not to have been contented with that, and then he takes £21,000, which was the circulation of the Bank of Mona, and he adds that in pencil—though he won't admit it—

to £714,000, and makes that £735,000. Then he begins and thinks—"Shall I put down £735,000 as the circulation of bank notes, or what sum "shall I put?" No, he does not seem contented with that, so the next thing he does is: he takes this £735,000, and deducts it from the true amount of circulation, £840,000, and brings out £105,000. Then he writes beneath, £105,000. But he is not pleased with that, and says—"Say make it "£100,000, instead of £105,000."

Now Morison did tell you that every word upon this sheet was dictated to him by Mr Stronach, and that Mr Stronach was looking over his shoulder, and that Mr Stronach said to him—"Say make that £100,000 less." That is not a sentence composed by Mr Morison himself, because we know his figures; he was there simply acting as the amanuensis or clerk of Mr Stronach. Can you believe that? You may, if you also believe something else he tells us. I asked, how falls it that it should be £100,000 less? He could give me no explanation. I asked him if this was the statement of the manager, and he said, "Yes;" and again, if the manager was looking over his shoulder and telling him to make it £100,000? "Yes," he said. Well, now, let us see what he did with this £100,000 less. What he does with this sum is this:—He goes away to the right-hand side again, about five inches up at the edge. Your Lordship will see in pencil there two figures—£840,000 and £100,000. There is written the word "off," which means, that you are to take off £100,000 from the £840,000, and he brings out to the margin in that way £740,000. Well, he looks at that a long time, and he is not quite satisfied with it. £740,000! he says; and he leaves that and tries another experiment, and the experiment is this, and it seems to have been the one which succeeded in the end. He goes away now to the right-hand side, to the column at the edge. You find there the figures I first referred to, £840,004. Well, there is deducted from that this time, £46,110. Now we are approaching the finale, and he brings out as the result £793,894. Now, where does he get the £46,110? We can see that too. It is the notes returned at exchange in Glasgow on the Thursday morning. You will see that immediately above the word "Circulation." This document was made up upon the Wednesday, and upon the Thursday morning, at the exchange of notes between the banks in Glasgow, he got back £46,110. A bright idea seems to have occurred to him that gets him out of all his difficulties. He says, "Now I'll tell you "what I will do; I will take the real genuine amount of £840,004, and I "will deduct these notes I got in on the Thursday morning." And he does that, leaving £793,896. Well there it is [pointing the jury to the balance-sheet]. Well, having got that, he leaves the right-hand side of the sheet. He is not pleased with them; it is too large. He wanted to see how he could get a little bit off in some way or other—to snip something off it. Well, we go from the right-hand side to the left, for this is somewhat vital, and there you will find in the third column of figures near the bottom, in black ink, £921,018. Now, that is the amount of gold and silver coin on hand. Well, what does the man do? He sets to work and he writes this out, in his own handwriting—"Why should this be so much?" He cannot comprehend that at all. And so, without more ado, after putting to himself that question, he goes away, and he deducts £30,000 from the actual true amount—£921,018, 0s. 2d.; and he brings out as the amount of gold and silver coin on hand, £891,018, 0s. 2d. That is the sum in the indictment. Look at the abstract page 6 of the indictment (see p. 29), under the head assets, and in the third division you will find that figure. Now that is the sum which this gentleman, Mr Morison, brings out by deducting £30.000 from the true amount of gold and silver coin on hand; and he brings out this sum of £891,018 as the amount of gold and silver coin on hand. And that is false, and he does so by deducting £30,000; and he does that, after having put to himself the question, which he has here recorded for our delight and for his own fame—"Why should this be so much?" Well then, after he had taken off this £30,000, what did he do with it? He went to the right-hand side of the sheet, and brought out £793,894. Well, where does he take the £30,000? He went from the left to the right side, and we find he brought out there £793,894—the result published in the abstract, page 6.

Now, gentlemen, whose handiwork was that? who was the author? who was it that said, "Make it less; why should this be so much?" who figured all that? Morison. And Morison was telling an untruth when he said that everything he did there was done by the direction of others. Morison did it, gentlemen. He says it was the manager. Gentlemen, I have often been impressed in criminal trials with the awful disadvantage under which a prisoner lies when his mouth is closed. I remember the time when, according to the law of evidence, a father could not speak in a court of justice in a case in which his son was interested, nor a son in a case in which his father was interested; and I remember the time when any person having the slightest pecuniary interest in a suit was excluded; but all these barbarous relics of ignorance have been swept away by the enlightened legislation of our own time. And I hope yet to see the day when a man who is accused shall be entitled to open his mouth in the witness-box, and tell his own story, and not remain a helpless log, to have his name and fame, his life's life, lied away. I hope yet to see the time when, if a prisoner shall not be compelled, at least he shall be competent to be a witness for himself. And I feel deeply the position in which I now stand, because, instead of putting the accused in the box and letting him tell his own story—how he had nothing in the world to do with this—I am compelled to go round and round about to endeavour to reach your minds and convictions, by a process of reasoning founded upon the working of this witness himself, in order to prove to you that, if there is anything wrong in that abstract, the first author of it was not any one of the accused, but Morison, the accountant. And with the perfect consciousness of that, we have a clue to all the inconsistencies—I shall not describe them in stronger terms—to all the defects of memory, to all the unveracities we heard from him. That is the explanation of them all. He thought it would tell against himself. He thought he might be brought in, and, I think, if any man should have been brought in as a person guilty of making up a false balance-sheet, it should have been this man. So, knowing that anything he said could not be contradicted by anybody, he said it was all done under the directions of the manager. I leave that portion of the case with you. I say that not one single statement of that man uncorroborated can be taken by you as true. He is convicted out of his own mouth, by his own admission, of having stated an untruth the first day, which he admitted the second; he is convicted, as I show you, of saying that what was done by him, and out of his own head, was done under the dictation of another. Therefore, the first point upon which you must make up your minds is this:—Assuming these balance-sheets to be false, did any one of the prisoners make them? It was no part of the manager's business to make the balance-sheets, nor was it any part of the directors' business. This figuring is the work of the accountant. It is the result of the books. Now, unless you can bring home to the prisoners at the bar the fabrication, the making of this balance-sheet, the first part of this indictment must fail. You are not entitled to infer that the manager and directors are responsible for it merely because they happened to be managers or directors. The knowledge of all this figuring, for example, which they never saw; the knowledge of all this working, by which a false entry is put on one side and a false one on the other—must be brought home to them. There is no proof of that. This paper is discovered in the Bank after the collapse. I looked with eagerness to the document of 1878, to see if I could get anything from it; but, alas! gentlemen, I found there nothing but the tails and noses of the figures, bits here and bits there, all carefully rubbed out. Who did that? You have no positive proof of who did it, but you may infer who had the motive to conceal the figuring, the remains of which are admitted by Mr Morison to have been his. For what purpose was the figuring with pencil scored out? You may infer that also when you see the character of the pencil calculations on the document of 1877.

Gentlemen, however, if it should come to this, that you are to hold Mr Stronach, whose handwriting is not upon that document, and whose connection with it is proved only by the uncorroborated testimony of this tainted witness—if you are to hold him responsible for the balance-sheet, is the balance-sheet false?

Now, gentlemen, this is where I was going to give you one or two figures. It is necessary that I should do so. In order to come really to an intelligent consideration of this question, you must see how the specific charges have been put. Will you be so good, gentlemen, as to look at the indictment at page 4? (See p. 27). I shall only take one year, 1876. The indictment says that the accused did "concoct or fabricate, or cause or procure to be "concocted and fabricated, a false and fictitious abstract balance-sheet or state-"ment of affairs, purporting to represent the true condition of the Bank's "affairs as at 7th June 1876, in the following or similar terms." And then, on page 4 (see p. 28), it is set forth—"which abstract, balance-sheet, or statement "of affairs was false and fictitious, and was known by you to be so, in the fol-"lowing particulars or parts thereof:—(1) The amount of deposits at the head "office and branches, and balances at the credit of banking correspondents "under Article 1, on the debtor side, was understated to the extent of "£1,006,216, 12s. 10d." And then look at page 3, and you will find that under the head of liabilities the first item is deposits amounting to £8,364,056, 18s. 5d. The specific charge against the accused is that this sum of eight millions was understated to the extent of £1,006,000. I will endeavour to make this matter as clear as possible. It was a matter which was carefully avoided by the Lord Advocate. He dwelt a great deal on generalities. He was very careful to prove to you that there was a difficulty in dealing with the four debtors. He was very careful to read to you the minutes showing that the directors had their cases frequently under consideration, and that therefore his inference was that the directors had perfect knowledge of their embarrassing condition. Alas! that was too true. It did not require all the dialectical skill of the Lord Advocate to prove what nobody denied. But it was not enough for him to prove knowledge of the embarrassed condition of these debtors in order to entitle him to conclude, as he did, by asking for a verdict of guilty. It was necessary that he should show, first, that the balance-sheets were false, and that they were false in the particulars that he has here specified on page 4 of the indictment. He did not even attempt this in his speech—he assumed it. He said, "It is proved to you by my accountants that all these "errors took place; and in particular I will take the first one, and there the "first item is understated to the extent of £1,006,216." That is how he put it. No doubt his accountants did state that. We had two of them—two young gentlemen from Glasgow, Mr Muir and Mr Hutton; and we had their evidence given in the ordinary and proper accountant fashion. They were perfectly clear and distinct that there was here an understatement, and they read off the figures as glibly as a juggler deals with his balls—£1,497,900, £2,500,000, and so on. No mortal man could cope with them, could not even take down their figures. An accountant is the most hard-mouthed skilled witness that I know, and he has you entirely at his command. He has all the books beside him, and you have not. You do not know the theory upon which he is to proceed, and it is quite impossible to cross-examine a man of that kind. When you want to ask him questions he rattles it off like this—"Two hundred and fifteen thousand millions"—and points to some book beside him which you can't reach. That is the kind of way in which Muir gave his evidence—in the old-accustomed fashion, adding to it an *animus* which really did excite one's dander. There was nothing that was error in the books! Oh, dear no, it is all falsification! Did the Lord Advocate ask him, "Well, what are the figures next year?" "Oh, £270,718" —that is the answer. Nothing more was wanted, but he must add, "Still going on." "What is it in 1877?" And the answer is—£415,000—still to the worse, you see, and taking it away from the general public and giving it to these people." So on he went. However, one came in the course of this rain of figures to understand the theory upon which the Crown was proceeding, and at once you got a clue to it—because we got no clue to it in the indictment. We were left perfectly helpless as to how those figures of a million and so forth were made up, and could not comprehend it, until the accountant appeared in the box; and then you got some information on the subject, and it altogether turns out to be this—what is called a fraud is simply the adoption of a system which does not commend itself to the enlightened and impartial mind of Mr Muir. What is called a fraud is, that in making up this abstract of accounts, the directors wanted to present to the shareholders the exact amounts that they were owing, and the exact amounts that were due to them. They were owing upon deposit accounts so many hundred thousands. There were due to them upon credit accounts so many hundred thousands. Well, instead of putting generally on one side the debts owing to them, and on the other side the debts due to them, what they did was this:—According as the balance turned out, they put it either to the debit or to the credit of the account. They put the balance—nothing more. Now, Mr Muir went on rattling away, telling us that this was understated upon the right hand side of the liabilities by £444,000, and this was understated on the left by so many hundred thousands, and so on. All that was perfectly true. If it is the only right way of keeping accounts to put down all your liabilities on the one side, and upon the other side all your assets—if that is the only system that can be adopted, and if the not following that system, as Mr Muir seems to think, is a fraud, then, undoubtedly, all that evidence was quite correct. That is not the system followed. The system followed is a system followed from the beginning of this Bank, at all events from as remote a time as its history has been traced. It is this,—we take a balance, if it is against the Bank we put it on one side, and if it is in favour of the Bank we put it on the other. Now, the whole of that sum of £1,006,000, which is said to be understated, is attributable simply to the system which we adopted in not putting down the totals, but the balances. That system, as I said, was a system which these men did not originate. They had it handed down to them by their predecessors unchallenged.

Gentlemen, I would have expected in a case of this kind, where the whole matter depends upon this question of putting in totals or putting in balances, that the Crown would have laid before you the practice of the other banks. How do they get up their reports? Not a word of that! It is left entirely upon the opinion of these young Glasgow accountants, Muir and Hutton. It is quite wrong, in their opinion, and the Lord Advocate seems to think that he has proved his case when he handed over that opinion to you. I have a great respect for these two gentlemen, a very great respect, but, at the same time, I would have a greater respect if, as I shall show you immediately, these gentlemen had not shown a true sleuth-hound kind of persistent pursuit, and being employed for the prosecution to get a conviction, used the strongest adjectives and the biggest substantives to bring out the result as false. I would have had a greater respect for them; greater respect for Mr Muir, if I did not see that he is ignorant of what he ought to know, or had wilfully shut his eyes to a view of the case which told against his own interest. Gentlemen, I say again that if the system which we followed is wrong, that should have been proved, and proved by bringing before you the manager of the Royal Bank, the manager of the Bank of Scotland, and the manager of the British Linen Company's Bank. They could have told us whether they followed our system, or the system of Muir and Hutton. If I convince you that that is the explanation of the whole of the alleged understatements in the accounts, there is an end of the case.

Now, gentlemen, I am not going to ask you to do much, but really and truly, the case is so important, that I must ask you to take down upon the back of your indictment the figures which constitute this £1,006,000. These are the figures which are referred to in Muir and Hutton's evidence, and perhaps your Lordship will also make a note of them. Now, gentlemen, this makes up the £1,006,000. Deposit accounts, £455,444; credit accounts, £147,468.

The LORD JUSTICE-CLERK—Where is it?

The DEAN OF FACULTY—Page 215: It is not all in the evidence of Muir; there are only seven lines of it, and I hope your Lordship will take a note of it.

The LORD JUSTICE-CLERK—Are these omissions?

The DEAN OF FACULTY—No; they are said to have been omitted altogether, and I am going to explain how the matter stands. Branches, £376,334; deposit accounts balance, £1346; correspondents' balances, £14,216; adjustment of interest, £11,405. Adding these together, you bring out the figures in this indictment, £106,216. Now, gentlemen, the first thing I have to explain, and which is charged against me, is this—the leaving out of these figures, £455,444. Muir puts that in his evidence (p. 183 F G) thus (see p. 211):—" (Q.) Will you refer again to the balance ledger No. 3. Is the " state of deposit accounts correctly given? (A.) No. The amount inserted " in the balance-ledger on the creditor side is £3233. That ought to be " £455,444. (Q.) Just explain how you come to that conclusion? (A.) " I find that that is the amount of deposits at the head office by looking at " the book Balances of Deposit Accounts, which is No. 59 of inventory; and " that book corresponds with the deposit ledger kept in the head office of the " Bank. (Q.) That book shows in separate columns both the balances due " to the Bank by overdrafts, and the balances due by the Bank to depositors? " (A.) It does. (Q.) These are crossed? (A.) Yes. (Q.) And the differ- " ence alone extended? (A.) Yes. (Q.) Do you think that is a correct " operation? (A.) Not except in cases where the debtor and creditor are " precisely the same. (Q.) Where there are cross accounts with the same " person or firm? (A.) Yes, and representing the same interest?" So, according to Mr Muir, this £455,444 is just simply a cross entry. Turn, gentlemen, to 130A.

The LORD JUSTICE-CLERK—What is it?

The DEAN OF FACULTY—This is the Abstract of accounts for the year 1876. The way in which this £455,444 is entered is this. The heading is—Abstract of Accounts, City of Glasgow Bank General Ledger, on Wednesday, 7th June 1876. Now, this document at the left side sets forth the names of the accounts and of the people who are debtors to the Bank, and the right-hand side sets forth the names of the people who are creditors of the Bank. Now, upon the right-hand side of this document there is entered the sum of £455,444, 5s. 10d. That is deposit accounts creditor balances. But on the opposite side it is entered by the debtor balance, £455,444. Why is that? The reason of it is this, that the whole of the balance is entered in the account. These two figures, the debtor and the creditor, neutralise one another. There is no use setting forth how much is at the debtor balance, and how much is at the creditor balance, if you really give the balance between the two. Now, we do that. The balance between the two is £507,433, and the £425,444 disappears from the account altogether. The only thing which is preserved is this balance of £507,433.

The LORD JUSTICE-CLERK—Where is that figure upon the abstract?

The DEAN OF FACULTY—Your Lordship will find it in black ink—£507,433. That is the only thing which remains,—the £455,444 disappears from the scene—it is entered on this side and then on that, the one entry equalising the other. The only thing that remains, as I have said, is the balance of £507,433.

The LORD JUSTICE-CLERK—Where is that sum, Mr Dean?

The DEAN OF FACULTY—On the scroll 128A, on the right-hand side, at the top. (See Appendix.) That scroll is made up from the weekly balance-sheet. This weekly balance-sheet is the handiwork of Mr Morison, the accountant. If your Lordship will please look at the page applicable to 7th June 1876, it brings out this matter very clearly. It is on the balance ledger. And this is the foundation of all the documents to be presented to the shareholders and the public; this is the balance-sheet laid by the accountant before the directors; this is the thing that they have read, and the thing that they sign. Now, in this balance-sheet Mr Morison does, upon the 7th June 1876, give us the amount of the balance at deposit account—interest receipts as they are called—but they are deposit receipts. How much is that balance? £507,433. This is the document that gives the real balances. It had nothing to do with how much is on the debtor side. It simply states the actual balances; and the balance is £507,433—the thing that appears in the abstract. Well, the £450,444—the first figure I gave you, which it is said we understated—is not in the balance ledger at all. It had nothing to do with it. It is simply an entry for which there was no use the moment the balance itself was given effect to.

Well, that is the first figure. The next is £147,468, the balance upon credit accounts. Well, that sum also, which we are accused of omitting, is not in the balance ledger—it is not there at all. I am going to deal with the credit account, and to show you why this £147,468 was not added as a thing that was due by the Bank, or due to the Bank. The figures £147,468 appear both on the right-hand side and on the left, both in the debtor and on the creditor accounts. Of course, therefore, they neutralise each other. And why is it that they are made to neutralise each other? Do they not represent any existing debt due to the Bank, or any existing liability due by it? They do not. The reason for it is that the balance upon the account is given credit for. The credit account is £3,467,000, and in that sum is included the sum of £147,000. Of course you wipe out the £147,000. It is of no more use when you have given effect to the balance of the credit account from whence it comes.

Well, that disposes of these two big figures, £455,000 and £147,000. The accountants, if they did not know, ought to have known that they arose in this manner, and that they were not understated. If we had stated them at all, and at the same time given effect to the balance, we would have committed a gross blunder; and if we had made such an error, these very accountants would no doubt very soon have pointed it out to us.

Well, the next thing I have to deal with is the sum of £376,334 under the head of branches. Now this is the sum referred to when his Lordship examined Muir, and brought out the figures making up £1,006,000. He was made to tell us that, and putting his and Hutton's evidence together, we find the result was to bring out the component parts of it. Amongst other things, he was examined as to this sum of £376,334 which I have given you. He says (see foot of p. 230) the true amount of the branch liabilities is £8,163,311, and in the scroll the figures representing that in red ink amount to £7,786,977. The difference understated is £376,334. "I cannot tell," he says, "what "that understatement consists of. That brings up the amount to the sum "stated in the indictment. I cannot tell what that understatement con-"sists of." Can't you, Mr Muir? Well, if you can't tell, it is a great change in your evidence, because it is patent on the face of the figures before you; and, if you can't tell what that understatement consists of, what kind of investigation did you make into these books, and how are we to believe you? Now, this £376,000, in all this confused muddle, is the thing that lies clearest upon the surface. This £376,000, which he says that these directors omitted to state, is just simply a cross-entry connected with the branches.

My Lord, if you will kindly look at the abstract of accounts of the Bank's branches for 1st June 1876, you will see that the entry we have got here is this—Cross accounts, Edinburgh branch, £361,000; Glasgow West End branch, about £5000—making in all, £376,334—being the thing that we are here dealing with. Now, gentlemen, what does that arise from? It arises from this. There was a customer of the Edinburgh branch—the North British Railway Company—and it had accounts in some of which it was creditor, and in others debtor; and there was one customer, the nature of whose transactions is told us by Mr Miller, the inspector of branches, at the Glasgow West End branch. And what the Bank did was this:—and nobody quarrels with them for that; even Mr Muir, with his usual zeal, could not say that is wrong—nay, he says it is quite right—when you are wanting to exhibit the state of the account of any particular customer, you take all his accounts in which he is a debtor or creditor, and deduct the one from the other, and the result tells you how he stands with you. Well, that is what is here done with this North British customer, and Mr Miller speaks of it in this way. There is the entry there under the head cross accounts, £376,334. After some further explanations, Mr Miller was asked—"Will you explain to the jury "what is the meaning of cross accounts? (A.) They belong entirely to the "North British Railway Company. The North British Railway kept several "accounts for their purposes. Some are debtor and creditor, bringing out "this, which was done by deducting the debtor from the creditor balance, and "treating it as one account." And he was asked—"Is that a perfectly proper "book-keeping operation? (A.) I think so." Then he says the amount brought out for 1876 was £376,000, which is the balance of the debtor and creditor account. You deduct the one from the other, and bring out the sum which we have here. Then he tells us of another case at the West End branch in Glasgow, and adds that the £376,334 in 1876 was applicable entirely to the account of the North British Railway, and he explains that this consisted of two accounts, the one general and the other interest and dividend account, and so on. Now, that is the history of the £376,000 which Mr Muir says he cannot make out.

The Lord Justice-Clerk—Was Muir not asked in any other place about it?

The Dean of Faculty—No, he was not.

Lord Mure—Have you any cross-examination of Muir on this point?

The Dean of Faculty—Yes.

Lord Mure—I don't see that you examine him at all.

The Dean of Faculty—I did not cross-examine him, because that was done to my hand by my friends, and there was no reason for going over the same ground.

The Lord Justice-Clerk—I asked Mr Muir expressly whether he could account for that sum, or say what it was made up of, and he said he could not. —What does Mr Hutton say about that?

The Dean of Faculty—Hutton's account of it is given in a single sentence at page 283 E. (See p. 274.) His opinion of the £376,000 is this:—"(Q.) "You are giving us what makes up the total of £1,006,000? (A.) Yes. "(Q.) I find the cross accounts have been deducted in error £376,334, "making up the sum contained in the indictment."

The Lord Justice-Clerk—Do you put that to him?

The Dean of Faculty—That is all he says. It is his opinion it is an error. Miller tells us it is right, and Morison tells us it is right; and even taking the theory of these men themselves, it is perfectly right. For there is nothing wrong whatever in crossing the accounts if the customer is the same person—is debtor and creditor in different accounts. The only thing they won't justify is this—the crossing where the customers were different persons, although it is the same sort of transaction. The Bank, for example, is not entitled to ascertain how much it owes on deposit money, how much it is creditor upon overdrafts; it cannot put the one against the other if the customers are different. I cannot for the life of me see, and I have devoted the whole force of my intellect to it, why that should be a wrong thing to do, if the object is simply to ascertain what is the real position of the Bank. It does not matter one brass farthing if the customers are different, if you only ascertain how much is due to you, and how much you owe. But Mr Hutton found out this thing which Mr Muir had not; and what are we to think of Muir's examination in regard to a patent thing like this which even an unlearned layman, and not a great big Glasgow accountant, could comprehend? That is the £376,000. That is the third figure I gave you. There is no harm in that, but that is one of the things I am accused of understating. Let us go on. The next thing I have to deal with is the £1346, 16s. 6d. That, gentlemen, is a very small sum.

The Lord Justice-Clerk—That is a balance is it not?

The Dean of Faculty—It is a balance which appears on the first paper, on the left-hand side. Then in the abstract, after writing off by opposite entries the various debtor and creditor summations, this balance remains of £1346, and it is a balance put upon the right side. I have not given the details. Now, that balance is a thing which appears in the weekly balance ledger, with an explanation. The figures £1346 won't be found in the weekly balance ledger, the reason being that between the making up of the abstract of accounts and the making up of the weekly balance ledger, there were certain operations by which the sum in the ledger was reduced from £3233 to the sum of £1346. The whole question is simply, Was that or was it not a balance? It was a balance, and, being so, I won't occupy your time longer about it.

The next thing I have to deal with is the £14,216, 15s. 2d. correspondents' balance. Now, gentlemen, it is said I ought to have added to the entry in this abstract of accounts of 1876. This also is one of the most extraordinary perversions, or, I should say, concealments of the truth, upon the part of those witnesses, that I have ever seen—the audacity of calling this a falsification, and imputing fraud to these men for what I am going to tell you. There was a sum due by foreign correspondents of £378,481; and there was also a sum due to foreign correspondents of £14,216. What was done in making up the abstract for the public was this:—The man deducted the £14,216 which the Bank owed from the £378,000 which was due to the Bank, and what they entered was the balance of £364,000, which is the figure that appears in the abstract No. 128. And these two men had the impudence to come here and tell us that this £14,216 has been omitted, and, according to them, fraudulently omitted, when you see it is given effect to—that it is simply a sum due by the Bank deducted from a sum due to the Bank, and the balance correctly stated. Now, that makes the fifth figure—

The Lord-Justice-Clerk—What explanation of that is given by the accountants?

The Dean of Faculty—Morison gives an account of it, my Lord, in his examination by the Lord Advocate, page 26 E. (See p. 115).

The Lord Justice-Clerk—He is against your view on that.

The Dean of Faculty—No; the question was "On the creditor side of "the abstract No. 130, what amount is there taken from the books and re-

"presented as due by the Bank to London, provincial, and foreign corre-"spondents? (A.) £378,481, 8s. 5d. (Q.) Is that sum correctly transferred "to the abstract No. 128? (A.) No. The amount there is £364,264, 13s. "3d., being a difference of £14,216, 15s. 2d. (Q.) How is that managed? "(A.) The lesser amount is simply the balance betwixt the different amounts." Well, then, that does not seem to suit the Lord Advocate, and he asks—"Was that in point of fact an understatement of indebtedness to that amount?" "Well, not of indebtedness"—the witness could not go further; but then some little courage was put into him, and the question is put again—"What? Eh? "To that extent?" "Well," it is replied, "if you look at it in that light it "was." He was quite willing to please the Lord Advocate. That is the whole account of it—it was simply a balance between the two amounts. What is wrong in that? and yet it is called fraud.

Well, the next thing I have to deal with, and it is the last, to make up the £1,006,216, is the £11,405 adjustment of interest. Now, gentlemen, the interest is simply a matter of calculation, and the representing this as an omission is also as audacious a piece of impudence as I think I ever heard attempted by a skilled witness—even by an accountant. The way that it is explained is just the same as in the case of the £14,216. The Bank owed interest, and the Bank was creditor in interest, and what is done is to put into this abstract, which is said to be false, the balance between the two.

The Lord Justice-Clerk—The same thing as in the other case.

The Dean of Faculty—It really appears so clear, my Lord, that I did think these witnesses might have had the candour to explain it. At page 130 the amount of interest due to the Bank was £78,115; the amount of interest due by the Bank was £11,405. Now, what is the wrong thing I am accused of? That I did not add this £11,405. How could I? What I put into my abstract was the difference between the two—namely, £66,709. I have gone over and have examined every item of which it is composed. I complain very bitterly that I have been obliged to do this at the end of the trial, and to get from the opposite side these details on which I alone could work, and give you that explanation. The indictment told me nothing. The men were in prison, and I had to grope my way about; and now, when this thing is probed to the bottom, we find it nothing else than this, that the system on which the two accountants work, and the system on which this Bank has worked from the very beginning, are different systems. That is only one of the items in the indictment. I promised that I would go through the whole of these specific charges. You can come to no satisfactory verdict, and form no intelligent conclusion—

The Lord Justice-Clerk—What was your answer, Dean, as to the £147,000?

The Dean of Faculty—It is the credit accounts—the credit balances.

The Lord Justice-Clerk—It is the same thing, then, originally.

The Dean of Faculty—The same thing.

Mr Balfour—It did not appear in the balance ledger.

The Dean of Faculty—It is included in the three millions, and does not appear in the balance ledger at all.

The Lord Justice-Clerk—Are these opposed to or in conformity with the balance ledger?

The Dean of Faculty—Entirely in conformity with the balance ledger. For example, £14,216 being the balance on foreign correspondents, which I am accused of understating; that is brought out in the balance ledger. Now, I have gone over every word of this charge. I am perfectly ready to stand examination even by these accountants upon it. I hope that I have made it intelligible to your minds, gentlemen of the jury, that the whole mistake—I call it no greater—arises just in assuming that their way is the right one, and mine is the wrong, both leading to the same result.

Look now to the second head in the libel—" The amount of Drafts out-" standing, and Drafts accepted by the Bank and its London agents, under " article 3, on the debtor side, was understated to the extent of £973,300 or " thereby." Now, you heard from Mr Balfour an explanation of the whole story of this, and I am not going to take up the parable again. I will just say one word about this £973,300. That was the sum which was put down in the cash book in the year 1873 by direction of Alexander Stronach. It entered into the general ledger as the sum due upon bills, and it is stated in the general ledger against which securities were held. Alexander Stronach left behind him the details to fill up the blank exhibiting how this debt is brought out. And these details are in existence, and were spoken to by Mr Morison. The Crown have got them, no doubt—they have got everything. Why have they kept back those details? Why have they not produced them now that we see they are going to found upon them? Why not produce them, and show us that Alexander Stronach had no foundation for a statement which he recorded in that book, that this was a debt against which security was held. I cannot understand that. There must be some reason for not disclosing it. It cannot be for the reason that it would tell in favour of the prisoners, because the object of the prosecution here is to obtain a conviction. What was the reason then? Was it that the details contained in these memoranda, of which the Crown have now got possession, would have justified Alexander Stronach in doing what he did in 1873, in putting this down as a sum to be taken out of the ordinary general run of accounts as fully secured. What the accounts were we do not know; not even the names of the accounts were contained in the memoranda—whether Morton, Fleming, Innes Wright, or some other of the six millions of debts, we cannot tell. I complain of that. I say there is a keeping back of light there which we ought not to suffer under. We ought to have had the whole thing disclosed as to this sum. I did not know about this, but the Crown did, and the Crown being masters of the situation, ought to have intimated to us what was the import of it, that we might have used it; and in order that it might have told in our favour—as its non-appearance induced me to conclude that it did. It appears, however, that in 1873, Alexander Stronach took this sum out of the general run of current accounts, and put it into a special account. Apparently, he did that without consulting anybody. There is no minute of the directors authorising it. The accountant is instructed by Stronach to do it, and he did it. Well, there it stands, apparently brought under nobody's notice, until some later period, as a sum to be dealt with apart, evidently, in the opinion of Alexander Stronach regarded as secured, and it was in 1873, 1874, 1875, 1876, and 1877, dealt with in the same way. It is deducted from bills outstanding as a thing to be treated by itself. The balance only is presented in the weekly balance-sheet, only after deducting this £973,000. That is done by the accountant. No change is adopted in the mode of treating it in the year 1876, when Robert Stronach became manager. It is dealt with by Mr Morison without any special instructions, although he tells us a lie there—I am sorry to have to use that word—although he does deflect from the truth in regard to this £973,000; for, as to 1876, he tells us first—" Though I put that down there, I put it down there by myself; I continued " the system that was in existence from 1873. I deducted it just as had " been done since its birth." But then, as he gets on, he picks himself up a little bit, and finds he is getting into this Serbonian bog of difficulties; and he is afraid to take a leap and assume the whole responsibility of doing this—of deducting the £973,000. He tells us the third time he is questioned about it—" It was Mr Potter and the manager that told me to deduct that " sum," although he had been deducting it in 1873, 1874, and 1875—although he did it then without any special instructions.

The LORD JUSTICE-CLERK—Does he say that he deducted it in 1875?

The DEAN OF FACULTY—He says he deducted it every week from June 1873, as it was sent to the manager and directors in that way. It is said in this second article of the indictment, on page 4, that the amount of outstanding drafts and acceptances was understated to the extent of £973,300. That depends altogether upon the way in which you look at that sum. It has been treated for five years not as a draft outstanding—not in reality as a thing that is secured—at all events secured in the mind of this very competent man,—the former manager of the Bank. Nobody's attention is particularly called at all to that sum; and when in 1876 the directors were called upon to exhibit to the world the condition of their Bank, what they did was simply to treat the entry as it had been treated before. Is that an intention of concealing from the public? There was no intention of concealing it from the public, or of misstating it with intent to defraud. Is that a purpose of misstating with the intent of defrauding, what they had no more hand in originating that than you or I? That man Morison, whose word I cannot believe, does say that upon one occasion he spoke to Robert Stronach about this £973,300, when Robert said, I suppose in a feeble and irritated way—"I don't know "anything about it; let it alone in the meantime; it was there when I came "into office;" and the disagreeable subject is passed by. Who is responsible for it? Did these men contrive this fine scheme out of their own heads, concealing from the public that they owed upon drafts to the extent of £973,000? It might have been on the responsibility of these directors, or any other body, in a civil action for damages. The sole question in a civil action is this—What are you impliedly or expressly liable for? You are liable in a civil action for your express covenants, or what you ought to do but did not do. You are liable for what you owe individually. You are liable in a civil action for what another man did in your name or you acquiesced in; but that is not what we are here dealing with. We are here dealing with the stern realities of criminal law, which require that proof of guilt shall be brought home to a man himself. An inference of guilt is a thing utterly abhorrent to the criminal law of Scotland. The doctrine of constructive guilt is the doctrine of tyrants,—it has been exploded and chased away from our jurisprudence altogether; and it is constructive guilt to bring in these men as responsible for the figures appearing in 1876.

Well, the third charge in this indictment is this:—"The amount of Bills of "local and country bills, credit accounts, and other advances, under article 1 "on the creditor side, was understated to the extent of £2,698,539, 10s. 4d., "or thereby." Well, now look at the creditor side, page 3 (see p. 28), and it is said that the amount of Bills of exchange, local and country bills, is £8,787,000, and it says that it is understated by the sum of £2,698,000. It is a very curious sort of thing this altogether. The usual mode in which a man pretends to deceive the world, or attempts to do it, is to pretend that he is a much greater man than he is—that he is very wealthy, and he cuts a dash amongst his acquaintances, professing to have a larger income than he has. But here is a Bank that is accused of understating its assets, and told that it ought to have set forth that it was richer by £2,698,000. That is composed in this wise. It is composed of our old friend the first figure of £1,006,000. It is composed of that, and then it is composed of the figure I have just dealt with, £973,300. Then it is composed of another figure, which I am going to refer to immediately, of £751,000. If you add these three figures together, with certain corrections, which will be found in Hutton's evidence (see p. 273), that brings out the sum contained in this third charge (p. 4) of £2,698,000. I have explained to you the £1,006,000; I have spoken also of the £973,300. The third figure is one that also comes under the fifth head at page 4, for it charges me with overstating the amount of Government stocks, &c., to the extent of £755,211. I am accused in article 3 of understating the amount of bills owing to me; and I am accused in article 5 of overstating to the same amount the amount of stock that was held by me. That is all. It is the same sum in both cases. It is not two charges—3 and 5. The Crown says that this £753,000 and £751,000 were really and truly bills which were owing to the Bank, and which, under article 5, they say I erroneously and wrongously called stocks. That has been already explained to you. Permit me, just in a few sentences, to repeat the explanation. In 1876, according to Morison, Mr Potter told him, when he was looking over the abstract, to bring down from the head of credit accounts three different accounts, making up that £751,000. Well, I do not know how the truth may stand on that—whether that is the notion of Mr Morison himself or not. We see how acute he was, how scheming he was in this matter of misrepresenting the notes in circulation, how neatly he takes £30,000 and carries it over from the one side to the other, and brings out these figures after trying three other schemes. Now, whether this idea of bringing the names down from the top to the bottom was Mr Morison's or Potter's, I don't know. I take it, *prima facie*, for granted, that the man who did it was the man who wrote it—the man who did it took it in in black ink first and showed it to Mr Potter, and to none else, till the whole thing was completed.

I can't tell you what I am told, gentlemen, because the prisoner's mouth is shut. I cannot even convey to you their story as to when they came to see this thing. I regret that bitterly, that I cannot get at the truth here except in this roundabout way; but I say there is no evidence whatever that the bringing down of these names from the credit account, and putting them down here, was not the suggestion of the ingenious mind who did the figuring of the abstract of 1877. But, gentlemen, is there in the thing itself the element of fraud such as to induce you to find not merely that it is wrong, but that it is criminally punishable? At that time, you may remember, in the year 1876, these three people—Smith, Fleming, & Co., Nicol Fleming, and Morton & Co.—were sailing before the wind; at all events Smith, Fleming, & Co., and Morton and Co., were in the full flush of prosperity; a rosy future was before them, and nobody doubted that they could get on in the future as they had got on in the past. Now, at that time it is proved to you that at least one-half of the debt of Smith, Fleming, & Co. was secured—one-half of it was secured by stocks. When, then, is a creditor entitled to treat stocks as absolutely his own? When the debt is not paid up, what was formerly held in security becomes his right. He is entitled to do that when the date of payment of the debt has come and gone, and the debt is not paid. What was formerly held by him in security then becomes his absolute right. Is there any proof that the stocks here mentioned, which were stocks as good as Government stocks—some of the stocks which they held—that these stocks were not held absolutely by the Bank at that time to the extent that is stated—in one case, Smith, Fleming, and Co., £200,000; in Nicol Fleming's, £100,000; and in the other, Morton and Company's, £450,000? I take it that this idea was Morison's at first, because he has so persistently defended it. All the inducements of cajolery, and speaking sweetly and gently to him by the Lord Advocate, had no effect in inducing him to alter the opinion to which he came. And the Lord Advocate, ascending to remonstrance, says, "Can you really justify this thing—the bringing down "of what is a credit account to the heading below?" and the man goes on to reiterate what he had said—"If stocks were held against that, I see no harm "in it." Says the Lord Advocate, ascending from remonstrance to indignation, "What do you mean by that? Is this not really and truly a credit account?" but again he says, "Well, I don't see anything wrong in it." But the poor soul at last, being driven into a corner, says, "Well, take your own way of it." But that is Morison's idea I am convinced, from the way in which he has defended it. And of all the things which are here challenged, I cannot for the life of me see that in this there is anything wrong. Private stocks were held against these sums of money which were only part of the debt owing to these debtors, and where is the proof that there was not? You point me to the ultimate realisation of these men's assets. Why, they are not realised yet. Smith, Fleming, & Co. is still in liquidation, and their properties in the East and in New Zealand and Australia are still unsold. So is Morton's, and therefore, for every one of these three sums if there were stocks held by the Bank, I cannot see that there was any harm in bringing them from the credit account to the place in which they are put.

Was that done with the intention to defraud is the question. If it be capable of an innocent interpretation, if it is capable of being construed in the way I suggest—that there was nothing so awfully wrong in it, that it was a correct and proper thing to do—then there is no criminality.

That deals with 3 and 5. The other article is article 4—"The amount of cash "on hand, viz., gold and silver coin, and notes of other banks, under article 3 "on the creditor side, was overstated to the extent of £29,095 or thereby." Well, the Crown must have been very hard put to it to make that a criminal charge. But I can easily understand it when I see the accountant's evidence on the subject. When questioned on this subject, this is what Morison said of it (see p. 134):—"(Q.) Does that sum of £29,000 represent your own notes, which "had been got in exchange for the notes of the other banks, between the "afternoon of Wednesday and the commencing of business on the Thus- "day, as you explained with reference to the £89,031? (A.) No. (Q.) "What is it? (A.) There is a reference here to it—'Notes remitted by "'branches.' (Q.) Was that sum remitted from the branches? (A.) I have "no doubt of it. (Q.) But were these notes then in the hands of the Bank? "(A.) They would be in transmission. (Q.) That means going from the "branches to the head office. (A.) Yes; and belonging to the head "office. (Q.) But when a note is passing from the branch to the head "office, it is in the hands of the Bank; it is not in circulation? (A.) "No. (Q.) Then if these notes were in that position, was it not a "perfectly proper deduction to make? (A.) I should say so. (Q.) If "you had stated these notes as in circulation, you would have stated what "was wrong if they were going between a branch and the head office? (A.) "That is my opinion." So that the whole of this charge is this: that we actually said that these notes, which were going through the Post Office from all the branches to the head office, were in my possession. They would be in my possession on Thursday morning at nine o'clock, and the Crown actually accuses me of understating—or is it overstating, for it does not much matter which to these accountants—overstating these notes that were in transit to the extent of £29,000. That is a crime, gentlemen of the jury!

Now, that is the whole of those specific charges, except 6 and 7—whether I made any earnings, and whether I had a reserve fund left. Now, as to whether I made any earnings, I represented that I made earnings. Quite true, I did; but there is no doubt about this fact, that I did make earnings to the extent of £70,000 yearly from the branches alone. That is clear gained money. Mr Miller told you that. Well, now, there is no doubt that there were accounts of very great magnitude, and that these were accounts that gave me very great anxiety. But still these were men of substance once and of great energy. I knew that the income of one of them —Smith, Fleming, & Co.—amounted for one or two years, between 1860 and 1870, to hundreds of thousands of pounds. How it does make one's mouth water, gentlemen, to hear such statements. Hundreds of thousands from their general trade. And then, besides, they had a commission business, which is just the surest of all kinds of business, once you have got a connection; and they had £93,000 a year from it. Glen Walker says £100,000, but we will take the lesser figure. They were men of such enormous incomes that, really and truly, if it had not been the disastrous times upon which we have fallen, there was no danger of that account. Now, why should I not do what Mr Hutton says is perfectly correct; and without his assistance we knew it ourselves. Why should I not calculate interest upon that, as a source of revenue upon which I was reasonably entitled to look? Take Morton, the possessor of vast estates in New Zealand and Australia, which are mortgaged to me,—now the best asset in the hands of the liquidators of this concern. Why should I not be entitled to look upon Morton as a source of revenue? It is said that no interest was paid upon those accounts. What did the accountant mean? Sums of money were paid in weekly, and daily, and monthly upon these accounts, and credited to them. Some years they got less, and then they gradually increased again; but still at what period is it that a man is bound to say—"Now that account is bad; I will place it in the suspense "account; I will never treat it more as a source of revenue?" That is matter of discretion. Are you to say that a man commits a fraud because he is hopeful, and entertains the most sanguine expectations from what his debtors had? Read the letters from Fleming which are printed here, and you find that during 1876-77-78, he held out to the directors the most splendid prospects. He was succeeding, he said, better than he had expected; but, alas! there next came something to dash away the glittering vision. The Collies' failure and the Duckworths' (their Liverpool agent's) failure came, and the vernal promise of prosperity is followed by the autumnal disappointment. So it ends. I think you must see that they at the outset regarded this as a good thing, and I think I am entitled to treat it in the manner I have done. What may be the ultimate outcome of that estate, or of Morton's estate, no man can tell. It depends altogether on the revulsion of trade, whenever that may come. So much for earnings. Well, they were entered in the books and dealt with. The persons by whom they were held were customers whose transactions were going on; and, therefore, I fail to see by what right the Crown prosecutor is entitled to say at that stage—"You must pause; you "must take the accounts of those men out of the class of good customers, "and put them into the class of doubtful; you must no longer apply the "earnings on that account to the payment of dividends; you must no longer "say you have dividends from him the moment you come to such and such "a day." So what but a moment before was good, right, and business-like, becomes criminal. I don't know any law for that. I say this was a matter entirely at the discretion of these people, and I say that that discretion they did not abuse.

That is also really the case with regard to the reserve. I stated that I had a reserve fund of £450,000, whereas in truth it had all melted away. Now, that altogether depends upon the ultimate realisation in one view; but it is not quite the question. The question was—Did I believe that it had melted away, and that the whole thing was in a condition of collapse? If I believed that all had gone, and irretrievable ruin was to follow, and then stated that it remained, that would be criminal. Did any of these unfortunate men do that? No, they did not. They kept their shares, and they have been ruined in consequence. Not one of them believed that the reserve fund was gone. Not one of them thought that the expectations which had been held out to them would prove unfruitful. They clung to this dismasted ship in the hope of being able to save her. Here they are, gentlemen, obliged to descend as ruined men, and begin the world again. The earnings of a long life-time are entirely gone, and the industry of it swallowed up. It is always a subject of solemn pity when we see a vast fortune lost; and when the last memorial of it is over, one has some sympathy and commiseration for its ruins and vestiges. Here are those men. They did not believe that the reserve fund was gone. They acted in a different manner, and we construe men's motives and their knowledge according to their actions.

Mr Stronach is not a man like any of the other gentlemen at the bar. He was not a merchant with vast connections in every country in the globe,—a merchant here and a merchant there; he occupied the humbler position of an official connected with this Bank. His own fortune when he became a shareholder was, as was proved by Mr Cowan, £11,000; and he loses everything; but he must submit to that like every person involved in this collapse. Notwithstanding the misery that the collapse of this Bank has entailed, it certainly would intensify its horrors if there were to be a conviction for a crime where there was really no criminality. It would not be asserting rational justice, but giving vent to the wild fury of exasperated feeling. The calamity is one which includes the largeness of national and all the individuality of private interests; and in writing its history, certainly it would be a sad thing if one had to say that a verdict was delivered against these men, whose conduct when analysed was compatible, it may be, with the purest innocence, as I think it is, and which, I think, is incompatible with, and cannot be construed into anything like guilt. I do say to you—Rise above the prejudices of society; do not put into your verdict the exasperated feelings that may arise from the misfortunes that have overtaken the shareholders in this Bank. Juries are men under rational influences and positive habits of thought. I do not ask you to do more than this—to give a fair consideration to what I have now laid before you in the analysis I have made of the charge brought by the Lord Advocate in the various specific particulars.

I do not go into the years 1877 and 1878, because they are upon the same lines and are capable of the same explanations as I have given. But I think I have done enough to show that if there is anything chargeable against these men, it is not the offence of falsifying a balance-sheet, but simply the offence of making up that balance-sheet upon a wrong system, or according to a principle not approved of by the prosecution.

Mr JAMIESON (a juryman)—May I ask, for the information of all the gentlemen of the jury, whether all the debtor and creditor balances in every book of the Bank for any year, when added up, correspond, and if the sums in the balance-sheet in the report issued by the directors to the shareholders agree with the balances so shown under the different headings and accounts of the Bank?

The LORD JUSTICE-CLERK—I refer you to counsel for that. [Addressing counsel]—What do you say?

The DEAN OF FACULTY—They do, my Lord.

The LORD JUSTICE-CLERK—I had understood from Mr Muir that his rectification of the balance-sheet did not affect the profit and loss and reserve, and the general state of the account, except in this way—that it represented the transactions on either side to be smaller than they actually were. I think that is a correct statement of it.

The SOLICITOR-GENERAL—That is our view of it.

Mr BALFOUR—The balances are all correct.

The LORD JUSTICE-CLERK—I shall make that clear when I come to address you. It is too late now to go on, and, besides, there are some considerations which the Dean of Faculty has suggested I should like to have a little time to go over. We shall meet to-morrow at twelve o'clock, and that, I think, will be the last day you will be detained.

Mr BALFOUR—We think we understand the question of the gentlemen of the jury, and if there is any doubt about it, we are quite prepared to show that the balances in the books all agree with the balances brought into the balance ledger and into the abstracts. The only difference is that, by Mr Muir's theory, you should bring in the totals. But if the principle of bringing in balances is right, the balances are all brought in correctly throughout. We are quite ready to show that. The balance ledger and the abstract of accounts correspond.

Eleventh Day—Friday, 31st January 1879.

THE LORD JUSTICE-CLERK'S CHARGE.

Gentlemen of the Jury—We are now nearing the close of this very long, painful, and important investigation. It has occupied a time, I believe, unexampled in the annals of this Court, as the occasion of it is without precedent in the history of the country. You have listened with attention, and have directed your minds and intelligence to evidence from witnesses lasting over this long time, and you have had your attention called to a great variety of documents, accounts, figures, balances, and results, which during that long period cannot fail to have perplexed you, as I must own they have perplexed me, and to leave you in considerable doubt as to what the result of the investigation was. I am glad, however, to think that as the case went on, and with the assistance of addresses from the bar on both sides, of which I can only say that they were well worthy of the renown of the body to which those gentlemen belong, and well worthy of the occasion on which they were delivered,—I am glad, I say, to think, now we have really approached the kernel of the question which is at issue before you, that I shall be able, within a reasonable compass, to winnow the case from a good deal of those surroundings which served to make it more intricate than it need have been, and to present for your consideration a few simple questions of fact which it remains for you to determine.

Something has been said by the counsel for the prisoners at the bar,—not too much nor too urgently pressed,—on two topics that cannot fail to be present to your minds. In the first place, the country is suffering under a great and unexampled calamity. This fabric, this joint-stock company of the City of Glasgow Bank, has met with an overwhelming catastrophe. Hundreds of families have been reduced from affluence or competence to poverty, and it is not wonderful that the feeling to which the learned counsel have alluded should have prevailed in many quarters—viz., a desire that the conduct of those in whose hands the calamity occurred, and under whose administration the institution was brought to ruin, should become the subject of judicial inquiry. That has been done. The inquiry has been full, and, as far as the Crown authorities could make it, complete. The whole facts connected with this most lamentable affair are now before you, and your verdict on it, whatever it may be, will undoubtedly command the respect to which it is entitled. On the other hand, gentlemen, there is no doubt that very large issues personal to the prisoners at the bar are in your hands. They are placed there,—persons who have during a long life held a high position, enjoying the respect and confidence of their friends and the community—placed now in hazard of fame and fortune, and position, and good name, and liberty. These are the issues no doubt which depend upon your verdict. But, gentlemen, I have mentioned these things, as you may well suppose, for the purpose of your laying them entirely aside. What may be thought of our proceedings, what may be thought of your verdict out of doors, can be of no moment whatever either to you or to me. We are to deal with this case as if there were no such external surroundings,—simply as a matter of proof and evidence, and to deal with it as we should with a case which excited no interest or sympathy in any quarter. Whether it be the one consideration or the other, they are equally foreign to the walls wherein we sit. We know of no such consideration save this—that the momentous issue which is now before you, must lead you, as it will lead me, to weigh still more scrupulously the facts that have been proved in the scales of even-handed justice, and to discard from our consideration every other topic.

Now, having said so much, let me commence my remarks by referring you to the questions that are raised in this indictment. It is an indictment which substantially contains three branches of imputation against the prisoners at the bar. The prisoners are the directors and the manager of the City of Glasgow Bank; and it was originally alleged against them, first that they had fabricated and falsified on three several occasions the balance-sheet for the year which they issued to the shareholders of the Bank,—that they had done so in certain particulars which are specified in the indictment. The second charge which the indictment contained was one directed against certain of the individual prisoners; and it was said that they, being directors, had availed themselves of their position as directors to obtain advances from the Bank in breach of their trust, and had embezzled the amount. The third charge was a charge of theft, for having improperly taken possession of bills sent to them for collection, and used them for the purpose of paying the debts of the Bank. Gentlemen, doubtless in any view which can be taken of it, these were very serious imputations indeed. However, the Lord Advocate, although we had sustained the relevancy of these two charges—and I need not go back to the views which were then expressed—after the evidence had been led, and looking to the facts at his command, and the expression of opinion which fell from us, came to the conclusion that his duty would be sufficiently discharged by abandoning the second and third charges, and confining his attention and yours to the three charges of fabricating these balance-sheets. Something, gentlemen, has been said regarding the course so followed by the public prosecutor. On that I have not a single remark to make. I have made it a rule from the bench never to form a judgment on the course followed by the public prosecutor in the exercise of the discretion which the law vests in him, for this simple reason, that the Court are not in possession of the information which would be necessary to form a judgment on that matter, and that the Lord Advocate exercises his discretion under a sense of his public responsibility, and may always be made responsible, although not to this Court. I cannot doubt, and I assume, that the grounds on which the Lord Advocate proceeded were grounds which, to his mind, were satisfactory. He is quite able to form an opinion, and quite able to maintain it; and therefore, gentlemen, I don't make a single remark on the course which has been followed, excepting to draw your attention to the fact that these two charges of embezzlement and theft are no longer presented to you for your consideration.

Laying, therefore, that matter aside, and addressing ourselves to the questions that are raised under the three charges, viz., the charges of falsifying the balance-sheets for the years 1876, 1877, and 1878, you will observe still further that the Crown have departed from the eighth head of the alleged falsification. The falsifications are alleged to have taken place in regard to eight specific sums. The last of these ran originally in this form—" Bad and " irrecoverable debts to an amount far exceeding the whole capital stock of " the Bank were included under Article I. on the creditor side, and so treated " as subsisting and available assets of the company." That item has been struck out, and the effect of that I may have occasion to say a word upon by-and-by. Now, gentlemen, you will observe that the charge which is made against these directors and the manager is " that you did, all and each or one " or more of you, wickedly and feloniously, with intent to defraud the mem-" bers of the said company and the public, for the purpose of concealing and " misrepresenting the true state of affairs of the company, concoct and fabri-" cate, or cause or procure to be concocted and fabricated, a false and ficti-" tious abstract balance-sheet or statement of affairs," and then follows the statement of affairs on page 3 (see p. 27); and then after the specification of the particulars, in which it is said that the balance-sheet was false (see p. 28), it is set out farther that the said prisoners did, each with intent to defraud, " use and utter the said false and fabricated abstract balance-sheet or state-" ment of affairs as true, well knowing it to be false and fabricated, and for " the purpose of concealing and misrepresenting the true state of the said " company's affairs." There is a similar charge in regard to the balance-sheets of 1877 and 1878, but I need not go over it in detail.

Now, gentlemen, that being the state of matters, there are three questions that arise on each of these three charges, and you must keep them clearly and distinctly in mind,—first, whether these balance-sheets are false; secondly, whether the prisoners, each of them or any of them, was in the knowledge that they were false; and thirdly, whether what they did with the balance-sheet—namely, the circulation and publication of the report with the balance-sheet—was with the intention of deceiving the shareholders and the public. These are three matters that will require to be very carefully kept in mind, and kept separate, during the whole course of the inquiry into which I now shortly propose to lead you.

But upon these three heads I shall make these general remarks. The prisoners at the bar are the directors and the manager of a joint-stock bank. You have heard a good deal about what the duties of a director of such an institution are; and from the views that were quoted to you by my learned friend Mr Trayner, as having been expressed by the Court in former cases, I have nothing to suggest in the way of dissent. A director is generally a man who has other avocations to attend to. He is not a professional banker. He is not expected to do the duty of a professional banker, as we all know. He is a man selected from his position, from his character, from the influence he may bring to bear upon the welfare of the bank, and from the trust and confidence which are reposed in his integrity and in his general ability. But I need not say that it is no part of his duty to take charge of the accounts of the Bank. He is entitled to trust the officials of the Bank who are there for that purpose, and as long as he has no reason to suspect the integrity of the officials, it can be no matter of imputation to him that he trusts to the statements of the officials of the Bank acting within the proper duties of the department which has been entrusted to them. You may assume that. It will not, however, follow from that, that where special circumstances arise to bring under the notice of the directors particular interests connected with the joint-stock company, there may not ensue an obligation of inquiry and an obligation of action which might not be necessarily inferred from the nature of the position which they hold. We must look this matter plainly in the face as it actually occurs in practical life. Remark has been made on the amounts—the extraordinary amounts disclosed in this case—amounts that take one's breath away as applied to ordinary commercial concerns; but we must not assume that in the inception of the sad history which we have had detailed here during the last fortnight there was anything abnormal whatever. Great mercantile success necessarily produces great mercantile transactions. Where you have merchants who count their profits by a hundred thousand pounds a year, they, of course, must have the same banking facilities that a man requires who only counts them by a thousand. The proportion will be larger, but the nature of them will be precisely the same; and it cannot be doubted that a bank that secures for its customers persons in that enormous scale of business, also secures for its shareholders unusually large profits. But then, gentlemen, with the magnitude of the transactions there comes a magnitude of danger also; for the merchant, although on that large scale, is subject, of course, to those fluctuations that have the effect of tying up a man's money temporarily, and depriving him of the use of it that he expected, and for these temporary occasions, of course, the millionaire, as well as the poorer merchant, requires or requests from those with whom he does his monetary transactions temporary assistance; and he gets it, with security that is reckoned to be, and is properly valued at, quite sufficient to keep the Bank safe. But then, gentlemen, comes the crash. A war, a famine, a drought, a strike, may make the whole of that edifice tumble down. The debt and the security go together. What is the Bank to do? Then it is that the unprofessional director finds himself face to face with an emergency which, beyond all question, it is difficult and hard to meet. The question for him then is,—is he to bring the Bank down by bringing down the debtor, or is he to carry on the debtor in the hope of the vessel getting into calmer water and righting herself in a smoother sea? We all know that that kind of question has been presented too often in our commercial experience. But, gentlemen, there is one rule which a director is bound to follow. In that, as in every case, honesty is the only policy, and neither the interests of the shareholders, nor the chances of recovering the debt, nor any of those considerations which doubtless, when one is in the middle of them, seem to be almost overwhelming, can for a moment justify or excuse or palliate the deliberate statement of what is known to be false.

I will not say what course the directors of this institution could or might have followed. All I can say is, that whatever their difficulties, and whatever their temptations, there is nothing in the circumstances in which they are placed which can in the least degree palliate the offence with which they are charged, if in reality they are found to be guilty of it. So much, gentlemen, for the offence.

Secondly, as to the knowledge of the directors,—as to their knowledge that these balance-sheets were fabricated. Now, what the prosecutor has undertaken to prove, and says that he has proved, is not that these directors were bound to know the falsity of the statements in the balance-sheets,—not that they lay under obligations to know it, not that they had the means of knowledge,—but that, in point of fact, they did know it; and that is what you must find before you can convict the prisoners of any part of the offences attributed to them. You must be able to affirm in point of fact, not that they had a duty and neglected it, not that they had the means of information within their power and failed to use them, but that, as a matter of fact, when that balance-sheet was issued, they knew that the statements contained in it were false. I say that, because there has been some phraseology used in the course of this trial that would seem to indicate that a constructive knowledge was all that was required for such a case. Constructive knowledge might be quite sufficient if we were dealing here simply with an action for civil debt or civil reparation; for what a man is bound to know he shall be held to have known. But that has no place at all when a man is charged with crime. His crime is his guilty knowledge, and nothing else. He is charged with personal dishonesty, and you must be able to affirm that on the evidence before you can convict him. But while I say that, gentlemen, I by no means mean to say that the knowledge which you must find must necessarily be deduced from direct evidence of it. You are not entitled to assume it; but you are entitled to infer that fact, as you are entitled to infer any other fact, from facts and circumstances which show and carry to your mind the conviction that the man when he circulated, or when he made that balance-sheet, knew that it was false. You must be quite satisfied, however, before you can draw that conclusion, not merely that it is probable, or likely, or possible that he knew, but that he did, in point of fact, know the falsehood of which he is accused.

Then, gentlemen, lastly, on the question of intent or motive—the fraudulent use only of this document,—for that is of the essence of the crime,—it is said to have been issued and circulated for the purpose of deceiving the shareholders and the public as to the true state of the Bank. Of that you must also be satisfied; for it would be of no moment that these statements were not in themselves accurate, unless they were put there for a fraudulent and dishonest purpose. It may be suggested that the end which the directors intended to serve was not to injure anyone; that their real object was in the meantime to keep the Bank afloat, until better times should relieve their securities and their debtors, and enable them to pay their way. Gentlemen, I have to tell you that so far from that being a sufficient defence, it is exactly the offence and the motive described in the indictment; because if they intended to give the Bank breathing time, by inducing the shareholders to imagine it was more prosperous than it was, then that is precisely the intent to deceive which is libelled in the indictment; for they put in hazard exactly the same interests which would have been imperilled if they had been actuated by the strongest and most malignant motive. The men who were induced to hold on, and the men who were induced to buy, are just ruined precisely as they would have been if that had been the result intended by the directors. Did they mean to deceive? If they meant to represent the Bank as being in a more prosperous condition than it was; and if they meant the shareholders to believe that, then they intended to run the risk of all the results that might follow from that deception. And, accordingly, I could not certainly say to you that even if you were satisfied that that was the real object which the directors had in view, it would tend in the slightest degree to take off from the motive or intent that is here libelled. On the other hand, you must be quite satisfied that there was an intention to deceive on the part of the prisoners before you can find them guilty. And, gentlemen, to conclude these general remarks, I can only say that the offence with which they are charged is not only a crime,—not only comes within the compass of the criminal law, but, if deliberately committed, is in truth a crime of very great magnitude. I need not say that the larger the interests committed to their charge, the more they were bound to absolutely honest administration.

And, gentlemen, having said those things, let us now turn to the first of these balance-sheets. And first, as to the falsehood, I have endeavoured, as far as I could, by assiduous attention to the evidence while it was being delivered, and also by devoting such spare time as I could to the comprehension of it, to arrive at some clear and definite result upon the figures submitted to you, and the arguments that have been raised upon them. I am not by any means confident that I have succeeded in that task; and I am the less solicitous about it, because I have no doubt at all that there are those of your number who are not unaccustomed to inquiries of this kind, or at least to deal with figures of a somewhat analogous kind. But it seems to me that the result of the evidence which we have has now reduced this case to a very simple issue. Mr Muir made out some states showing the results of his evidence in regard to the different balance-sheets, and I have requested that copies should be made for the jury, because it will greatly shorten my exposition of the evidence in regard to that matter, and will show you at a glance the result of the evidence of Mr Muir in regard to the alleged falsification of the balance-sheets. There are three of them,—one applicable to each year (see pp. 232, 233, and 234.) I intended them, however, more to assist your private deliberations after I have finished my remarks, than to be the subject of comment at present. [They are handed to the jury.] These documents are simply the result of Mr Muir's evidence, and they show the alleged overstatements and the alleged understatements brought into a very clear and intelligible form.

I shall begin with the balance-sheet of 1876; and first let me call your attention to what Mr Morison described as the mode in which these balance-sheets, or abstracts rather, which are ultimately reported to the shareholders, are made up. The head office keeps its own books—its weekly balance book and its general balance ledger; and when a balance is to be struck, there is obtained from the branches a statement of the balances on their accounts, and the accountant, having received from the inspector of branches his statement of balances, goes over the whole and makes up a general balance-sheet showing the result of the Bank's transactions. In the balance ledger of the Bank these transactions are entered, showing the balance on the year. He explained to you that he took the balance as appearing upon the last weekly balance-sheet; that he read over the items to the directors, who had the balance ledger before them, and that they checked how far the entries in the balance ledger corresponded with what was read to them by the accountant, Mr Morison, from the weekly states and other documents. And then that balance is abstracted. Mr Morison makes up his abstract; he has it revised, as he explained, by the manager; and then it is laid before the directors and adopted. The weekly balance book contains the balances at the head office from week to week—I may leave the branches out of view in the meantime,—the last weekly balance is the one taken for the entry of the balance in the balance ledger; and then the balance ledger is the foundation, but only the foundation, of the abstract which is laid before the shareholders of the Bank. That is proved to be the course of procedure.

Now, it is said that this balance-sheet is defective in seven particulars, and those seven particulars consist of sums which are said to have been overstated or understated for the purpose of deceiving the public. I shall, meanwhile, speak of the first five of these subdivisions. The first is the amount of Deposits, which is said to be understated by one million odds; the second is the amount of Drafts outstanding, which are said to be understated; third, the amount of Bills of exchange, said to be understated; and then you have overstatements, on the other side, consisting of £29,000 Cash on hand, and £753,000 of investments. Now, you have had a long and anxious inquiry, and a great deal of most acute and powerful observation on the items contained in these five articles of the indictment. But I am glad, for your convenience, to think that, in the view which I take of this matter, it will not be necessary for me to dwell, at all events at any length, on any but two of these sums, which were the subject of dispute. It was observed from the bar, and observed quite rightly and correctly, that these alleged overstatements and understatements consist of two classes,—one class is at variance with the books, and the other class which is in conformity with the books. Now, in the meantime, if you please, I shall confine myself entirely to two of these alleged misstatements, misrepresentations, or falsifications which are not in conformity with the books. I think you will see immediately the reason of that observation. These two falsifications or misrepresentations are two that you have heard a great deal about, and which it will not be necessary for me to explain to you in any great detail. The balance-sheet, it is said, contains on both sides the sum of £973,000 as a deduction from the transactions of the year. It also contains, under the head of Government securities, the sum of £751,000. £751,000 was the original sum, but it is raised to £753,000 in this particular article. It contains that sum included under Government securities and other investments, which in reality ought to have been placed in the credit accounts. And the first matter that I shall ask your attention to—and you will find it to be one of very great moment in this inquiry,—is, putting aside altogether for the present the criticism on the other items contained in these specified charges, to consider these two alleged misrepresentations by themselves, and let us see how the evidence applies to them.

Gentlemen, I take the sum of £973,000 first; and it is right that you should understand what will come out still more clearly when I go to the other charges, that the charge under these heads is not so much of falsifying results, as of falsifying amounts. The sides of the account will balance precisely in the same way after the operation, which was alleged to be performed, had been performed as it would before. But in regard to this £973,000, its effect is simply this—to represent the transactions of the Bank on floating debt to be just a million less than it was. Gentlemen, it is said that this sum of £973,000 was introduced into the books, and that it was to be found in the weekly balance book and in the balance ledger; and that is quite true, and if that had been consistently followed out, it would have been a very important fact. But the main thing in this sum of £973,000 for you to consider—for it is entirely in your hands—is, was there any truth or honesty in that sum? Did it ever represent anything? There is not a vestige or a trace of it in the general books of the Bank; and you have the evidence of Mr Morison, and the evidence of Mr Muir, and the evidence of every man who has looked at the books, and the entire silence of those who could have cleared it up, which corroborate beyond all question (at least you must consider whether it does or does not), the fact that this sum of £973,000, whoever is responsible for it, is in truth an interpolation without any substance on which to rest. I shall read to you what Mr Morison says about it. I shall have occasion to remark upon his evidence afterwards, as much comment has been made upon it; but, in the meantime, I shall refer you to what he says as to what he knew about this, and if Mr Morison can tell us no more, I think you may assume that there was no more to be told. He was asked—"Why was the sum of "£973,000 deducted from the foreign and colonial credits? (A.) Because "there was a credit account to that extent. (Q.) Did you get instructions "from anybody to deduct it? (A.) No; it was in the ledger. (Q.) Why did "you put it in the ledger? (A.) In June 1873 there was an entry made by "the instruction of the late manager, Mr Alexander Stronach, which appears "in the book titled City of Glasgow Bank Cash Book, private No. 6, extracts "from which are contained in No. 2A. I made that entry; it is in the follow-"ing terms:—'Foreign and colonial credits No. 2, the following credits to be "'retired as they mature, and debited under the respective accounts to credit "'a/c No. 2, against which securities are now held by the Bank, and in pro-"'cess of realisation and payment of the proceeds—£973,000.'" That entry does unquestionably occur in the private ledger which is referred to. Mr Morison proceeds—"That deduction from foreign and colonial credits "was carried on in the books and in the balance-sheets from year to year "thereafter down to 1878 inclusive, without any change being made. There "was a note written by the late manager giving the particulars of that deduc-"tion, but I never got the particulars." Then he is asked, "Was it a right "deduction?" and he says, "I would not like to say so." Now, gentlemen, the fact unquestionably remains that that entry having been made by Alexander Stronach in 1873, there is not a trace in the books of any such sum being represented by securities or by anything else. It is for you to judge, but the question is, whether it was not a sum written off without there being anything to represent it, in consequence of the fear that the manager then had that the transactions of the Bank would be considered too large for their position, and his anxiety to reduce the apparent amount. Gentlemen, I am not desirous at all of casting imputations on the memory of men who can no longer defend themselves, but the fact remaining that nobody can account for that sum of £973,000 is certainly one from which you are entitled to draw your own inferences. It is unfortunately only too true that in 1873 we have, in the correspondence under Alexander Stronach's own hand, the fact of his intense solicitude about the advances which had been given, which, it is plain from his own letters, he had not taken the directors into counsel about, for he says so in the plainest terms. You will consider, therefore, whether it can be doubted that that sum of £973,000 was not a correct, but was a false deduction from the transactions of the Bank. You will find it in the slip that I have given you, placed on either side of the account. It makes no difference at all upon the ultimate result. The difference it does make, and the difference intended, according to the prosecutor, it is for you to say if you adopt it—was to diminish the amount of the liabilities or the contingencies of the Bank by the amount of £973,300. I say nothing at this moment as to who is responsible for that. The first question you have to consider is, whether you are satisfied that that is a false deduction.

The second question relates to the sum of £751,000, which Mr Morison says was taken out of the amount of the credit advances, and was inserted in the balance-sheet among the Government and other securities, the meaning of which is, according to the allegation, that it was taken out of those credit advances which were dependent for their realisation on the debtors to whom the advances had been made and represented that sum—amounting to three-quarters of a million—as being invested in securities for behoof of the Bank. Gentlemen, these are not indifferent things. If a man borrows or obtains upon overdraft an advance of one or two thousand pounds, that is one thing; if the Bank invests its surplus profits to the extent of one or two thousand pounds in Government or other securities, that is a totally different thing. It is not an advance; it is a transaction of an entirely different kind. Now, it is said, and that you must assume as true, for there have been no evidence led on the other side to impugn that result, although there have been strong comments made in regard to it—I say, assuming that this ought to have been charged against the debtors in the advances—that is to say, in their name—as expected assets coming from debtors to whom advances had been made, it is impossible to say that it is consistent with any imaginable principle of stating accounts, to take that out of the account in which it stood in the books, and to place it where it did not stand as a Government security, or a security of any kind. Nor would it make the smallest difference, I think you will be of opinion, whether security had been taken for the advance or not. The fact remained that it was not an investment. That was not the banking term for it, nor did it express the nature of the transaction. It was an advance—whether an advance on security, or an advance without security, is of no moment. It was under the right title in the books; it comes under the wrong title in the balance-sheet.

Now, gentlemen, it is for you to consider that, and be satisfied about it; but it has this element, which is very important, that there is no such entry in the book under the account or the title under which it appears in the abstract; and that, therefore, the alteration which was made on the abstract makes the abstract disconform to the books. In the view which I take of this case that is most important; for it is one thing to say, "You made up this " abstract from the books, but the books were wrong," and quite another thing to say, "You had the books in your hand, and you deliberately altered what " you found there, making it not only inaccurate itself, but disconform to the " accurate entry which you had before you when you made it." And therefore, gentlemen, upon the first question, whether these two sums of £973,000 and £751,000 were entered falsely in this balance-sheet for 1876, you will consider whether the evidence has satisfied you that such was the fact.

Gentlemen, there have been a variety of other sums called in question in this balance-sheet, and after a good deal of evidence, and a good deal of discussion, it has at last come to this, that these sums which are called in question are accurately taken from the books,—I mean from the books from which they ought to have been taken—the balance ledger and the weekly balances. It would have saved a good deal of trouble if it had been brought out a little more clearly at first; but the complaint really is this, that these are not balances, but differences; and that instead of giving the credit and debit balance of the accounts to which they relate, more than one account is taken, and they are set against each other; and where the Bank is debtor on one account and creditor in another, then only the difference is inserted in the balance ledger, instead of both sides of the account. Now that is all. There is no controversy as to figures. There is no controversy as to the truth of the sums in question. There is no controversy that that is the balance of these cross accounts. The controversy relates to this, whether it was properly entered, not so much in the balance-sheet as in the balance ledger. Gentlemen, I by no means say that if this entry in the balance ledger was an erroneous entry to the knowledge of the directors, they are not guilty of falsifying the balance-sheet if they transfer that erroneous entry to the balance-sheet. But you will at once see that it makes a very different kind of allegation from that which was the subject of my former remarks. It may be quite true,—I think we are bound to hold that it is true, because such evidence as we have from Mr Muir and Mr Hutton unquestionably points at that result,—that these balances ought not to have been carried into the balance ledger in that way, but that both sides of the accounts should have been taken. That may have been the correct form of bookkeeping, and therefore, if that was so, then you may say that, to that extent, the balance-sheet does not truely represent the balance which ought to have been entered in a different way in the balance ledger. I must own, gentlemen, and I don't hesitate to tell you that I should have been much better satisfied if the true nature of the crime alleged had been more clearly evinced in the indictment, because in those cases it must be manifest to you that the true falsification was of the books and not of the balance-sheet. But I don't think it necessary to go into that at any length, because, if it came to this question of bookkeeping, the next question would be, is there evidence to show that this was done with a fraudulent intent? and in order to ascertain that, it would have been necessary, in my view, to have shown not that in this particular year the abstract balances were so carried down, but to have shown what the ordinary practice of the Bank was, and that it was departed from with an object. I am unable to judge whether the crossing of particular accounts is or is not a proper banking operation in the balance ledger of the bank itself. I can conceive cases in which it might be convenient; but, on the other hand, it might be the instrument of great fraud, as it is said to be here. That appears to me to be doubtful, but it is entirely in your hands. You may dismiss altogether the controversy about the figures. They are there at your hand, and all I have to tell you about them is, that these are the true balances, or rather the rectification of the two sides of the account. And, accordingly, it is quite unnecessary that you should pursue the investigation into the figures which has formed the subject of so much remark from the bar. The real question is whether you can say, in the first place, upon the evidence that you have, as a matter that has been demonstrated to your satisfaction, that to carry the balances of separate accounts into the balance ledger, and not the two sides of the account, is a false operation; and in the second place, whether you think the evidence sufficient to show that that was done in these three years, with the fraudulent object of it being copied by the accountant of the Bank into the balance-sheet, and promulgated by the directors. The question of how far the directors were in the knowledge of it relates to a subsequent part of the inquiry. But on the whole matter, gentlemen, it rather seems to me, —I don't withdraw it from your consideration,—but it seems to me that it will lighten your labours, and really relieve you of some amount of obscurity which may still hang over this troublesome part of the case, if you dismiss it from your mind. If on the first two branches, which I have referred to, you shall find that the abstract balance-sheet was falsified to the extent of a million and three-quarters, it does not seem to me that we need engage in bookkeeping controversies, or that you need pay any great regard to these other less important items. Some of them are large beyond a doubt; but you will consider the whole of that matter.

Before going farther, I may make a remark on the two balance-sheets for 1877 and 1878. There is a very remarkable entry in the balance-sheet for 1877; and probably you will come to be of opinion that it has a very strong bearing on some of the remarks which fell from my learned friend, the Dean of Faculty, in his very admirable address of yesterday. The £973,000 does not appear on the balance-sheet of 1877; but instead of that there are some new entries which had never appeared before, and which made up a sum somewhat larger, amounting to £1,300,000. This is spoken to both by Mr Morison and by Mr Muir; and they both say the same thing about it; indeed, you will find it in the red ink balance-sheet for 1877, on which I am going to say a word by-and-by. But Mr Muir is asked, "In the scroll abstract or draft for 1877, does "the £963,000 appear as before?" and he says, "No, in neither 127 nor "131 does it appear. [131 is the red ink scroll.] The amount of Bills payable "account, after having the £973,000 deducted, is carried into this ledger, but "it has been scored out, as if some new idea had occurred to them,—another "way of doing it; and I find in No. 131 a pencil jotting which shows the new "method that was adopted of falsifying the accounts. (Q.) Of something "substituted for the £973,000? (A.) Yes. (Q.) What is substituted? (A.) "I find opposite the words "Bills payable" entered £2,683,348. That is "wrong to the extent of £2300. Then from that sum is deducted cash "lodged on D/A, £94,368; anticipations, £527,940; S. F. & Co., £552,704; "and J. N. F., £158,000—together £1,333,012, 19s. 1d.; difference, "£1,350,335, which was the sum stated in the published balance-sheet." (I should have reminded you under my remarks on the balance of 1876 that the £751,000 taken out of the credit advances and placed under Government securities was a part of the debt due by these three firms, Smith, Fleming, and Co., James Nicol Fleming, and James Morton & Co. That has a considerable bearing on some other parts of the case, and I shall have occasion to speak of it afterwards). Here we have the interpolation in a new form; that is to say, the £973,000 does not appear, but these three items appear, amounting together to £1,350,000, including cash on deposit account, £94,000; anticipations, £527,000; brought down from Smith, Fleming, & Co., £552,000; and from Nicol Fleming, £158,000. Gentlemen, you will consider the effect of the fact of that alteration on the balance-sheet. Morison says, "There "were no entries made for these alterations. They were not made from any "entries or any heading in the books." Then he is asked, "Are they purely "fictitious?" and he says, "There are no entries for them. (Q.) Then are "they fictitious entirely? (A.) So far as I know." So, gentlemen, whoever made that entry, or made up that balance-sheet, was certainly of opinion at that time that the sum of £973,000 ought not to enter the balance-sheet, and that those other sums ought to enter the balance-sheet. You will consider what effect that fact has when you come to consider whether the sum of £973,000 was or was not an entry believed to be honest. I pass over the other items; they are so analogous to those of 1876 that they don't require more observation from me, although you will keep in mind all that has been addressed to you from both sides of the bar on that subject. In the year 1878 the sum of £973,000 again appears,—also a fact not without its significance. But in that balance-sheet there is a sum of £200,000 added for what is called reserve gold, which, it is said by Morison, and apparently there is no dispute about it, was purely fictitious, and was, in fact, taken off the debt of Smith, Fleming, and Co. These are the falsifications and fabrications to which I think your attention had better be, if not confined, at all events, chiefly directed.

But then, gentlemen, I approach the much more delicate and difficult question,—who is responsible for that false statement in the balance-sheet? And in this instance, as regards those two sums, and, indeed, as regards all that I have spoken to, we are not without information, provided it is information on which you can rely, in regard both to the manner in which the alteration or falsification was made, and the object of it. And this leads me now, gentlemen, to deal with the account which Morison gives of this matter; and I must ask you to give to the subject, which I am now about to enter on, your most anxious attention, because it truly depends on the credibility of the witness, and that is so eminently a matter for you,—so entirely a matter within your province, that you will require to make up your minds upon it with caution, and care, and intelligence, but to come to a conclusion on that question whether you think Morison's evidence is to be relied on or not. A great deal hangs upon it, and I must now address myself to it. Gentlemen, it cannot fail to have struck you—it struck me very painfully—a painful incident in a very painful proceeding,—that of all these officials of the Bank,—and I am bound in justice to the accused to say so,—Mr Leresche was the only one who did not come here to admit that he had committed a fraud. Of Mr Leresche's evidence, I am bound to say that it was given with great candour, with great sincerity, and I think was in every way worthy of credit. I did not intend to include Mr Miller in my observations—but the three subordinate officials. Mr Miller's evidence was in the highest degree creditable to him. Nothing could have been clearer or more explicit. But, gentlemen, Mr Morison came here to say that he himself was the man who perpetrated this fraud, no doubt, as he says, at the instigation or by the direction of his superiors, but that he did it. Morris, Stronach's confidential clerk, admitted to you that in keeping the private ledger he valued James Nicol Fleming's securities at par,—he said, in order to make the thing square, without any authority, and without the slightest foundation for the entry. And then you have, I regret to say, the fact brought out that another witness, Turnbull, admitted that in his return of the gold in the Bank coffers for 1878 he stated it at, I think, twice the amount that was actually there. Gentlemen, I think I should not, in the discharge of my duty, avoid remarking on that matter. It is impossible, in any inquiry of this kind, not to feel and not to express the reprobation which acts of that kind deserve. Nor does it make it at all better that they were the servants of a man that they say wished them to betray their trust and falsify the accounts. The same excuse might be open to every official in any position of life. And therefore, gentlemen, you will take along with you that element, and it is not without its importance in this matter. But, gentlemen, at the same time, the prosecution can only work with the materials which are open to it. It might have been impossible to detect this fraud without the evidence of some one who had complicity with it. And although the observation made by some of the counsel for the prisoners is one not to be lightly treated in regard to the nature of the avowal and confession which Morison had to make, you will recollect that still it is a question for yourselves, and that which satisfies your minds on the fact is that which is evidence of the fact in the case. Now, gentlemen, I must fairly own that this evidence of Morison in some respect stands on a very insecure and unsatisfactory basis. I shall read to you a few passages from his evidence if you desire it, or probably I can state it quite accurately, unless you would rather hear his words.

A Juror—If you state it, my Lord, it will be quite sufficient.

The Lord Justice-Clerk—When Mr Morison was first in the witness-box, I certainly took up the impression, although he did not say it absolutely, and was not altogether consistent in his statement,—I understood that what he said was this:—He first described the mode in which the balance-sheets were made up, as to getting in the balances from the branches, and then he made up a scroll abstract. That scroll abstract he wrote out in black ink, and took it to the manager. He said it was arranged that the manager and Mr Potter should meet and go over that abstract, and that they did so, and that, in consequence of their instructions, he made the entry of £973,000, or rather that he made the entry of the sum of £751,000. He admitted afterwards that he had taken the figure from the balance ledger. He said he made the red ink alterations on the black ink scroll which he had taken with him, and then from that he made out the clean copy of the balance-sheet for the directors. But, gentlemen, it turned out that there was no foundation at all for that statement, as far as the particular document was concerned. I rather think the Crown originally supposed, as I certainly supposed, that the document with the red ink markings on it was the original scroll—the one which he took to the meeting with Potter and Stronach,—and that the red ink marks were the alterations which Potter and Stronach directed to be made. And that would have made a very clear case of it as far as his evidence was concerned. But, gentlemen, he did not stand to that; and after a good deal of confusion—I don't think it necessary to use a stronger word, because, in my opinion, Morison was a very confused witness—I don't think he kept his presence of mind well in the witness-box; he was agitated, and, moreover, he was not by any means a willing witness for the Crown; I think there were plain indications of that; but at last it came to this, that that was not the document which he took to the meeting; that the red ink marks were not put on at that time; and at last he said he remembered that he destroyed the black ink scroll which he took to the meeting. And therefore, gentlemen, you may discard that evidence altogether, except for this purpose: you have a copy of the scroll, and it is not difficult to see what was in the mind of the man who made up these alterations—whether he did that by direction or not by direction, you see the fact. The Dean of Faculty yesterday most ingeniously went through what he said was a demonstration that Morison was really the author of all these alterations himself. His argument was chiefly confined to the scroll of 1877, but you heard it—it was very ingenious, very powerfully put, and you will consider what effect it produced upon your own minds; but this, at all events, is certain, that the theory with which the Crown started upon Morison's evidence gave way, and that whoever made these alterations, or rather, whoever instructed them to be made, the document now produced is not the original document which Morison presented, as he alleged. There is a little more, gentlemen, before I come to the main and direct question here. I asked Morison how Potter and Stronach, who he said gave these directions at that meeting, got the figures. He said they had no figures and no books, and that he had to go and get the information and the particulars of Bills payable, and also to get the details of the credit advances, in order, he said, to see if any deduction could be made from them, and that he went and got information from the other officials. I suppose none was available; but it certainly would have been satisfactory if there had been some collateral evidence from these officials about this matter. There is no doubt the evidence of the abstract itself, which, as far as corroboration is concerned, is strong corroboration of the *res gestæ*,—the substance of what Morison speaks to. The fact that the balance-sheet was altered is a very strong circumstance in support of the allegation which Morison makes; but still, as upon his evidence a very important matter hangs, it certainly would have been to be desired, if Morison really went from the meeting to the officials, that some corroborative evidence of that should have been at hand. Now, gentlemen, I have made the observations I thought right in the direction of the defence, on Morison's testimony. But upon the main matter of fact he was clear enough, that he had a meeting with Stronach and with Potter, and that they directed him to make that alteration of the £751,000. The question is, whether that carries conviction to your minds,—and I need not say that in regard to Potter it is of the most vital consequence. If you believe Morison—if you think his evidence satisfactory and conclusive,—if you think it is sufficient on which to find that Mr Potter was not only cognisant of that falsification, but directed it, then I need not say that there is no alternative in this matter. And thus, on that question of the £751,000, it rests upon the evidence of Morison; but if his evidence is believed, then Stronach and Potter directed that alteration. If, on the other hand, you should think that Morison's evidence is not to be implicitly relied upon, then Potter will remain in the same position as the other prisoners at the bar in relation to those two sums.

But, gentlemen, what are we to say of Stronach's position in regard to this particular part of the imputation? You have evidence from Morison that the £973,000 had been the subject of conversation with him. He called his attention to it standing in the book at one time, and Stronach said it was there before he came, and that it had better not be meddled with; and that he said in 1878 that he hoped that would be the last time that he would require to make such an entry. Of course, these matters depend on the same question of credibility as the others to which I have referred; but even if Morison had not said so,—even if you had no proof that Stronach was aware of that sum of £973,000 which was there, and which he inherited from his predecessor, you could hardly fail to infer that an entry of that kind in the private cash-book was known to the manager. I don't say that the mere duty to know would convict him of knowing, but it is for you to consider whether it is or is not proof of the fact that he was cognisant of that £973,000 entry, that it stood in that private cash-book, and that there was no entry of any kind or description which could be found in any of the books to justify or explain it. Gentlemen, that is a matter on which you also, painful as it is, must make up your minds. I shall say no more about it on that part of the case. It is a matter entirely in your hands. If you shall be of opinion that the evidence is not sufficient, even against Stronach, that any such meeting took place, or that he knew that the alteration had been made, then, of course, you will give him the benefit of any doubt that rests upon your minds on that subject. But it must be plain to you that the position of the manager of the Bank is entirely different from that of the directors, and that things that you could not infer as matters of fact as regards the directors, it may be that you find yourselves compelled to infer in regard to the man who was professionally charged with the knowledge and the keeping of the whole accounts of the Bank.

Now, gentlemen, there is a third point. Whether Potter was or was not cognisant of this,—whether the evidence is sufficient against Stronach or not, what is to be said of the other directors as regards these sums? On that matter, gentlemen, I don't think it necessary to trouble you much. For my own part, I do not see that the knowledge of these two fabricated entries is brought home to them,—at least I do not know any of the evidence which leads to the conclusion that they knew that that sum of £953,000 was a fictitious entry, or that they knew that the sum of £751,000 was transferred from the one account to the other. You had it explained by Morison that when he went over the weekly balances, and read them over to the directors, they checking the entries in the balance ledger, he only read the balances, and did not read the details, and, in particular, that he did not read the sum of £973,000, and did not read the sum of £751,000, so that, in their operations in making up the balance-sheet, there is no special knowledge traced to them of either the one entry or the other. And the same observation, if it were necessary to enlarge upon it, would apply with still more force to those entries which not only appeared in the balance ledger, but which are so far supported by the whole system of bookkeeping. Even supposing it were the case that the crossing of these accounts, and the taking of their difference as representing a balance, were not true banking, or were not consistent with bookkeeping,—nay, even that it was done with a fraudulent intent, I do not see that in the circumstances that we have heard, the other prisoners, apart from Potter and Stronach, are necessarily involved in it. You are the judges of it, but that is the impression that I have formed upon the evidence. If you think otherwise, of course you will give effect to your view.

Now, gentlemen, so much for the first branch of this case, which, as I have already said, I think truly resolves practically into the question whether these two sums were or were not inserted in the balance-sheet falsely, and in the knowledge of the defenders that they were so inserted falsely. But then comes the question of the object or motive; and here, I think, you must keep in mind what has been explained frequently in the course of the trial, but still what it is rather difficult to apprehend, that the mode of deception is said to have been, not to make the balance false, but to make the materials for striking the balance false, so that the public and the shareholders, and the London banks should believe that the amount which the Bank had out at hazard was less than in reality it was, and that their assets were better secured than in reality they were. That was the motive, or the imputed motive, of putting in the sum of £973,000, and for transferring the £751,000 from the doubtful category of advances into the certain category of investments or securities. And therefore, on that part of the question, if you are satisfied upon the falsehood, and secondly, on the authors of the falsehood, I do not think on the last of these that there is much room for doubt. And that, gentlemen, concludes the first part of my observations on this important case. And to sum up the matter as it stands now, it appears to me that the main gravamen of the charge which is made against these two prisoners consists of their falsifying the balance-sheet in the two respects that I have mentioned; and that, you will observe, applies to all the three years; for it certainly does not make it better, but makes it considerably worse that that £973,000 was missed out of the second of the three balance-sheets, and a separate but equally false sum inserted. And in regard to the knowledge of the directors and the motive, you will consider whether you think that Mr Morison's evidence is sufficient to fix Mr Potter with the part which he is said to have played in regard to this matter. If it is sufficient, then there can be no question as to the object with which the alteration was made. It is in vain to say that it was an innocent alteration, if, in point of fact, it was done in the way that Morison suggests. If you should think his evidence sufficient, and I cannot tell you that it is not evidence on which you are entitled to judge, for, as I have said, it is corroborated by the balance-sheet itself, and by these scrolls very strongly —if you should think it sufficient, then I fear that Mr Potter is implicated in this matter. But, on the other hand, you will keep in mind that there have been the most serious imputations upon that testimony; you have heard it, and I have made the observations that I think right upon it. You will consider whether these observations had or had not foundation, or whether the foundation which you think they had is sufficient to discredit his testimony. You will see it is a very serious matter, and you will, I have no doubt, give it serious attention. Then, as regards Stronach, that arises in different circumstances. If you shall be of opinion that the entry of £973,000 was a fraudulent entry, you will consider whether Stronach's knowledge of it, even without Morison's evidence, is not liable at all events to a very strong presumption, or inference rather, arising from the circumstances, and whether with Morison's evidence you can have much doubt that he was cognisant of that entry. And as to the other sum of £751,000, you must judge for yourselves. You have heard the case. Stronach was the man who ought to have checked these accounts. It is possible, if you don't believe Morison, that the £751,000 might have escaped his observation, charged though he was with the Bank's books. But that is all in your hands. I don't think that I can add to the materials that you have by any further observations on this branch of the case.

I have now concluded the observations which I think it necessary to address to you on the first five subdivisions of the charges in regard to the abstract balance-sheets of 1876, 1877, and 1878. They are substantially the same, and excepting in the particulars that I have already mentioned, the observations which apply to the year 1876 are equally applicable to the other years. But there remain two charges in the indictment—two subdivisions of the narrative, or specification of the particulars, in which these abstract balance-sheets were falsified and fabricated. The last of them, as I have said, as to the bad and irrecoverable debts, is no longer a subject for inquiry. That is to say, the public prosecutor does not allege that the directors were in the knowledge that there were bad and irrecoverable debts beyond those specified in the abstract. But he says in article 6 and article 7, that the earnings of the Bank during the year were overstated under the head of profit and loss to the extent of £125,763, and then he says that the reserve fund to the extent of £450,000 was also overstated. We may dismiss the reserve fund, because the reserve fund, as I understand it, and as was explained to you, consists of the excess of the profit and loss account; that is to say, whatever is not divided as dividend is carried into the reserve fund. The real question raised here is whether the amount stated to the credit of profit and loss was or was not a false entry in the knowledge of the directors, for a fraudulent object. Gentlemen, this part of the case has given me a great deal of anxiety, in relation to the proper function that I and my colleagues have to discharge. It was objected, and I am now taking up the observations which Mr Asher made, and made very powerfully, in the course of his address,—it was objected to the indictment before you were sworn that the eighth charge was bad, because it did not contain a specification or enumeration of the debts said to be bad and irrecoverable, but not made allowance for in the abstract balance-sheet. On that objection no judgment was pronounced; but the public prosecutor struck the charge out of the indictment; and the result of that was, as I have said, that he precluded himself from alleging that bad and irrecoverable debts to a larger extent, in the knowledge of the directors, were given credit for. The trial proceeded, and the objection was also extended to Nos. 6 and 7, because, said the counsel for the prisoners, "You "cannot allow the prosecutor to go to proof that the earnings of the Bank "were less, for that is just another way of proving that so many more debts "were bad and irrecoverable." Well, manifestly, we could not sustain that objection, because it did not appear on the face of the indictment that the earnings of the Bank might not have been falsified and fabricated, although there were no bad and irrecoverable debts. We could not exclude the evidence; and, on the other hand, we declined to exclude the evidence as to bad and irrecoverable debts, although the charge founded upon it was withdrawn, because it was necessary that you should know what the true state of the Bank was, which the directors wished to conceal. But now it is said, and I am not quite sure that that was the original conception when the evidence began,—that the debts to which No. 6 refers were not bad and irrecoverable, but that they were debts which, at all events, were temporarily unprofitable, and that, therefore, the interest upon them ought to have been carried, not into the profit and loss account, but the debts themselves, and the interest charged on them, should have been carried to suspense account, and ought not to have been entered into the profit and loss account, until the debts again became profitable and advantageous. It is said that the earnings of the Bank in that way were swelled by the amount of the interest upon these outstanding debts, whereas, in the knowledge of the directors, not only had the interest not been paid, but in all probability it might never be paid. Now it has been said, and I am very far from saying that there was not force in the observation, that that is in another shape reviving the question about bad and irrecoverable debts. But on the best consideration I can give to that question, with the assistance of their Lordships, I have come to be of opinion, that even if the objection had been taken upon article 6, that it did not specify the particular debts, I should not, in a question of that kind, have felt myself bound to hold the indictment irrelevant. The objection is substantially this, that profits were alleged in this abstract balance-sheet, and credit was taken for an amount of profit, which, in point of fact, never were earned. That is a different thing from saying that there were bad and irrecoverable debts. But if the directors of a bank allege that they have profits when they know that they have none, I am not prepared to say that it is necessary that there should be a specification of the particulars which might have led to the representation of profit. It is enough to allege that there were none, and to prove it. I must own that the indictment is not conceived in that respect in the terms in which I think it should for clearness and distinctness have been expressed. If the Crown meant to say that these debts, although not bad and irrecoverable, were still of so contingent a nature that they could not with propriety be carried into profit and loss, I think it would have been better if that had appeared more distinctly upon the face of the indictment.

But, gentlemen, with that observation,—and the only weight it can receive, so far as you are concerned, is that you should hold the Crown very strictly to the proof of what they now undertake to establish,—I must now proceed to consider how far there is any ground for the allegation that this abstract balance-sheet was fabricated or falsified in respect of the entry to profit and loss, which stands in article 6 of the abstract, page 3 of the indictment (see p. 28). Gentlemen, this leads us into another and a larger field of inquiry. We have hitherto been considering simply the mode in which this balance-sheet of 1876 and the other balance-sheets were made up. The question that is now raised is of a different description. It is not denied that in the books of the Bank the profit and loss stood precisely as it is represented in the abstract balance-sheet. That account of profit and loss was prepared by the proper officials of the Bank, and during these three years the same course has been followed in regard to the amount carried to it; while it is not denied that the interest on the debts I am now going to speak of does, in point of fact, form part of the apparent surplus which appears in the account of profit and loss, although that could not be ascertained on the face of the balance ledger. Now, I am going to show you shortly how, in point of fact, those debts on which interest is so charged and carried to profit and loss stood; and then we must go on to inquire what was the proper mode of dealing with them, what the intent with which they were dealt with, and what the knowledge of the directors themselves. Gentlemen, the accountants spoke of eight accounts as being accounts that were material in this investigation; but it appears to me that it would be more accurate and quite sufficient for our purpose to confine our attention to four of the eight, for four of the eight absorb nine-tenths of the whole amount of the alleged deficiency. They are the accounts of James Morton & Co., Smith, Fleming, & Co., James Nicol Fleming, and Innes Wright & Co. You have the amounts which stood at their respective debits in the evidence of Mr Muir, and I shall shortly state to you what they were. In 1878, Morton & Co. were due £2,173,000; Smith, Fleming, & Co. were due £1,900,000 in round numbers; James Nicol Fleming was due £1,200,000; and Innes

Wright & Co. were due £485,000. So that the whole amount is as near as may be four millions and a half. Interest was charged on these accounts, and it is the interest charged on these accounts that is the subject of this challenge on the part of the Crown. Gentlemen, the history of these four accounts is undoubtedly a very remarkable one. As I said in the outset of my observations, the mere amount of loss is not quite the test of the character of the transactions on which the loss was created. You must look at the extent of the operations as well as the extent of the loss, and see what, in point of fact, was the origin of those remarkable and extraordinary advances being given to those four debtors.

I shall begin with Smith, Fleming, & Co. Mr Fleming was examined, and he gave his evidence with singular clearness and lucidity,—with great candour I think you will admit,—and the story that he told had a certain flavour of romance about it, but it was a very remarkable history of the career of a Scottish merchant. He said that when he and his brother entered into business, or were in business, in 1863, they were counting their profits, as he expressed it, by hundreds of thousands a-year; and that was a business which apparently was not mere speculation, but was that solid class of business which consists in commission agency. It seems that between 1863 and 1870 they had suffered very much by the failure of a Liverpool correspondent; and although he was actually making £93,000 a-year for the three years previous to 1870, Mr Fleming came to Glasgow in that year, having had some connection with the City of Glasgow Bank before, and told Alexander Stronach that unless he was assisted he had resolved to stop payment. He tells us that his loss was not created at all by the debt to the Bank, which amounted to something like £150,000; but it was a debt created by the failure of his Liverpool correspondent, and that £500,000 would be necessary to set him afloat again. Gentlemen, Alexander Stronach, in an evil hour for himself and for the Bank, set his face against the resolution of John Fleming to stop payment, and promised that the Bank would support him. I think there is evidence that Mr Potter was also in counsel in that matter, and at that time I think James Nicol Fleming was a director of the Bank. Well, gentlemen, it was proposed to John Fleming, much against the grain, that a new firm should be created in Liverpool, and that the bills drawn by John Fleming, and accepted by the new firm, should be discounted by the Bank, and in that way credit to the amount of £500,000 should be created. John Fleming did not much like that, and he said he did not expect that it would succeed, but still he renounced the intention of suspending payment, and agreed to go into the proposal with great reluctance, for he says that he was, in fact, hurt and irritated by the proposition that was made, that he left the room, and he thinks he was brought back by Potter. Gentlemen, as to what the inducement was on the part of Alexander Stronach to take this strong step in regard to one of the Bank customers, we are left entirely in the dark. The Bank was covered, so John Fleming says; and the mere fact of his suspension of payment would have led to no loss, or, at least, only to an insignificant loss. He said distinctly that his debt to the Bank was covered by securities, and what interest beyond that there existed on the part of Alexander Stronach to prevent the stoppage of John Fleming & Co. does not appear. But this does appear in the subsequent correspondence, that he took a great interest in the two Flemings—that he evidently was anxious to promote their interests, and prevent their ruin; and that interest he showed very clearly by his subsequent proceedings. It was arranged, therefore, on the part of the Bank at that time, that a credit of £500,000 should be raised in the way that I have described. The way is not very material to the present question. But, gentlemen, it appears quite clearly that from that day forward Alexander Stronach began a course of concealed advances to John Fleming,—concealed from his own directors,—for you have that alluded to over and over again in the correspondence of Alexander Stronach; and it is possible that you may find in that the secret of the entry about which so much has been spoken; for his letters in 1873 and 1874 are those of a man who is overwhelmed with a burden that he cannot shake off. But that these debts were not disclosed at that time to the directors, is clear from his own statement. And so the matter goes on, until in 1875 Mr Robert Stronach is appointed in his place. In that year Mr Robert Stronach was appointed manager of the Bank. He was most reluctant to accept the office. I don't wonder that he was. He says in his letter to the directors that Alexander Stronach had withheld his confidence from him. I think that very likely; but I think, at the same time, that he can hardly have failed to see very good reason for the disinclination which he evinced. He says, and there is evidence of that elsewhere, that James Morton & Co. had promised to pay £400,000 in diminution of their debt if he would become the manager of the Bank, and he did become manager on a condition; and that is a condition to which I shall immediately ask your attention. But such was the state of matters in 1875, before the first of those years when John Fleming's affairs came to a crisis. He had still a large commission business. I think there is evidence that he made £50,000 a-year by his own personal commission business, besides his partner's; but these old debts still hung round him; the Bank were pressing, and accordingly he came to an arrangement in August 1875, which was the commencement of a career of irregular operations on the part of the Bank, which ultimately assumed still larger dimensions. The result of that arrangement in 1875 was this: the Bank agreed to give up so much of their interest and commission, and to reduce the interest from 5 to 3½ per cent., with a corresponding reduction in the commission which they charged; they were to advance £100,000, which was to be secured upon shares to be purchased by the Bank in the Otago Land Company, the rate of interest in the colony being apparently so much in advance of that at home, that it was calculated that by that manipulation a considerable saving would be effected. When all that was done, it was calculated by John Fleming—and he told you that he thought his calculation an accurate one—that he would be able to pay the whole interest and commission chargeable by the Bank, and £25,000 a-year in reduction of the principal debt. In that way, in 1875, it was calculated that in fourteen years one half of the debt would be entirely extinguished. Gentlemen, that arrangement was made by the directors of the Bank at that time, and the shares were purchased, the £100,000 of credit was obtained, the interest was reduced, but, unfortunately, the £25,000 a-year was not realised, and was not paid. And in the end,—for there is not much in the interval between 1875 and 1878,—it turned out that the debt of John Fleming, instead of being diminished, was largely increased. It was £1,300,000 in 1875 when this arrangement was made, and, as I have told you, in 1878 it was £1,960,000, and that is the figure at which it ultimately remained. There was a meeting in 1878, after the balance-sheet had been prepared and published, but apparently that was too late to be of any moment in this inquiry. And that is the history of one of these debts. The amount is about two millions.

The second of the debtors, James Nicol Fleming, had a career very similar. He was a director of the Bank, and he resigned in 1874. He also had been a successful man in his day, but at the date which we are speaking of—between 1870 and 1875—things had gone greatly against him, and it is proved by his own clerk that he had lost all the capital with which he started, and therefore had nothing but borrowed money to trust to. He had a large commission business, and he had very large schemes afloat. He was making, even later than that, £20,000 a-year, but then these old encumbrances were still round him, and in 1875 he was owing the Bank £1,005,000. There were securities doubtless held for that, but that was the sum at which he stood in the books of the Bank. Gentlemen, it is needless to disguise that when Robert Stronach succeeded to the management of this Bank, he succeeded to a very anxious and troublesome legacy. These debts were none of his creating. There were advances made by the directors afterwards, but these were as a drop compared with the accumulation which existed; and when he succeeded, therefore, to the office of manager, he succeeded his relative, who had been going on with a system of concealed advances until they reached that very serious and alarming amount. Mr Hunter, who was also examined before you, and whose evidence was of the clearest and most satisfactory kind, described to you the negotiations that took place to see whether some means could not be found of enabling James Nicol Fleming, who still had a large and valuable connection, to go on. The result was that Mr Hunter recommended Stronach to get rid of this account as soon as he could. And accordingly, in 1875, the account was put into liquidation,—by which is meant that the account is no longer to go on, that there are to be no further operations upon it, but that the securities are to be realised and placed to the credit of the account. In the meantime James Nicol Fleming started a new Indian and Australian concern, by which he hoped, along with the securities which the Bank held, to be able to redress his balance. Some little time after that the Bank lighted upon a scheme which was explained to you in detail, and which I don't mean to go into at any length, but which, beyond all doubt, was beyond the pale of regular banking. But as I have said to you before, and I think it necessary to tell you again, we are not concerned here at all with the question whether the proceedings of the directors in these matters were beyond their contract or within their contract. We are dealing with the question of personal dishonesty, and not of civil liability; and although this scheme that I am now going to describe might be subject to great observation in any question in regard to civil right, or the rights of securities obtained under it, that is not a matter that can affect this case, or the charge that is now made, except as part of the history of the case. But so it is that Mr Potter had very large and valuable connections in Australia. Mr Glen Walker seems to have been brought into counsel at this period of the Bank's history, and the result of the whole matter was this, that the Bank undertook, through Mr Glen Walker, to make purchases in New Zealand or Australia—in New Zealand, I think—of land which was to be held in property by the Bank, or at least for them, in the hope and expectation that the rise in the value of that land, which they thought to be pretty secure, in a few years would wipe off the indebtedness of James Nicol Fleming. And in the meantime, they proposed to carry on the operations by a system of double discount,—by drawing bills upon the Bank which were to be accepted by the Bank and then discounted, and before the currency of these bills expired another set of bills was put in the circle, the discount being used to retire them. Gentlemen, some questions have arisen in regard to these bills, but with these I do not think it necessary to trouble you. It was a question of accounting which Mr Muir raised as to whether, when both the sets of bills were discounted, and the proceeds paid into the Bank, it created one debt or two. In the view that I have taken it is not necessary that we should decide that matter, though undoubtedly I should have thought that Mr Muir's view of it was right. The main matter is this, that that singular and very irregular proceeding was adopted—for a Bank is incorporated not for the purpose of buying land or speculating in land, but for the proper and legitimate objects of banking,—I say such was the proceeding, and such was the endeavour that the Bank made to shake themselves clear of this unfortunate encumbrance.

Now, gentlemen, the third debtor was James Morton. We have heard very little about him, and I have it not in my power—because there was not evidence to enable me to do it—to explain to you the fluctuations and vicissitudes of that account; but it was one of the largest, and it ended with a balance of £2,170,000. What the operations upon it had previously been, we have had no evidence to show; and for my own part, I should certainly have preferred that we had seen Mr Morton or some one connected with the firm, because it is plain from the correspondence, which I don't weary you by going over, that all these firms were intimately connected, and that Potter, Wilson, & Co., and Lewis Potter & Co., and Morton, and Innes Wright, and the two Flemings, had more or less business concerns together, and were in fact, to a certain extent, in the same interest.

The fourth account stands in a singular position, and we have very little information about it also. You will recollect the evidence about it; I shall have to refer to it before I conclude. But the fourth account was the account of John Innes Wright & Co., which amounted, in 1878, to £485,000,—nearly half a million. It had not increased materially since Mr Wright became a director in 1875, but you had his partner Mr Paul, who told you plainly that the other partner, Scott, managed the whole financial affairs of the company, that he never could get an account from him, that he was entirely and absolutely ignorant of the amount of the advances from the Bank, and he was not even able, at the time that he was examined, to give a clear financial history of the affairs of the firm. And I may here take the opportunity of saying, that it appeared to me that Mr Guthrie Smith succeeded in showing that the balance which comes out in 1878, which is nearly £100,000 larger than that of 1877, was truly not on a proper company account at all. £33,000 of it, he said, was the result of a wool lien,—a transaction between Glen Walker & Co. under the arrangement which had been made. £46,000 of it arose in this way,—in a way which, in this particular matter, can scarcely be an element against Mr Wright; for Scott had been entrusted by the Bank, not in the way of an advance for his personal benefit, but entirely as attorney or agent for the Bank itself, to discount the Bank's acceptances and remit to them the discount. Scott did not do so, and was a defaulter to the extent of £46,000. Whatever importance may be attached to that fact now, I think it only right to say that I think it was satisfactorily established. I shall say a word upon Mr Wright's personal interest in that matter by-and-by.

Now, gentlemen, there you see were four accounts, the balances on which amounted altogether to four millions and a half. And how were they secured? That is a question on which our information is imperfect, because these securities have not been realised, and their value has not been ascertained. It is but fair to the defenders to say, that although these accounts were of enormous amount, at the same time the earning power of John Fleming & Co. and James Nicol Fleming, and Morton & Co., that is to say, their business connection,—their knowledge of the trade in which they were embarked, the confidence which foreign merchants had in them, still remained as a valuable asset, if it could only be made available. So say the defenders, and I think they established that. They then say that John Fleming was quite confident, in 1875, that he would be able to pay the interest, and would also in fourteen years be able to clear off the main part of the debts due to the Bank, and that he had no doubt at all, if he confined himself to his proper commission business, he could without difficulty clear off that debt and start again without encumbrance. Nor was he alone in that, for if I don't mistake, some observation of the same kind was made by Mr Hunter. On the other hand, in regard to the account of James Fleming & Co., Mr Glen Walker was very confident that in the end, if he had gone on, the New Zealand and Australian lands would become of immense value. And perhaps they may also say that the fact of the stoppage, which in truth did not directly result from these debts, has depreciated the securities, as of course it would, far below what they might have been valued at if the Bank had been going on, and their debtors consequently allowed to go on too. Now, gentlemen, so stands that part of the case.

There are four questions which then arise for your consideration. First, did the directors—the prisoners at the bar—know the condition of these accounts? Second, if they did know it, what was the proper mode of dealing with them in the balance-sheets which were to be laid before the shareholders? Third, were the directors personally aware of the mode in which the accounts were dealt with in the Bank? And lastly, supposing that they didn't know these things directly, had they such information as must have put them in bad faith to state that amount of profit as having been earned within the year?

Gentlemen, in regard to the first of these questions, viz., the knowledge of the directors generally, and of Stronach, the manager, as to the state of these accounts, I don't think that that is a matter which, taken as a general statement, can be doubted. I don't say that they knew the details of accounts in 1878; perhaps not either in 1876 or 1877; but you heard in the course of the evidence, and there is no denial of the fact, that Robert Stronach would not take office until he had somebody to share with him the anxiety of this horrible legacy that had been left him by his predecessor, and although the accounts are not named in the letter which has been read to you more than once, he distinctly says—"I take office on the condition that the directors "will look into these old accounts, and will take measures in order to their "liquidation," And, gentlemen, they did take measures. I thought the remarks of the Dean of Faculty very well founded upon that matter. They were not debts of their incurring. They had no responsibility about them. They were debts which were incurred by the former manager, without their knowledge; but, as the Dean of Faculty has said, they set to work manfully to devise some means of lightening the burden for the Bank, and removing it from the shoulders of the shareholders. Up to that point there is nothing to say against what they did. And here I take the opportunity of saying that I think the remarks on the part of the prosecutor as to the course which they followed in their deliberations—now that we see all round this matter—were pressed somewhat more strongly than the facts altogether warranted. I don't think the directors wanted to postpone the evil day in this matter. A postponement for four months—as appears in one of the minutes —was not an unreasonable thing, looking to the large ventures that were still unascertained. I don't think that the fact that Mr Leresche was asked to leave the room when these matters were discussed argued anything; for what were the directors doing but endeavouring to make arrangements by which the debt should be liquidated? I think it is no part of this case, and you may dismiss that from your minds altogether,—at least I think so, that there was any hidden conspiracy on the part of the directors to ruin the Bank for their own advantage. There was nothing of that kind. The charge of crime against the directors is of a different description altogether, and the motive is different too. But the importance of the inquiry that I am now going into is the fact that the directors, as a body and individually, were in the cognisance of the fact that the debts were so doubtful that it was necessary to take some step for the purpose of bringing them into shape.

Gentlemen, in regard to the secretary being present at the meetings, of course every bank has its own more secret deliberations,—its own more difficult and delicate accounts,—and we are not going to press hardly upon gentlemen who have such a herculean task to perform as to clear off debts amounting to about four millions, which they had not incurred themselves. For my own part, as far as that is concerned, I think every one must sympathise with the difficulty of the position. But then, gentlemen, most undoubtedly in 1875, the directors, when they set their shoulders to the task, must have been aware of the position in which these debts stood. In 1875 they made the arrangement with John Fleming. Well, John Fleming says he expected that that would enable him to pay £25,000 a-year, after paying the interest and the commission. The directors may have thought so. It is for you to consider what was the true conclusion that ought to have been derived from that position. At the same time, the arrangement was one that obliged the Bank to go out of its ordinary course, and to take shares in a trading company in Australia, which undoubtedly was not the ordinary procedure, nor an ordinary course to follow under the Bank contract. And that went on. There are a variety of meetings. I am not going to trouble you by reading the minutes over again. I will only say this, that I think the result of them all is that Mr Stronach did do what he said he intended to do,—that he brought the state of the accounts before the directors, and they took up the accounts. They seem to have settled the arrangement with John Fleming in 1875, and in 1876 they put James Nicol Fleming into liquidation. There he remained, and as far as that account is concerned, I don't find in the minutes that anything took place until the land speculation of Glen Walker came up. Beyond all question,—it is needless to disguise it,—this was not legitimate banking, although it might be the most likely way of relieving themselves of their advances. This land speculation led to farther advance, to double sets of bills accepted by the Bank for that purpose,—all most irregular banking unquestionably, and all most certainly foreshadowing the ruin that ultimately came. It was possible, undoubtedly, that if the commercial crisis had passed over, and a sudden rush of advance on securities had taken place, and the cloud which has been overhanging this country for so many years had dispersed—it was within the chapter of accidents that things would have come right. In short, they were precisely in the position that I have described to you in the outset of my remarks, and were brought face to face with it. They had, perhaps, the alternative of either closing the Bank doors, or doing what, in point of fact, was done. But between these two things there could be no legal choice at all. They had a deficit of four millions, though covered by securities which still remained doubtful. No doubt if they stopped and closed the Bank doors, or took away their assistance, the securities would crumble into nothing, and it might be a dead loss to the shareholders; and so it would. But, in the meantime, the question is whether they were aware of the state of these accounts at the date of the first of these balance-sheets. I think, gentlemen, without holding that they were aware of all the steps and proceedings in regard to the accounts; without knowing how the arrangement of 1875, in John Fleming's instance, had succeeded; without knowing whether the New Zealand speculation was a profitable or promising one or not, they did know that these large accounts were outstanding, and that the realisation of them was still a matter of question. So much for the first of these questions. It is not of any importance to go into the question who was present at this meeting, and who was present at that. The conclusion that I think you will come to is, that there was enough known to the Bank board to fix the general knowledge of the position of the accounts on all the directors.

But then, gentlemen, comes the next question. It is conceded by the Crown, and the Crown have no power to withhold the concession, that they do not say that the directors knew these debts to be bad and irrecoverable. I don't think they were bad and irrecoverable. I think that was not the category under which they should have been classed. I think they were very hazardous. But in the question whether they are to be sent to the suspense account or to be carried in the ordinary way into profit and loss, there arises a question very much for you. It is, as the counsel said, to a certain extent a matter of opinion. I should have said, that looking to the position in which the accounts stood, the only safe way for the shareholders was, in the meantime, not to calculate on their being profitable. But you must keep in mind what the ordinary practice is; and it is this; when a debt is bearing interest, the interest on it when charged in the account is carried to profit and loss, whether it be paid or not, provided there is a reasonable prospect that it will be paid. And, accordingly, Mr Hutton explained that if these large accounts had been only for a year, he would have seen nothing wrong in carrying the interest to profit and loss: but he said, if the interest has not been paid for several years, then he would think it wrong to do anything but put it in suspense account. Gentlemen, that is a matter, in the first place, as a matter of proper banking, which you must decide. It was said by the counsel for the prisoners, and said truly, that some of these accounts which are said to have been properly the subjects of suspense accounts were, in point of fact, not in that position. It does appear that in 1876 James Morton & Co. paid up £80,000 of the principal debt, and that of course included the payment of the previous interest. It also appears, I think, that Innes Wright & Co., in one year, did the same. The smaller accounts of Matthew, Buchanan, and Co., and Glen Walker & Co., are liable to the same observation. They were not dormant accounts; and apparently, from John Fleming's account, the advances which he got between 1875 and 1878 were, to a certain extent, covered by securities which were actually paid in. Now, that is what the defenders say, and I have thought it right to bring it under your notice. You have heard the evidence, and you can judge for yourselves. What they substantially say is this, that in 1875 and 1876 the accounts of the two Flemings were not materially in hazard, and might have done very well if the Bank had been able to go on; and that therefore there was nothing which compelled the directors to go out of the ordinary course, and to carry the interest upon these debts to suspense account. Now, gentlemen, if you shall think that that was clearly a matter of opinion, and that although your own opinion is the proper and true opinion as regards the administration of the Bank, if you shall yet think that the opposite course could have been followed in good faith, although wrongly—even foolishly—then you cannot find that there was any fraudulent intent in carrying this sum to the credit of profit and loss. But if you shall think that, looking to the circumstances as you have heard them detailed, no prudent man—no man in his senses—would have held out that sum of £125,000 as profit made in the year, if it truly consisted of nothing but the interest on these debts which had never been paid, then I am afraid that will come to be a serious matter, and that is a matter that really I must leave entirely in your hands. It is right to say, however, that during 1878 £74,000 of profit was realised by the branches alone. That, however, applies to the next point that I am going to refer to. If you shall think that the directors ought not to have carried this to profit and loss, but, on the contrary, must have known that they were wrong in doing so, I don't know, gentlemen, what you are to make of the fact that they actually increased the dividend that year over the year before. But, gentlemen—and this brings me to the testing and the touching point of that part of the case—this sum of £125,000 stands in the book at the credit of profit and loss; and of course when the balance was made up, what the officials of the Bank were bound to do, and were wont to do, was to take the balance, transcribe it first into the balance ledger, and then pass it into the abstract balance-sheet. That is the ordinary course. When the directors saw the £125,000 at the credit of profit and loss, it did not appear, on the face of that document, how that £125,000 was entered in the books; and it is said—and that is really the most important consideration on this head that you have—it is said, it is quite true the directors may have known all about these accounts, but they had no reason to suppose that when the books of the Bank were balanced, and £125,000 of profit was shown, any part of that or the whole of it consisted of interest on these accounts. They did not know how the accounts were dealt with in the books, but they were entitled to assume, as they could not be constantly examining the books, that the officials of the Bank had not played them false.

Gentlemen, that is the defence of the directors on this part of the case. The observations that I have made about the manager, I am afraid, apply to this part of the case also; and I am afraid I must add another remark in regard to Mr Potter, because, although the other directors, the members of committees, and those present at board meetings when these accounts were overhauled, might after all have a very slight and shadowy acquaintance with the details of the accounts and the details of the arrangements, I am afraid,—and it is only right that I should say so, and I regret to say it,—that Mr Potter throughout, from first to last, apart altogether from his position as a director of the Bank, was cognisant of all the proceedings that were taken for the purpose of liquidating the debts of these firms. I am far from imputing that to Mr Potter as of itself derogatory to him. I am going to make a remark upon the personal position of all the seven prisoners at the bar before I conclude. Only I fear that it will hardly be possible for Mr Potter to say that he was not aware of the position of the accounts. It is another question,—and that is for you to consider,—whether, although he knew the position of the accounts intimately, he was aware that the profit and loss was struck after crediting the amount of interest on these accounts.

But, gentlemen, there is a concluding question, and with that I shall very nearly terminate the observations which I have to make. Apart from Potter and Stronach, do you think that, in 1876, 1877, and 1878, any of the directors of this Bank thought that a dividend of 12 per cent., or a profit of £125,000, had been earned from the business? If you should come to be of opinion that the position of the accounts was such, in their knowledge, that whatever the details of the accounts might have been, that was a result which could not possibly be accurate, then I fear you have a serious duty before you. I have stated to you, as fairly as I am able, the grounds upon which I think your judgment must proceed. If you think there are the means of discrimination between the prisoners, you are quite entitled to use your own judgment on that matter. It certainly strikes one now, at the end of the day, as not a favourable fact in this case that with all the knowledge which the directors had, and the actual fact of these liabilities before them, that knowledge found no expression whatever in their balance-sheet. At the same time, I have only to repeat that what you have to find is not general suspicion or impression, but you must be satisfied that they knew that this statement, like the others, was unfounded in fact, and that it was fraudulently made.

Gentlemen, I said that before I concluded I should think it right to make an observation upon each of the prisoners at the bar, and in the first place on the case of Mr Stewart. Now it is quite certain that Mr Stewart was on more than one occasion brought into direct communication with the actors in the matters that I have referred to. John Fleming said he had never seen him, but I think Mr Hunter or Mr Glen Walker said they had; and it is also certain that Mr Stewart went over the draft of the report for 1878 and compared it with the abstract. Gentlemen, I don't put much stress upon that any more than I put much stress upon the fact that a man sits in the chair at a board meeting, hears things read, and takes part in the formal business. I don't put much stress upon it, unless it had been shown that Mr Stewart really was perfectly informed as to the matters with which they were dealing. Mr Potter stood in a different position, for he understood the whole of the negotiations quite well. But, in the meantime, I am talking of Mr Stewart, and as far as his personal actings are concerned, while I think you cannot relieve him of the knowledge of the general position of these accounts, probably he was not particularly conversant with their details; and as to the books of the Bank, you certainly cannot charge him with any knowledge of them at all. I think it right to say that I don't wonder that Mr Stewart's counsel rather protested against the allegations that were originally made in the indictment; and I think it right in justice to him to call attention to the fact, that not only could it not have been said, as the case turned out, that he had been guilty of embezzling the funds of the Bank, but, in point of fact, he was a man in such circumstances that he was able, out of his means, to have paid his obligations to the Bank twice over. I think that is a fair observation to make on the part of Mr Stewart. On the other hand, while I bring that before you, you will not forget that if you are of opinion that all the directors were aware generally of the position of these accounts, I have already gone over the views that occur to me as to the result of that knowledge.

As to Mr Potter, I have made some observations upon his knowledge and proceedings already; but there are one or two remarks that I think it is only reasonable and right to make. If you believe Mr Morison that Mr Potter was a party to the falsification of the abstract balance of 1876, it is impossible to disguise the gravity of the offence thereby committed. In regard to the rest, I think it is quite true that Mr Potter was very cognisant of all these matters from beginning to end, and on the whole I am not disposed to think that he was acting for any particular benefit of his own. The Bank was not in advance to him substantially; he was a man worth £16,000 a year, quite able to meet any liability that could come upon him at that time; and moreover, it is so far in his favour, and in favour of the confidence of the directors in these firms, that it does appear that his son, John Potter, had proposed to join the firm of Smith, Fleming, & Co. just at the very crisis, and in the very middle of their embarrassments. That is a fact, and it is only due to the prisoner to say so. I have read through the correspondence very carefully, and I have not found in any portion of it any indication of a personal interest,—I mean a corrupt personal interest, on the part of Mr Potter; but, on the contrary, I have seen several indications of good feeling and friendliness.

As to the case of Mr Salmond, I think he has established that when the negotiations about the adjustment of the balance-sheets were going on in the months of June and July, in these three years he was for the most part out of Scotland for the benefit of his health. Whether he has absolutely established such an *alibi* as would have enabled him to escape in a trial of a different kind is not quite the question. But I think you may give some weight to the fact that he was not at hand for consultation. He was not there. He not only could not consult, but he could not be consulted, because he was not at home. I don't think it necessary to go into the particular details which were so clearly explained by his counsel; and no very specific observations were made against that view by the Lord Advocate, who rather seemed to say that that was not the kind of plea that could be very available in an inquiry like this. Gentlemen, you must consider that. Lord Mure reminds me of an incident in the history that I gave you, where John Fleming writes to Robert Stronach to warn him that he had seen Salmond in communication with Mr Potter, and to warn him not to be too communicative to Salmond if he should speak on the subject. That was at the time there was a proposal that John Potter should join the firm.

The DEAN OF FACULTY—That was a letter to Alexander Stronach.

The LORD JUSTICE-CLERK—The letter bears to be to Robert Stronach, but the witness Fleming corrected that, and said it was written to Alexander. It is of no moment to which of them it was written; the point is as it affects Salmond.

Gentlemen, in regard to Taylor, there was evidence led that he was quite above the world; and although his indebtedness to the Bank was considerable —to the extent of some £70,000—he had had a large business,—he had had large operations on the Bank—debits and credits—and that there was nothing in his position which should have given him any object whatever in being a party to a fraud for any possible personal advantage that he could get from it.

The account of John Innes Wright & Co. is certainly not a satisfactory element. Mr Wright became a director when James Nicol Fleming retired; and his partner, Mr Paul, told him that he should not take the office. I think you must be quite satisfied, and I fear Mr Wright must be quite satisfied, that that judgment was perfectly sound. It was not desirable that the partner of a firm indebted in over £300,000 to the Bank should be a director. On the other hand, it does seem, as I have already said, that the financial affairs of the firm were not in his hands at all, and his personal advances from the Bank were nothing, excepting the price advanced to purchase his qualification as a director.

Mr Inglis states in his own vindication that he was resident in Edinburgh, and not a Glasgow man at all; that he did his best to attend the meetings of the board, and that he neither did nor could undertake to investigate the details of any of the accounts. As to the advances which appear in the indictment, there is no allegation now made that these were improperly obtained, and his counsel chose to rest his view on this, that he was not bound to enter into Mr Inglis' private pecuniary affairs, if no charge was made on that subject.

As regards Mr Stronach, their is no doubt that the weight of this blow comes very heavily upon him. His position, unquestionably, was a very painful and a difficult one; but that will not, as I have said more than once, in any degree remove the consequences of the truth of such a charge from his shoulders. Mr Salmond was, I think, the largest shareholder amongst the directors, and he held his shares to the end. So did Mr Stronach, and so did Mr Taylor. And, indeed, there is nothing in the conduct of the prisoners at the bar to indicate that they were making ready to quit a falling house, or that they were making preparations for a catastrophe that they thought was at hand. Mr Stronach had quite means enough to meet any advances that he had received, and, indeed, it was proved that he has been able to pay the first call now due upon his shares.

Gentlemen, I have now discharged the very painful duty that has been imposed upon me, and which has now occupied our time and attention for so many days. I have never, since I had a seat on the bench, experienced so much feeling of pain, of regret—I had almost said of mortification. The circumstances that we have been inquiring into have a large significance outside these walls. I need not allude to them again. But I have only in conclusion to say, as I said at the beginning, that we have nothing but an ordinary duty to perform here, which is to weigh the evidence that has been led, and to come to the conclusion that right, and justice, and conscience dictate. You will give the prisoners the benefit of every reasonable doubt, as all prisoners are entitled to have. You will take into view their character, as you would take into view the character of any prisoner accused of a crime at this bar. But if you shall be satisfied that the prosecutor has established his charge, then you will deliver the verdict which your conscience may dictate; and whether your verdict be to convict or to acquit, it will be enough for you, doubtless, that your own consciences approve; but I think I may safely say that, be it what it may, it will carry with it the respect and the approbation of the country.

The jury retired at ten minutes to four, and returned into Court at a quarter to six o'clock.

The LORD JUSTICE-CLERK—Gentlemen, what is your verdict?

The FOREMAN OF THE JURY (Mr JAMIESON)—The jury unanimously find the panels Lewis Potter and Robert Summers Stronach guilty of the charges as libelled; and find the panels John Stewart, Robert Salmond, William Taylor, Henry Inglis, John Innes Wright, guilty of using and uttering a false abstract balance-sheet or statement of the affairs of the City of Glasgow Bank.

The LORD JUSTICE-CLERK—Then, gentlemen, you will formally find the four panels who are charged with embezzlement not guilty, and the panels charged with theft not guilty, those charges having been withdrawn.

The VERDICT was recorded as follows:—"The jury unanimously find the "panels, Lewis Potter and Robert Summers Stronach, guilty of the first, "second, and third charges, as libelled, and find them not guilty of the "remaining charges; and find the panels, John Stewart, Robert Salmond, "William Taylor, Henry Inglis, and John Innes Wright, guilty of using and "uttering, as libelled, under the first, second, and third charges, and find them "not guilty of all the remaining charges."

The LORD JUSTICE-CLERK (to the Jury)—I have to thank you for the great attention you have paid to this very important case; and to announce that in respect of your service on this occasion, you will not again be required to act as jurymen for the next five years.

The LORD JUSTICE-CLERK then intimated that sentence would be pronounced to-morrow, at half-past ten o'clock.

Twelfth Day.—Saturday, 1st February 1879.

The LORD JUSTICE-CLERK, addressing Lewis Potter and Robert Stronach, said,—Lewis Potter, Robert Stronach, the jury, after a long investigation, and after full deliberation, have found you guilty on the first branch of the three charges of falsifying and fabricating the balance-sheets of the Bank. I think it is proper to say, in explanation of the sentence which must now follow upon that verdict, that, had the other two charges contained in the indictment, or either of them, been proved to the jury, it would have imposed upon us the duty of inflicting a very severe punishment, because not only would these charges have inferred a crime of very great magnitude, but they would have brought into the case the element of personal advantage as the motive of the act which you committed; and I am desirous to say that, as the case now stands, the act which was done by both of you did not necessarily involve, and probably was not actuated by, any design or desire of personal advantage, but was a criminal act committed, as you thought, for the benefit of the Bank. That does not remove it from the category of crime,—very far from it,—but it does remove from the crime of which you have been convicted the element, as I have said, of corrupt personal motive for personal ends. That consideration has weighed with the Court in the sentence which I am now to pronounce, being short of one of penal servitude. The sentence of the Court on you, Lewis Potter, and on you, Robert Stronach, is that you be imprisoned for the period of eighteen calendar months.

The LORD JUSTICE-CLERK (addressing the other prisoners)—The jury have found all of you guilty, not of fabricating or falsifying the balance-sheets, but of uttering and publishing them, knowing them to be false. We have considered also your case, and looking to the crime of which you have been convicted, and the distinction that may be drawn between you and the other two prisoners, and considering that you have been in jail now since the month of October, the sentence of the Court is that you be further imprisoned for eight calendar months.

The LORD JUSTICE-CLERK added—It has been represented to me that, in my observations in charging the jury yesterday, I made some remarks upon the officials of the Bank that might be misunderstood. Some of the gentlemen who were witnesses, at least one who was a witness at the trial—I mean Murdoch—it has been said, might possibly feel hurt, and might be injured if my remarks were intended to apply to him; and I wish it, therefore, to be clearly understood that in the remarks that I made about the officials of the Bank, I referred to three of the witnesses, viz., Morison, the accountant; Morris, the private clerk; and Turnbull, who gave the false return to the Inland Revenue.

APPENDIX.

APPENDIX II.

REPORT by Messrs KERR, ANDERSONS, MUIR, & MAIN, Chartered Accountants, Glasgow, and Messrs M'GRIGOR, DONALD, & CO., Solicitors, Glasgow, in reference to BALANCE-SHEET of the CITY OF GLASGOW BANK, as at 1st October 1878.

ON the 2d instant we were instructed by the Directors of the City of Glasgow Bank to prepare a balance-sheet of the Bank, as at 1st October 1878, to be submitted to the shareholders on the earliest possible day.

For reasons that will sufficiently appear in the course of this report, we have felt it necessary to prefix to this balance-sheet a statement explanatory of the system adopted by us in preparing it, and of the leading points in which it contrasts with the balance-sheet issued by the Board of Directors as of 5th June last.

On receipt of the instructions referred to, we at once proceeded to make an investigation of the books at the head office of the Bank, and gave directions for the necessary statements and returns being procured from the branches. For the first few days it was extremely difficult to make any real progress. The immediate result of the stoppage of the Bank was, as might be expected, a temporary disorganization of the working staff, and, besides, the incessant demands made upon us to reply to enquiries, and to advise as to questions calling for immediate decision, greatly interfered with the steady prosecution of the investigation.

By the afternoon of the 4th instant, however, we became satisfied, from what we had even then learned of the position of the Bank, that there was no reasonable probability of its being able to resume business, and, with the view of protecting the interests of the shareholders, we reported to the directors that it was not advisable to delay any longer calling them together. It seemed to us to be of less importance that an exhaustive examination of the books should take place (a matter which would have involved weeks, if not months of delay), than that a vidimus, however rough, showing, even approximately, the *real* state of matters should be laid before the shareholders, in order that they should have the power of at once deciding on the course to be followed, and, if they should see fit, of appointing competent parties with the requisite authority to preserve and administer what remained of the Bank's property and assets. In the ordinary case, the resolutions passed at such a meeting of shareholders would have required confimation, involving altogether a delay of four weeks, but by taking advantage, as has been done (under the advice of counsel), of the 3d sub-section of the 129th section of the Companies Act, 1862, a fortnight will have been saved in the event of liquidation being resolved on.

The time at our disposal has thus been proportionately abridged, and we have not aimed at producing anything like an exhaustive examination of particular details, which, under the circumstances, would have proved utterly futile. We have, at the same time, been careful to indicate below the various elements of uncertainty which appear to us to attach to individual items on each side of the balance-sheet. In framing this balance-sheet and report, no avoidable delay has been incurred, and the work has been proceeded with as rapidly as was consistent with the circumstances, which demanded the fullest investigation possible, independent altogether of data voluntarily submitted to us.

The books which more immediately came under our cognisance, as containing a record of the transactions of the Bank, were as follows:—

1. Discount ledgers and abstracts thereof; showing, in detail, all the current bills discounted at the head office, with the exception of those having not more than seven days to run.

2. Deposit ledgers and interest receipt registers; containing the accounts of all depositors who are creditors of the Bank on current or deposit accounts, or debtors to the Bank on cash overdrafts.

3. Credit ledgers; containing a record of the cash credits granted by the Bank, whether secured, partially secured, or wholly unsecured.

4. Returns from the various branches, 133 in number; containing, as regards these branches, the same information as the foregoing books supply with regard to the head office.

5. General ledgers and abstracts thereof; showing the results of the business of the Bank upon discounts, interests, and commission. These ledgers also contain an account raised out of profit and loss account to the amount of £450,000 as a reserve fund against losses, and a contingent account having at the credit a sum of £18,036, 11s. 9d., and consisting of the accumulation of certain other sums set aside from time to time out of the profit and loss account.

6. Balance books; which contain a complete statement of the balances in the general ledgers, and which were annually docquetted by the directors, or a majority of their number.

7. Abstract of accounts made up annually, in which the yearly result of the transactions recorded in the Bank books are brought into a focus, and from which the printed balance-sheet issued to the shareholders is epitomised.

8. Registers of securities held by the Bank, of which one was kept by the law secretary, and another, containing a record of securities held against advances on certain special accounts, by the private clerk of the manager.

9. Cashier's ledger, containing a record of notes issued, or in reserve, and of coin in possession of the Bank.

10. Circulation ledger, containing a daily record of the Bank's circulation, the coin on hand at the head office and branches, and of the monthly average, and from which the weekly returns forwarded to Government were made up.

Besides the above, we have incidentally examined, as occasion seemed to require, many of the other books necessary for the carrying on of the business of the Bank, such as tellers' cash books and jotting books, and monthly and weekly abstracts of individual accounts made up by the private clerk of the manager, besides drafts of the more recent abstracts of accounts (No. 7 above referred to), and memoranda and jottings by the late manager of the Bank.

We have likewise availed ourselves of all the information we could procure from the sub-officials of the Bank, which has been readily, and we believe frankly and fully, accorded to us.

At an early stage in our inquiry, it became apparent that questions seriously affecting the course of management by the directors and manager of the Bank were involved in the investigation; and we have felt it our duty, while soliciting from these gentlemen explanations as to certain particular items, to bring under their notice the serious nature of the questions referred to. In most instances we were told that the explanations we invited related to points which were as new and as startling to the parties interrogated as to ourselves.

We shall now proceed to refer to certain items in our detailed statement of liabilities and assets which seem to call for special explanation or remark.

I.—LIABILITIES.

D. Acceptances by the Bank past due or current.

In the general ledger of the Bank there is an account under the heading of "Bills "Payable," which, on June 4th, 1873, showed a balance at the debit of the Bank of £2,128,686, 11s. 9d. In the cash book under the same date is the following entry, creating and forming the single entry in a new account entitled "Bills Payable "Account, No. 2."

"Bills Payable Account, No. 2. To the following accounts under acceptance of "this date to be retired by the Bank under special arrangement with the parties of "date 1st June 1873, against which certain securities are now held by the Bank "and in process of realisation and payment of proceeds, £973,300."

There is likewise in the general ledger another account entitled "Foreign and "Colonial Credits," which on June 4th showed a balance at the credit of the Bank of £2,132,452, 2s. 3d. In the cash book under the same date, the following entry was also made, creating and forming the single entry in a new account entitled "Foreign "and Colonial Credits, No. 2."

"Foreign and Colonial Credits, No. 2. For the following credits to be retired as "they mature, and debited under the respective accounts to Credit Accounts, No. 2, "against which securities are now held by the Bank and in process of realisation "and payment of the proceeds, ... £973,300."

No details were specified under either of these headings, and the slump sums were carried to the general ledger, and there simply entered as "to cash per cash "book," and "by cash per cash book," respectively.

In the weekly balance book this £973,300 is entered and deducted from the "bills payable" account, and from the "foreign and colonial credits" account, the balances being carried to the balance book annually docquetted by the directors.

Since 1873 this system has been regularly adhered to, the sum of £973,300 having been annually deducted from each of these accounts.

In the printed balance-sheet issued by the board for this year, the sums at the credit and debit of these accounts respectively are included, the one under the head of "bills outstanding due or with a currency not exceeding twenty-one days, and "drafts accepted by the Bank and its London agents on account of home and "foreign constituents," and the other under "bills of exchange, local and country "bills, credit accounts, and other advances upon security."

The consequence of this has been, that the shareholders have been led to believe,—

(*a*) That the Bank had lent on foreign and colonial credits less than was the fact, by the amount of... ... ... £973,000

(*b*) That the Bank had accepted fewer bills payable than was the fact, to the amount of £973,000

E. Bills parted with.

Of the £149,435, 9s. of bills entered under this head, we have reason to believe that £64,595, 12s. 9d., although handed to the Bank for collection or retention, have been forwarded to London, and either discounted or placed to the credit of a "No. "2 Account" with the London Joint Stock Bank, which was held by that Bank, as a security for any advances under which they might come to the City of Glasgow Bank.

II.—ASSETS.

A. Cash.

	£	s.	d.
The amount of gold and silver in the hands of the cashier at the head office on the 1st inst., as entered in the cashier's ledger, which appears to have been correctly kept, was	£231,500	0	0
To this falls to be added the amount in the hands of the tellers at that date, ascertained from their cash books and jotting books,	12,156	6	0
And at the branches, ascertained from the register of notes and specie in hand at branches, ...	49,889	0	0
Making in all, ...	£293,545	6	0

The coin at the branches is, however, only returned once a week, and the above item of £49,889 consequently represents what was actually in hand at the 28th September.

	£	s.	d.
As the authorised circulation of the Bank was only	£72,921	0	0
The addition of this	293,545	6	0
Would only have justified an issue of...	£366,466	6	0
But the circulation of the previous Saturday, as vouched by the circulation ledger, was	604,196	0	0

The explanation of the discrepancy is to be found in the circulation ledger itself, from which it appears that since the commencement of this year, it had been the habit to add to the weekly return of bullion made to Government under 8 and 9 Victoria, cap. 38, an imaginary sum, less or more, according to the emergencies of the period, beginning with £60,000 under the first week in January, and fluctuating weekly, until, on the 21st September, when the last return was made, it reached £300,000. The additions thus made are openly and regularly entered in the circulation ledger in smaller figures, over the amount of gold really in hand at Glasgow.

The summations of the entries in this ledger, vitiated by these additions, were weekly returned to Government, and the Bank have thus, under the 14th section of the Act, become subject to very heavy penalties, which, however, under the circumstances, we have not thought it right to bring into the balance-sheet.

B. Balances on Current Accounts for Credits and Overdrafts considered good.

We have recovered the draft of the abstract of accounts for 1878. In it there is an entry taken from the general ledger, under the heading "Credit Accounts, *Dr.* "Balance, £2,009,752, 11s. 2d." In the revision of this draft, it would appear that, to lessen the apparent amount of this account, the sum of £926,724 was deducted from its total, and transferred from the first head of the abstract, under which it was grouped, to the third head, under the new headings, "Credit Accounts, Nos. 1, "3, and 4, Balance." A further reduction of £200,000 was made from the same account by transferring that amount to a new entry under head No. 3 in the abstract, entitled "reserve gold."

As all accounts grouped in the abstract under head No. 1, are in the printed balance-sheet included under the heading "Bills of exchange, local and country "bills, credit accounts, and other advances upon security," and all accounts under head No. 3, under the heading "Cash in hand," and entered under two divisions, viz. :—"Gold and silver coin, and notes of other banks at head office and branches," and "Government stocks, Exchequer bills, railway and other stocks and debentures, "and balances in hands of banking correspondents," the practical result of this was that the shareholders have been led to believe,—

(*a*) That the Bank had lent upon credits less than was the fact, by the amount of £1,126,764

(*b*) That the Bank had in their hands good securities belonging to themselves absolutely, more than was the fact, by 926,764

(*c*) That the Bank had in their cash chest more reserve gold than was the fact, by 200,000

C. Bills on Hand.

After deduction of all bills believed to be bad, amounting to £307,416, 15s. 7d., a deduction of £5 per cent. has been made from the balance of bills on hand at the head office, and of £2 per cent. from the balance of country bills sent to the head office, which it is believed will cover any reasonable risk of loss. No deduction has been made from exchange bills, or bills received for collection.

E. Business Premises of the Bank.

The premises belonging to the Bank in Virginia Street and Glassford Street (the latter in course of erection), the Gorbals branch office, and the offices at Greenock, Paisley, and Edinburgh, have been valued for us by Mr Thomas Binnie at £98,340. It has, of course, been impossible to overtake a detailed valuation of all the branch premises belonging to the Bank throughout the country; but from an estimate prepared by him, founded on the original cost of these, the population of the towns in which they are situated, and the fact that a considerable number will fall to be taken over by other banks as places of banking business, we have felt justified in putting down their probable value at £100,775, 4s. 9d.

Heritable Property in Glasgow.

The items under this heading have been taken from a record in the books of properties practically belonging to the Bank. To a large extent we have taken these at the valuations in the books, but in many instances where sales have been effected, or satisfactory information furnished to us, we have rectified these valuations. In this case the amount brought out by us exceeds the amount in the books by £10,407, 11s. 9d.

Heritable Property in the Colonies.

These properties, consisting of lands in New Zealand (North Island) and Australia, have been entered at the price which the Bank have paid for them within the last two years.

They comprise:—

(1.) 40,024 acres of freehold land in the province of Poverty Bay, purchased in October 1877, on a Government title, at 12s. 6d. per acre, and 11,808 acres of leasehold land adjoining, with the stock thereon, the lease being for eighteen years, and the price £11,628. Since the purchase of the freehold, £3433 has been expended in the purchase of stock. Since the acquisition of the leasehold, the bank agents were in course of acquiring from the natives the freehold right thereof, and have expended towards this a further sum of £1350. The balance is in the hands of the agents, or in materials purchased for the use of the station.

We consider that we are entitled to take this at least at the cost price, as we believe it would realise that now, and besides, it has the prospect of materially increasing in value.

(2.) The property in New South Wales and Queensland, the cost of which we are informed has been £368,000, including outlay on improvements and stocking. Of this there appears to have been paid by the acceptances of the Bank, which are still current, £130,000, the balance of £238,000 being met by the promissory notes of Mr Walker, the agent, who alleges that the Bank are bound to relieve him of this amount, but as we have not as yet been able to verify this statement, and have consequently not put this item into the liabilities, we have estimated the value of this asset at the £130,000 above referred to.

F. Furniture.

A rough estimate of the value of the furniture at the head office has been made for us by Messrs Hutchison & Dixon. The value of furniture at the branches has been based, as far as possible, on reports from the several branches.

G. Shares and Debentures in other Companies, apart from Shares in the New Zealand and Australian Land Company (Limited), held absolutely by the Bank.

Under this item we have included all the various items we have been able to discover which are embraced under the two following headings in the abstract of accounts from which the balance-sheet of June last was framed.

	£	s.	d.
"Railway and other stocks and debentures, ...	£1,023,699	7	10"
"General securities' stocks, ...	67,475	16	10"
In all, ...	£1,091,175	4	8

The items are as follows:—In the beginning of the year the Bank held $2,910,000, in 7 per cent. Bonds of $1000 each of the Western Union Railway of America, which, from information received from New York, we value at 75 per cent., representing £436,500. On the 18th May last, bonds representing $1,500,000 were sent by the Bank to the General Credit and Discount Company, London, for the purpose of raising money thereon, and on these £90,000 was raised, the balance being retained "for further instructions."

We have accordingly valued this item as follows:—

	£	s.	d.
$2,910,000 at 75 per cent., ...	£436,500	0	0
Less advance, ...	90,000	0	0
	£346,500	0	0
Besides these the Bank hold of the stock or shares of the Western Union Railway, $1,992,340 = £398,468 sterling at par, but which, from the information we have received, is only worth	11,950	0	0
They further hold in connection with the above railway company (who have the option of purchasing it under arbitration), the property of the Racine Warehouse and Dock Company, acquired at a cost of $300,000, but which we are advised is now worth only $30,000, or	6,000	0	0
They also hold 3273 shares of $100 each in the Milwaukee and St Paul Railway, which, at 31 per cent., the present selling price, represent $101,463, or	20,292	0	0
They hold, besides, the following shares, which we have put down at the present market value:—			
180 share Marabella Iron Ore Company, ...	495	0	0
150 shares Glasgow Jute Company, ...	0	0	0
£85,000 Grand Trunk Railway of Canada, ordinary, ...	5,525	0	0
430 shares Erie Railway preferred capital, 7 per cent., ...	2,279	0	0
£10,000 Grand Trunk Railway of Canada, 3d preference,	1,187	10	0
18 shares Upper Assam Tea Company, ...	1,840	0	0
In all, ...	£396,068	10	0

H. Government Stocks.

These in the abstract balance-sheet of June last are put down as—

Government Stocks, No. 1,	... ...	£1,857 6 6 and
Government Stocks, No. 2,	... ...	7,751 15 9
In all,	... ...	£9,609 2 3

The stocks answering to this description, so far as we are aware, held by the Bank, consist of East India Government 4 per cent. promissory notes, in two lots of 10,000 and 50,000 rupees respectively, which, at 1s. 9d., give ... £5,250 0 0
And £2000 British 3 per cent. annuities, worth, say, ... 1,857 6 6

In all, ... £7,107 6 6

Estimated Value of Securities held against Bad Debts.

The total amount represented by bad debts, which we, as at October 1st, have estimated at £7,345,357, 15s. 6d., the Bank have been in the habit of treating in the balance-sheets as an available asset.

Among the debtors included under this head are four, of which, owing to the magnitude of the amounts, we think it right to append separate notes.

	LIABILITIES.		PROBABLE VALUE OF SECURITIES HELD.		DEFICIT.
I.	£2,320,591 18 9	...	£688,184 19 11	...	£1,632,406 18 10
II.	1,864,627 2 4	...	452,582 12 9	...	1,412,044 9 7
III.	1,142,987 18 4	...	310,532 17 7	...	832,455 0 9
IV.	464,186 19 5	...	71,135 6 9	...	393,051 12 8

This deficit, however, is exclusive of any return that may be received from the estates of the debtors themselves, or from the estates of parties who have suspended payment, but against whom the Bank will have a ranking in regard to these debts.

It would appear that up to the time when the books of the Bank were put into our hands, no attempt had been made to value the securities held in reference to these four assets (any more than the other securities held by the Bank), which are entered in the security ledger at sums which appear to have been indicated by the debtors themselves. It was upon a statement of these accounts, in which, as we are informed, these securities were accepted at the latter figure, that the banks, consulted before the stoppage, resolved that it would not be expedient to assist the City Bank. Since then, the examination we have instituted into the real value of the securities, superficial as it has necessarily been, has shown that the estimate thus put upon them was enormously exaggerated, and it is by no means improbable that our own estimate is beyond the mark, as the Bank's title to much of what we have entered as good is of a very imperfect description.

Life Policies.

The Bank held life policies against the debts which we have dealt with as bad for an amount in all of £611,051, 13s. 5d. These have been entered at the surrender value, £74,014, 14s. 11d. The annual premiums due upon them amount to £17,214, 14s. 8d.

Shares in New Zealand and Australian Land Company (Limited).

Under this item are included all the shares of the New Zealand and Australian Land Company (Limited), to which the Bank appear to have right. The position of the Bank in regard to a large number of these shares is not so satisfactory as might be desired, many of the transfers not being completed, but it is believed that their right to the whole can be vindicated.

We have dealt with the Bank as holding £219,052 of A preference stock, and £912,079 of ordinary stock. The preference stock being 4 per cent. stock, we have taken it at £80 = £175,242. As to the ordinary stock we have had some difficulty. It yields at present only 3 per cent.; but its main value is prospective, and we do not believe that voluntary sellers would be disposed to part with it under par. If held for a period of years, it will in all probability realise a much higher figure; but again, were so large a quantity forced on the market at once, it is difficult to say what, on an average, it might bring. On the whole, we have thought it reasonable to value the ordinary stock, for the purpose of the present statement, at £80, like the preference, which gives £729,662,—or in all, £904,904.

It is right to mention that, besides this sum, there are a number of shares in this company belonging to parties whose liabilities to the Bank are so heavy that nearly the whole proceeds will probably fall into the funds of the Bank. The amount of such shares we make out to be £9406 preference, and £76,770 ordinary,—in all, £86,176, which, at £80, gives a possible additional asset of £68,941.

Heritable Properties held in security.

To the extent of £176,320, this item is composed of the value of properties at Rangoon, Kurrachee, &c., as to which we have acted upon the best information we have been able to receive. We cannot, however, declare that in any case the title of the Bank to these securities is at all satisfactory.

It is hardly necessary for us to say that, in making this item, we have not had it in our power to avail ourselves of the assistance of professional valuators.

The various items specially above referred to will go far to explain the difference between the results brought out by the balance-sheet of June last, and the estimate of assets and liabilities now submitted.

We must, however, in addition explain, that two items are entered in the abstract of accounts from which the June balance-sheet was prepared, as assets, which we have been obliged to reject *in toto*. One of these is a sum of £280,000, entered as an asset under the head of suspense account, and which we have found it necessary to include in our estimate of bad debts; the other a sum of £96,294, 3s. 6d., entered as an asset under the head of Credit Account, No. 2, but which is made up of balances so hopelessly bad, that, as we are informed, they were specially removed under this heading to prevent the possibility of interest being calculated on them from year to year.

We are fully conscious of the numerous defects in the present statement, and we cannot but anticipate that many errors and omissions may become apparent from day to day. The valuations conducted, as we have been forced to conduct them, in most cases without the aid of skilled valuators, and under the urgency of continued and increasing pressure, can hardly fail to be very incomplete; but we believe that those who are most conversant with the nature and details of such a duty as has been imposed upon us, will be most ready to make allowance for, and to excuse the imperfections of, the results.

As the form in which the statement of liabilities and assets has been prepared is different from that of the printed annual balance-sheets, we have thought it right to append an abstract of the results at which we have arrived under the headings adopted in the latter, and, for the convenience of comparison, we have placed above it a copy of the balance-sheet which was laid before the shareholders at their meeting on 3d July last.

(Signed) KERR, ANDERSONS, MUIR, & MAIN,
Chartered Accountants.

M'GRIGOR, DONALD, & CO.,
Solicitors.

GLASGOW, 18*th October* 1878.

ABSTRACT BALANCE-SHEET, AS AT 5TH JUNE 1878.

As issued by the Bank, and submitted to Annual Meeting, 3d July 1878.

Liabilities.

I.	Deposits at the head office and branches, and balances at the credit of banking correspondents,		£8,102,001 0 4
II.	Bank notes in circulation in Scotland and the Isle of Man,		710,252 0 0
III.	Drafts outstanding, due, or with a currency not exceeding 21 days, and drafts accepted by the Bank and its London agents on account of home and foreign constituents,		1,488,244 18 6
	Liabilities to the public,		£10,300,497 18 10
IV.	Capital account,	£1,000,000 0 0	
V.	Reserve fund,	450,000 0 0	
VI.	Profit and loss,	142,095 12 10	
	Liabilities to partners,		1,592,095 12 10
			£11,892,593 11 8

Assets.

I.	Bills of exchange, local and country bills, credit accounts, and other advances upon security,		£8,484,466 9 2
II.	Advances on heritable property, and value of bank buildings and furniture at head office and branches,		265,324 9 0
III.	Cash on hand—viz., gold and silver coin and notes of other banks at head office and branches,	£845,963 1 0	
	Government stocks, Exchequer bills, railway and other stocks and debentures, and balances in hands of banking correspondents,	2,296,839 12 6	
			3,142,802 13 6
			£11,892,593 11 8

ABSTRACT BALANCE-SHEET, AS AT 1ST OCTOBER 1878.

Prepared in conformity with subjoined State of Liabilities and Assets.

Liabilities.

I.	Deposits at the head office and branches, and balances at the credit of banking correspondents,	£8,798,788 13 4
II.	Bank notes in circulation in Scotland and the Isle of Man,	863,403 0 0
III.	Drafts outstanding, due, or with a currency not exceeding 21 days, and drafts accepted by the Bank and its London agents on account of home and foreign constituents,	2,742,105 14 11
		£12,404,297 8 3

Assets.

I.	Bills of exchange, local and country bills, credit accounts, and other advances upon security,		£5,996,792 3 0
II.	Advances on heritable property, and value of bank buildings and furniture at head office and branches,		211,074 10 8
III.	Cash on hand—viz., gold and silver coin and notes of other banks at head office and branches,	£418,363 16 4	
	Government stocks, Exchequer bills, railway and other stocks and debentures, and balances in hands of banking correspondents,	587,083 7 0	
			1,005,447 3 4
	Balance, being Loss,		5,190,983 11 3
			£12,404,297 8 3

NOTE.—To the above balance of loss,	£5,190,983 11 3
Falls to be added the capital,	1,000,000 0 0
Making the total loss,	£6,190,983 11 3

BALANCE-SHEET, 1ST OCTOBER 1878.

LIABILITIES.

I. ORDINARY, viz. :—				
(A) Bank Notes in the Hands of the Public,		£863,403 0 0		
*(B) Current Deposit Accounts, viz. :—				
1. At head office,	£361,544 19 1			
2. At branches,	2,203,525 1 11			
		2,565,070 1 0		
*(C) Interest Receipts, viz. :				
1. At head office,	£485,132 3 8			
2. At branches,	5,345,135 15 1			
		5,830,267 18 9		
(D) Acceptances by the Bank—Current,		2,742,105 14 11		
(E) Bills Lodged with the Bank and Collected or Parted with, viz. :—				
1. At head office,	£143,630 8 0			
2. At branches,	5,805 0 3			
		149,435 9 0		
(F) Balances due to other Banks and Banking Correspondents—				
1. At head office,	£157,906 11 10			
2. At branches,	2,492 0 0			
		160,398 11 10		
(G) Dividends past due to Shareholders,		4,519 4 0		
(H) Due Stamp Office for Duties—				
1. Head office,	£10 11 11			
2. Branches,	24 14 8			
		35 6 7	£12,315,235 6 1	
II. CONTINGENT:—				
(I) Customers' Bills Re-discounted by the Bank and expected to become bad in the Hands of the Discounters,			89,062 2 2	£12,404,297 8 3

NOTE.—*Another contingent liability is the possible cost of Re-exchange of Foreign Bills.*

* *In consequence of the limited time at disposal, interest has not been credited upon the deposit accounts and interest receipts for the period between 5th June and 1st October 1878, neither has interest been debited to the overdrafts and credit accounts for the same period.*

ASSETS.

I. ESTIMATED GOOD :—				
(A) Cash—				
(*a*) Gold—				
1. At head office,	£236,840 10 0			
2. At branches,	38,043 10 0			
		£274,884 0 0		
(*b*) Silver and copper—				
1. At head office,	£7,679 17 11			
2. At branches,	39,189 6 5			
		46,869 4 4		
(*c*) Notes and cheques of other banks—				
1. At head office,	£18,496 0 0			
2. At branches,	78,114 12 0			
		96,610 12 0	£418,363 16 4	
(B) Balances on Current Accounts for Credits and Overdrafts considered Good—				
1. At head office,		£526,825 11 4		
2. At branches,		1,253,009 3 11		
			1,779,834 15 3	
(C) Bills on Hand—Considered good—				
(*a*) Current—Discounted by the Bank; viz.:				
1. At head office,	£1,073,011 2 8			
2. At branches,	984,666 16 0			
		£2,057,677 18 8		
(*b*) Past Due—Discounted by the Bank ; viz.:				
1. At head office,	£91,863 9 9			
2. At branches,	49,422 8 1			
		141,285 17 10	2,198,963 16 6	
(D) Balances due by other Banks and Banking Correspondents—				
1. At head office,		£176,932 16 10		
2. At branches,		210 2 7		
			177,142 19 5	
(E) Heritable Property—				
(*a*) Business premises of the Bank—				
1. At head office,	£34,500 0 0			
2. At branches,	164,615 4 9			
		£199,115 4 9		
Carry forward,		£199,115 4 9	£4,574,305 7 6	

Brought forward,		£199,115 4 9	£4,574,305 7 6	
(*b*) Other property held by the Bank—				
1. In Glasgow,	£98,259 8 0			
2. In the Colonies,	176,500 0 0			
		274,759 8 0		
			473,874 12 9	
(F) Furniture—				
1. At head office,		£526 1 0		
2. At branches,		11,433 4 11		
			11,959 5 11	
(G) Shares and Debentures in other Companies—apart from Shares in the New Zealand and Australian Land Company (Limited)—held absolutely by the Bank,			396,068 10 0	
(H) Government Stocks,			7,107 6 6	
(I) Miscellaneous Assets—				
1. At head office,		£5,495 11 3		
2. At branches,		1,268 19 10		
			6,764 11 1	
				£5,470,079 13 9

Note.—*Between the evening of the 1st and morning of the 2d October there would be in transit to the pay offices letters of credit purchased by customers, and on the other hand exchange and other vouchers, consisting of, for example, the cheques of other Banks honoured on 1st October at Branches of the City Bank. The full extent of these operations will, it is estimated, result in a balance in favour of the City of Glasgow Bank of about £140,000.*

II. ESTIMATED VALUE OF SECURITIES HELD AGAINST BAD DEBTS—*

1. At head office—			
(*a*) Shares in New Zealand Land Company (Limited),	£904,904 0 0		
(*b*) Shares in companies other than New Zealand and Australian Land Company (Limited),	126,074 15 0		
(*c*) Heritable Securities,	378,776 6 8		
(*d*) Life Policies,	74,014 14 11		
(*e*) Produce,	71,750 0 0		
(*f*) Shipping,	38,308 6 7		
(*g*) Bills and Promissory Notes,	92,497 13 6		
(*h*) Miscellaneous,	11,000 0 0		
		£1,697,325 16 8	
2. At branches—			
(*a*) Heritable,	£30,097 2 10		
(*b*) Life Policies,	13,333 2 3		
(*c*) Shares in other companies,	1,658 12 10		
(*d*) Shipping,	300 0 0		
(*e*) Miscellaneous,	519 8 8		
		45,908 6 7	
			1,743,234 3 3
III. BALANCE, BEING DEFICIENCY,			5,190,983 11 3
			£12,404,297 8 3

* The above securities are held against the following debts, which are estimated bad. It is to be noted, however, that against other debts due to the Bank it holds a large quantity of securities which do not appear above, the debts against which these are held being considered good.

1. Head office—(*a*) Current accounts for credits and overdrafts estimated bad,		£6,899,912 2 1	
(*b*) Discounted bills on hand, current,	do.	194,856 18 8	
(*c*) Do. do., past due,	do.	77,752 12 10	
			£7,172,521 13 7
2. At branches—(*a*) Current accounts for credits and overdrafts estimated bad,		£128,028 18 4	
(*b*) Discounted bills on hand, current,	do.	14,913 15 0	
(*c*) Do. do. past due,	do.	19,893 8 7	
			162,836 1 11
Total estimated bad debts,			£7,335,357 15 6

The Assets will be increased and the loss proportionally diminished by whatever dividends are received from the estates of the debtors and obligants in respect of the above bad debts.

COMMERCIAL PRINTING COMPANY, EDINBURGH.

ABSTRACT OF ACCOUNTS IN THE CITY OF GLASGOW BANK'S GENERAL LEDGER ON WEDNESDAY, 6th JUNE 1877

	TITLES OF ACCOUNTS	DEBTOR.	CREDITOR.	Dr. BALANCES.	TOTAL.
	Deposit Accounts Dr Balances	449692 16 10	449692 16 10		
I.	HEAD OFFICE—Local Bills,	857543 9 5			
	Country Bills,	167934 1 9			
	Bills of Exchange,	55218 17 5			
	Bills Received for Collection,	2449 2			
	Bills Remitted,	483728 9 7			
	Past Due Bills,	187044 17 5			
	Suspense Accounts,	300000			
	Instalment and Composition Bills,	2832 12			
	Contingent Account,	348629 16 5	176628 19 2		
	City of Glasgow Bank Stock,	1806987 10 6			
	Credit Accounts (Balance per General Ledger),	220683 5 8	220683 5 8		
	Credit Accounts (Cr. Balances),	1500			
	~~Assurance Suspense~~	98848 8 11			
	Heritable Property Account,	1710048 2			
	Foreign and Colonial Credits,	1499 12 2			
	Stamps Accounts,	30887 1			
	Adjusting Account of Interest—(Interest due by Customers),	950 14 4			
	Officers' Guarantee Fund—(Loan),	2000			
	Notes and Outfit—(Stock on hand),	1100			
	Stationery—(Stock on hand),	8000			
	Expenses / Credit Accounts No 2	96617 14 2			
	Credit Accounts No 2 Cr Balances	59 16	5916		
	Credit Accounts No 3	870142 3 11			
	Credit Accounts No 4				
		8509285 11 11	688064 17	7621218 14 3	
	BRANCHES—Local Bills,	1170475 3 7			
	Bills Received for Collection,	52880 8 2			
	Country and Exchange Bills, £646.877.19.8		121183 15 9		
	Bills Lodged,	449221 12 8			
	Past Due Bills,	14797 14 6			
	Bad and Doubtful Debts,	1426 11 1			
	Suspense Accounts (Dr. Balances),		5061 7 1		
	Suspense Accounts (Cr. Balances),		9533 9 1		
	Contingent Accounts,				
	Credit Accounts (Balance per Weekly Abstract Book),	859514 3 6			
	Credit Accounts (Cr. Balances),	154584 7 10			
	Deposit Accounts (Dr. Balances),	468159 3			
	Adjusting Accounts of Interest—(Interest due by Customers),	1386 4 4			
	Stamps Accounts,	54 14 4		2.687519 6	
	Law Charges Accounts,				
	Deposit Accounts Dr Balances Special	15241 16 5	131224 1 11		
II.	HEAD OFFICE—Property Account—(Head Office),	49862 4 11			
	Do. —(Branches),	128502 8		178364 12 11	
	BRANCHES—Property Accounts,	22576 6 7			
	New Premises Accounts,	10861 11 11			
	Fixtures and Furniture Accounts,			33437 18 6	211802 11 5
III.	HEAD OFFICE—Gold and Silver Coin on hand—Cash Chest,	590500			
	Do. Do. —Tellers,	25254 7 6			
	Notes of other Banks on hand—Tellers,	89 153		655156 7 6	
	BRANCHES—Gold and Silver Coin on hand,				
	Notes of other Banks on hand,		2358661 12 8	921018 2	
	HEAD OFFICE—Government Stocks—No. 1,	1857 6 6			
	Government Stocks—No. 2,	771 15 9			
	Railway and other Stocks and Debentures,	1,023694 7 10			
	London, Provincial, and Foreign Correspondents (Dr. Balances),	290648 4			
	Do. Do. (Dr. Balances, ₩ Weekly Abstract Book),	44611 19 1			
	General Securities, Stocks,	67498 7 11			
		100300			
		200875	2187542 1 1		
	BRANCHES—Agents, Gyps, & Co.	3547	3547	2187896 8 1	21089148 3

Difference betwixt Head office & Branch Balances

	TITLES OF ACCOUNTS.	DEBTOR.	CREDITOR.	Cr. BALANCES.	TOTAL.
I.	HEAD OFFICE—Deposit Accounts (Balance per General Ledger),		3548813		
	Deposit Accounts (Dr. Balances),	449692 16 10	449692 16 10		
	Interest Receipts,		553580 7 7		
	Credit Accounts (Cr. Balances),	220683 5 8	220683 5 8		
	Bankers' Balances,		7765		
	Dividends due Shareholders,		4689 11		
	Unaccepted Bill Account,		21,123		
	Tellers' Suspense Account,		67 4		
	Bills Lodged,		436401 15 9		
	London, Provincial, and Foreign Correspondents (Cr. Balances),				
	Do. Do. (Cr. Balances, ₩ Weekly Abstract Book),		224438 18		
	Adjusting Account of Interest—(Interest due to Customers),		1108816 2		
	Credit Lodged against Drafts on Branch		251911 19 11		
	Credit Accounts No 2 Cr Balances	5916	5916		
		670455 18 6	13767221 9 2	706287 8	
	Credit Accounts Cr Balances Special		12052 18 7		
	BRANCHES—Deposit Accounts (Balance per Weekly Abstract Book),		2,210007 18 4		
	Deposit Accounts (Dr. Balances),		468159 3		
	Interest Receipts,		5236800 6 6		
	Credit Accounts (Cr. Balances),		154584 7 10		
	Adjusting Accounts of Interest—(Interest due to Customers),		69616 8 8		
	Credit Cheques,		1584 5 10		
	Unaccepted Bill Accounts,		58 18 4		
	~~Bankers Balances~~ Head Office,		4341		
			8175077 1		
	Cross Accounts: Edinburgh Board, West End Branch	268692 8 3			
		5150 5			
		273842 13 3	8117507 7	17883664 13	10858995 14 6
	Other Accounts, viz.: ~~Deposit Accounts Dr Balances~~ ~~Credit Accounts Cr Balances~~				
II.	HEAD OFFICE—City of Glasgow Bank Issue Account,		2111290		
	BRANCHES —Bank of Man Do.		30000	2141290	
	HEAD OFFICE—Company's Notes on hand—Cash Chest,	273000			
	Do. —Tellers,	337100		610100	
	BRANCHES —Company's Notes on hand,		693186	1303286	
III.	HEAD OFFICE—Bills Payable,				
	BRANCHES—Drafts at a Currency not yet due				
	Drafts at a Currency above days,				
IV.	HEAD OFFICE—Capital Account,			1000000	
V.	HEAD OFFICE—Reserve Fund,			450000	
VI.	HEAD OFFICE—Profit and Loss,			148501 12 6	1598501 12 6
					12208265 7 2

ABSTRACT OF ACCOUNTS IN THE CITY OF GLASGOW BANK'S GENERAL LEDGER ON WEDNESDAY, 5th JUNE 1878.

TITLES OF ACCOUNTS.	DEBTOR.	CREDITOR.	Dr. BALANCES.	TOTAL.
I. HEAD OFFICE—Local Bills,	766675 19 8			
Country Bills,	1364836 15			
Bills of Exchange,	764575 16 5			
Bills Received for Collection,	222818 10			
Bills Remitted,	375958 13 1			
Past Due Bills,	179417 7			
Suspense Account,	280000			
Instalment and Composition Bills,	127 5 4			
Contingent Account,				
City of Glasgow Bank Stock,	444434 15 6	12103 5 7		
Credit Accounts (Balance per General Ledger),	3009752 11 2	[illegible]		
Credit Accounts (Cr. Balances),	346336 6 9	346336 6 9		
Deposit Accounts (Dr. Balances),	[illegible]	440738 10 9		
Heritable Property Account,	38696 7 7			
Foreign and Colonial Credits,	2381252 18 6	973300		
Stamps Accounts,	1471 6 7			
Adjusting Accounts of Interest—(Interest due by Customers),	37230 11 7			
Officers' Guarantee Fund—(Loss),	912 3 11			
Notes and Outfit—(Stock on hand),	2091 7 8			
Stationery—(Stock on hand),	1500			
Tellers' Suspense Account,				
Branch Preliminary Expenses	7500			
Income Tax	1000			
Credit Accounts No. 2	46244 3 6			
Credit Accounts No. 3, No. 4	[illegible]	[illegible]		
	9583949 18 8	[illegible]	6225681 9 15 7	
BRANCHES—Local Bills,	4047609 9			
Bills Received for Collection,	843743 11 9			
Country and Exchange Bills, £598705. 6. 5				
Bills Lodged,		127874 19 7		
Past Due Bills,	45648 17 3			
Bad and Doubtful Debts,	18498 13 9			
Suspense Accounts (Dr. Balances),	10109 10 9			
Suspense Accounts (Cr. Balances),		463 12 6		
Contingent Accounts,		1180 8 2		
Credit Accounts (Balance per Weekly Abstract Book),	835472 16 2			
Credit Accounts (Cr. Balances),	31493 19 3			
Deposit Accounts (Dr. Balances),	465885 18			
Adjusting Accounts of Interest—(Interest due by Customers),				
Stamps Accounts,	1471 19 3			
Law Charges Accounts,	1771 15 1			
Remittances Outstanding between Branches, Correspondents, and Head Office,	108353 3 10	[illegible]		
Deposit Accounts (Dr. Balance per Weekly Abstract Book)	924315 9			
	[illegible]	[illegible]	[illegible]	
Cash Accounts, viz.— Edinburgh Branch		148939 18 11	8355660 13 1	
West End Branch		5150 5		
			154090 3 11	8481466 9 2
Heritable Property Account				
II. HEAD OFFICE—Property Account—(Head Office),	33312 3 3			
Do. —(Branches),	138520 3 1		171832 6 4	
BRANCHES—Property Accounts,	22062 3 9			
New Premises Accounts,				
Fixtures and Furniture Accounts	10429 18 11		33492 2 8	265324 9
III. HEAD OFFICE—Gold and Silver Coin on hand—Cash Chest,	538500			
Do. Do. —Tellers,	23313 6 11			
Notes of other Banks on hand—Tellers,	34810	596623 6 11		
Remittances transit H. Co. & Head office				
BRANCHES—Gold and Silver Coin on hand,	111705 8 3			
Notes of other Banks on hand,	[illegible]	1400786 8 3	[illegible]	
HEAD OFFICE—Government Stocks—No. 1,	1857 6 6			
Government Stocks—No. 2	7771 15 9			
Railway and other Stocks and Debentures,	1022699 7 10			
London, Provincial, and Foreign Correspondents (Dr. Balances),	245568 15 6			
Do. Do. (Dr. Balances, ℔ Weekly Abstract Book),	2344412			
General Securities—Stocks,	67475 16 10			
Credit Accounts No. 1 Balance, No. 3 Do., No. 4 Do.	[illegible]	2296591 14 5		
BRANCHES—Prescott, Grote, & Co.,	24718 1		2296839 12 6	3142502 13 6
				£ 18892593 11 8

TITLES OF ACCOUNTS.	DEBTOR.	CREDITOR.	Cr. BALANCES.	TOTAL.
I. HEAD OFFICE—Deposit Accounts (Balance per General Ledger),		3895914 8	3494698 5 5	
Deposit Accounts (Dr. Balances),	440738 10 9	440738 10 9		
Interest Receipts,		477785 3 3		
Credit Accounts (Cr. Balances),	346336 6 9	346336 6 9		
Bankers' Balances,		14657		
Dividends due Shareholders,		4174 4 3		
Unstamped Bill Account,		15 18 6		
Tellers' Suspense Account,		3 12 4		
Bills Lodged,		80864 2		
London, Provincial, and Foreign Correspondents (Cr. Balances),				
Do. Do. (Cr. Balances, ℔ Weekly Abstract Book),		2344412		
Adjusting Accounts of Interest—(Interest due to Customers),		9825 2 10		
Cash lodged agt Bank acceptances		16599 2 6		
	[illegible]	[illegible]	6613781 16	
BRANCHES—Deposit Accounts (Balance per Weekly Abstract Book),		1860635 7 5		
Deposit Accounts (Dr. Balances),		465885 18		
Interest Receipts,		5153421 11 1		
Credit Accounts (Cr. Balances),		31493 19 3		
Adjusting Accounts of Interest—(Interest due to Customers),		75474 4 3		
Credit Cheques,		901 17 4		
Unstamped Bill Accounts,		39 18 4		
Remittances Outstanding between Branches, Correspondents, and Head Office,				
Bank Balances		5026		
Credit Accounts (Balance per Weekly Abstract)		1883 17 1		
		7594712 12	7594712 12 4	
Cash Accounts, viz.— Edinburgh Br.	148939 18 11			
West End Br.	5150 5	154090 3 11	7440622 8 10	
			154090 3 11	14102001 . 4
II. HEAD OFFICE—City of Glasgow Bank Issue Account,		2163790		
BRANCHES —Bank of Mona Do.		32000	2195790	
HEAD OFFICE—Company's Notes on hand—Cash Chest,	411500			
Do. —Tellers,	164871	576371		
BRANCHES —Company's Notes on hand,		820136	1396507	
III. HEAD OFFICE—Bills Payable. Rec. Circular to Head office, to Branches, Remittances in Transit		41085, 47946	15031	716732
Head office Bills Payable	973300	2881252 18 6		
		[illegible]		[illegible]
BRANCHES—Drafts at a Currency under days,				10301497 18 10
Drafts at a Currency above days,				
IV. HEAD OFFICE—Capital Account,			1000000	
V. HEAD OFFICE—Reserve Fund,			450000	
VI. HEAD OFFICE—Profit and Loss,			142095 12 10	1592095 12 10
				£18892593 11 8

ABSTRACT OF ACCOUNTS IN THE City of Glasgow Bank's GENERAL LEDGER ON ~~TUESDAY~~ Wednesday 7th June, 1876.

TITLES OF ACCOUNTS.	DEBTOR.	CREDITOR.	Dr. BALANCE.
I. Bills of Exchange, Local & Country Bills, Credit Accounts and other advances on Security			
Bills Discounted,	927 117 11 8		
Country Bills,	152 315 15 4		
Bills of Exchange,	112 205 15 9		
~~Bills in Transit,~~			1,191 639 2 9
~~Cash Vouchers Remitted,~~			
Bills Received for Collection,	1676 12 1		
Bills Remitted,	430 102 14 7		431 779 6 8
Past Due Bills,	248 500 13 6		
Bad and Doubtful Debts,	50 000		
~~Transferred and Compromised Debts,~~			
Contingent Account, 1	10 749 3 11		
2			
3	309 247 17 5		309 247 17 5
4			
City of Glasgow Bank Stock	356 825 7		
General Stock			
Credit Accounts, Balance	2 715 914 14 11		
~~Credit Accounts (Cr. Balances),~~			
~~Deposit Accounts (Dr. Balances),~~			
Heritable Property Account,	119 541 15 4		
Foreign and Colonial Credits,	1 304 873 17 1		
Stamps Accounts,	1 708 13 4		
Adjusting Account of Interest—(Interest due by Customers),	66 709 10 9		
Officers' Guarantee Fund—(Loan),	988 4 4		
Notes and Outfit—(Stock on hand),	2 500		
Stationery—(Stock on hand),	1 200		
~~Suspense Accounts,~~ Preliminary Expenses	1 500		
Income Tax	2 000		4 510 756 16 4
~~Cross Accounts—Cheque Bills,~~			6 573 423 3 2
~~Interest Receipts, "In Trust, &c."~~		Dr. No. 1	[illegible]
			8 787 804 17 9
II. Advances on Heritable Property and Value of Bank Buildings and Furniture			
Head Office, &c.,	96 410 1 3		
Branches,	126 127 17 5		222 537 18 8
		Dr. No. 2	[illegible]
III. Cash on hand			
Company's Notes on hand—Cash Chest,	168 500		
—Tellers,	268 868		
Gold and Silver Coin on hand—Cash Chest,	535 500		
—Tellers,	28 263 10 6		
Notes of other Banks on hand—Tellers,	87 471		1,088 602 10 6
		Dr. No. 3 & 4	
Government Stocks—No. 1,	1857 6 6		
Government Stocks—No. 2,	7751 15 9		
Railway Stocks and Debentures,	1,023 908 6 11		
~~London, Provincial, and Foreign Correspondents,~~	364 264 13 3		
Royal Bank Credit	65 451 14 2		
South Western [illegible]	200 875		
[illegible]	100 300		
[illegible]	450 600		
Notes Remitted by Branches			
	2,215 008 16 7	29 095	2,185 913 16 7
			10,010 477 8 11

TITLES OF ACCOUNTS.	DEBTOR.	CREDITOR.	Cr. BALANCE.
I. Deposits at the Head Office & Branches & Balances at the credit of Banks Correspondents			
Deposit Accounts, Balance	1346 16 6		
~~Deposit Accounts (Dr. Balances),~~			
Interest Receipts,		507 433 1 2	
~~Credit Accounts (Cr. Balances),~~			506 086 4 8
~~Cross Accounts—Cheque Dues,~~			
Interest Receipts, "In Trust, &c."			
Bankers' Balances,		30 029	
Dividends due Shareholders,		3517 10 10	
Unstamped Bill Account,		21 18 8	
Tellers' Suspense Account,		86 7 4	
Bills Lodged,		30 376 12 11	
~~London, Provincial, and Foreign Correspondents,~~			
~~Adjusting Account of Interest—Interest due to Customers,~~			
Cash lodged against Drafts handed to Branches		16 962 1 3	
Dr. No. 2			
Circulation			
Office [illegible] £3,056,790			
			70 993 11
			577 079 15 8
II. Bank Notes in Circulation in Scotland and the Isle of Man		Dr. No. 1	
Issued, Balance,			
Returned	4843 710	6879 500	2036 790
III. Drafts outstanding, &c., and with a currency			
Bills Payable, No. 1		2288 673 17 1	
Bills Payable, No. 2	973 300		1,315 373 17 1
IV. Capital Account			Dr. No. 4
Stock Account,		2288 673 17 1	
		973 300	
		1,315 373 17 1	1,000 000
V. Reserve Fund			Dr. No. 5
Reserve Fund,	183 432 4 8		
	143 421 4 5		
	326 853 9 1		
	988 520 3	1,315 373 17 1	450 000
VI. Profit and Loss			Dr. 6
Profit and Loss,			136 365 10 3
Branches—Balance, Balance			4,494 868 5 11
Branches	4537 630 18 10		
Head office	4444 868 5 11		
Remittances in course of transmission	32 752 7 11		£10,010 477 8 11

ABSTRACT OF ACCOUNTS IN THE CITY OF GLASGOW BANK'S GENERAL LEDGER ON WEDNESDAY, 6th JUNE 1877.

	TITLES OF ACCOUNTS.	AMOUNT.	AMOUNT.	Dr. BALANCE.
I.	Local Bills,	1887543 4 5		
	Country Bills,	167934 1 9		
	Bills of Exchange,	85218 17 5		
	Bills on demand,		1,140696 8 7	
	Cash Vouchers Remitted,			
	Bills Received for Collection,	2499 2		
	Bills Remitted,	4827?? 9 7	486227 9 9	
	Past Due Bills,	187044 17 5		
	Suspense Account,	300000		
	Instalment and Composition Bills,	2832 12		
		489877 9 5		
	Contingent Account,	17628 19 2	4?2248 10 3	
	Credit Accounts No 2 Cr Balances	59 16		
	Income Tax	1500		
	City of Glasgow Bank Stock,	398629 16 5		7621218 14 3
	Credit Accounts No. 1 (Balance per General Ledger),	1,806987 10 6		
	Do. No. 2 Do.	96617 14 2		
	Do. No. 3 Do.	870142 3 11		
	Do. No. 4 Do.	494852 5		
	Credit Accounts No. 1 (Cr. Balances),	1220683 5 8		
	Deposit Accounts (Dr. Balances),	2449692 16 10		
	Heritable Property Account,	98848 8 11		
	Foreign and Colonial Credits,	1710048 2		
	Stamps Accounts,	1499 12 2		
	Adjusting Account of Interest—(Interest due by Customers),	30862		
	Officers' Guarantee Fund—(Loan),	930 14 4		
	Notes and Outfit—(Stock on hand),	2000		
	Stationery—(Stock on hand),	1100		
	Tellers' Suspense Account, Preliminary Expenses	8004	6197412 4 2	
			8241654 12 9	
	Cross Accounts, viz.—			
	Credit Accounts Cr Balances	1220683 5 8		
	Deposit Accounts Dr Balances	2449692 16 10		
	Credit Accounts No 2 Cr Balances	59 16	670435 18 6	~~7621218 14 3~~
				7227805 15 2
II.	Property Account—(Head Office),	49862 4 11		
	Do. —Branches,	128502 8		~~178364 12 11~~
				2?1364 12 11
III.	Company's Notes on hand—Cash Chest,	273000		
	—Tellers,	337100	610100	
	Gold and Silver Coin on hand—Cash Chest,	570500		
	—Tellers,	75754		
	Notes of other Banks on hand—Tellers,	39402 7 6	685156 7 6	
			1,295256 7 6	
	Government Stocks—No. 1,	1857 6 6		
	Government Stocks—No. 2,	7751 15 9		
	Railway and other Stocks and Debentures,			
	London, Provincial, and Foreign Correspondents (Dr. Balances),	225644 7 10		
	Do. Do. (Dr. Balances, ℔ Weekly Abstract Book),	44611 19 7		
	General Securities—Stocks,	67198 7 11		
	Stocks £200,275 / 100,500 / 450,600 / £751,775		1435767 1 1	2731023 8 7
				~~£10530606 15 9~~
				10173193 16 8

	TITLES OF ACCOUNTS.	AMOUNT.	AMOUNT.	Cr. BALANCE.
I.	Deposit Accounts (Balance per General Ledger),	35488 13		
	Deposit Accounts (Dr. Balances),	1449692 16 10		
	Interest Receipts,	553580 7 2		
	Credit Accounts (Cr. Balances),	2220683 5 8		
	Credit Accounts No 2 Cr Balances	59 16		
			1,259504 18 8	
	Bankers' Balances,	7765		
	Dividends due Shareholders,	4089 11		
	Unstamped Bill Account,	71 12 5		
	Tellers' Suspense Account,	6 17 4		
	Bills Lodged,	43640 15 9		
	London, Provincial, and Foreign Correspondents (Cr. Balances),			
	Do. Do. (Cr. Balances, ℔ Weekly Abstract Book),	22493 18		
	Adjusting Account of Interest—(Interest due to Customers),	11008 16 2		
	Cash Lodged against Drafts to Customers at Branches	28191 19 11		
			117718 6	
			1,376722 14 2	
	Cross Account, viz.—			
	Deposit Accounts – Dr Balances	1449692 16 10		
	Credit Accounts – Cr Balances	2220683 5 8		
	Credit Accounts No 2 – Cr Balances	59 16	670435 18 6	706287 8
II.	Issue—Balance,			2,111290
III.	Bills Payable,		2683 346	~~2,707748 2~~
				1,350335 1 1
IV.	Capital Account,			1,000000
V.	Reserve Fund,			450000
VI.	Profit and Loss,			148501 12 6
	Balance—Branches,			4406780 2 5
				~~£10530606 15 9~~
				£10,173193 16 8